CW00797657

GBN

BINGS LIMITED

Telephone:
2617 Central

Telegrams:
Geebeeyen London

25 ROPEMAKER STREET

LONDON E. C.

SOLE VENDORS IN THE UNITED KINGDOM OF THE GOODS OF

BING BROS. A.-G., NUREMBERG

BAVARIA

The Development of the Firm of

BING BROTHERS A.-G., NUREMBERG

since the year 1895 shewing number of Staff employed.

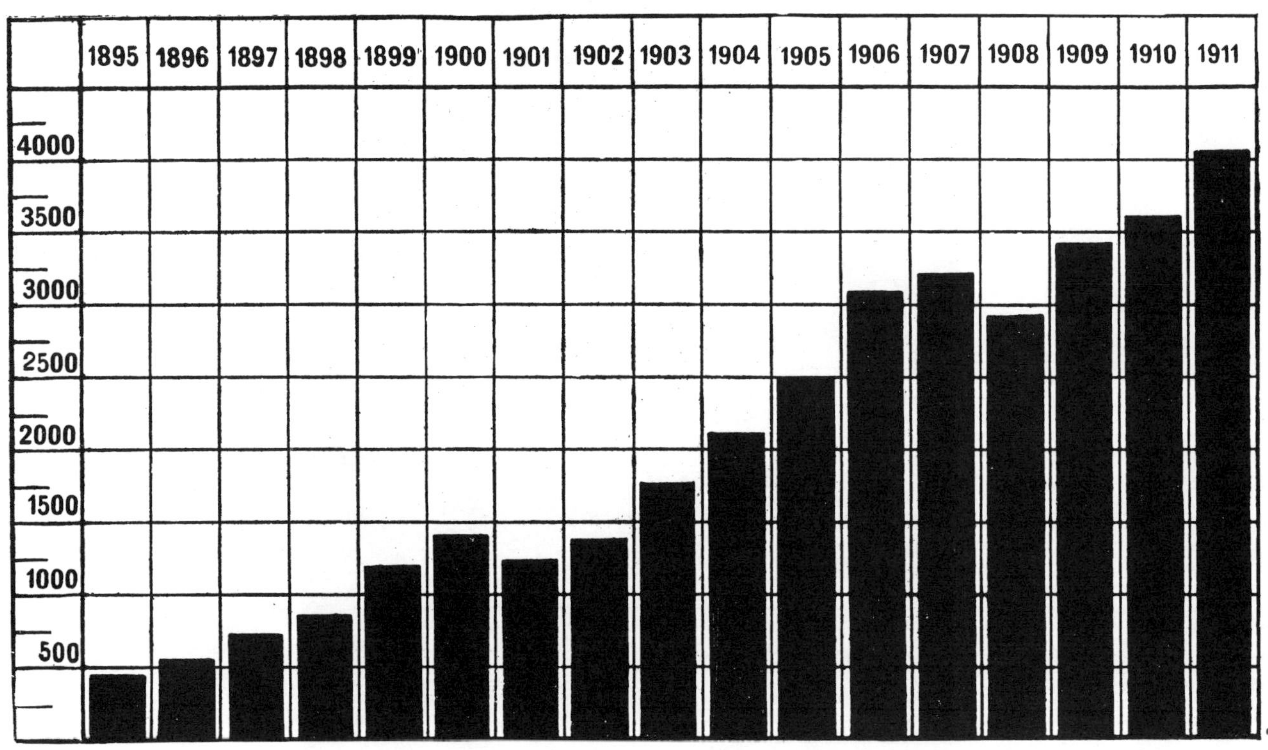

First edition published in 2001
by New Cavendish Books
3 Denbigh Road, London W11 2SJ
Tel. 44 20 72296765 Fax. 44 20 77920027
E-mail: narisa@new-cav.demon.co.uk
www.newcavendishbooks.com

ISBN 1 872727 75 1

Printed and bound in Thailand
by Amarin Printing & Publishing Co., Ltd. (Plc)

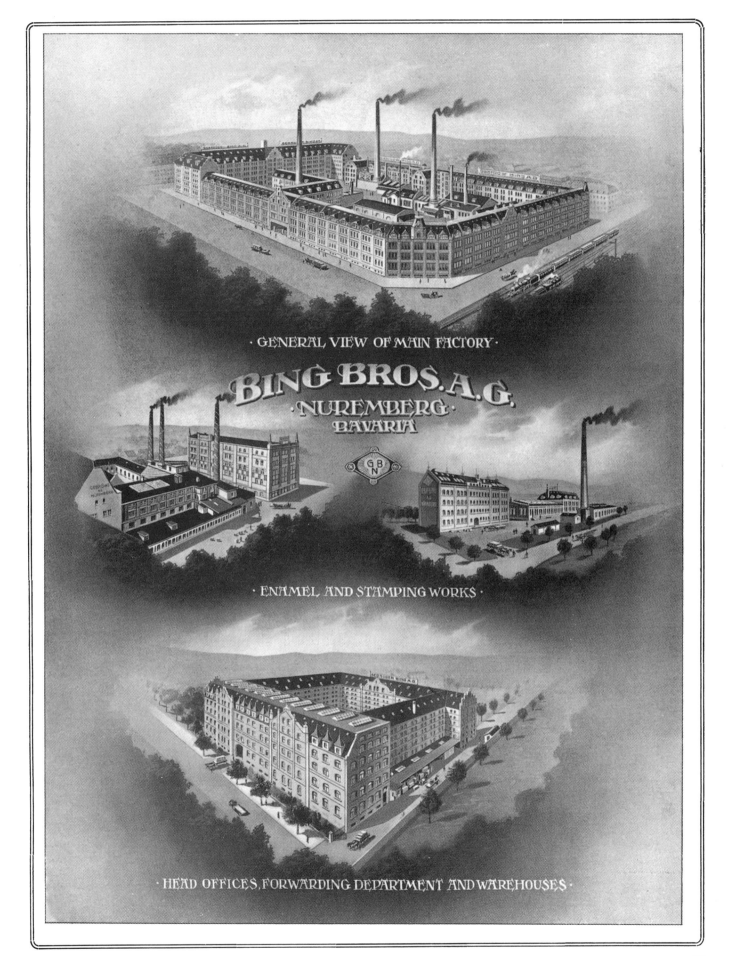

· GENERAL VIEW OF MAIN FACTORY ·
BING BROS. A.G.
· NUREMBERG ·
BAVARIA
G B N
· ENAMEL AND STAMPING WORKS ·
· HEAD OFFICES, FORWARDING DEPARTMENT AND WAREHOUSES ·

Permanent Show Rooms

of

BING BROS., A.-G.
NUREMBERG

BAVARIA

in

LONDON E. C.:	25 Ropemaker Street
NEW-YORK:	381 to 385 Fourth Avenue
BERLIN S. W.:	"Ritterpalast" Ritterstrasse 79
HAMBURG:	Neuer Wall 69
PARIS:	19 Rue Béranger
BRUSSELS:	99 Boulevard Anspach
MILAN:	17 Via S. Maria Fulcorina
AMSTERDAM:	Keijzersgracht 37
BARCELONA:	Pelayo 7
ZURICH:	Uraniastrasse 11
PFORZHEIM:	westl. Karl-Friedrich-Strasse 6
MUNICH:	Neuhauser Strasse 20

At the Leipzig Fair "Koenigshaus" Markt 17/I

SPECIAL PRICE LIST

of

INSTRUCTIVE MECHANICAL, OPTICAL AND ELECTRICAL

TOYS

EDITION 1912

NOTES AND TERMS

PREVIOUS LISTS CANCELLED

The issue of this list cancels all others.

NEW ACCOUNTS

First transactions should be accompanied by Cash or Trade References.

BREAKAGES

Goods are forwarded at the risk of the consignee. When taking in goods we advise you to sign for same as „not examined". We cannot be held responsible for any claims unless we are advised within 7 days after receipt of goods.

RETURNS

All goods are carefully checked before leaving the works. We therefore cannot accept Returns under ordinary circumstances; if however it appears, that a mistake has been made on our side, or if there is any other substantial reason for returning goods, it is necessary under all circumstances to correspond about this and come to an arrangement with us before returning such goods.

GOODS

Goods supplied to the Trade only, no Catalogues are sent to private persons.

ELECTROS

Electros can be supplied for every line; these will be charged for at cost, and the full value will be refunded as soon as we receive the Electros back.

STEAM ENGINES

HOT AIR ENGINES

STATIONARY ENGINES

ELECTRIC GENERATING PLANTS

MODELS

FITTINGS

Model Steam Engines.

The following illustrations have been made as large as possible, so as to convey a very clear idea of the various designs and also to show the fittings better. — The illustrations are reproduced from original photographs. — All details, measurements etc. of the various lines will be found in the accompanying description.

Vertical Steam Engines

with oscillating cylinders.

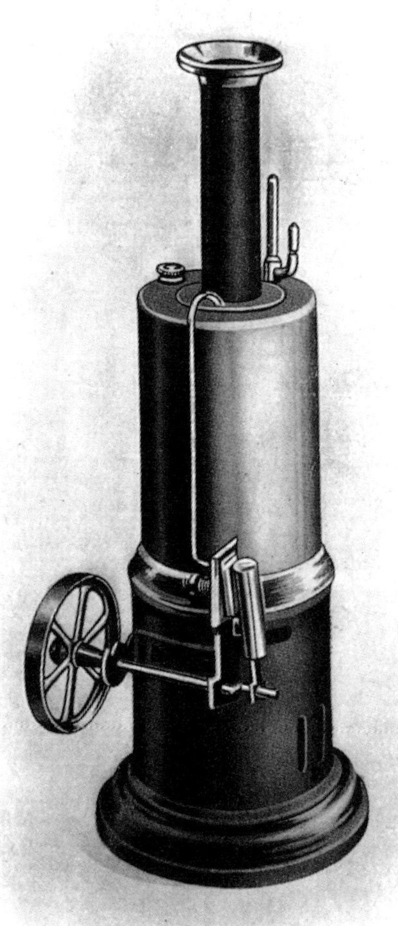

130/12

130/15

Model Steam Engine, good quality, with brass boiler, made of one piece, oscillating brass cylinder, safety valve, reliably working, mounted on metal base, nicely japanned.

No.	Full height incl. chimney	Diameter of Boiler	Length of Boiler			each
130/10	$7^7/_8$ in.	$1^3/_4$ in.	$2^1/_2$ in.	without steam whistle	with round base	**1/7**
„ **/11**	$7^7/_8$ „	$1^3/_4$ „	$2^1/_2$ „	with „ „	„ „ „	**2/2**
„ **/12**	$9^1/_2$ „	2 „	$2^7/_8$ „	„ „ „	„ „ „	**2/9**
„ **/13**	$10^1/_2$ „	$2^1/_4$ „	$3^1/_4$ „	„ „ „	„ square „	**3/10**
„ **/14**	$11^1/_2$ „	$2^3/_8$ „	$3^5/_8$ „	„ „ „	„ „ „	**5/5**
„ **/15**	$12^1/_2$ „	$2^3/_4$ „	$3^7/_8$ „	„ „ „	„ „ „	**7/2**

Fine Model Steam Engines

with oscillating cylinders.

130/31—36

Strong Steam Engine brass boiler **blue oxydised and finely polished,** made of one piece with steam whistle, best oscillating nickelled brass cylinder, safety valve, **finely nickelled fittings,** monnted on cast base, nicely japanned.

No.	Full height incl. chimney	Diameter of Boiler	Length of Boiler	Finish		each
130/31	$9^3/_4$ in.	2 in.	$2^3/_4$ in.	. . . .	with spring safety valve	**5/2**
„ **/32**	11 „	$2^3/_8$ „	$3^1/_8$ „	. . . .	„ „ „ „	**7/2**
„ **/33**	$12^3/_4$ „	$2^5/_8$ „	$3^1/_4$ „	with water gauge glass	„ „ „ „	**9/6**
„ **/34**	14 „	$2^3/_4$ „	$3^3/_4$ „	„ „ „ „	„ „ „ „	**12/—**
„ **/35**	15 „	$2^7/_8$ „	$4^1/_8$ „	„ „ „ „	„ „ „ „	**14/6**
„ **/36**	$17^1/_4$ „	$3^1/_4$ „	$4^1/_2$ „	„ „ „ „	with lever safety valve and vapour lamp	**17/—**

Fine Model Steam Engines with oscillating cylinders and reversing gear.

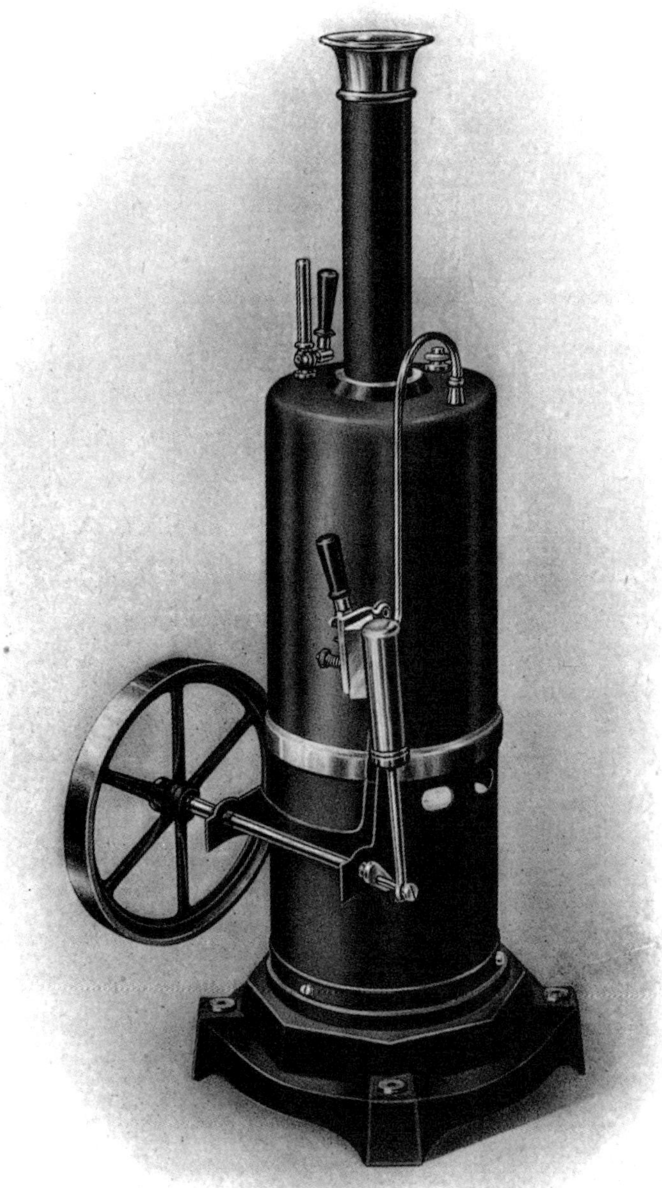

130/45

Strong Steam Engine with oxydised brass boiler made of one piece, with steam whistle, best oscillating nickelled brass cylinder with reversing lever for forward and backward movement, with safety valve, fittings finely nickelled, mounted on cast base finely japanned.

No.	Full height incl. chimney	Diameter of Boiler	Length of Boiler	Finish		each
130/41	$9^3/_4$ in.	$2^1/_8$ in.	$2^3/_4$ in.	. . . .	with spring safety valve	**6/—**
" **/42**	11 "	$2^3/_8$ "	$3^1/_8$ "	. . . .	" " " "	**8/4**
" **/43**	$12^3/_4$ "	$2^5/_8$ "	$3^1/_4$ "	with water gauge glass	" " " "	**11/—**
" **/44**	14 "	$2^3/_4$ "	$3^3/_4$ "	" " " "	" " " "	**13/8**
" **/45**	15 "	$2^7/_8$ "	$4^1/_8$ "	" " " "	" " " "	**16/4**
" **/46**	$17^1/_4$ "	$3^1/_4$ "	$4^1/_2$ "	" " " "	with lever safety valve and vapour lamp	**19/—**

Fine Model Steam Engines

with fixed cylinders and reversing gear.

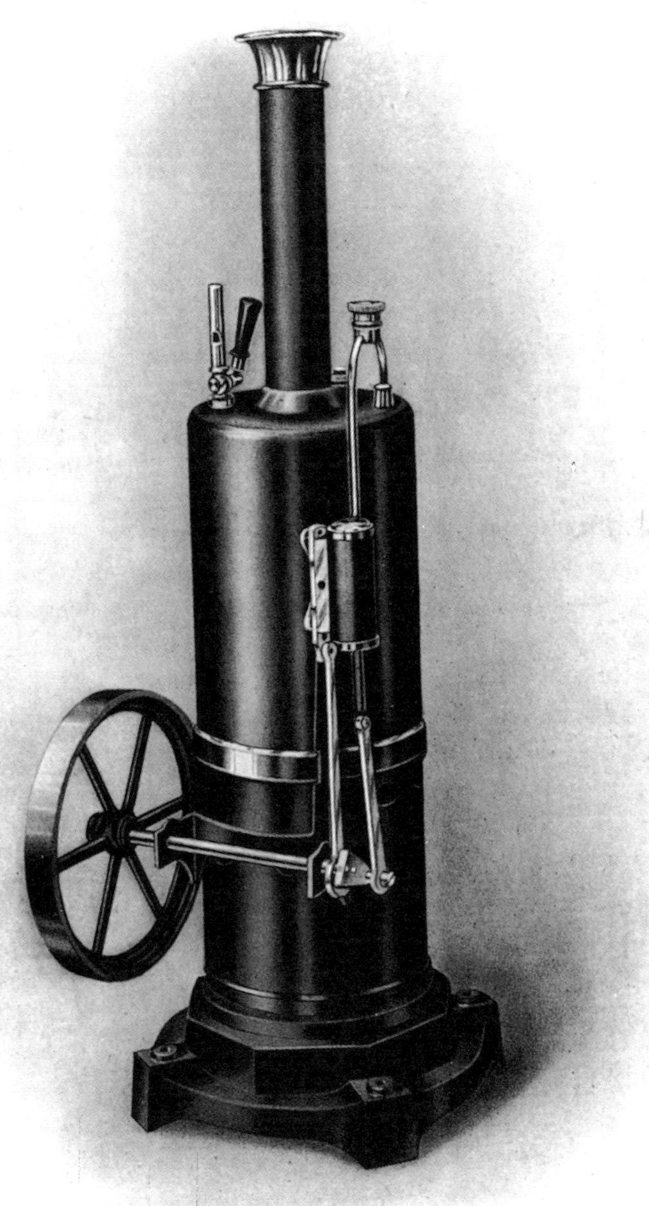

130/54

Fine Model Steam Engine with oxydised brass boiler and steam whistle, with fixed cylinder, **with Slip Excentric Reversing Gear,** will work in whatever direction the wheel is started, with safety valve, all fittings finely nickelled, mounted on cast base finely japanned.

No.	Full height incl. chimney	Diameter of Boiler	Length of Boiler	Finish		each
130/51	9¾ in.	2 in.	2¾ in.	. . . .	with spring safety valve	**7/4**
„ **/52**	11 „	2⅜ „	3⅛ „	. . . .	„ „ „ „	**10/—**
„ **/53**	12¾ „	2⅝ „	3¼ „	with water gauge glass	„ „ „ „	**12/6**
„ **/54**	14 „	2¾ „	3¾ „	„ „ „ „	„ „ „ „	**14/8**
„ **/55**	15 „	2⅞ „	4⅛ „	„ „ „ „	„ „ „ „	**16/10**
„ **/56**	17¼ „	3¼ „	4½ „	„ „ „ „	with lever safety valve and vapour lamp	**21/—**

New Range of

Fine Model Steam Engines

with fixed cylinders and brass fittings.

Steam Engine with brass boiler, mat finish, fixed cylinder with new improved tubular slide valve, flywheel with groove cut in and with extra pulley wheel (small) at the side of the large flywheel, particularly suitable for driving small Dynamos, all fittings of fine brass, mat finish, base and bearings for the fittings in cast iron finely japanned, with vapour spirit lamp.

No.	Full height incl. chimney	Diameter of Boiler	Length of Boiler	Diameter of Fly wheel		each
130/331	12¼ in.	2⅝ in.	3⅞ in.	3½ in.	with water gauge glass	**17/—**
„ **/332**	13½ „	2⅞ „	4¼ „	3⅞ „	„ „ „ „	**20/—**
„ **/333**	14¾ „	3⅛ „	4¾ „	4¼ „	„ „ „ „	**24/—**
„ **/334**	16½ „	3½ „	5¼ „	4¾ „	„ „ „ „	**28/6**

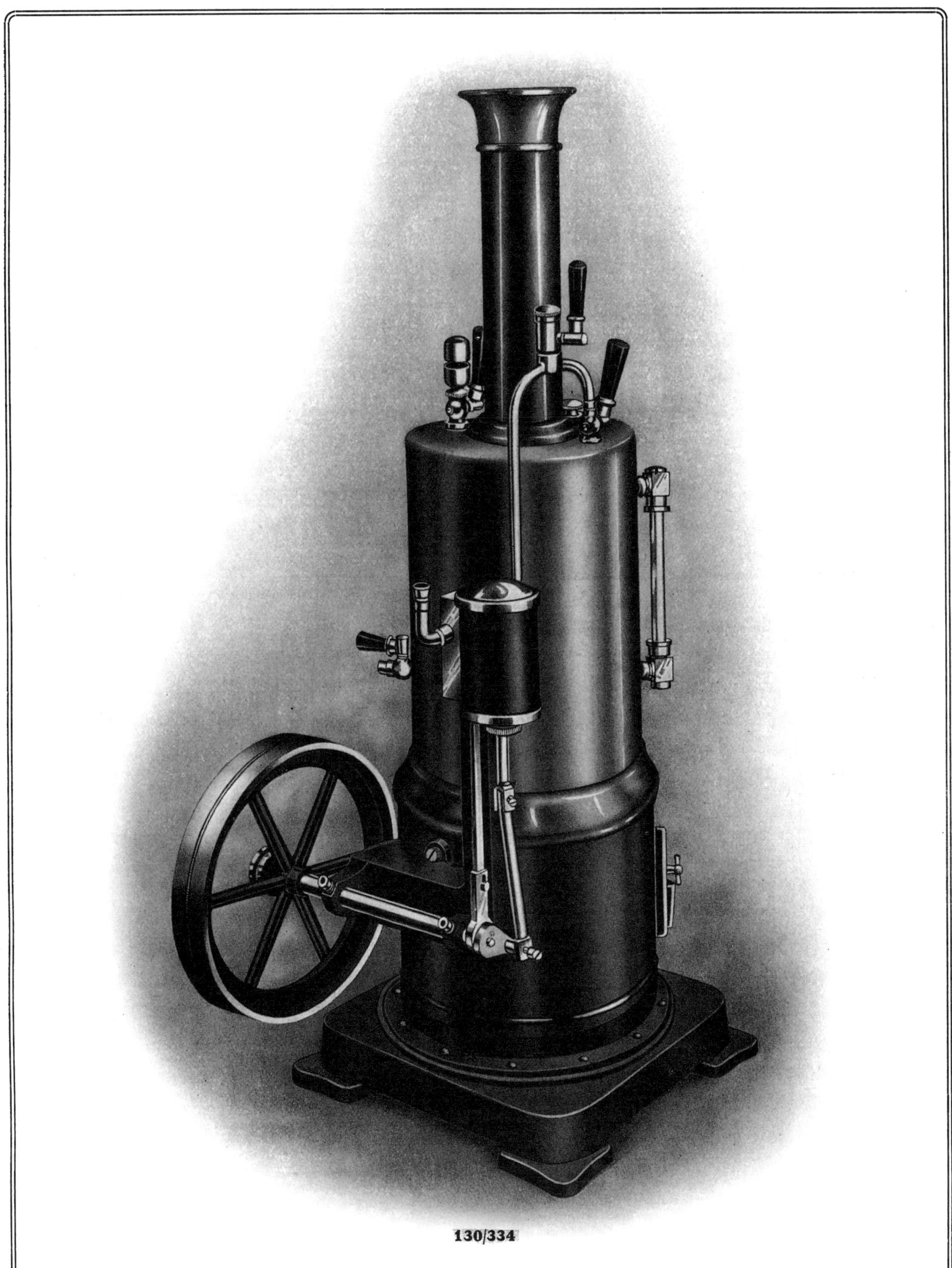

130/334

Superior Vertical Steam Engines.

New Original Design

oxydised brass boiler with fixed cylinder, and new improved tubular slide valve, with complete fittings, all superior quality, with vapour spirit lamp.

No.	Full height incl. chimney	Diameter of Boiler	Diameter of Fly Wheel			each
130/111	12 in.	$2^3/_8$ in.	$3^1/_8$ in.	without feed pump	without governor	**19/—**
„ **/112**	13 „	$2^3/_4$ „	$3^1/_2$ „	„ „ „	„ „	**26/6**
„ **/113**	$14^3/_4$ „	$3^1/_8$ „	$3^7/_8$ „	with „ „	with „	**41/6**
„ **/114**	$16^1/_2$ „	$3^1/_2$ „	$4^1/_4$ „	„ „ „	„ „	**53/—**
„ **/115**	$18^1/_4$ „	$3^7/_8$ „	$4^3/_4$ „	„ „ „	„ „	**68/—**
„ **/116**	$20^3/_4$ „	$4^1/_2$ „	$5^1/_4$ „	„ „ „	„ „	**87/—**

130/114

High Class Vertical Steam Engine

extra heavy make

with fixed cylinder, new improved tubular slide valve, oxydised brass boiler, with complete fittings, all superior quality, with vapour spirit lamp.

No.	Full height incl. chimney	Diameter of boiler	Diameter of Fly Wheel			each
130/95	$14^1/_4$ in.	$3^1/_2$ in,	$3^7/_8$ in.	with feed pump	with governor	**67/—**
„ **/96**	16 „	$3^7/_8$ „	$4^1/_2$ „	„ „ „	„ „	**84/—**
„ **/97**	$17^1/_4$ „	$4^1/_2$ „	$5^1/_4$ „	„ „ „	„ „	**102/—**

130/97

Horizontal Steam Engines

very good value.

130/204

Steam Engine with oscillating brass cylinder, blue oxydised brass boiler, mounted on stamped metal base finely japanned (imitaton tiles)

No.	Full height incl. chimney	Base		each
130/203	$6^7/_8$ in.	$5^1/_2 \times 5^1/_2$ in.	. . . .	**3/8**
„ **/204**	$7^1/_2$ „	$6^1/_4 \times 6^1/_4$ „	superior finish	**4/6**

Horizontal Model Steam Engine.

130/205

Steam Engine, with oscillating brass cylinder, oxydised brass boiler with safety valve and steam whistle, fly wheel mounted on cast stand, with dummy governor, the whole engine mounted on metal base, finely japanned (imitation tiles).

No.	Full height incl. chimney	Base	Length of Boiler	each
130/205	$7^7/_8$ in.	$7^1/_8 \times 7^1/_8$ in.	$3^1/_2$ in.	**6/—**

Reliable, Strong Steam Engines

Factory Type Engine

with fixed slide valve cylinder, brass boiler in blue oxydised steel casing, with safety valve and finely nickelled fittings, steam jet oiler with stamped chimney (imitation brickwork) mounted on strong wooden base with fine stamped coloured metal plate (imitation tiles).

No.	Full height incl. chimney	Base			each
130/271	$12^1/_4$ in.	$10^3/_8 \times 5^1/_4$ in.	. . . .	. . . .	**11/4**
„ **/272**	$13^3/_4$ „	$13^1/_2 \times 6^1/_4$ „	with bell steam whistle	with steam pressure gauge	**17/2**
„ **/273**	15 „	15 $\times 6^7/_8$ „	„ „ „ „	„ „ „ „	**22/8**

130/273

Superior Steam Engines

improved pattern, with oscillating brass cylinder and reversing gear, blue oxydised brass boiler, safety valve, steam whistle and stamped chimney (imitation brickwork), all fittings finely nickelled, mounted on strong wooden base with fine stamped coloured metal plate (imitation tiles).

No.	Full height incl. chimney	Base	Boiler length	Boiler diameter	Finish	each
130/211	9¼ in.	6½×6½ in.	3⅛ in.	1½ in.	without water gauge glass " outlet tap	**7/6**
" **/212**	10⅜ "	6⅞×6⅞ "	3⅞ "	1¾ "	without water gauge glass " outlet tap	**9/—**
" **/213**	11¼ "	7⅝×7⅝ "	3⅞ "	2⅞ "	with water gauge glass without outlet tap	**11/4**
" **/214**	12½ "	8½×8½ "	4⅞ "	2⅛ "	with water gauge glass without outlet tap	**13/8**
" **/215**	13½ "	11¼×9⅝ "	5⅞ "	2⅛ "	with water gauge glass, outlet tap, steam dome and vapour spirit lamp	**22/8**

130/215

Superior Horizontal Steam Engines

with fixed slide valve cylinder, new improved finish

with blue oxydised brass boiler, all fittings finely nickelled and highly polished, with stamped chimney, imitation brickwork, mounted on strong wooden base with fine stamped coloured metal plate (imitation tiles).

No.	Full height incl. chimney	Base	Boiler		Description	each
			length	diameter		
130/231	9¼ in.	6½×6½ in.	3⅛ in.	1½ in.	without water gauge glass with steam whistle	**8/4**
„ **/232**	10 „	6⅞×6⅞ „	3⅞ „	1¾ „	„ „ „ „ „ „ „	**9/2**

Reversible

(Slip Eccentric Reversing Gear)

without lever, will work in whatever direction the fly wheel is started.

No.	Full heigth incl. chimney	Base	Boiler		Description	each
			length	diameter		
130/233	11¼ in.	7⅝×7⅝ in.	3⅞ in.	2⅞ in.	with water gauge glass, with steam whistle	**12/6**
„ **/234**	12½ „	8½×8½ „	4⅞ „	2⅛ „	„ „ „ „ „ „ „	**15/2**
„ **/235**	13 „	11½×9¾ „	5⅞ „	2⅛ „	with water gauge glass, with outlet tap, steam dome, bell steam whistle and vapour spirit lamp	**25/—**
„ **/236**	18¼ „	13¾×13 „			with water gauge glass, outlet tap, steam dome, bell steam whistle and vapour spirit lamp	**33/—**

130/235

Superior Model Steam Engines (Twin Engines)

with oscillating cylinders.

130/222

Horizontal Steam Engines with 2 oscillating cylinders and reversing gear blue oxydised brass boiler, safety valve, steam whistle, stamped chimney (imitation brickwork), all fittings finely nickelled, mounted on strong wooden base with fine stamped coloured metal plate (imitation tiles).

No.	Full height incl. chimney	Length of Boiler	Diameter of Boiler	Base		each
130/221	$10^1/_4$ in.	$3^7/_8$ in.	$1^3/_4$ in.	9×9 in.	without water gauge glass	**17/8**
„ **/222**	13 „	$4^7/_8$ „	$2^1/_{16}$ „	$9^3/_8$×11 in.	with „ „ „	**21/—**

Superior Model Steam Engines (Twin Engines)

with fixed cylinders.

130/242

Fine Horizontal Steam Engine with 2 fixed cylinders, blue oxydised brass boiler, safety valve, steam whistle, stamped chimney (imitation brickwork), all fittings finely nickelled, mounted on strong wooden base with fine stamped coloured metal plate (imitation tiles).

No.	Full height incl. chimney	Length of Boiler	Diameter of Boiler	Base		each
130/241	$12^1/_2$ in.	$4^3/_4$ in.	$2^1/_8$ in.	9×9 in.	without water gauge glass	**19/4**
" **/242**	$13^1/_2$ "	$6^1/_8$ "	$2^3/_8$ "	$9^3/_8$×11 in.	with " " "	**23/—**

Horizontal Model Steam Engine

Model of a slide-valve Engine with fixed cylinder

with large casing and Dummy slide valve action, large fly wheel, blue oxydised brass boiler, with water gauge glass, starting and outlet tap, with steam bell whistle, all fittings highly nickelled, mounted on base of sheet-iron finely japanned.

No.	Full height incl. chimney	Length of Boiler	Diameter of Boiler	Diameter of Fly wheel	Base	each
130/120	$18^1/_2$ in.	$7^1/_4$ in.	$2^3/_4$ in.	$4^3/_4$ in.	$12^3/_4 \times 12^3/_4$ in.	**34/—**

130/120

Superior Model Steam Engine, Best Make

greatly improved

with finest fixed cylinder, tubular slide valve, blue oxydised brass boiler, safety valve, bell steam whistle, steam jet oiler, water gauge, outlet- and Starting tap, vapour spirit lamp, chimney stamped, imitation brickwork, finely japanned, steam exhaust through chimney. All fittings finely nickelled, engine mounted on iron base the whole mounted upon a wooden base with finely stamped coloured metal plate. With feed pump and reversing gear.

No.	Full height incl. chimney	Diameter of Boiler	Length of Boiler	Diameter of Fly wheel	Base		each
130/301	13 3/4 in.	2 1/8 in.	5 7/8 in.	3 1/2 in.	10 5/8×9 3/8 in.	without governor	**42/—**
„ **/302**	16 1/2 „	2 3/4 „	7 1/2 „	4 1/8 „	12 3/4×19 3/4 „	with „	**59/—**
„ **/303**	19 „	3 1/2 „	9 „	4 3/4 „	14 3/4×14 1/4 „	„ „ 1 outlet tap and three way cock	**86/—**

130/303

Fine Model Steam Engine

with fixed cylinder

new improved tubular slide valve, with regulating screws and crank guide, feed pump with three way cock, large fly wheel, outlet and starting tap, blue oxydised brass boiler with wide nickelled bands, water gauge glass, bell steam whistle, steam dome, governor, lever safety valve, steam jet oiler vapour spirit lamp, fire door, outlet for condensed water, stamped and japanned chimney, imitation brickwork, exhaust steam passes through chimney, all fittings well finished and highly nickelled, mounted on strong wooden base, with japanned metal plate (imitation tiles).

No.	Full height incl. chimney	Diameter of Boiler	Length of Boiler	Diameter of Fly wheel	Base		each
130/280	19 in.	$2^3/_4$ in.	$7^1/_2$ in.	$4^3/_4$ in.	$13^3/_4 \times 12^3/_4$ in.	with feed pump	**58/—**

130/280

Superior, extra strong Steam Engine
(Twin Engine)

with 2 extra large oscillating brass cylinders, blue oxydised brass boiler, lever safety valve, bell steam whistle steam jet oiler, water gauge, starting tap, governor and fire door, vapour spirit lamp, stamped chimney (imitation brickwork) all fittings finely nickelled, engine mounted on iron base the whole on wooden base, with coloured metal plate (imitation tiles), exhaust steam passes through chimney.

No.	Full height incl. chimney	Diameter of Boiler	Length of Boiler	Base		each
130/225	19 in.	$3^1/_2$ in.	9 in.	$16^1/_2 \times 14^1/_2$ in.	with governor	**72/—**

130/225

Superior Model Steam Engine

Model of a compound engine with high and low pressure, double action cylinders, boiler blue oxydised brass, built into stamped boiler house, imitation brickwork with gallery and steps; all fittings finely nickelled and finished dull steel, with feed pump and three way cock, exhaust steam passes through chimney, with projecting water gauge glass, lever safety valve, bell steam whistle and governor.

No.	Full height incl. chimney	Diameter of Boiler	Length of Boiler	Diameter of Fly wheel	Base	each
130/300	20 in.	$3^1/_8$ in.	$7^1/_2$ in.	$5^1/_4$ in.	$15^3/_4 \times 16^1/_2$ in.	**116/—**

130/300

Extrafine Model Steam Engines

fixed vertical cylinders with tubular slide valve, vertical engine with gallery and steps, with fine blue oxydised brass boiler in stamped boiler house (imitation brickwork), with vapour spirit lamp, feed pump and three way cock, with governor, with highly finished and nickelled fittings, lever safety valve, water gauge glass, steam pressure gauge, steam jet oiler, and steam dome, exhaust steam passing through chimney, mounted on strong wooden base with coloured metal plate (imitation tiles).

No.	Full height incl. chimney	Diameter of Boiler	Length of Boiler	Diameter of Fly wheel	Base	each
130/321	19¾ in.	3⅛ in.	7½ in.	4¼ in.	15×15¾ in.	**160/—**
„ **/322**	23 „	3½ „	8½ „	4¾ „	17×19 in.	**232/—**

130/322

New Highest Class Model Steam Engine

particularly suitable for driving Dynamos.

Very strong and Extra Powerful very best Make and Finish.

Boiler of sheet iron, welded, tested for a pressure of 90 lbs per □ inch (ordinary pressure is 45 lbs per □ inch). Cylinder with new valve motion, large fly wheel, feed pump, correct working Pressure Gauge, steam whistle, lever safety valve, steam dome, water gauge glass, starting tap, 2 outlet taps, large steam jet oiler with tap, new extra powerful Paraffin-vapour lamp (D. R. G. M.), best fittings, superior make and finish throughout. Exhaust steam passes through chimney, mounted on strong base with coloured metal plate.

No.	Full height incl. chimney	Length of Boiler	Diameter of Boiler	Diameter of Fly wheel	Base	each
130/345	30 in.	12¾ in.	5⅝ in.	8¼ in.	21¾×21¾ in.	**432/—**

The same Engine, but with brass boiler made seamless of one piece, ends screwed on, cylinder with tubular slide valve, (see illustrations a. foot.), otherwise the same finish as above described Engine 130/345.

No.	Full height incl. chimney	Length of Boiler	Diameter of Boiler	Diameter of Fly wheel	Base	each
130/341	22½ in.	10¼ in.	4⅞ in.	5⅞ in.	17¼×17¼ in.	**180/—**
„ **/342**	27 „	11⅜ „	5½ „	7½ „	19¾×19¾ „	**280/—**

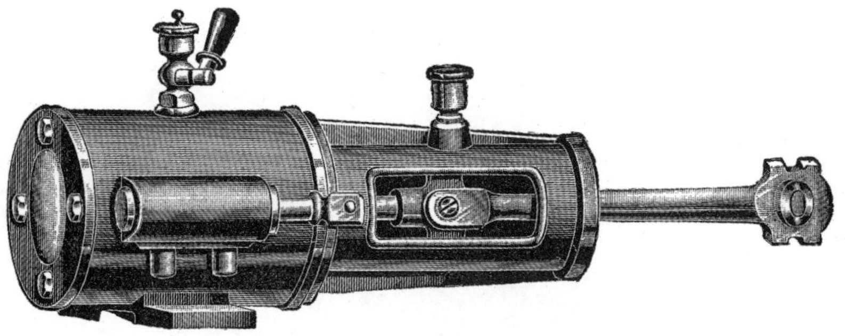

130/345

Dynamo Plants, Electric Lighting Outfits
Steam Engines,
coupled with Dynamos generating electric light

Absolutely reliable. *Large capacity.*

with blue oxydised brass boiler, with oscillating cylinder, all fittings finely nickelled, with safety valve, water gauge glass, steam jet oiler, starting tap, vapour spirit lamp, with electric lamp. Capacity of dynamo 4 Volt, 0,2 Ampères, if 4000 revolutions per minute are made, with oil can and screwdriver. The Steam Engine can be disconnected from the dynamo to work models.

No.	Full height inkl. chimney	Diameter of Boiler	Height of Boiler	Base		each
130/510	11 in.	$2^1/_4$ in.	$6^1/_4$ in.	$10^3/_8 \times 4^7/_8$ in.	with steam whistle	**22/—**
„ **/511**	$11^3/_8$ „	$2^3/_4$ „	$6^7/_8$ „	$12^3/_4 \times 5^1/_2$ „	with bell steam whistle	**28/—**

13064 Spare electric lamps fitting above engines . . . . doz. **13/—**

For **single** dynamos for connection with any steam engine see section: **ELECTRICAL TOYS.**

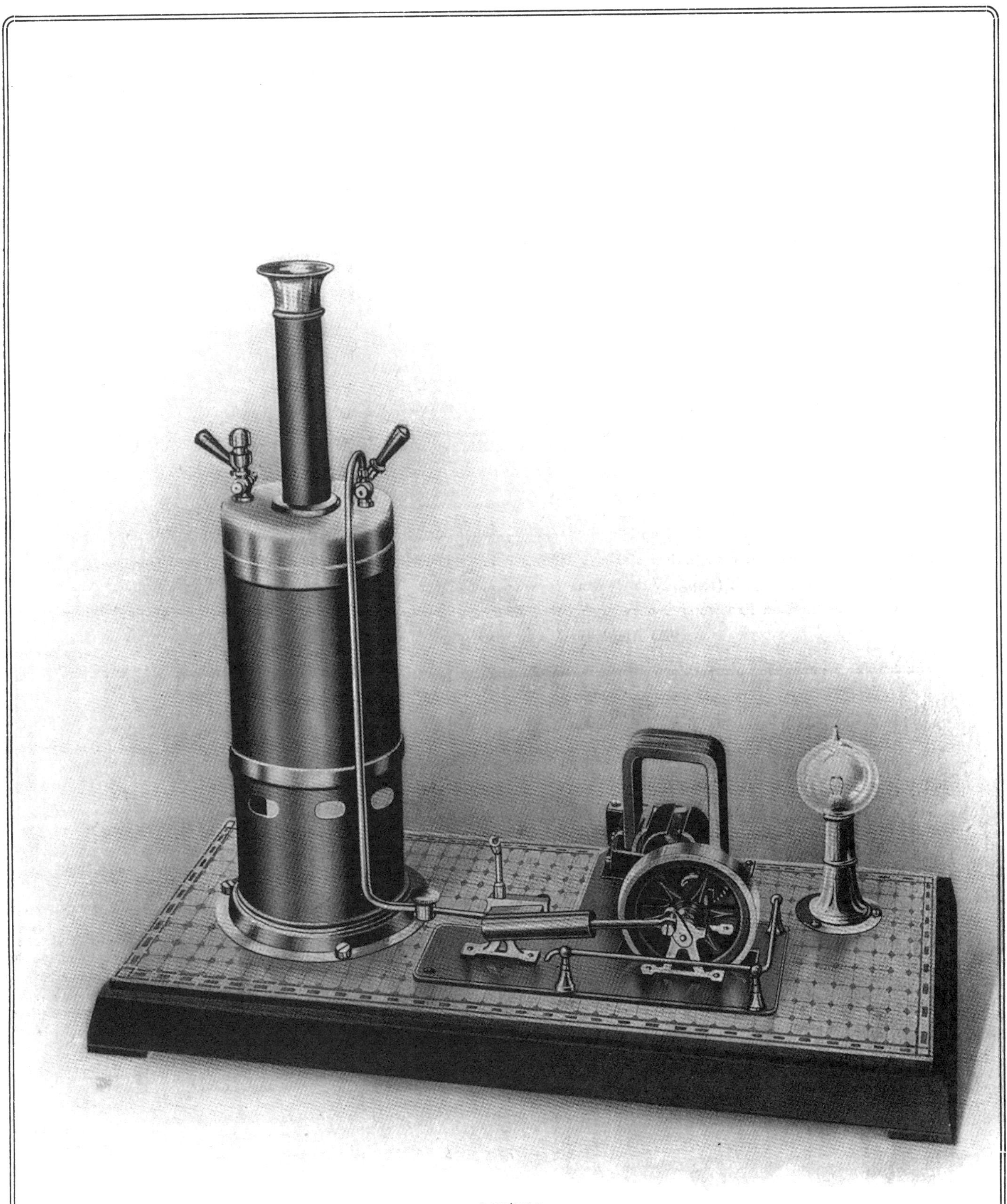

130/511

Dynamo Plants, Electric Lighting Outfits
Steam Engines,
coupled with Dynamos generating electric light

Absolutely reliable. *Large capacity.*

with blue oxydised brass boiler, fixed upright high speed engine, with improved slide valve cylinders with regulating screws and finely nickelled fittings, bell steam whistle, starting tap, steam jet oiler, outlet tap, safety valve, water gauge glass and vapour spirit lamp. With dynamo (can be disconnected) electric lamp (4 Volt) on nickelled stand, with switch, mounted on fine wooden base, with coloured metal plate (imitation tiles). Capacity of dynamo 4 Volt; 0,25 Ampères, if 4000 revolutions are made,

No.	Full height incl. chimney	Diameter of Boiler	Height of Boiler	Base		each
130/521	$13^1/_4$ in.	$3^1/_8$ in.	$7^7/_8$ in.	$15^1/_4 \times 7$ in.	. . . .	**38/6**
„ **/522**	$14^1/_4$ „	$3^1/_8$ „	$7^7/_8$ „	$16^3/_4 \times 7^7/_8$ „	with lever safety valve fire door and disconnecting switch	**50/—**
„ **/523**	$15^1/_8$ „	$3^1/_2$ „	$8^3/_4$ „	$18^1/_4 \times 8^1/_2$ „	with lever safety valve fire door and disconnecting switch	**62/—**

13064 Spare electric globes fitting above engines . . . . doz. **13/—**

For single dynamos for connection with any steam engine see section: **ELECTRICAL TOYS.**

130/523

Dynamo Plants, Electric Lighting Outfits
Steam Engines,
coupled with Dynamos generating electric light

Absolutely reliable. *Large capacity.*

with fine blue oxydised brass boiler, fixed cylinder, with tubular slide valve. Dynamo (can be disconnected), 1 electric lamp (4 Volt) on nickelled stand, switch and 2 pole clamps, so that the current can be used for other purposes, mounted on fine wooden base, with coloured metal plate (imitation tiles).

Capacity of Dynamo 4 Volt 0,25 Ampères.

A beautiful most instructive toy. *Very good value.*

No.	Full height incl. chimney	Length of Boiler	Diameter of Boiler	Base	each
130/541	$13^1/_2$ in.	$5^7/_8$ in.	$2^1/_8$ in.	$11\times9^3/_8$ in.	**30/6**
„ **/542**	15 „	$6^7/_8$ „	$2^5/_8$ „	$12^3/_8\times11$ „	**38/—**

130/542

Dynamo Plants, Electric Ligthing Outfits
Steam Engines,
coupled with Dynamos

Absolutely reliable. *Large capacity.*

with new powerful Engine, with improved slide valve cylinders, fine blue oxydised brass boiler with complete fittings, correctly indicating steam pressure gauge, dynamo in superior finish, mechanical parts of the engine all finely polished, base etc. mat black japanned, with driving belt, connecting engine and dynamo, with switch and pole clamps for conducting the electric current produced by the dynamo. All fittings highly nickelled. Boiler house and chimney stamped (imitation brickwork), with feed pump, three way cock, lever safety valve, bell steam whistle, steam jet oiler, steam dome, fire door, vapour spirit lamp, with heater for feed water on chimney, exhaust steam passes through chimney, mounted on strong wooden base with finely japanned metal plate.

No.	Full height incl. chimney	Diameter of Boiler	Length of Boiler	Diameter of Fly Wheel	Base		each
130/381	$16^5/_8$ in.	$2^3/_4$ in.	$7^1/_2$ in.	$4^1/_4$ in.	$13^3/_4 \times 13^1/_2$ in.	with water gauge glass	**80/—**
„ **/382**	$19^1/_4$ „	$3^1/_2$ „	$9^5/_8$ „	$5^1/_4$ „	$15^3/_4 \times 15^3/_4$ „	„ „ „ „	**114/—**
„ **/383**	22 „	$4^5/_{16}$ „	$10^5/_8$ „	$6^1/_8$ „	$17^3/_4 \times 17^3/_4$ „	with water gauge glass superior finish	**159/—**

130/383

Stationary Steam Engines.

Over Type Engines.

130/584

Steam Engines, with blue oxydised boiler, fixed double action cylinder and finely nickelled fittings.

No.	Full height incl. chimney	Length of Boiler	Diameter of Boiler	Diameter of Fly wheel	Base	each
130/581	$8^1/_2$ in.	$6^3/_4$ in.	$2^1/_8$ in.	$2^7/_{16}$ in.	$7^1/_2 \times 3^7/_8$ in.	**9/—**
„ **/582**	$9^3/_8$ „	$7^1/_2$ „	$2^3/_8$ „	$2^3/_4$ „	$8^1/_4 \times 4^1/_8$ „	**11/8**
„ **/583**	$10^1/_4$ „	8 „	$2^5/_8$ „	$3^1/_8$ „	$8^7/_8 \times 4^1/_4$ „	**14/10**
„ **/584**	$11^3/_8$ „	9 „	$2^7/_8$ „	$3^3/_4$ „	$9^3/_8 \times 4^3/_4$ „	**17/10**

High class Stationary Steam Engines

technically perfect and elegantly finished.

Over Type Engines.

130/606

With fine fixed slide valve cylinder, steam jet oiler, safety valve, water gauge glass, steam whistle, large fine iron fly wheel, exhaust steam passing through chimney (imitating smoke) with excellent vapour lamps mounted on elegant wooden base. All fittings are highly finished, screwed and nickelled, ironparts finely japanned with oilcan and screwdriver.

No.	Full height incl. chimney	Diameter of Boiler	Length of Boiler	Base			each
130/601	11 in.	$3^1/_2$ in.	$7^5/_8$ in.	$4^3/_4 \times 8^5/_8$ in.	. . . .	. . . .	**26/—**
„ **/602**	12 „	$2^3/_4$ „	$8^1/_2$ „	$4^7/_8 \times 10^1/_2$ „	with outlet tap, stop tap and bell steam whistle	. . . .	**35/8**
„ **/603**	$13^1/_4$ „	$3^1/_8$ „	$9^1/_2$ „	$5^7/_8 \times 11^3/_4$ „	with feeding pump, three way cock, outlet tap, stop tap and bell steam whistle	governor and lever safety valve	**50/6**
„ **/604**	$15^3/_4$ „	$3^1/_2$ „	$10^3/_8$ „	$6^1/_2 \times 13^1/_2$ „	do. and fine water gauge	do.	**65/—**
„ **/605**	$16^1/_4$ „	$3^7/_8$ „	$11^3/_4$ „	$6^7/_8 \times 15$ „	„ „ „ „ „	do.	**86/—**
„ **/606**	17 „	$4^1/_2$ „	$13^3/_4$ „	$7^1/_2 \times 16^3/_4$ „	„ „ „ „ „	do. and steam pressure gauge	**104/—**

Steam Traction Engines.

130/733

Steam Traction Engine with safety valve, fixed slide valve cylinder, steam whistle and flame guard, blue oxydised brass boiler and heavy fly wheel.

No.	Full height incl. chimney	Length of Boiler	Diameter of Boiler		each
130/731	$9\frac{3}{4}$ in.	$6\frac{5}{8}$ in.	$1\frac{15}{16}$ in.	without outlet tap, without steam whistle, without water gauge	**15/4**
„ **/732**	$11\frac{5}{8}$ „	$7\frac{7}{8}$ „	$2\frac{5}{16}$ „	with „ „ „ „ „ „ „ „	**19/—**
„ **/733**	$13\frac{1}{2}$ „	9 „	$2\frac{3}{4}$ „	„ „ „ with bell „ „ with „ „	**22/8**

Steam Rollers.

New Improved Models
very realistic.

130/742

Steam Roller, with reversing gear, running backward and forward, with oscillating brass cylinder, safety valve, steam whistle and flame guard. With blue oxydised brass boiler and solid fly wheel.

No.	Full height incl. chimney	Total length	Width	each
130/741	$6^1/_2$ in.	$9^3/_8$ in.	$4^1/_8$ in.	**14/—**
„ **/742**	$7^1/_2$ „	$10^5/_8$ „	$4^7/_8$ „	**19/—**

Extra powerful Hot Air Engines

with deplacer and working cylinder fitted into each other.

By this important improvement a considerably higher power is attained, as the utilisation of the heat effect with this system is raised to the highest perfection.

135/16

Hot Air Engines with deplacer and working cylinder fitted into each other, excellent working, cooling ribs without water cooling, bearings screwed, with extraordinary power, socle finely polychrome japanned, all fittings finely nickelled, mounted on elegant wooden base.

No.	Full height incl. chimney	Base	Deplacer and working cylinder fitted into each other		each
135/11	7½ in.	8⅝×3¼ in.	with 1 deplacer and 1 working cylinder		**5/2**
„ **/12**	9½ „	8⅝×3½ „	„ 2 „ „ 2 „ „		**9/8**
„ **/15**	9¼ „	10⅜×5⅛ „	„ 1 „ „ 1 „ „	with reversing gear for forward and backward movement	**8/—**
„ **/16**	12½ „	10⅝×5½ „	„ 2 „ „ 2 „ „	with reversing gear for forward and backward movement	**13/8**

Extra powerful Hot Air Engines.

135/22

Hot Air Engines, with the deplacer and working cylinder fitted into each other, excellent working, without water cooling, with extraordinary power, socle cast iron, finely japanned, fittings highly nickelled, mounted on elegant wooden board, covered with coloured metal plate (imitation tiles).

No.	Full height incl. chimney	Base	Deplacer and working cylinder fitted into each other	each
135/21	9 in.	$10^1/_4 \times 4^3/_4$ in.	with 1 working cylinder and 1 deplacer	**13/—**
„ **/22**	$12^3/_4$ in.	$10^1/_4 \times 5^1/_4$ „	„ 2 „ „ „ 2 „	**20/6**

Extra powerful Hot Air Engines.

135/32

with deplacer and working cylinder fitted into each other, excellent working, without water cooling, with extraordinary power, socle cast iron, finely japanned, fittings highly nickelled, mounted on elegant wooden board, covered with coloured metal plate (imitation tiles).

No.	Full height incl. chimney	Base	Deplacer and working cylinder fitted into each other		each
135/31	$13^3/_4$ in.	$14^1/_2 \times 6^1/_4$ in.	with 1 working cylinder and 1 deplacer	with vapour lamp	**28/6**
„ **/32**	$13^3/_4$ „	$14^1/_2 \times 7^7/_8$ „	„ 2 „ „ „ 2 „	„ „ „	**44/—**

Vertical Hot Air Motor.

135/50

Hot Air Motor with 2 deplacers and 2 working cylinders, suitable for driving show pieces, mounted on cast iron base.

No.	Full height	Base	Diameter of Fly wheel		each
135/50	14 in.	$8^1/_4 \times 4^1/_2$ in.	$3^7/_8$ in.	with vapour lamp	**42/—**

Hot Air Engine

with fan (Ventilator).

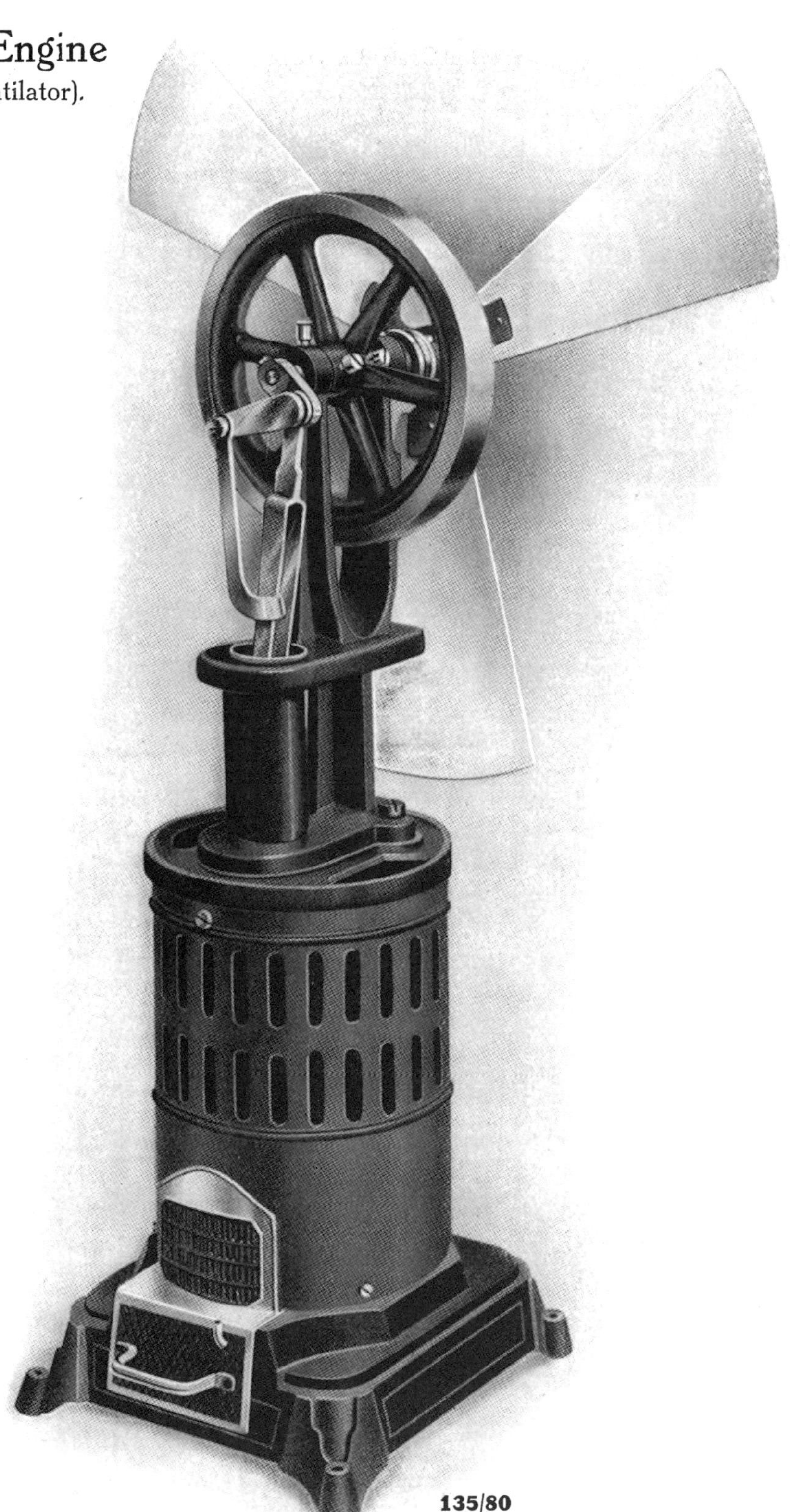

135/80

Deplacer and working cylinder fitted into each other, body and base, made of cast iron, blades of fan made of aluminium, with special pulley wheel for driving models.

No.	Full height incl. fan	Base	Diameter of Fly wheel		each
135/80	17 in.	$4^7/_8 \times 4^7/_8$ in.	$3^7/_8$ in.	with vapour lamp	**32/8**

Hot Air Engine

extrafine and strong

135/41

with deplacer and working cylinder, fitted into each other (new patent gear), spirit lamp with vaporiser, cooling ribs, without water cooling, socle cast iron finely japanned, fittings highly nickelled, mounted on solid wooden base.

No.	Full height incl. chimney	Diameter of Fly Wheel	Base		each
135/41	$16^3/_4$ in.	$6^1/_4$ in.	$15^3/_4 \times 6^1/_4$ in.	with vapour lamp	**94/—**

Fine Hot Air Motor.

Extra large, very powerful engine

specially suitable for working show pieces, extrafine finish, with 2 deplacers, 2 working cylinders, 2 large fly wheels (4 in. diam.), cogwheel gearing (increasing the speed), 3 speed pulley wheel and large spirit lamp (burning abt. 3 hours).

No.	Full height incl. chimney	Base	Diameter of Fly wheel	each
135/60	17 in.	$16^1/_4 \times 11^1/_4$ in.	4 in.	**66/—**

135/60

Model Explosion Motor

for gas or benzine

4 cycle, fitted with adjustable accelerating sparking gear (electric ignition), regulating the revolutions of the fly wheel, developing extraordinary power, suitable for driving dynamos, to produce electric light, or as motoric power for driving working models. As current resource for the ignition any 4 Volt accumulator is suitable (for accumulators see section "Electrical Toys").

No.	Full height	Base	Capacity	revolutions per minute	each
130/950	16½ in.	16½×13¾ in.	about ⅓ H P.	2000	**390/—**

Dynamo

producing electric current for lamps or motors, wires and connection clamps distinctly arranged, generating either continuous or alternating current, recommended for instructive purposes.

No.	Full height	Base	Capacity	revolutions per minute	each
130/960	4¾ in.	12×7⅞ in.	65 Volt 0,8 Ampère	2500	**140/—**

Rotating Electro-magnetic Disk

for experiments in connection with above dynamo (an iron disk in accordance with the revolutions made by the dynamo and the induction thereby generated will turn at an increasing speed) very interesting and instructive experiment.

No.	Full height	Base	each
130/970	2¼ in.	6¼×6¼ in.	**16/—**

130/950

130/960

130/970

Steam Engines with Models.

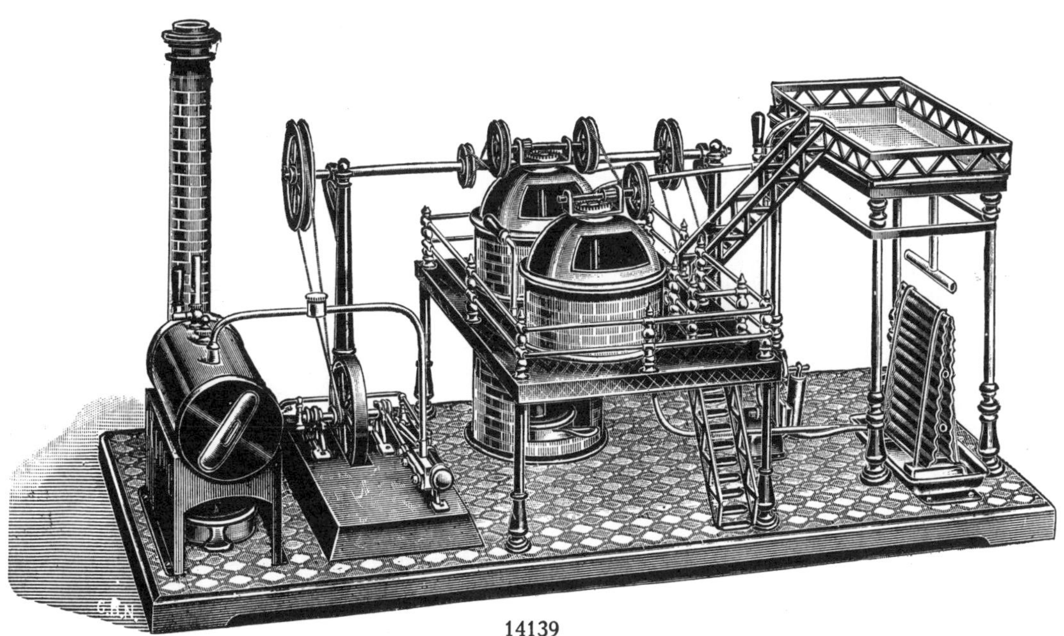

14139

14139 **Brewery, worked by steam,** mounted on firm wooden base with coloured metal plate (imitation tiles), **Superior steam engine** with fixed slide valve cylinder, oxidised brass boiler, safety valve, steam whistle, water gauge glass, all fittings finely nickelled, chimney stamped and finely japanned (imitation brickwork). **Brewery** nicely japanned, exceedingly well finished; all machinery, which is used in a brewery, is exactly reproduced, such as the mash-charger, mash-cooler, brewing-vat &c. &c. with copper fittings. Boiler of steam engine 2 in. diam., $4^1/_8$ in. long, fly wheel $2^1/_2$ in. diam., complete set $19^1/_2$ in. long, 9 in. wide, $10^5/_8$ in. high . . . . . . each **52/—**

13934

13934 **Factory,** complete with **Steam Engine** and **Models,** consisting of: **Steam engine** with oscillating brass cylinder, brass boiler in oxidised casing, safety valve and steam whistle. The shafting works: **1 lathe, 1 grindstone, 1 drilling machine** and **1 hammer,** pulley wheels adjustable with wedges, mounted on wooden board, $16^1/_2$ in. long, $8^3/_4$ in. wide, $12^1/_2$ in. high . . . . each **40/—**

Steam Engines with Models.

10340

10381

10340 **Steam Engine** (with steam whistle) **working Water Mill with Forge,** Base 12 in. long, 5 1/2 in. wide, 9 in. high . . . . each **4/6**

10381 **Steam Engine working Fountain,** Base 13 3/4 in. long, 6 3/4 in. wide, 10 in. high . . . . „ **5/8**

10253

10253 **Revolving Steam Crane with Vertical Steam Boiler.** high speed Steam Engine with oscillating cylinder, reversing gear, water gauge, steam whistle, safety valve, mounted on finely stamped japanned base (imitation brickwork) boiler house and crane to be turned by means of handle on the base, 13 5/8 in. long, 5 1/4 in. wide, total height 12 5/8 in. . . . . each **16/4**

New Working Models for Steam Engines.

9956/466 9956/467 9956/468 9956/469 9956/470 9956/471

9956/466	**Circular Saw,** $3^1/_2$ in. high	doz. **5/—**
„ **/467**	**Grindstone,** $3^1/_2$ in. high	„ **5/—**
„ **/468**	**Polishing Buff,** $3^1/_2$ in. high	„ **5/—**
„ **/469**	**Drilling Machine,** $4^1/_2$ in. high	„ **5/6**
„ **/470**	**Hammer,** $4^3/_4$ in. high	„ **5/6**
„ **/471**	**Eccentric Press,** $4^3/_4$ in. high	„ **5/6**

9956/399

9956/390

9956/228

9956/319 and 305

9956/399	**Windmill,** japanned, 6 in. high	doz. **6/4**
„ **/390**	„ „ $5^1/_4$ in. high	„ **9/8**
„ **/228**	„ fine polychrome, japanning, $6^1/_2$ in. high	„ **11/—**
„ **/319**	**Water Mill with Forge,** fine polychrome japanning, $4^1/_2$ in. long, $4^1/_2$ in. high	„ **12/—**
„ **/305**	„ „ „ „ „ „ „ 7 „ „ $5^1/_4$ „ „	„ **19/—**

9956/472

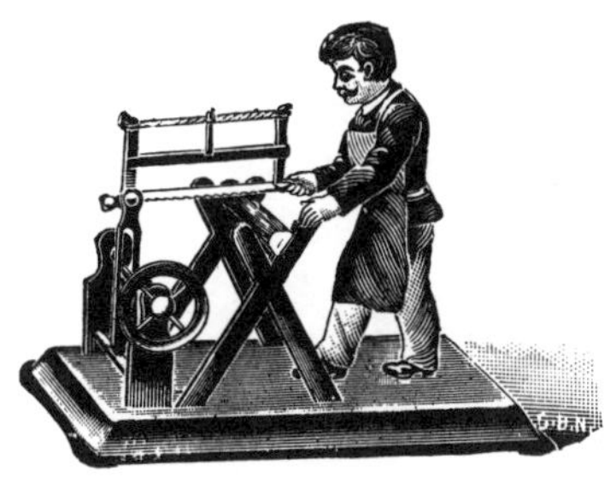

9956/472

9956/142 and 143

9956/472	**A Range of Models,** showing workmen at their work, 6 different patterns, japanned $4^1/_2$ in. high	doz. **9/2**
„ **/142**	**Dredges,** finely japanned, $5^1/_4$ in. high	„ **8/—**
„ **/143**	„ „ „ 6 „ „	„ **9/6**

Working Models, japanned.

9956/127

9956/216

9956/296

9956/127	**Wheel Dredge** with 4 buckets, $6\frac{3}{4}$ in. long, $5\frac{1}{2}$ in. high	doz. **18/—**
„ **/216**	**Dredge, strong make,** with 3 buckets, best finish, $6\frac{1}{2}$ in. long, $8\frac{1}{4}$ in. high	„ **19/—**
„ **/296**	**Dredge** with 4 buckets, 8 in. long, 8 in. high	„ **21/—**

9956/391

9956/473

9956/229

9956/391	**Windmill** with Hammer, 6 in. high	doz. **18/—**
„ **/473**	**Dredge** with Hammer, 7 in. high, $5\frac{1}{4}$ in. long, $4\frac{3}{4}$ in. wide	„ **17/—**
„ **/229**	**Windmill,** strong make, fine polychrome japanning, $9\frac{1}{2}$ in. high	„ **18/—**

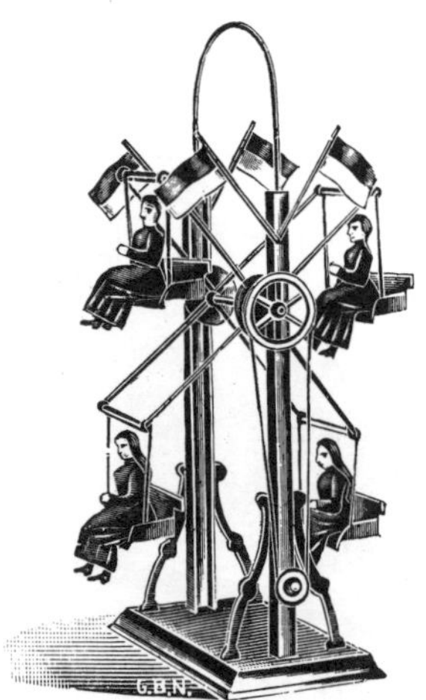
9956/239

9956/495 and /275

9956/301

9956/239	**The Big Wheel** with 4 figures, 12 in. high	doz. **17/6**
„ **/495**	**Organ Grinder** in fine polychrome japanning with Swiss Musical Box, $5\frac{1}{4}$ in. high, with 8 Notes	„ **30/6**
„ **/275**	„ „ „ „ „ „ „ „ $5\frac{1}{4}$ „ „ „ 22 „	„ **52/—**
„ **/301**	**The Big Wheel** with 4 seats and figures, $12\frac{1}{2}$ in. high	„ **34/—**

Models for Steam Engines etc.

from original drawings, humorous, richly coloured on tin, 4¼ in. high, 4 in. wide.

8743/2

8743/6

8743/8

8743/2 **Porter,** moving arm . . . . doz. **9/6**
„ **/6** **Wood Chopper,** chopping wood . . . . „ **9/6**
„ **/8** **Old Man,** catching flies . . . . „ **9/6**

8743/10

8743/11

8743/12

8743/10 **Peasant Woman,** feeding hens and ducks (ducks moving heads) . . . . . . doz. **9/6**
„ **/11** **Musician,** moving arm, with music (revotina) . . . . „ **11/4**
„ **/12** **Organ Grinder,** moving arm, with music (revotina) . . . . . . „ **11/4**

9956/474

9956/475

9956/476

9956/477

9956/474 **Taylor,** moving head and arm . . . . doz. **17/—**
„ **/475** **Cobbler's Boy,** moving head and arm . . . . „ **18/—**
„ **/476** **Cobbler,** moving head and arm . . . . „ **18/—**
„ **/477** **Tinker,** moving head and arm . . . . „ **18/—**

Working Models (Machinery).

9956/222

9956/94

9956/96

9956/304

9956/222 **Polishing Buff,** cast pillar, finely japanned, $3^1/_2$ in. high . . . . . doz. **6/10**
„ **/94** **Circular Saw,** fine polychrome japanning, $4^1/_2$ in. long, 3 in. wide, $3^1/_2$ in. high . . . . . „ **6/10**
„ **/96** **Grindstone,** fine polychrome japanning, $4^1/_2$ in. long, 3 in. wide, 4 in. high . . . . . „ **9/2**
„ **/304** **Forge Hammer,** fine polychrome japanning, $5^1/_4$ in. long, $2^3/_4$ in. wide, $2^3/_4$ in. high . . . . . „ **9/—**

9956/183

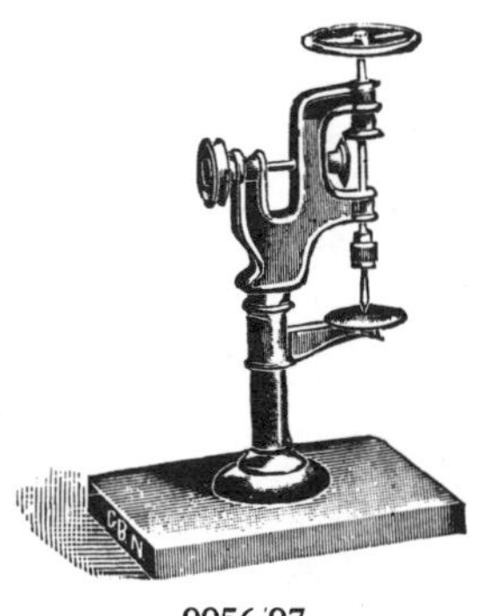

9956/97

9956/95

9956/178

9956/183 **Fan** with 3 nickelled blades on cast pillar, 5 in. high . . . . . doz. **9/—**
„ **/97** **Drilling Machine,** strongly by finished, finely japanned, $5^1/_2$ in. high . . . . . „ **11/—**
„ **/95** **Circular Saw** in fine polychrome japanning, $5^1/_2$ in. long, 4 in. wide, 4 in. high . . . . . „ **11/—**
„ **/178** **Crushing Mill,** finely japanned. $5^1/_4$ in. long, $2^3/_4$ in. wide, $4^3/_4$ in. high . . . . . „ **19/—**

9956/223

9956/303

9956/328

9956/327

9956/223 **Quick Hammer,** strong finish, $4^1/_2$ in. long, $2^3/_4$ in. wide, $4^3/_4$ in. high . . . . . doz. **18/—**
„ **/303** **Hammer,** fine polychrome japanning with corrugated roof, $5^1/_2$ in. long, 4 in. high . . . . . „ **19/—**
„ **/328** **Circular Saw,** cast stand, nickelled table, 3 in. high, $3^1/_4$ in. wide . . . . . „ **11/—**
„ **/327** **Drilling Machine,** cast stand, boring table finely nickelled, $4^1/_2$ in. high, $3^1/_4$ in. wide . . . . . „ **18/—**

Models of Machine Tools

built up from castings.

9956/169

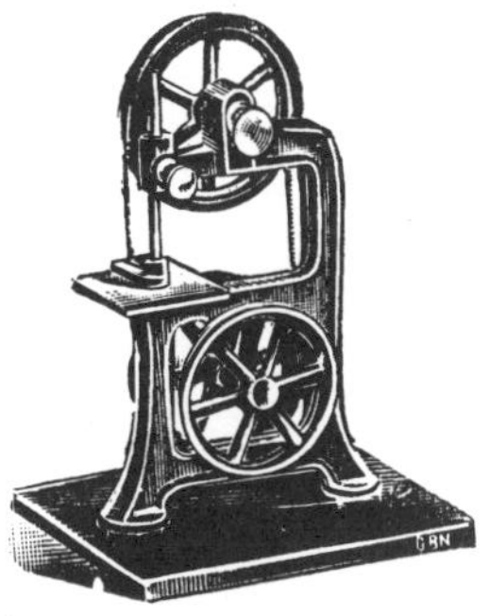

9956/13

9956/478

9956/11

9956/169 **Eccentric Press,** strong finish, 5 in. high . . . . doz. **21/—**
" **/13** **Band Saw,** heavy make, $4\frac{3}{4}$ in. high . . . . " **27/4**
" **/478** **Lathe,** heavy make, $4\frac{1}{2}$ in. long, $2\frac{3}{4}$ in. wide, 4 in. high . . . . " **17/—**
" **/11** **Lathe,** heavy make with table and tools, $4\frac{3}{4}$ in. long, $2\frac{3}{4}$ in. wide, 4 in. high . . . . " **21/—**

Working Models with Moving Figures.

(Figures in polychrome japanning, Models painted.)

9956/347

9956/116

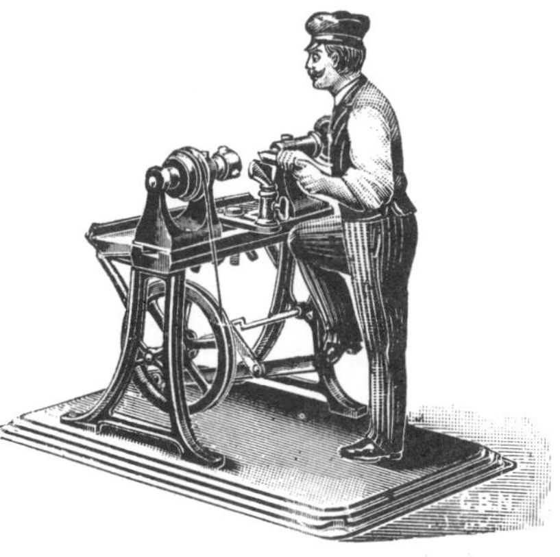

9956/27

9956/347 **Sawyer,** 5 in. high . . . . doz. **10/6**
" **/116** **Sawyer,** 5 " " . . . . " **18/—**
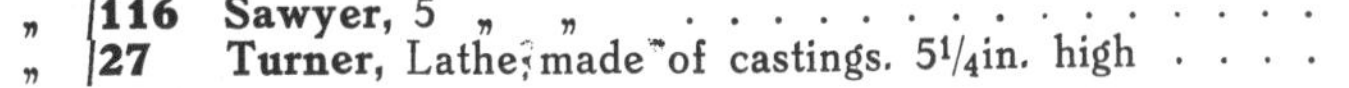
" **/27** **Turner,** Lathe, made of castings. $5\frac{1}{4}$in. high . . . . " **28/6**

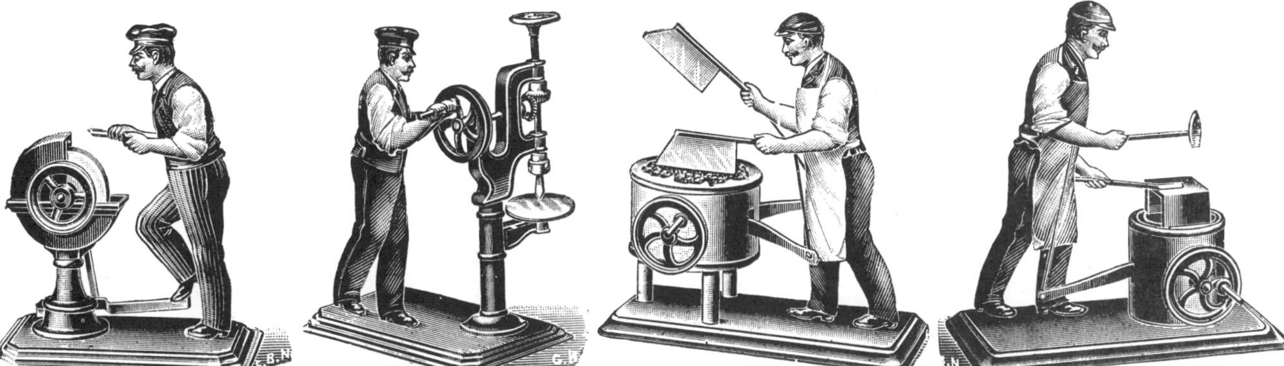

9956/25 9956/115 9956/423 9956/352

9956/25 **Grinder,** Grindstone made from castings, $5\frac{1}{4}$ in. high . . . . doz. **18/—**
" **/115** **Driller,** finely japanned, $5\frac{1}{4}$ in. high . . . . " **18/—**
" **/423** **Butcher,** $5\frac{1}{4}$ in. high . . . . " **19/—**
" **/352** **Smith,** $5\frac{1}{4}$ in. high . . . . " **19/—**

A New Range of Good Working Models of Machine Tools

built up from castings, finely japanned, Fittings finely nickelled, polished wood base.

For suitable Shaftings see Page 83—86.

9956/455

9956/456

9956/458

9956/455	**Grindstone,** $3^3/_4$ in. high	doz. **19/—**
„ **/456**	**Drilling Machine,** $4^1/_2$ in. high	„ **26/—**
„ **/458**	**Circular Saw,** $3^1/_4$ in. high	„ **32/—**

9956/457

9956/459

9956/457	**Eccentric Press,** 5 in. high	doz. **34/6**
„ **/459**	**Quick Hammer,** $4^3/_4$ in. high.	each **3/—**

9956/461

9956/462

9956/461	**Band Saw,** with adjustable tension, $5^1/_4$ in. high	each **3/8**
„ **/462**	**Lathe,** with tools, 4 in. high	„ **4/2**

High-class Working Models

built up from castings, finely japanned, fittings highly nickelled, correctly working, very useful for instructive purposes.

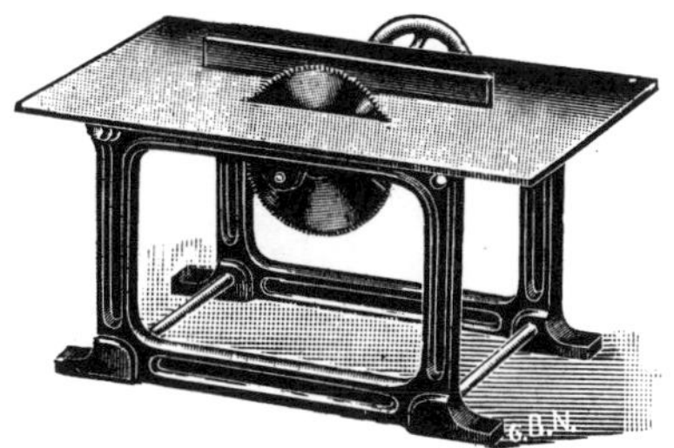

9956/430 to /432

9956/446 and /447

9956/442 and /443

9956/430	**Circular Saw** with removable table and adjustabel guide rail, fine steel saw and pulley wheel $4^{1}/_{2}$ in. long, $3^{1}/_{8}$ in. wide	each **3/6**
„ **/431**	do. $6^{1}/_{2}$ in. long, $4^{3}/_{8}$ in. wide	„ **5/4**
„ **/432**	do. 8 in. long, $5^{1}/_{2}$ in. wide	„ **7/10**
„ **/446**	**Polishing Machine** with 2 speed pulleys, $3^{1}/_{2}$ in. high, diam. of disc 2 in.	„ **3/10**
„ **/447**	do. $4^{3}/_{4}$ in. high, diam. of disc $2^{3}/_{4}$ in.	„ **6/10**
„ **/442**	**Horizontal Polishing Machine** with pulley wheels, $4^{1}/_{8}$ in. high, $2^{3}/_{4}$ in. diam. of polishing disc	„ **5/4**
„ **/443**	do. $5^{1}/_{8}$ in. high, $7^{1}/_{2}$ in. diam. of polishing disc	„ **11/8**

9956/444 and /445

9956/441

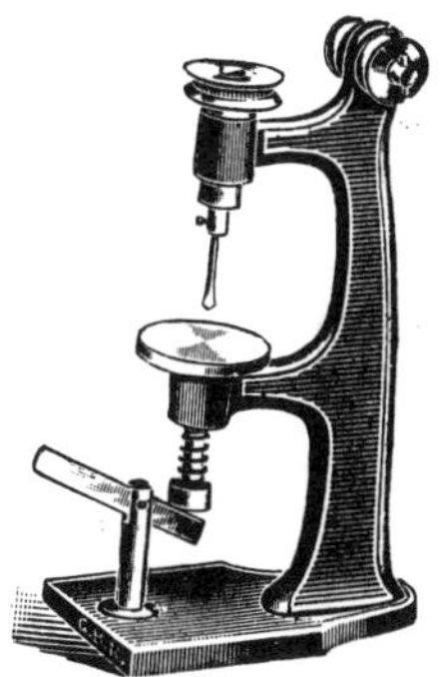

9956/201

9956/444	**Vertical Polishing Machine** with movable rest and pulley wheels, $4^{1}/_{2}$ in. high, $2^{3}/_{8}$ in. diam. of polishing disc	each **7/4**
„ **/445**	do. $6^{1}/_{4}$ in. high, $2^{3}/_{4}$ in. diam. of polishing disc	„ **15/10**
„ **/441**	**Grindstone,** finely japanned, $5^{1}/_{8}$ in. high, diam. of Grindstone 5 in.	„ **3/6**
„ **/201**	**Drilling Machine** with vertical and horizontal pulley wheels, movable table on spring with drill bit, $4^{3}/_{8}$ in. high	„ **3/2**

High-class Working Models

built up from castings, finely japanned, fittings highly nickelled correctly working, very useful for instructive purposes.

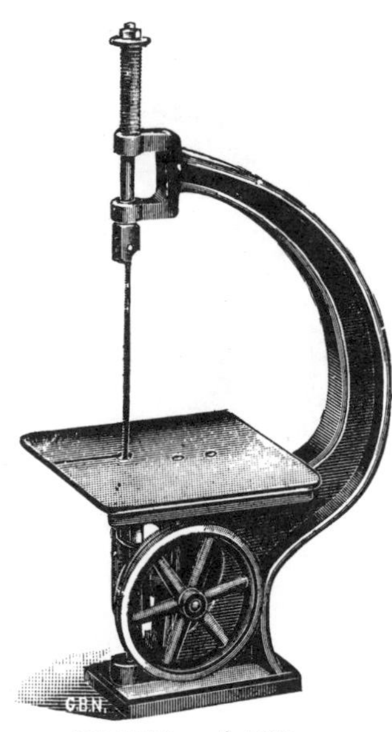

9956/428 and /429

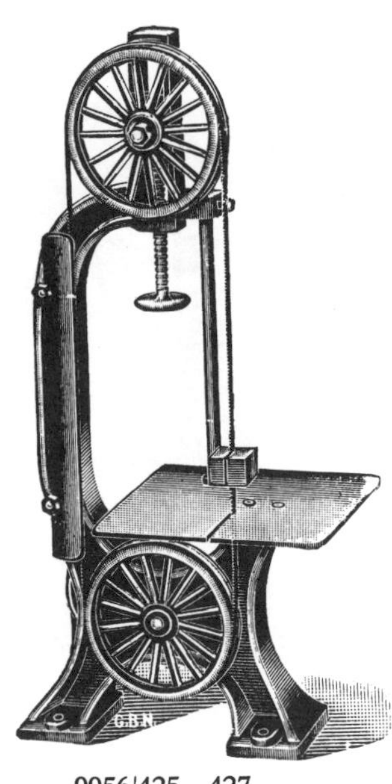

9956/425—427

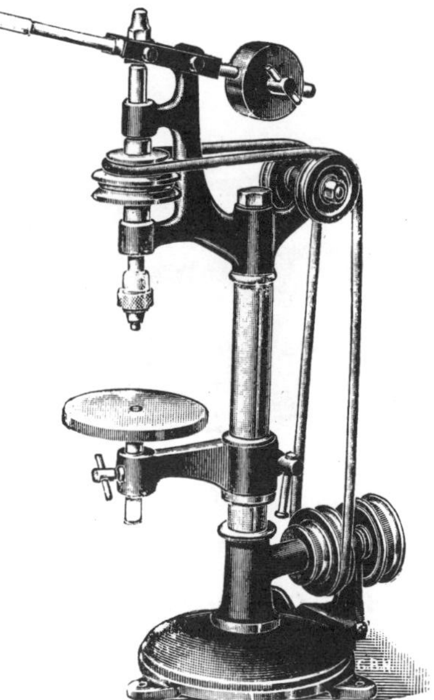

9956/439 and /440

9956/428	**Fret Saw,** for Fretwork, with adjustable tension, $7\frac{1}{2}$ in. high	each **5/8**
„ **/429**	„ „ „ „ „ „ „ $10\frac{1}{2}$ „ „	„ **9/10**
„ **/425**	**Band Saw,** with guide wheels, screw, adjustable wheels, adjustable tension, $7\frac{3}{4}$ in. high	„ **7/4**
„ **/426**	„ „ „ „ „ „ „ „ „ „ $9\frac{1}{2}$ „ „	„ **9/10**
„ **/427**	„ „ „ „ „ „ „ „ „ „ $11\frac{1}{4}$ „ „	„ **17/—**
„ **/439**	**Sensitive Drills,** with conical speed pulley, $9\frac{1}{2}$ in. high	„ **13/4**
„ **/440**	„ „ „ „ „ „ 13 „ „	„ **30/6**

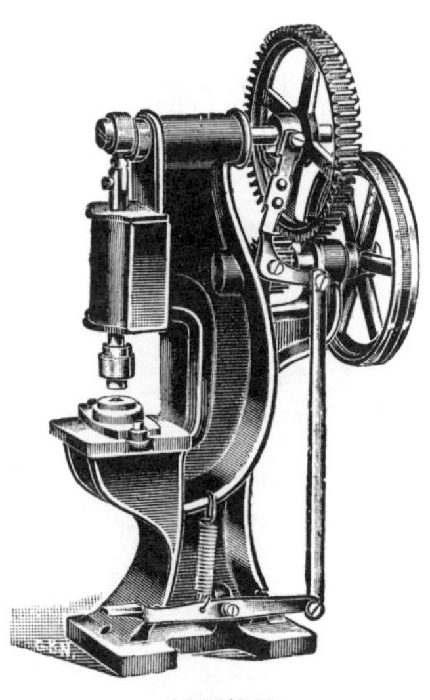

9956/240

9956/435

9956/192

9956/240	**Eccentric Press,** with cog wheel gearing, foot clutch, fine steel stamp. All parts screwed, $6\frac{7}{8}$ in. × 4 in.	each **11/8**
„ **/435**	**Triple Vertical Saw,** with 3 saws, $7\frac{1}{4}$ in. high	„ **15/4**
„ **/192**	**Eccentric Press,** fine model of the Machine used in the principal Toy Factories, $6\frac{7}{8}$ in. × 4 in.	„ **23/8**

High-class Working Models

built up from castings, finely japanned, fittings highly nickelled, correctly working, very useful for instructive purposes.

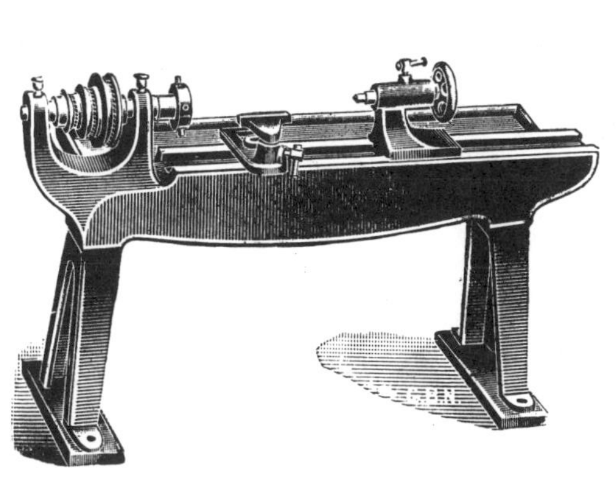

9956/437

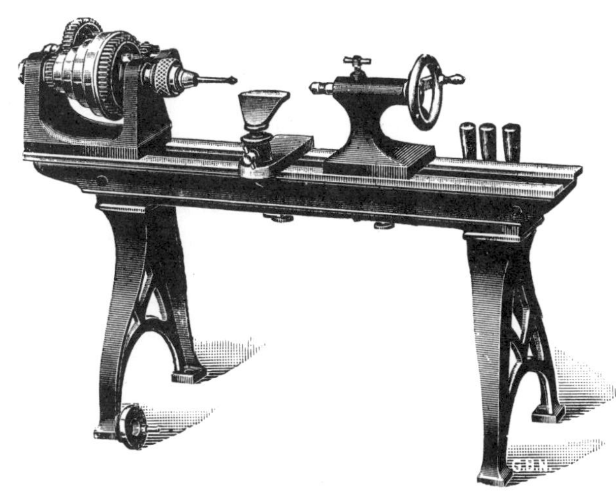

9956/438

9956/437 **Lathe** with three speed pulley, mandrel fitted inside, adjustable head stock with mandrel and rest, oilers in bearings, wooden table, exact finish, $5^1/_8$ in. high, $8^3/_4$ in. long . . . . each **11/6**

„ **/438** **Model Back-Geared Lathe,** three speed pulley, mandrel fitted inside, adjustable head stock, with mandrel and rest, oilers in bearings, wooden table with tools, 8 in. high, 12 in. long . . „ **30/6**

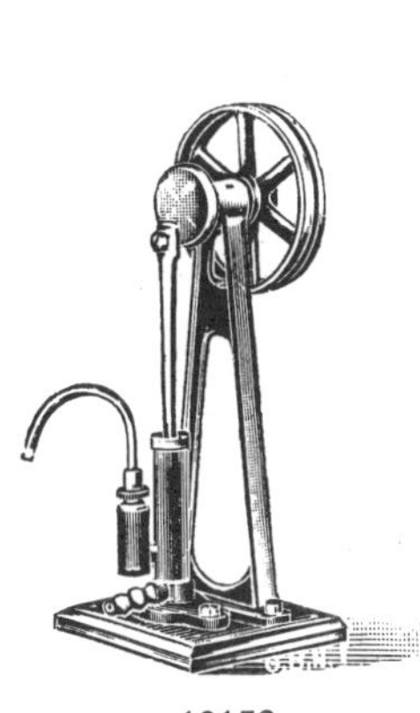

10153

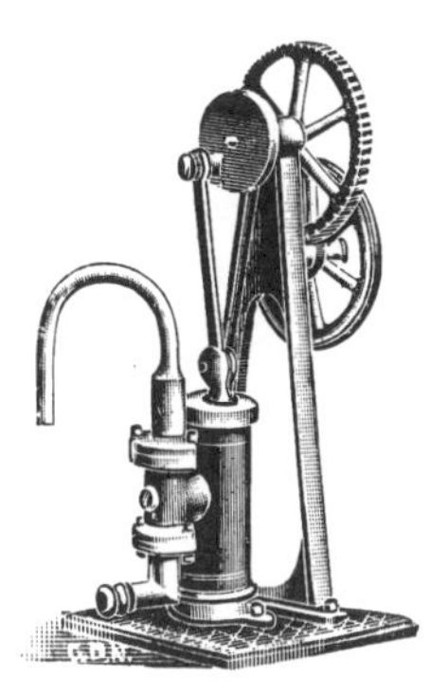

9655

9956/433

10153 **Feed Pump,** highly finished, cast iron stand, pump solid brass, finely japanned, $5^1/_2$ in high . . . . . . each **6/4**

9655 **Feed Pump,** cast iron stand, pump solid brass with cog wheel gear, all parts screwed . . . . „ **13/8**

9956/433 **Horizontal Saw** with screw attachment, to lower the saw while working, $7^1/_8$ in. high, 10 in. long, 3 in. wide „ **13/8**

„ **/434** „ „ „ „ „ „ „ „ „ „ „ 10 „ „ $12^3/_4$ „ „ $3^3/_4$ „ „ „ **20/6**

Large Model Veneer Saw

built up from castings finely japanned, fittings highly nickelled, correctly working, very useful for instructive purposes.

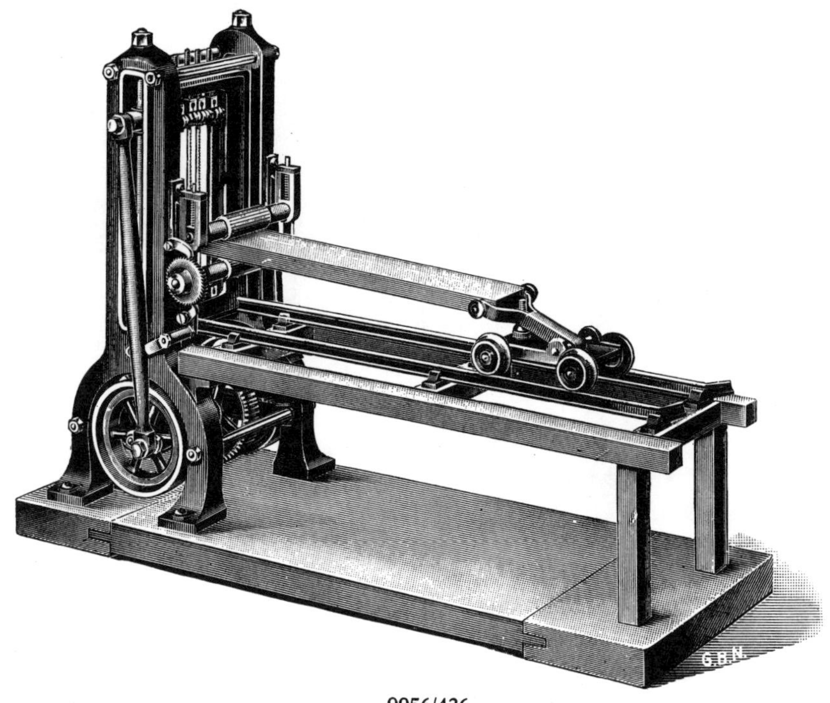

9956/436

9956/436 **Large Veneer Saw** with 4 saws, automatic action, specially geared for light running, $15\frac{1}{2}$ in. long, $6\frac{1}{2}$ in. wide, $11\frac{1}{4}$ in. high . . . . each **50/—**

Model Printing Presses

for Steam Engines etc. or to be worked by hand.

9956/302

9956/377

9956/302 **Rotary Printing Press,** specially geared for easy run with any Steam Engine, Motor etc., finely japanned, with 1 roll of paper, 1 set of rubber types and bottle of printing ink, $6\frac{1}{4}$ in. long, $4\frac{1}{4}$ in. wide, 4 in. high . . . . each **8/—**

8092 Extra India Rubber Types, 60 letters and 10 blocks with pincers . . . . per doz. set **12/—**

8093 Violet Printing Ink . . . . doz. bottles **3/—**

9956/377 **New Rotary Printing Press,** Quick rotation, though easy to work, finely japanned, complete with set of rubber types, roll of paper and bottle of ink, $8\frac{3}{4}$ in. long, $4\frac{3}{4}$ in. wide, $3\frac{3}{4}$ in. high . . . . each **15/10**

10246 Set of rubber types consisting of 60 types, 10 blocks and 1 pair of tweezers . . . . each set **3/—**

8093 Violet Ink . . . . doz. bottles **3/—**

New Comical Working Models.

Figures with original movements.

9956/378

9956/379

9956/380

9956/378 Tailors shop with 3 moving figures, $8^3/_4$ in. long, $3^3/_4$ in. wide, $6^3/_8$ in. high . . . . each **4/10**
„ **/379 Shoemakers Workshop** with 2 moving figures, $8^3/_4$ in. long, $3^1/_4$ in. wide, $6^3/_8$ in. high . . . . . . „ **4/10**
„ **/380 Tinkers Workshop** with 2 moving figures, $8^3/_4$ in. long, $3^1/_4$ in. wide, $6^3/_8$ in. high . . . . „ **4/10**

9956/353

9956/355

9956/358

9956/353 Carpenters at Work, $5^1/_8$ in. high, $7^1/_8$ in. long, $5^1/_8$ in wide . . . . each **2/4**
„ **/355 Blacksmiths at Work,** $5^1/_8$ in. high, $7^3/_4$ in. long, $3^3/_8$ in. wide . . . . „ **2/6**
„ **/358 Wheel Wrights at Work** with revolving wheel, $5^3/_8$ in. high, $7^3/_4$ in. long, $3^3/_4$ in. wide . . . . . . „ **3/2**

Mechanical Working Models

of good workmanship, with moving figures, finely japanned.

9956/359

9956/357

9956/360

9956/359 **Forging Press,** $8\frac{1}{2}$ in. high . . . . each **3/2**
„ **/357** **Joiner with Pendulum Saw,** $7\frac{1}{8}$ in. high, $6\frac{3}{8}$ in. × $6\frac{3}{8}$ in base . . . . „ **3/2**
„ **/360** **Pile Driver at Work,** $14\frac{1}{4}$ in. high, $6\frac{1}{4}$ in. × $6\frac{1}{4}$ in. base . . . . „ **3/10**

9956/365

9956/366

9956/362

9956/365 **Wheelwright,** $6\frac{3}{8}$ in. high, $6\frac{7}{8}$ in. long . . . . each **3/10**
„ **/366** **Chaff Cutter,** $7\frac{1}{8}$ „ „ $5\frac{1}{8}$ „ „ . . . . „ **3/10**
„ **/362** **Street Pavers,** Figures $5\frac{3}{8}$ in. high, Base $6\frac{3}{8}$ in. × $6\frac{3}{8}$ in. . . . . „ **3/10**

9956/389

9956/389

Horizontal Saw,

with carriage on rails, with wood block

$5\frac{3}{4}$ in. high, $4\frac{7}{8}$ in. wide, 8 in. long . . . . each **3/2**

Mechanical Working Models

of good workmanship, with moving figures, finely japanned.

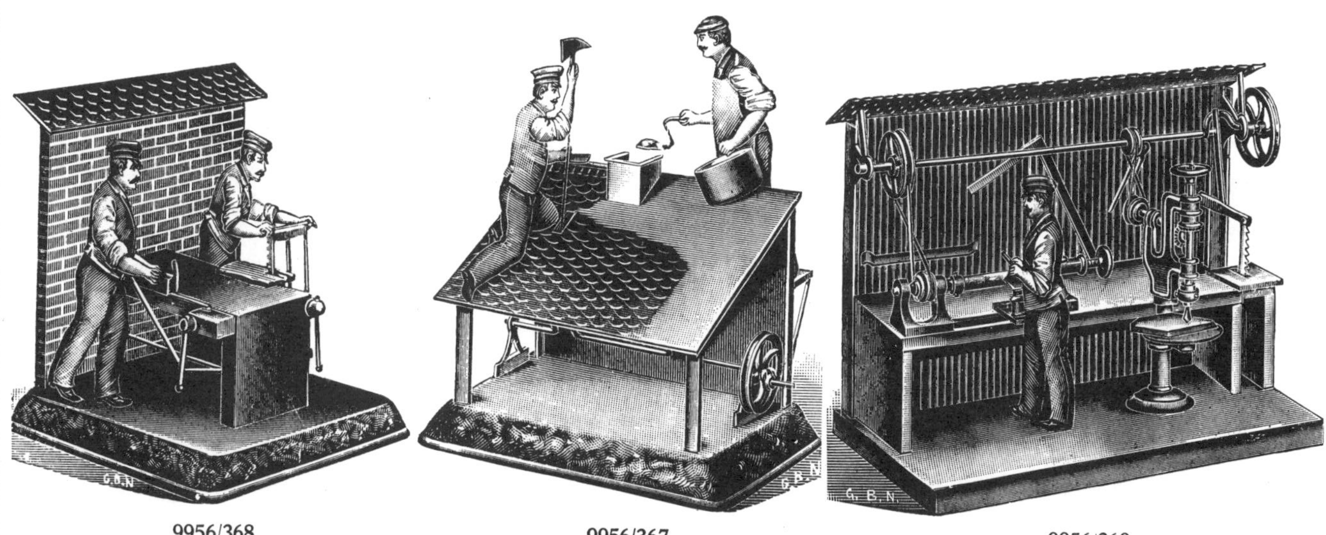

9956/368 9956/367 9956/369

9956/368 **Joiners at Work,** Sawing and planing, $6^1/_2$ in. high, $6^1/_8$ in. wide, $6^1/_8$ in. long . . . . each **4/10**

„ **/367** **Builders at Work,** total height $8^1/_2$ in., base $7^1/_8$ in. $\times$ $5^1/_4$ in. „ **4/10**

„ **/369** **Mechanical Workshop** with Figure, Shafting, Saw, Drilling Machine and Lathe, all movable, $6^1/_8$ in. high, $5^3/_4$ in. wide, 10 in. long . . . . „ **6/2**

9956/167

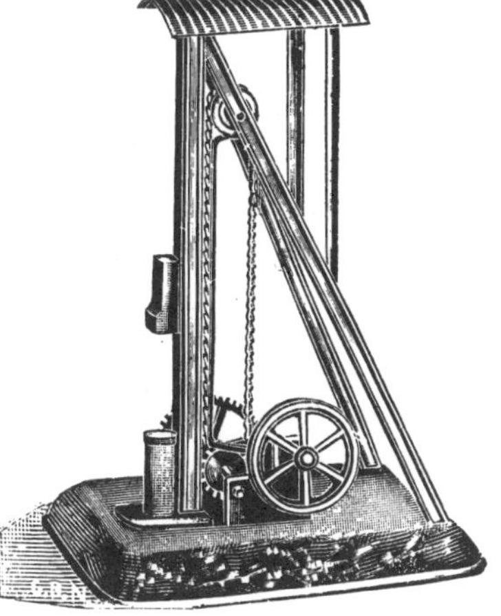

9956/213

9956/285

9956/167 **Smithy** (can be used as showpiece) with 2 movable figures and bellows, 8 in. long, $4^1/_2$ in. wide, $8^1/_4$ in. high . . . . each **6/2**

„ **/213** **Pile Driver,** very strong finish with cog gearing, 10 in. high . . . . „ **4/—**

„ **/285** **Forge,** finely japanned with corrugated tin roof, 7 in. long, $4^3/_4$ in. wide . . . . „ **3/—**

Working Models

of good workmanship, finely japanned.

9956/354

9956/180

9956/356

9956/354 Windmill with Saw, $6^1/_4$ in. high, $3^3/_8$ in. wide, $7^1/_4$ in. long . . . . each **2/4**

" **/180 Dredge,** superior, strong finish, finely japanned with 2 buckets, $6^1/_8$ in. long, $8^1/_4$ in. high . . . . . " **2/6**

" **/356 Mill with Stamping Machine, Windmill with 2 stampers,** 10 in. high, $5^3/_8$ in. wide, $7^1/_4$ in. long " **3/—**

9956/334

9956/363

9956/306

9956/334 Dredge, finely japanned with arrangement for lifting the ballast and throwing it into the funnel $5^1/_2$ in. high, 4 in. wide, $5^1/_2$ in. long . . . . each **3/2**

" **/363 Windmill with Stamping Machine** (Crushing Mill) with 4 stampers, alternating action, $6^1/_4$ in. high, $3^1/_2$ in. wide, 10 in. long . . . . " **3/10**

" **/306 Dredge with Sandmill,** original, strongly finished, 7 in. long, $7^3/_4$ in. high, $3^1/_8$ in, wide . . . . . " **4/2**

Working Models of Superior Quality

finely japanned.

9956/181

9956/289

9956/181 Dredge with Windmill, strong make, finely japanned with 3 buckets, 9 in. long, 10 in. high . . . each **4/2**

„ **/289 Coal Mine,** very original, extra fine, effective finish, plastically stamped and finely japanned, with Engine House, winding shaft with gear and signal bell, moving barrow men, in front, underground working miners (moving), 15¾ in. long, 8 in. wide, 9 in. high . . . . „ **12/6**

9956/337

9956/337 New Dredging Machine, original finish, with raising scoop and tilting chute, with transmission and sand cart, 9⅛ in. high, 10 in. long, 3½ in. wide . . . . each **4/10**

9956/338

9956/338 New Dredging Machine, original finish, with reversing scoop, tilting chute, transmission and sand cart, 11 in. high, 14¾ in. long, 2½ in. wide . . . . . . each **7/10**

Working Models of Superior Quality

finely japanned.

9956/299

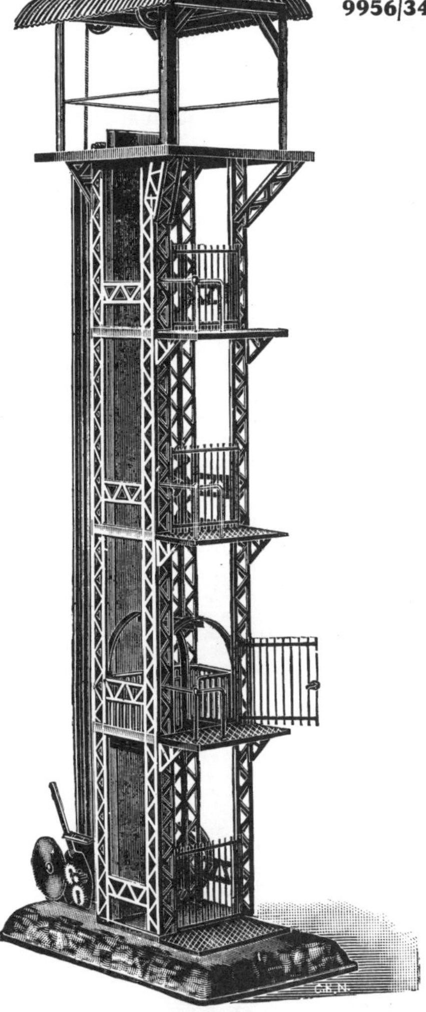

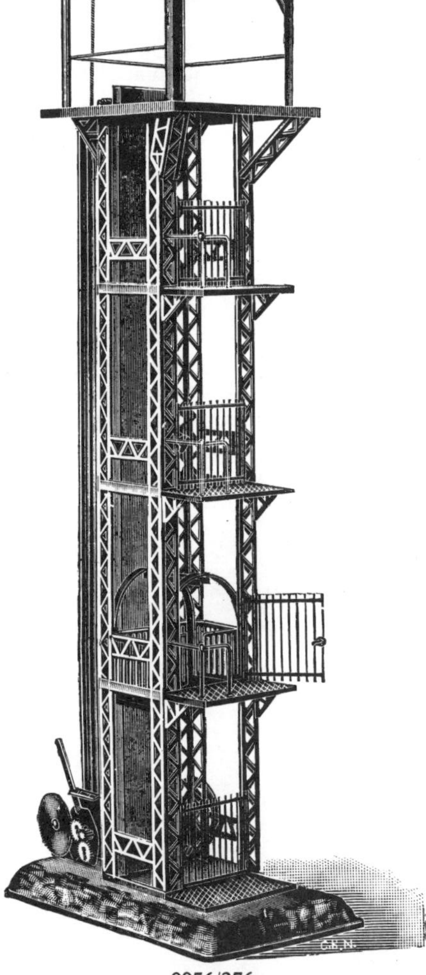

9956/340

9956/299 **Crane,** finely japanned, on metal base, with corrugated tin roof, also to be worked by hand, continuously raising and lowering vessel (endless chain) crane can be turned, $5^{1}/_{2}$ in. long, $8^{1}/_{4}$ in. high doz. **18/—**

9956/340 **Endless Chain Carrier,** with 3 packages, $8^{1}/_{4}$ in. high, $12^{3}/_{8}$ in. long, $4^{1}/_{8}$ in. wide each **5/4**

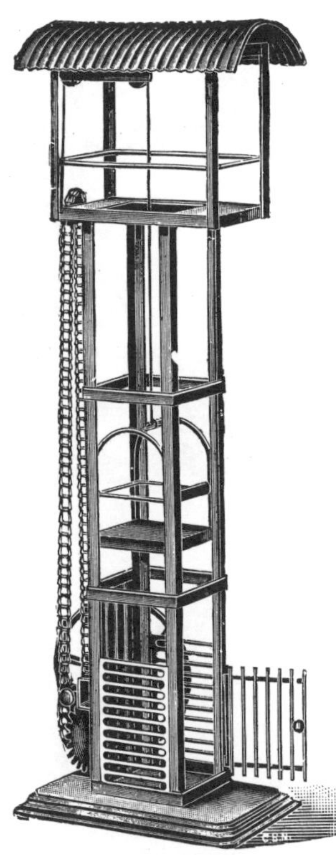

9956/300 9956/376 9956/375

9956/300 **Large Crane,** finely japanned, imitation iron construction, with corrugated tin house, with 3 gear lever for either raising or lowering the goods, or for free run of the wheel, with handle for turning the crane in any direction, total height 17 in. . . . . each **9/6**

„ **/376** **Passenger Lift,** extra large size, well finished, with 4 landings, Mechanical reversing gear for moving upwards and downwards, constructed so as to stop at each floor; Platforms and doors at each floor, 27 in. high . . . . „ **20/—**

„ **/375** **Passenger Lift,** with automatic reversing gear for moving upards and downwards, $14^{5}/_{8}$ in. high . . „ **5/2**

New Working Models of Superior Quality

finely japanned.

10355

10355 **Crane on stamped base** (imitation brickwork) with double action, one action to raise or to lower the load and the other to turn the crane round, with disconnecting lever, 8¼ in. high . . . . each **5/8**

9956/494

9956/490

9956/88

9956/494	**Pump,** finely japanned, with 2 spouts, 7 in. long, 3½ in. wide, 5¼ in. high	doz. **17/—**
„ **/490**	„ „ „ stamped imitation brickwork, 5½ in. high	„ **18/—**
„ **/88**	„ „ „ „ „ „ 7 „ „	each **3/—**

9956/422

9956/484

9956/279

9956/422	**Fountain,** finely japanned, 5¼ in. wide, Basin 3½ in. diam.	each **3/—**
„ **/484**	**Ornamental Fountain,** modern design, finely japanned, 9½ in. high	„ **4/6**
„ **/279**	„ „ very effective finish, finely japanned and stamped in brickwork imitation, with strong pump, 3 lions heads with continuous waterspouts and 2 flowerpots, 5⅛ in. high, 8 in. diam.	„ **8/—**

Artistic Designs of Model Fountains

Easy Working.

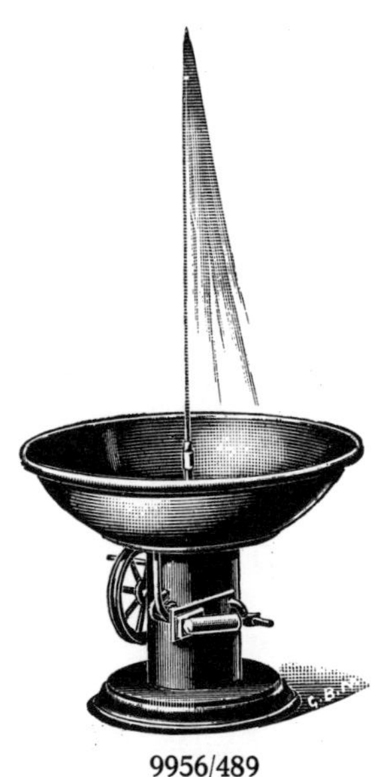

9956/489

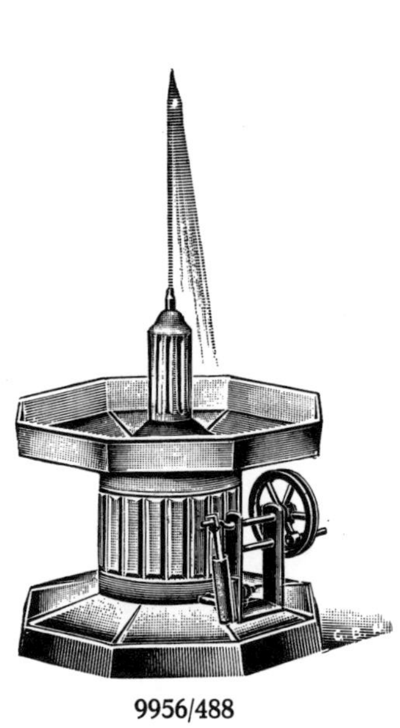

9956/488

9956/491—493

9956/489	**Fountain,** finely japanned, with strong pump, $4\frac{3}{8}$ in. high, $5\frac{1}{4}$ in. diam.	doz.	**23/—**
„ **/488**	**Octagon-Fountain,** finely japanned, with strong pump, $6\frac{3}{4}$ in. high, $6\frac{1}{4}$ in. diam.	each	**5/2**
„ **/491**	**Fountains,** finely japanned, with strong pump, $5\frac{1}{4}$ in. high, $6\frac{1}{2}$ in. diam.	„	**2/10**
„ **/492**	„ „ „ „ „ „ 6 „ „ 8 „ „	„	**4/6**
„ **/493**	„ „ „ „ „ „ $6\frac{3}{4}$ „ „ $9\frac{1}{2}$ „ „	„	**6/6**

9956/485

9956/486- 487

9956/485	**New Ornamental Fountain,** superior finish, with strong pump, basin $5\frac{3}{4}$ in. square	each	**3/10**
„ **/486**	„ „ „ „ „ „ „ „ $7\frac{3}{4}$ in. square	„	**5/8**
„ **/487**	„ „ „ „ „ „ „ „ $9\frac{1}{2}$ „ „ with 3 sprays coming out	„	**7/6**

Working Model Windmills

of Superior Quality.

9956/381

9956/382

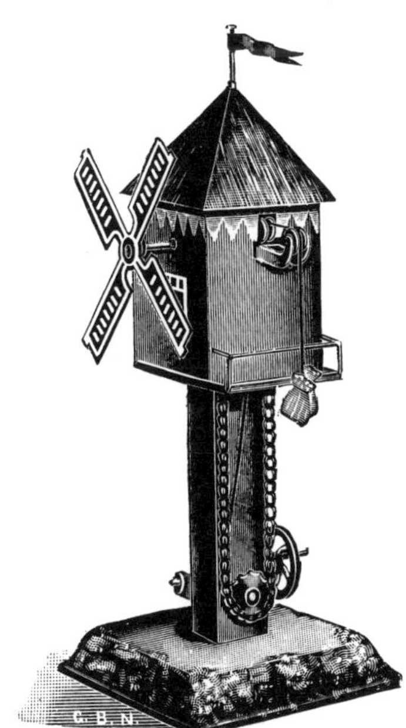

9956/364

9956/381 **Windmill with Music,** fine polychrome japanning, $8^3/_4$ in. high (without Flag) . . . . each **2/—**

„ **/382** „ „ **Dredger,** „ „ „ $10^5/_8$ „ „ „ „ . . . . „ **5/8**

„ **/364** „ „ **Crane,** „ „ „ 11 „ „ . . . . „ **3/10**

9956/419

9956/420

9956/421 *Very Original!*

9956/419 **Windmill,** finely japanned, $8^3/_4$ in. high . . . . each **4/10**

„ **/420** „ **with Sandmill,** finely japanned, $10^5/_8$ in. high . . . . „ **7/10**

„ **/421** „ mechanical, very original and amusing. While the mill is working, the miller cannot be seen, but as soon as the mill stops working he appeares perplexed at the window to see what is wrong; then disappears again, when the mill proceeds working, finely japanned, 13 in. high . . . . „ **14/6**

Scenic Working Models

of Superior Quality.

9956/70

9956/326

9956/70 **Water Mill,** finely japanned, with water basin, brass pump with water wheel, can also be worked by hand, $6^{1}/_{2}$ in. long, $6^{1}/_{4}$ in. wide, $4^{3}/_{4}$ in high . . . . each **4/4**

„ /326 **Cottage and Parish Pump,** realistic design, fine polychrome japanning, brass pump, producing continuous stream of water, $7^{7}/_{8}$ in. high, 11 in. long, $7^{7}/_{8}$ in wide . . . . „ **6/—**

9956/325

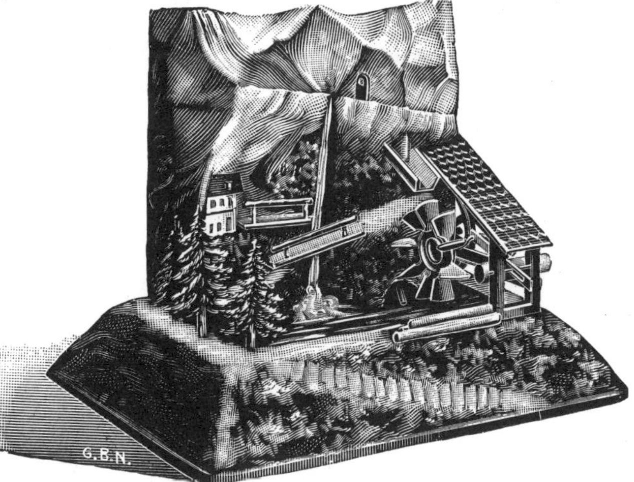

9956/185

9956/325 **The Old Mill,** very effective finish, finely japanned, strong pump work with oscillating brass cylinder and water wheel, height $5^{1}/_{2}$ in., length $9^{7}/_{8}$ in., width 6 in. . . . . each **5/8**

„ /185 **Water Mill,** very effective finish, plastically stamped and finely japanned, strong pumpwork with brass cylinder air chamber, weir, waterfall, outlet to the mill wheel with movable saw, very original, 11 in. long, 8 in. wide, $8^{1}/_{4}$ in. high . . . . „ **10/—**

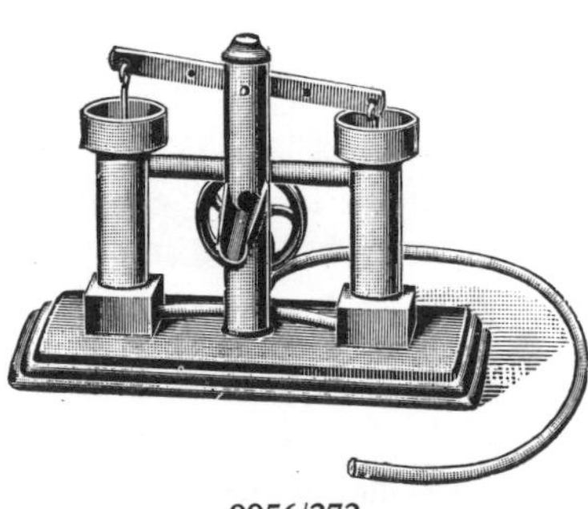

9956/373

9956/374

9956/373 **Double Action Pump,** without receptacle for water finely japanned, $5^{1}/_{4}$ in. long, $2^{3}/_{4}$ in. wide, $3^{3}/_{4}$ in. high each **3/2**

„ /374 „ „ „ with receptacle for water finely japanned . . . . „ **4/10**

Working Model of Domestic Machinery.

Superior Quality.

9956/175

9956/280

9956/281

9956/175 Turnip-cutter with 3 knives, finely japanned, $4\frac{1}{4}$ in. long, 4 in. high . . . . doz. **18/—**
" **/280 Chaff-cutter** with 2 knives, finely japanned, $5\frac{3}{4}$ in. long, 3 in. high . . . . " **19/—**
" **/281 Trashing Machine,** finely japanned, $5\frac{3}{4}$ in. long, $3\frac{3}{4}$ in. high . . . . each **2/6**

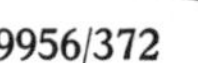

9956/372

9956/282

9956/372 Grinding Mill with Trough, 2 pairs of Grinding Rollers with press spring and receiving receptacle, $4\frac{1}{2}$ in. high . . . . each **2/10**
" **/282 Corn refining Mill** with moving sieve, finely japanned, $6\frac{1}{4}$ in. long, 4 in. high . . . . " **3/2**

Special

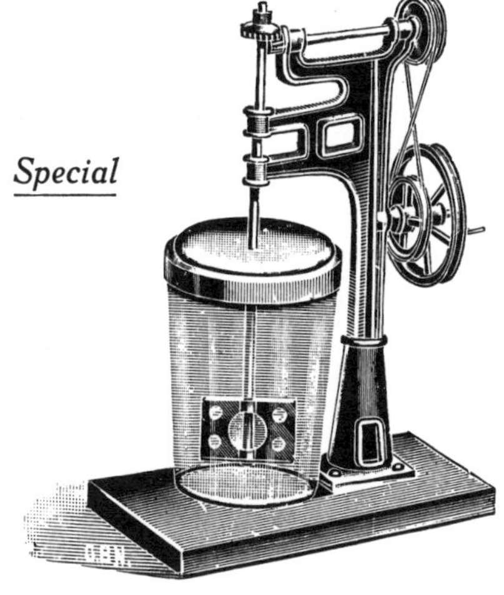

9956/212

9956/424

9956/212 Butter churn, cast iron stand, finely japanned, with glass butter-tub, suitable for practical use, 6 in. long, 8 in. high . . . . each **3/4**
" **/424 Coffee Roaster** with roasting barrel and spirit lamp, $6\frac{3}{4}$ in. long, 4 in. wide, 4 in. high . . . . . . " **2/4**

Working Models of Domestic Machinery

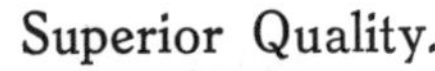

Superior Quality.

9956/324

9956/329

9956/330

9956/324 **Mixing Machine,** (for confectionery etc.) finely japanned with removable tinned bowl and tinned whisk, height $5^{1}/_{4}$ in. . . . . doz. **25/4**

„ **/329** **Centrifugal Drying Machine,** very fine finish, with quickly revolving drum, height $3^{3}/_{8}$ in. length $6^{1}/_{4}$ in. „ **38/—**

„ **/330** **Mangle,** very fine finish, with spring rollers height $4^{1}/_{2}$ in., length $5^{1}/_{2}$ in. . . . . „ **38/—**

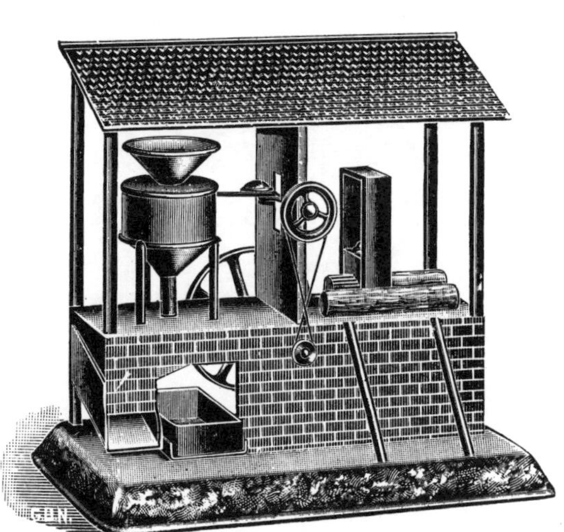

9956/370

9956/388

9956/370 **Grinding-and Saw Mill,** well finished, with mill-course, separating sieve and Veneer Saw, $8^{7}/_{8}$ in. high, $5^{3}/_{4}$ in. wide, 10 in. long . . . . each **7/10**

„ **/388** **Windmill with Sandmill and Dredging Machine,** finely japanned, complete height 13 in., base 10 in. long, $5^{1}/_{2}$ in. wide . . . . „ **6/10**

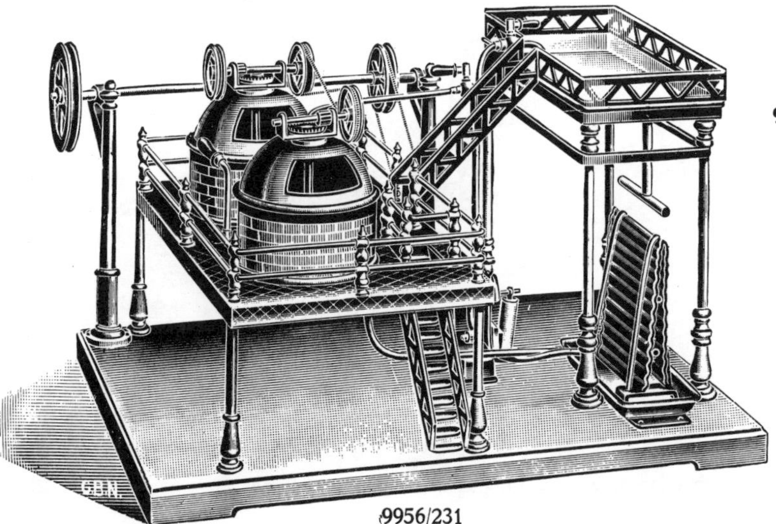

9956/231

9956/231 **Fine Model Brewery,** highly japanned, elegantly finished with copper fittings, all the machinery, which is connected with a brewery, is exactly imitated, such as mash-charger, mash-cooler, brewing-vat etc., mounted on fine wooden base with coloured metal plate (imitation tiles), 14 in. long, 9 in. wide, 11 in. high . . . . . . each **31/—**

Working Models

Special line.

9956/350 Sewing Machine of thoroughly good finish and exact workmanship, guaranteed to work perfectly. This model can also be worked by hand for which purpose a handle is attached to the wheel. A clamp to screw on to table supplied with every machine.

Measurements: $4^{8}/_{4}$ in. high, 4 in. long doz. **23/—**

9956/350

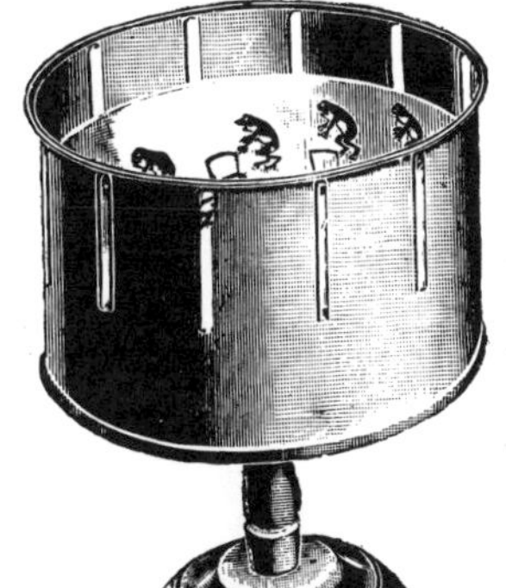

8913

Zoetropes (Living Pictures) Russian Iron Drum on wooden stand, with practical picture holder, with 6 strips = 12 coloured pictures.

8913/1	$4^{1}/_{4}$ in diam.	doz.	**15/—**
„ /2	$5^{1}/_{4}$ „ „	„	**19/—**
„ /3	$6^{1}/_{4}$ „ „	each	**2/6**
„ /4	$7^{1}/_{4}$ „ „	„	**3/6**
„ /5	$9^{1}/_{2}$ „ „	„	**4/8**

Model Roundabouts.

9956/412

9956/413

9956/414 and /415

9956/416 and /417

9956/418

Model Roundabouts, finely japanned for use as models or by hand with Music, light Weight and Finish.

9956/210	with 3 Figures, $7^{1}/_{2}$ in. high, $4^{1}/_{4}$ in. diam.	doz.	**9/6**
„ **/412**	„ 3 „ on horses $9^{1}/_{2}$ in. high, $4^{1}/_{4}$ in. diam.	„	**18/—**
„ **/413**	„ 3 „ „ „ 11 „ „ $5^{1}/_{8}$ „ „	„	**28/—**
„ **/414**	„ 3 „ „ „ $12^{8}/_{4}$ „ „ $5^{1}/_{2}$ „ „	each	**3/2**
„ **/415**	„ 3 „ „ „ 15 „ „ $6^{1}/_{2}$ „ „	„	**3/10**
„ **/416**	„ 4 „ „ „ 16 „ „ $7^{1}/_{8}$ „ „	„	**5/4**
„ **/417**	„ 4 „ „ „ and 3 lamps, $17^{1}/_{2}$ in. high, $8^{1}/_{8}$ in. diam.	„	**6/2**
„ **/418**	„ 4 „ „ „ 4 „ 20 „ „ $9^{1}/_{2}$ „ „	„	**8/—**

Very Attractive Show Models

easy to work either by hand or with Steam Engines etc.

Strong make, finely japanned.

9956/483

9956/483 **Scenic Railway,** very original, with transmission, endless chain gear and 2 carriages. While one of the cars is pulled up the other runs down the „Figure 8" Measurements: 13 in. high, without flag, length of rail abt. 2 feet, 12 in. . . . . price complete each **12/6**

9956/336

9956/336 **Working Model: „Figure 8 Railway" or „Scenic Railway".** Very original, with transmission, endless chain gear and 2 carriages; (Whilst the one carriage is taken upwards the other one runs down the form of the „Figure 8"), with complete outfit, finely japanned, 16 in. high, length of track about $11^{1}/_{2}$ feet each **23/—**

10300 **Same as above, with Electric Motor,** (for low current) . . . . „ **30/6**

Model Workshop Shaftings

of strong make.

9956/341

9956/341 **Shafting** with 4 pulley wheels on japanned metal base, $6^1/_4$ in. long, 3 in. wide, $2^3/_4$ in. high . . . . doz. **9/8**

9956/342

9956/342 **Shafting** with 6 pulley wheels on japanned metal base, $7^3/_4$ in. long, $3^1/_2$ in. wide, $2^3/_4$ in. high . . . . . doz. **14/—**

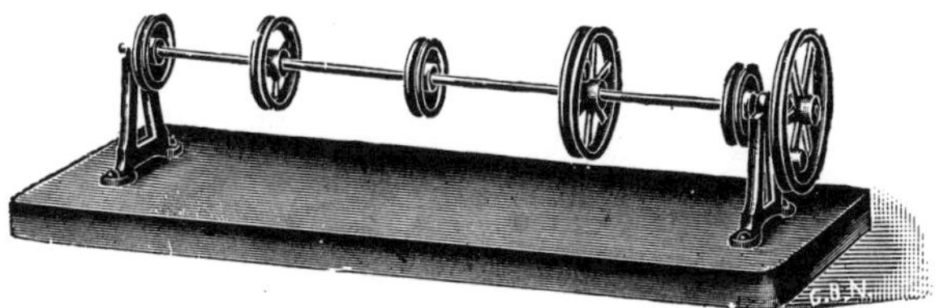

9956/343

9956/343 **Shafting** on strong wooden base with 6 pulley wheels, 10 in. long, $2^3/_4$ in. high doz. **17/6**

9956/344

9956/344 **Shafting,** mounted on solid wooden base, with 8 pulley wheels, $17^3/_4$ in. long, $2^3/_4$ in. high doz. **26/6**

9956/265

9956/267

9956/265 **Workshop Shafting** with 2 strong cast pillars and 4 pulley wheels, mounted on strong wooden board, 8 in. long, $7^3/_4$ in. high . . . . doz. **19/—**

„ **/267** **Workshop Shafting** with 2 strong cast pillars and 4 pulley wheels, mounted on strong wooden base, 10 in. long, 8 in. high . . . . doz. **25/4**

Model Workshop Shaftings

of strong make.

9956/321

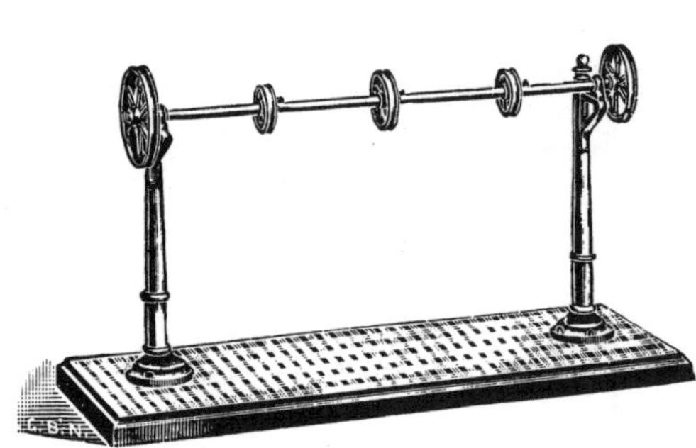

9956/120

9956/321 **Workshop Shafting** with 3 strong cast pillars and 8 pulley wheels, mounted on strong wooden base, $17^3/_4$ in. long, 8 in. high . . . . each **3/10**

" **/120** **Workshop Shafting** with 2 cast iron pillars, finely japanned, with 5 adjustable pulley wheels, fastened with wedges, mounted on strong wooden base, $12^3/_4$ in. long, $7^1/_4$ in. high . . . . each **4/4**

9956/121

9956/121 **Workshop Shafting with 3 cast iron pillars,** finely japanned, with 9 adjustable pulley wheels fastened with wedges, mounted on strong wooden board, $27^1/_2$ in. long, $7^1/_4$ in. high . . . . . . each **7/10**

Corner Shaftings

finely japanned, plastically stamped (imitation brickwork) 2 Speeds.

9956/345

9956/346

9956/345 **Shafting** with 2 low bearings, finely japanned and stamped (imitation brickwork) 3 pulley wheels on one side, 4 on the other, 2 speeds, $3^1/_4$ in. high, $6^1/_2$ in. long . . . . doz. **27/4**

" **/346** **Shafting** with 2 stands, finely japanned and stamped, (imitation brickwork) 6 pulley wheels, on each side; 2 speeds, $8^1/_4$ in. high, $6^1/_4$ in. long, $5^3/_8$ in. wide . . . . each **3/10**

New Model Workshop Shaftings (low patterns)

of superior quality with finely nickelled pulley wheels.
Polished Wood Base — Grey castings — Nickel Fittings.

9956/465

9956/465 **Shafting** with 2 supports, finely japanned, with 3 nickelled pulley wheels, mounted on strong wooden base finely polished $5^1/_2$ in. long, 3 in. wide, 4 in. high . . . . doz. **23/—**

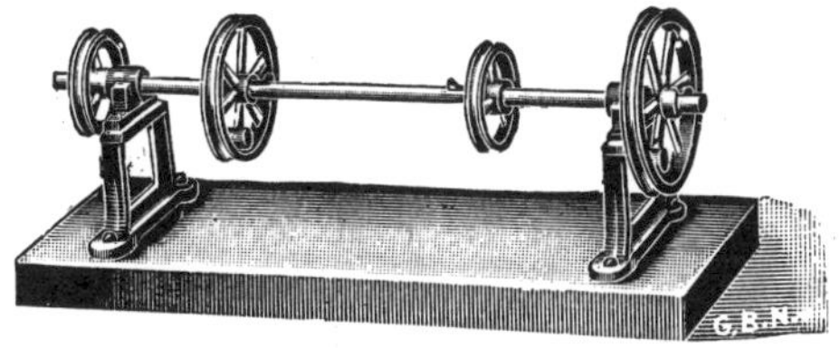

9956/480

9956/480 **Shafting** with 2 supports, finely japanned, with 4 nickelled pulley wheels, mounted on strong wooden base, finely polished, 8 in. long, $2^3/_4$ in. wide, 3 in. high . . . doz. **28/6**

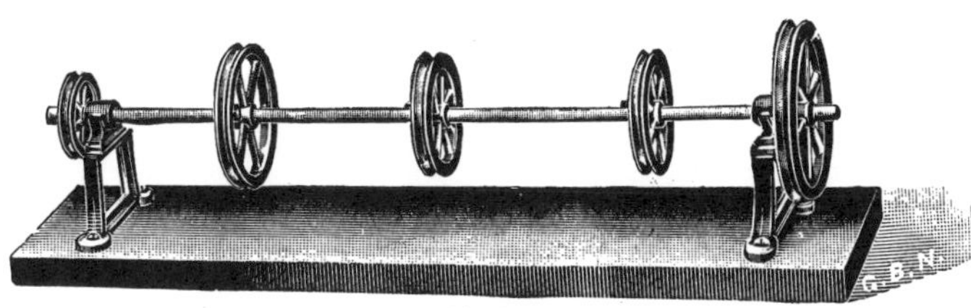

9956/481

9956/481 **Shafting** with 2 supports, finely japanned with 5 nickelled pulley wheels, mounted on strong wooden base, finely polished 12 in. long, 3 in. wide, $3^1/_4$ in. high each **3/2**

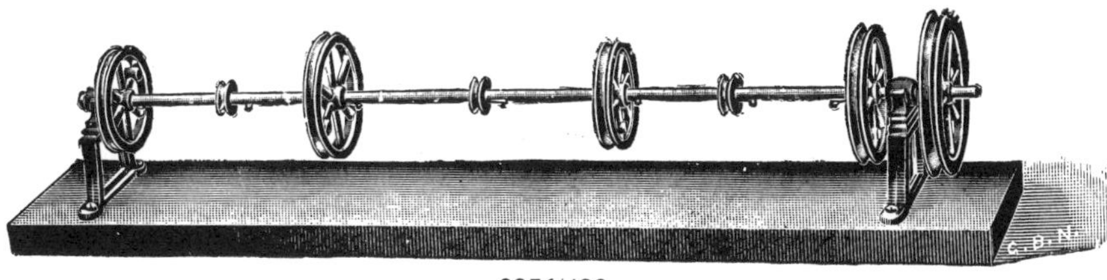

9956/482

9956/482 **Shafting** with 2 supports finely japanned, with 8 nickelled pulley wheels mounted on highly polished wooden base each **4/10**

9956/463

9956/463 **Two Speed Pulleys** with 2 supports, finely japanned, with nickelled wheel and 2 speed pulley, mounted on finely polished wooden base $4^1/_2$ in long, $2^3/_4$ in. wide, $2^3/_4$ in. high doz. **13/8**

9956/464

9956/464 **Three Speed Pulley** with 2 supports, finely japanned, with nickelled wheel and 3 speed pulley, mounted on finely polished wooden base, $4^1/_2$ in. long, $2^3/_4$ in. wide, $3^1/_4$ in. high . . doz. **19/—**

Model Workshop Shaftings

built up from castings, finely japanned, nickelled wheels, mounted on strong wooden boards.

9956/448 9956/451

9956/448 **Shafting** with 2 cast iron columns and 4 adjustable pulley wheels, fastened with wedges, $9\frac{1}{2}$ in. long, $4\frac{3}{8}$ in. high . . . . each **4/4**

" **/451** **Shafting** with 3 cast iron columns and 9 adjustable pulley wheels, fastened with wedges, $33\frac{1}{2}$ in. long, $4\frac{3}{4}$ in. high . . . . each **12/8**

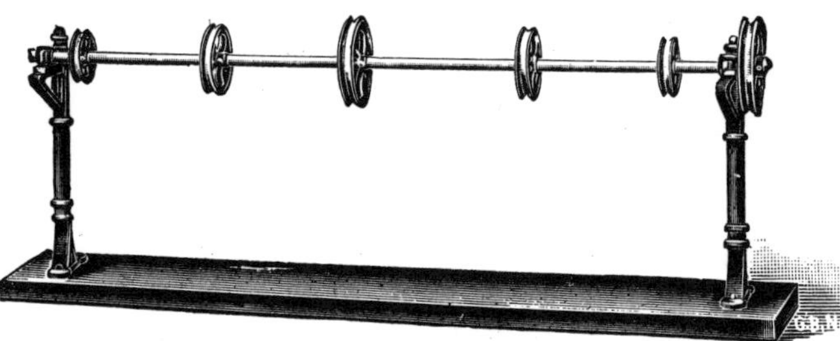

9956/449

9956/449 **Shafting** with 2 cast iron columns and 6 adjustable pulley wheels, fastened with wedges, 19 in. long, $7\frac{1}{8}$ in. high, each **7/8**

9956/450

9956/450 **Shafting** with 2 cast iron columns and 7 adjustable pulley wheels, fastened with wedges, $19\frac{3}{4}$ in. long, $10\frac{1}{8}$ in. high . . . . each **12/—**

9956/453

9956/453 **Shafting, extra large,** with 3 cast iron columns and 11 pulley wheels, fastened with wedges; with attachment on lower columns with 2 pulley wheels, 47 in. long, 10 in. high . . . . each **33/—**

Fittings for Model Steam Engines.

6587 — 8468 and 8653 — 7322 and 7344

6587	**Steam Whistle,** brass, plain, 1¼ in. high	doz.	**3/4**

Steam Whistles with polished wooden handle and bush

8468/00	brass, 1¼ in. high	doz.	**7/—**
„ /0	„ 1⅝ „ „	„	**7/6**
„ /1	„ 2 „ „	„	**11/—**
8653/00	nickelled, 1¼ in. high	„	**8/—**
„ /0	„ 1⅝ „ „	„	**8/6**
„ /1	„ 2 „ „	„	**12/—**

Bell Whistles with polished wooden handle and bush

7322/1	brass, 1⅜ in. high	doz.	**11/—**
„ /2	„ 1½ „ „	„	**12/8**
7344/1	nickelled, 1⅜ in. high	„	**12/4**
„ /2	„ 1½ „ „	„	**14/2**

8467 and 8652 — 6599

Outlet Taps with bush

8467/0	brass, ¾ in. long	doz.	**6/—**
„ /1	„ ⅞ „ „	„	**6/10**
8652/0	nickelled, ¾ in. long	„	**6/10**
„ /1	„ ⅞ „ „	„	**8/4**

Qutlet Tap, four-cornered

6599	nickelled, ⅞ in. long	doz.	**11/2**

8466 and 8644 — 6374 and 6391

Starting Taps (Connecting cocks)

8466	brass, ⅞ in. long	doz.	**8/4**
8644	nickelled, ⅞ in. long	„	**9/2**

Starting Taps (Connecting cocks) with tube connection

6374	brass, 1½ in. long	doz.	**12/4**
6391	nickelled, 1½ in. long	„	**13/8**

6921 — 7067

Three way Tap, four-cornered

6921	nickelled, 1½ in. long	doz.	**17/—**

Model Regulator as used in Locomotives with 3 tubes starting from it, accurately made of brass, nickelled

7067/1	9/16×9/16 in.	doz.	**24/—**
„ /2	¾×¾ „	„	**36/—**

8874 and 8445 — 6404 and 8483

Tube Connections with pipe-end

8874	brass, complete	doz.	**9/4**
8445	nickelled, complete	„	**11/8**

6404/0	**Filling Screws** with bush, brass	„	**2/—**
„ /1	„ „ „ „ „	„	**3/2**
8483/0	„ „ „ „ nickelled	„	**2/8**
„ /1	„ „ „ „ „	„	**3/10**

Bush Rings with thread inside

9429/00	brass, thread 3/16 in.	gross	**17/4**
„ /0	„ „ ¼ „	„	**17/4**
„ /1	„ „ 5/16 „	„	**17/4**
8487/00	nickelled, thread 3/16 in.	„	**18/6**
„ /0	„ „ ¼ „	„	**18/6**
„ /1	„ „ 5/16 „	„	**19/—**

9429 and 8487 — 8780 and 8783

Packing Rings (Washers)

8780	glaze paste board suitable for all Engines and fittings	gross	**2/4**
8783	India rubber, for safety valves	„	**2/6**

Fittings for Model Steam Engines.

6949 | 7323 and 7352 | 8485 and 8661 | 6953

Spring Safety valves with bush,

6949	brass, smal size	doz.	**2/8**
7323	brass polished, medium size	„	**4/4**
7352	nickelled, medium size	„	**5/2**
8485	brass, medium size	„	**4/8**
8661	nickelled, medium size	„	**6/4**
6953	large, finely nickelled	„	**6/4**

8486/2 nickelled

8486/2 **Lever Safety Valve** with sliding weight, finely nickelled, $2\frac{3}{4}$ in. long . . . . doz. **15/6**

6961

6961 **Lever Safety Valve** with tube connection in right angle and sliding weight, finely nickelled, $2\frac{3}{4}$ in. long . . . . doz. **18/—**

7081

7081 **Lever Safety Valve** with drop-weight, brass finely nickelled, $2\frac{3}{4}$ in. long . . . . . . doz. **15/6**

7358/1 | 7358/3 | 7359 | 7358/2 | 7041

Oil Cups for Steam Engines

7358/1	brass, finely nickelled, small size . . .	gross	**22/6**
„ **/2**	„ „ „ medium size . .	„	**29/6**
„ **/3**	„ with celluloid cup, large size . .	doz.	**6/2**

7359 **Steam jet oiler** for fixed cylinders, to be fitted on steam pipes . . . . doz. **4/6**

7041 **Oiler with tap** finely nickelled, 1 in. long doz. **17/—**

13313/2 | 10142

13313/2 **Steam Pressure Gauge** correctly indicating up 2 atmospheres (1 Atm. = 15 lbs. per square inch), brass highly nickelled with bush, $1\frac{11}{16}$ in. high . . . . each **4/10**

10142 **Steam Pressure Gauge** guaranteed for correctly indicating up to 3 atmospheres (1 Atm. = 15 lbs. per square inch) technically perfect finish

10142/2	diam. $\frac{3}{4}$ in.	each	**6/10**
„ **/2½**	„ 1 „	„	**7/—**
„ **/3**	„ $1\frac{3}{16}$ „	„	**7/2**
„ **/4**	„ $1\frac{5}{8}$ „	„	**7/4**

Fittings for Model Steam Engines.

7361

7353 and 7354

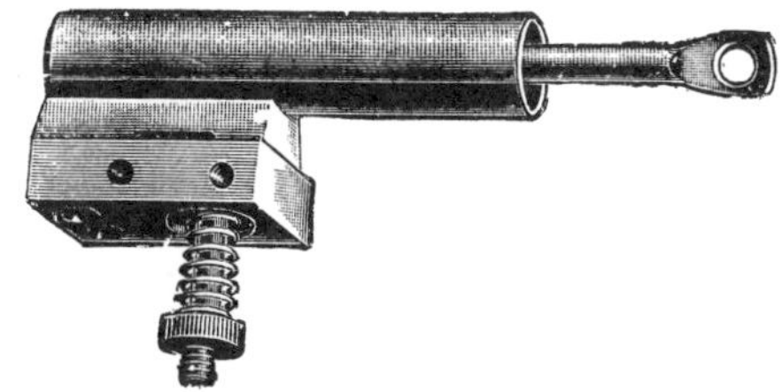

8168 and 8211

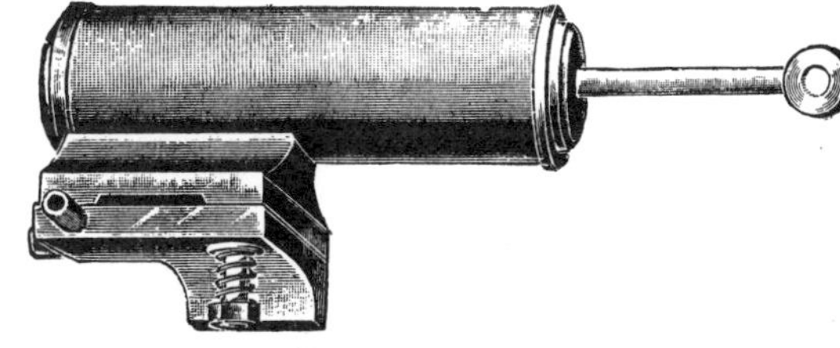

extra large 7340 Brass
„ „ 7410 finely nickelled

Oscillating Steam Cylinder, strong finish with piston, fixing plate, spring and screw

No.		bore	length of cylinder	stroke	
7361	Brass polished,	bore 5/16 in.,	lenght of cylinder 13/16 in.,	stroke 9/16 in.	doz. **12/—**
7353/1	„ „	„ 5/16 „	„ „ „ 13/16 „	„ 9/16 „	„ **13/2**
„ /2	„ „	„ 3/8 „	„ „ „ 1 1/4 „	„ 9/16 „	„ **15/—**
7354/1	„ nickelled,	„ 5/16 „	„ „ „ 13/16 „	„ 9/16 „	„ **14/—**
„ /2	„ „	„ 3/8 „	„ „ „ 1 1/4 „	„ 9/16 „	„ **17/—**
8168/1	„ polished,	„ 5/16 „	„ „ „ 1 9/16 „	„ 1 1/8 „	„ **19/6**
„ /2	„ „	„ 3/8 „	„ „ „ 1 3/4 „	„ 1 1/4 „	„ **24/—**
„ /3	„ „	„ 1/2 „	„ „ „ 1 3/4 „	„ 1 3/8 „	„ **30/—**
8211/1	„ nickelled,	„ 5/16 „	„ „ „ 1 9/16 „	„ 1 1/8 „	„ **22/—**
„ /2	„ „	„ 3/8 „	„ „ „ 1 3/4 „	„ 1 1/4 „	„ **26/6**
„ /3	„ „	„ 1/2 „	„ „ „ 1 3/4 „	„ 1 3/8 „	„ **32/6**
7340	„ polished,	„ 3/4 „	„ „ „ 3	„ 1 1/8 „	each **6/2**
7410	„ nickelled,	„ 3/4 „	„ „ „ 3	„ 1 1/8 „	„ **7/—**

8715 for vertical engines

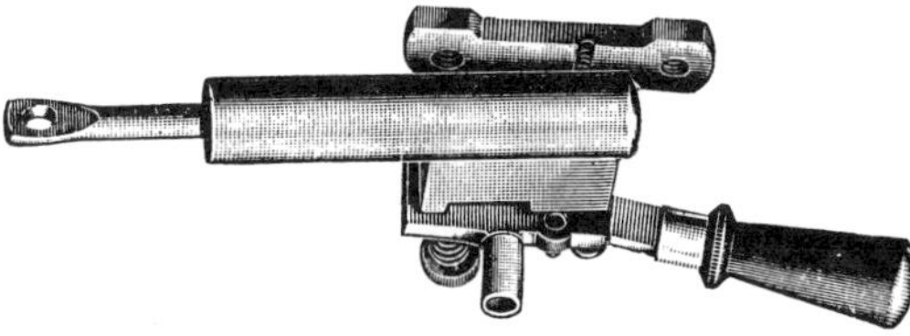

8717 for horizontal engines

Steam Cylinder, brass nickelled, oscillating, strong finish, with piston, fixing plate, spring and screw

size	1	2	3	
Core	5/16	5/16	3/8	in.
length of cylinder	1 5/8	1 11/16	1 11/16	„
8714 not reversing . . . each	**1/6**	**2/—**	**2/6**	
8715 with reversing lever „	**3/—**	**3/—**	**3/6**	

size	1	2	3	
Core	5/16	5/16	3/8	in.
length of cylinder	1 5/8	1 11/16	1 11/16	„
8716 not reversing . . . each	**2/—**	**2/6**	**3/—**	
8717 with reversing lever „	**3/—**	**3/6**	**4/—**	

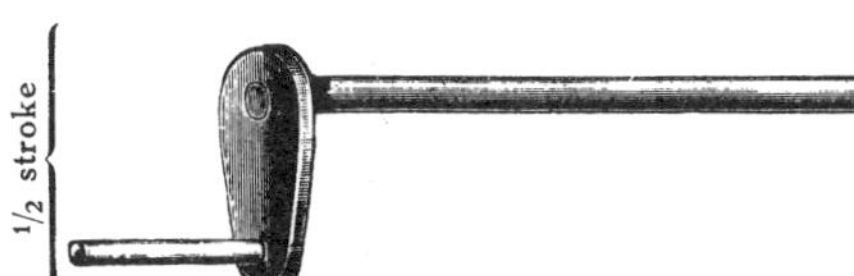

6303

8161

6328

6329

6303 Shafts and Crank sfor oscillating cylinders

size	1	2	3	4
stroke	1/2	5/8	3/4	15/16 in.
doz.	**2/2**	**2/8**	**3/2**	**3/10**

8161 Cranks, for oscillating cylinders

size	1	2	3	4
stroke	1/2	5/8	3/4	15/16 in.
	gross **17/—**	doz. **2/—**	**2/6**	**3/—**

Springs and Nuts, for oscillating cylinders

6328 Springs . . . . . . gross **9/4**
6329 Nuts . . . . „ **7/8**

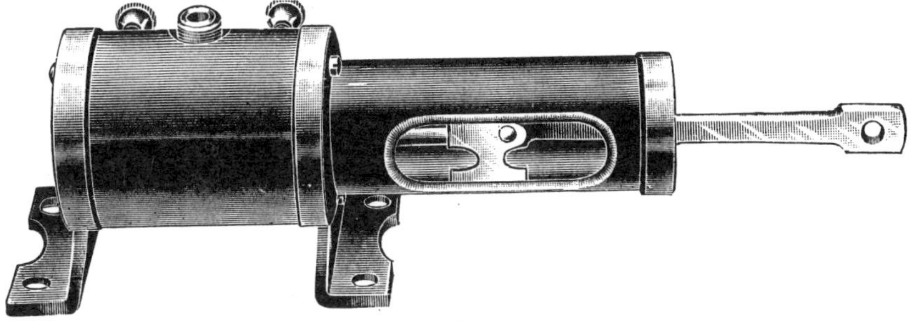

8396

8396 Fixed Steam Cylinder, large, with improved double action slide valve, moving on rollers, guide bar and regulating screws, bore of cylinder 9/16 in., length of cylinder with stroke 5 3/4 in. . . . . each **9/6**

Fittings for Model Steam Engines.

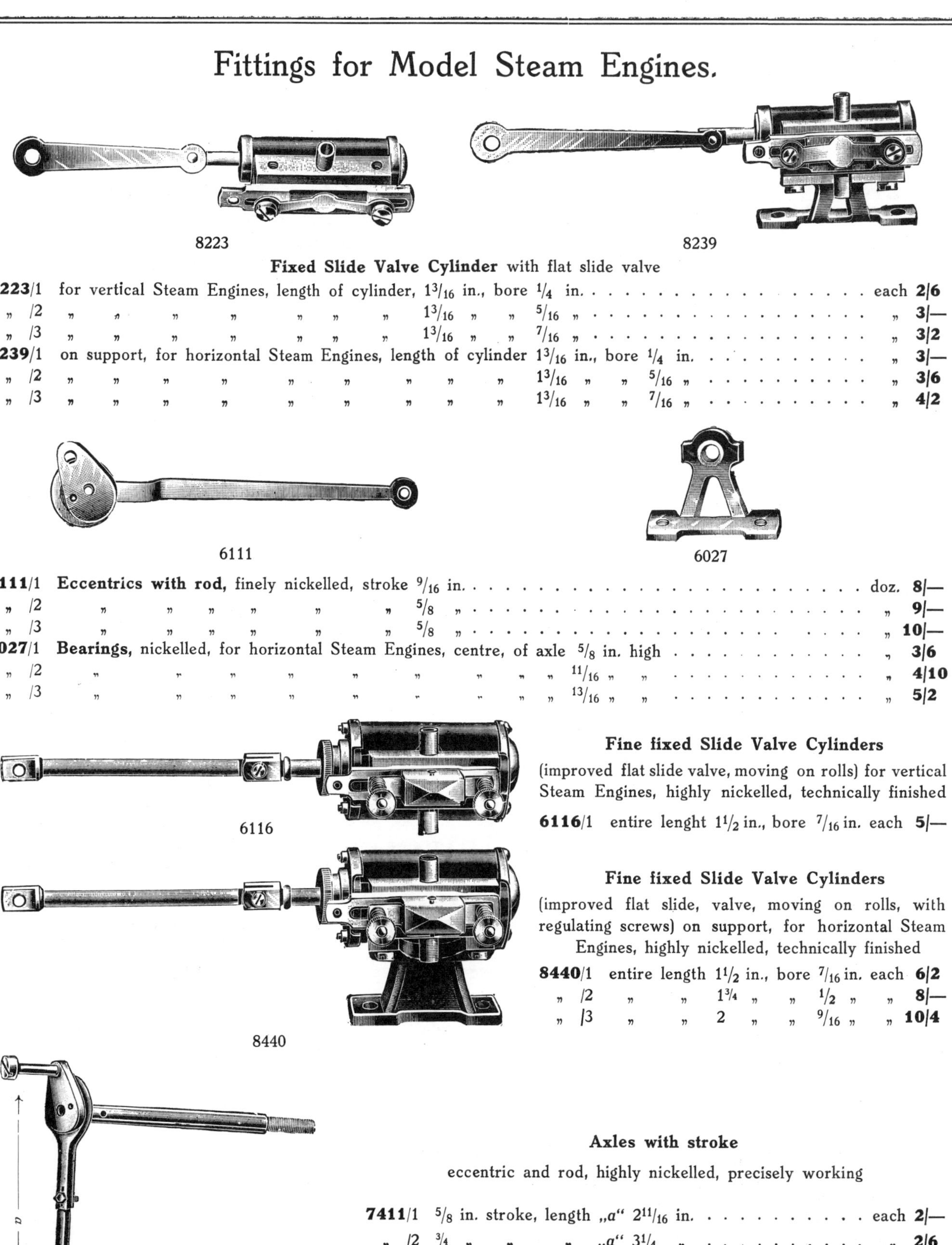

8223 8239

Fixed Slide Valve Cylinder with flat slide valve

8223/1	for vertical Steam Engines, length of cylinder, $1^3/_{16}$ in., bore $^1/_4$ in.	each **2/6**
„ /2	„ „ „ „ „ „ „ $1^3/_{16}$ „ „ $^5/_{16}$ „	„ **3/—**
„ /3	„ „ „ „ „ „ „ $1^3/_{16}$ „ „ $^7/_{16}$ „	„ **3/2**
8239/1	on support, for horizontal Steam Engines, length of cylinder $1^3/_{16}$ in., bore $^1/_4$ in.	„ **3/—**
„ /2	„ „ „ „ „ „ „ „ „ $1^3/_{16}$ „ „ $^5/_{16}$ „	„ **3/6**
„ /3	„ „ „ „ „ „ „ „ „ $1^3/_{16}$ „ „ $^7/_{16}$ „	„ **4/2**

6111 6027

6111/1	**Eccentrics with rod,** finely nickelled, stroke $^9/_{16}$ in.	doz. **8/—**
„ /2	„ „ „ „ „ „ $^5/_8$ „	„ **9/—**
„ /3	„ „ „ „ „ „ $^5/_8$ „	„ **10/—**
6027/1	**Bearings,** nickelled, for horizontal Steam Engines, centre, of axle $^5/_8$ in. high	„ **3/6**
„ /2	„ „ „ „ „ „ „ „ „ $^{11}/_{16}$ „ „	„ **4/10**
„ /3	„ „ „ „ „ „ „ „ „ $^{13}/_{16}$ „ „	„ **5/2**

6116

Fine fixed Slide Valve Cylinders

(improved flat slide valve, moving on rolls) for vertical Steam Engines, highly nickelled, technically finished

6116/1 entire lenght $1^1/_2$ in., bore $^7/_{16}$ in. each **5/—**

8440

Fine fixed Slide Valve Cylinders

(improved flat slide, valve, moving on rolls, with regulating screws) on support, for horizontal Steam Engines, highly nickelled, technically finished

8440/1	entire length $1^1/_2$ in., bore $^7/_{16}$ in.	each **6/2**
„ /2	„ „ $1^3/_4$ „ „ $^1/_2$ „	„ **8/—**
„ /3	„ „ 2 „ „ $^9/_{16}$ „	„ **10/4**

7411

Axles with stroke

eccentric and rod, highly nickelled, precisely working

7411/1	$^5/_8$ in. stroke, length „a“ $2^{11}/_{16}$ in.	each **2/—**
„ /2	$^3/_4$ „ „ „ „a“ $3^1/_4$ „	„ **2/6**
„ /3	$^{15}/_{16}$ „ „ „ „a“ $3^5/_8$ „	„ **3/—**

Fittings for Model Steam Engines.

7080 right hand

7070 left hand

Fixed Double action Slide Valve Cylinder for Steam Engines, Traction Engines and Steam Locomotives
with tubular slide valve and reversing gear.

7080/1	Right hand, bore of cylinder $3/8$ in.	each	**4/—**
„ /2	„ „ „ „ „ $7/16$ „	„	**5/—**
„ /3	„ „ „ „ „ $1/2$ „	„	**6/—**
„ /4	„ „ „ „ „ $9/16$ „	„	**7/—**
„ /5	„ „ „ „ „ $5/8$ „	„	**8/—**
„ /6	„ „ „ „ „ $11/16$ „	„	**10/—**
„ /7	„ „ „ „ „ $3/4$ „	„	**13/—**
7070/1	Left hand, bore of cylinder $3/8$ „	„	**4/—**
„ /2	„ „ „ „ „ $7/16$ „	„	**5/—**
„ /3	„ „ „ „ „ $1/2$ „	„	**6/—**
„ /4	„ „ „ „ „ $9/16$ „	„	**7/—**
„ /5	„ „ „ „ „ $5/8$ „	„	**8/—**
„ /6	„ „ „ „ „ $11/16$ „	„	**10/—**
„ /7	„ „ „ „ „ $3/4$ „	„	**13/—**

6355

6334

6335

6355/0	**Eccentrics with rod** for tubular slide valves on locomotives (left and right), 3 in. long	doz.	**20/—**
„ /1	„ „ „ „ „ „ „ „ „ „ „ $3\,5/8$ in. long	„	**21/6**
„ /2	„ „ „ „ „ „ „ „ „ „ „ $4\,1/4$ „ „	„	**27/6**
6334	Screws fitting above	gross	**12/—**
6335/1	**Connecting Rods** for Locomotives, highly nickelled, 2 in. long	doz.	**3/10**
„ /2	„ „ „ „ „ „ $2\,3/16$ in. long	„	**4/10**
„ .3	„ „ „ „ „ „ $3\,1/8$ „ „	„	**5/8**

7073/1 **Crank** (cast) **with screw**

7073/1	$5/16$ in. long	doz.	**20/—**
„ /2	„ same, $3/8$ in. wide	„	**24/—**
„ /3	„ „ $1/2$ „ „	„	**28/—**
„ /4	„ „ $5/8$ „ „	„	**34/—**
„ /5	„ „ $3/4$ „ „	„	**42/—**

7073

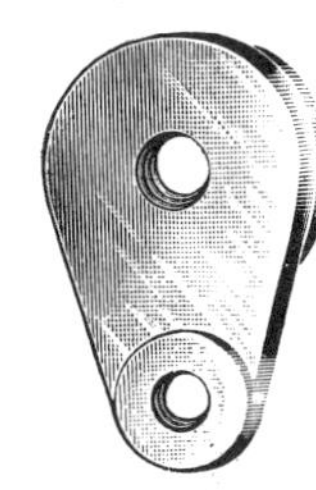

7494

7494 **Crank,** extra large, brass $5/8$ in. wide, $1\,1/4$ in. high each **3/6**

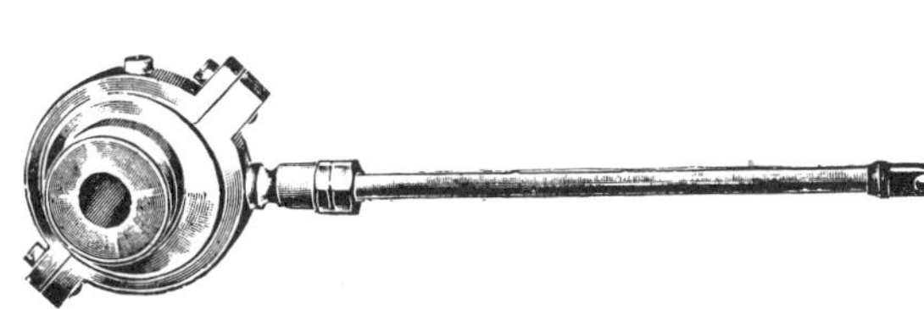

7079

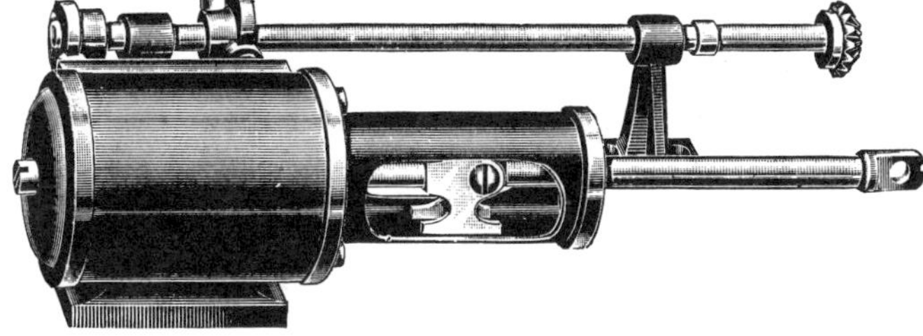

7071/1—3

7079/1	**Eccentrics,** 2 parted with rod for feeding pumps, extra large, best workmanship, diam. of eccentric $7/8$ in., length from centre to centre $7/16$ in. efficiency $1/8$ in.	each	**8/—**
„ /2	Same in the following measurements, diam. of eccentric $1\,1/8$ in. length, from centre to centre $9/16$ in., efficiency $1/8$ in.	each	**11/—**
7071/1	**Steam Cylinder with valve motion,** technically perfect, finely nickelled parts, diam. of piston $9/16$ in., length of crank $5/8$ in. distance between centre of crank and of cylinder $4\,5/8$ in.	each	**14/—**
„ /2	Same, diam. of piston $11/16$ in., length of crank $3/4$ in., distance between centre of crank and of cylinder $5\,3/4$ in.	„	**20/—**
„ /3	„ „ „ „ $13/16$ „ „ „ „ 1 „ „ „ „ „ „ „ „ „ $6\,3/4$ „	„	**30/—**

Fittings for Model Steam Engines.

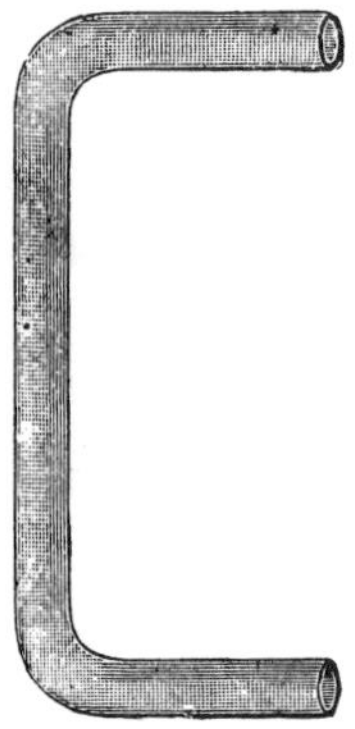

No.	Description		Price
7766/1	**Water Gauge Glasses,** Glases only, 1 in. long	gross	**19/—**
„ /2	„ „ „ „ „ $1^{5}/_{16}$ „	„	**22/—**
„ /3	„ „ „ „ „ $1^{13}/_{16}$ „	„	**26/—**

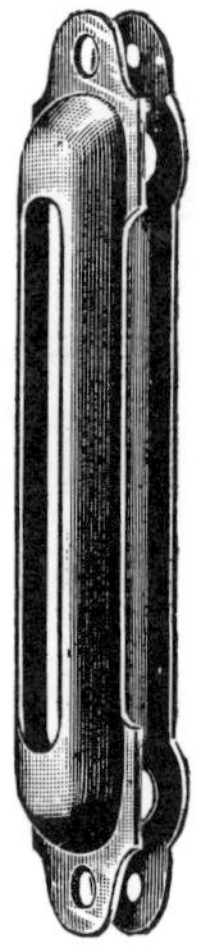

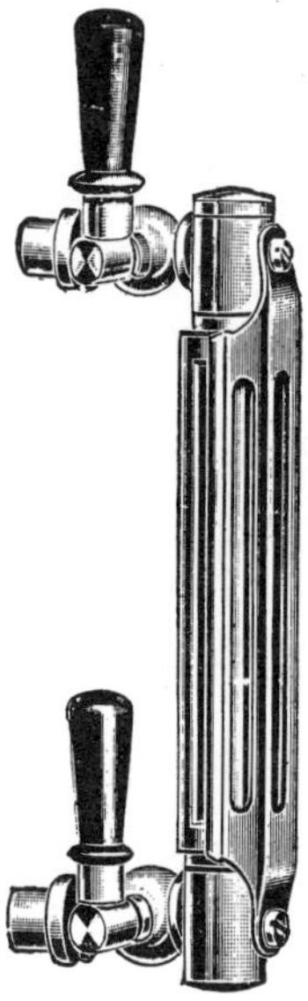

Casings for above water gauge glasses, consisting of: bottom-casing black burnished, top-casing finely nickelled

No.			Price
7910/1		gross	**26/—**
„ /2		„	**31/6**
„ /3		„	**38/—**
7936	**Washers** for above	„	**3/2**
8475	**Water Gauge Glasses** complete, with 2 taps, bush, washers and casing, brass polished, $3^{5}/_{8}$ in. long	each	**3/6**
8654	do. brass finely nickelled, $3^{5}/_{8}$ „ „	„	**4/—**
8482	water gauge glasses only, for 8475 and 8654	gross	**14/6**

7766 7910 8475 and 8654

No.	Description	Length	Hole dist.		Price
13309/1	**Water Gauge Glasses** with 2 holes cut,	$1^{9}/_{16}$ in. long.,	hole dist. 1 in.	doz.	**3/10**
„ /2	do.	2 „ „	„ „ $1^{5}/_{16}$ „	„	**4/6**
„ /3	do.	$2^{7}/_{16}$ „ „	„ „ $1^{7}/_{8}$ „	„	**5/—**

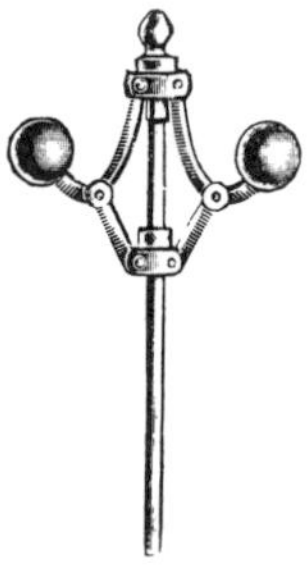

13309

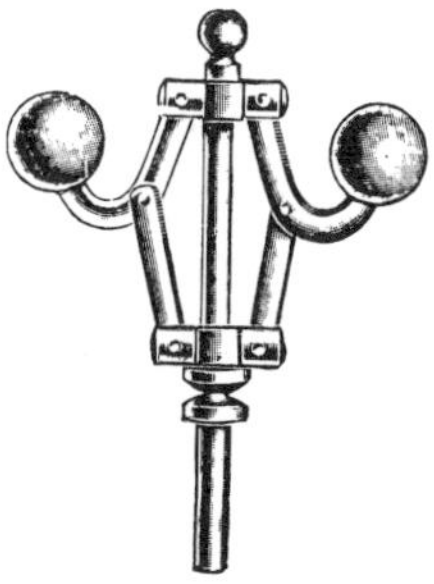

No.	Description		Price
8455	**Governor** composition casting, with support, $2^{5}/_{16}$ in. high	doz.	**4/6**
8480	**Governor,** finely nickelled with centrifugal balls, movable on curved rod, 2 in. high	doz.	**15/4**
8495	**Governor** with cased top, brass finely nickelled, with support, $2^{1}/_{2}$ in. high	doz.	**27/4**

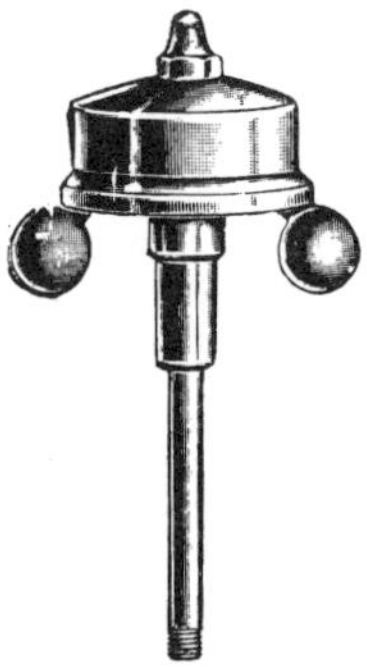

8455 8480 8495

Seamless Tubing

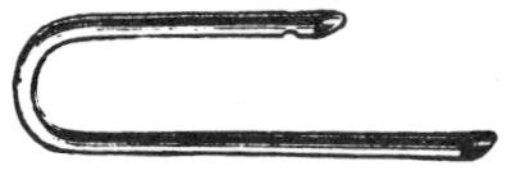

No.			Price
9004/25	brass	per doz. meters	**10/6**
„ /28	„	„ „ „	**12/8**
„ /30	„	„ „ „	**12/8**
„ /35	„	„ „ „	**15/—**
„ /40	„	„ „ „	**17/—**
„ /45	„	„ „ „	**17/—**
„ /50	„	„ „ „	**19/—**

9004 and 8665

No.			Price
8665/25	nickelled	per doz. meters	**12/8**
„ /28	„	„ „ „	**12/8**
„ /30	„	„ „ „	**15/—**
„ /35	„	„ „ „	**17/—**
„ /40	„	„ „ „	**17/—**
„ /45	„	„ „ „	**19/—**
„ /50	„	„ „ „	**21/—**

Bearings cast iron **rough, without hole**

No.			Price
8404/1	Centre of shaft $^{13}/_{16}$ in. high	doz. pairs	**6/4**
„ /2	„ „ „ $1^{1}/_{16}$ „ „	„ „	**8/6**

do. cast iron, **japanned, with hole**

No.			Price
8852/1	Centre oft shaft $^{13}/_{16}$ in. high.	„ „	**10/6**
„ /2	„ „ „ $1^{1}/_{16}$ „ „	„ „	**15/—**

Bearings with detachable top, cast iron, **rough, without hole**

No.			Price
8892	Centre of shaft $1^{1}/_{16}$ in, high	each pair	**1/4**

do. Cast iron, **japanned, with hole**

No.			Price
8895	Centre of shaft $1^{1}/_{16}$ in. high	„ „	**4/2**

Bearings solid, cast iron, **rough, without hole**

No.			Price
8941/1	Centre of shaft $^{18}/_{16}$ in. high	doz. pairs	**8/6**
„ /2	„ „ „ 1 „ „	„ „	**12/—**
„ /3	„ „ „ $^{18}/_{16}$ „ „	„ „	**15/—**

do. solid, cast iron, **japanned, with hole**

No.			Price
9043/1	Centre of shaft $^{13}/_{16}$ in. high	„ „	**18/—**
„ /2	„ „ „ 1 „ „	„ „	**24/6**
„ /3	„ „ . $1^{3}/_{16}$ „ „	„ „	**33/8**

8404 and 8852 8892 and 8895

8941 and 9043

Extra large, fine Fittings, strong and elegant finish

brass, finely nickelled, dull.

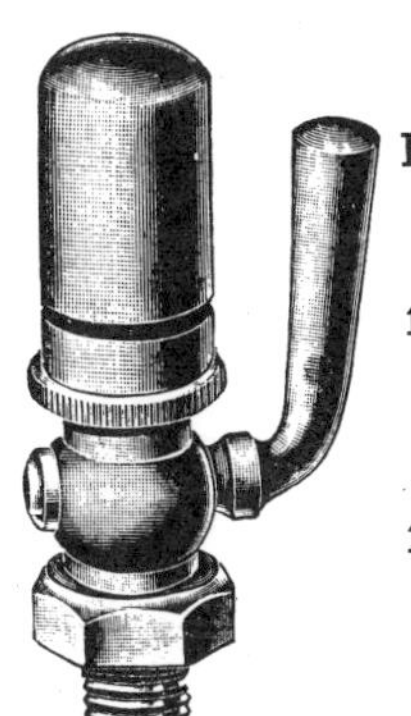

Bell Steam Whistle with boiler screw (hexagonal)

10259/1 2 in. high, screw thread 7,5 mm each **2/10**

10259/2 $2^3/_4$ in. high, screw thread 10 mm each **3/10**

10259

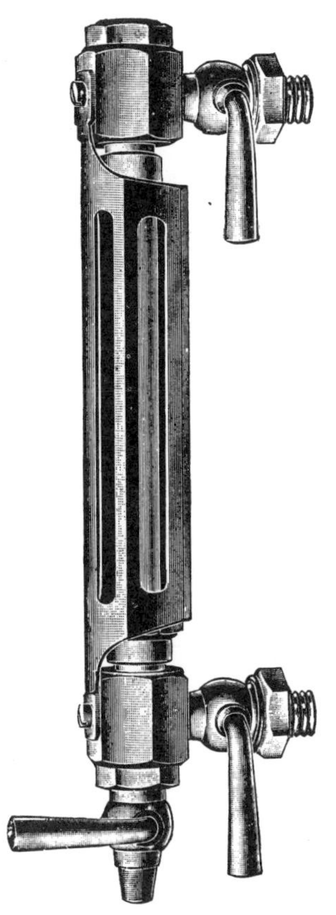

10257

Watergauge Glass
2 taps with screws (hexagonal) and outlet tap and casing

10257/1 $5^3/_4$ in. long, thread 7 mm each **11/8**

„ /2 $7^1/_2$ in. long, thread 10 mm each **15/4**

10261

Closing Screw (hexagonal)

10261/1 diam. of screw $^3/_4$ in., thread 10 mm . . doz. **13/8**

„ /2 diam. of screw $1^1/_8$ in., thread 12,5 mm . . doz. **20/6**

Waste pipe
wiih 2 pipe-couplings (stuffing box)

10260/1 2 in. long, diam. of pipe 4 mm, boring 2 mm each **2/10**

10260/2 $2^3/_8$ in. long, diam. of pipe 7 mm, boring 2,5 mm each **3/10**

10260

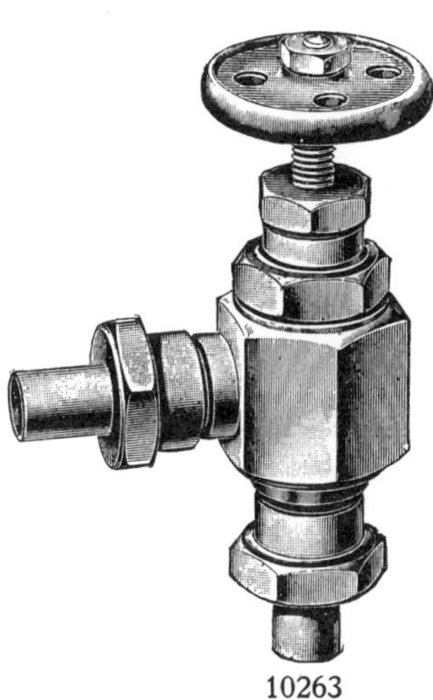

10263

Regulating Valve Tap
with 2 couplings (stuffing box)

10263/1 2 in. long, diam. of pipe 4 mm, boring 2 mm, each **5/—**

„ /2 3 in. long, diam. of pipe 7 mm, boring 2,5 mm, each **6/10**

10266

Steam Stop Cock
with boiler screw and 1 pipe coupling (stuffing box)

10266/1 $1^3/_4$ in. long, thread 7,5 mm, diam. of pipe 4 mm, boring 2 mm . . . . . . each **2/8**

„ /2 $2^1/_4$ in. long, thread 10 mm, diam. of pipe 7 mm, boring 2,5 mm . . . . . each **3/10**

10267

Pressure Gauge Tap
with screw

10267/1 $1^3/_8$ in. high, thread 7,5 mm doz. **22/8**

„ /2 $1^3/_4$ in. high, thread 10 mm doz. **31/6**

10265

Outlet Tap with boiler screw

10265/1 $1^1/_4$ in. long, thread 7,5 mm, boring 2 mm . . doz. **25/4**

„ /2 $1^5/_8$ in. long, thread 10 mm, boring 2,5 mm . . doz. **34/—**

Extra large, fine Fittings, strong and elegant finish

brass, finely nickelled, dull

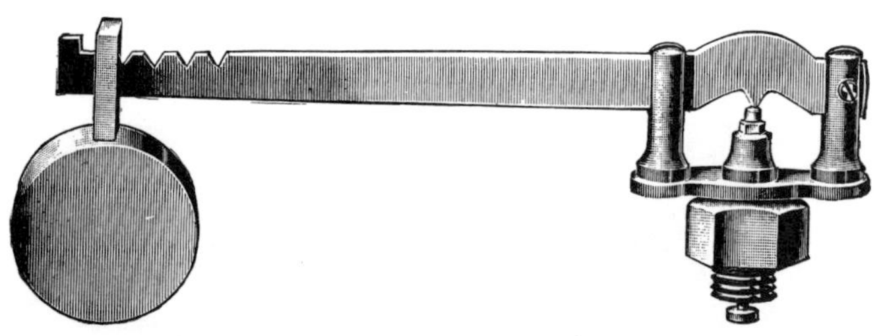

10258

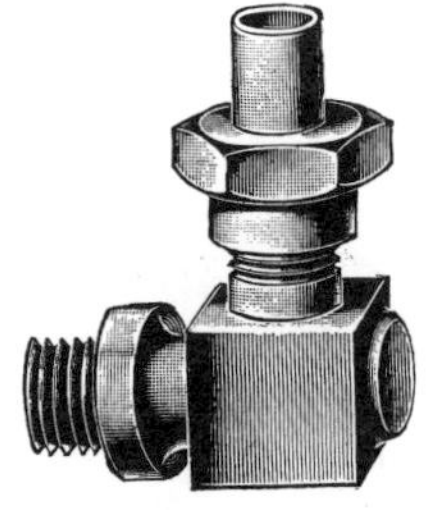

10262

10258/1	**Lever Safety Valve** with boiler screw and valve cone, length 5 in., thread 10 mm	each **3/10**
„ /2	„ „ „ „ „ „ „ „ „ „ $6^1/_8$ „ „ 12,5 „	each **5/4**
10262/1	**Boiler Tube** with boiler screw and socket joint, $1^1/_2$ in. long, diam. of tube 4 mm, boring 2 mm . .	doz. **36/6**
„ /2	„ „ „ „ „ „ „ „ $1^3/_4$ „ „ „ „ „ 7 „ „ 2,5 „ . .	each **4/4**

10264

10238 and 10239

10264/1	**Three Way Tap** with boiler screw and 2 socket joints, $1^5/_8$ in. long, thread 7,5 mm, diam. of tube 3 mm	doz. **36/6**
„ /2	„ „ „ „ „ „ „ „ 2 „ „ 2 „ „ „ 10 „ „ „ „ 4 „	each **4/4**
10238	**Flywheels** extra large, cast iron, 30 mm wide diam. 210 mm, cast iron rough	each **4/10**
10239	„ „ „ „ „ 30 „ „ „ 210 „ „ „ turned, with hole.	each **14/2**

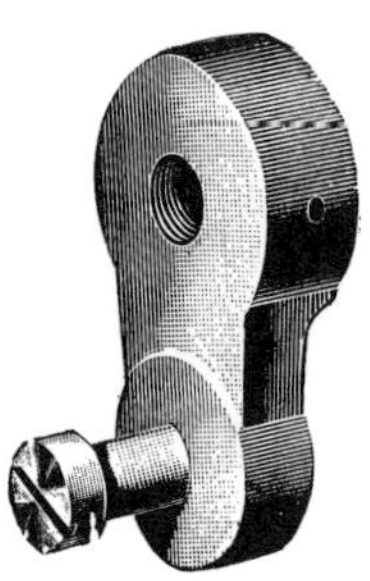

7073

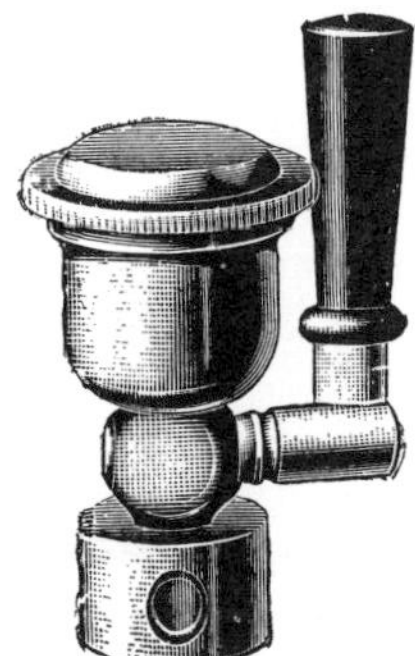

7074

7073/4	**Crank** made of castings with screw, $^9/_{16}$ in.	doz. **34/—**
„ /5	„ „ „ „ „ „ $^{11}/_{16}$ „	„ **42/—**
„ /6	„ „ „ „ „ „ $^7/_8$ „	„ **54/—**
7074	**Oiler** made of brass casting with tap $1^9/_{16}$ in. high	„ **28/—**

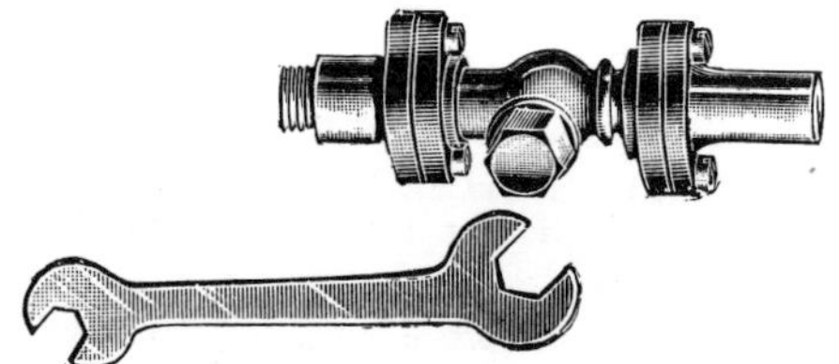

7377

7377 **Closing Tap,** extra large brass, with flanges and spanner to screw on the nut, tap $2^1/_2$ in. long . . . . each **5/6**

Extra large, fine Fittings, Strong and elegant Finish.

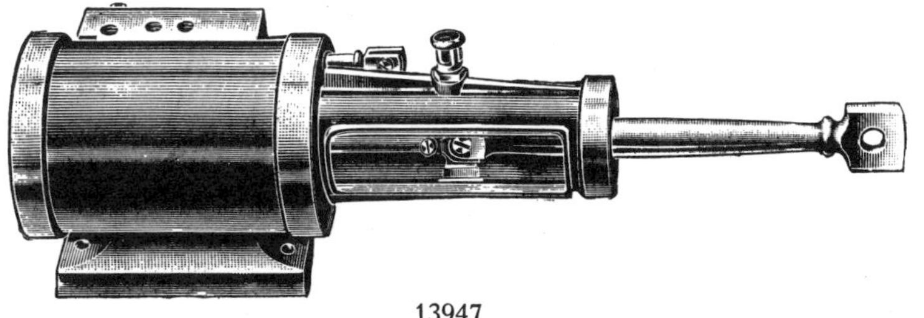

13947

13947 Fixed Steam Cylinder,

extra large, with slide valve, technically perfect, brass with screwed bottom, with guide bar, strong piston rod, oiler etc.

diam. of piston 1 in., entire length 8 in.

each **76/—**

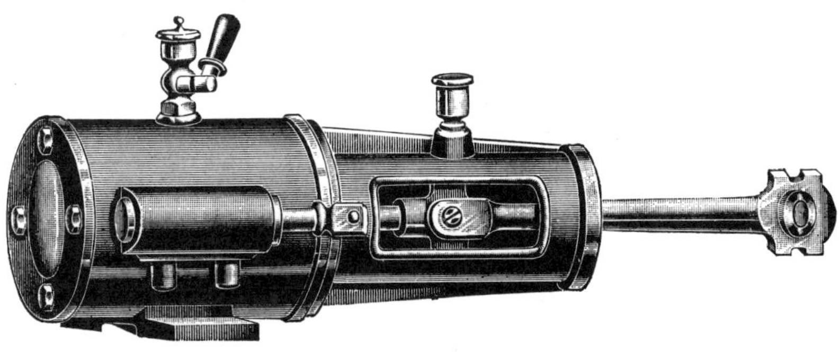

7069

7069 Fixed Steam Cylinder

technically perfect made of brass castings, with guide bar and tubular slide valve

size	1	2
diam. of piston	1	$1^1/_4$ in.
length of stroke	$1^1/_4$	$1^7/_{16}$ „
distance from centre of stroke to centre of cylinder	$5^1/_2$	$5^3/_4$ „
each	**60/—**	**90/—**

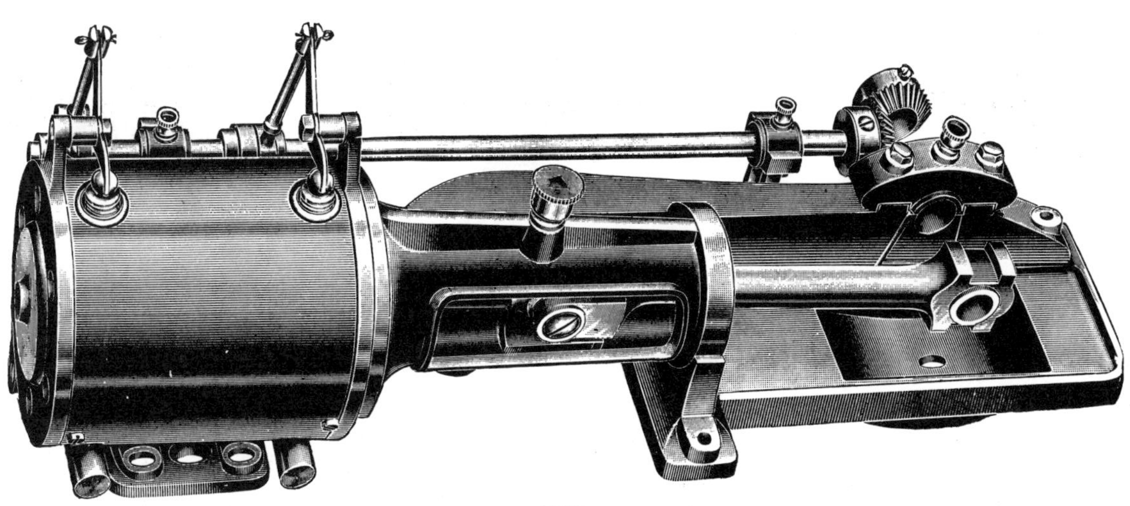

7072

7072 Model Steam Cylinder with valve motion, extra large, finish technically perfect throughout, with screwed bottom, guide bar, massive piston rod, oiler etc., diam. of piston $1^3/_8$ in., entire length of stroke $1^3/_4$ in., distance from centre of cylinder to centre of axle $8^1/_4$ in. . . . . each **140/—**

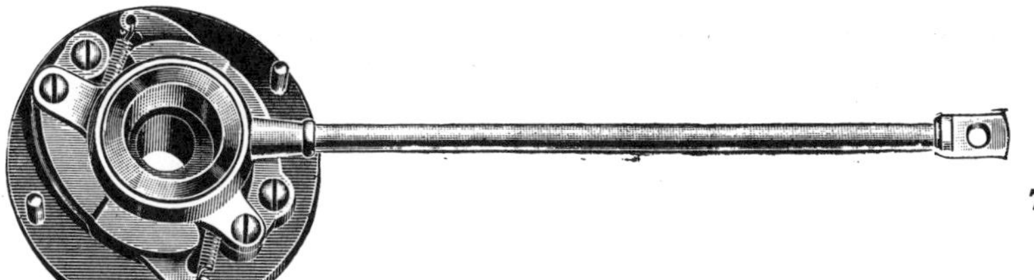

7075/1 and /2

Axle Regulator with adjustable Eccentric Ring

7075/1 diam. of disc $1^5/_8$ in., length $4^1/_4$ in. each **10/—**

„ /2 diam. of disc 2 in., length $5^1/_2$ in. each **14/—**

Best Fittings for Model Steam Engines

strong and heavy make, extra large.

7076/2

Model Governor
correctly working

7076/1 $4^1/_4$ in. high, without regulator each **7/—**

„ /2 $4^1/_2$ in. high, with regulator each **11/6**

„ /3 $5^1/_2$ in. high, with regulator each **15/6**

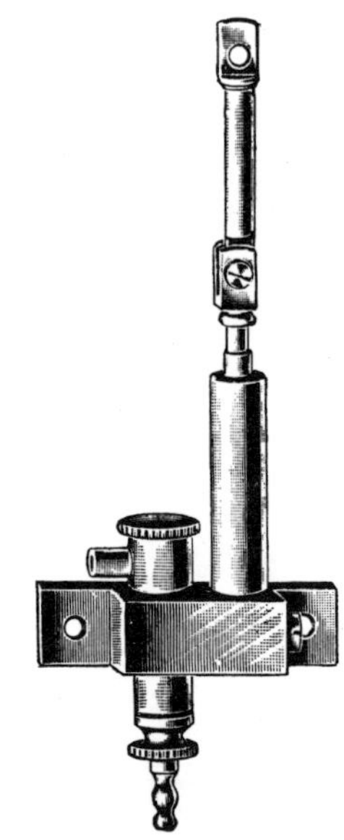
9341

9341 Boiler Feeding Pump
for Traction Engines
with tap and india rubber tube
highly nickelled
each **6/—**

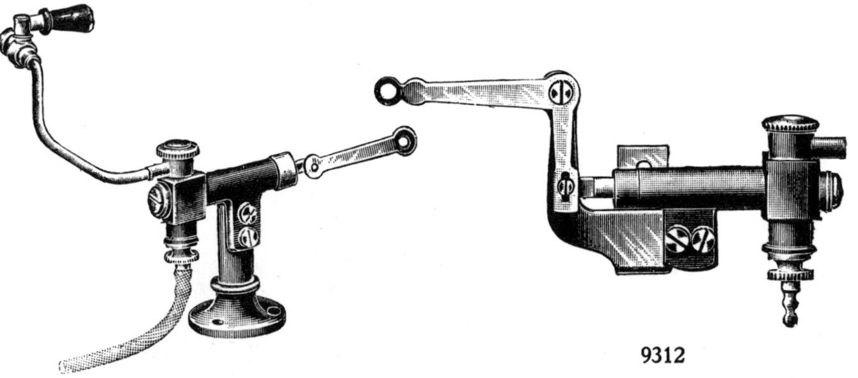
9247 9312

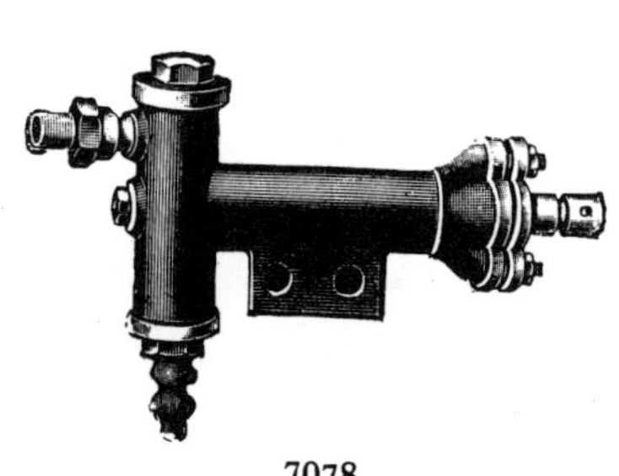
7078

9247/0 **Boiler Feeding Pump** with lever gear, for horizontal Steam Engines, with stand, tap and India-rubber tube, highly nickelled, bore $^3/_{16}$ in. . . . . . each **6/—**
„ /1 do. do. „ $^3/_{16}$ „ . . . . . „ **6/—**
„ /2 do. do. „ $^3/_{16}$ „ . . . . . „ **6/—**
9312 do. with lever gear, for horizontal Steam Engines, with tap, India rubber tube, and fastening plates, highly nickelled, bore $^3/_{16}$ in. . . . . . each **6/4**
7078 do. of superior workmanship for $^3/_{16}$ in. pistons of horizontal engines . . . . „ **10/—**

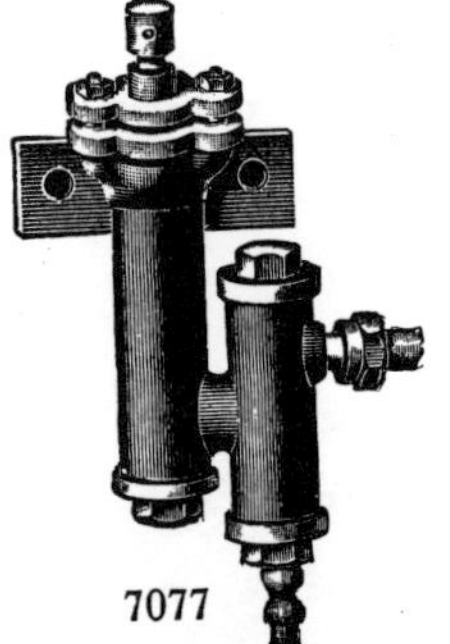
7077

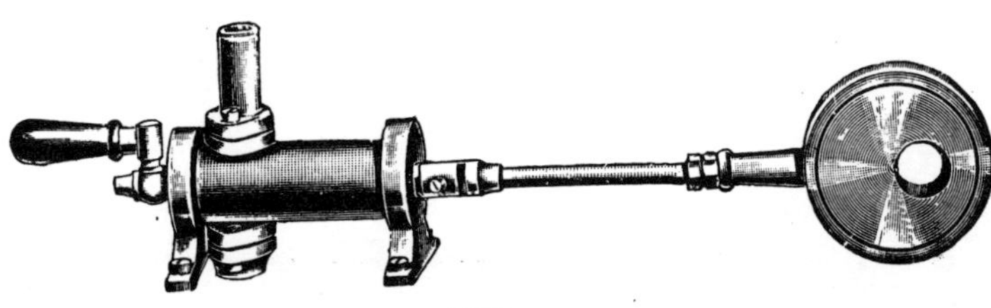
7350

7077 Boiler Feeding Pump of superior workmanship for $^3/_{16}$ in. pistons of vertical engines . . . . each **10/—**
7350 Feeding Pump, extra large, brass, eccentric stroke and flanges, tube-connection and pipe-end, length of cylinder $1^3/_4$ in., bore $^5/_{16}$ in. . . . . . each **26/6**

Wheels for Locomotives and Engines.

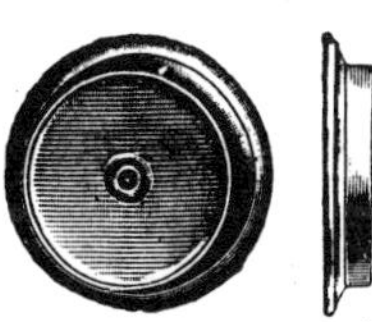

7304

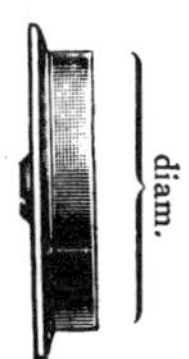

9499

9034

7304/0	**Flanged Wheels** with axle hole, stamped sheet iron, black, outer diam., $1^{1}/_{16}$ in.	gross	**19/—**
„ /1	„ „ „ „ „ „ „ „ „ „ „ „ $1^{1}/_{2}$ „	„	**26/—**
9499/1	„ „ „ „ „ cast lead, solid, diam. of flange $^{13}/_{16}$ in.	„	**8/6**
„ /2	„ „ „ „ „ „ „ „ „ „ „ $^{7}/_{8}$ „	„	**11/—**
„ /3	„ „ „ „ „ „ „ „ „ „ „ $1^{7}/_{16}$ „	„	**27/6**
„ /4	„ „ „ „ „ „ „ „ „ „ „ $1^{11}/_{16}$ „	„	**39/—**
9034/0	„ „ „ „ „ solid cast lead with stroke, diam. of flange $1^{1}/_{8}$ in.	doz.	**3/—**

9395

Flanged Wheels for Locomotives
iron, turned, with axle hole and thread, without stroke

9395/1	diam. of flange $^{3}/_{4}$ in.	doz.	**2/2**
„ /2	„ „ „ $^{11}/_{16}$ „	„	**3/2**
„ /3	„ „ „ 1 „	„	**4/4**
„ /4	„ „ „ $1^{1}/_{8}$ „	„	**5/4**
„ /5	„ „ „ $1^{5}/_{16}$ „	„	**6/—**
„ /7	„ „ „ $1^{5}/_{8}$ „	„	**8/—**
„ /8	„ „ „ $1^{7}/_{8}$ „	„	**9/—**
„ /10	„ „ „ $2^{7}/_{16}$ „	„	**10/—**
„ /12	„ „ „ $2^{7}/_{8}$ „	„	**12/8**

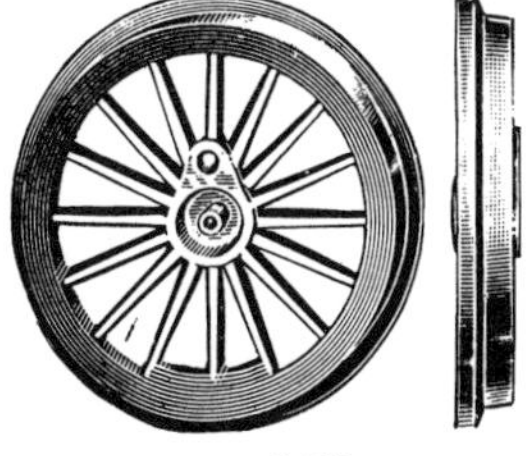

9423

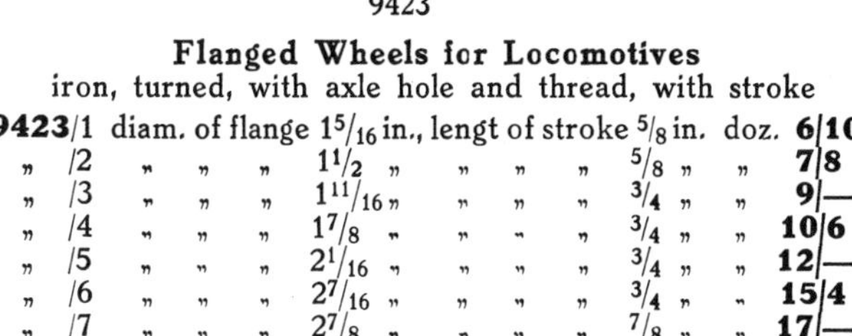

Flanged Wheels for Locomotives
iron, turned, with axle hole and thread, with stroke

9423/1	diam. of flange $1^{5}/_{16}$ in., lengt of stroke $^{5}/_{8}$ in.	doz.	**6/10**
„ /2	„ „ „ $1^{1}/_{2}$ „ „ „ „ $^{5}/_{8}$ „	„	**7/8**
„ /3	„ „ „ $1^{11}/_{16}$ „ „ „ „ $^{3}/_{4}$ „	„	**9/—**
„ /4	„ „ „ $1^{7}/_{8}$ „ „ „ „ $^{3}/_{4}$ „	„	**10/6**
„ /5	„ „ „ $2^{1}/_{16}$ „ „ „ „ $^{3}/_{4}$ „	„	**12/—**
„ /6	„ „ „ $2^{7}/_{16}$ „ „ „ „ $^{3}/_{4}$ „	„	**15/4**
„ /7	„ „ „ $2^{7}/_{8}$ „ „ „ „ $^{7}/_{8}$ „	„	**17/—**

8496/0—1 and 7431/1

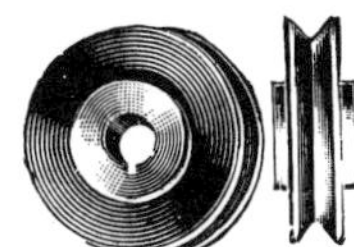

8496/2—3 and 7431/2—3

8496/4—8 and 7431/4—8

Pulley Wheels, cast lead

	size	0	1	2	3	4	5		6	7	8	
	diam.	$^{5}/_{8}$	$^{11}/_{16}$	$^{13}/_{16}$	1	$1^{3}/_{16}$	$1^{9}/_{16}$		2	$2^{3}/_{8}$	$2^{3}/_{4}$	in.
8496	without groove: gross	**8/8**	**14/—**	**17/4**	**18/—**	**23/—**	**24/—**		**26/—**	**38/—**	**52/—**	
7431	with groove: „	—	**16/—**	**20/6**	**20/6**	**26/—**	**30/—**	doz.	**3/—**	**3/2**	**5/2**	

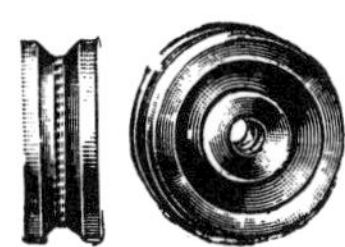

9211

8490

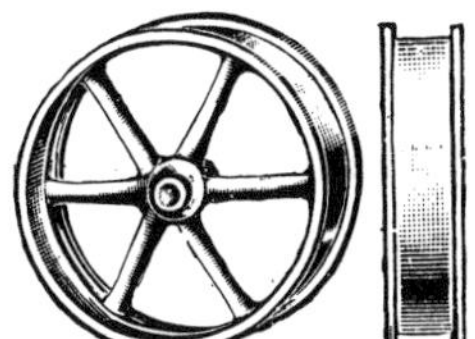

8494

9211/1	**Brass Pulley Wheels,** finely nickelled for round driving band or belt, diam. $^{5}/_{8}$ in.	doz.	**5/—**
„ /2	„ „ „ „ „ „ „ „ „ „ „ „ $^{13}/_{16}$ „	„	**7/6**
„ /3	„ „ „ „ „ „ „ „ „ „ „ „ 1 „	„	**14/6**
„ /4	„ „ „ „ „ „ „ „ „ „ „ „ $1^{3}/_{8}$ „	each	**4/2**
8490/1	**Driving Wheels,** cast iron, with groove, turned, diam. $1^{3}/_{16}$ in.	doz.	**5/2**
„ /2	„ „ „ „ „ „ „ „ „ $1^{9}/_{16}$ „	„	**6/4**
„ /3	„ „ „ „ „ „ „ „ „ $1^{7}/_{8}$ „	„	**8/6**
8494/1	**Pulley Wheels,** cast lead, with axle hole, diam. $1^{3}/_{4}$ in.	gross	**26/—**
„ /2	„ „ „ „ „ „ „ „ $2^{9}/_{16}$ „	doz.	**3/6**

Fly Wheels and Fittings for Shaftings.

8502

Fly Wheels

cast lead, with axle hole and boss

size	0	1	$1^{1}/_{2}$	2	3	4	5	6	7	8
diam.	$1^{3}/_{8}$	$1^{5}/_{8}$	$1^{3}/_{4}$	2	$2^{9}/_{16}$	$2^{7}/_{8}$	$3^{1}/_{8}$	$3^{3}/_{4}$	$4^{3}/_{8}$	$4^{15}/_{16}$ in.
8502 gross	**22/—**	**27/4**	**30/6**	doz. **2/10**	**4/—**	**4/10**	**9/—**	**16/—**	**18/—**	**20/—**

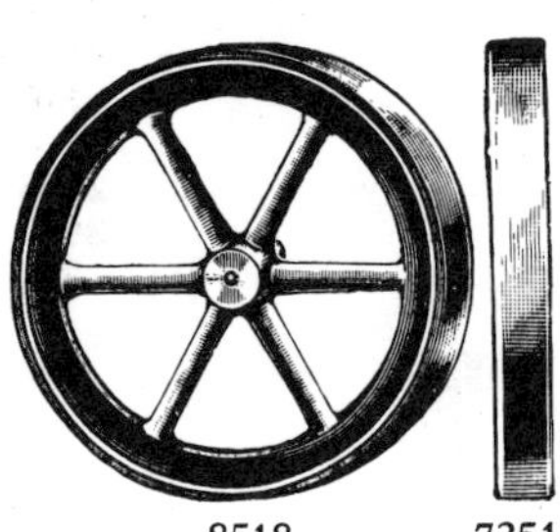

8518 7351

Fly Wheels,

solid, cast iron

	size	1	2	3	4	5	6	7	8	9
	diam.	$2^{1}/_{2}$	3	$3^{1}/_{4}$	$3^{11}/_{16}$	$4^{1}/_{16}$	$4^{7}/_{16}$	$4^{3}/_{4}$	$5^{1}/_{2}$	$6^{1}/_{4}$ in.
8518	rough, without hole, doz.	**4/—**	**4/10**	**7/6**	**8/—**	**9/—**	**12/—**	**12/8**	**16/6**	**28/—**
7351	turned, with hole, with threads „	**9/6**	**12/4**	**17/4**	**18/—**	**20/—**	**26/6**	**31/6**	**43/6**	each **6/4**

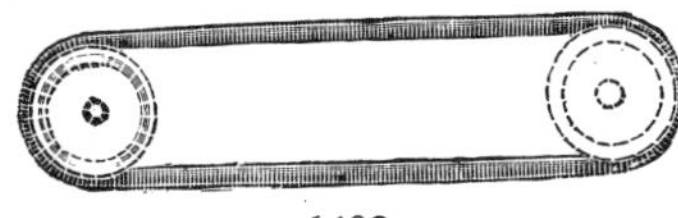

6408

6408/1 **Driving Band,** spiral, made of brass, spiral $^{1}/_{16}$ in. diam. . . . . doz. meters **2/8**
„ /2 „ „ „ „ „ „ $^{3}/_{32}$ „ „ . . . . „ „ **3/10**
„ /3 „ „ „ „ „ „ $^{1}/_{8}$ „ „ . . . . „ „ **5/2**

Fittings for Shaftings.

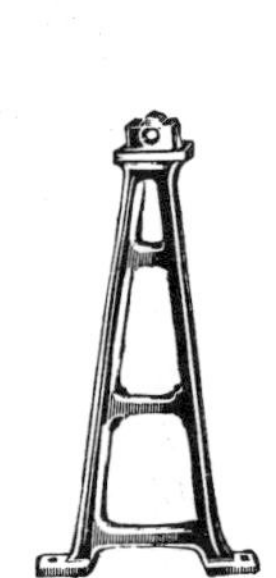

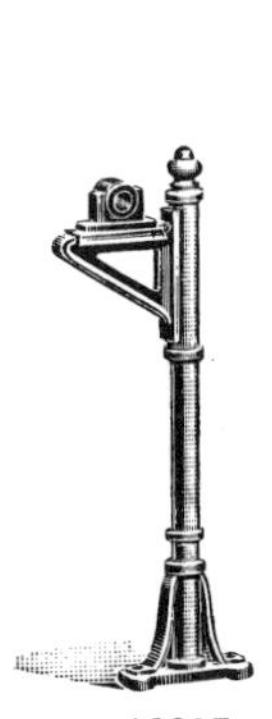

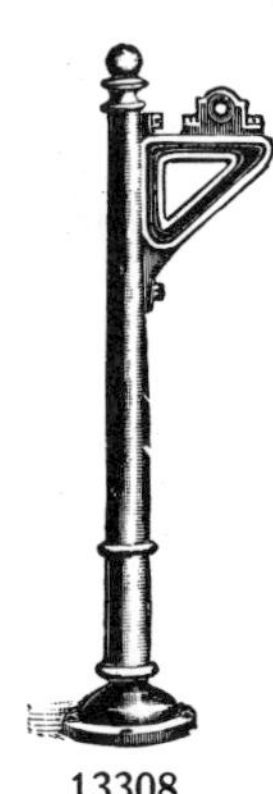

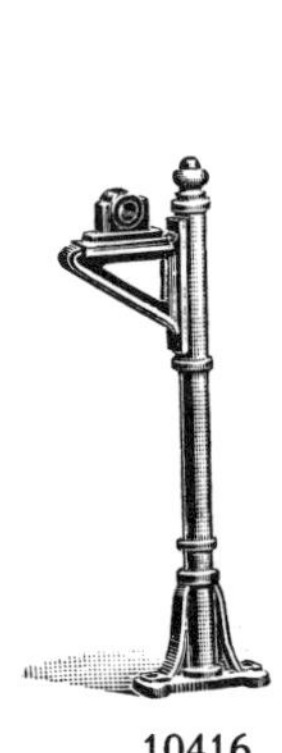

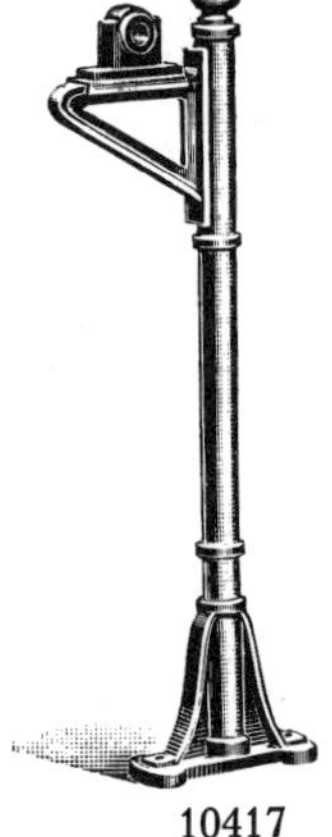

9242 9012 13307 13308 10416 10417

9242 **Shafting Support,** composition casting, 7 in. high . . . . doz. **4/10**
9012 „ „ „ $6^{1}/_{4}$ „ „ . . . . „ **6/—**
13307/1 do. cast iron, rough, without hole, $6^{1}/_{4}$ in. high . . . . „ **6/10**
„ /2 „ „ „ japanned and bronzed, with hole, $6^{1}/_{4}$ in. high . . . . „ **11/2**
13308/1 do. „ „ rough, without hole, $8^{1}/_{2}$ in. high . . . . „ **15/—**
„ /2 „ „ „ japanned and bronzed, with hole, $8^{1}/_{2}$ in. high . . . . „ **26/—**
10416/1 do. „ „ rough, $5^{3}/_{4}$ in. high. . . . . „ **6/—**
„ /2 „ „ „ japanned, with hole, $5^{3}/_{4}$ in. high . . . . „ **12/—**
10417/1 do. „ „ rough, $8^{3}/_{4}$ in. high. . . . . „ **18/—**
„ /2 „ „ „ japanned, with hole, $8^{3}/_{4}$ in. high . . . . „ **24/—**

7309

7309 **Shafts,** iron, $^{3}/_{16}$ in. diam., with groove, in pieces of 1 meter (about 39 in.) . . . . doz. meters **8/6**

7422

7422 **Wedges** for fixing wheels on shaftings . . . . gross **5/—**

Fittings for Locomotives and Railway Carriages.

7368 7371 7374 7373 7382/1

7368/0	**Buffers** cast lead, black oxidised, $^{9}/_{16}$ in. long	gross	**13/10**
„ /1	„ „ „ „ „ „ $^{3}/_{4}$ „ „	„	**19/—**
7371/0	„ „ „ „ „ „ $^{5}/_{8}$ „ „ , plate $^{1}/_{4}$ in. diam.	„	**12/—**
„ /1	„ „ „ „ „ „ $^{13}/_{16}$ „ „ „ $^{3}/_{8}$ „ „	„	**18/—**
7374/1	„ cast lead body, japanned, with nickelled brass buffer, $^{3}/_{4}$ in. long	doz.	**5/—**
„ /2	„ „ „ „ „ „ „ „ „ 1 „ „	„	**6/10**
7373/0	„ brass, finely polished, $^{5}/_{8}$ in. long, plate $^{1}/_{4}$ in. diam.	„	**3/6**
„ /1	„ „ „ „ $^{13}/_{16}$ „ „ „ $^{3}/_{8}$ „ „	„	**4/6**
„ /2	„ „ „ „ $^{15}/_{16}$ „ „ „ $^{7}/_{16}$ „ „	„	**6/—**
7382/1	„ brass finely nickelled **with spring**, $^{9}/_{16}$ in. long	„	**10/—**

9087 6338 6342

9087/0	**Coupling Hooks** for locos and carriages gauge 0	gross sets	**6/4**
„ /1	„ „ „ „ „ „ „ 1	„ „	**12/8**
6338/0	„ „ „ „ „ „ „ 0	gross	**13/8**
„ /1	„ „ „ „ „ „ „ 1	„	**22/—**
6342	„ „ „ „ „ „ „ 2—4, **solid brass hook** with **brass eye**	„	**6/4**

6354 6349/1 6349/2 6349/3 9118 9177

6354	**Locomotive Lanterns**, cast lead, oxidised, $^{15}/_{16}$ in. heigh	doz.	**3/—**
6349/1	„ „ „ „ „ with reflctor, $1^{3}/_{16}$ in. high	„	**3/—**
6349/2	„ „ „ „ „ „ „ $1^{1}/_{4}$ „ „	„	**6/4**
6349/3	„ „ „ „ „ „ „ $1^{7}/_{16}$ „ „	„	**9/6**
9118	„ „ „ „ „ „ „ and lens, $1^{9}/_{16}$ in. high	„	**9/—**
9177	„ „ cast lead, finely oxidised, with nickelled reflector, **electric** lamp with small bulb, $1^{3}/_{16}$ in. long	each	**2/6**

Spirit Lamps for Steam Engines and Steam Locomotives.

9411

8216

8217

9557/1 and /2

9557/3—5

9411	**Cheap Spirit Lamp,** $1^3/_{16}$ in. diam., 1 in. high		gross	**18/—**
8216/00	**Spirit Lamps,** tin, round, with 1 burner diam. $1^7/_{16}$ in., high $1^3/_{16}$ in.		doz.	**2/8**
„ /0	„ „ „ „ „ 1 „ „ $1^9/_{16}$ „ „ $1^3/_{16}$ „		„	**3/—**
„ /1	„ „ „ „ „ 1 „ „ $1^9/_{16}$ „ „ $1^1/_8$ „		„	**3/2**
„ /2	„ „ „ „ „ 1 „ „ $1^3/_4$ „ „ 1 „		„	**3/6**
„ /3	„ „ „ „ „ 1 „ „ $1^3/_4$ „ „ $1^3/_8$ „		„	**4/4**
„ /4	„ „ „ „ „ 1 „ „ $2^1/_8$ „ „ $1^3/_8$ „		„	**5/—**
„ /5	„ „ „ „ „ 1 „ „ $2^1/_2$ „ „ $1^5/_8$ „		„	**6/2**
8217/1	**Spirit Lamps,** tin, round, with 2 burners, diam. $1^3/_4$ in., high $1^1/_8$ in.		doz.	**4/4**
„ /2	„ „ „ „ „ 2 „ „ $1^3/_4$ „ „ $1^3/_8$ „		„	**4/10**
„ /3	„ „ „ „ „ 2 „ „ $2^1/_2$ „ „ $1^3/_8$ „		„	**5/2**
„ /4	„ „ „ „ „ 2 „ „ $2^1/_2$ „ „ $1^5/_8$ „		„	**6/2**
„ /5	„ „ „ „ „ 2 „ „ $3^1/_2$ „ „ $1^3/_4$ „		„	**7/6**
9557/1	**Spirit Lamps with Vaporiser,** (Gas generating lamps) diam. $1^3/_4$ in., high $1^1/_4$ in.		„	**9/—**
„ /2	„ „ „ „ „ „ „ „ $1^3/_4$ „ „ $1^1/_2$ „		„	**10/6**
„ /3	„ „ „ „ „ „ „ „ $2^1/_8$ „ „ $1^3/_4$ „		„	**12/—**
„ /4	„ „ „ „ „ „ „ „ $2^1/_8$ „ „ $1^3/_4$ „		„	**12/6**
„ /5	„ „ „ „ „ „ „ „ $2^1/_2$ „ „ 2 „		„	**15/—**

Spirit Vapor Lamp, nickelled

10397/1 and 2

No.	long	wide	high	with		Price
10397/1	$3^1/_2$ in. long,	$1^3/_4$ in. wide,	$1^3/_8$ in. high,	with 1 burner	doz.	**24/—**
„ /2	4 „	„ $1^3/_4$ „	„ $1^5/_8$ „	„ „ 1 „	„	**24/—**
„ /3	$5^1/_4$ „	„ $2^1/_4$ „	„ 2 „	„ „ 2 burners	each	**3/6**
„ /4	6 „	„ $2^1/_2$ „	„ $2^1/_4$ „	„ „ 3 „	„	**4/6**
„ /5	7 „	„ $2^1/_2$ „	„ $2^1/_4$ „	„ „ 3 „	„	**5/—**

Spirit Vapor Lamps, nickelled with fire door

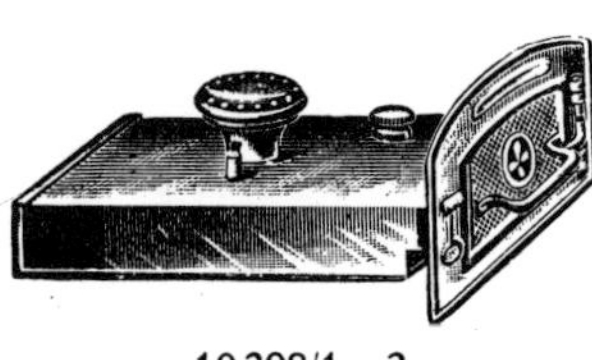
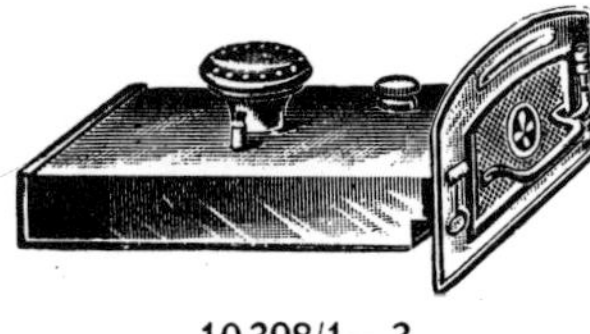
10398/1—3

No.	long	wide	high	with		Price
10398/1	4 in. long,	2 in. wide,	$1^5/_8$ in. high,	with 1 burner	each	**2/6**
„ /2	$4^1/_2$ „	„ $1^3/_4$ „	„ $1^1/_2$ „	„ „ 1 „	„	**2/6**
„ /3	$4^3/_4$ „	„ 2 „	„ $1^7/_8$ „	„ „ 1 „	„	**3/—**
„ /4	$4^3/_4$ „	„ $1^7/_8$ „	„ $1^3/_8$ „	„ „ 2 burners	„	**3/—**
„ /5	$5^1/_4$ „	„ 2 „	„ $1^7/_8$ „	„ „ 2 „	„	**3/6**
„ /6	6 „	„ $2^1/_4$ „	„ $1^3/_4$ „	„ „ 2 „	„	**4/—**

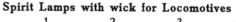

Spirit Lamps with wick for Locomotives

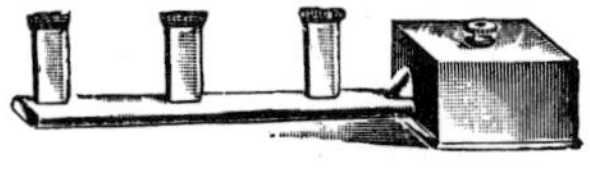
10401 tin, retinned

	10401/0	1	2	3	4	5
entire length	$4^3/_4$	$5^1/_8$	$5^1/_2$	$5^3/_4$	$5^1/_2$	$7^3/_4$ in.
height	$^7/_8$	$^{13}/_{16}$	$^{13}/_{16}$	$^{11}/_{16}$	$^7/_8$	1 in.
container . .	$^{13}/_{16}\times{}^3/_4$	$1^3/_{16}\times1^3/_8$	$1^3/_8\times{}^{13}/_{16}$	$1^3/_{16}\times1^7/_8$	$2^1/_8\times1$	$1^3/_{16}\times2^3/_{16}$ in.
flame . . .	0,08	0,12	0,12	0,08	0,08	0,12 in.
doz.	**9/—**	**11/6**	**10/6**	**9/6**	**9/6**	**14/6**

Spirit Vapor Lamps, nickelled with 1 gas tube

10399/1 and 2

10399/1	length „a“ $4^1/_8$ in.	height 1 in.	container $1^3/_8\times1^1/_2$ in.	each	**2/6**
„ /2	„ „a“ $4^1/_2$ „	„ $^{13}/_{16}$ „	„ $1^{13}/_{16}\times1^3/_{16}$ „	„	**3/—**

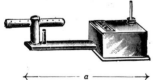

Spirit Vapor Lamps, nickelled with 2 gas tubes

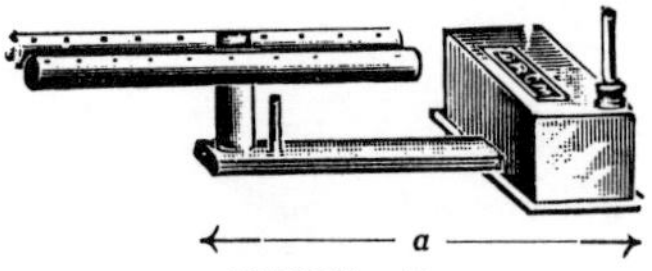
10400/1—7

	10400/1	2	3	4	5	6	7
length „a“ .	$4^1/_8$	$4^3/_4$	6	$6^3/_4$	$4^3/_4$	6	$6^1/_2$ in.
height . . .	$1^1/_8$	1	1	1	$1^1/_4$	$1^3/_8$	$1^5/_8$ in.
container	$1^1/_2\times1^1/_2$	$1^7/_8\times1^7/_8$	2×2	$2^1/_4\times2^1/_4$	$1\times2^3/_4$	$1^1/_4\times3^1/_8$	$1^3/_4\times3^1/_4$ in.
each	**2/6**	**3/—**	**3/6**	**4/—**	**4/6**	**5/—**	**7/—**

Accessories for Toys driven by Steam.

9021

9021/1	**Wicks** round,	1/4 in. diam.	doz. meters	**2/10**
„ /2	„	„ 5/16 „	„ „	**3/10**
„ /3	„	„ 3/8 „	„ „	**5/2**
„ /4	„	„ 1/2 „	„ „	**6/10**

9028

9028 **Wick,** flat, 1/2 in wide (5''') doz. meters **2/4**

10017

10041/1

10041/2

10017	**Oil funnel,** small, without handle	gross	**18/—**
10041/1	**Water funnels,** without handle	„	**12/8**
10041/2	„ „ with handle	„	**29/6**

8521

10042

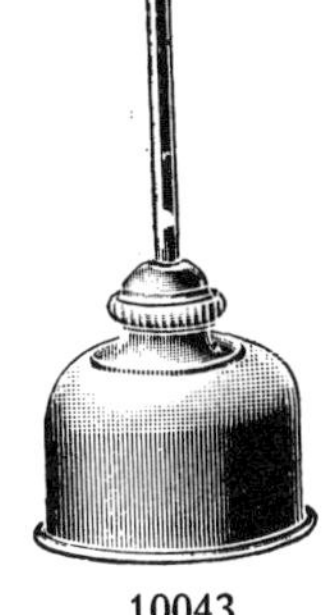
10043

10044

8521	**Measure** tin, $1^3/_4$ in. diam.	gross	**12/8**
10042	„ graduated, tin, $2^3/_8$ in. high, $1^3/_8$ in diam.	doz.	**3/6**
10043	**Oiler** tin, with brass top to unscrew $1^5/_8$ in.	„	**5/10**
10044	**Oil Cup** filled with finest Machine Oil	„	**7/4**

10045

10045 **Screw Driver,** $3^3/_4$ in. long . . . . . . gross **12/8**

10046

10046 **Oil brush,** $3^3/_8$ in. long . . . . . . doz. **5/10**

10047

10047 **Fire poker,** 4 in. long . . . . . . gross **12/8**

STEAM LOCOMOTIVES

STEAM TRAINS

Model Steam Locomotives

English Types.

Our Steam Locomotives are so widely known for absolute reliability from the cheapest to the best that they need no further comment. They are well modelled and the lettering and lining is correct.

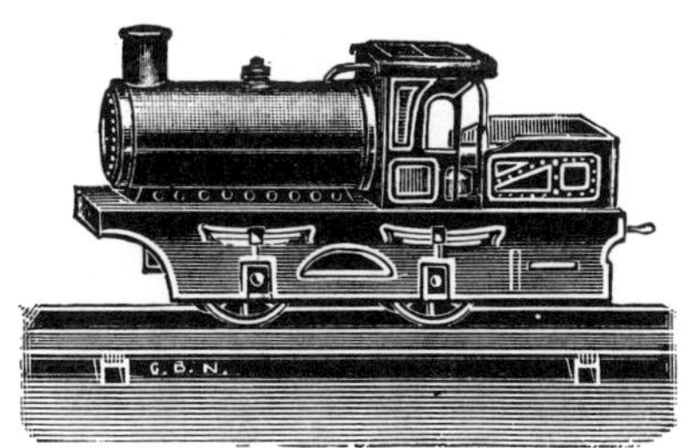

30592/0	30593/0
M. R.	L.N.W.R.

Gauge 0 = $1^3/_8$ in.

30592/0 } **Steam Tender Loco** (Force Locomotive) with oscillating brass cylinder, stamped frame, polished brass
30593/0 } boiler and safety valve, $7^1/_2$ in. long . . . . each **3/10**

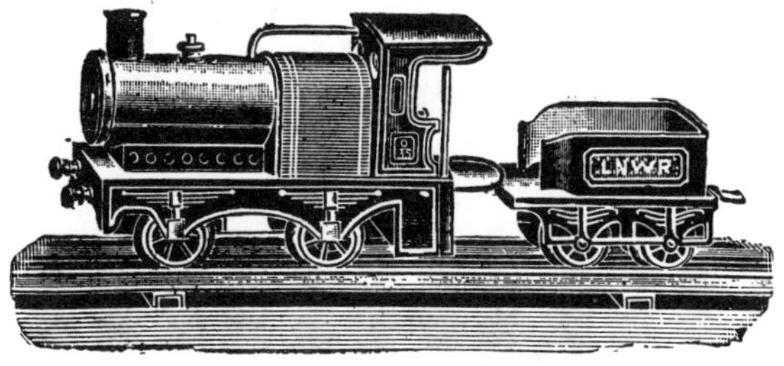

31592/0	31593/0
M. R.	L.N.W.R.

Gauge 0 = **$1^3/_8$** in.

31592/0 } **Steam Loco with Tender** (Force Locomotive) stamped frame, polished brass boiler, oscillating brass
31593/0 } cylinder and safety valve, $10^3/_4$ in. long (includ. tender) . . . . complete with tender each **5/6**

29592/0	29593/0
M. R.	L.N.W.R.

Gauge 0 = **$1^3/_8$** in.

29592/0 } **Steam Loco with Tender** (Force Locomotive) stamped frame, polished brass boiler, oscillating brass
29593/0 } cylinder, safety valve and steam whistle, excellent working model, $11^3/_4$ in. long (includ. tender)
complete with tender each **7/4**

Improved Models of Steam Locomotives.

Gauge 0 = $1^3/_8$ in.

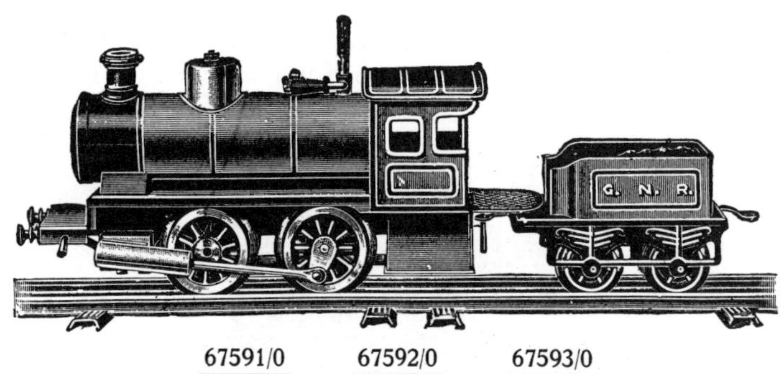

67591/0	67592/0	67593/0
G. W. R.	M. R.	L. N. W. R.

Special Value.

67591/0
67592/0
67593/0 **Steam Locomotive with Tender,** painted in the correct colours of the respective Railway Companies. This loco is fitted with 2 oscillating outside cylinders, steam dome, steam whistle, flame guard and safety valve; the boiler and the wheels are japanned, $11^5/_8$ in. long (includ. tender) . . . . complete with tender each **9/6**

39591/0	39592/0	39593/0
G. W. R.	M. R.	L. N. W. R.

Correct colouring, lettering and lining.

39591/0
39592/0
39593/0 **Steam Locomotive with Tender,** exact working model with finely japanned brass boiler, with 2 oscillating cylinders, steam dome, hand rails, steam whistle, flame guard, safety valve and 4 large japanned driving wheels, $13^1/_4$ in. long (includ. tender) . . . . complete with tender each **14/8**

13762/0

Made in M. R. G. N. R. L. N. W. R. colours; correctly painted lettered and lined.

13762/0 **Steam Pilot Loco, with Reversing Gear** finely japanned in assorted colours with oscillating brass cylinder and cog wheel gear to increase the power, steam whistle, safety valve and our special flame guard. All fittings are of solid brass finely japanned. The boiler, cab and all other parts are finely painted. The loco throughout is of heavy make . . . . each **17/10**

Improved Models of Steam Locomotives.

Gauge 0 = $1^1/_8$ in.

60591/0	60592/0	60593/0
G. W. R.	M. R.	L. N. W. R.

Correctly coloured, lettered and lined.

60591/0
60592/0
60593/0

Fine Steam Locomotive with Tender with fixed slide valve cylinders and with Slip Eccentric Reversing Gear with 2 fixed slide valve cylinders, finely japanned brass boiler, 4 large, finely nickelled flanged wheels, steam dome, bell steam whistle, **improved lubricating device built in the smoke box** and safety valve. Loco with flame guard and highly finished fittings; with Spirit Vapor Lamp, Tender finely japanned; $13^5/_8$ in. long

each **22/—**

28592/0	28593/0	28594/0
M. R.	L. N. W. R.	G. N. R.

Correctly painted, lettered and lined

28592/0
28593/0
28594/0

Improved, highly finished, Steam Locomotive with Tender with automatic reversing gear

Perfect Model, fitted **with Stephensons Link Motion Reversing Gear;** 2 fixed slide valve cylinders with tubular slide valves, accurately finished, finely japanned brass boiler, highly nickelled flanged wheels, steam dome, bell steam whistle, safety valve and **improved lubricating device built in the smoke box.** Loco with highly finished fittings, with new **gas generating Spirit Lamp,** improved flame guard, including Tender $14^3/_4$ in. long

each **32/6**

66591/0	66592/0	66593/0
G. W. R.	M. R.	L. N. W. R.

Correctly painted, lettered and lined

66591/0
66592/0
66593/0

New Model Express Steam Loco Entirely reconstructed and brought up to date.

This is the first really good model of an 8 wheeled Steam Locomotive in this small gauge 0.

With 2 fixed cylinders and reversing gear japanned brass boiler and best fittings, steam dome, **new flame guard,** safety valve, **new improved steam jet oiler** holding a large quantity of oil, which continually oils the working cylinders), with **new gas generating lamp,** tender with imitation coal, $14^1/_2$ in. long incl. tender

each **45/6**

Model Express Steam Locomotive

Gauge 0 = $1^3/_8$ in.

160/1595

160/1595 Continental Express Locomotive of the Latest Type well modelled, with fixed cylinders, cross-head, starting tap, spirit vapor lamp. Boiler made of brass finely painted in black. All fittings are of best make.

Entire length incl. tender 21 in. each **61/—**

It is advisable to let these long stretched engines run on our easy curves 36389/0 illustrated on page 196 *of this catalogue.*

Constructional Steam Locomotives

Gauge 0 = $1^3/_8$ in.

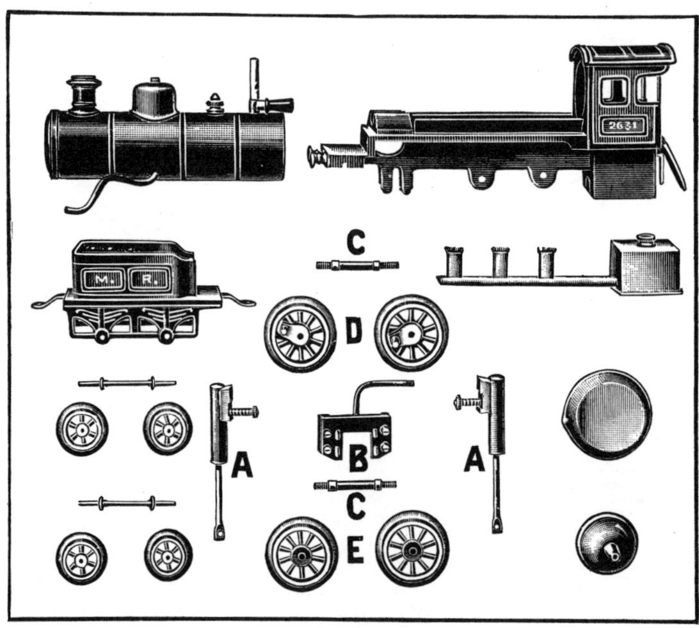

M 3415/0

M 3415/0 Complete Set of Finished Parts for Constructing Steam Locomotives gauge 0 = $1^3/_8$ in.
Set complete as illustration, consisting of all the parts as shown, when fitted up complete makes a splendid Model Steam Locomotive and Tender, packed in strong red cardboard box, assorted in M. R. & L. N. W. R. colours . . . . each set **13/—**

Improved Models of Steam Locomotives

Gauge 1 = $1^7/_8$ in.

67591/1	67592/1	67593/1
G. W. R.	M. R.	L. N. W. R.

Correctly painted, lettered and lined

67591/1
67592/1
67593/1 **Steam Locomotive with Tender** excellent working model with 2 oscillating cylinders, finely japanned brass boiler and best fittings, steam dome, steam whistle, flame guard, safety valve and japanned flanged wheels; . . . . including tender $14^3/_8$ in. long each **15/4**

30592/1	30593/1
M. R.	L. N. W. R.

Correctly painted lettered and lined

30592/1
30593/1 **Steam Tender Locomotive** (Force Locomotive) **with reversing gear,** oscillating cylinder, painted brass boiler, steam dome and steam whistle

$10^1/_2$ in. long each **18/8**

74592/1	74593/1
M. R.	L. N. W. R.

Correctly painted lettered and lined

74592/1
74593/1 **New improved and enlarged Model of Steam Locomotive with Tender** exact working model wi!h finely japanned brass boiler, with 2 oscillaling cylinders, steam dome, hand rails, steam whistle, flame guard, safety valve and 4 large finely japanned wheels; length incl. tender $16^1/_2$ in. each **21/6**

New Model Steam Locomotives

Improved and enlarged patterns.

13762/1

Made in G. N. R. and L. N. W. R. colours
Correctly painted lettered and lined.

Gauge 1 = $1^7/_8$ in.

13762/1 **Steam Tender Locomotive** with **reversing gear,** boiler and frame finely painted, with oscillating brass cylinder and cog wheel gear to increase the power, finely nickelled flanged wheels nickelled imitation piston rods, steam whistle, safety valve and steam dome, with flame guard, all fitings finest brass, 11 in. long, each **27/—**

60592/1	60593/1
M. R.	L.N.W.R.

correctly painted, lettered and lined.

60592/1
60593/1 **Fine Steam Locomotive with Tender with fixed slide valve cylinders and with Slip Eccentric Reversing gear** finely finished, with 2 fixed slide valve cyilnders, finely japanned brass boiler, 4 large, finely nickelled flanged wheels, 2 steam exhaust pipes, steam jet oiler, hand rails, steam dome, safety valve, steam whistle. Loco with flame guard and new **improved gas generating lamp;** all fittings highly finished. Tender finely japanned; including Tender $17^1/_2$ in. long . . . . each **29/—**

28592/1	28593/1	28594/1
M. R.	L.N.W.R.	G. N. R.

correctly painted lettered and lined.

28592/1
28593/1
28594/1 **Improved, highly finished Steam Locomotive with Tender with automatic reversing gear.** Most perfect model, fitted **with Stephensons Link Motion Reversing gear;** with 2 fixed slide valve cylinders with tubular slide valves, finely japanned brass boiler, highly nickelled flanged wheels, steam dome, bell steam whistle, starting tap, safety valve, hand rails and **improved lubricating device built in the smoke box.** All Fittings accurately finished, Loco with new **gas generating lamp,** with flame guard; including Tender $18^3/_4$ in. long . . . . each **42/—**

Improved Models of Express Steam Locomotives.

Entirely reconstructed and brought up to date.

Gauge 1 = $1^7/_8$ in.

66591/1

made in:	66591/1 G. W. R.	66592/1 M. R.	66593/1 L. N. W. R.

Correctly coloured, lettered and lined.

Steam Loco, elegantly japanned, with **reversing gear,** 2 fixed slide valve cylinders, accurately finished water gauge glass, japanned brass boiler and best fittings, steam whistle, steam dome, **improved flame guard** (to prevent the burning of the finely japanned frame parts) safety valve, **improved steam jet oiler** (holding a large quantity of oil, which continually oils the working cylinders) with starting tap, exhaust steam passing through the funnel, tender with imitation coal, 16. in long incl. tender . . . . each **72/—**

63593/1

L. & N. W. R. Express Steam Locomotive

finest finish and elegantly japanned, 2 fixed slide valve cylinders with tubular slide valves and guide bars, **with automatic reversing gear** (can be worked automatically from the rails or from the cab) with steam regulator to start or stop the engine, with finely japanned brass boiler and finely nickelled fittings, water gauge glass and bell steam whistle, **with feed-pump** (guaranteed for good working), **extra water supply carried in the tender,** with tubes to the feed-pump, large **gas generating vapour lamp** (burning abt. 20 min.) **with improved flame guard** (to prevent the burning of the finely japanned frame parts), tender with imitation coal, whole length incl. tender $24^1/_2$ in., height 7 in.

63593/1 **L. & N. W. R. colour** (London & North Western Railway) complete with tender . . . . each **98/—**

Model Steam Locomotives.

13345/2 J

Gauge 2 = $2^1/_8$ in.

13345/2 **Steam-Locomotive** (Tank or Pilot Locomotive) with reversing gear, 2 fixed slide valve cylinders, flame guard, 8 highly nickelled flanged wheels, oxidised brass boiler, bell steam whistle, safety valve, steam dome, starting tap, exhaust steam passing through the funnel imitating the smoke of the locomotive $12^1/_2$ in. long . . . . **42/—**

Steam Express Locomotives

with Reversing gear

2 fixed slide valve cylinders with guide bars, most accurately finished, 8 highly nickelled flanged wheels with connecting rods, japanned brass boiler, with flame guard, bell steam whistle, safety valve, water gauge, 2 domes, brass hand-rails, starting tap and steam jet oiler, **steam passing through the funnel** imitating the smoke of the locomotive, brass spring buffers and head lamp, tender with imitation coal, strong axle bearings, $24^1/_2$ in. long incl. tender.

Gauge 3 = $2^5/_8$ in.,

33594/3

33594/3 **Gauge 3 = $2^5/_8$ in., G. N. R., Express Loco** (Great Northern Railway), on 4 axles = 8 wheels complete with tender each **54/6**

33595/3 **Gauge 3 = $2^5/_8$ in., L. & S. W. R., Express Loco** (London & South Western Railway), on 4 axles = 8 wheels complete with tender each **54/6**

Complete Steam Trains on Rail

in strong cardboard boxes.

Steam Trains with Force Locomotive 30592/0
finely japanned, with stamped frame, polished brass boiler, 7 in. long.

Gauge 0 = $1^{3}/_{8}$ in.

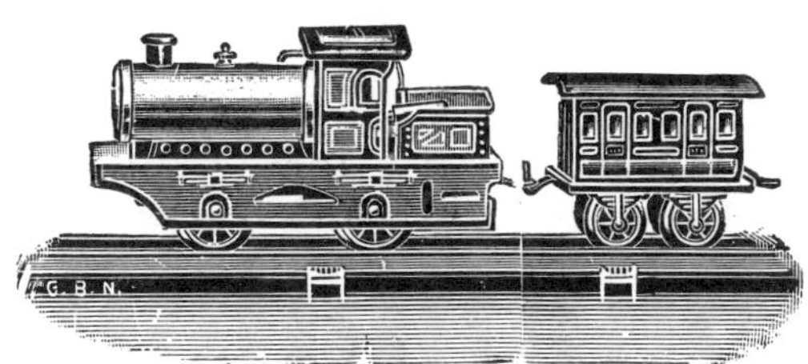

30092/000

30092/000 **M. R. train** (Midland Railway), consisting of: Locomotive, 1 passenger car and ◎ round rail formation = 6 rails, complete length of train $11^{1}/_{2}$ in. . . . . each **6/10**

30093/000 **L. & N. W. R. train** (London & North Western Railway), same as above . . . . „ **6/10**

30092/0

30092/0 **M. R. train** (Midland Railway), consisting of: Locomotive, 2 passenger cars and 1 guard's van, and oval rail formation = 8 rails. complete length of train 20 in. . . . . each **9/4**

30093/0 **L. & N. W. R. train** (London & North Western Railway), same as above . . . . „ **9/4**

31092/0

31092/0 **M. R. Steam train,** consisting of: Force Locomotive 31592/0 (finely japanned, with stamped frame, polished brass boiler and safety valve, incl. tender $10^{3}/_{4}$ in. long), 2 passenger cars and 1 guards van and oval rail formation = 8 rails, complete length of train $23^{1}/_{2}$ in. . . . . each **10/4**

31093/0 **L. & N. W. R. Steam train,** same as above . . . . „ **10/4**

Steam-Trains

specially suited for Window Attractions.

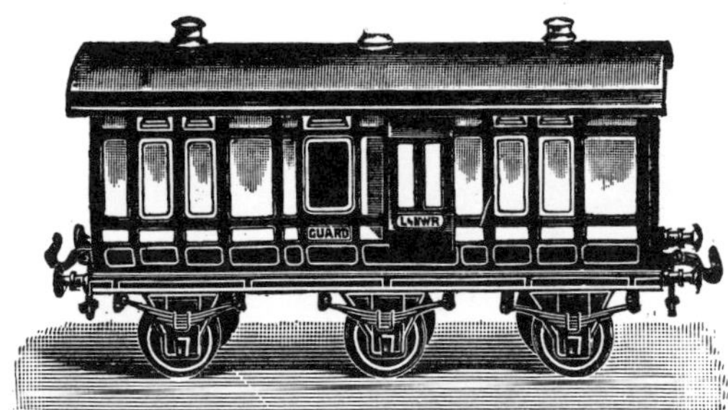

Correct Models
of
English Railways.

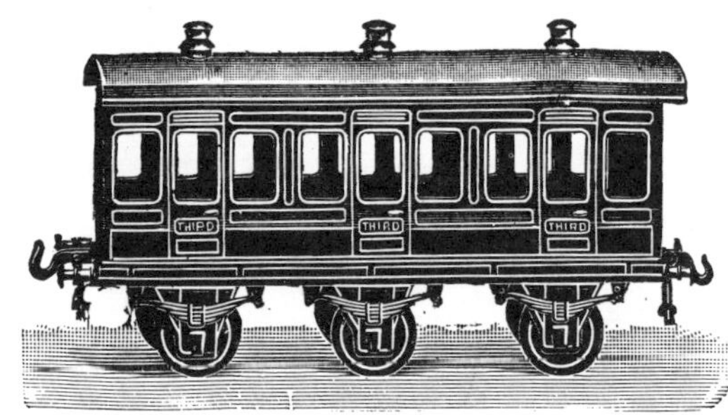

Gauge 2 = $2^{1}/_{8}$ in.

Model Suburban Steam Train with reversing gear. Consisting of: Steam Locomotive, elegant finish, with 8 highly nickelled flanged wheels, 2 long Model Passenger Cars, finely japanned on 3 axles, with large oval set of rails = 18 pieces. Length of train: 36 in. Measurements of track: 7 feet 9 in. × 4 feet 3 in. . . . . at £ **3.—.—**

Gauge 3 = $2^{5}/_{8}$ in. M. R.

Model Steam Express Train with reversing gear. Consisting of: Extra fine Steam Locomotive, modern type, with Tender, imitation coal, 2 finely japanned long Model Express Passenger Cars, on 3 axles, 1 long Model Express Guard's Van, finely japanned, on 3 axles, with large oval set of rails = 18 pieces. Length of train: 65 in. Measurements of track: 7 feet 10 in. × 4 feet 4 in. . . . . at £ **4. 4.—**

BOATS

FIRE ENGINES
FIRE ESCAPES
GUNS
FLYING MACHINES

Clockwork Boats.

Good finish and with new fittings.

Strong reliable Clockwork Movements.

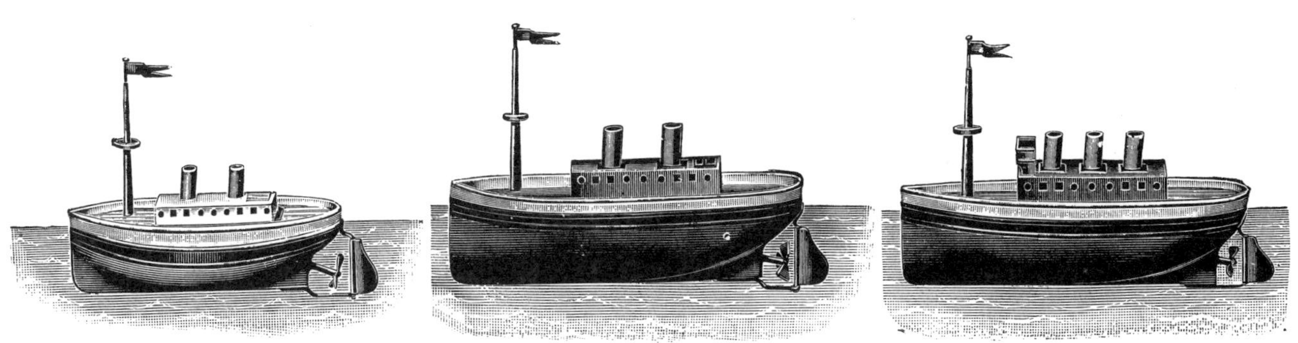

155/321 155/322 155/323

Ocean Liners, with strong Clockwork Movements.

155/321	finely japanned, with 2 funnels, $6\frac{1}{4}$ in. long	doz.	**19/—**
„ **/322**	„ „ „ 2 „ $7\frac{1}{2}$ „ „	„	**29/6**
„ **/323**	„ „ „ 3 „ $8\frac{3}{4}$ „ „	each	**3/4**

155/324

155/325

155/324	finely japanned, with 4 funnels, $10\frac{1}{4}$ in. long	each	**5/4**
„ **/325**	„ „ „ 4 „ $12\frac{1}{2}$ „ „	„	**8/6**

Ocean Liners

modelled after the famous Cunard Liner „Mauretania".

155/343 and 353

Ocean Liners, finely japanned and richly fitted, with superior Clockwork-Movements

Superior Quality! *Latest Type!* *Best Make and Finish!*

155/341	driven by clockwork, $16^1/_2$ in. long	each	**17/2**
„ **/342**	„ „ „ 20 „ „	„	**22/8**
„ **/343**	„ „ „ with 4 lifeboats, 25 in. long	„	**39/8**
„ **/344**	„ „ „ „ 6 „ $32^1/_2$ in. long	„	**68/—**
„ **/351**	„ „ steam, $16^1/_2$ in. long	„	**18/—**
„ **/352**	„ „ „ 20 „ „	„	**24/—**
„ **/353**	„ „ „ with 4 lifeboats $25^1/_2$ in. long	„	**40/—**

155/350

Ocean Liner, highly japanned and very richly fitted, with 10 lifeboats, with superior Clockwork Movement

Superior Quality! *Latest Type!* *Best Make and Finish!*

155/350 39 in. long . . . . each **102/—**

Motor Boats with best Clockwork Movements finely japanned.

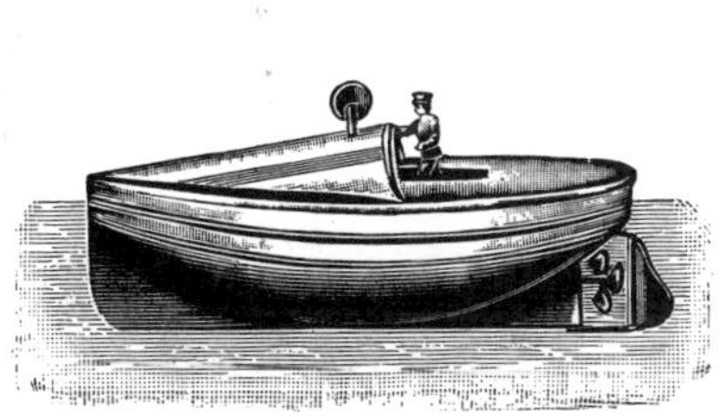

155/22

155/31

155/21 **Motor Boats,** $6^{1}/_{4}$ in. long . . . . doz. **18/—**
„ /22 „ „ with rudder, $7^{1}/_{2}$ in long . . . . „ **29/—**
„ /23 „ „ „ „ $8^{1}/_{2}$ „ „ . . . . „ **38/—**
„ /31 „ „ with figure, $10^{1}/_{4}$ „ „ . . . . each **5/4**
„ /32 „ „ „ „ 15 „ „ . . . . „ **7/8**
„ /33 „ „ „ „ $19^{3}/_{4}$ „ „ . . . . „ **11/8**

155/34

155/34 **Motor Boat,** finely japanned, with figure, $23^{1}/_{2}$ in. long . . . . each **15/4**

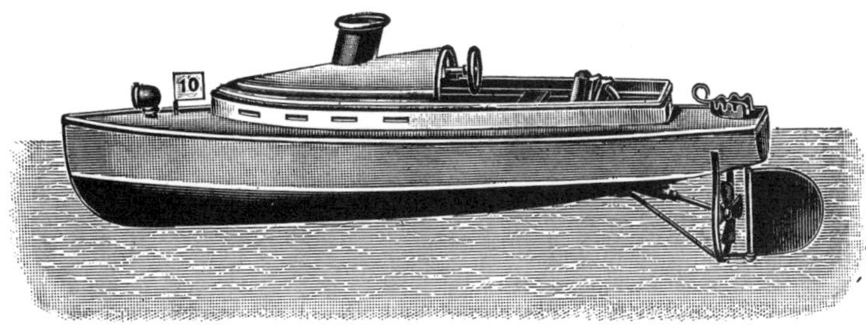

155/35 and 36

Steam Motor Racing Boats, good design, finely japanned, with brass steam boiler and oscillating brass cylinder
155/35 Hull 18 in. long . . . . each **13/8**
„ /36 „ 22 „ „ . . . . „ **20/—**

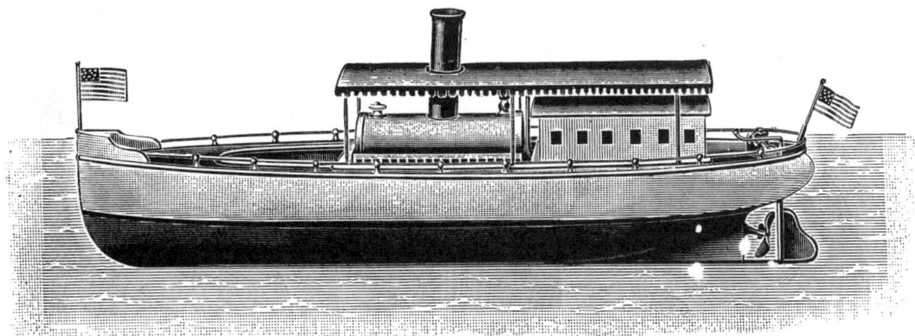

155/42

Turbine Steam Boats, finely japanned, with polished brass boiler and well working turbine engine
155/41 $12^{3}/_{4}$ in. long . . . . each **6/10**
„ /42 $15^{3}/_{4}$ „ „ with awning . . . . „ **10/6**
„ /43 20 „ „ „ „ . . . . „ **16/10**

Paddle Steamer.

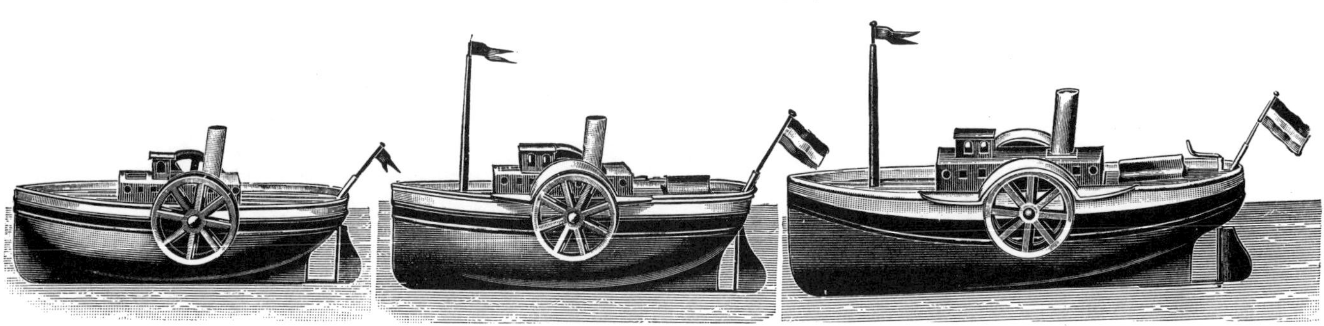

155/361 155/362 155/363

Paddle Steamers, with strong Clockwork Movements

155/361	finely japanned, 7 1/2 in. long	each	**3/—**
/362	" " 8 3/4 " "	"	**3/10**
/363	" " 10 1/4 " "	"	**5/10**

New Sailing Yachts, self steering (D. R. G. M.).

155/312

Important: These boats cannot sink. Through an ingenious arrangement the action of the wind upon the sails causes the rudder to be deflected according to the strength of the breeze encountered.

Brightly coloured, best finish, smart models

155/312	18 in. long, 20 in. high incl. sail	each	**9/10**
/313	20 1/2 " " 20 1/2 " " " "	"	**17/10**
/314	26 3/4 " " 24 " " " "	"	**30/—**

Divers.

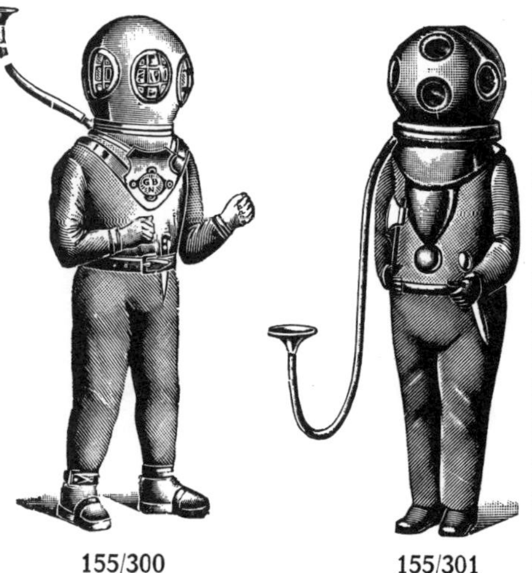

155/300 155/301

Divers, finely japanned.

These divers are a very useful addition to our range of boats. They dive into the water and rise to the surface again by air being blown into the rubber tube.

155/300	5 1/8 in. high	doz.	**15/—**
/301	8 1/4 " "	"	**30/—**

The Navy

Submarines.

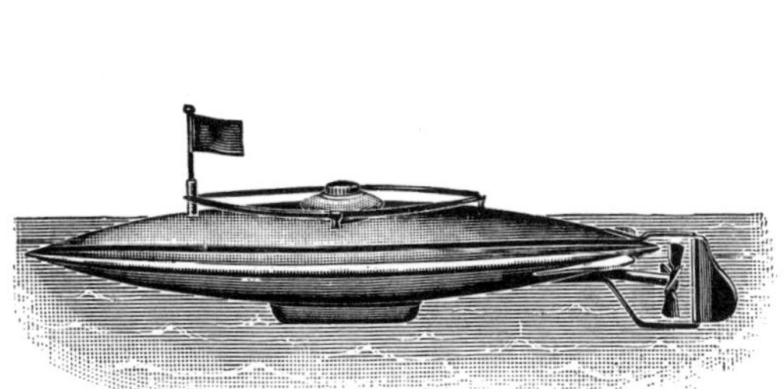

155/100

155/190—192

155/100 **Model Submarines,** alternately diving and rising to the surface, imitating in a sursprising manner the movements of the large prototypes, finely japanned, with strong clockwork, working excellently, packed in handsome box, $10\frac{1}{4}$ in long . . . . doz. **40/—**

155/100$\frac{1}{2}$ do. $13\frac{1}{2}$ in long . . . . each **7/10**

155/190 **New Model Submarines,** with improved upper works, correct Models of the latest Types, alternately diving and rising to the surface, $10\frac{1}{4}$ in. long . . . . each **4/8**

with new construction to dive and rise to the surface again or only for running on the surface

155/191 $11\frac{7}{8}$ in. long . . . . each **11/6**

„ **/192** 17 in. long . . . . „ **22/8**

New Range of Gun Boats

with best Clockwork Movements.

155/431

155/432

155/431 **Gun Boat,** finely japanned, with 2 funnels, 2 guns, $7\frac{1}{4}$ in. long . . . . doz. **19/—**

„ **/432** „ „ „ „ 3 „ 2 „ $8\frac{3}{4}$ „ „ . . . . each **19/—**

Correct Naval Grey.

155/433

155/433 **Gun Boat,** finely japanned, with 3 funnels and 2 guns, $10\frac{1}{2}$ in. long . . . . each **4/6**

Correct Naval Grey.

New Armoured Cruisers

modern type, with 4 funnels, complete with large and small ordnance, highly japanned.

155/442

155/441	**New Armoured Cruiser, driven by Clockwork,** 17 in. long	each **15/—**
„ **/442**	„ „ „ „ „ „ $21^1/_4$ in. long with 2 lifeboats	„ **25/6**
„ **/452**	„ „ „ „ „ **Steam,** $21^1/_4$ in. long . . . „ 2 „	„ **25/6**

Latest Type, 4 funnelled, accurate details, large and small guns faithfully reproduced, also bridge and lifeboats, good outlines.

155/444

155/443	**New Armoured Cruiser, driven by Clockwork,** $25^1/_4$ in. long with 2 lifeboats	each **36/—**
„ **/444**	„ „ „ „ „ „ $29^1/_5$ „ „ „ 2 „	„ **47/—**
„ **/453**	„ „ „ „ „ **Steam,** $25^1/_4$ in. long with 2 lifeboats	„ **36/—**

Latest Type, 4 funnelled, large und small guns faithfully reproduced also bridge und lifeboats and other accurate details, good outlines.

New Armoured Cruisers.

Modern Type, with 4 Funnels, with complete set of large and small guns, best Make and Finish accurate Details in every respect, bridge, lifeboats, etc., good outlines.

155/446

155/445	**New Armoured Cruiser** driven by Clockwork, $33^1/_4$ in. long, with 4 lifeboats	each	**62/—**
„ /446	„ „ „ „ „ „ $37^1/_4$ „ „ „ 4 „	„	**82/—**
„ /455	„ „ „ „ „ steam, $33^1/_4$ „ „ „ 4 „	„	**62/—**

Automatically Firing Gun Boats.

155/383

After winding up the clockwork, the boat is put on the water. It will go straight ahead for some distance, then, as if intending to attack an enemy, will suddenly fire a shot. After this, the boats sizes 1 and 2 will sail on in a circle whilst boat size 3 will turn round and steer back to its original starting place.

New Automatically firing Gun Boats finely finished and elegantly japanned, with excellent quality clockwork and automatic steering gear.

155/381	with 1 gun, $11^3/_4$ in. long	each	**9/2**
„ /382	„ 1 „ $15^3/_4$ „ „	„	**14/2**
„ /383	„ 2 guns, firing 2 shots at intervals, $19^1/_4$ in long	„	**20/6**

Model Dreadnoughts.

155/112

155/111 **Dreadnought with strong reliable Clockwork Movements,** finely japanned, correct naval grey, $11^3/_4$ in. long . . . . each **6/—**

155/112

Dreadnought with strong reliable Clockwork Movements,
finely japanned, correct naval grey, with conning tower and bridge

155/112	$15^3/_4$ in. long	each	**9/—**
„ **/113**	$19^3/_4$ „ „	„	**13/8**

New Series of Model Super Dreadnoughts.

155/114

Model Super Dreadnought with Clockwork
modelled after H. M. S. Bellerophon, correct colours and accurate details throughout

155/114	$11^3/_4$ in. long with 1 propeller	each	**7/10**
„ **/115**	$15^3/_4$ „ „ „ 1 „	„	**12/8**
„ **/116**	$19^3/_4$ „ „ „ 3 propellers	„	**19/10**

Model Super Dreadnoughts

Superior Quality and Finish. Extra strong and powerful Clockwork Movements.

155/204

155/204 **Model Super Dreadnought** with extra strong clockwork, modelled after H. M. S. Bellerophon, superfine japanning, correct colouring and accurate details throughout, 26 in. long . . . . each **63/—**

155/205

155/205 **Model Super Dreadnought** with best clockwork movement, modelled after H. M. S. Bellerophon, superfine japanning, correct colouring and accurate details throughout, $33^1/_2$ in. long . . . . each **105/—**

Torpedo Boats and Destroyers.

155/141

New Torpedo Boats with strong **Clockwork Movements,** exact models, finely japanned in grey

155/141	$10\frac{1}{2}$ in. long, Torpedo Boat Model	each **4/8**
/142	$12\frac{1}{2}$ " " " " "	" **6/10**
/143	17 " " " " "	" **10/6**
/144	23 " " " " "	" **15/10**

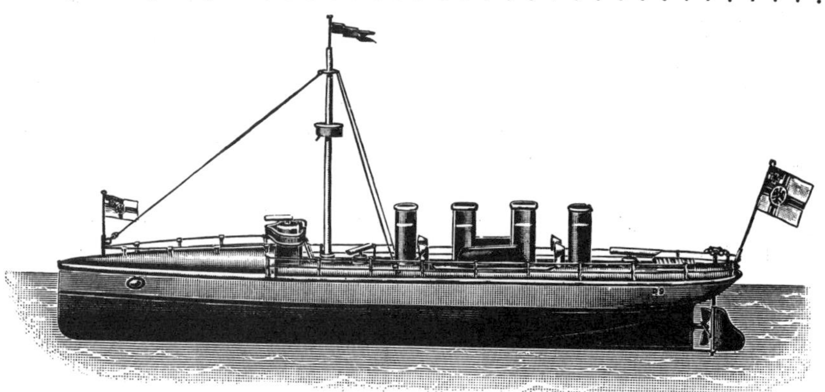

155/151

New Destroyers

155/151	with superior **Clockwork Movement,** $23\frac{1}{2}$ in. long with torpedo tube and lifeboats	each **22/—**
/152	" " " " $27\frac{1}{2}$ " " " " " lifeboats and anchor	" **32/6**
/551	driven by steam, $23\frac{1}{2}$ in. long with torpedo tube and life-boats	" **23/—**
/552	" " " $27\frac{1}{2}$ " " " " " " " and anchor	" **32/—**

155/153

Large Destroyer, finely japanned, typical narrow shape, torpedo tubes, lifeboats and 2 anchors

155/153	$39\frac{1}{2}$ in. long, driven by strong superior Clockwork	each **62/—**
/553	$39\frac{1}{2}$ " " " " steam	" **60/6**

Houseboat,

completely fitted, finely japanned and richly furnished.

With chinese lanterns, flower-pots, hammocks, flags and pennons, with stamped windows, small boat, boat ladder and life-buoys

13662/1 $13^1/_2$ in. long, 6 in. wide, $11^1/_2$ in. high each **12/—**

Mechanisms to build into Boats.

11623

Clockwork-Motor with strong spring

11623/1	2	3	4	
$5^1/_4$	$6^1/_4$	$6^7/_8$	$7^1/_8$	in. long
$1^7/_8$	$2^1/_2$	3	3	in. wide
$3^1/_2$	4	$5^1/_8$	$5^7/_8$	in. high
each **4/—**	**6/—**	**12/—**	**14/—**	

11625

Steam Boiler with Engine, Boiler of brass with oscillating cylinder

11625/1	2	3	4	
$5^1/_4$	$6^1/_4$	$6^7/_8$	$7^1/_8$	in. long
$1^7/_8$	$2^1/_8$	3	3	in. wide
$3^1/_8$	$3^1/_8$	$3^1/_2$	$4^1/_4$	in. high
each **4/—**	**6/—**	**8/—**	**10/—**	

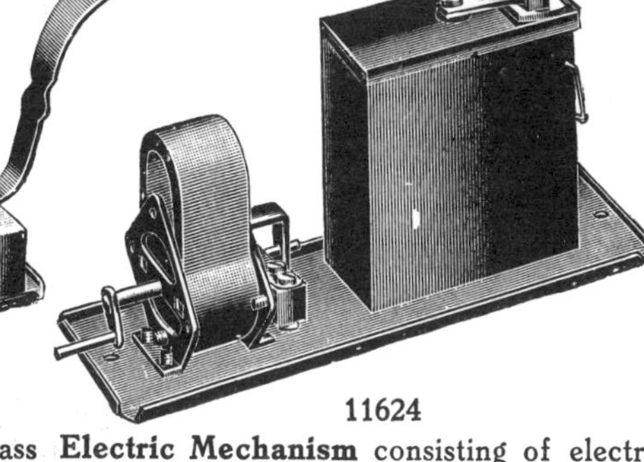

11624

Electric Mechanism consisting of electr. Motor with casing for battery and battery

11624/1	2	3	
$5^1/_4$	$6^1/_4$	$6^7/_8$	in. long
$1^7/_8$	$2^1/_8$	3	in. wide
$3^3/_8$	$3^3/_8$	$3^3/_8$	in. high
each **9/—**	**10/—**	**16/—**	

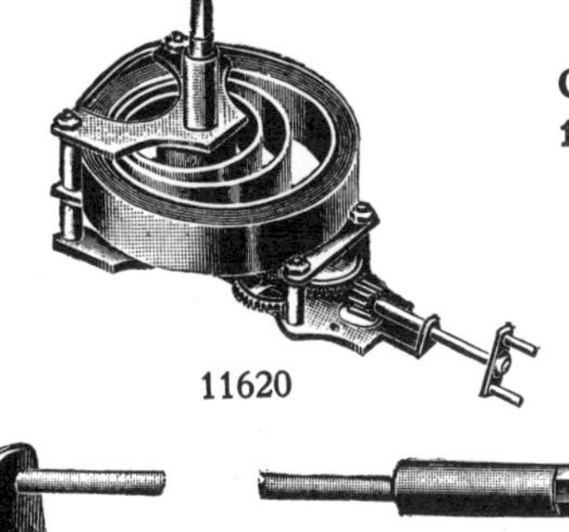

11620

Clockwork Motors for Boats, thoroughly good finish

11620/1, $3^7/_8$ in. long, $1^1/_2$ in. width, $1^3/_8$ in. high doz. **22/—**

„ /2, $5^1/_8$ „ „ $2^3/_4$ „ „ $2^7/_8$ „ „ each **6/—**

„ /3, $6^1/_4$ „ „ $3^3/_4$ „ „ $5^7/_8$ „ „ „ **12/—**

11622

Propeller with stuffing box, shaft and bearings

11622/1, $6^1/_2$ in. length doz. **6/—**

„ /2, 8 „ „ „ **8/6**

„ /3, $9^3/_4$ „ „ „ **12/—**

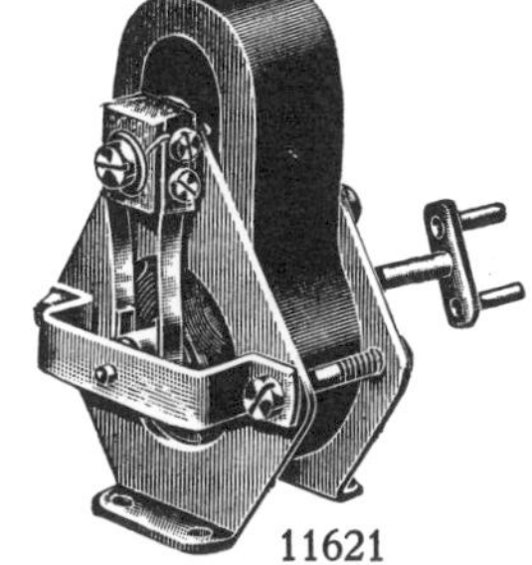

11621

Electr. Motors for Boats, in Aluminium casings

11621/1, $2^1/_2$ in. high each **5/8**

„ /2, $2^7/_8$ „ „ „ **9/6**

Accessories for Boats.

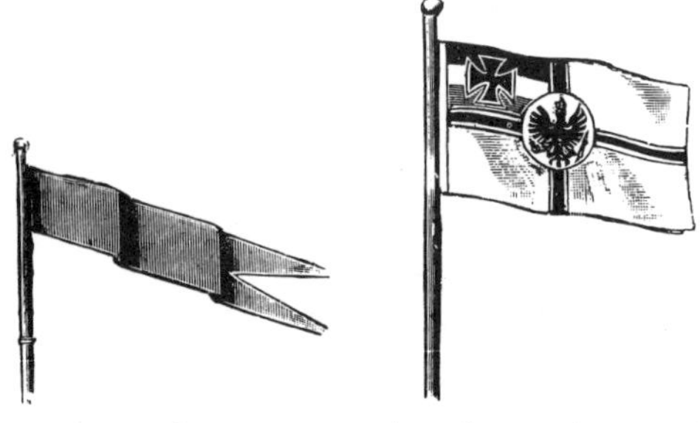

13436/1 sheet 13436/2 sheet and 11614 silk

Flags, japanned

13436/1	**Pennons,** $1^{5}/_{8}$ in long	gross	**8/6**
„ /2	**Flags** of different Nations, 1 in. long, simple . . .	„	**12/—**
„ /3	„ „ „ „ $2^{1}/_{8}$ in. long, best finish,	doz.	**2/10**
11614	„ „ silk, of different Nations, 2 in. long . . .	„	**17/—**

13472

13473/1

13473/2

13472	**Ship Anchors,** $^{3}/_{4}$ in high, composition casting . .	gross	**10/6**
13473/1	„ $1^{3}/_{16}$ „ „ „ „ black oxidised	„	**24/—**
„ /2	„ $1^{3}/_{4}$ „ „ composition casting, black oxidised	doz.	**3/—**

10426

10426/1	**Propeller for Boats,** plain tin, 1 in.	gross	**4/—**
„ /2	„ „ „ „ „ $1^{1}/_{4}$ „	„	**6/—**
„ /3	„ „ „ „ „ $1^{1}/_{2}$ „	„	**7/—**
„ /4	„ „ „ „ „ $1^{3}/_{4}$ „	„	**10/—**
„ /5	„ „ „ „ „ $2^{1}/_{4}$ „	„	**18/—**

11615/1

11615/2

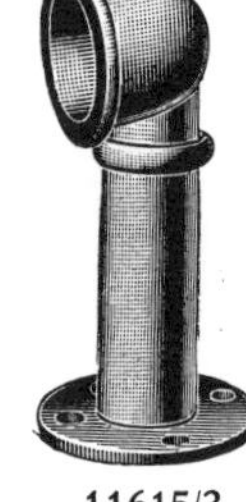

11615/3

11615/1	**Ship Ventilators,** cast lead, finely japanned, $^{5}/_{8}$ in. high,	doz.	**2/6**
„ /2	„ „ „ „ „ 1 „ „	„	**4/—**
„ /3	„ „ „ „ „ $1^{1}/_{2}$ „ „	„	**4/6**

13437

13437/1	**Life Boats,** tin, finely japanned, with eyes, $2^{1}/_{4}$ in. long	doz.	**6/—**
„ /2	„ „ „ „ „ „ $2^{3}/_{4}$ „ „	„	**7/6**

10276

10276/1	**Boat Sledges,** on wheels with wave-like movements, fine polychrome japanned, $9^{1}/_{2}$ in. long . .	doz.	**8/6**
„ /2	do. 12 in. long	„	**11/—**
„ /3	do. 14 „ „	.	**12/—**

Accessories for Boats.

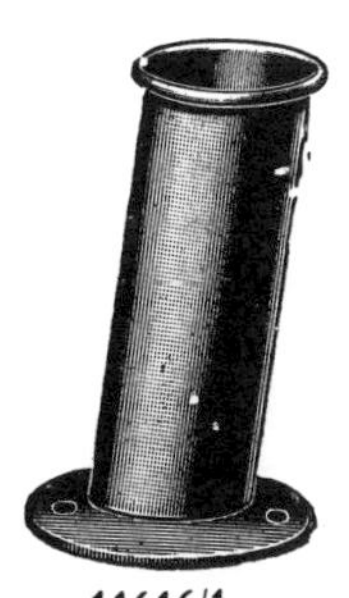
11616/1

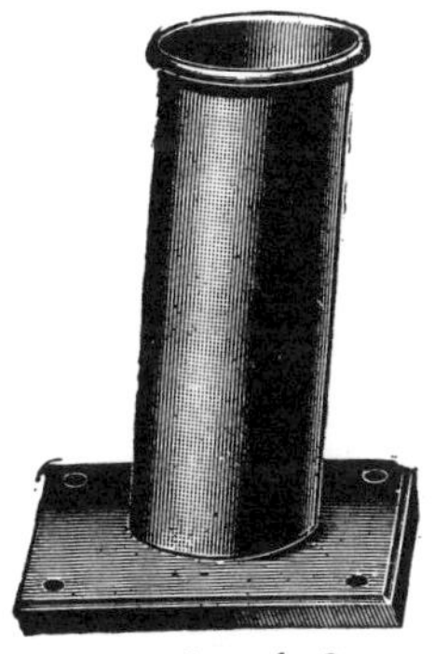
11616/2 and /3

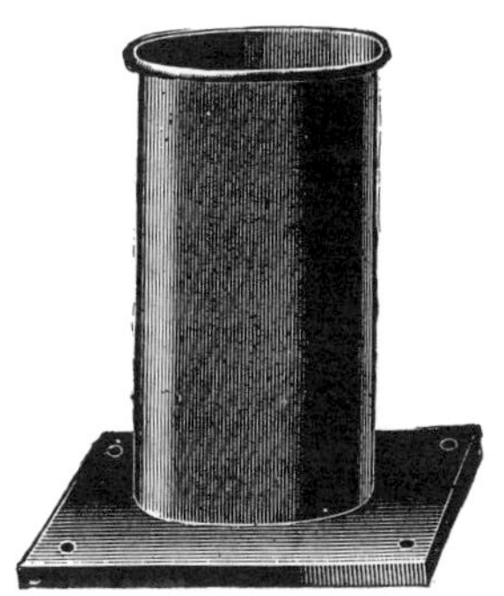
11617

11616/1	**Funnels for Boats,** finely black japanned, round	$1\frac{3}{4}$ in. high	doz.	**5/—**
„ /2	„ „ „ „ „ „ „	$2\frac{1}{4}$ „ „	„	**6/—**
„ /3	„ „ „ „ „ „ „	$2\frac{3}{4}$ „ „	„	**7/—**
11617/1	„ „ „ „ „ „ oval	$1\frac{3}{4}$ „ „	„	**6/—**
„ /2	„ „ „ „ „ „ „	$2\frac{1}{4}$ „ „	„	**7/—**
„ /3	„ „ „ „ „ „ „	7 „ „	„	**8/6**

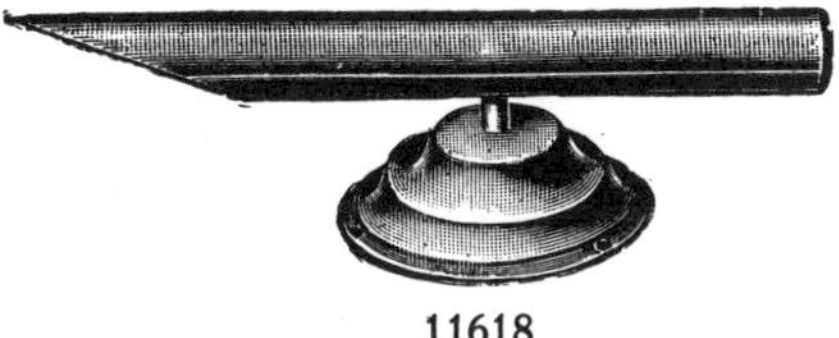
11618

Torpedo-Tube, turning, finely nickelled, stand japanned

11618/1	$1\frac{5}{8}$ in. long	doz.	**5/—**
„ /2	$2\frac{5}{8}$ „ „	„	**7/—**
„ /3	3 „ „	„	**9/6**

11619

Naval Gun, composition, casting

11619/1	tube $1\frac{3}{4}$ in. long	doz.	**8/6**
„ /2	„ $3\frac{3}{8}$ „ „	„	**14/—**

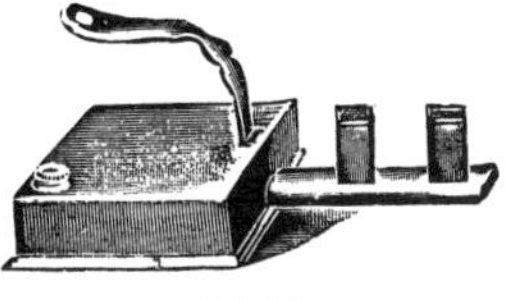
13439

Spirit Lamps for steam boats, tin, with filling screw and **2** burners

13439/1	4 in. long,	1 in. wide	doz.	**8/—**
„ /2	$4\frac{1}{2}$ „ „	$1\frac{1}{4}$ „ „	„	**9/6**
„ /3	$5\frac{1}{2}$ „ „	$1\frac{3}{4}$ „ „	„	**11/—**
„ /4	$6\frac{3}{4}$ „ „	2 „ „	„	**12/8**

13443/1

13443/2

13443/1	**Ship Figures,** composition casting, 6 figures on a card, for Passenger Boats	doz. cards	**9/—**
„ /2	„ „ „ „ 6 „ „ „ „ „ War Ships	„ „	**9/—**

Fire Pumps and Fire-Escapes.

156/20

Fire Pumps, very strong and elegant finish
with strong brass pumpwork, continual jet, finely japanned, with india rubber hose and mouth piece

156/20	length of waggon (without shaft), $7^1/_4$ in., height $3^3/_4$ in., with single pump			each	**4/2**
„ **/21**	„ „ „ „ „ $8^1/_4$ „ „ $4^1/_4$ „ „ double „			„	**5/10**
„ **/22**	„ „ „ „ „ $10^5/_8$ „ „ 6 „ „ „ „			„	**8/—**
„ **/23**	„ „ „ „ „ $12^5/_8$ „ „ $7^1/_8$ „ „ „ „			„	**9/8**
„ **/24**	„ „ „ „ „ $14^5/_8$ „ „ $7^7/_8$ „ „ „ „			„	**12/6**
„ **/25**	„ „ „ „ „ 17 „ „ $9^3/_4$ „ „ „ „			„	**16/—**

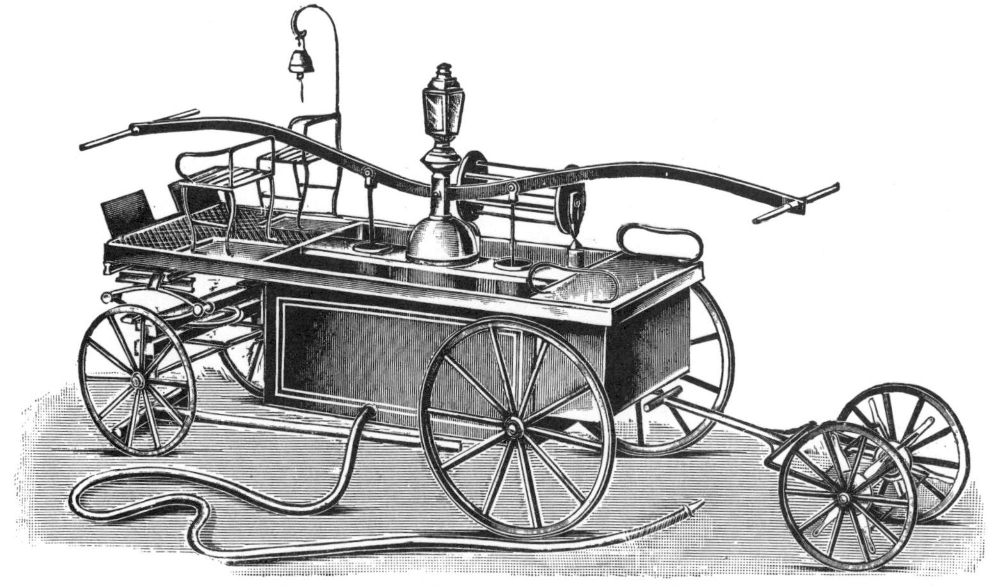

Fire pump 156/31 with hose waggon 156/41

Superior Fire Pumps, strong finish and finely japanned, with continual jet, with excellent, ground **brass pumpwork,** very powerful, with lantern to burn, windlass for hose and long india rubber hose with mouth piece

156/31	length of waggon (without shaft) $14^5/_8$ in., height $10^1/_4$ in. (without hose waggon)	each	**22/6**
„ **/32**	„ „ „ „ „ $18^1/_2$ „ „ $11^1/_2$ „ „ „ „ „	„	**30/6**
„ **/33**	„ „ „ „ „ $22^1/_2$ „ „ 13 „ „ „ „ „	„	**42/—**

Hose Waggon with windlass and india rubber hose with mouth piece

156/41	fitting fire pumps 156/31	doz.	**24/8**
„ **/42**	„ „ „ „ /32 and 33	each	**4/4**

India Rubber Hose fitting Fire Pumps

13348/5	$^3/_{16}$ in. diam., $^1/_{16}$ in. thick	per doz. meters	**6/4**
„ **/6**	$^1/_4$ „ „ $^1/_{16}$ „ „	„ „ „	**8/6**

Salvage Corps and Fire Escapes.

156/80

156/82

Salvage Corps very elegant and strong finish, finely japanned, with ladders and tool box, lantern and bell

156/80 with **4 small ladders,** 2 pails and 4 figures, $9^1/_2$ in. long, (without shaft), 4 in. wide, $6^1/_4$ in. high. . . each **9/6**

„ **/81** with **2 large ladders,** 2 hooks, 2 pails and 5 figures, 10 in. long, (without shaft), $4^1/_4$ in. wide, $7^1/_8$ in. high „ **13/4**

„ **/82** with **1 mechanical Fire Escape, 3 ladders, 1 hand pump,** (very powerful), **2** hooks and 5 figures, $11^3/_4$ in. long (without shaft), 6 in. wide, $14^1/_4$ in. high . . . . „ **23/—**

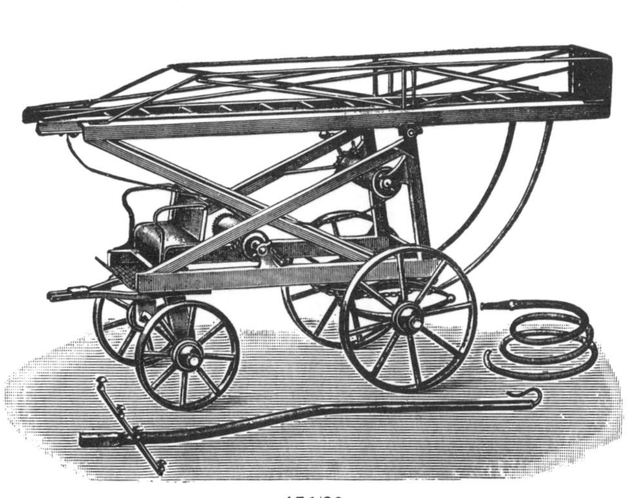

156/90

156/100

156/90 **Mechanical Fire Escape, adjustable** (for upright position of the ladder), $25^1/_2$ in. high, (measured at full height). . . . . each **15/4**

Mechanical Fire Escapes on wheels, strong finish finely japanned

156/100 **Fire Escapes,** 23 in. high (measured at full height) . . . . each **6/—**

„ **/101** „ „ $30^3/_4$ „ „ „ „ „ „ . . . . „ **8/6**

Motor Fire Engines

with strong clockwork.

156/116

156/116 **Fire Brigade,** consisting of: Motor salvage corps, motor fire-escape, motor fire engine and 5 figures, motor ambulance car with Chauffeur, finely japanned, packed in elegant boxes, box' 14 in. long, $8^1/_4$ in. wide each set **6/6**

156/110

156/111

156/112

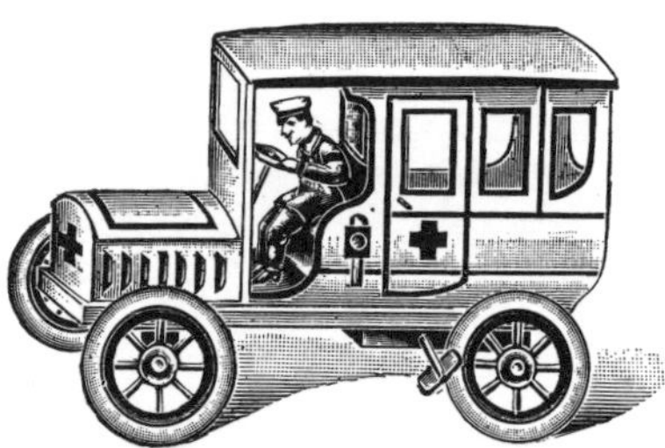

156/113

156/110 **Motore Fire Engine,** in strong finish, finely japanned with bell and 1 figure adjustable for straight and circular run, $6^1/_8$ in. long, $2^3/_4$ in. wide . . . . doz. **18/—**

„ **/111** **Mechanical Fire Escape** with figure and bell, escape can be raised and lowered, turned and extended, good clockwork, adjustable for straight and circular run, finely japanned, $6^1/_4$ in. long, 12 in. high (at full heigth) doz. **18/—**

„ **/112** **Motor Salvage Corps** with 3 figures and bell, good clockwork, adjustable for straight and circular run, finely japanned, $6^1/_8$ in. long, $2^3/_4$ in. wide . . . . doz. **18/—**

„ **/113** **Motor Ambulance Car** with good Clockwork Movement, adjustable for straight and circular run, with driver, $5^1/_8$ in. long, $3^1/_2$ in. high . . . . doz. **9/—**

Motor Fire Engines, Escapes &c.

with extra strong Clockwork, finely japanned.

156/162/1 156/162/3

Motor Fire Engines, with strong Clockwork Movements, with air chamber, hose and figures, reservoir, wheels with rubber tyres, front axle adjustable, for straight and circular run, with exchange gear, either to drive the wheels or the pump, with brake and bell, sounding while running.

156/161/1	10¼ in. long, 4⅛ in. wide, 5¼ in. high	each **13/6**
„ **/162**/1	12⅜ „ „ 4¾ „ „ 6¼ „ „	„ **22/—**

Motor Fire Escape, with strong Clockwork with 3 actions; one to put the ladder into an upright position, the other to swing the ladder round into any direction required and the third to extend the ladder, with bell sounding while running, brake, bell and figures, wheels with rubber tyres, front axle adjustable for straight and circular run.

156/161/3	30 in. long with ladder extended, 4 in. wide 5¼ in. high	each **9/2**
„ **162**/3	36 „ „ „ „ „ 4¾ „ „ 6¼ „ „	„ **15/6**

156/162/2 156/162/4

Motor Salvage Corps, with strong Clockwork with brake, 4 ladders, hose windlass, bell and figures, wheels with rubber tyres, front axle adjustable for straight and circular run; giving a bell signal while running.

156/161/2	10¼ in. long, 3⅞ in. wide, 4¾ in. high	each **8/—**
„ **/162/2**	12 „ „ 4¾ „ „ 6⅛ „ „	„ **14/—**

Motor Ambulance, with strong clockwork finely polychrome japanned, wheels with rubber tyres, with Chauffeur, doors to open, with brake, front axle adjustable for straight and circular run.

156/161/4	7⅞ in. long, 5 in. wide, 5¼ in. high	each **3/6**
„ **/162**/4	9⅞ „ „ 4¾ „ „ 6 „ „	„ **5/—**

Artillery Guns.

157/50—54

Modern Field Guns, thoroughly good finish **to shoot India rubber shells by means of caps — absolutely without danger** — with improved arrangement for sighting, lever to fire the gun, ammunition holder, finely japanned, with India rubber shells and brush.

157/50	$10^1/_4$ in. long, $4^1/_8$ in. high	each	**5/4**
„ /51	$13^1/_2$ „ „ $5^1/_8$ „ „	„	**7/—**
„ /52	$15^7/_8$ „ „ $6^1/_4$ „ „	„	**9/2**
„ /53	$17^7/_8$ „ „ $7^1/_2$ „ „	„	**11/6**
„ /54	$21^3/_4$ „ „ $8^3/_4$ „ „	„	**16/—**
6649	India rubber shells for gun 157/50	gross	**7/4**
6641	„ „ „ „ „ „ /51—54	„	**7/4**

157/40

157/31 and 32

157/40 **Modern Quick-Firing Gun** finely finished, **to shoot India rubber shells by means of caps — absolutely without danger,** with adjustable arrangement for sighting, to fire mechanically, with armoured shield, to turn in any direction, finely japanned with India rubber shells . . . . . each **11/8**

6641 India rubber shells extra . . . . . gross **7/4**

Coast Guard Guns finely finished, **to shoot India rubber shells by means of caps — absolutely without danger** — with adjustable arrangement for sighting, to fire mechanically, ammunition holder, with India rubber shells and and brush, finely japanned

157/31	$8^1/_4$ in. long, $4^1/_2$ in. high	each	**5/4**
„ /32	$11^1/_2$ „ „ $5^1/_8$ „ „	„	**6/8**
6641	India rubber shells extra	gross	**7/4**

The Little Showman.

10120 I. At the fair

Very original. *Splendid value.*

„The Little Showman". Very entertaining toy.

Illustration I
shows the Traction Engine stationary, driving the roundabout, using the car as base.

Illustration II
shows the Traction Engine drawing the car containing the roundabout, taken to pieces.

All parts finely japanned, Engine with strong clockwork, nicely boxed.

Traction Engine $7^1/_2$ in. long, $4^1/_2$ in. high
Car $5^1/_2$ in. long, 4 in. high.
Roundabout $4^1/_2$ in. high

each **5/—**

10120 II. On the road.

New Travelling Menagery.

Very original.

10196

Menagery Van with Traction Engine, most entertaining toy

10196 **Traction Engine** with strong clockwork and brake, fine polychrome japanning; **van** with doors to open and 3 felt animals, very droll; traction engine and van with adjustable front axle for straight and circular run; Traction Engine 7 in. long, $4^1/_4$ in high, Van $9^1/_4$ in. long, $4^3/_4$ in. high . . . . each **5/—**

Bing's Famous Model Aeroplanes.

Practically Indestructible!

Good Models!

These Aeroplanes are made of best steel spring wire covered with real silk material and are in a sense elastic, in as much as they rebound, when coming into contact with an obstruction. The way, the propeller is started is simplicity itself and all parts are strong and reliable.

Full instructions &c. supplied with every machine. The Aeroplanes will fly for about 50 yards horizontally or about 15 yards straight upwards.

11582 Model "Wright"

Starting handle.

This starting handle is supplied with every Flying Machine.

11582 Double Decker Model "Wright Bros.", $12^1/_4$ in. wide, with starting handle . . . . each **6/4**

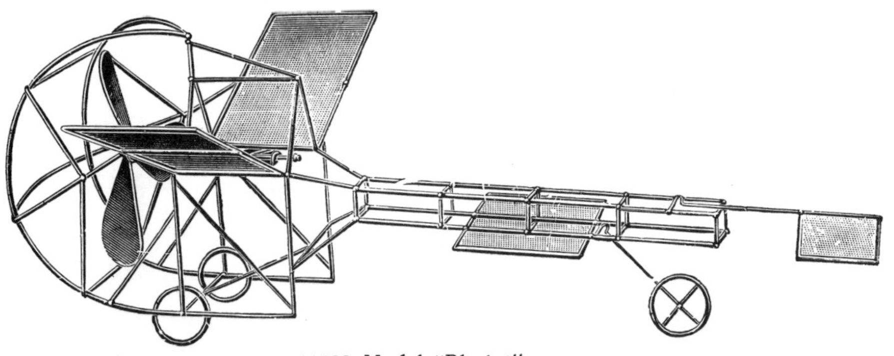

11588 Model "Bleriot"

11588 Single Decker Model "Bleriot", $12^1/_4$ in. wide, with starting handle each **8/6**

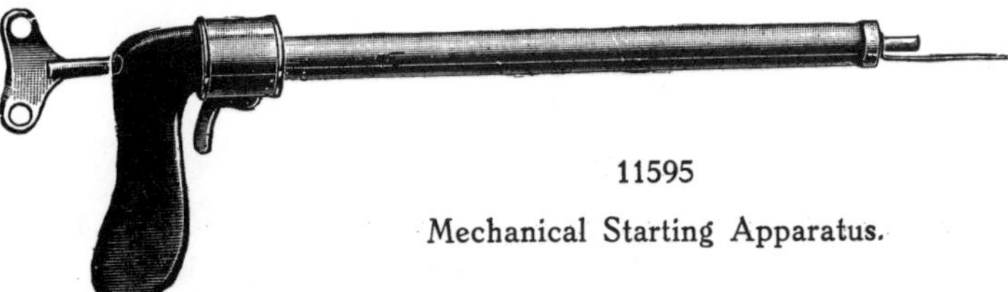

11595

Mechanical Starting Apparatus.

11595 Aerona Gun, mechanical starting apparatus, suitable for above flying machines, with very strong spring, to be wound up with key, 21 in. long each **5/—**

With the aid of this mechanical starting apparatus the Flying Machines can easily be shot off and at the same time fly a considerable distance.

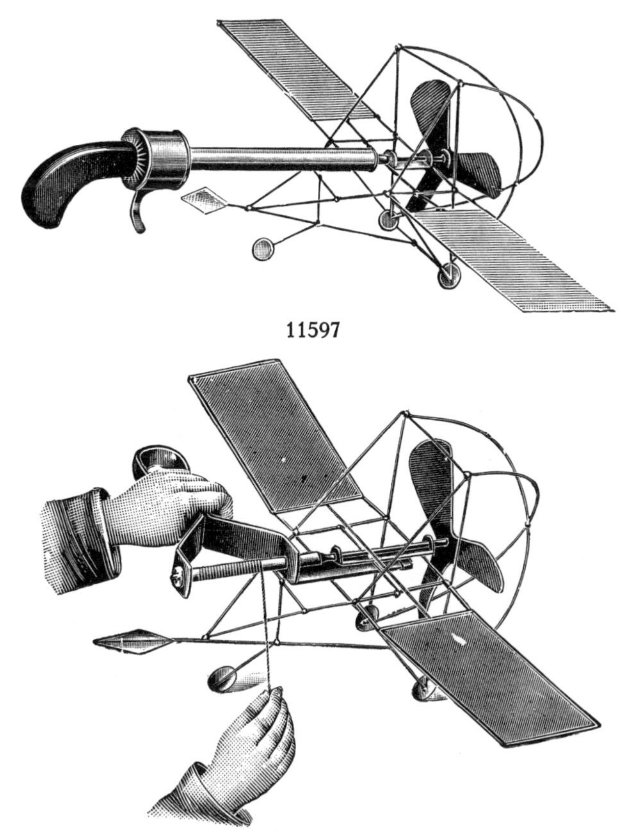

11597

11612

11597 "Aerona" Revolver Aeroplane.

D. R. G. M.

The construction of this Aeroplane is on the lines of our well-known "Aerona" Flying Machines. It is made of Steel Spring Wire, jointed in such a manner as to render it practically indestructible.

The Planes are made of Aluminium, so as to get a minimum of weight and a maximum of stability. One of the principal New Features is the Mode of Propulsion, which is as follows: —

The Aeroplane is put on to the end of the Barrel of a Mechanical Revolver, and the release of the Trigger causes a Coil Spring in the Barrel to unwind rapidly, thus launching the Aeroplane on its flight.

Pistol with strong spring, finely nickelled, Aeroplane of excellent steel wire, with Aluminium planes, width $14^{1}/_{4}$ in. . . . . each set **4/8**

11612 "Aerona" Aeroplane

with starting handle.

Also this Aeroplane is made of steel spring wire, the planes covered with ligth strong silk.

The balancing is carefully regulated in the manufacture.

A starting handle is supplied with every machine.

It is worked like an ordinary top, wound up by a length of string.

The pulling off sets the propeller into quick rotation thus launching the machine on its flight, $14^{1}/_{4}$ in. wide . . . . each set **4/6**

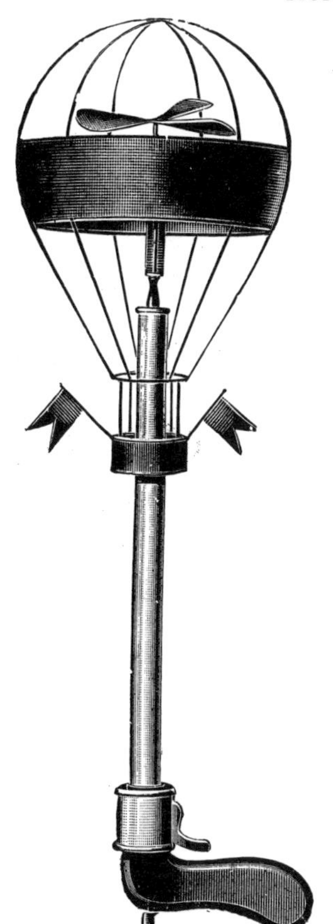

11596

Attractive Novelty!

D. R. G. M.

11596 "Aerona" Balloon.

The balloon by means of the mechanical starting apparatus (in the shape of a carbine) is shot into the air in a vertical direction; with the help of a propeller it rises to a considerable height and then descends slowly to the ground.

Starting apparatus with very strong spring, barrel finely nickelled to be wound up with key.

Balloon of high class quality steel wire with silk covering and silk flags, 7 in. diam., $11^{3}/_{4}$ in. high, Pistol 21 in. long . . . . each **11/—**

11595 Shooting Apparatus (gun) **extra** . . . . each **5/—**

The Aerona Revolver D. R. G. M.

Will shoot a propeller either horizontally or vertically. Through an ingenious and simple arrangement the revolver is cocked, the propeller is fixed on to the end of the barrel and the trigger gently pulled.

══ ***Astonishing effect!*** ══

The propeller or butterfly will fly a distance of about 25—30 yards, thereby describing curves in an original manner.

Absolutely without danger!

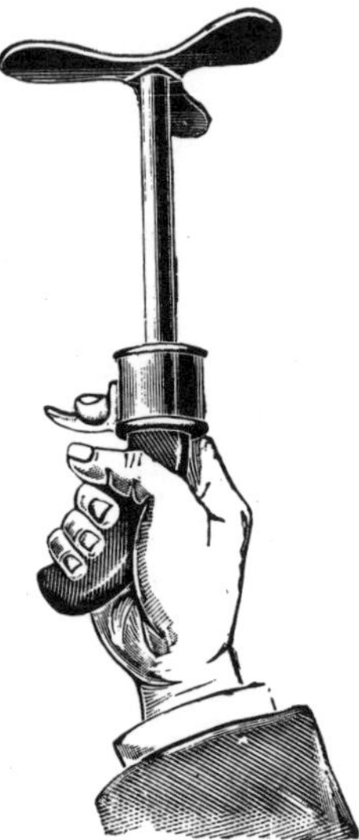

Simplicity itself! ***Absolutely reliable!***

11591

11591 **Aerona Revolver** in strong, elegant finish, finely nickelled, complete with 2 celluloid propellers, nicely packed in elegant cardboard box. $13\frac{1}{2}$ in. × $7\frac{1}{4}$ in. doz. sets **30/6**

11592 **Propellers extra,** made of celluloid in assorted colours, 12 pieces in a box, per doz. boxes each containing 12 propellers **38/—**

11599

Very Original! ***Very Original!***

11599 The Butterfly Revolver.

══ **Large Size.** ══

D. R. G. M.

Consisting of: finely nickelled pistol, 3 large celluloid butterflies, assorted colours, nickely packed in elegant cardboard box. 15 in. × 10 in. . . . . each set **3/5**

11598 **Propeller butterflies extra,** made of celluloid in assorted colours, 6 pieces in a box, per box of 6: **2/10**

11630

11630 Aerona-Balloon

with Revolver.

══ ***Original Novelty!*** ══

The Aerona-Balloon is made of coloured celluloid and fitted with a basket. By means of the Revolver the Balloon is shot off up to a considerable height. The set is nicely packed in elegant cardboard box, $11\frac{1}{4}$ in. long, $6\frac{1}{2}$ in. wide, doz. sets **44/—**

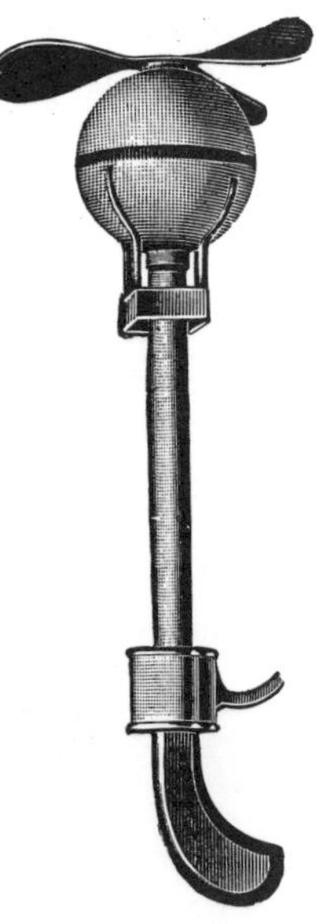

MOTOR CARS

Motor Garages with Motor Cars.

11635 and 11634

11637 and 11636

Motor Garage made of fine polychrome printed cardboard, with door to open with one Model Taxi Cab for straight and circular run, with strong clockwork, finely polychrome japanned. Garage $6^1/_4$ in. deep, 4 in. front, $4^1/_8$ in. high

11635 packed $^1/_2$ doz. in a box . . . . doz. **9/8**
11634 „ each in a box . . . . „ **11/—**

Double Motor Garage made of fine polychrome printed cardboard, with door to open, containing 2 Motor Cars as shown, for straight and circular run, with strong reliable Clockwork Movements, fine polychrome japanned. Garage $6^1/_4$ in. deep, $7^1/_2$ in. wide, $4^1/_2$ in. high

11637 packed $^1/_4$ doz. in a box . . . . doz. **19/6**
11636 „ each in a box . . . . „ **21/—**

New Models of Motor Cars

in fine polychrome japanning.

10386

13177

Motor Car front axle adjustable for straight and circular run

10386 $5^7/_8$ in. long, $3^7/_8$ in. wide, $3^7/_8$ in. high . . . . doz. **9/—**

Motor Car with rubber tyres and plastic seats, front axle adjustable for straight and circular run, with tin figure

13177/0 6 in. long, $3^1/_4$ in. wide, 3 in. high . . . . doz. **17/6**
„ /1 $6^3/_4$ „ „ $3^3/_4$ „ „ $3^1/_2$ „ „ . . . . „ **27/6**

$10384/1^1/_2$

10384/2

Model Taxi Cab with strong reliable Clockwork, adjustable for straight and circular run, with Chauffeur

10384/1 $5^1/_8$ in. long, $2^3/_4$ in. wide, $3^1/_2$ in. high, doors not to open . . . . doz. **8/6**
„ $/1^1/_2$ $5^1/_8$ „ „ $2^3/_4$ „ „ $3^1/_2$ „ „ „ to open . . . . „ **9/6**
„ /2 $6^3/_4$ „ „ $2^1/_8$ „ „ $4^1/_4$ „ „ „ „ „ . . . . „ **19/6**

Models of Fine Motor Cars.

10384/3

10384/4

Motor Cabs

in fine polychrome japanning, with strong clockwork, doors to open, Chauffeur, front axle adjustable for straight and circular run.

10384/3	$7\frac{7}{8}$ in. long,	$3\frac{1}{2}$ in. wide,	$4\frac{3}{4}$ in. high	doz. **30/—**
„ /4	$9\frac{7}{8}$ „ „	$4\frac{1}{2}$ „ „	$5\frac{1}{4}$ „ „	„ **46/—**
„ /$4\frac{1}{2}$	$9\frac{7}{8}$ „ „	$4\frac{1}{2}$ „ „	$5\frac{1}{4}$ „ „	„ **48/—**

10385/1

10385/2

Motor Cabs

in fine polychrome japanning, with strong clockwork, rubber tyres, doors to open, with brake, front axle adjustable for straight and circular run.

10385/1	$7\frac{7}{8}$ in. long,	4 in. wide,	$5\frac{1}{4}$ in high	doz. **42/—**
„ /2	$9\frac{3}{4}$ „ „	$4\frac{3}{4}$ „ „	$5\frac{7}{8}$ „ „	each **5/6**

30234/00

30234/0 and 1

Motor Bus

in fine polychrome japanning, with strong clockwork, adjustable for straight and circular run with up to date advertisements.

30234/00	7 in. long,	$4\frac{1}{2}$ in. high		doz. **18/—**
„ /0	10 „ „	$5\frac{1}{2}$ „ „	with brake	„ **39/—**
„ /1	$12\frac{3}{4}$ „ „	$6\frac{1}{4}$ „ „	„ „	each **5/2**

New Motor Cars

finely japanned with strong regulated clockwork, brake at driver's seat, extra strong rubber tyres, plastic seats, chassis, very elegantly finished, chauffeur. Front axle adjustable for straight and circular run.

10191/1

10191/4

New Series of 2 seated Motor Cars

10191/1	7 in. long, $3^1/_2$ in. wide, $3^3/_8$ in. high	. . . .	each	**4/4**
„ /2	$7^7/_8$ „ „ 4 „ „ 4 „ „	. . . .	„	**4/10**
„ /3	$10^1/_4$ „ „ $5^1/_8$ „ „ 5 „ „	. . . .	„	**8/6**
„ /4	11 „ „ $5^1/_2$ „ „ $5^3/_8$ „ „	. . . .	„	**12/—**

10192/2

10332 with electric lights

New 4 seated Open Touring Cars with wind screens

10192/1	$7^1/_2$ in. long, $3^1/_2$ in. wide, $3^1/_2$ in. high	. . . .	each	**6/2**
„ /2	$8^1/_4$ „ „ 4 „ „ $3^3/_4$ „ „	. . . .	„	**7/10**

New Model Motor Brougham

with 2 electric head lights, the light of which is supplied by a dry battery; body finely japanned, with strong clockwork movement, rubber tyres, brake, front axle adjustable for straight and circular run

10332	$9^7/_8$ in. long, $4^3/_4$ in. wide, $5^3/_4$ in. high	. . . .	each	**10/2**
10219/2	dry battery fitting above Car	. . . .	doz.	**14/—**

Models of Fine Motor Cars with Clockwork.

10375/1 10375/2 and 3

New series of 4 seated open Touring Cars of the Latest Type

finely painted and elegantly finished, with strong clockwork, rubber tyres and plastic seats, with brake, front axle adjustable for straight and circular run.

10375/1	$9^1/_2$ in. long, $3^7/_8$ in. wide	each	**8/6**
„ /2	$12^3/_8$ „ „ $5^7/_8$ „ „	„	**16/—**
„ /3	$15^1/_2$ „ „ $6^1/_8$ „ „	„	**28/6**

10376/1 and 2

10376/3 and 4

Model Motor Limousine of the Latest Type

finely painted and very elegantly finished, with extra strong clockwork, bevelled glass windows, rubber tyres, doors made to open and plastical seats, with brake, front axle adjustable for straight and circular run, with Chauffeur.

10376/1	$10^1/_2$ in. long, $4^1/_2$ in. wide	each	**12/6**
„ /2	$13^1/_8$ „ „ $5^1/_2$ „ „	„	**21/—**
„ /3	$16^1/_4$ „ „ $6^1/_8$ „ „	„	**34/—**
„ /4	$18^5/_8$ „ „ $7^1/_8$ „ „	„	**45/6**

Motor Cars finely finished with Clockwork.

14001/2

Superior open Touring Cars

finely hand japanned with extra strong regulated clockwork, brake to be worked from Chauffeurs seat, extra strong rubber tyres, plastical seats, bonnet, elegant and thoroughly good finish throughout, front axle adjustable for straight and circular run, with glass wind screen (sizes 2 and 3 with bevelled glass)

with Motor horn sounding, when the car is in motion

14001/1, $10^5/_8$ in. long., $5^1/_8$ in. wide	each	**15/—**
„ /2, $12^1/_4$ „ „ $5^1/_2$ „ „	„	**20/6**
„ /3, $14^1/_2$ „ „ $6^3/_4$ „ „	„	**31/6**

Motor Goods Vans (Lorries)

highly finished with extra strong clockwork.

10350/1 and 2 — 10351/1 and 2

best finish, with strong clockwork, with sacks and tarpaulin adjustable for straight and circular run

10350/1 $8^1/_4$ in. long, $3^1/_2$ in. wide . . . . . each **4/—**

„ /2 with rubber tyres, 11 in. long, $4^1/_4$ in. wide . . . . . „ **7/6**

for carrying sand with tilting arrangement, highly japanned, adjustable for straight and circular run, wheels with rubber tyres

10351/1 12 in. long, $3^1/_2$ in. wide . . . . . each **8/10**

„ /2 15 „ „ $4^1/_4$ „ „ . . . . . „ **15/6**

10352/1 and 2

10352/1 **Motor Goods Van with Trailer,** $18^1/_4$ in. long, $3^1/_2$ in. wide . . . . . each **13/6**

„ /2 „ „ „ „ „ 25 „ „ $4^1/_4$ „ „ . . . . . „ **23/6**

14412/2

Motor Delivery Vans

with driver, best finish, with strong clockwork and various packages, adjustable for straight and circular run, doors to open.

14412/1	with tin wheels, $6^3/_4$ in. long, $3^1/_4$ in. wide . . . . each	**3/10**
„ /2	with India rubber wheels, $8^3/_4$ in. long, $4^1/_2$ in. wide . . . . each	**7/4**
„ /3	with 2 lanterns, steering gear and brake, wheels pneumatic tyres, 12 in. long, $5^1/_2$ in. wide . . . . each	**14/6**

14480/0

Auto-Garage

tin stamped and japanned (brickwork imitation) with corrugated tin roof, lattice windows, work-table and vice.

14480/0 with 1 doorway, $9^1/_2$ in. wide, 11 in. deep, 7 in. high each **6/4**

13103

Chauffeurs finely japanned

13103/6	$2^1/_2$ in. high	doz.	**2/4**
„ /7	$2^3/_4$ „ „	„	**3/4**
„ /8	$3^1/_4$ „ „	„	**4/—**
„ /10	4 „ „	„	**7/4**
„ /11	$4^1/_4$ „ „	„	**9/6**
„ /13	$5^1/_8$ „ „	„	**10/—**
„ /15	6 „ „	„	**14/—**

10394

10395

10396

Tin wheels, stamped polychrome japanned

10394/1	outside diamet.	$1^3/_8$ in.	doz.	**—/8**
„ /2	„ „	$1^5/_8$ „	„	**1/—**
„ /3	„ „	$1^3/_4$ „	„	**1/4**

Tin wheels, stamped, japanned **with rubber tyres**

10395/1	outside diamet.	$1^3/_8$ in.	doz.	**1/8**
„ /2	„ „	$1^7/_{16}$ „	„	**2/—**
„ /3	„ „	$1^3/_4$ „	„	**3/6**
„ /4	„ „	$1^{15}/_{16}$ „	„	**5/—**
„ /5	„ „	$2^3/_{16}$ „	„	**5/6**
„ /6	„ „	$2^3/_8$ „	„	**7/—**
„ /7	„ „	$2^7/_{16}$ „	„	**9/—**
„ /8	„ „	$2^7/_{16}$ „	„	**9/—**
„ /9	„ „	$2^{15}/_{16}$ „	„	**13/6**
„ /10	„ „	$3^3/_4$ „	„	**19/6**

Rubber Tyres extra fitting these wheels

10396/1	inside diamet.	$1^1/_{16}$ in.	doz.	**—/8**
„ /2	„ „	$1^5/_{16}$ „	„	**1/—**
„ /3	„ „	$1^7/_{16}$ „	„	**2/—**
„ /4	„ „	$1^9/_{16}$ „	„	**3/—**
„ /5	„ „	$1^9/_{16}$ „	„	**3/6**
„ /6	„ „	$1^3/_4$ „	„	**4/—**
„ /7	„ „	$1^3/_4$ „	„	**5/—**
„ /8	„ „	$1^{15}/_{16}$ „	„	**6/—**
„ /9	„ „	$1^{15}/_{16}$ „	„	**10/—**
„ /10	„ „	$2^9/_{16}$ „	„	**12/—**

CLOCKWORK TRAINS

RAILWAY ACCESSORIES

Superior Clockwork Springs

of best quality and fitting all our Clockwork Locomotives.

Notice.

Clockwork Springs.

The quality of the springs depends upon the material used as well as upon the tempering of the springs. We on principle manufacture springs of the very best and finest steel only, and the hardening of same is also accomplished through a well tried process, gained from many years of experience. In spite of all it will sometimes occur that springs split or break without any apparent cause. Rust easily forms on springs, thus decaying the steel, therefore all toys with springs ought to be kept in dry rooms.

In case a spring should break, it can easily be remedied by fitting in a new one; this process is very simple and by adhering to the following instructions, it can be done without taking the works to pieces. These instructions will be very welcome to many of our customers.

Instructions

for fitting new springs in the works of Locomotives, without taking the works to pieces.

1. In the first instance remove the broken spring by lifting the outstanding top-ring of the spiral of the spring with a screwdriver, so far that the spring can be grasped by the hand or otherwise be fastened by means of a vice. At the same time by turning the peg *C* with the key in the opposite direction, the spring is wound out, until that end which is hooked on to the pillar *B* can be bent open and thus one part of the broken spring be removed. The other part of the spring is taken out by lifting the hook *D.*

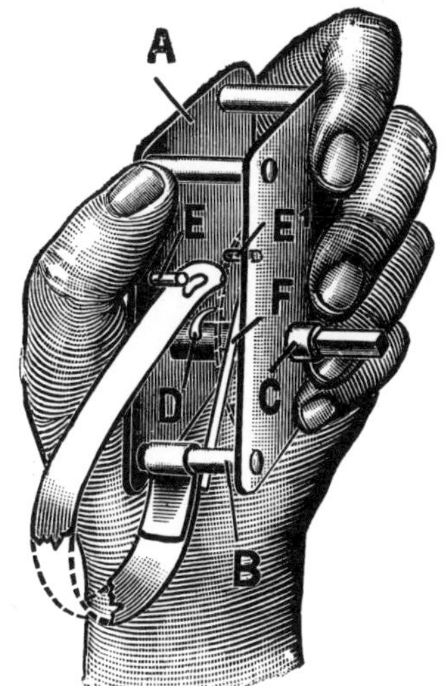

2. It must be carefully kept in mind for the later fitting in of the new spring, **to which pillar of the works the spring had been fastened, before,** and it is also necessary to note **the direction in which the spring itself was hooked in,** as otherwise **the works would turn in the wrong direction.**

3. Before the new spring is fitted, it must be well oiled with acid-proof oil; the winding peg also has to be oiled.

4. To fit the new spring, hang the eyelet end on hook *D* which is on the winding peg *C* as shown in the illustration. The hook is then pressed a little down with a pair of flat pincers in order to prevent any slipping out of the spring. The spring itself has now to be fitted round the winding key which can easily be done, as the spring on this end is annealed and soft.

5. Now the opposite end of the spring is hung round pillar *B* and is also pressed with a pair of flat pincers. On strong springs there is also at this end a rivet hole and it is advisable in this case to rivet the end of the spring.

6. The clockwork is now to be wound up with the key whereby the spring easily and quickly winds itself in. The works should be held at that side which is opposite to the one where the spring is wound in (see illustration).

7. In the works are small points *E*, E^1 and *F*, between which the spring has to lie. If the spring is properly fitted is has to be nearer to pillar *A* than to point *F.*

Price list of Springs for our Clockwork Locomotives.

No. of Locomotives	44590/0	45590/0	51590/0	42590/0	68590/0	75590/0	52590/0	59590/0
No. of Spring	14760/179 a	—/178 b	—/197	—/256	—/198	—/198	—/198	—/258
Price of Spring	doz. **2/—**	**3/—**	**4/—**	**5/—**	**—/6**	**6/—**	**6/—**	**7/6**

No. of Locomotives	77590/0	78590/0	47590/0	49590/0	48590/0	50590/0	57590/0	65590/0
No. of Spring	14760/258	—/259	—/270	—/262	—/264	—/196	—/252	—/178 c
Price of Spring	doz. **7/6**	**11/—**	**12/—**	**14/—**	**15/—**	**15/—**	**15/—**	**3/—**

No. of Locomotines	76590/0	56590/0	70590/1	71590/1	72590/1	73590/1	49590/1	62590/1	76590/1
No. of Spring	—/196	—/199	14760/260	—/266	—/263	—/265	—/261	—/251	—/200
Price of Spring	doz. **15/—**	**16/—**	**9/6**	**13/—**	**15/—**	**20/—**	**30/—**	**40/—**	**50/—**

Popular Priced Clockwork Trains on Lines.

P 2/1

14983 **Clockwork Train,** consisting of: Loco, tender and 1 passenger car, all finely japanned in English colours, with round rail formation ◎ = 5 rails, 10 in. diam., length of train $8^1/_2$ in. . . . . doz. **10/—**

English Models of Clockwork Trains

with our well known reliable clockwork movements, patent regulator and brake; japanned and lettered in the exact colours of the respective Railway Companies.

Locomotive with tender $7^1/_4$ in. long, Car 4 in. long.

44092/000

44092/000	**44093**/000	**44094**/000	**44098**/000
M. R.	L.N.W.R.	G. N. R.	Lancashire & Yorkshire

Train, consisting of: loco with tender and 1 passenger car, with round rail formation ◎ = 5 rails, small gauge $1^1/_8$ in., complete length of train 11 in. . . . . doz. **18/—**

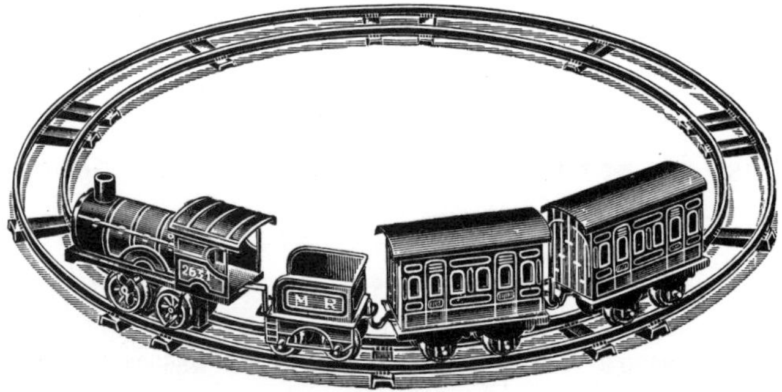

44092/00

44091/00	**44092**/00	**44093**/00	**44098**/00
G. W. R.	M. R.	L. N. W. R.	Lancashire & Yorkshire

Train, consisting of: loco with tender and 2 passenger cars, with round rail formation ◎ = 5 rails, small gauge $1^1/_8$ in., complete length of train 15 in. . . . . doz. **19/6**

English Models of Clockwork Trains

with strong Clockwork, Patent Regulator and Brake; loco, tender and carriages finely japanned in the exact colours of the respective railway companies. Train packed in nicely printed cardboard box with elegant label.

Gauge 00 = $1^1/_8$ in.

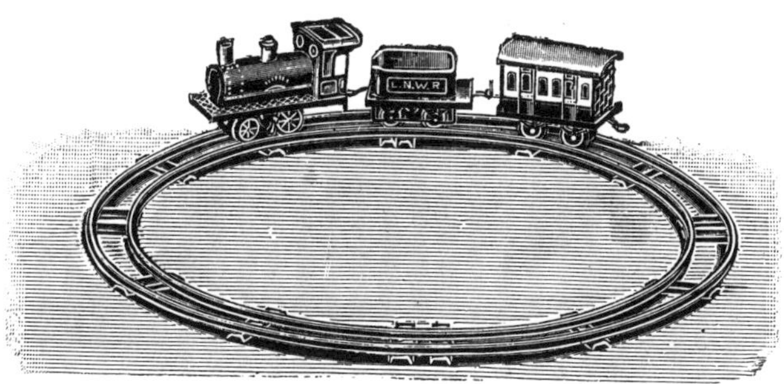

65091/000	**65093**/000
G. W. R. colour	L. N. W. R. colour

Train consisting of: Loco with brake to be worked from the cab, tender and 1 passenger car, with circle of rails = 4 rails incl. brake rail, length of complete train $14^1/_2$ in. . . . . doz. **24/—**

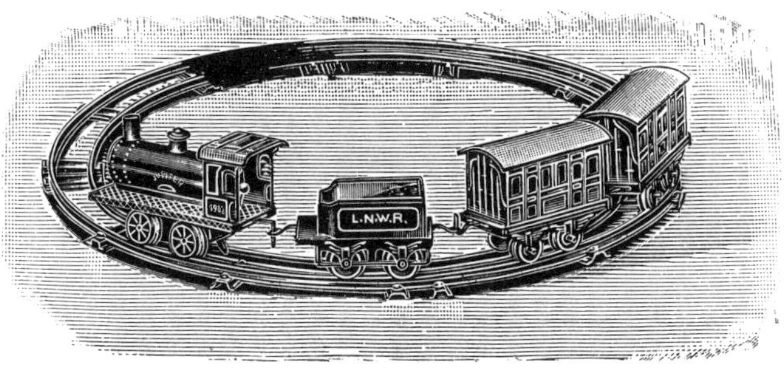

65091/00	**65093**/00
G. W. R. colour	L. N. W. R. colour

Same Train as above, but with 2 passenger cars, length of train $18^1/_2$ in. . . . . doz. **27/—**

English Models of Clockwork Trains.

Locos fitted with strong Clockwork, Patent Regulator and Brake, trains packed in strong, red cardboard boxes.

Gauge 0 = $1^{3}/_{8}$ in.

The gauge is measured from centre to centre of the top of the rails.

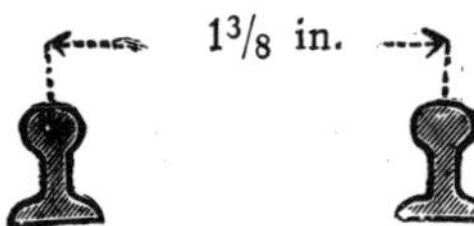

Locomotive with tender . $9^{3}/_{4}$ in. long
Car . . . . $4^{3}/_{4}$ „ „

45092/000	**45093**/000	**45094**/000	**45098**/000
M. R.	L. N. W. R.	G. N. R.	Lancashire & Yorkshire

consisting of: **Locomotive** with **strong clockwork, patent regulator,** with **brake** to be worked from the rail or from the cab, **tender** and **1 passenger car,** japanned and lettered in the exact colours of the respective railway companies, with circle set of rails ◎ = 4 rails incl. brake rail, length of complete train $14^{1}/_{2}$ in. . . . . . doz. **28/—**

45091/00	**45092**/00	**45093**/00	**45098**/00
G. W. R.	M. R.	L. N. W. R.	Lancashire & Yorkshire

Same train as above with **2 passenger cars** and oval set of rails ⬭ = 6 rails incl. brake rail (4 curved and 2 short straight rails), length of complete train $18^{3}/_{4}$ in. . . . . doz. **34/—**

45092/0	**45093**/0	**45094**/0	**45098**/0
M. R.	L. N. W. R.	G. N. R.	Lancashire & Yorkshire

Same train as above, with **2 passenger cars** and **1 guard's van,** with oval set of rails ⬭ = 6 rails incl. brake rail (4 curved and 2 long straight rails), length of complete train $23^{1}/_{2}$ in. . . . . doz. **42/—**

English Models of Clockwork Trains.

Special Value!

Our Cheapest Reversing Train. Loco fitted with strong Clockwork, Regulator and Reversing Gear.

Train packed in strong, red cardboard box.

Gauge 0 = $1^{3}/_{8}$ in.

Locomotive with tender $10^{1}/_{2}$ in. long, Car $4^{3}/_{4}$ in. long.

51091/000

51091/000	**51092**/000	**51093**/000
G. W. R.	M. R.	L. & N. W. R.

consisting of: Locomotive with strong clockwork and patent regulator, reversing gear (wich also acts as brake) to be worked from the cab, tender with imitation coal and 1 passenger car, japanned and lettered in the exact colours of the respective Railway Companies, with circle set of rails ◎ = 4 rails, length of complete train 15 in. . . . . doz. **42/—**

51091/00

51092/00	**51093**/00	**51094**/00
M. R.	L. & N. W. R.	G. N. R.

Same Train as above with 2 passenger cars and oval set of rails ⬭ = 6 rails, length of complete train $19^{1}/_{2}$ in.
each **4/6**

English Models of Clockwork Trains.

Special Value!

Locos fitted with extra strong clockwork and Patent Regulator.
Train packed in strong red cardboard box.

Gauge 0 = $1^3/_8$ in.

42091/000	**42093**/000
G. W. R.	L. N. W. R.

Train consisting of: Loco with brake to be worked from the rail or from the cab, tender and 1 passenger car with circular set of rails = 4 rails incl. brake rail, length of complete train $14^1/_2$ in. . . . . each **3/9**

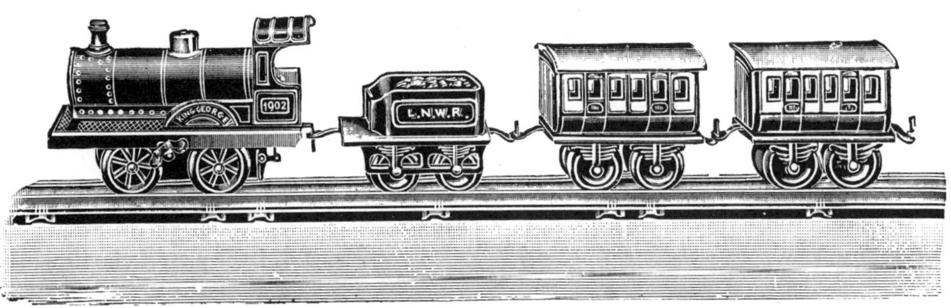

42091/00	**42093**/00
G. W. R.	L. N. W. R.

Same Train as above, but with 2 passenger cars, with oval set of rails = 4 curved and 2 straight rails incl. brake rail, length of complete train 19 in. . . . . each **4/9**

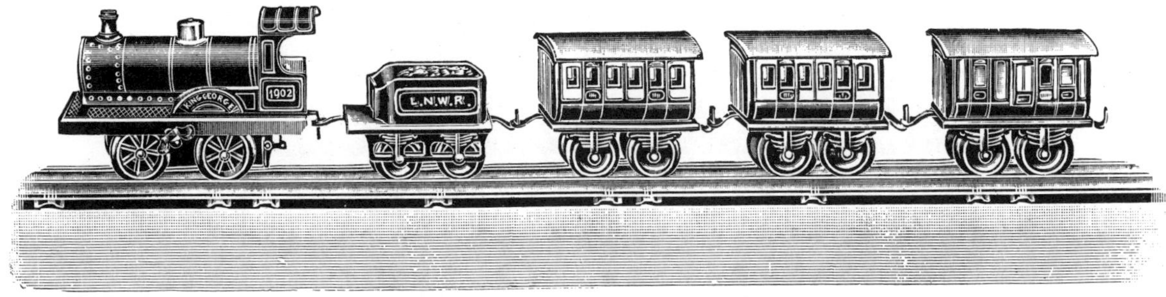

42091/0	**42093**/0
G. W. R.	L. N. W. R.

Same Train as described above but with 2 passenger cars and 1 guards van, with large oval set of rails = 4 curved and 4 straight rails. Complete train $23^1/_2$ in. long . . . . each **5/10**

New Series of English Model Clockwork Trains

fitted with strong Clockwork with Reversing Gear, Brake and Regulator, packed in strong red cardboard boxes.

Gauge 0 = $1^{3}/_{8}$ in.

Locomotive with Tender 10 in. long, Car $4^{3}/_{4}$ in. long.

68092/000	**68093**/000	**68094**/000
M. R.	L. N. W. R.	G. N. R.

consisting of: Locomotive with strong Clockwork and Regulat or, **automatic Brake** to be worked from the rail or from the cab, **Reversing gear** and 1 passenger car with **doors to open** japanned and lettered in the exact colours of the respective Railway Companies, with circle set of rails = 4 rails incl. brake rails, length of complete train $14^{3}/_{4}$ in. . . . . each **6/—**

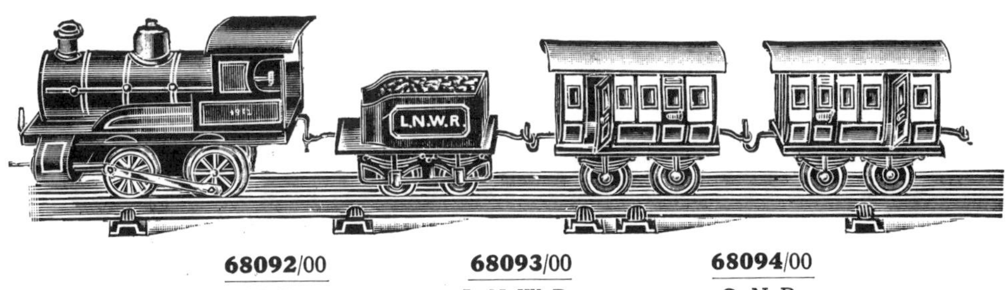

68092/00	**68093**/00	**68094**/00
M. R.	L. N. W. R.	G. N. R.

Same Train as above with 2 passenger cars and oval set of rails = 6 rails including brake rails, **carriages** with **doors to open,** length of complete train, $19^{1}/_{2}$ in. . . . . each **7/4**

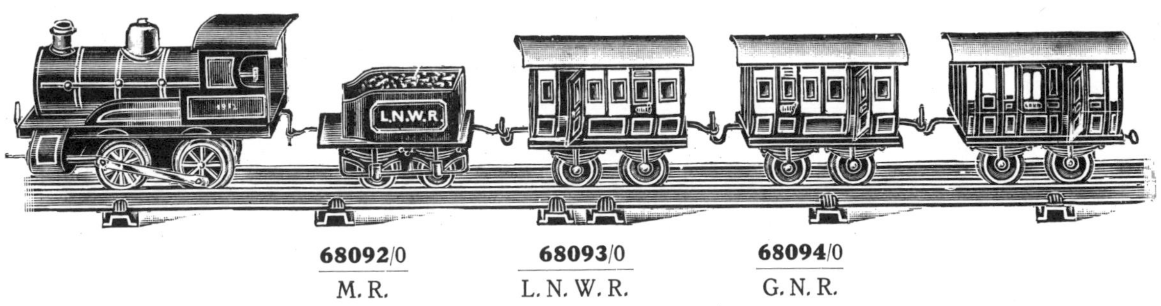

68092/0	**68093**/0	**68094**/0
M. R.	L. N. W. R.	G. N. R.

Same Train as above with 2 passenger cars and 1 guards van all with **doors to open,** with large oval set of rails = 8 rails incl. brake rail, length of complete train, 24 in. . . . . each **8/6**

New Series of English Model Clockwork Trains.

Fine Locos with extra strong Clockwork and Patent Regulator, with brake and automatic reversing gear.

Packed in strong, red cardboard boxes.

Trains fitted with brake and our new automatic reversing gear by means of which the train can be reversed from the rail or from the drivers place.

At the same time, the special rail supplied with these trains can be used as a brake rail simply by shifting the position of the stop catch

Gauge 0 = $1^3/_8$ in.

Locomotive with tender $10^5/_8$ in. long, Car $5^1/_8$ in. long.

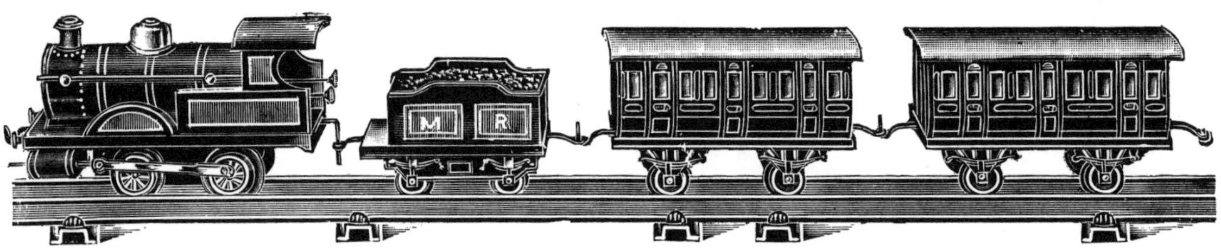

77092/00	**77093**/00	**77094**/00
M. R.	L. N. W. R.	G. N. R.

Train, consisting of: Fine loco with **powerful** clockwork and patent regulator, with brake and automatic reversing gear, both either to be worked from the rail or from the cab, with piston rods guide bars and finely finished fittings, tender with imitation coal and 2 long express passenger cars, oval set of rails (oval) = 6 curved and 2 straight rails incl. special automatic reversing and brake rail; length of complete train 23 in. . . . . each **9/10**

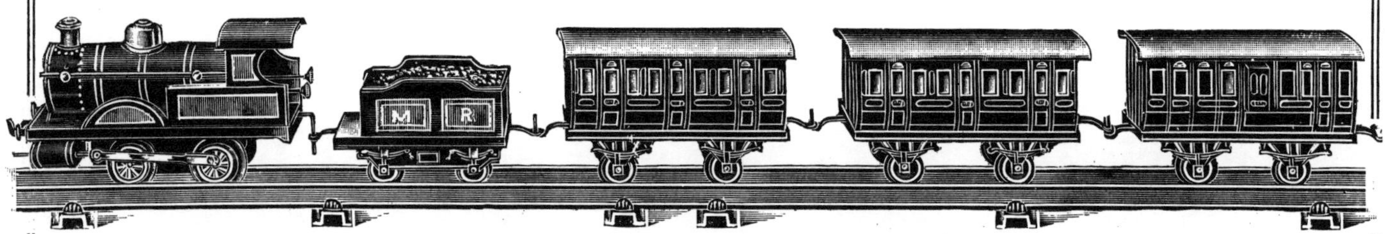

77092/0	**77093**/0	**77094**/0
M. R.	L. N. W. R.	G. N. R.

Same train as described above with 2 passenger cars and 1 guards van, large oval set of rails (oval) = 6 curved and 4 straight rails including special automatic reversing and brake rail, length of complete train 29 in. . . . . . . each **11/4**

New Series of English Model Clockwork Trains.

Fine Locos with superior clockwork and Patent Regulator, with brake and automatic Reversing Gear, packed in strong red cardboard boxes.

Trains fitted with brake and our new automatic reversing gear by means of which the train can be reversed from the rail or from the driver's place. At the same time, the special rail supplied with these trains can be used as a brake rail simply by shifting the position of the stop catch.

Gauge 0 = $1^3/_8$ in.

Locomotive with tender $10^1/_2$ in long
Car . . . . $4^7/_8$ „ „

78092/00	**78093**/00	**78094**/00
M. R.	L. N. W. R.	G. N. R.

Train consisting of: Locomotive with extra powerful clockwork and regulator, brake and **automatic reversing gear** both to be worked from the rail or from the cab, with nickelled fittings, tender with imitation coal and 2 new long model express passenger cars with 4 compartments, japanned, lettered and lined in the exact colours of the respective Railway companies, with oval set of rails (⬭) = 8 rails including special automatic reversing and brake rail, length of complete train 23 in. . . . . each **13/4**

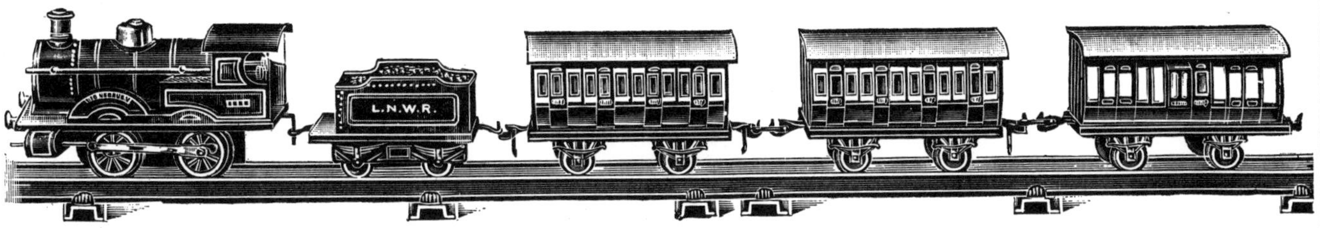

78092/0	**78093**/0	**78094**/0
M. R.	L. N. W. R.	G. N. R.

Same train as described above with 2 new model cars and 1 new model guards van, with large oval set of rails (⬭) = 10 rails incl. special automatic reversing and brake rail, length of complete train $28^3/_4$ in. . . . . . . each **15/4**

English Models of Clockwork Express Trains.

High Class Quality with Superior Clockwork Movements.

Improved Locos fitted with excellent strong Clockwork, Patent Regulator and Brake.

Gauge 0 = $1^{3}/_{8}$ in.

Locomotive with tender $12^{1}/_{4}$ in. long, Car $6^{1}/_{4}$ in. long.

47093/000

L. N. W. R.

Express Train, consisting of: Locomotive in fine, elegant finish, with extra strong, powerful clockwork, patent regulator, with brake to be worked from the rail or from the cab; bogie-wheels and connecting rods, 4 axles = 8 wheels, tender with imitation coal and 1 long model express passenger car, with circle set of rails = 6 rails incl. brake rail, length of complete train $18^{1}/_{4}$ in. . . . . each **8/4**

47093/00

L. N. W. R.

Same Train as above with 2 long model express passenger cars and oval set of rails = 8 rails incl. brake rail, length of complete train $24^{1}/_{2}$ in. . . . . each **9/10**

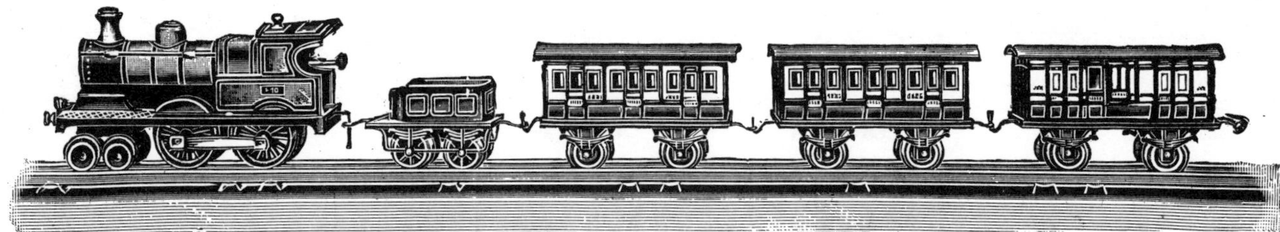

47093/0

L. N. W. R.

Same Train as above with 2 long model express passenger cars and 1 model express guard's van, with large oval set of rails = 10 rails incl. brake rail . . . . each **11/6**

English Models of Clockwork Express Trains.

High Class Quality, Superior Clockwork Movements.

Improved Locos with excellent strong Clockwork, Patent Regulator, Brake and Reversing Gear.

Gauge 0 = $1^3/_8$ in.

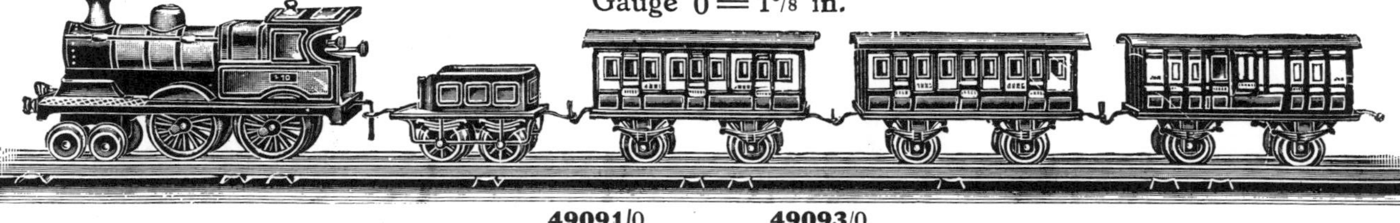

49091/0 G. W. R. **49093/0** L. N. W. R.

Express Train consisting of: Fine elegantly finished locomotive, with extra strong, powerful clockwork and patent regulator, automatic brake, to be worked from the rail or from the cab and reversing gear, on 4 axles = 8 wheels, tender with imitation coal, 2 long model express passenger cars and 1 model express guard's van, with oval set of rails ⬭ = 10 rails incl. brake rail, packed in strong cardboard box; locomotive with tender $12^1/_4$ in. long, car $6^1/_4$ in. long, length of complete train 31 in. . . . . . each **13/8**

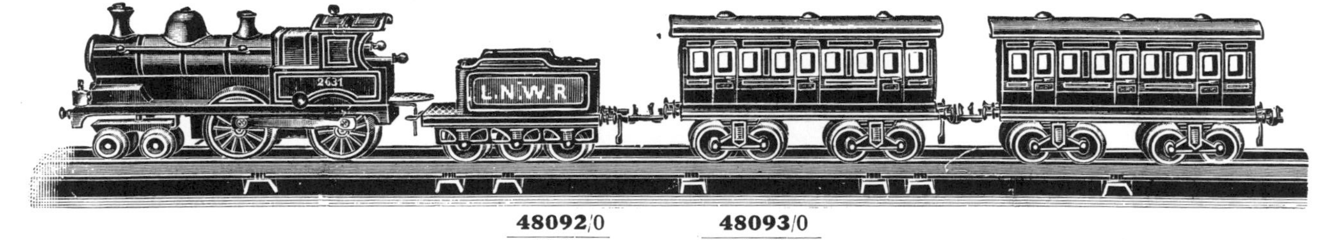

48092/0 M. R. **48093/0** L. N. W. R.

Express Train consisting of: Extra fine express locomotive, elegant finish, with strong, powerful clockwork and patent regulator, automatic brake, to be worked from the rail or from the cab and reversing gear, on 4 axles = 8 wheels, tender with imitation coal and 2 fine model bogie express passenger cars, japanned and lettered in the exact colours of the L. & N. W. R. Co., with oval set of rails ⬭ = 10 rails incl. brake rail, packed in strong cardboard box; locomotive with tender 15 in. long, car 8 in. long, length of complete train $31^1/_2$ in. long . . . . . each **17/10**

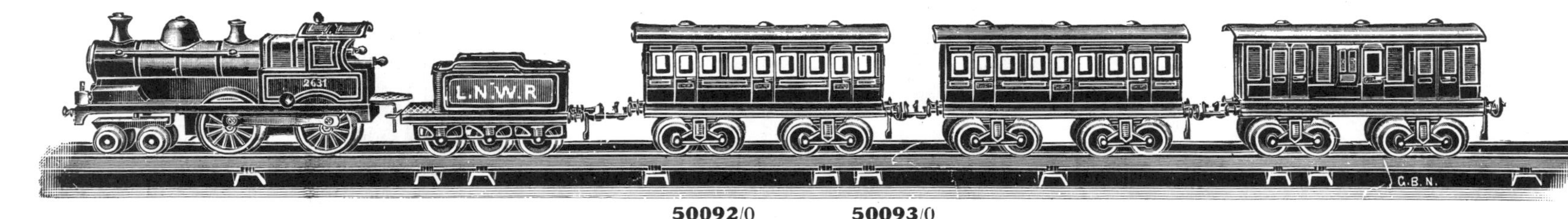

50092/0 M. R. **50093/0** L. N. W. R.

Express Train consisting of: Locomotive in fine, elegant finish, with very powerful clockwork and patent regulator, brake and new automatic reversing gear, to be worked from the rail or from the cab, on 4 axles = 8 wheels, tender with imitation coal, 2 fine model bogie express passenger cars and 1 model bogie express guard's van, japanned and lettered in the exact colours of the L. & N. W. R. Co., with large oval set of rails ⬭ = 12 rails incl. special automatic reversing and brake rails, packed in strong cardboard box. Locomotive with tender 15 in. long. car 8 in. long, length of complete train 39 in. . . . . each **22/—**

New Series of English Model Clockwork Trains

with strong Clockwork Movements.

Gauge 1 = $1^{7}/_{8}$ in.

Locomotive with tender $12^{1}/_{2}$ in. long
Car . . . . 6 " "

70191/000	**70193**/000
G. W. R.	L. N. W. R.

consisting of: Locomotive with strong regulated clockwork and automatic brake which is worked from the rail or from the cab, tender and 1 passenger car, japanned and lettered in the exact colours of the respective Railway Companies, with circular set of rails ◎ = 6 rails incl. brake rail . . . . complete train 19 in long each **7/6**

70191/00	**70193**/00
G. W. R.	L. N. W. R.

Same train as described above with 2 passenger cars and oval set of rails ⬭ = 8 rails incl. brake rail
complete train $25^{1}/_{2}$ in long **9/6**

New Series of English Model Clockwork Trains

with strong Clockwork Movements.

Gauge 1 = $1^{7}/_{8}$ in.

71192/00	**71193**/00
M. R.	L. N. W. R.

Train, consisting of: Locomotive with strong clockwork and automatic brake which is worked from the rail or from the cab, tender and 2 passenger cars japanned and lettered in the exact colours of the respective Railway Companies with oval set of rails = 10 rails incl. brake rail, complete train 27 in. long . . . . each **11/10**

71192/0	**71193**/0
M. R.	L. N. W. R.

Same Train as described above with 2 passenger cars and 1 guards van, large oval rail formation = 12 rails incl. brake rail complete train 34 in. long . . . . each **13/10**

72192/00	**72193**/00
M. R.	L. N. W. R.

Automatic Reversing Train with tender and 2 passenger cars oval rail formation = 12 rails incl. special automatic brake and reversing rail, complete train 27 in. long . . . . each **16/6**

New Series of Clockwork Express Trains

Good Models, Superior Clockwork Movements.

Trains fitted with brake and our automatic reversing gear by means of which the train can be reversed from the rail or from the driver's place At the same time, the special rail supplied with these trains can be used as a brake rail, simply by shifting the position of the stop catch.

Gauge 1 = $1^{7}/_{8}$ in.

Locomotive with tender $16^{1}/_{2}$ in. long
Car . . . . 6 „ „

73192/00	**73193**/00
M. R.	L. N. W. R.

Train, consisting of: Locomotive with extra strong clockwork and patent regulator with brake and **automatic** reversing gear, tender and 2 passenger Cars with doors to open, japanned and lettered in the exact colours of the respective Railway companies, oval set of rails (⊂⊃) = 12 rails incl. automatic brake and reversing rail
complete train 29 in. long each **22/—**

73192/0	**73193**/0
M. R.	L. N. W. R.

Same train as described above with 2 passenger cars and 1 guards van with doors to open, large oval rail formation (⊂⊃) = 14 rails incl. special automatic brake and reversing rail . . . . complete train 35 in. long each **25/—**

English Model Express Clockwork Trains.

Thoroughly good Finish, Superior Clockwork Movements.

Trains fitted with excellent clockwork, brake and our automatic reversing gear by means of which the train can be reversed from the rail or from the driver's place. At the same time, the rail supplied with these trains can be used as a brake rail simply by shifting the position of the stop catch.

Gauge 1 = $1^{7}/_{8}$ in.

Locomotive with tender $16^{1}/_{2}$ in. long, Car 10 in. long.

49192/00 M. R.   **49193**/00 L. N. W. R.

Express Train, consisting of: Locomotive with extra strong clockwork and patent regulator, with brake and automatic reversing gear to be worked from the rail or from the cab, loco on 3 axles = 6 wheels incl. 1 pair of bogie wheels, tender, 2 long model express passenger cars, japanned and lettered in the exact colours of the respective Railway Companies, with oval set of rails ⬭ 12 rails incl. special automatic reversing and brake rail, packed in strong cardboard box with pamphlet "The little Railway Engineer", length of complete Train 36 in. . . . . . each **29/6**

49192/0 M. R.   **49193**/0 L. N. W. R.

Same Train as above with 2 long model express passenger car and 1 model express guards van, japanned and lettered in the exact colours of the respective railway companies with large oval rail formation ⬭ = 12 rails incl. special automatic reversing and brake rail, complete train 46 in. long . . . . . each **35/—**

Superior Clockwork Express Trains

with High Class Clockwork Movements.

With Automatic Reversing Gear. — Carriages with doors to open.

Trains fitted with excellent clockwork, brake and our new automatic reversing gear by means of which the train can be reversed from the rail or from the driver's place. At the same time, the rail supplied with these trains can be used as a brake rail simply by shifting the position of the stop catch.

Gauge 1 = $1^7/_8$ in.

Locomotive with tender $16^3/_4$ in. long, Car $11^1/_2$ in. long.

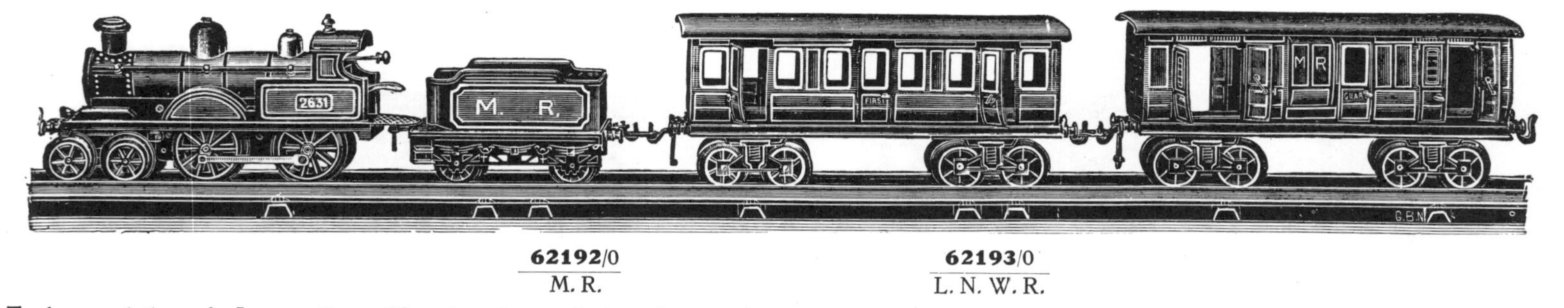

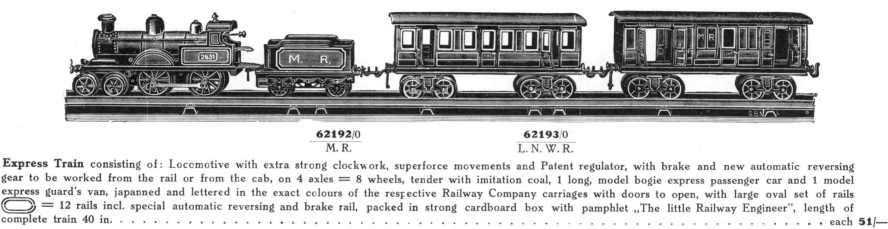

62192/0 M. R. — **62193**/0 L. N. W. R.

Express Train consisting of: Locomotive with extra strong clockwork, superforce movements and Patent regulator, with brake and new automatic reversing gear to be worked from the rail or from the cab, on 4 axles = 8 wheels, tender with imitation coal, 1 long, model bogie express passenger car and 1 model express guard's van, japanned and lettered in the exact colours of the respective Railway Company carriages with doors to open, with large oval set of rails ⬭ = 12 rails incl. special automatic reversing and brake rail, packed in strong cardboard box with pamphlet „The little Railway Engineer", length of complete train 40 in. . . . . each **51/—**

Best Finish, handpainted! ***Slow and Fast Movement!***

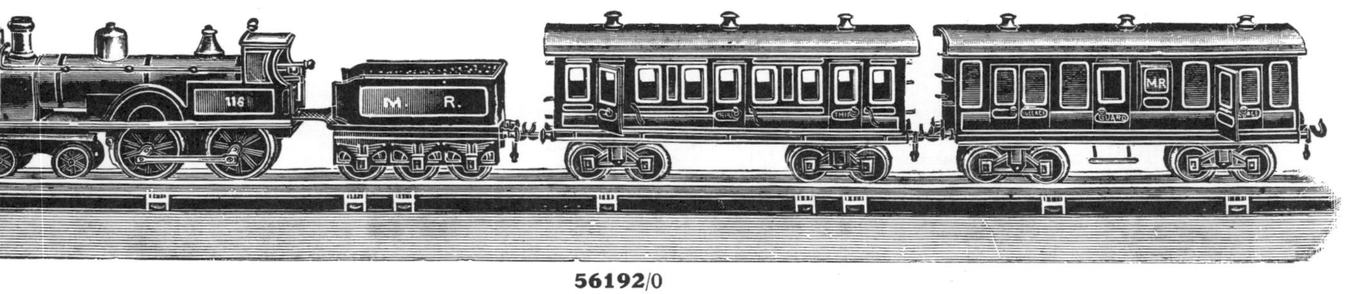

56192/0 M. R.

Express Train consisting of: Locomotive, fine elegant finish, with extra strong powerful clockwork and patent regulator, lever for fast and slow movement, with brake and new automatic reversing gear to be worked from the rail or from the cab, on 4 axles = 8 wheels, tender with imitation coal, 1 model bogie express passenger car and 1 model bogie express guard's van, japanned and lettered in the exact colours of the Midland Railway Company, carriages with doors to open, with large oval set of rails ⬭ 12 rails incl. special automatic reversing and brake rail, packed in strong cardboard box with pamphlet „The little Railway Engineer", length of complete train 52 in. . . . . each **82/—**

New English Models of Clockwork Trains

with various rail formations, Locos fitted with strong clockwork and regulator.

Gauge 0 = $1^3/_8$ in.

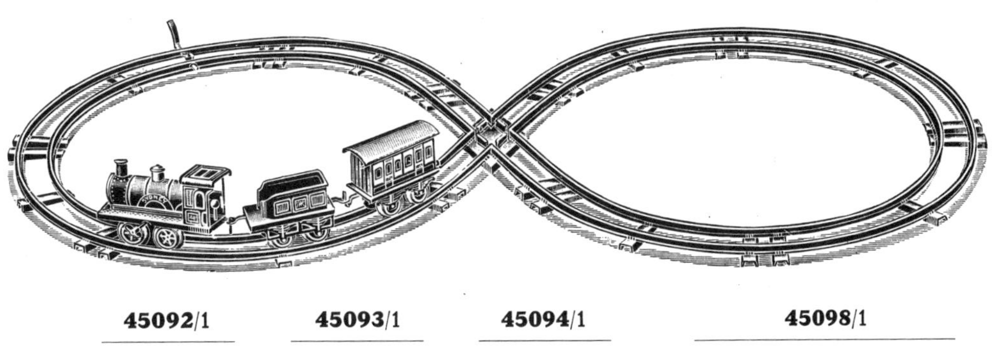

45092/1	**45093**/1	**45094**/1	**45098**/1
M. R.	L. N. W. R.	G. N. R.	Lancashire & Yorkshire R.

consisting of: **Locomotive** with **strong clockwork** and **regulator, automatic brake** to be worked from the rail or from the cab, **tender** and **1 passenger car,** japanned and lettered in the exact colours of the respective Railway Companies, with ∞ rail formation ∞ = 1 crossing and 8 rails incl. brake rail, loco with tender $9^3/_4$ in. long, car $4^3/_4$ in. long, length of complete train $14^1/_2$ in. . . . . each **5/—**

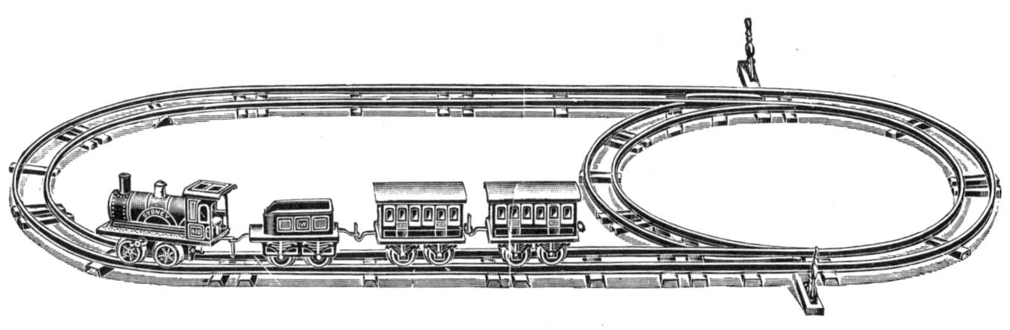

45091/2	**45092**/2	**45093**/2	**45098**/2
G. W. R.	M. R.	L. N. W. R.	Lancashire & Yorkshire R.

Same train as above with 2 passenger cars, large rail formation with 2 points and 9 rails incl. brake rail, length of complete train 19 in. . . . . each **7/2**

Train Combinations.

Trains and Accessories produced from Original Models.

Gauge 0 = $1^3/_8$ in.

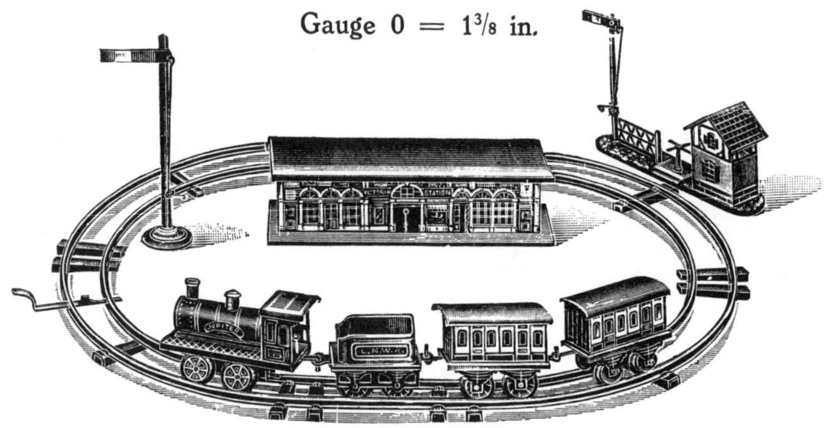

30253—30255

30250	**30251**	**30252**
M. R.	L. N. W. R.	G. N. R. colour

Train, consisting of: Locomotive with strong clockwork, regulator and brake, tender, 1 passenger car, japanned and lettered in the exact colours of the respective Railway Companies, watchman's house and signal, with circle set of rails ◎ = 4 rails incl. brake rail, packed in strong cardboard box, length of complete train $14^1/_2$ in. . . . . each **3/8**

30253	**30254**	**30255**
M. R.	L. N. W. R.	G. N. R.

Train, consisting of: Locomotive with strong clockwork, regulator and brake, to be worked from the rail or from the cab, tender and 2 passenger cars, japanned and lettered in the exact colours of the respective Railway Companies, with station, watchman's house with barriers and signal, and 1 separate signal, with oval set of rails ⬭ = 6 rails incl. brake rail, packed in strong cardboard box, length of complete train 19. in. . . . . . . each **6/—**

Gauge 0 = $1^3/_8$ in.

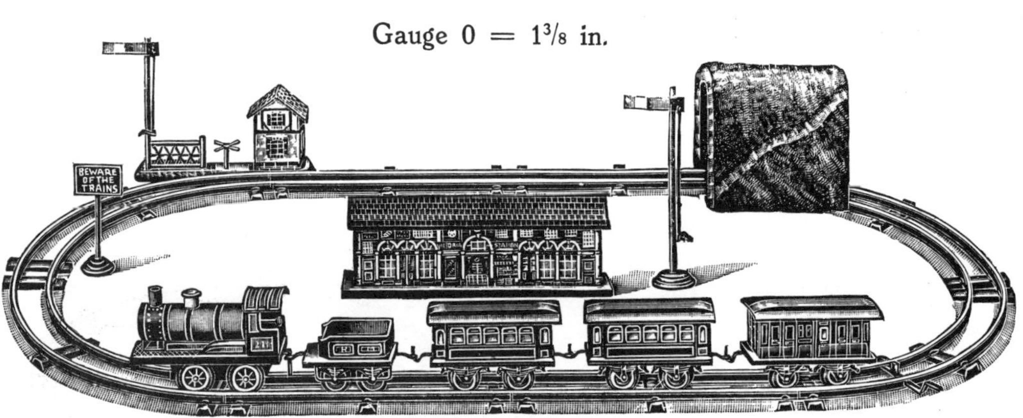

30258 and 30259

30256	**30257**
G. W. R.	L. N. W. R.

Train, consisting of: Locomotive with extra strong clockwork, automatic brake to be worked from the rail or from the cab, tender, 2 long passenger cars, japanned and lettered in the exact colours of the respective Railway Companies, with tunnel, warning plate, watchman's house with barriers and signal, 1 separate signal, with oval set of rails ⬭ = 6 rails incl. brake rail, packed in strong cardboard box, length of complete train $19^1/_2$ in. . . . . . each **8/6**

30258	**30259**
G. W. R.	L. N. W. R.

Train, consisting of: Locomotive with extra strong clockwork, regulator, with automatic brake, to be worked from the rail or from the cab, tender, 2 long passenger cars and 1 guard's van, japanned and lettered in the exact colours of the respective Railway Companies, with station, tunnel, warning board, watchman's house, with barriers and signal and 1 separate signal, with large oval set of rails ⬭ = 8 rails incl. brake rail, packed in strong cardboard box, length of complete train 24 in. . . . . each **11/—**

Combination Train

with large variety of accessories, in fine polychrome japanning.

Gauge 0 = $1^3/_8$ in.

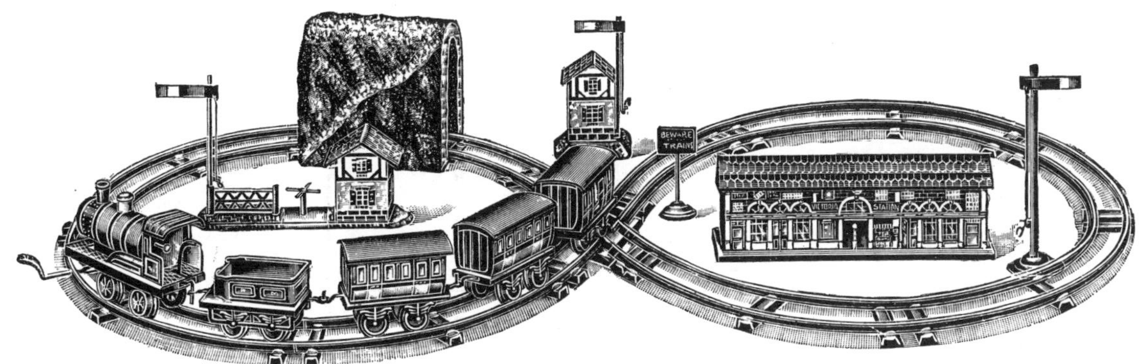

30260

G. W. R. and L. N. W. R. assorted.

30260 **Train,** consisting of: Locomotive with extra strong clockwork and regulator, automatic brake to be worked from the rail or from the cab, tender, 2 passenger cars and 1 guard's van, japanned and lettered in the exact colours of the G. W. R. Co., with station, tunnel, warning board, watchman's house with barriers and signal, and 1 separate signal, with ∞ rail formation = 1 crossing and 8 rails incl. brake rail, length of complete train 24 in. . . . . each **13/6**

M **3426** **Combination Train,** consisting of: Locomotive with strong clockwork and Patent Regulator, with automatic brake to be worked from the rail or from the cab with tender, 2 passenger cars, railway station, indicator, semaphor, trolley, guards lamp, bell punch and tickets, oval set of rails mounted on slopes in very realistic painting. The Set is nicely got up and packed in a strong red carboard box. . . . . each set **15/—**

Mountain Railway (Cog Wheel Action).

Gauge 0 = $1^3/_8$ in.

14460

14460 **Mountain Railway,** strong finish, excellently working, consisting of: Locomotive with strong clockwork and brake, 1 passenger car with platform, with oval set of rails (⊂⊃) = 10 rails, (4 straight rails with racks and 6 curved rails), with pillars of various height, length of complete train 12 in. . . . . each **16/10**

Correct English Model of Goods Train.

Gauge 0 = $1^{3}/_{8}$ in.

M 3452/0

M 3452/0 Goods Train consisting of: Locomotive with strong clockwork, regulator and automatic brake which is worked from the rail or from the cab, reversing gear; 3 open goods trucks in assorted colours, all finely japanned, with oval set of rails (oval) = 8 rails incl. brake rail; length of complete train 30 in. . . each **8/—**

Fine Model of English Mail Bag Train.

Gauge 1 = $1^{7}/_{8}$ in.

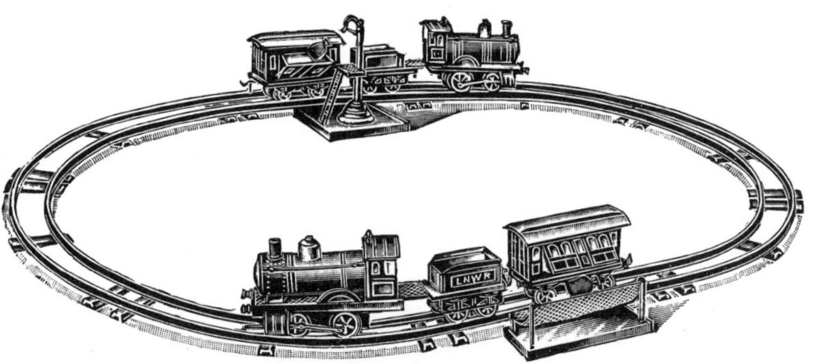

M 3413/1

M 3413/1 English Mail Train consisting of loco with powerful clockwork and brake, tender and mail van, japanned and lettered in the exact colours of the M. R. Co. with oval set of rails (oval) = 10 rails incl. brake rail, delivery platform and receiving net each with rail attached, with post bags . . . . complete each **33/—**

Clockwork Trains

specially suited for Window Attractions.

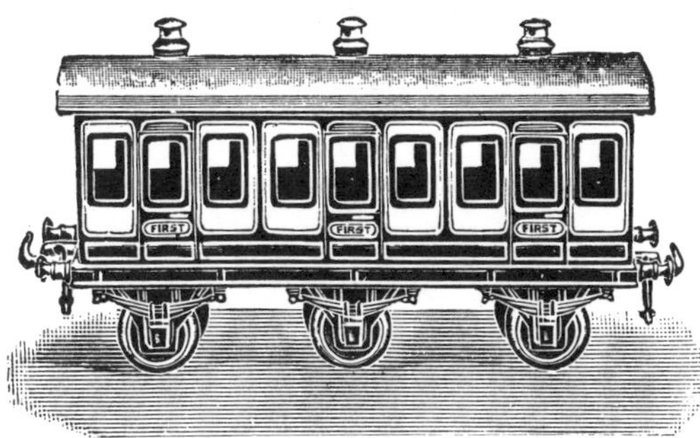

Marvellous Value!

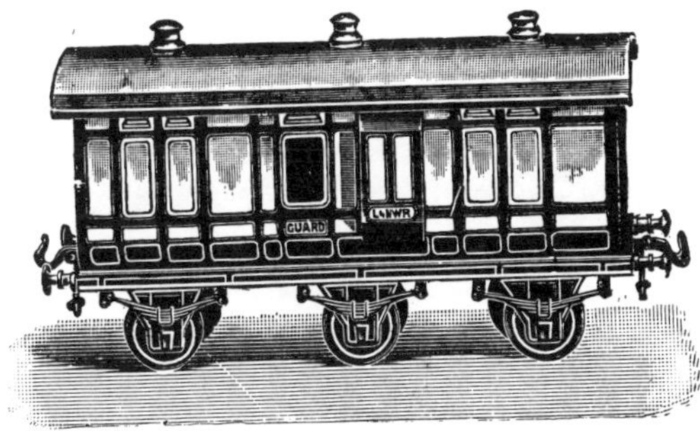

Gauge 3 = $2^5/_8$ in. Model Suburban Train with reversing gear.

Consisting of: Clockwork Locomotive of superior workmanship throughout with extra powerful clockwork mechanism with reversing gear, with 2 long model passenger cars on 3 axles with large oval set of rails = 18 pieces; made in Midland and L. & N. W. colours. Length of train 4 feet, measurement of track 7 feet 10 in. × 4 feet, 4 in.

17392/00	**17393**/00
M. R.	L. & N. W. R.

complete set **72/—**

Gauge 4 = 3 in. Model Express Train with reversing gear.

Consisting of: Clockwork Locomotive of superior workmanship throughout, with extra powerful clockwork mechanism with reversing gear, with 2 long model passenger bogie carriages on 4 axles = 8 wheels with 8 hinged doors to open, inside richly fitted up, with seats, racks &c. and 1 model guards van made in the same fashion, with large oval set of rails = 22 rails, made in L. & N. W. R. and L. S. W. R. colours. Length of train 6 feet, 10 in., measurement of track 9 feet, 10 in.

17493/0	**17495**/0
L. & N. W. R.	L. S. W. R.

complete set **144/—**

Models of English Electric Trams

with regulated clockwork and Brake

exact Models as seen in London, Liverpool, Manchester and Glasgow etc.

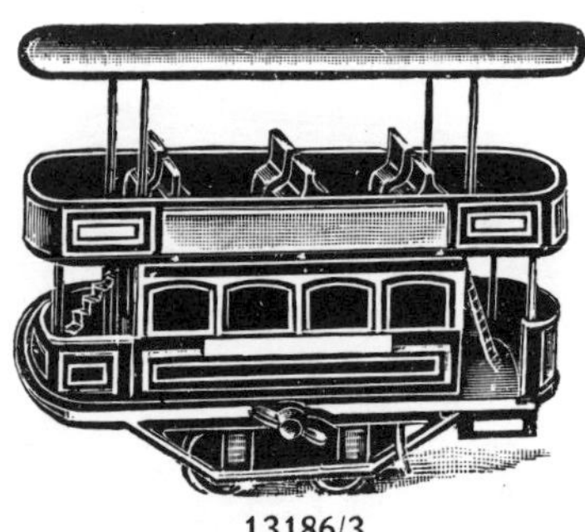

13186/3

14435

Carpet Tram with strong clockwork, fitted with seats and stairs, roof detachable finely japanned.

13186/3 $9^1/_2$ in long, $6^3/_4$ in. high . . . . each **4/8**

Tram, with extra strong clockwork, for running on floor (Carpet), in fine japanning, high class finish with patent regulator and brake

14435/0 Gauge 0 = $1^3/_8$ in., car $7^1/_4$ in. long, $2^3/_4$ in. wide, $5^1/_4$ in. high . . . . each **6/—**

„ /1 „ 1 = $1^7/_8$ „ „ $8^3/_4$ „ „ $3^1/_4$ „ „ $5^3/_4$ „ „ . . . . „ **8/—**

Gauge 00 = $1^1/_8$ in.

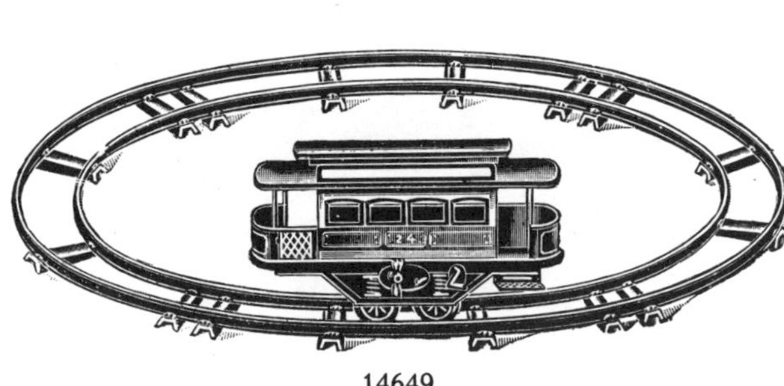

14649

Gauge 00 = $1^1/_8$ in.

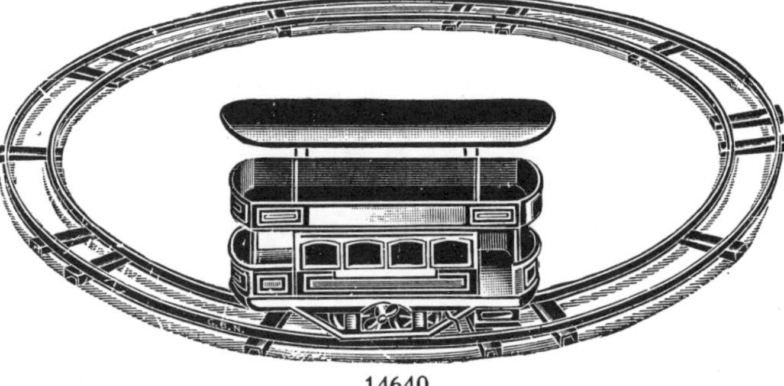

14640

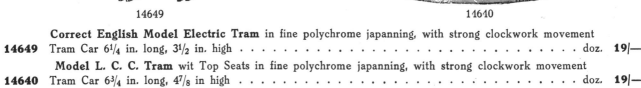

Correct English Model Electric Tram in fine polychrome japanning, with strong clockwork movement

14649 Tram Car $6^1/_4$ in. long, $3^1/_2$ in. high . . . . doz. **19/—**

Model L. C. C. Tram wit Top Seats in fine polychrome japanning, with strong clockwork movement

14640 Tram Car $6^3/_4$ in. long, $4^7/_8$ in high . . . . doz. **19/—**

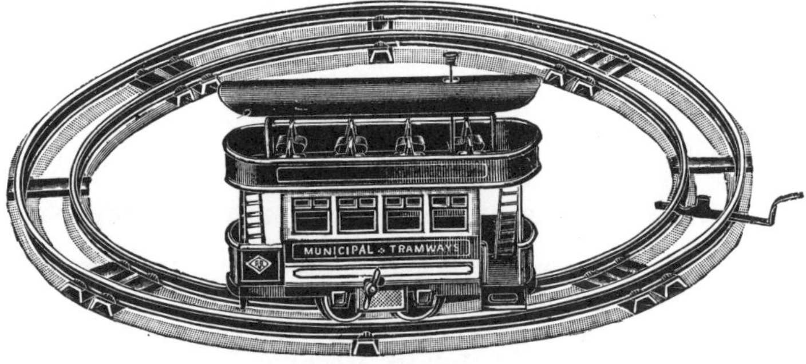

10244

Gauge 0 = $1^3/_8$ in.

Model Tram with strong reliable Clockwork Movement in fine polychrome japanning with circle of rails with brake

10244 Tram $7^1/_2$ in. long, $5^3/_4$ in. high packed in red cardboard box . . . . doz. **57/—**

Carpet Trains without Clockwork.

Paked in strong red cardboard boxes.

30226/2

M 2787/1 **Carpet Train** without clockwork, consisting of: Loco, tender and 1 goods truck, japanned in assorted colours: G. W. R., M. R., L. N. W. R. and G. N. R., car 4 in. long, length of complete train 11 in. . . . doz. **7/—**

30226/2 **Same Train** as above with 1 passenger car and 1 goods truck, car 4 in. long, length of complete train 15 in. . . . doz. **9/8**

30228/6

30227/4 **Carpet Train** without clockwork, consisting of: Tenderloco, 3 passenger cars and 1 goods truck, finely japanned in assorted colours G. W. R., M. R., L. N. W. R. and G. N. R., car 4 in. long, length of complete train 23 in. . . . doz. **17/6**

30228/6 **Same Train** as above, but with Loco, separate Tender, 4 passenger cars and 2 goods trucks, length of complete train $32\frac{3}{4}$ in. . . . doz. **25/4**

30228/8 **Same Train** as above, with 5 passenger cars and 3 goods trucks, length of complete train 41 in.. . doz. **30/—**

Street Rollers.

6574 13639/0 13639/1

6574 **Traction Engine,** with good clockwork, adjustable for straight and circular run, finely japanned, $4\frac{1}{2}$ in. long, 4 in. high . . . doz. **9/8**

13639/0 **Street Roller** with good clockwork, adjustable for straight and circular run, finely japanned, 5 in. long, 4 in. high . . . doz. **9/8**

13639/1 **Street Roller strong regulated clockwork,** adjustable for straight and circular run, finely japanned, $6\frac{1}{2}$ in. long, $4\frac{1}{4}$ in. high . . . doz. **18/—**

Large Sized Carpet Goods Train.

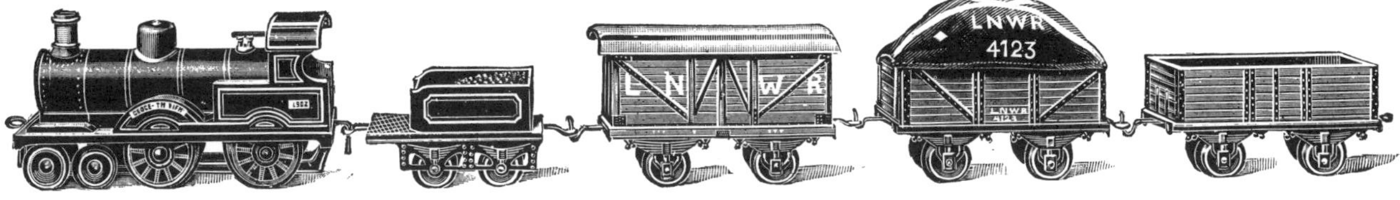

M 3416

M 3416 **Carpet Train** without clockwork thorougly good finish with 3 various trucks. This train being made in a specially large scale, all little details are correctly carried out. Complete Length 41 in. . . . . . each **9/—**

The smallest Train in the world.

A Perfect Miniature Train.

30267/0

This is a perfect Model of a L. & N. W. R. Express on a very small Scale.

Length of Loco with Tender . . . . $5^1/_8$ in.
„ „ Carriage . . . . $3^3/_8$ „
„ „ entire Train . . . . 21 „

The Train consists of Locomotive, Tender, 3 Passenger Carriages and 1 Guard's van. It is a perfect replica of the well known L. & N. W. R. Expresses from Euston to Birmingham, Manchester, Liverpool, Glasgow etc.

30267/0 Packed in handsome box, $12^1/_2$ in. $\times$ 3 in. . . . . doz. **18/—**

Carpet Locos with reliable Clockwork Movements

finely japanned, elegantly finished.

14489/0

14489/1

14489/3—4

14489/0	$5^3/_8$ in. long,	$3^3/_8$ in. high		doz.	**9/8**
„ /1	$7^7/_8$ „	„ $4^1/_2$ „ „		„	**17/6**
„ /3	$9^1/_2$ „	„ 5 „ „	with bell	each	**3/2**
„ /4	12 „	„ $5^3/_4$ „ „	„ „	„	**5/—**

New English Models of Clockwork Locomotives.

Correctly painted, lettered and lined in accordance with the respective Railway Companies Colours.

Gauge 0 = $1^3/_8$ in.

45590/0

Locomotive fitted **with very strong Clockwork, patent regulator and brake,** to be worked from the cab or from the rail, japanned and lettered in the correct colours of the respective Railway Companies. Loco incl. tender $10^1/_2$ in. long.

Loco with tender complete doz. **19/—**

	45592/0	**45593**/0	**45594**/0	**45598**/0	
made in	M. R.	L. & N. W. R.	G. N. R.	L. & Y. R.	colours.

Reversing gear.

51592/0

Locomotive with strong clockwork and patent regulator, with reversing gear and brake, to be worked from the cab or rail, with tender, japanned and lettered in the exact colours of the respective Railway Companies. Loco incl. tender $10^1/_2$ in. long.

Loco with tender complete doz. **29/6**

	51592/0	**51593**/0	**51594**/0	
made in	M. R.	L. & N. W. R.	G. N. R.	colours.

42590/0

Locomotive with strong clockwork and patent regulator, with automatic brake to be worked from the cab or from the rail, with tender, japanned and lettered in the exact colours of the respective Railway Companies. Loco incl. tender $11^1/_2$ in. long.

Loco with tender complete doz. **33/8**

	42591/0	**42593**/0	
made in	G. W. R.	L. & N. W. R.	colours.

Reversing gear.

75593/0

Tank-Locomotive with **strong Clockwork** and patent regulator with automatic brake and reversing gear. Well modelled engine, lettered and lined in the correct colours of the respective Railway Companies. 7 in. long. . . . . doz. **42/—**

	75593/0	**75594**/0	
made in	L. & N. W. R.	G. N. R.	colours.

New English Models of Clockwork Locomotives.

Gauge 0 = $1^3/_8$ in.

Reversing gear.

52593/0

Locomotive with **strong clockwork** and patent regulator, with automatic brake, to be worked from the cab or from the rail, reversing gear and tender, japanned and lettered in the exact colours of the respective Railway Companies, loco incl. tender $10^1/_2$ in. long

Loco with tender complete each **3/8**

52591/0	**52593/0**
made in G. W. R.	L. &. N. W. R. colour

Reversing gear.

68593/0

Locomotive with **strong clockwork** and patent regulator, with automatic brake, to be worked from the cab or from the rail, reversing gear and tender, japanned and lettered in the exact colours of the respective Railway Companies, loco incl. tender 10 in. long

Loco with tender complete each **4/6**

68592/0	**68593/0**	**68594/0**
made in M. R.	L. & N. W. R.	G. N. R. colours

Automatic reversing gear.

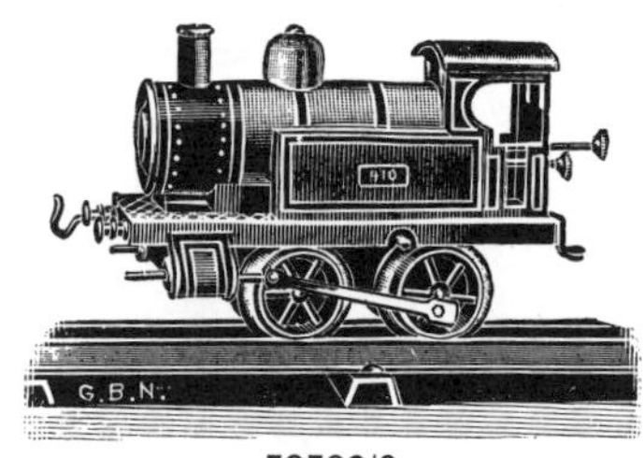

59593/0

59593/0 L.N.W.R. **Pilot (Tender) Locomotive** with **extra strong clockwork**, with superforce movement and patent regulator, with brake and new automatic reversing gear, both either to be worked from the rail or from the cab, nickelled piston rods and fittings, body finely japanned, $5^3/_4$ in. long . . . . each **5/10**

Automatic reversing gear.

77590/0

Fine Locomotive with **powerful clockwork** and patent regulator with brake and new automatic reversing gear, either to be worked from the rail or from the cab, with piston rods and finely nickelled fittings, tender with imitation coal, length incl. tender $11^1/_2$ in.

Loco with tender complete each **5/10**

77592/0	**77593/0**	**77594/0**
made in M. R.	L. N. W. R.	G. N. R. colours

Automatic reversing gear.

78593/0

Locomotive with **extra strong powerful clockwork** and patent regulator, with brake and automatic reversing gear by means of which the loco can be reversed from a special rail or from the driver's place, with nickelled fittings, tender with imitation coal, japanned and lettered in the exact colours of the respective Railway Companies, loco incl. tender 12 in. long

Loco with tender complete each **7/10**

78592/0	**78593/0**	**78594/0**
M. R,	L. N. W. R.	G. N. R. colour

Models of English Express Locomotives.

Gauge $0 = 1^3/_8$ in.

Reversing gear.

49593/0

49593/0 **Express Locomotive** with **superforce movement,** on 4 axles = 8 wheels incl. bogie wheels, in fine elegant finish, with extra strong clockwork and patent regulator with brake to be worked from the rail or from the cab, reversing gear, tender with imitation coal, japanned and lettered in the exact colours of the respective Railway Companies, loco incl. tender $12^1/_4$ in. long.. . Loco with tender complete each **9/ –**

	49591/0	**49593**/0	
made in	G. W. R	L. & N. W. R.	colour

Automatic reversing gear.

57593/0

57593/0 **Express Locomotive** with **superforce movement,** on 3 axles = 6 wheels incl. bogie wheels in fine elegant finish with **extra strong** clockwork and patent regulator, with brake and **new automatic** reversing gear both either to be worked from the rail or from the cab, brass fittings, hand rails and piston rods, tender with imitation coal, japanned and lettered in the exact colours of the L. N. W. R. Railway Company, loco incl. tender 13 in. long. Loco with tender complete each **17/—**

Scale Model.

London & North Western Railway,
Express Locomotive "George the Fifth" No. 2663.

Gauge 0 = $1^{3}/_{8}$ in.

Will run over old sharp radius as well as over new large radius curves.

Will run over old sharp radius as well as over new large radius curves.

76593/0

The "George the Fifth" 4—4—0 class of Locomotive is considered to be the "Premier" Locomotive of Englands "Premier" Line, and its introduction among our range of clockwork driven Models will no doubt be appreciated by all Model Railway Enthusiasts.

Frames and Superstructure are made of best tinned steel plate stamped out with powerful press tools.

The Clockwork Movement is one of superior workmanship throughout, combining a maximum of pulling power with long run at an even speed. It is fitted with automatic reversing gear and brake, both can be worked from the cab or from the rail.

Enamelled and lined in correct L. & N. W. R. colours.

76593/0 Loco with Tender $16^{3}/_{4}$ in. long . . . . complete with tender each **11/6**

NB. This loco does not have to have large radius rails, but will run satisfactorily on the old sharp radius rails as well as on the new large radius rails.

Finest Express Locomotives.

Automatic Reversing Gear.

56593/0

Finest Express Locomotive with best powerful clockwork and patent regulator, with brake and new automatic reversing gear by means of which the loco can be reversed from a special rail or from the cab, on 4 axles = 8 wheels incl. bogie wheels, tender with imitation coal, hand painted and lettered in the exact colours of the respective Railway Companies. Loco incl. tender 12 in. long. . . . . Loco with tender complete each **26/—**

56592/0	**56593**/0
made in M. R.	L. N. W. R. colours.

6 coupled Express-Locomotive, latest type.

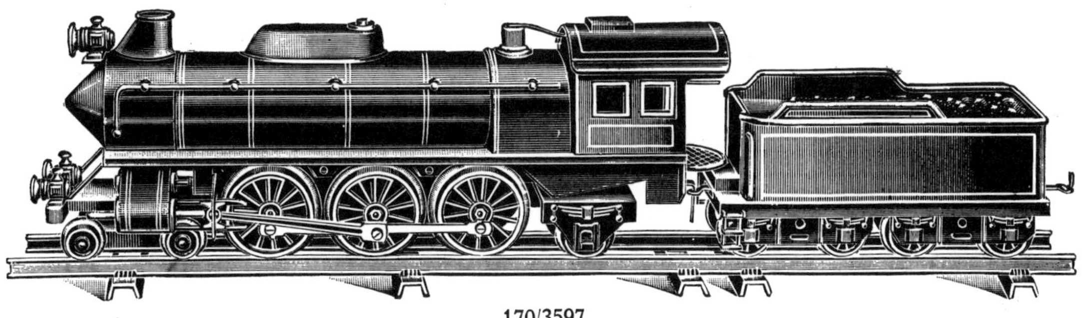

170/3597

This Model is an exact reproduction of the latest 6 coupled Engines introduced on the Continental Lines. It is fitted with automatic brake and automatic reversing gear and is the first Model of an 0 gauge Engine, which can be made to run **slow and fast.** Enamelling and finish of fittings is of the very best quality.

170/3597 Gauge 0 = $1^3/_8$ in., loco incl. tender $18^3/_4$ in. long . . . . Loco with tender complete each **46/—**

New Series of English Model Clockwork Locomotives
with strong Clockwork Movements.

Gauge 1 = $1^7/_8$ in.

70593/1

Locomotive with strong regulated clockwork and automatic brake, which is worked from the rail or from the cab, japanned and lettered in the exact colours of the respective Railway Companies, loco incl. tender $12^1/_2$ in. long

Loco with tender compl. each **5/—**

70591/1	**70593/1**
G. W. R.	L. N. W. R.

71592/1

Locomotive with strong clockwork and automatic brake, which is worked from the rail or from the cab, japanned and lettered in the exact colours of the respective Railway Companies, loco incl. tender $14^1/_2$ in long

Loco with tender compl. each **7/—**

71592/1	**71593/1**
M. R.	L. N. W. R.

Automatic reversing gear.

72592/1

Locomotive with strong clockwork, automatic reversing gear, which is worked from the rail or the cab and automatic brake, japanned and lettered in the exact colours of the respective Railway Companies, loco incl. tender $14^1/_2$ in. long

Loco with tender compl. each **9/—**

72592/1	**72593/1**
M. R.	L. N. W. R.

Automatic reversing gear

73592/1

Locomotive with extra strong clockwork and patent regulator with brake and automatic reversing gear, which is worked from the rail or the cab, with tender, japanned and lettered in the exact colours of the respective Railway Companies, loco incl. tender $16^1/_2$ in. long

Loco incl. tender compl. each **13/—**

73592/1	**73593/1**
M. R.	L. N. W R.

New English Models of High Class Clockwork Express Locomotives.

Gauge 1 = $1^7/_8$ in.

With brake and automatic reversing gear.

Express Locomotive with extra strong clockwork, superforce movement and patent regulator, with brake and **automatic reversing gear** to be worked from the cab or by means of a special reversing rail, which — at the same time — can be used as brake rail simply by shifting the position of the stop catch, tender with imitation coal, japanned and lettered in the exact colours of the respective Railway Companies, loco incl. tender $16^1/_2$ in. long.

Loco with tender complete each **18/6**

49592/1	**49593/1**
made in M. R.	L. N. W. R. colours.

With brake and new automatic reversing gear.

Superior Express Locomotive with powerful clockwork, patent regulator, with brake and new automatic reversing gear, to be worked from the cab or by means of a special reversing rail, which — at the same time — can be used as a brake rail simply by shifting the position of the stop catch, tender with imitation coal, japanned and lettered in the exact colours of the respective Railway Companies, loco incl. tender $16^1/_2$ in. long.

Loco with tender complete each **28/—**

62593/1
made in L. N. W. R. colour.

Scale Model.

London & North Western Railway, Express Locomotive "George the Fifth" No. 2663.

Gauge $1 = 1^7/_8$ in.

Will run over old shard radius as well as over new large radius curves.
Will run over old sharp radius as well as over new large radius curves.
2663

76593/1

The "George the Fifth" 4—4—0 class of Locomotive is considered to be the "Premier" Locomotive of Englands "Premier" Line and its introduction among our range of Clockwork driven Models will no doubt be appreciated by all Model Railway Enthusiasts.

Frames and Superstructure are made of best tinned steel plate, stamped out with powerful press tools.

The Clockwork Movement is of the very best make and finish throughout combining a maximum of pulling power with long run at an even speed. It is fitted with automatic Reversing gear and brake and with a 2 speed Gear for fast and slow run, both Reverse and brake Gears can be worked from the cab or from the rail.

Enamelled and lined in correct L. & N. W. R. colours.

76593/1 Loco with tender $22^1/_2$ in. long . . . . Loco with Tender complete each **63/—**

6 coupled Express-Locomotive, latest type.

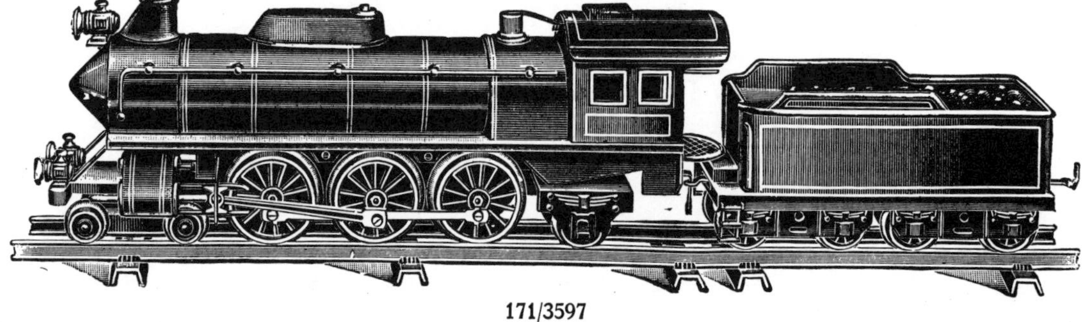

171/3597

This Model is an exact reproduction of the latest 6 coupled Engines introduced on the Continental Lines. It is fitted with automatic brake and automatic reversing gear, with slow and fast movement. Enamelling and finish of fittings is of the very best quality.

171/3597 Gauge $1 = 1^7/_8$ in., loco incl. tender $23^3/_4$ in. long. . . . . loco with tender complete each **92/—**

Models of English Railway Locomotives

highly finished and japanned in the colours of the different Railway Companies.

Gauge 3 = $2^5/_8$ in.

17592/3

Finest Express Locomotive, with extra powerful clockwork, superforce movement and patent regulator, with brake, reversing gear, lever for fast and slow movement, piston rods with guide bars, 2 brass domes and brass hand-rails, tender with imitation coal, loco incl. tender 25 in. long . . . . loco with tender complete each **45/—**

17592/3	**17593**/3	**17594**/3	**17595**/3
M. R.	L. N. W. R.	G. N. R.	L. & S. W. R.

Gauge 4 = 3 in.

17594/4

Finest Express Locomotive, with extra powerful clockwork, superforce movement and patent regulator, with brake, reversing gear, lever for fast and slow movement, piston rods with guide bars, 2 brass domes and brass hand-rails, tender with imitation coal, loco incl. tender 25 in. long, japanned, lettered and lined in the exact colours of the respective Railway Company . . . . loco with tender compl. each **55/—**

17592/4	**17593**/4	**17594**/4	**17595**/4
M. R.	L. N. W. R.	G. N. R.	L. & S. W. R.

Models of English Railway Carriages

highly finished and japanned in the colours of the different Railway Companies.

Railway Carriages

well japanned and highly finished, fitting trains and locomotives for steam, clockwork and electricity.

52793/0 and 71793/1

52893/0 and 15892/1

Passenger Cars, finely japanned

Gauge 0 = $1^{3}/_{8}$ in.	—	**52792**/0	**52793**/0	**52794**/0	car 4 in. long,	doz. **6/—**
„ 1 = $1^{7}/_{8}$ „	**71791**/1	—	**71793**/1	—	„ 6 „ „	„ **15/—**
	G. W. R.	M. R.	L. & N. W. R.	G. N. R.	colour	

Luggage Vans, finely japanned

Gauge 0 = $1^{3}/_{8}$ in.	**52892**/0	**52893**/0	**52894**/0	car 4 in. long	doz. **6/—**
„ 1 = $1^{7}/_{8}$ „	**15892**/1	**15893**/1	**15894**/1	„ 6 „ „	„ **15/—**
	M. R.	L. & N. W. R.	G. N. R.	colour	

54791/0 and 46792/1

54891/0 and 46892/1

Passenger cars, finely japanned, with 4 hinged doors to open

Gauge 0 = $1^{3}/_{8}$ in.	**54791**/0	**54792**/0	**54793**/0	car 4 in. long	doz. **9/10**
„ 1 = $1^{7}/_{8}$ „	—	**46792**/1	**46793**/1	„ 6 „ „	„ **31/6**
	G. W. R.	M. R.	L. & N. W. R.	colour	

Luggage cars, finely japanned, with 2 hinged doors to open

Gauge 0 = $1^{3}/_{8}$ in.	**54891**/0	**54892**/0	**54893**/0	car 4 in long	doz. **9/10**
„ 1 = $1^{7}/_{8}$ „	—	**46892**/1	**46893**/1	„ 6 „ „	„ **31/6**
	G. W. R.	M. R.	L. & N. W. R.	colour.	

Models of English Railway Carriages

highly finished and japanned in the colours of the different Railway Companies.

Fine Express Railway Carriages,

well japanned and highly finished, fitting trains and locomotives with steam, clockwork and electricity.

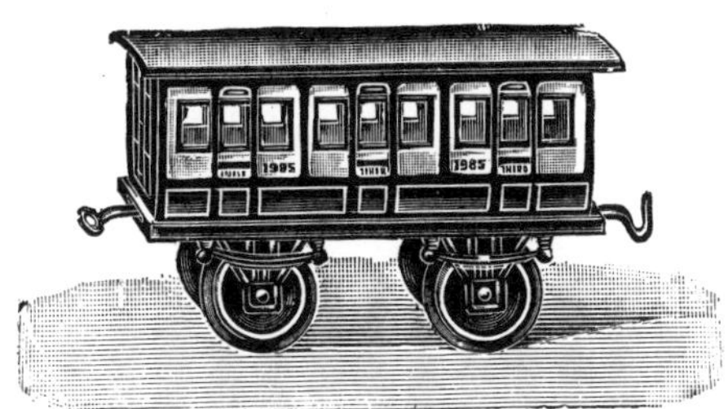

47791/0 and 1

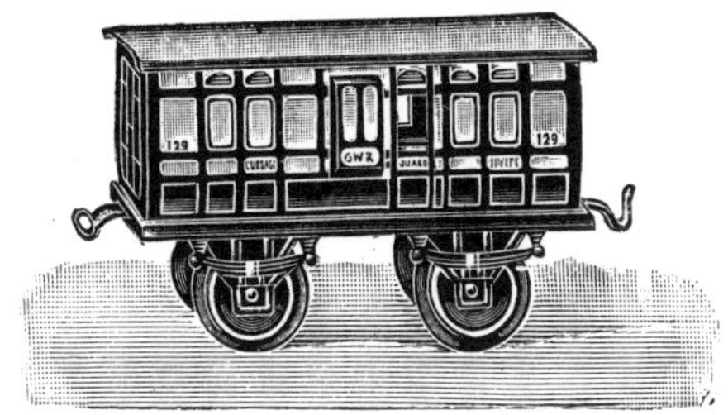

47891/0 and 1

Express Passenger Cars, finely japanned

Gauge	G. W. R.	M. R.	L. & N. W. R.	G. N. R.	L. & S. W. R.	colours	
Gauge $0 = 1\frac{3}{8}$ in.	**47791**/0	**47792**/0	**47793**/0	—	—	car $5\frac{1}{4}$ in. long . . .	doz. **9/10**
„ $1 = 1\frac{7}{8}$ „	—	**47792**/1	**47793**/1	**47794**/1	**47795**/1	„ $9\frac{1}{2}$ „ „ . . .	„ **36/—**

Express Luggage Vans, finely japanned

Gauge	G. W. R.	M. R.	L. & N. W. R.	colour	
Gauge $0 = 1\frac{3}{8}$ in.	**47891**/0	**47892**/0	**47893**/0	car $5\frac{1}{4}$ in. long	doz. **9/10**
„ $1 = 1\frac{7}{8}$ „	—	„ /1	„ /1	„ $9\frac{1}{2}$ „ „	„ **36/—**

New Series of Model Carriages and Vans

Made to Scale for Gauge 0

with Four Compartments and all Doors to open

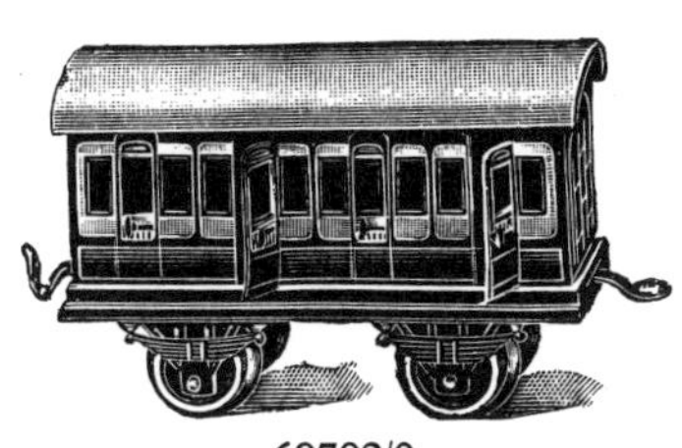

69792/0

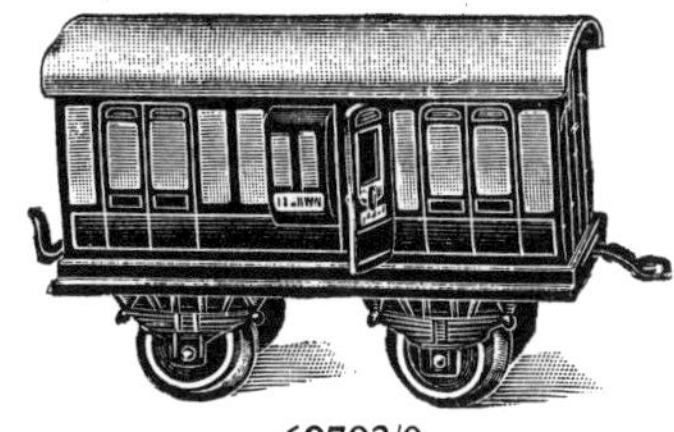

69793/0

Important New Line $5\frac{1}{4}$ in. long

Gauge $0 = 1\frac{3}{8}$ in.

	M. R.	L. & N. W. R.	
Passenger Cars	**69792**/0	**69793**/0	doz. **17/—**
Guards Vans	**69892**/0	**69893**/0	„ **17/—**

Fine Models of Express Bogie Carriages

with doors to open.

56792/0 and 1

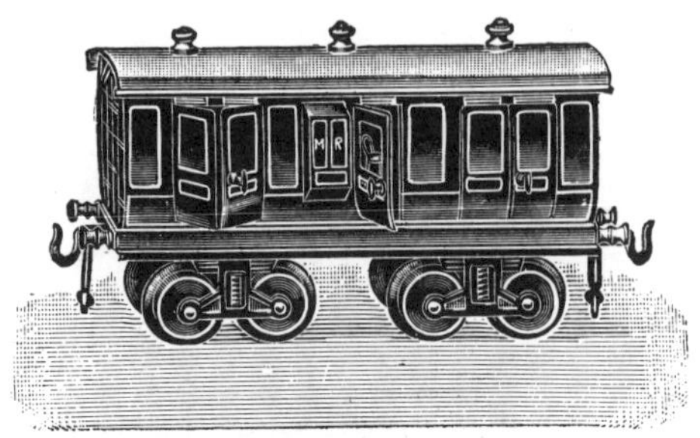

56892/0 and 1

Express Bogie Coaches with 6 hinged doors **to open,** on 4 axles = 8 wheels

Gauge	M. R.	L. & N. W. R.	G. N. R. colour		
Gauge 0 = $1^{3}/_{8}$ in.	**56792**/0	**56793**/0	**56794**/0	car $6^{1}/_{2}$ in. long	each **3/—**
„ 1 = $1^{7}/_{8}$ „	„ /1	„ /1	—	„ $11^{1}/_{2}$ „ „	„ **7/6**

Express Bogie Luggage Vans with 6 hinged doors **to open,** on 4 axles = 8 wheels

Gauge	M. R.	L. & N. W. R.	G. N. R. colour		
Gauge 0 = $1^{3}/_{8}$ in.	**56892**/0	**56893**/0	**56894**/0	car $6^{1}/_{2}$ in. long	each **3/—**
„ 1 = $1^{7}/_{8}$ „	„ /1	„ /1	—	„ $11^{1}/_{2}$ „ „	„ **7/6**

Correct Models of 6 coupled Passenger Cars and Guards Vans

best handpainted finish.

Gauge 1 = $1^{7}/_{8}$ in.

16792/1

16892/1

Express Passenger Cars, finely japanned

Gauge	M. R.	L. N. W. R.	G. N. R.	L. S. W. R. colour	
Gauge 1 = $1^{7}/_{8}$ in.	**16792**/1	**16793**/1	**16794**/1	**16795**/1	. . . . . each **6/—**

Express Luggage Vans, finely japanned

Gauge	M. R.	L. N. W. R.	G. N. R.	L. S. W. R. colour	
Gauge 1 = $1^{7}/_{8}$ in.	**16892**/1	**16893**/1	**16894**/1	**16895**/1	. . . . . each **6/—**

Extra fine English Express Bogie Carriages

fitting trains and locomotives for steam and clockwork.

Gauge 1 = $1^7/_8$ in.

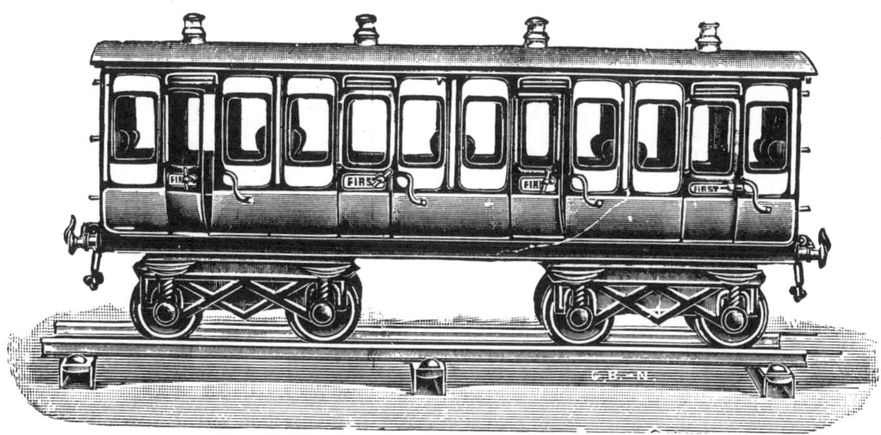

17793/1

Express Coaches, finely japanned, on 4 axles = 8 wheels, with 8 hinged doors to open, fitted with plastic seats (imitation cushions) and hat racks, spring buffers &c., top to open, 13 in. long . . . . each **10/—**

17792/1	**17793**/1	**17794**/1	
M. R.	L. &. N. W. R.	G. N. R.	colour

Gauge 1 = $1^7/_8$ in.

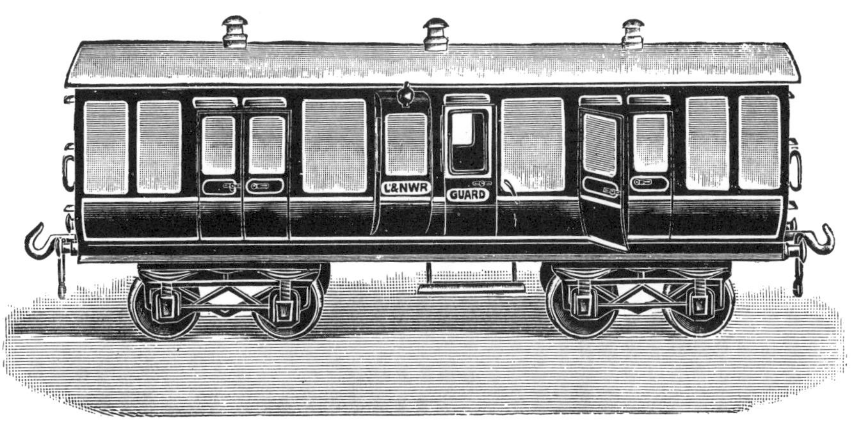

17893/1

Express Brake and **Guard's Van,** finely japanned, on 4 axles = 8 wheels, with 6 doors to open, 13 in. long each **10/—**

17892/1	**17893**/1	**17894**/1	
M. R.	L. &. N. W. R.	G. N. R.	colour.

Models of English Railway Carriages

highly finished and japanned in the colours of the different Railway Companies.

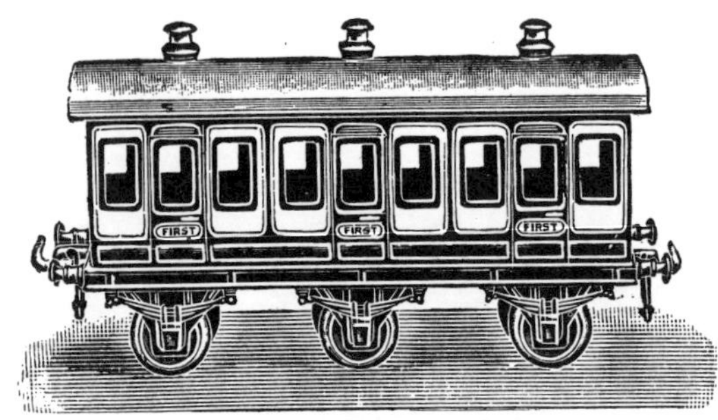

Express Passenger Car

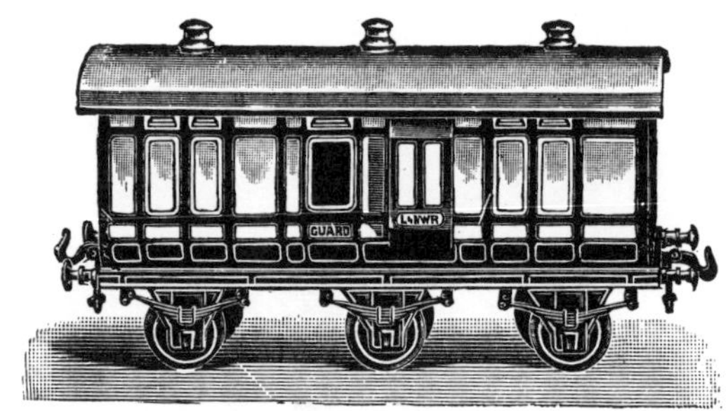

Express Luggage Vans

Gauge 3 = $2\frac{5}{8}$ in.

16792/3	**16793**/3	**16794**/3		**16892**/3	**16893**/3	**16894**/3	
M. R.	L. N. W. R.	G. N. R.	colour	M. R.	L. N. W. R.	G. N. R.	colour
each **6/—**	**6/—**	**6/—**		each **6/—**	**6/—**	**6/—**	

Gauge 4 = 3 in.

16792/4	**16793**/4	**16795**/4		**16892**/4	**16893**/4	**16895**/4	
M. R.	L. N. W. R.	L. S. W. R.	colour	M. R.	L. N. W. R.	L. S. W. R.	colour
each **7/—**	**7/—**	**7/—**		each **7/—**	**7/—**	**7/—**	

Extra Fine English Express Bogie Carriages

fitting trains and locomotives for steam and clockwork.

Gauge 4 = 3 in.

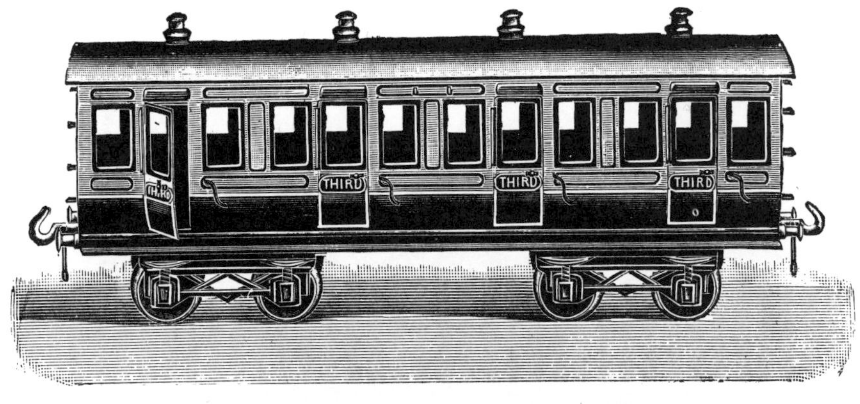

Express Coaches finely japanned on 4 axles = 8 wheels with hinged doors to open, fitted with plastic seats (imitation cushions) and hat racks, spring buffers etc. top to open.

19 in. long.

17792/4	**17793**/4	**17795**/4	colour
M.R.	L.N.W.R.	L.S.W.R.	

each **23/—**

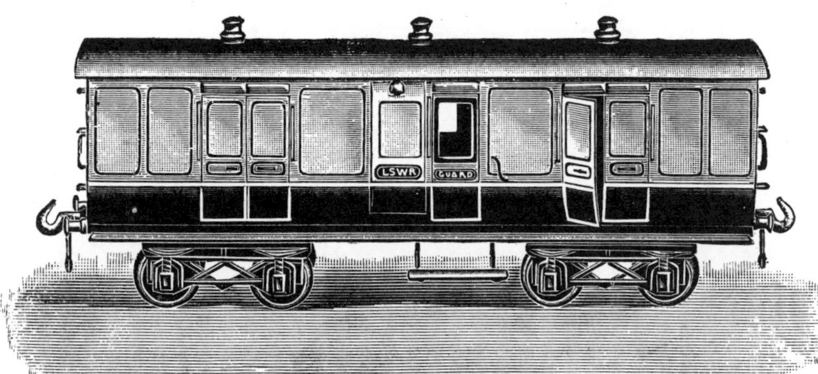

Express Brake and Guard's Vans, finely japanned, on 4 axles = 8 wheels, with 6 doors to open.

19 in. long.

17892/4	**17893**/4	**17895**/4	
M.R.	L N.W.R.	L.S.W.R.	colour

each **23/—**

Express Bogie Carriages

fine polychrome japanning, on 4 axles = 8 wheels.

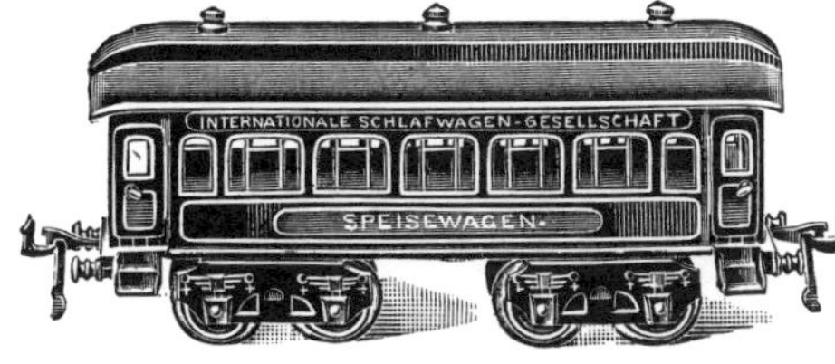

10241/0

Dining Car

10241/0 Gauge 0 = $1^{3}/_{8}$ in., $8^{7}/_{8}$ in. long. . . . . each **3/2**
„ /1 „ 1 = $1^{7}/_{8}$ „ $13^{3}/_{4}$ „ „ . . . . „ **6/—**

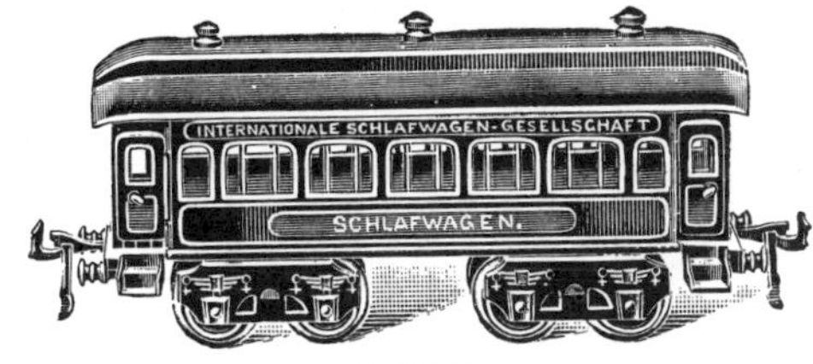

10242/0

Sleeping Car

10242/0 Gauge 0 = $1^{3}/_{8}$ in., $8^{7}/_{8}$ in. long. . . . . each **3/2**
„ /1 „ 1 = $1^{7}/_{8}$ „ $13^{3}/_{4}$ „ „ . . . . „ **6/—**

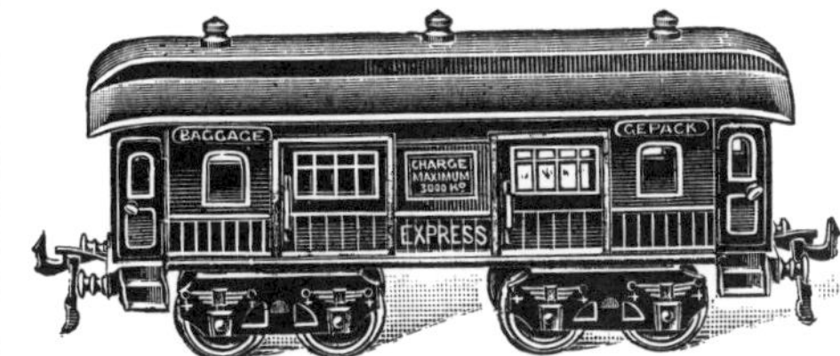

10243/0

Luggage Van

10243/0 Gauge 0 = $1^{3}/_{8}$ in., $8^{7}/_{8}$ in. long. . . . . each **3/2**
„ /1 „ 1 = $1^{7}/_{8}$ „ $13^{3}/_{4}$ „ „ . . . . „ **6/—**

13556/1

Express Dining Cars

with Corridors, doors to open, complete Furnishing and Figures

13556/0 Gauge 0 = $1^{3}/_{8}$ in., $8^{3}/_{4}$ in. long . . . each **4/8**
„ /1 „ 1 = $1^{7}/_{8}$ „ $13^{7}/_{8}$ „ „ . . . . „ **9/6**

13638/1

Express Sleeping Cars

with Corridors, doors to open, Figures and complete Furnishing as Passenger and Sleeping Cars (small beds &c.)

13638/0 Gauge 0 = $1^{3}/_{8}$ in., $8^{3}/_{4}$ in. long . . . each **4/8**
„ /1 „ 1 = $1^{7}/_{8}$ „ $13^{7}/_{8}$ „ „ . . . . „ **10/6**

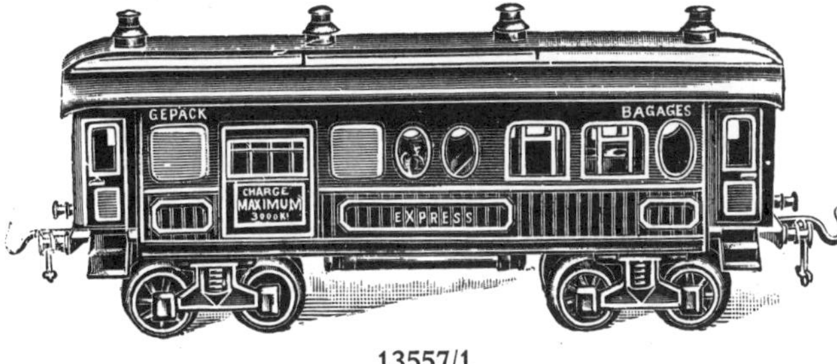

13557/1

Corridor Express Mail and Luggage Cars

doors do open, Figures (Post Officials) and complete Furnishing (sorting boards &c.)

13557/0 Gauge 0 = $1^{3}/_{8}$ in., $8^{3}/_{4}$ in. long . . . each **4/8**
„ /1 „ 1 = $1^{7}/_{8}$ „ $13^{7}/_{8}$ „ „ . . . . „ **9/6**

Extra long Express Bogie Carriages.

(Pullman Cars.)

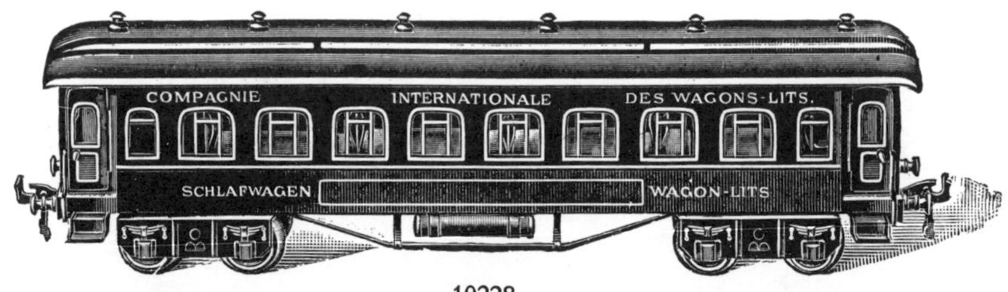

10228

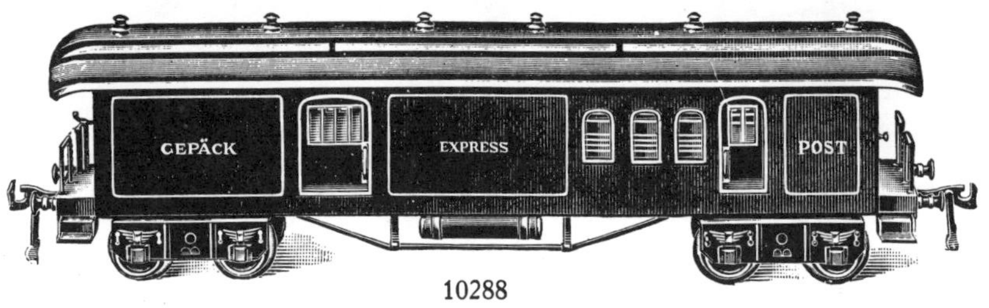

10288

finely hand japanned, with bogie wheels (4 axles = 8 wheels) and with inside fittings (Pullman Cars) for large rail formations.

10286/0	**Dining Car,**	gauge 0 = $1^3/_8$ in.,	$12^5/_8$ in. long	each	**12/4**
„ /1	„	„ „ 1 = $1^7/_8$ „	$19^3/_4$ „ „	„	**23/2**
10228/0	**Sleeping Car,**	„ 0 = $1^3/_8$ „	$12^5/_8$ „ „	„	**13/4**
„ /1	„	„ „ 1 = $1^7/_8$ „	$19^3/_4$ „ „	„	**24/6**
10288/0	**Luggage Van,**	„ 0 = $1^3/_8$ „	$12^5/_8$ „ „	„	**11/8**
„ /1	„	„ „ 1 = $1^7/_8$ „	$19^3/_4$ „ „	„	**21/8**

Elegant finish on 4 axles = 8 wheels, doors to open, imitation gas tank.

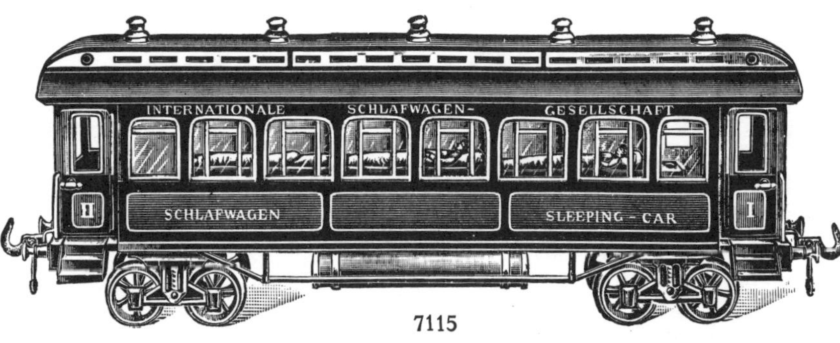

7115

With complete Furnishing inside and figures, finely hand japanned (Pullmann Cars).

Dining Car

7114/0	gauge 0 = $1^3/_8$ in.,	$8^7/_8$ in. long	each	**8/6**
„ /1	„ 1 = $1^7/_8$ „	$13^3/_4$ „ „	„	**16/—**
„ /4	„ 4 = 3 „	$21^3/_4$ „ „	„	**44/—**

Sleeping Car

7115/0	gauge 0 = $1^3/_8$ in.,	$8^7/_8$ in. long	each	**8/6**
„ /1	„ 1 = $1^7/_8$ „	$13^3/_4$ „ „	„	**16/—**
„ /4	„ 4 = 3 „	$21^3/_4$ „ „	„	**44/—**

Elegant finish on 4 axles = 8 wheels, doors to open, imitation gas tank.

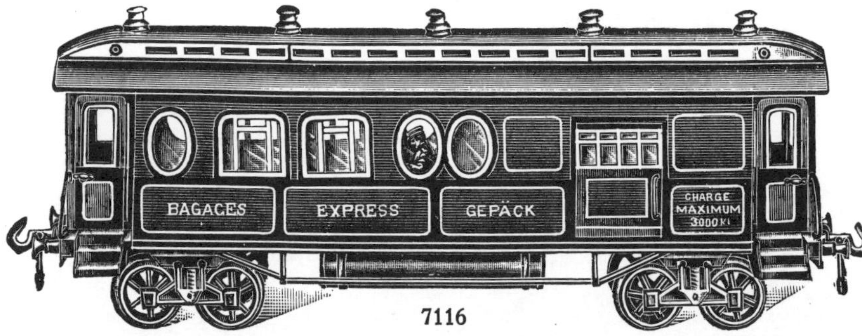

7116

With complete Furnishing inside and figures, finely hand japanned (Pullmann Cars).

7116/0	**Mail and Luggage Van,**	gauge 0 = $1^3/_8$ in.,	$8^7/_8$ in. long	each	**8/6**
„ /1	„ „ „ „	„ 1 = $1^7/_8$ „	14 „ „	„	**16/—**
„ /4	„ „ „ „	„ 4 = 3 „	$21^3/_4$ „ „	„	**44/—**

English Railway Goods Trucks

finely finished and japanned in the colours of the different Railway Companies.

M 1360/0

M 1361/0

M 1360/0	**Goods Trucks,** finely japanned, gauge	$0 = 1^3/_8$ in.,	M. R. Truck,	$4^3/_4$ in. long	doz. **9/—**
„ /1	„ „ „ „ „	$1 = 1^7/_8$ „	„ „ „	$6^5/_8$ „	„ **18/—**
M 1361/0	„ „ „ „ „	$0 = 1^3/_8$ „	G. N. R. Truck,	$4^3/_4$ „	„ **9/—**
„ /1	„ „ „ „ „	$1 = 1^7/_8$ „	„ „ „ „	$6^5/_8$ „	„ **18/—**

M 1384/0

M 1385/0

M 1384/0	**Goods Trucks,** finely japanned, gauge	$0 = 1^3/_8$ in.	L. & N. W. R. Truck,	$4^3/_4$ in. long	doz. **9/—**
„ /1	„ „ „ „ „	$1 = 1^7/_8$ „	„	$6^5/_8$ „ „	„ **18/—**
M 1385/0	„ „ „ „ „	$0 = 1^3/_8$ „	L. & S. W. R. „	$4^3/_4$ „ „	„ **9/—**
„ /1	„ „ „ „ „	$1 = 1^7/_8$ „	„ „	$6^5/_8$ „ „	„ **18/—**

M 3414/0

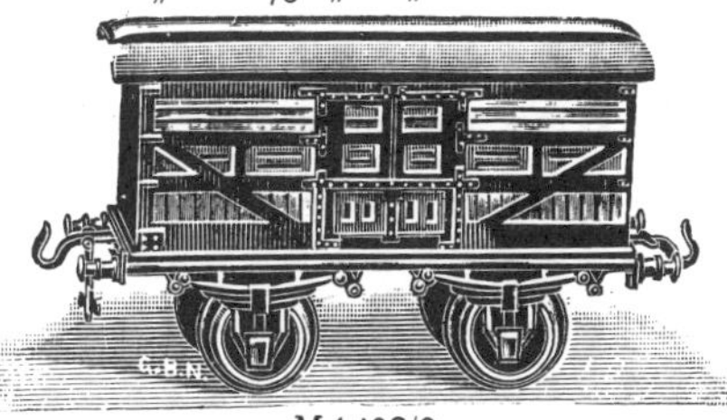
M 1408/0

M 3414/0	**Goods Trucks,** finely japanned, gauge	$0 = 1^3/_8$ in.,	L. N. W. R., Goods Van,	$4^3/_4$ in. long	doz. **9/—**
„ /1	„ „ „ „ „	$1 = 1^7/_8$ „	„ „ „	7 „ „	„ **18/—**
M 1408/0	„ „ „ „ „	$0 = 1^3/_8$ „	„ Cattle Truck,	$4^3/_4$ „ „	„ **9/—**
„ /1	„ „ „ „ „	$1 = 1^7/_8$ „	„ „	7 „ „	„ **19/—**
M 1407/1	„ „ „ „ „	$1 = 1^7/_8$ „	M. R. Cattle Truck,	7 „ „	„ **19/—**

M 1359

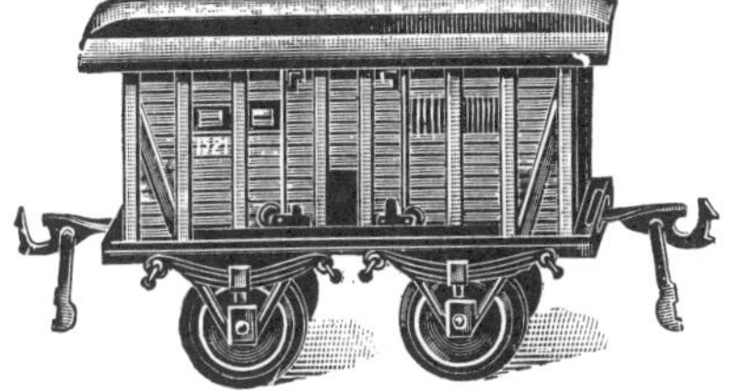
10159/0

M 1359/0	**Petroleum Waggons,** very realistic japanning,	Gauge	$0 = 1^3/_8$ in.,	$4^3/_4$ in. long	doz. **9/—**
„ /1	„ „ „ „ „	„	$1 = 1^7/_8$ „	$6^5/_8$ „ „	„ **19/—**
10159/0	**Goods Van,** finely japanned,	„	$0 = 1^3/_8$ „	$4^3/_4$ „ „	„ **9/—**
M 1365/1	„ „ „ „ with lettering: "Fish Van",	„	$1 = 1^7/_8$ „	7 „ „	„ **18/—**

Assorted Railway Goods Trucks

finely finished and japanned.

10114/1

7784/0

14467/1

10114/0 **Goods Truck** in fine polychrome japanning, Gauge 0 = $1^{3}/_{8}$ in., $3^{3}/_{8}$ in. long . . . . . doz. **8/6**
„ /1 „ „ „ „ „ „ „ 1 = $1^{7}/_{8}$ „ 6 „ „ . . . . . „ **15/6**

Long Wood Truck improved finish, finely japanned, with movable beam and chain
7784/0 Gauge 0 = $1^{3}/_{8}$ in., $3^{1}/_{4}$ in. long . . . . „ **8/6**
„ /1 „ 1 = $1^{7}/_{8}$ „ $5^{1}/_{4}$ „ „ . . . . „ **18/—**

14467/0 **Truck loaded with timber** in fine polychrome japanning, Gauge 0 = $1^{3}/_{8}$ in., $5^{1}/_{4}$ in. long . . . . . „ **9/10**
„ /1 „ „ „ „ „ „ „ „ „ 1 = $1^{7}/_{8}$ „ 8 „ „ . . . . . „ **20/—**

10365/1

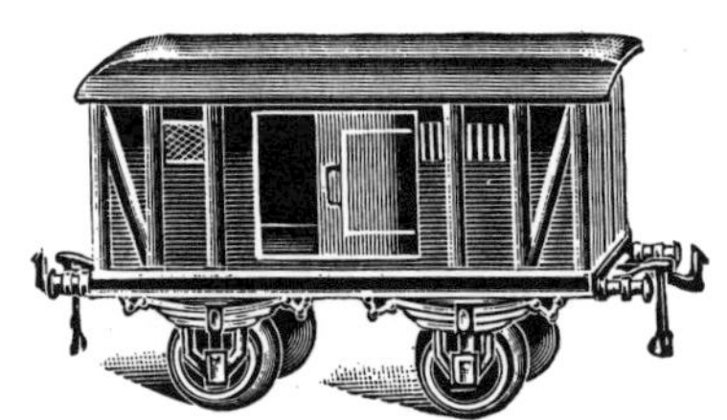

10328/0 and 1

10118/1

10365/0 **Crane Truck** in fine polychrome japanning, Gauge 0 = $1^{3}/_{8}$ in., $3^{5}/_{16}$ in. long. . . doz. **10/6**
„ /1 „ „ „ „ „ „ „ 1 = $1^{7}/_{8}$ „ $5^{3}/_{4}$ „ „ . . . „ **17/—**

10328/0 **Goods Truck** with doors to open, „ 0 = $1^{3}/_{8}$ „ $4^{3}/_{4}$ „ „ . . . „ **11/—**
„ /1 „ „ „ „ „ „ „ 1 = $1^{7}/_{8}$ „ $7^{7}/_{16}$ „ „ . . . „ **24/—**

10118/0 **Goods Truck** with brake house, in fine polychrome japanning, „ 0 = $1^{3}/_{8}$ „ $3^{3}/_{4}$ „ „ . . . „ **11/—**
„ /1 „ „ „ „ „ „ „ „ „ „ 1 = $1^{7}/_{8}$ „ 6 „ „ . . . „ **19/—**

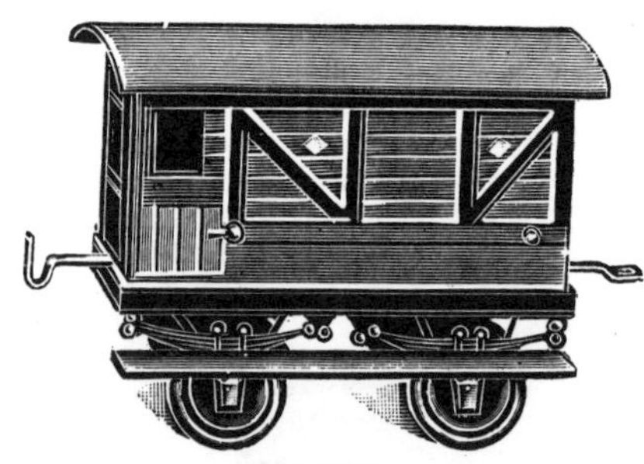

M 3420/0

10125/0

8356/0

M 3420/0 **Goods Brake Van** Gauge 0 = $1^{3}/_{8}$ in., $3^{3}/_{8}$ in. long . . . . . . doz. **9/10**
„ /1 „ „ „ „ 1 = $1^{7}/_{8}$ „ $4^{3}/_{4}$ „ „ . . . . „ **17/—**

10125/0 **Beer Car** with sliding doors, fine polychrome japanning, „ 0 = $1^{3}/_{8}$ „ $3^{1}/_{4}$ „ „ . . . . doz. **12/8**
„ /1 „ „ „ „ „ „ „ „ „ „ 1 = $1^{7}/_{8}$ „ $5^{1}/_{4}$ „ „ . . . . „ **25/4**

8356/0 **Tilting Car** finely japanned. new construction, „ 0 = $1^{3}/_{8}$ „ $3^{1}/_{4}$ „ „ . . . . „ **15/4**
„ /1 „ „ „ „ „ „ „ 1 = $1^{7}/_{8}$ „ $5^{1}/_{4}$ „ „ . . . . each **2/6**

Series of Loaded Trucks

complete with Tarpaulins.

Correct Models, most realistic, loaded with small sacks.

M 3409.0

Gauge 0 = $1^3/_8$ in.

M 3408/0 = M. R. colour
M 3409/0 = G. N. R. „
M 3410/0 = L. & N. W. R. „
M 3411/0 = L. & S. W. R. „

$4^3/_4$ in. long, finely japanned

doz. **18/—**

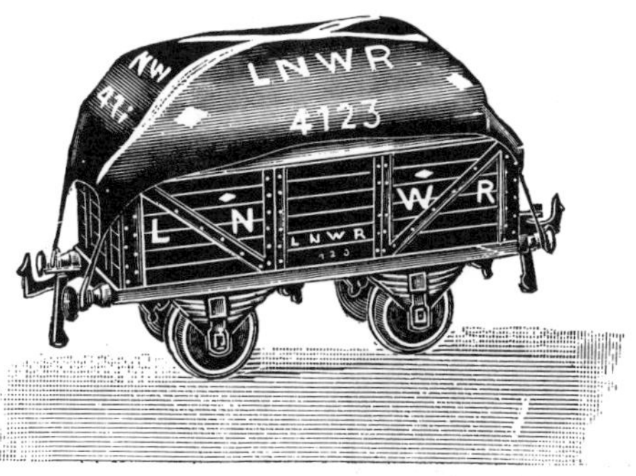

M 3410/1

Gauge 0 = $1^7/_8$ in.

M 3408/1 = M. R. colour
M 3409/1 = G. R. N. „
M 3410/1 = L. & N. W. R. „
M 3411/1 = L. & S. W. R. „

$6^5/_8$ in. long, finely japanned

doz. **31/6**

Complete with Tarpaulin and loaded with 6 small Sacks.

Assorted Railway Goods Trucks.

M 3418/0

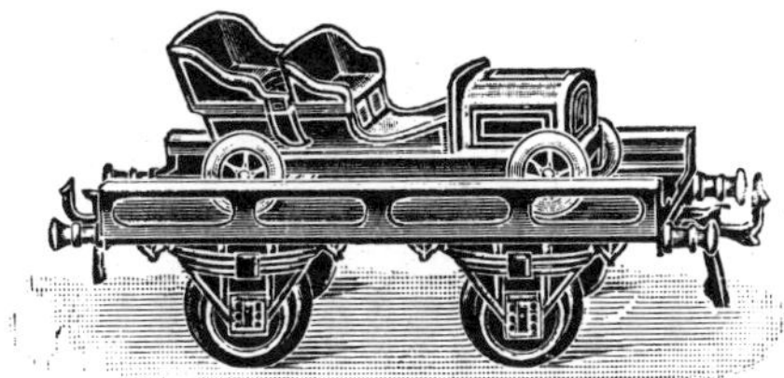

M 3418/1

10113/0

M 3418/0 **Motor Traffic Truck,** gauge 0 = $1^3/_8$ in., $4^1/_2$ in. long . . . . . doz. **17/—**
„ /1 „ „ „ „ 1 = $1^7/_8$ „ $8^1/_4$ „ „ . . . . . „ **36/—**

Goods Van, with brake house and sliding door, in fine polychrome japanning

10113/0 Gauge 0 = $1^3/_8$ in., 4 in. long . . . . . „ **15/6**
„ /1 „ 1 = $1^7/_8$ „ $5^1/_4$ in. long . . . . . „ **27/4**

Assorted Railway Goods Trucks

finely finished and japanned.

10121/1

9681/1

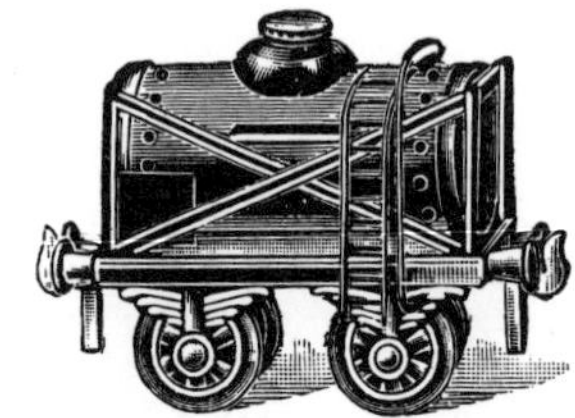

9176/0

Cattle Truck with Animals with 2 compartments, fine polychrome japanning

10121/0	Gauge 0 = $1^3/_8$ in., $3^1/_4$ in. long	doz.	**18/—**
„ /1	„ 1 = $1^7/_8$ „ $5^1/_4$ „ „	each	**2/10**
9681/0	**Covered Goods Truck,** finely japanned, with cloth covering, Gauge 0 = $1^3/_8$ in., $3^1/_4$ in. long	doz.	**16/6**
„ /1	„ „ „ „ „ „ „ „ „ 1 = $1^7/_8$ „ $5^1/_4$ „ „	each	**2/10**
9176/0	**Petroleum Waggon,** finely japanned, „ 0 = $1^3/_8$ „ $3^1/_4$ „ „	doz.	**19/—**
„ /1	„ „ „ „ „ 1 = $1^7/_8$ „ $5^1/_4$ „ „	each	**2/8**

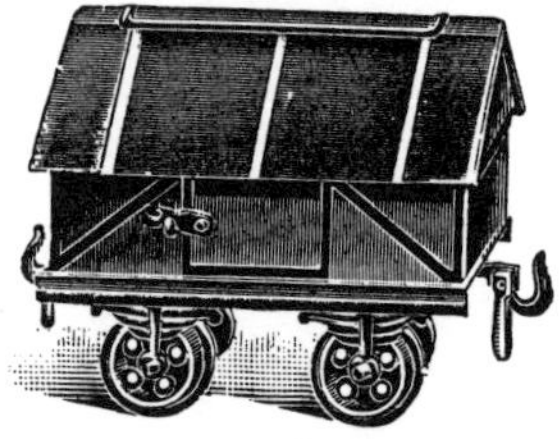

9686/0

9184/1

7084/1

Lime Waggon with 2 side doors and 2 flap doors, finely japanned

9686/0	Gauge 0 = $1^3/_8$ in., $3^1/_4$ in. long	doz.	**19/—**
„ /1	„ 1 = $1^7/_8$ „ $5^1/_4$ „ „	each	**2/8**
9184/0	**Gas Waggon,** finely japanned, Gauge 0 = $1^3/_8$ in., $3^1/_4$ in. long	doz.	**16/6**
„ /1	„ „ „ „ „ 1 = $1^7/_8$ „ $5^1/_4$ „ „	each	**2/4**
7084/0	**Timber Truck,** „ „ „ 0 = $1^3/_8$ „ $3^1/_4$ „ „	doz.	**16/6**
„ /1	„ „ „ „ „ 1 = $1^7/_8$ „ $5^1/_4$ „ „	each	**2/6**

14466/1

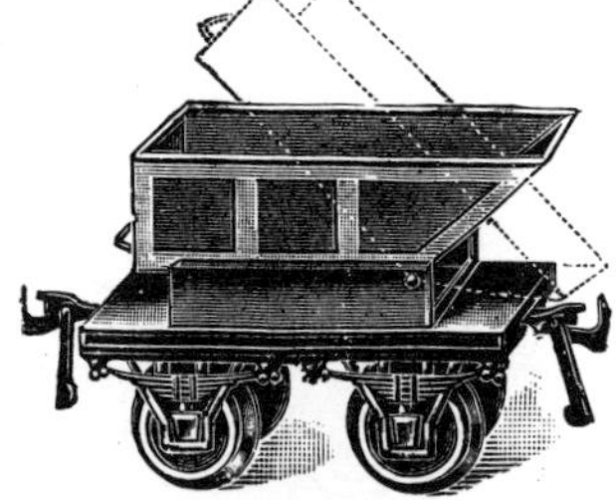

10256/0

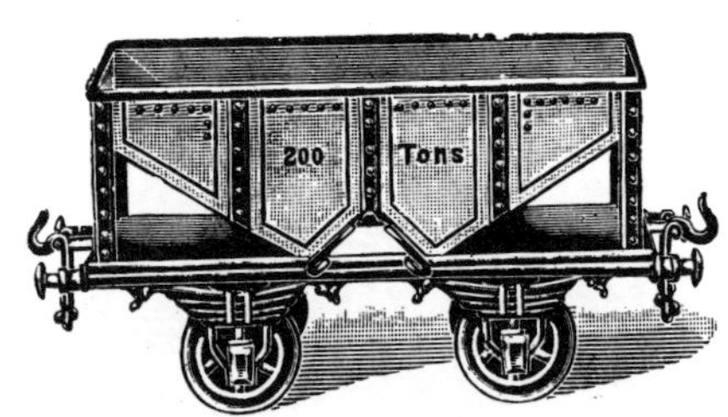

13668/1

14466/0	**Coal Truck** with imitation coal, finely hand-japanned, Gauge 0 = $1^3/_8$ in., $5^3/_4$ in. long	doz.	**19/—**
„ /1	„ „ „ „ „ „ „ „ 1 = $1^7/_8$ „ $8^1/_4$ „ „	„	**30/—**
10256/0	**New Tilting Car,** revolving, finely japanned by hand, „ 0 = $1^3/_8$ „ $3^3/_8$ „ „	„	**20/6**
„ /1	„ „ „ „ „ „ „ „ „ 1 = $1^7/_8$ „ $4^3/_4$ „ „	„	**29/6**

Coal Truck with 2 doors in bottom of car to empty the truck, finely hand-japanned

13668/0	Gauge 0 = $1^3/_8$ in., $4^1/_2$ in. long	doz.	**25/—**
„ /1	„ 1 = $1^7/_8$ „ $7^3/_4$ „ „	„	**40/—**

Assorted Railway Goods Trucks

finely finished and japanned.

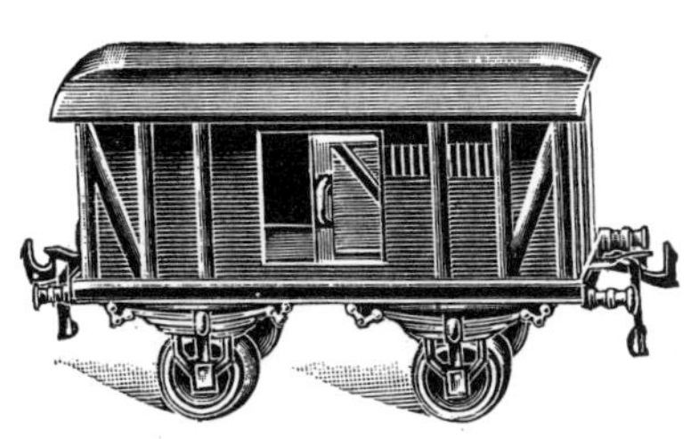

7019/1

9193

6307/1

Horse Transport Van, finely japanned, with sliding doors and fittings, with 2 pewter horses

7019/0 Gauge 0 = $1^{3}/_{8}$ in., $4^{1}/_{2}$ in. long . . . . each **2/8**
„ /1 „ 1 = $1^{7}/_{8}$ „ 6 „ „ . . . . „ **4/8**

Furniture Transport Car, finely japanned, with japanned furniture car with inscription

9193/0 Gauge 0 = $1^{3}/_{8}$ in., $3^{1}/_{4}$ in. long . . . . each **2/10**
„ /1 „ 1 = $1^{7}/_{8}$ „ $5^{1}/_{4}$ „ „ . . . . „ **4/4**

Tank Waggon with guard's seat, figure and outlet tap, finely hand-japanned

6307/0 Gauge 0 = $1^{3}/_{8}$ in., $4^{3}/_{4}$ in. long . . . . each **2/8**
„ /1 „ 1 = $1^{7}/_{8}$ „ $6^{1}/_{4}$ „ „ . . . . „ **4/2**

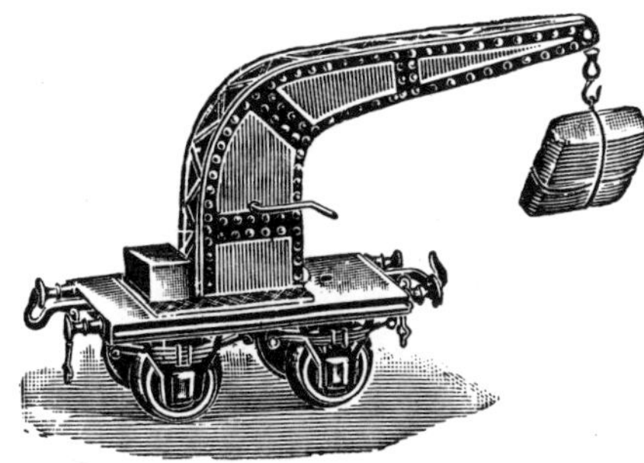

13806/1

10297/1

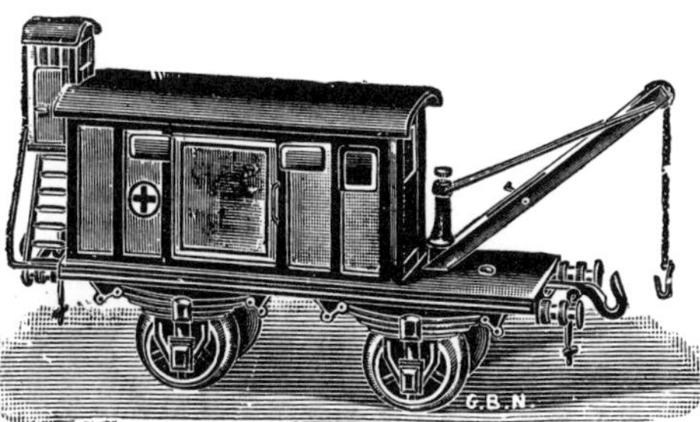

14473/1

Crane Truck, finely japanned, with mechanical windlass, turnable, with movable counter-weight to balance the load

13806/0 Gauge 0 = $1^{3}/_{8}$ in., $5^{7}/_{8}$ in. long . . . . each **2/10**
„ /1 „ 1 = $1^{7}/_{8}$ „ $8^{7}/_{8}$ „ „ . . . . „ **4/2**

10297/0 **Acid Waggon** with 4 Acid Bottles, finely japanned, Gauge 0 = $1^{3}/_{8}$ in., 6 in. long . . . . each **3/—**
„ /1 „ „ „ 4 „ „ „ „ „ 1 = $1^{7}/_{8}$ „ $8^{1}/_{8}$ in. long . . . . „ **4/10**

Ambulance- or Tool Car with Crane with guard's seat, adjustable crane, sliding doors, fine hand-japanning

14473/0 Gauge 0 = $1^{3}/_{8}$ in., $6^{1}/_{2}$ in. long . . . . doz. **37/—**
„ /1 „ 1 = $1^{7}/_{8}$ „ $8^{3}/_{4}$ „ „ . . . . each **4/8**

14465/1

10319/1

10285/0

Snow-Plough Car with snow plough moved by the axles of the wheels, with sliding doors, finely hand-japanned

14465/0 Gauge 0 = $1^{3}/_{8}$ in., $6^{1}/_{2}$ in. long . . . . doz. **44/—**
„ /1 „ 1 = $1^{7}/_{8}$ „ $9^{1}/_{2}$ „ „ . . . . each **6/6**

10319/0 **Beer Waggon** with 2 barrels, finely japanned, Gauge 0 = $1^{3}/_{8}$ in., 6 in. long . . . . each **3/10**
„ /1 „ „ „ 2 „ „ „ „ 1 = $1^{7}/_{8}$ „ $8^{1}/_{8}$ in. long . . . . „ **5/10**

New Crane Truck with mechanical crane, corrugated tin house, turning on swivel, finely japanned by hand

10285/0 Gauge 0 = $1^{3}/_{8}$ in., $4^{3}/_{4}$ in. long, $7^{1}/_{8}$ in. high . . . . each **4/10**
„ /1 „ 1 = $1^{7}/_{8}$ „ $5^{3}/_{4}$ „ „ 9 „ „ . . . . „ **6/—**

Assorted Railway Goods Trucks

on 4 axles

finely finished and japanned.

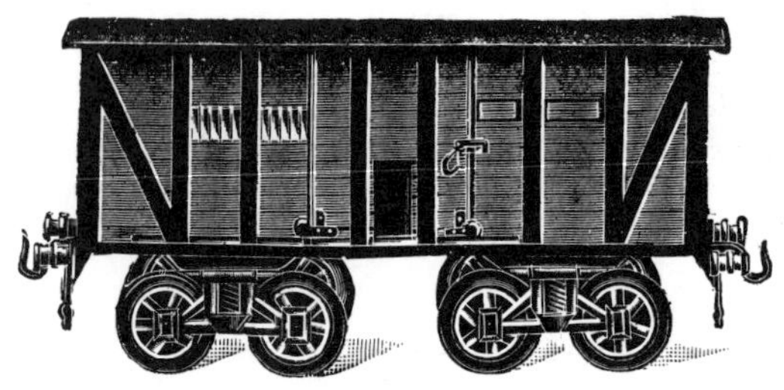

14200/1

14120/1

Goods Truck for Fast Traffic fine polychrome japanning, on 4 axles = 8 wheels on bogie carriages

14200/0 Gauge 0 = $1^{3}/_{8}$ in., $6^{3}/_{4}$ in. long . . . . doz. **19/—**

„ /1 „ 1 = $1^{7}/_{8}$ „ $10^{1}/_{4}$ „ „ . . . . „ **38/—**

Timber Truck finely hand-japanned on 4 axles = 8 wheels on bogie carriages, loaded with wooden boards

14120/0 Gauge 0 = $1^{3}/_{8}$ in., $6^{1}/_{2}$ in. long . . . . doz. **24/—**

„ /1 „ 1 = $1^{7}/_{8}$ „ $9^{3}/_{4}$ „ „ . . . . each **3/4**

14472/2

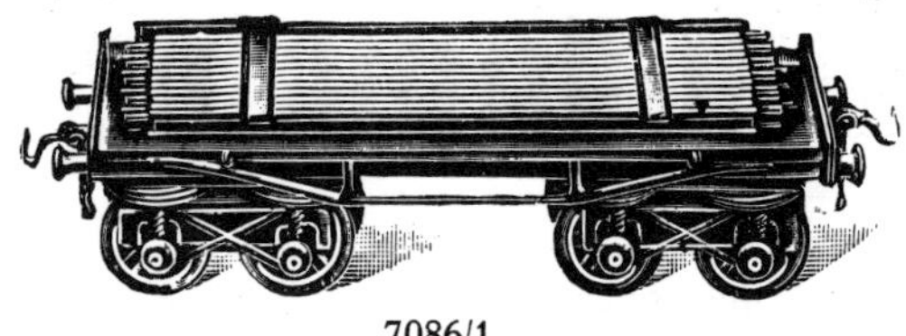

7086/1

14472/0 **Truck, loaded with Fibre** on bogie wheels, finely hand-japanned, Gauge 0 = $1^{3}/_{8}$ in., 7 in. long . . doz. **25/4**

„ /1 „ „ „ „ „ „ „ „ „ „ 1 = $1^{7}/_{8}$ „ 10 „ „ . . „ **42/—**

Rail Truck finely japanned on 4 axles = 8 wheels on bogie carriages, with single lines for self-mounting

7086/0 Gauge 0 = $1^{3}/_{8}$ in., 7 in. long . . . . each **2/8**

„ /1 „ 1 = $1^{7}/_{8}$ „ 10 „ „ . . . . „ **4/10**

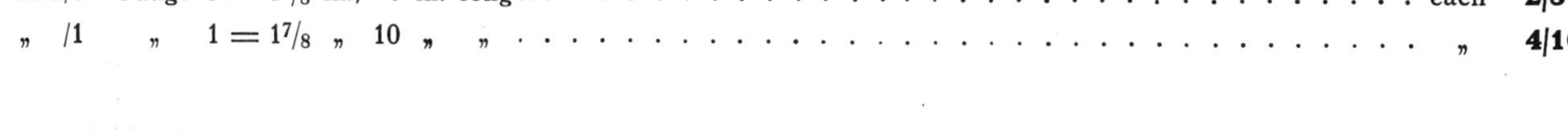

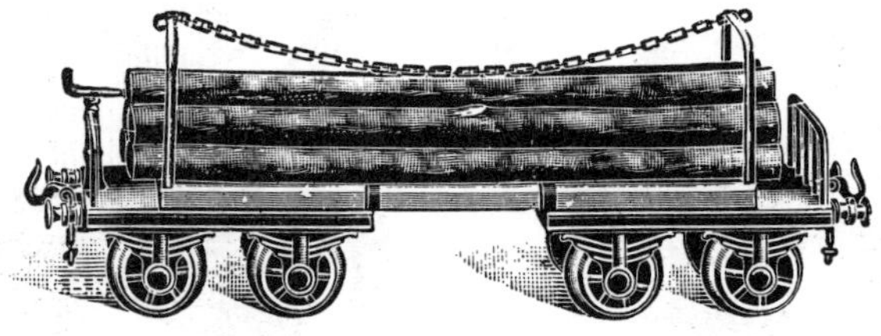

14470/1

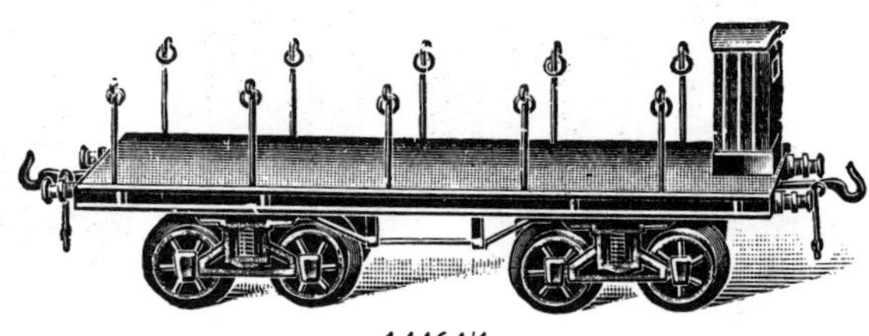

14464/1

14470/0 **Extension Truck,** loaded with Timber, finely hand-japanned, Gauge 0 = $1^{3}/_{8}$ in., 9 in. long . . doz. **37/—**

„ /1 „ „ „ „ „ „ „ „ 1 = $1^{7}/_{8}$ „ 12 „ „ . . each **4/10**

14464/0 **Platform Waggon** with small brake house, finely hand-japanned, „ 0 = $1^{3}/_{8}$ „ 9 „ „ . . „ **3/2**

„ /1 „ „ „ „ „ „ „ „ „ 1 = $1^{7}/_{8}$ „ 12 „ „ . . „ **5/—**

Assorted Railway Goods Trucks

on 4 axles

finely finished and japanned.

13811/1

14469/1

Coal Truck, finely stamped and japanned on 4 axles = 8 wheels on bogie carriages, with doors to open

13811/0	Gauge 0 = $1^3/_8$ in., $9^1/_2$ in. long	each	**3/6**
„ /1	„ 1 = $1^7/_8$ „ $11^3/_4$ „ „	„	**5/—**

Fish Van, finely japanned by hand, on 4 axles = 8 wheels on bogie carriages, with sliding doors

14469/0	Gauge 0 = $1^3/_8$ in., 9 in. long	„	**4/10**
„ /1	„ 1 = $1^7/_8$ „ 12 „ „	„	**6/10**

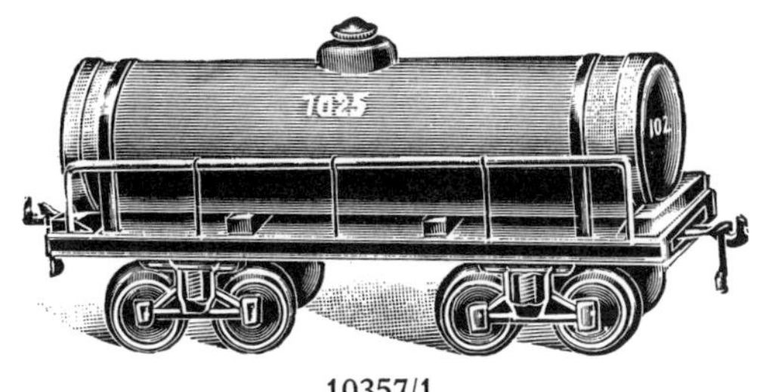

10357/1

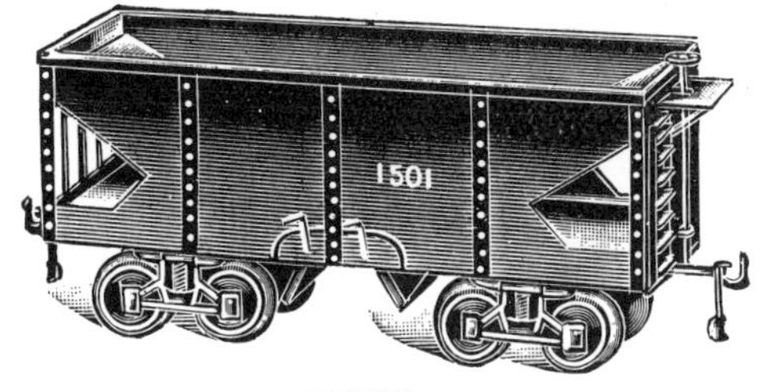

10358/1

Petrol Tank Waggon, finely japanned with filling screw at the top

10357/0	Gauge 0 = $1^3/_8$ in., $7^1/_8$ in. long	doz.	**52/—**
„ /1	„ 1 = $1^7/_8$ „ $10^1/_2$ „ „	each	**7/—**

Coal Truck with 2 openings at the bottom for dropping the load

10358/0	Gauge 0 = $1^3/_8$ in., $7^1/_8$ in. long	doz.	**57/—**
„ /1	„ 1 = $1^7/_8$ „ $10^1/_2$ „ „	each	**7/6**

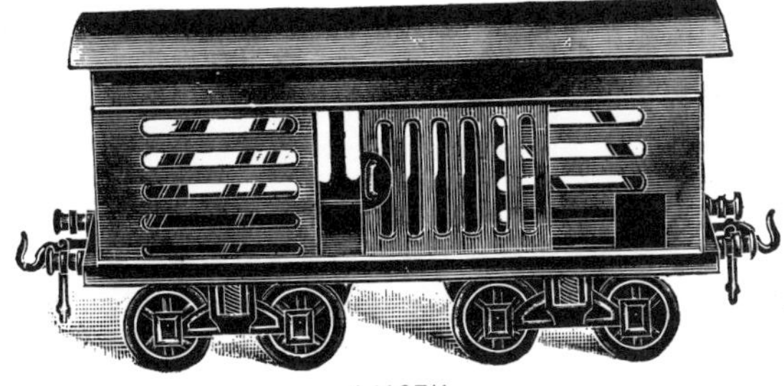

14137/1

Cattle Truck, finely hand-japanned on 4 axles = 8 wheels on bogie carriages, with sliding doors

14137/0	Gauge 0 = $1^3/_8$ in., 7 in. long	each	**6/—**
„ /1	„ 1 = $1^7/_8$ „ $9^3/_4$ „ „	„	**9/—**

English Railway Carriages, Trucks, Mail Cars &c.

constructed from original models, highly finished and japanned in the colours of the different Railway Companies.

Accessory for Shunting Trains.

Gauge 0 = $1^{3}/_{8}$ in.

The slip-off carriage.

37693/0

Set, consisting of: 1 Passenger Car, 1 Luggage Van and 1 special rail for detaching the cars, length of car 5 in. By means of the special rail it is possible to detach the carriages from each other without touching them, whilst the train is passing. This set can be attached to any 0 Gauge railway track.

37692/0 M. R. Shunting set . . . . each **2/—**
37693/0 L. & N. W. R. Shunting set . . . . „ **2/—**

Royal English Mail.

Receives and delivers Post Bags automatically can be attached to any part of the rail system, made on the principle of the system employed by the Railway Companies.

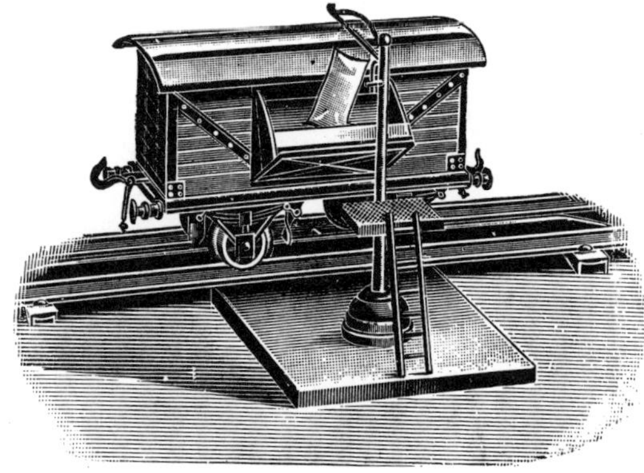

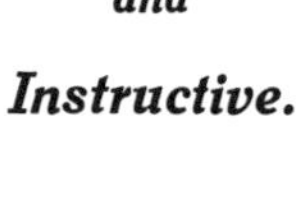

M 1367

Receiving Net

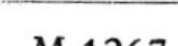

M 1367

Delivery Platform

Gauge 1 = $1^{7}/_{8}$ in.

M 1367/1

M. R. colour

Automatic Mail Bag Set, consisting of: Royal Mail Van, $6^{7}/_{8}$ in. long, Delivery Platform with rail attached $14^{1}/_{2}$ in. long, Receiving Net with rail attached $14^{1}/_{2}$ in. long, with Post Bags, complete in strong card-board box . . . . each **16/—**

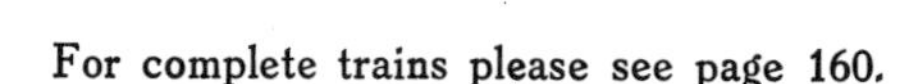

For complete trains please see page 160.

Rails.

These rails are manufactured by a patented process and are remarkable for their extraordinary durability.

They are made in the following gauges

Gauge	$0 = 1\frac{3}{8}$ in.	$1 = 1\frac{7}{8}$ in.	$2 = 2\frac{1}{8}$ in.	$3 = 2\frac{5}{8}$ in.	$4 = 3$ in. width
length of rail	10	14	$14\frac{1}{4}$	$14\frac{1}{2}$	$14\frac{1}{2}$
diameter of circle	$19\frac{1}{2}$	36	$55\frac{3}{4}$	$55\frac{3}{4}$	73 in.
	6	8	12	12	16 pieces to cirle

For rails with alternating pegs and Reform Rails with extra large Radius see page 196.

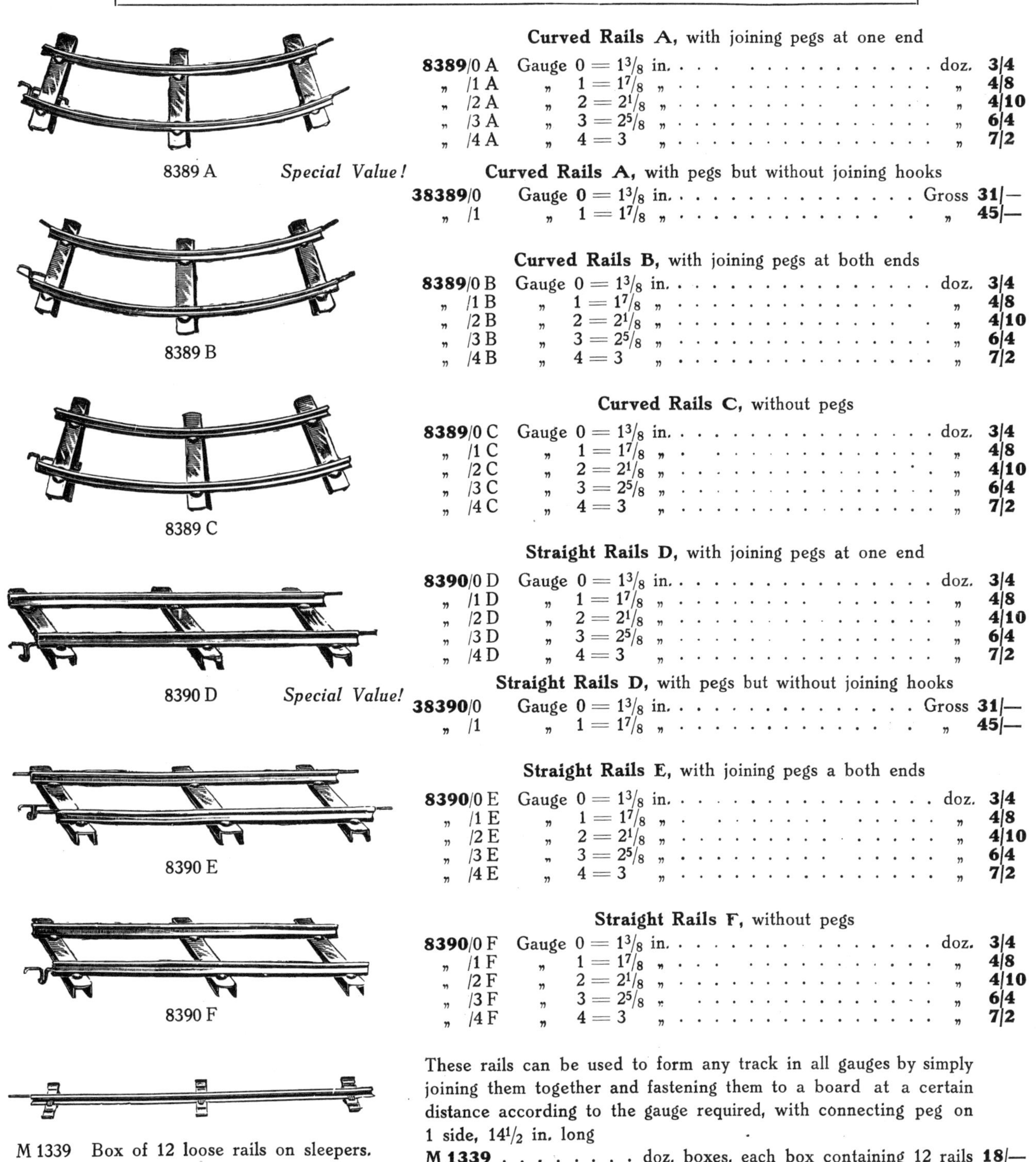

8389 A *Special Value!*

8389 B

8389 C

8390 D *Special Value!*

8390 E

8390 F

M 1339 Box of 12 loose rails on sleepers.

Curved Rails A, with joining pegs at one end

8389/0 A	Gauge $0 = 1\frac{3}{8}$ in.	doz.	**3/4**
„ /1 A	„ $1 = 1\frac{7}{8}$ „	„	**4/8**
„ /2 A	„ $2 = 2\frac{1}{8}$ „	„	**4/10**
„ /3 A	„ $3 = 2\frac{5}{8}$ „	„	**6/4**
„ /4 A	„ $4 = 3$ „	„	**7/2**

Curved Rails A, with pegs but without joining hooks

38389/0	Gauge $0 = 1\frac{3}{8}$ in.	Gross	**31/—**
„ /1	„ $1 = 1\frac{7}{8}$ „	„	**45/—**

Curved Rails B, with joining pegs at both ends

8389/0 B	Gauge $0 = 1\frac{3}{8}$ in.	doz.	**3/4**
„ /1 B	„ $1 = 1\frac{7}{8}$ „	„	**4/8**
„ /2 B	„ $2 = 2\frac{1}{8}$ „	„	**4/10**
„ /3 B	„ $3 = 2\frac{5}{8}$ „	„	**6/4**
„ /4 B	„ $4 = 3$ „	„	**7/2**

Curved Rails C, without pegs

8389/0 C	Gauge $0 = 1\frac{3}{8}$ in.	doz.	**3/4**
„ /1 C	„ $1 = 1\frac{7}{8}$ „	„	**4/8**
„ /2 C	„ $2 = 2\frac{1}{8}$ „	„	**4/10**
„ /3 C	„ $3 = 2\frac{5}{8}$ „	„	**6/4**
„ /4 C	„ $4 = 3$ „	„	**7/2**

Straight Rails D, with joining pegs at one end

8390/0 D	Gauge $0 = 1\frac{3}{8}$ in.	doz.	**3/4**
„ /1 D	„ $1 = 1\frac{7}{8}$ „	„	**4/8**
„ /2 D	„ $2 = 2\frac{1}{8}$ „	„	**4/10**
„ /3 D	„ $3 = 2\frac{5}{8}$ „	„	**6/4**
„ /4 D	„ $4 = 3$ „	„	**7/2**

Straight Rails D, with pegs but without joining hooks

38390/0	Gauge $0 = 1\frac{3}{8}$ in.	Gross	**31/—**
„ /1	„ $1 = 1\frac{7}{8}$ „	„	**45/—**

Straight Rails E, with joining pegs a both ends

8390/0 E	Gauge $0 = 1\frac{3}{8}$ in.	doz.	**3/4**
„ /1 E	„ $1 = 1\frac{7}{8}$ „	„	**4/8**
„ /2 E	„ $2 = 2\frac{1}{8}$ „	„	**4/10**
„ /3 E	„ $3 = 2\frac{5}{8}$ „	„	**6/4**
„ /4 E	„ $4 = 3$ „	„	**7/2**

Straight Rails F, without pegs

8390/0 F	Gauge $0 = 1\frac{3}{8}$ in.	doz.	**3/4**
„ /1 F	„ $1 = 1\frac{7}{8}$ „	„	**4/8**
„ /2 F	„ $2 = 2\frac{1}{8}$ „	„	**4/10**
„ /3 F	„ $3 = 2\frac{5}{8}$ „	„	**6/4**
„ /4 F	„ $4 = 3$ „	„	**7/2**

These rails can be used to form any track in all gauges by simply joining them together and fastening them to a board at a certain distance according to the gauge required, with connecting peg on 1 side, $14\frac{1}{2}$ in. long

M 1339 . . . . doz. boxes, each box containing 12 rails **18/—**

Half and Quarter Rails.

The **half and quarter Rails** help to simplify the forming of complicated rail formations. If a figure cannot be completed by using a whole rail, the short ones will be found a good help.

The half rails and quarter rails are made in the following gauges:

Gauge	0	1	2	3	4	
Width	1 3/8	1 7/8	2 1/8	2 5/8	3	inches
Length of half rails	5	7	7 1/4	7 1/4	7 1/4	"
Length of quarter rails	2 1/2	3 1/4	3 1/2	3 1/2	3 1/2	"

and differ according to how the joining pegs are arranged.

When ordering it is therefore necessary to state which **gauge** and whether **form** A, B, C, D, E or F is required.

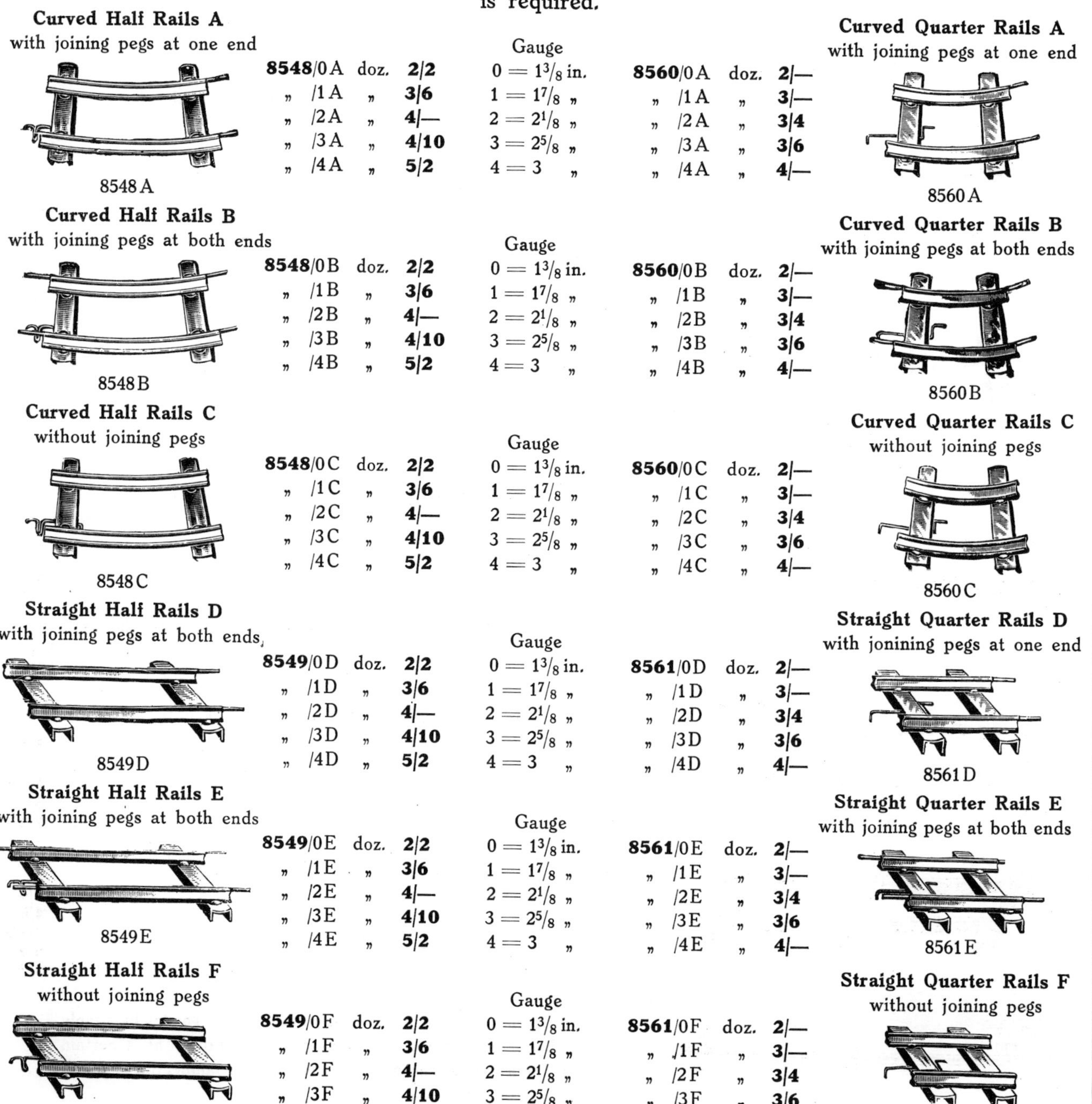

Curved Half Rails A with joining pegs at one end — 8548 A
Curved Quarter Rails A with joining pegs at one end — 8560 A

			Gauge			
8548/0A	doz.	**2/2**	0 = 1 3/8 in.	**8560**/0A	doz.	**2/—**
" /1A	"	**3/6**	1 = 1 7/8 "	" /1A	"	**3/—**
" /2A	"	**4/—**	2 = 2 1/8 "	" /2A	"	**3/4**
" /3A	"	**4/10**	3 = 2 5/8 "	" /3A	"	**3/6**
" /4A	"	**5/2**	4 = 3 "	" /4A	"	**4/—**

Curved Half Rails B with joining pegs at both ends — 8548 B
Curved Quarter Rails B with joining pegs at both ends — 8560 B

			Gauge			
8548/0B	doz.	**2/2**	0 = 1 3/8 in.	**8560**/0B	doz.	**2/—**
" /1B	"	**3/6**	1 = 1 7/8 "	" /1B	"	**3/—**
" /2B	"	**4/—**	2 = 2 1/8 "	" /2B	"	**3/4**
" /3B	"	**4/10**	3 = 2 5/8 "	" /3B	"	**3/6**
" /4B	"	**5/2**	4 = 3 "	" /4B	"	**4/—**

Curved Half Rails C without joining pegs — 8548 C
Curved Quarter Rails C without joining pegs — 8560 C

			Gauge			
8548/0C	doz.	**2/2**	0 = 1 3/8 in.	**8560**/0C	doz.	**2/—**
" /1C	"	**3/6**	1 = 1 7/8 "	" /1C	"	**3/—**
" /2C	"	**4/—**	2 = 2 1/8 "	" /2C	"	**3/4**
" /3C	"	**4/10**	3 = 2 5/8 "	" /3C	"	**3/6**
" /4C	"	**5/2**	4 = 3 "	" /4C	"	**4/—**

Straight Half Rails D with joining pegs at both ends — 8549 D
Straight Quarter Rails D with jonining pegs at one end — 8561 D

			Gauge			
8549/0D	doz.	**2/2**	0 = 1 3/8 in.	**8561**/0D	doz.	**2/—**
" /1D	"	**3/6**	1 = 1 7/8 "	" /1D	"	**3/—**
" /2D	"	**4/—**	2 = 2 1/8 "	" /2D	"	**3/4**
" /3D	"	**4/10**	3 = 2 5/8 "	" /3D	"	**3/6**
" /4D	"	**5/2**	4 = 3 "	" /4D	"	**4/—**

Straight Half Rails E with joining pegs at both ends — 8549 E
Straight Quarter Rails E with joining pegs at both ends — 8561 E

			Gauge			
8549/0E	doz.	**2/2**	0 = 1 3/8 in.	**8561**/0E	doz.	**2/—**
" /1E	"	**3/6**	1 = 1 7/8 "	" /1E	"	**3/—**
" /2E	"	**4/—**	2 = 2 1/8 "	" /2E	"	**3/4**
" /3E	"	**4/10**	3 = 2 5/8 "	" /3E	"	**3/6**
" /4E	"	**5/2**	4 = 3 "	" /4E	"	**4/—**

Straight Half Rails F without joining pegs — 8549 F
Straight Quarter Rails F without joining pegs — 8561 F

			Gauge			
8549/0F	doz.	**2/2**	0 = 1 3/8 in.	**8561**/0F	doz.	**2/—**
" /1F	"	**3/6**	1 = 1 7/8 "	" /1F	"	**3/—**
" /2F	"	**4/—**	2 = 2 1/8 "	" /2F	"	**3/4**
" /3F	"	**4/10**	3 = 2 5/8 "	" /3F	"	**3/6**
" /4F	"	**5/2**	4 = 3 "	" /4F	"	**4/—**

Rails.

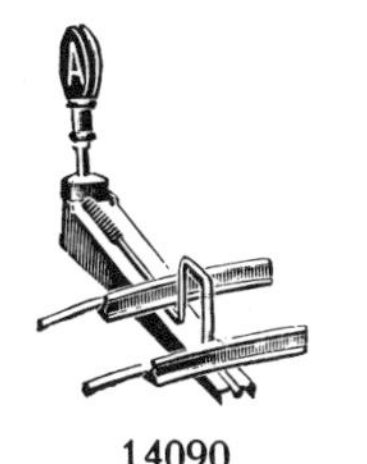

14090

Brake Rails

plain finish, cheap, with arrangement to work the brake of the locomotive, can be inserted without disturbing the rail formation

14090/0 Gauge 0 = $1^3/_8$ in. . . . . . doz. **5/8**
„ /1 „ 1 = $1^7/_8$ „ . . . . . „ **6/4**

7300 DA

Straight Brake Rails

plain, with arrangement to work the brake of the locomotive

7300/0 DA Gauge 0 = $1^3/_8$ in. . . . . . doz. **6/10**
„ /1 DA „ 1 = $1^7/_8$ „ . . . . . „ **8/4**

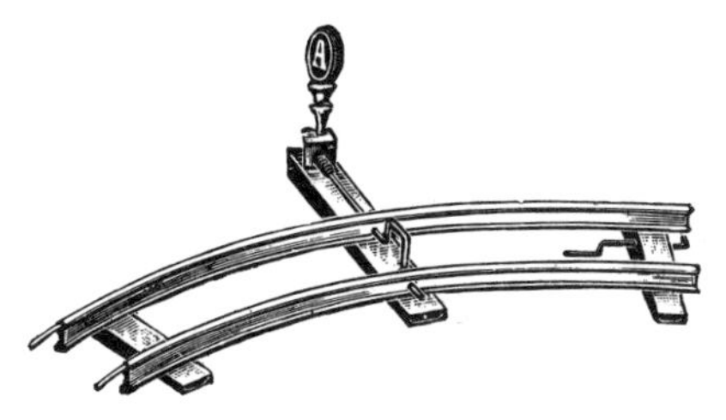

6945 AA

Curved Brake Rails

plain, with arrangement to work the brake of the locomotive

6945/0 AA Gauge 0 = $1^3/_8$ in. . . . . . doz. **6/10**
„ /1 AA „ 1 = $1^7/_8$ „ . . . . . „ **8/4**

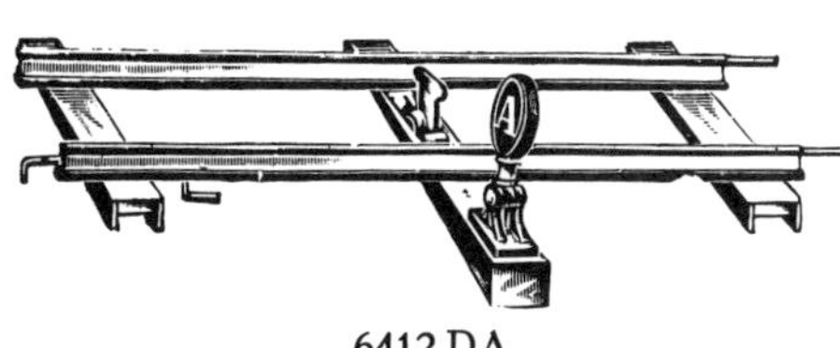

6412 DA

Straight Brake Rails

with arrangement to work the brake of the locomotive

6412/0 DA Gauge 0 = $1^3/_8$ in. . . . . . doz. **14/8**
„ /1 DA „ 1 = $1^7/_8$ „ . . . . . „ **18/6**
„ /2 DA „ 2 = $2^1/_8$ „ . . . . . „ **20/—**

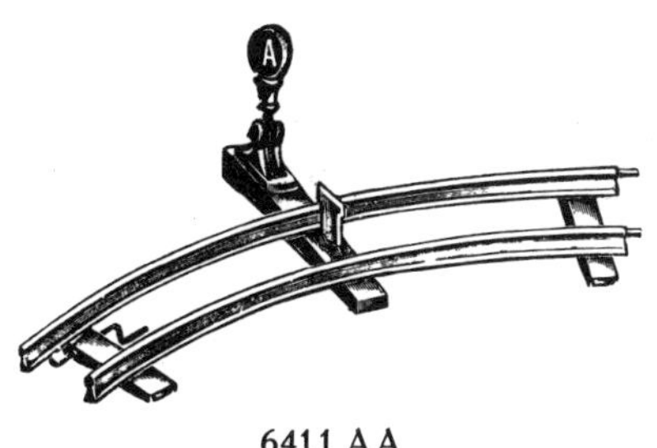

6411 AA

Curved Brake Rails

with arrangement to work the brake of the locomotive

6411/0 AA Gauge 0 = $1^3/_8$ in. . . . . . doz. **14/8**
„ /1 AA „ 1 = $1^7/_8$ „ . . . . . „ **18/6**
„ /2 AA „ 2 = $2^1/_8$ „ . . . . . „ **20/—**

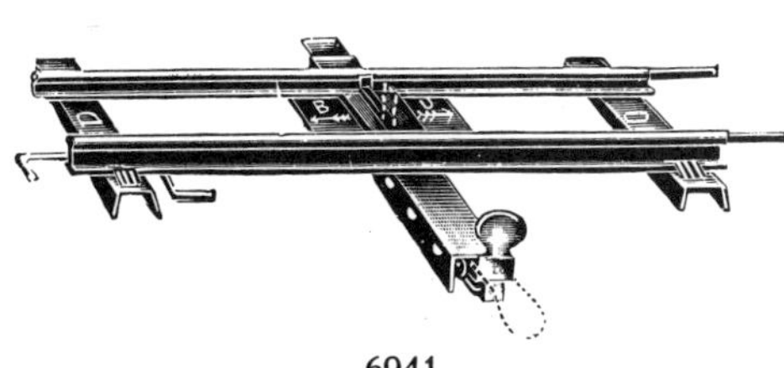

6941

Straight Automatic Brake Rails

with arrangement to work the brake of the locomotive as well as the automatic reversing gear

6941/0 Gauge 0 = $1^3/_8$ in. . . . . . doz. **11/6**
„ /1 „ 1 = $1^7/_8$ „ . . . . . „ **15/8**

in simpler finish:

6946/0 Gauge 0 = $1^3/_8$ in. . . . . . doz. **8/6**
„ /1 „ 1 = $1^7/_8$ „ . . . . . „ **13/—**

Crossings and Points.

13614 and 8391

13236

13614/0	**Acute Angled Crossings,**	Gauge 0 =	$1^3/_8$ in.	doz.	**14/2**
„ /1	„ „ „	„ 1 =	$1^7/_8$ „	„	**19/6**
8391/2	„ „ „	„ 2 =	$2^1/_8$ „	each	**2/8**
„ /3	„ „ „	„ 3 =	$2^5/_8$ „	„	**3/10**
„ /4	„ „ „	„ 4 =	3 „	„	**3/10**
13236/0	**Right Angled Crossings**	„ 0 =	$1^3/_8$ „	doz.	**16/4**
„ /1	„ „ „	„ 1 =	$1^7/_8$ „	„	**20/—**
„ /2	„ „ „	„ 2 =	$2^1/_8$ „	„	**24/8**
„ /3	„ „ „	„ 3 =	$2^5/_8$ „	each	**3/6**
„ /4	„ „ „	„ 4 =	3 „	„	**3/6**

13642

13643

13642/0	**Left Hand Point,** plain finish,	Gauge 0 =	$1^3/_8$ in.	doz.	**16/6**
„ /1	„ „ „ „ „	„ 1 =	$1^7/_8$ „	„	**25/4**
13643/0	**Right Hand Point,** plain finish	„ 0 =	$1^3/_8$ „	„	**16/6**
„ /1	„ „ „ „ „	„ 1 =	$1^7/_8$ „	„	**25/4**

8392

Best Quality!

8393

8392/0	**Left Hand Point,** extra strong finish, with turning lanterns,	Gauge 0 =	$1^3/_8$ in.	doz.	**32/6**
„ /1	„ „ „ „ „ „ „ „ „	„ 1 =	$1^7/_8$ „	„	**42/—**
„ /2	„ „ „ „ „ „ „ „ „	„ 2 =	$2^1/_8$ „	„	**44/—**
„ /3	„ „ „ „ „ „ „ „ „	„ 3 =	$2^5/_8$ „	each	**4/8**
„ /4	„ „ „ „ „ „ „ „ „	„ 4 =	3 „	„	**4/8**
8393/0	**Right Hand Point,** exta strong finish, with turning lanterns	„ 0 =	$1^3/_8$ „	doz.	**32/6**
„ /1	„ „ „ „ „ „ „ „ „	„ 1 =	$1^7/_8$ „	„	**42/—**
„ /2	„ „ „ „ „ „ „ „ „	„ 2 =	$2^1/_8$ „	„	**44/—**
„ /3	„ „ „ „ „ „ „ „ „	„ 3 =	$2^5/_8$ „	„	**4/8**
„ /4	„ „ „ „ „ „ „ „ „	„ 4 =	3 „	„	**4/8**

Points.

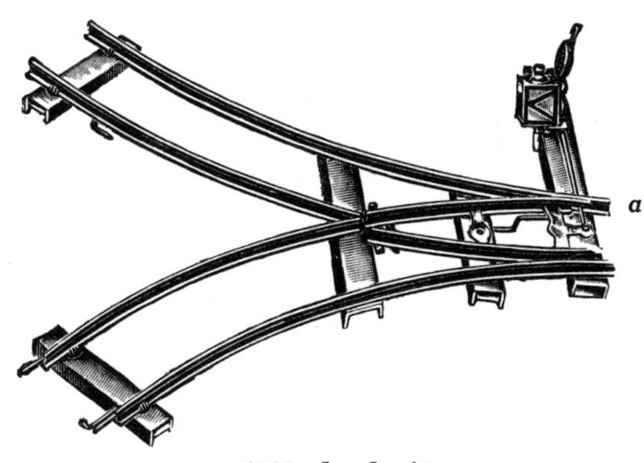

6732 Ia. Quality

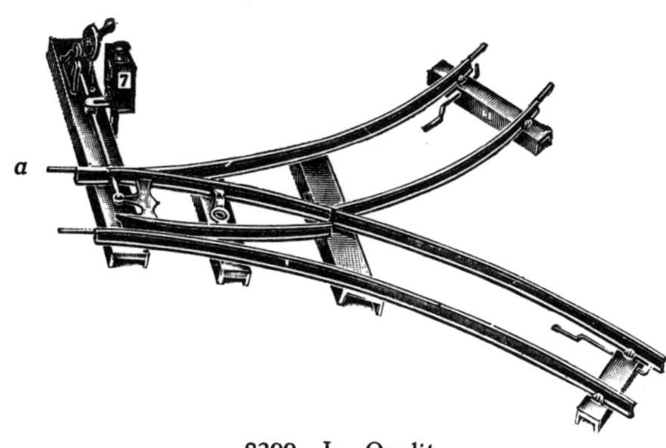

8399 Ia. Quality

Best Quality!

Symmetric Double Points, with 2 curved rails and turning lantern

6732/0	without joining pegs at the end *a*,	Gauge $0 = 1^{3}/_{8}$ in.	doz.	**32/6**
„ /1	„ „ „ „ „ „ *a*	„ $1 = 1^{7}/_{8}$ „	„	**42/—**
„ /2	„ „ „ „ „ „ *a*	„ $2 = 2^{1}/_{8}$ „	each	**3/8**
„ /3	„ „ „ „ „ „ *a*	„ $3 = 2^{5}/_{8}$ „	„	**4/8**
„ /4	„ „ „ „ „ „ *a*	„ $4 = 3$ „	„	**4/8**
8399/0	with joining pegs at the end *a*	Gauge $0 = 1^{3}/_{8}$ in.	doz.	**32/6**
„ /1	„ „ „ „ „ „ *a*	„ $1 = 1^{7}/_{8}$ „	„	**42/—**
„ /2	„ „ „ „ „ „ *a*	„ $2 = 2^{1}/_{8}$ „	each	**3/8**
„ /3	„ „ „ „ „ „ *a*	„ $3 = 2^{5}/_{8}$ „	„	**4/8**
„ /4	„ „ „ „ „ „ *a*	„ $4 = 3$ „	„	**4/8**

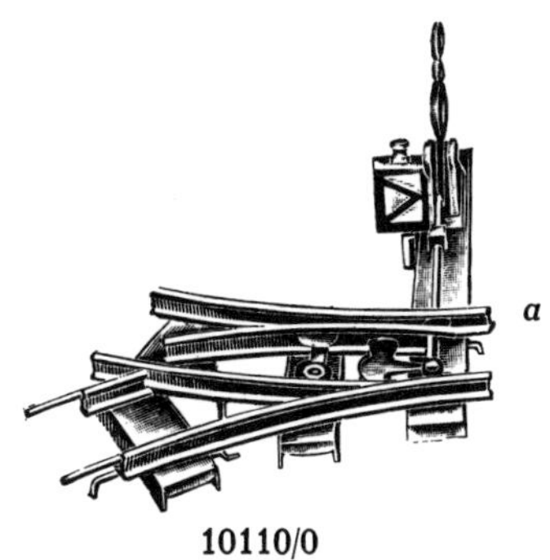

10110/0

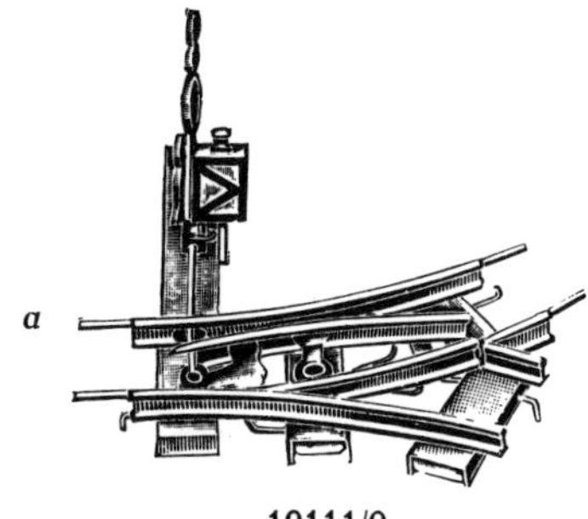

10111/0

Short Symmetric Double Switch, with 2 curved rails and turning lantern

10110/0	with joining pegs at the end *a*	Gauge $0 = 1^{3}/_{8}$ in.	doz.	**25/—**
„ /1	„ „ „ „ „ „ *a*	„ $1 = 1^{7}/_{8}$ „	„	**37/—**
10111/0	without joining pegs at the end *a*,	Gauge $0 = 1^{3}/_{8}$ „	doz.	**25/—**
„ /1	„ „ „ „ „ „ *a*	„ $1 = 1^{7}/_{8}$ „	„	**37/—**

Switches.

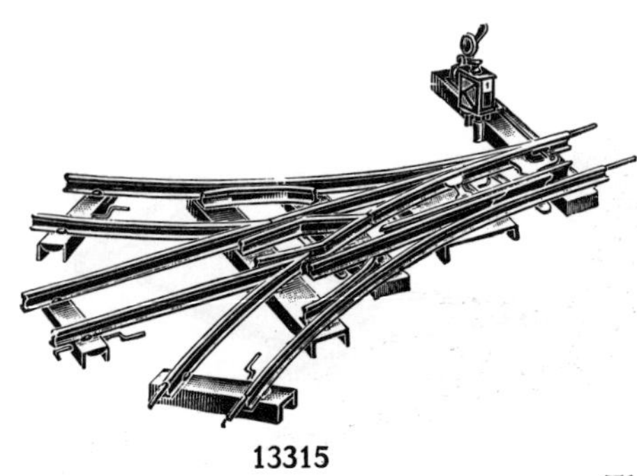

13315

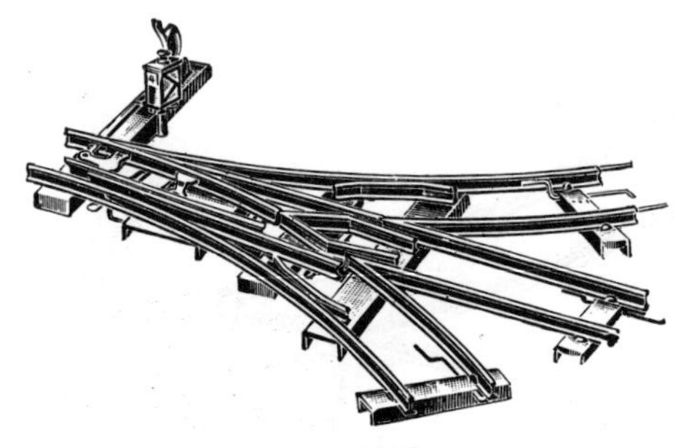

13235

Three Way Points

with 2 curved and 1 straight rail, with turnable lantern

with joining pegs at the end *a*				without joining pegs at the end *a*			
13315/0	Gauge 0 = $1^3/_8$ in.	each	**5/2**	**13235**/0	Gauge 0 = $1^3/_8$ in.	each	**5/2**
„ /1	„ 1 = $1^7/_8$ „	„	**6/2**	„ /1	„ 1 = $1^7/_8$ „	„	**6/2**
„ /2	„ 2 = $2^1/_8$ „	„	**7/2**	„ /2	„ 2 = $2^1/_8$ „	„	**7/2**

By combining three way points 13315 and 13235 a three way Crossing can be formed.

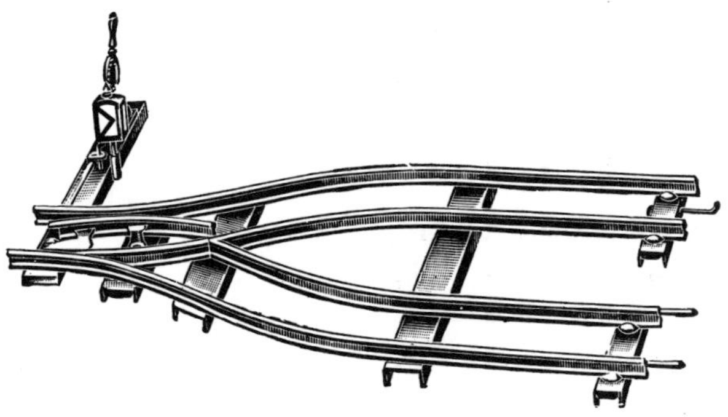

14006

Parallel Symmetric Points

with turning lantern

14006/0 Gauge 0 = $1^3/_8$ in. . . . . each **3/10**

„ /1 „ 1 = $1^7/_8$ „ . . . . „ **5/4**

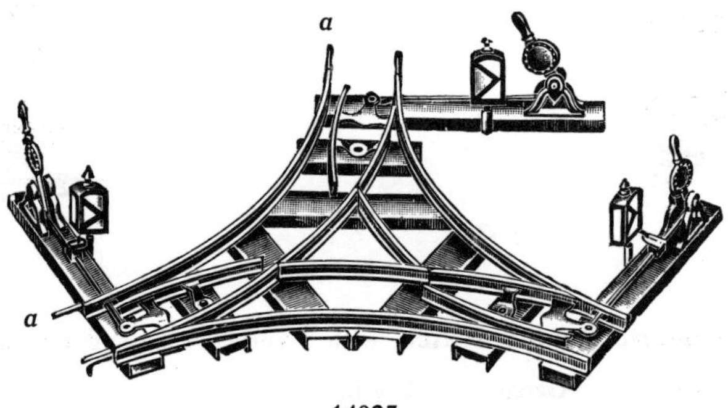

14035

Star Switches

with 3 levers and 3 turning lanterns (joining pegs at the ends *a*)

14035/0 Gauge 0 = $1^3/_8$ in. . . . . each **7/—**

„ /1 „ 1 = $1^7/_8$ „ . . . . „ **10/6**

Paralell Points and Turn Tables.

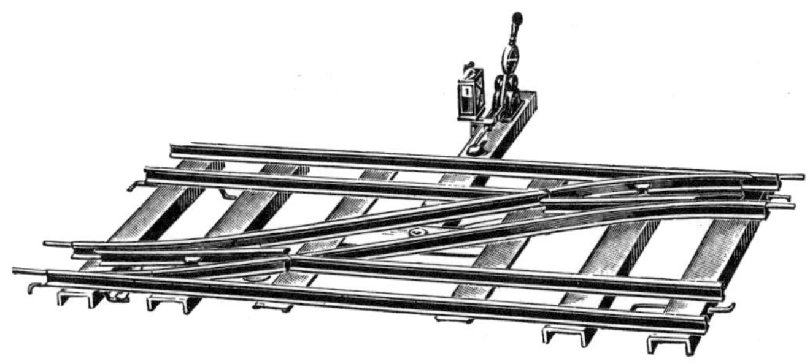

9221 left

Parallel Point, left

with 1 lever and 1 turning lantern, joining pegs at one side

9221/0	Gauge 0 = $1^{3}/_{8}$ in.	each	**5/4**
„ /1	„ 1 = $1^{7}/_{8}$ „	„	**6/6**
„ /2	„ 2 = $2^{1}/_{8}$ „	„	**7/10**

wifh 2 levers and 2 lanterns

9221/3	Gauge 3 = $2^{5}/_{8}$ in.	each	**11/8**
„ /4	„ 4 = 3 „	„	**13/8**

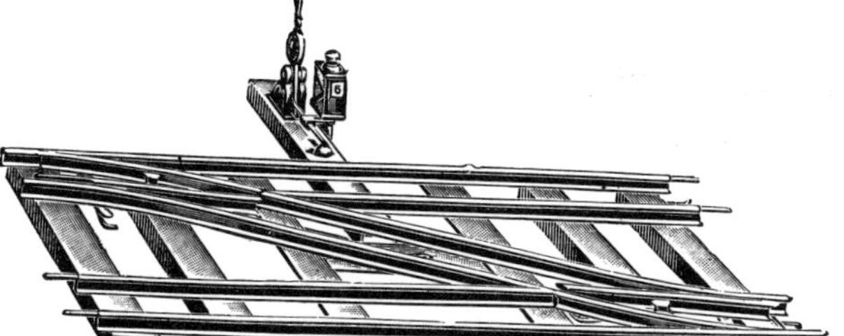

14367 right

Parallel Points, right

with 1 lever and 1 turning lantern, with joining pegs at one side

14367/0	Gauge 0 = $1^{3}/_{8}$ in.	each	**5/4**
„ /1	„ 1 = $1^{7}/_{8}$ „	„	**6/6**
„ /2	„ 2 = $2^{1}/_{8}$ „	„	**7/10**

with 2 levers and 2 lanterns

14367/3	Gauge 3 = $2^{5}/_{8}$ in.	„	**11/8**
„ /4	„ 4 = 3 „	„	**13/8**

9625

Parallel Crossing Points.

By using these crossing points original rail formations on comparatively little space can be obtained. Designs for all formations given with each piece.

With 1 central lever

9625/0	Gauge 0 = $1^{3}/_{8}$ in.	each	**11/2**
„ /1	„ 1 = $1^{7}/_{8}$ „	„	**15/—**

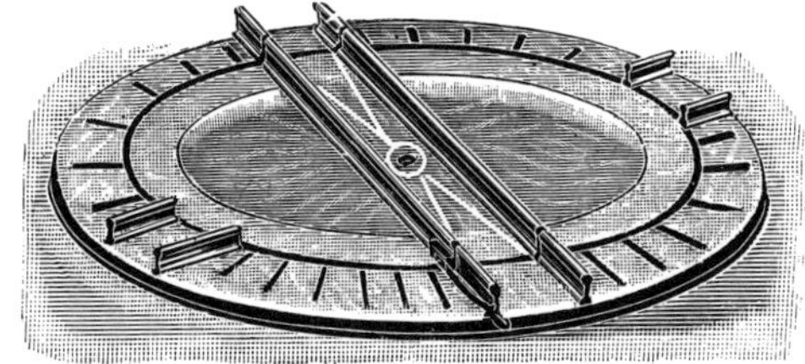

14089

Turn Table

plain finish, in fine polychrome japanning

14089/0	Gauge 0 = $1^{3}/_{8}$ in.	doz.	**17/6**
„ /1	„ 1 = $1^{7}/_{8}$ „	„	**27/4**

Best Quality.

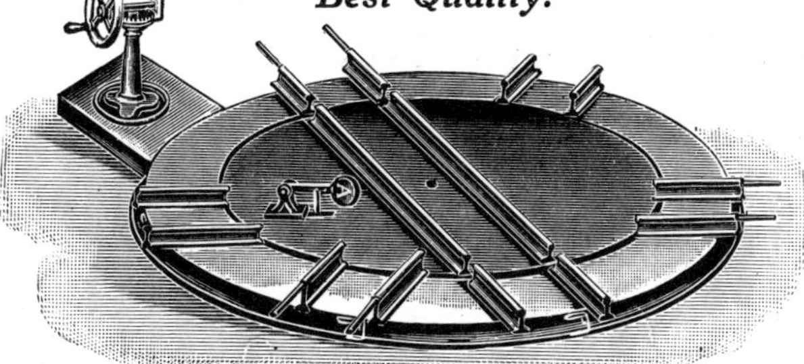

7617

Turn Table

with mechanism for turning, with rail attachments

7617/0	Gauge 0 = $1^{3}/_{8}$ in.	each	**5/—**
„ /1	„ 1 = $1^{7}/_{8}$ „	„	**10/4**

New Large Radius Rails.

Points and Crossings for the large Radius.

The enlarged Radius is of particular value for Clockwork and Steam Locomotives and Trains, as smoothest possible running is warranted by the reduced friction against these rails. The alternating pegs have the advantage that one kind only each of straight or curved rails is required for constructing any rail formation without guide.

Large Radii Rails with Alternating Pegs.

8397/0	Gauge 0 = $1^3/_8$ in., curved, 12 pieces to circle, 4 ft. outside diam., with joining hook	doz.	**3/8**
8398/0	„ 0 = $1^3/_8$ „ straight, 12 „ „ „ 4 „ „ „ „ „ „	„	**3/8**
8397/1	„ 1 = $1^7/_8$ „ curved, 16 „ „ „ 6 „ „ „ „ „ „	„	**4/8**
8398/1	„ 1 = $1^7/_8$ „ straight, 16 „ „ „ 6 „ „ „ „ „ „	„	**4/8**
36389/0	„ 0 = $1^3/_8$ „ curved, 12 „ „ „ 4 „ „ „ without „ „	gross	**38/6**
36389/1	„ 1 = $1^7/_8$ „ „ 16 „ „ „ 6 „ „ „ „ „ „	„	**46/—**

Points for the large Radius with Alternating Pegs.

10456/0	Gauge 0 = $1^3/_8$ in., left hand Point	each	**3/6**
10457/0	„ 0 = $1^3/_8$ „ right „ „	„	**3/6**
10456/1	„ 1 = $1^7/_8$ „ left „ „	„	**4/2**
10457/1	„ 1 = $1^7/_8$ „ right „ „	„	**4/2**

Crossings for the large Radius with Alternating Pegs.

10458/0	Gauge 0 = $1^3/_8$ in., with acute angle	doz.	**21/—**
„ /1	„ 1 = $1^7/_8$ „ „ „ „	„	**28/—**

Ordinary Sharp Curved Rails with Alternating Pegs.

By means of these new rails with alternating pegs any rail formation may be put together without any guide being required.

9609/0	Gauge 0 = $1^3/_8$ in., length of rail $10^1/_4$ in., **Curved Rail,** diam. of cirle 20 in.	doz.	**2/10**
„ /1	„ 1 = $1^7/_8$ „ „ „ „ $13^3/_4$ „ „ „ „ „ „ 36 „	„	**4/—**
9610/0	„ 0 = $1^3/_8$ „ „ „ „ $10^1/_4$ „ **Straight Rail**	„	**2/10**
„ /1	„ 1 = $1^7/_8$ „ „ „ „ $13^3/_4$ „ „ „	„	**4/—**

Engine Sheds.

10231

Engine Shed for 2 Locomotives, fine japanning, plastically stamped.

10231/0	Gauge 0 = $1^{3}/_{8}$ in.,	$8^{1}/_{4}$ in. high,	9 in. deep,	$9^{1}/_{2}$ in. wide	. . . .	each	**4/10**
„ /1	„ 1 = $1^{7}/_{8}$ „	$10^{1}/_{4}$ „ „	17 „ „	$12^{1}/_{4}$ „ „	. . . .	„	**9/10**

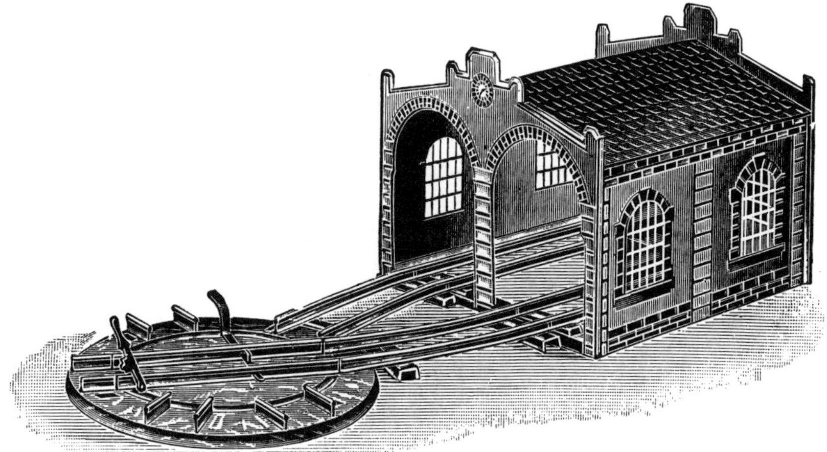

10232

Engine Shed for 2 Locomotives, with Turntable detachable with brake arrangement and switch, fine japanning, plastically stamped.

10232/0	Gauge 0 = $1^{3}/_{8}$ in.,	Shed $8^{1}/_{4}$ in. high,	9 in. deep,	$9^{1}/_{2}$ in. wide	. . . .	each	**6/10**
„ /1	„ 1 = $1^{7}/_{8}$ „	„ $10^{1}/_{4}$ „ „	17 „ „	$12^{1}/_{4}$ „ „	. . . .	„	**12/10**

6166

Engine Shed for 1 Locomotive, imitation brickwork, finely japanned, with swing door, corrugated roof, single line with brake arrangement.

6166/0	Gauge 0 = $1^{3}/_{8}$ in.,	Shed $6^{3}/_{8}$ in. high,	$6^{3}/_{4}$ in. wide,	10 in. deep	. . . .	each	**4/10**
„ /1	„ 1 = $1^{7}/_{8}$ „	„ 8 „ „	$7^{3}/_{4}$ „ „	$15^{3}/_{4}$ „ „	. . . .	„	**8/—**

Engine Sheds.

Engine Shed for 2 Locomotives, imitation brickwork, finely japanned with swingdoors, corrugated roof, symmetrical switch with brake arrangement before each door.

6167/0 Gauge 0 = $1^3/_8$ in. Shed, $7^1/_8$ in. high, $8^1/_4$ in. wide, $9^1/_2$ in. deep . . . . each **10/6**
„ /1 „ 1 = $1^7/_8$ „ „ 9 „ „ 11 „ „ $15^3/_4$ „ „ . . . . „ **18/6**

Engine Shed for 3 Locomotives, with detachable Turntable, plastically stamped and finely japanned, imitation brickwork, with plastic windows.

10294/0 Gauge 0 = $1^3/_8$ in., 8 in. high, 20 in. wide, $7^1/_2$ in. deep . . . . complete including turntable each **15/4**

Engine Shed for 3 Locomotives, with detachable Turntable, plastically stamped and finely japanned, imitation brickwork, with plastic windows.

10268/0 Gauge 0 = $1^3/_8$ in., $8^1/_2$ in. high, $21^3/_4$ in. wide, $12^1/_2$ in. long . . . . complete with turntable each **27/—**
„ /1 „ 1 = $1^7/_8$ „ 10 „ „ 29 „ „ $17^3/_4$ „ „ . . . . „ „ „ „ **38/—**

Railway Stations.

13813/1

13813/1 **Railway Station** stamped, in fine polychrome japanning, with advertisements, correct in every detail $15^1/_8$ in. long, $4^3/_8$ in. high, $4^3/_8$ in. wide . . . . . doz. **18/—**

10234/0

Stations
in fine, polychrome japanning, with stamped roof (imitation tiles) and cut-out windows; fitted for lighting with candles.

13846/0

10234/0 without inscription, 9 in. long, $7^1/_2$ in. high, $4^1/_4$ in. wide . . . . . doz. **27/4**

13846/0 „ „ $11^1/_4$ „ „ 11 „ „ $4^3/_8$ „ „ . . . . . each **4/—**

10198/1

10198/2

10198/1 **Railway Station** in fine polychrome japanning with fence and sliding gates and dummy arc lamp, $9^3/_4$ in. long, $5^1/_2$ in. wide. $7^1/_4$ in. high . . . . . doz. **38/—**

10198/2 **Railway Station** in fine polychrome japanning, plastically stamped, with cut-out windows (registered), fitted for lighting with candles, fence with sliding gates, dummy arc lamp, $13^3/_4$ in. long, $8^1/_4$ in. wide, $8^1/_4$ in. high doz. **63/—**

Railway Stations.

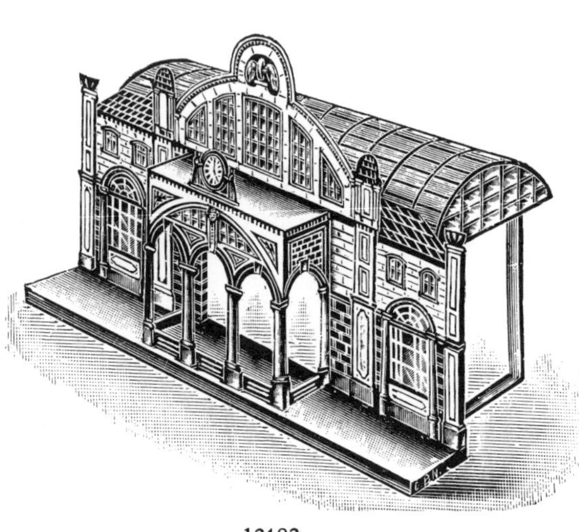

13183

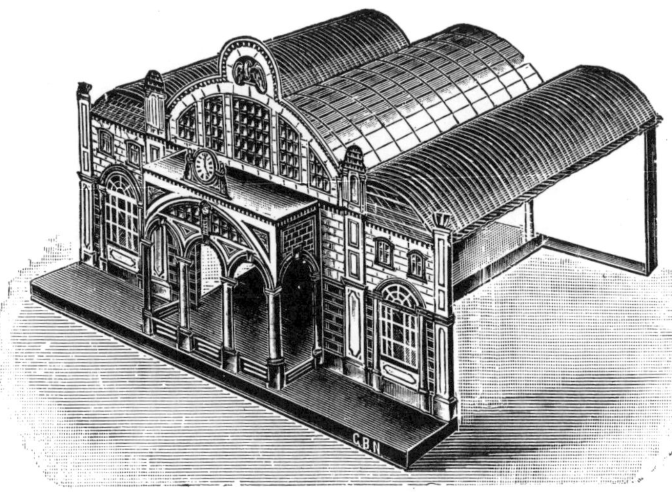

13184

13183 **New Railway Station** in fine polychrome japanning with platform and hall, fitted for lines going through the station, $13^1/_2$ in. long, 7 in. wide, $8^1/_2$ in. high . . . . each **3/2**

13184 **New Railway Station** (Terminus Station) in fine polychrome japanning with platform, hall fitted for 2 lines, $13^1/_2$ in. long, 12 in. wide, $8^1/_2$ in high . . . . each **5/—**

7042

7063

7042 **Railway Station,** plastically stamped, imitation brickwork, with stamped roof, plastic windows and doors, fitted for lighting with candles, 10 in. long, $6^1/_2$ in. wide, $10^1/_4$ in. high . . . . each **5/—**

7063 **Railway Station,** plastically stamped, imitation brickwork, with stamped roof, plastic windows and doors, 2 halls with corrugated roofs, fitted for lighting with candles, 15 in. long, $6^1/_4$ in. wide, $11^3/_4$ in high . . . . . . each **9/—**

Railway Stations,

plastically stamped, finely japanned.

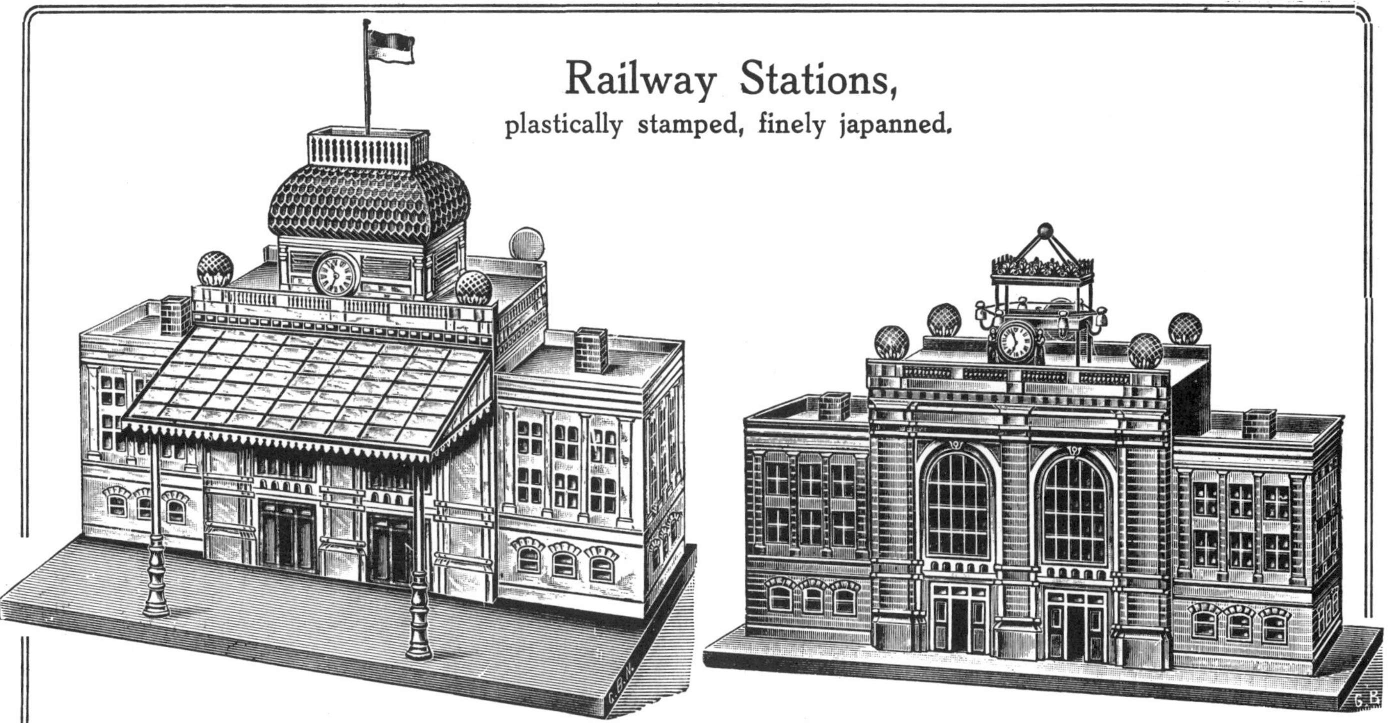

13953 10148

Fine Railway Station in fine polychrome japanning, plastically stamped, white imitation marble, finest decorative finish, with stamped cut-out windows and doors, with dome, platform with imitation glass shelter roof, fitted for lighting with candles.

13953 $14^1/_2$ in. long, $13^3/_8$ in. high . . . . each **12/8**

Railway Station, white, nicely decorated, fine polychrome japanning, plastically stamped, cut-out windows and doors, fitted for lighting with candles.

10148 15 in. long, $5^1/_8$ in. wide, $10^1/_4$ in. high . . . . each **8/—**

7065 11574

Fine Railway Station, plastically stamped, fine imitation brickwork, with datachable corrugated front roof, plastic windows and doors, fitted for lighting with candles.

7065 $13^3/_4$ in. long, 8 in. wide, $11^3/_4$ in. high . . . . each **10/6**

Fine Railway Station, plastically stamped and finely japanned, hall with corrugated roof, fitted for lighting with candles with inside-fittings (Ticket Office, Tables, Seats, Figures).

11574 $13^3/_4$ in. long, $8^3/_4$ in. wide, $10^1/_4$ in. high . . . . each **17/—**

New Series of Model English Stations.

Two Important New Items.

New.

30272/1

New.

30272/2

Realistic Models of the Average English Railway Station executed as shown, sizes right for 0 Gauge Trains, with a large number of advertisement plates in the correct positions and other accurate details.

30272/1	21 5/8 in. long,	5 in. wide,	6 1/8 in. high	doz.	**60/—**
„ /2	26 1/2 „	„ 5 3/4 „	„ 7 1/4 „ „	„	**84/—**

Perfect Model of an English Wayside Station.

A very fine Line. ***Fills a long felt want.***

30266

30266 **Correct English Railway Station** in fine polychrome japanning, with finely painted advertisements in correct colours, signboards, doors to open, to light up with candles. 42 1/2 in. long, 8 1/2 in. wide, 6 1/2 in. high each **13/8**

This model is designed exactly to scale to fit the standard 0 Gauge Trains, the platform will be found to be just the correct height and everything else in exact proportion.

Railway Stations

plastically stamped, finely japanned.

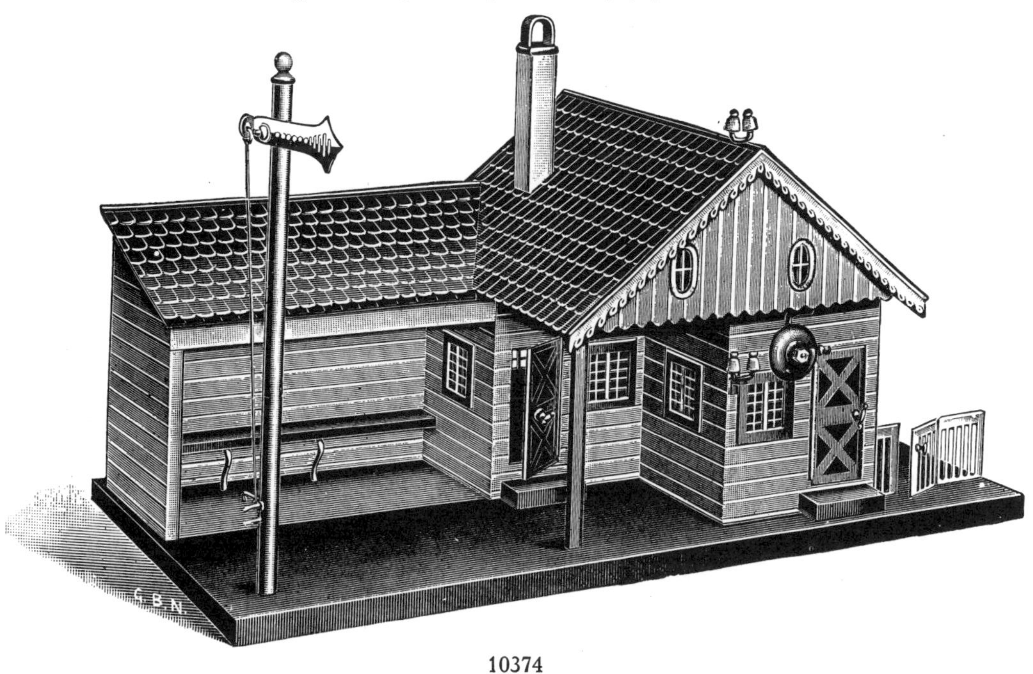

10374

10374 **Country Railway Station,** well japanned, with waiting room, 1 signal, 1 signal bell, doors to open, fitted for lighting, with candles, $16^3/_4$ in. long, $11^3/_8$ in. deep, $12^1/_2$ in. high . . . . each **19/—**

13175

13175 **Fine Railway Station,** highly japanned and stamped, with waiting room, with corrugated roof fitted for lighting, with candles, with fittings inside (ticket office seats, table etc.), with barrier, signal bell etc., $16^3/_4$ in. long, $11^1/_2$ in. wide, 13 in. high. . . . . each **28/6**

Railway Stations, plastically stamped, finely japanned.

10236 **Railway Station,** plastically stamped, well japanned, imitation rough sand stone, very effective, fitted for lighting with candles; with figures and silk flags.
Base: 23¼ in. long, 8¼ in. wide, 12¼ in. high (without flags) each **24/8**

10237 **Railway Station,** plastically stamped, finely japanned, imitation rough sand stone, very effective, fitted for lighting with candles, with figures and silk flags.
29¾ in. long, 11 in. wide, 13¾ in. high (without flags) each **38/—**

Superior Railway Station.

13130

Extra fine large Station, with mechanical Signal Bell imitation brickwork, realistic painting with stamped roofs, embossed coloured glass windows, fitted for lighting with candles, 2 sheltered halls, 1 arc lamp to light, figures and signal bell with strong clockwork

13130 26 in. long, 16 in. high . . . . each **59/—**

Railway Platforms.

13873/0

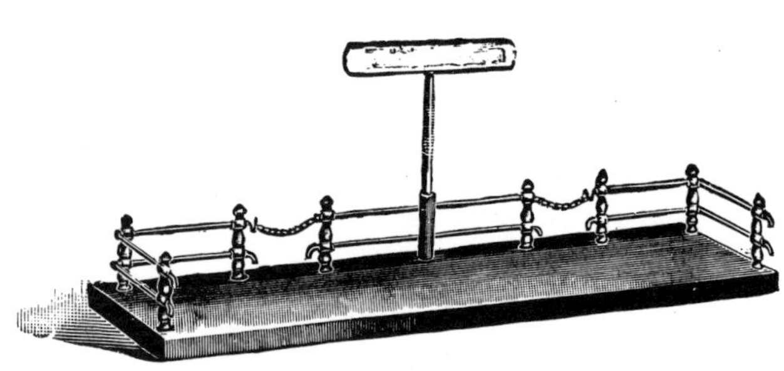

13450

13873/0	**Platform,** finely japanned, with barriers and 2 seats, $9^1/_4$ in. long, $4^3/_4$ in. high	each	**2/5**
13450 E	„ „ „ „ figures, $13^1/_2$ „ „ $3^1/_2$ „ wide	„	**3/2**

10345/1

10345/1 **Platform,** finely japanned with corrugated roof with figures, 12' in. long, $5^1/_4$ in. high . . . . each **5/4**

10345/2

10345/2 **Platform,** finely japanned, with corrugated roof and figures, $15^3/_4$ in. long, $6^7/_8$ in. high . . . . . . each **7/6**

Railway Platforms.

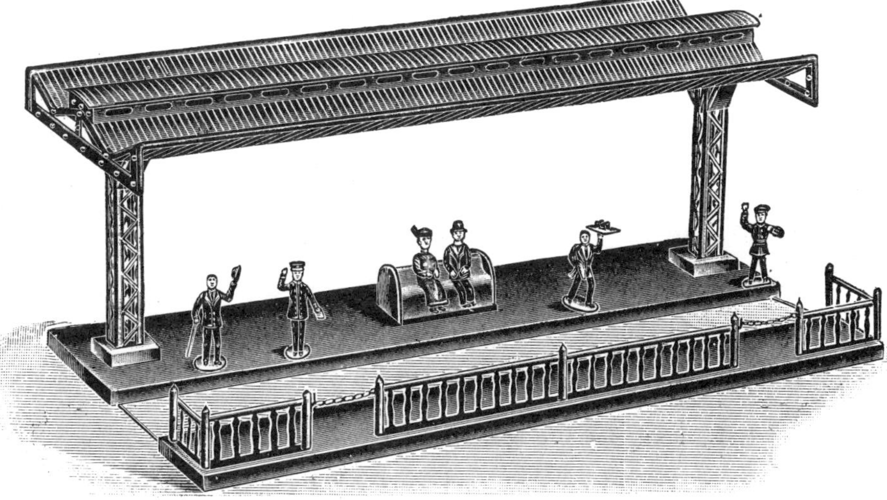

10345/3 **Platform,** finely japanned, with corrugated roof, seats and figures, 19$^{3}/_{4}$ in. long, 7$^{1}/_{4}$ in. high . . . each **11/4**

10345/4 **Platform,** finely japanned, with corrugated roof, seats, lamps and figures, 23$^{3}/_{4}$ in. long, 8$^{5}/_{8}$ in. high . . each **18/—**

10345/5 **Platform,** finely japanned, with corrugated roof, with buffet, lamps and figures, 27$^{1}/_{2}$ in. long, 10$^{1}/_{2}$ in. high . . . . each **24/6**

Level Crossings and Barriers.

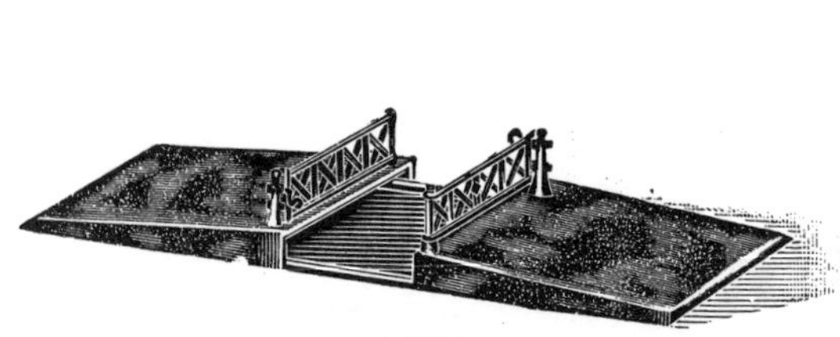

10189

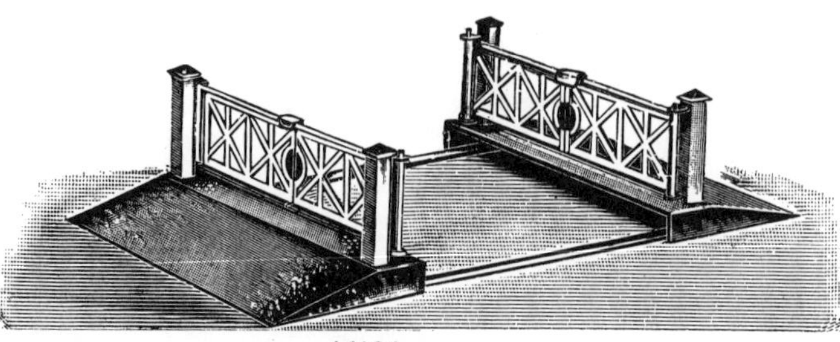

14134

10189 **Railway Crossing** with 2 movable barriers fitting all gauges, fine polychrome japanning, 14 in. long, $4^1/_2$ in. wide doz. **17/6**

14134 **Railway Crossing,** finely japanned, doors to open, fitting all gauges, 8 in. long . . . . each **5/8**

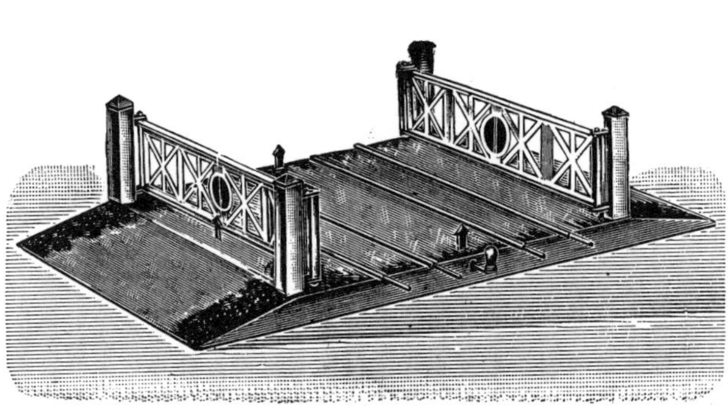

30209

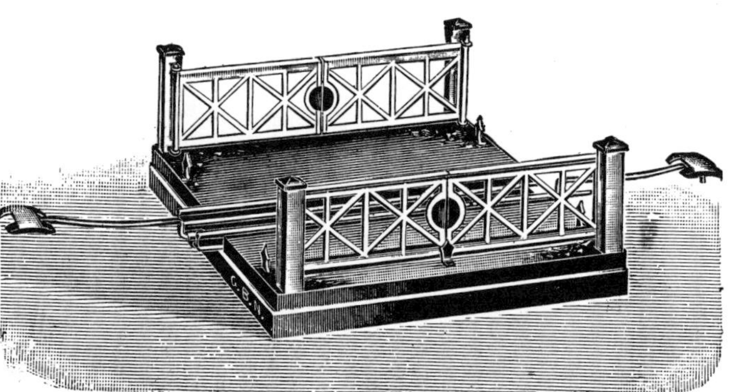

14135/1

30209 **Correct Model of an English Railway Crossing,** finely japanned, doors to open by means of a lever, to be worked by hand, not automatic, fitting gauge 0, size $14^3/_4 \times 8^3/_4$ in. . . . . each **8/—**

14135/1 **Railway Crossing,** finely japanned, **barriers opening automatically** through the passing train touching the contact. Gauge 1 = $1^7/_8$ in. . . . . each **13/10**

8785

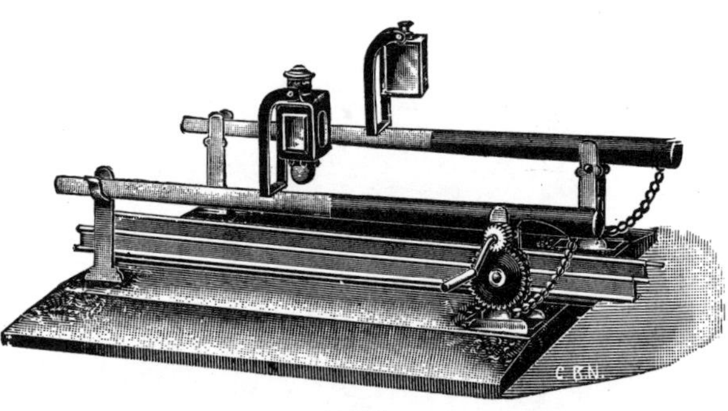

10337

Barriers with double bars and mechanical arrangement to raise the bars, finely japanned

8785/0 Gauge 0 = $1^3/_8$ in. . . . . each **4/4**

„ /1 „ 1 = $1^7/_8$ „ . . . . „ **6/10**

Barriers with double bars and mechanical arrangement to raise same, with 2 signal lanterns fitted for lighting, finely japanned, rails adjustable to fit, 0 Gauge trains = $1^3/_8$ in. and 1 Gauge trains = $1^7/_8$ in.

10337 $9^3/_4$ in long, $11^1/_2$ in. wide . . . . each **6/10**

Signal Boxes.

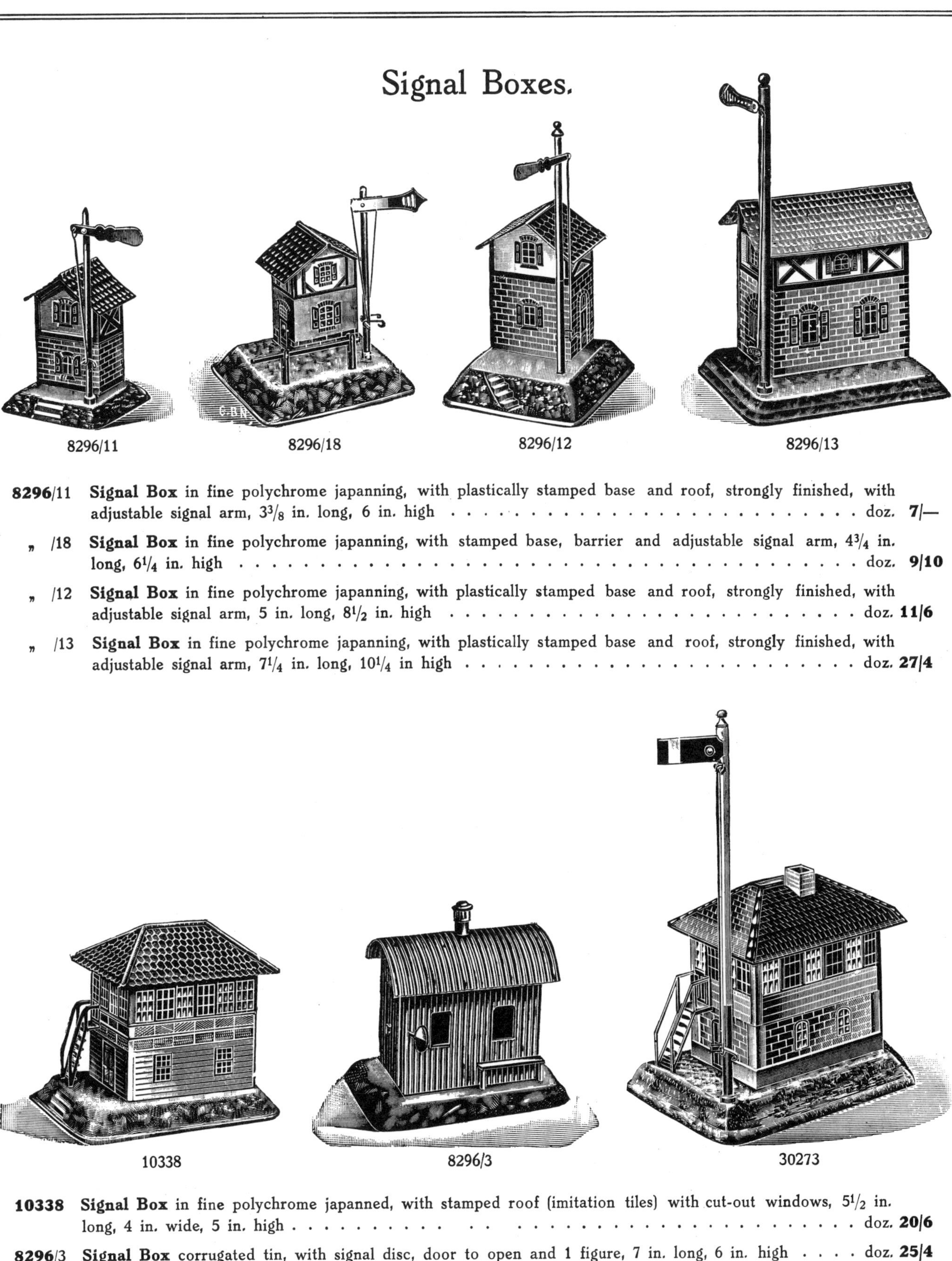

8296/11 8296/18 8296/12 8296/13

8296/11 **Signal Box** in fine polychrome japanning, with plastically stamped base and roof, strongly finished, with adjustable signal arm, $3\frac{3}{8}$ in. long, 6 in. high . . . . doz. **7/—**

„ /18 **Signal Box** in fine polychrome japanning, with stamped base, barrier and adjustable signal arm, $4\frac{3}{4}$ in. long, $6\frac{1}{4}$ in. high . . . . doz. **9/10**

„ /12 **Signal Box** in fine polychrome japanning, with plastically stamped base and roof, strongly finished, with adjustable signal arm, 5 in. long, $8\frac{1}{2}$ in. high . . . . doz. **11/6**

„ /13 **Signal Box** in fine polychrome japanning, with plastically stamped base and roof, strongly finished, with adjustable signal arm, $7\frac{1}{4}$ in. long, $10\frac{1}{4}$ in high . . . . doz. **27/4**

10338 8296/3 30273

10338 **Signal Box** in fine polychrome japanned, with stamped roof (imitation tiles) with cut-out windows, $5\frac{1}{2}$ in. long, 4 in. wide, 5 in. high . . . . doz. **20/6**

8296/3 **Signal Box** corrugated tin, with signal disc, door to open and 1 figure, 7 in. long, 6 in. high . . . . doz. **25/4**

30273 **Signal Box** correct english Model, with plastically stamped roof, cut-out windows, fitted for lighting with candles, with adjustable signal, $6\frac{3}{4}$ in. long, $5\frac{1}{8}$ in. wide, $6\frac{1}{4}$ in. high . . . . doz. **36/—**

Signal Boxes.

10186

8296/25

8296/24

10186 **New Signal Box, good Model** fine polychrome japanning with plastically stamped roof, cut-out windows, fitted for lighting with candles, 6¾ in. long, 5⅛ in. wide, 6¼ in. high . . . . doz. **35/6**

8296/25 **Signal Box,** finely polychrome japanned with plastically stamped base and stamped roof (imitation tiles) with automatic signal disc, which turns, as soon as the train touches the contact, 7⅛ in. long, 5¼ in. wide, 6¼ in. high . . . . doz. **29/6**

8296/24 **Signal Box,** in fine polychrome japanning, with automatic signal bell, ringing as soon as the train touches the rail, 4¾ in. long, 4¾ in. wide, 6¼ in. high . . . . each **3/8**

8296/16

8296/19

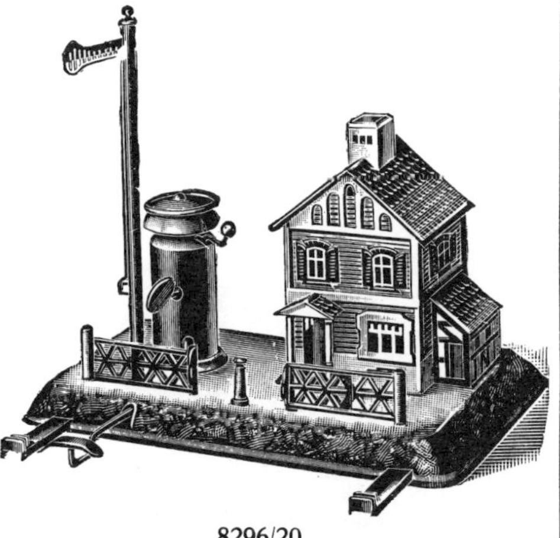

8296/20

8296/16 **Signal Box,** plastically stamped and finely handjapanned, with automatically working signal bell, 8½ in. long, 6 in. wide, 6¼ in. high . . . . each **4/10**

8296/19 **Signal Box,** in fine polychrome japanning, with plastically stamped base and stamped roof, with automatically working bell. As soon as the train touches the signal contact on the rail, the signal bell rings automatically. 7¼ in. long, 5¼ in. wide, 6½ in. high . . . . each **5/—**

8296/20 **Signal Box,** fine polychrome japanning, with Signal, with automatic bell, to be worked from the rails. House in very effective finish. 10 in. long, 8 in. wide, 6½ in. high (without Signal) . . . . each **6/8**

Signal Boxes.

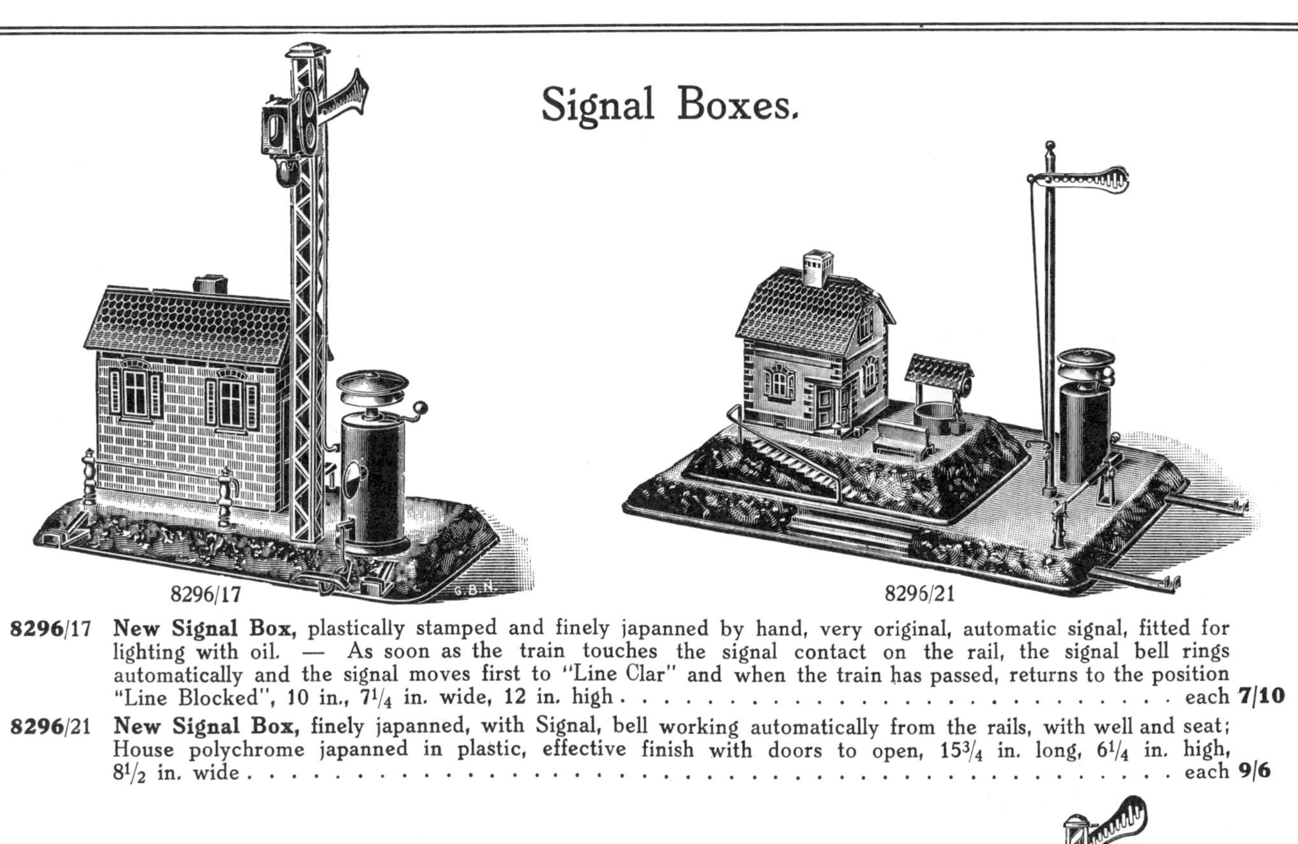

8296/17 8296/21

8296/17 **New Signal Box,** plastically stamped and finely japanned by hand, very original, automatic signal, fitted for lighting with oil. — As soon as the train touches the signal contact on the rail, the signal bell rings automatically and the signal moves first to "Line Clar" and when the train has passed, returns to the position "Line Blocked", 10 in., $7^1/_4$ in. wide, 12 in. high . . . . each **7/10**

8296/21 **New Signal Box,** finely japanned, with Signal, bell working automatically from the rails, with well and seat; House polychrome japanned in plastic, effective finish with doors to open, $15^3/_4$ in. long, $6^1/_4$ in. high, $8^1/_2$ in. wide . . . . each **9/6**

8296/9 **Signal Box,** mechanical, finely japanned, very original, with signal bell, signal (2 arms) and barrier, $9^1/_4$ in. long, $10^1/_2$ in. high . . . . each **16/—**

By turning the crank the signal bell is started, the watchman steps out of the house, the signal arm goes up, the barrier is closed and the watchman salutes the passing train. Then the signal drops, the barrier goes up and the watchman returns to the house. The whole arrangement is worked automatically.

8296/9

8296/22

8296/23

8296/22 **New Signal Box,** finely japanned, with automatic signal and bell, both working from the rails; House in plastic effective finish, with doors to open, Signal to light up, 14 in. long, $8^1/_2$ in. wide, $7^1/_4$ in. high (with signal) each **11/6**

„ /23 **New Signal Box,** finely polychrome japanned, with Signal; House in plastic, effective finish, with doors to open to be lit by electricity (dry battery), $8^1/_2$ in. long, 6 in. wide, 6 in. high . . . . each **8/8**

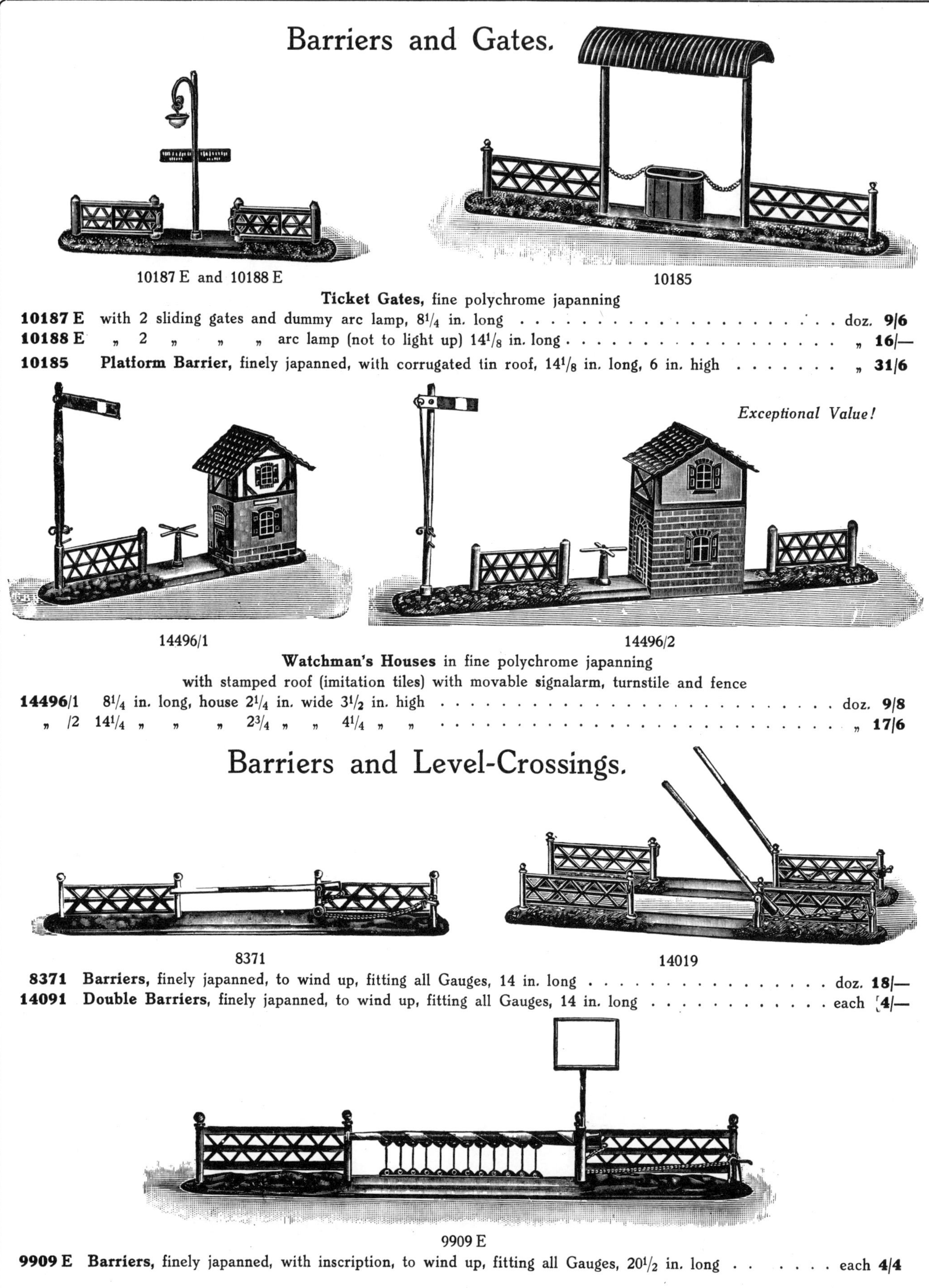

Barriers and Gates.

10187 E and 10188 E

10185

Ticket Gates, fine polychrome japanning

10187 E with 2 sliding gates and dummy arc lamp, $8^{1}/_{4}$ in. long . . . . doz. **9/6**

10188 E „ 2 „ „ „ arc lamp (not to light up) $14^{1}/_{8}$ in. long . . . . „ **16/—**

10185 **Platform Barrier,** finely japanned, with corrugated tin roof, $14^{1}/_{8}$ in. long, 6 in. high . . . . „ **31/6**

Exceptional Value!

14496/1

14496/2

Watchman's Houses in fine polychrome japanning
with stamped roof (imitation tiles) with movable signalarm, turnstile and fence

14496/1 $8^{1}/_{4}$ in. long, house $2^{1}/_{4}$ in. wide $3^{1}/_{2}$ in. high . . . . doz. **9/8**

„ /2 $14^{1}/_{4}$ „ „ „ $2^{3}/_{4}$ „ „ $4^{1}/_{4}$ „ „ . . . . „ **17/6**

Barriers and Level-Crossings.

8371

14019

8371 **Barriers,** finely japanned, to wind up, fitting all Gauges, 14 in. long . . . . doz. **18/—**

14091 **Double Barriers,** finely japanned, to wind up, fitting all Gauges, 14 in. long . . . . each **14/—**

9909 E

9909 E **Barriers,** finely japanned, with inscription, to wind up, fitting all Gauges, $20^{1}/_{2}$ in. long . . . . each **4/4**

Foot Bridges.

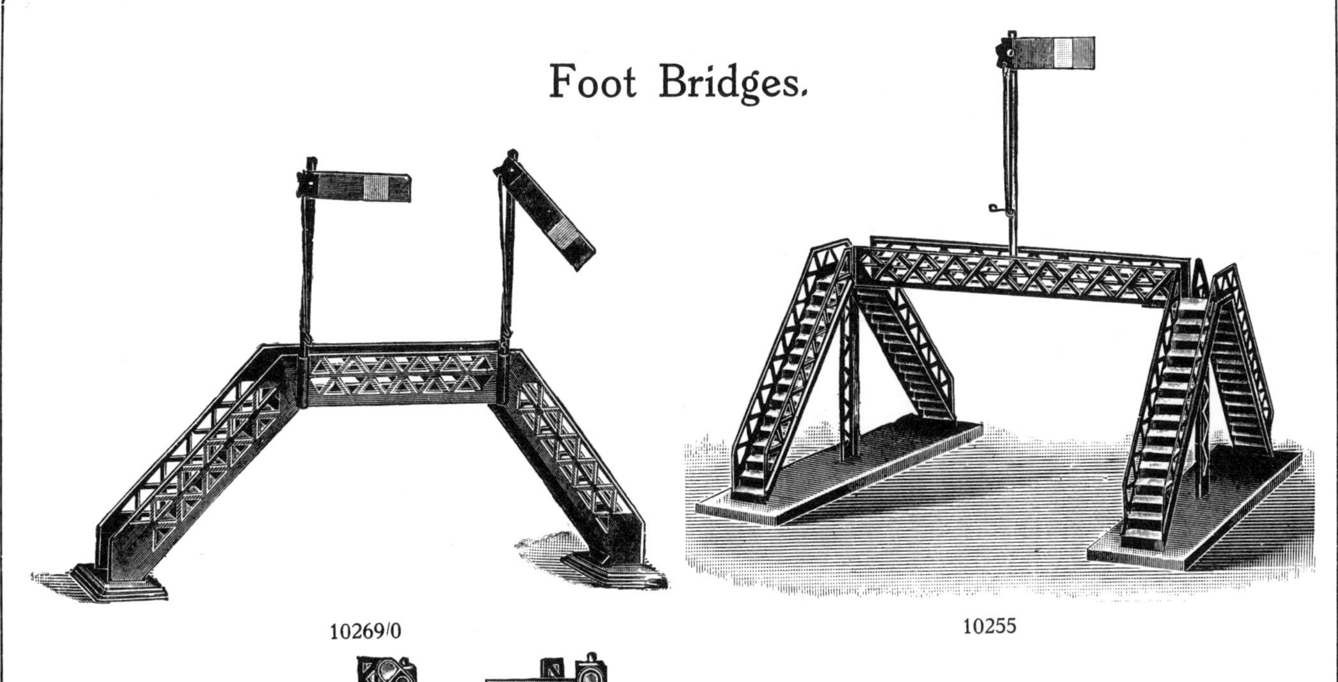

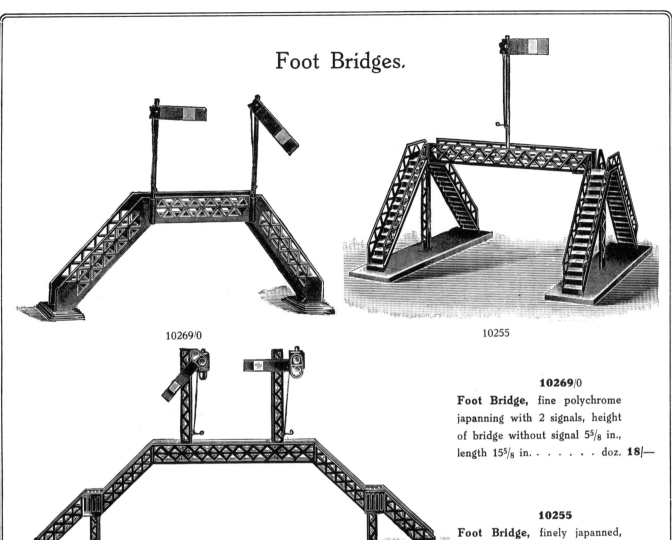

10269/0 10255

30268

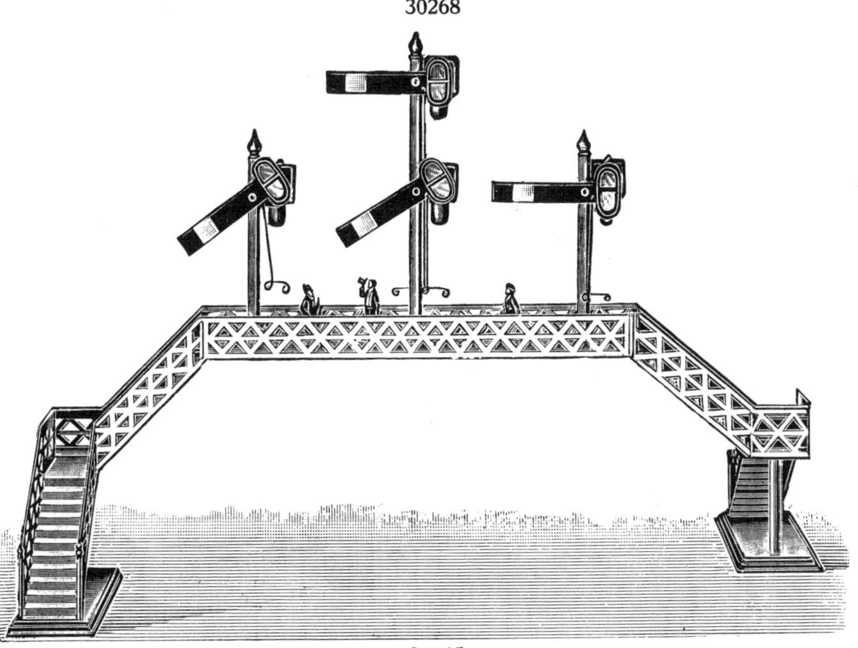

30245

10269/0

Foot Bridge, fine polychrome japanning with 2 signals, height of bridge without signal $5\frac{5}{8}$ in., length $15\frac{5}{8}$ in. . . . . . . doz. **18/—**

10255

Foot Bridge, finely japanned, height of bridge without signal $6\frac{3}{4}$ in., length 13 in. . . . each **4/10**

30268

Model Foot Bridge with 2 posts and signals with 2 lamps to burn oil with green and red spectacles, $8\frac{1}{4}$ in. high, 28 in. long, each **6/—**

30245

Foot Bridge, strong finish, finely japanned, imitation girder work, with 3 signal posts and 4 movable signal arms, 6 lanterns fitted for lighting, with red and green glasses, with 3 figures, $24\frac{1}{2}$ in. long, $16\frac{1}{4}$ in. high . . . . each **9/6**

Goods Stations.

10115

10370/1

10115 **Goods Station** with sliding door and loading platform, fine polychrome japanning, $10^1/_4$ in. long, $3^1/_8$ in. wide, $3^1/_2$ in. high . . . . doz. **17/6**

10370/1 **Goods Station,** plastically stamped (imitation brickwork) with stamped roof with sliding door and loading platform, $8^3/_4$ in. long, $4^1/_4$ in. wide, $5^1/_2$ in. high . . . . each **5/2**

10361

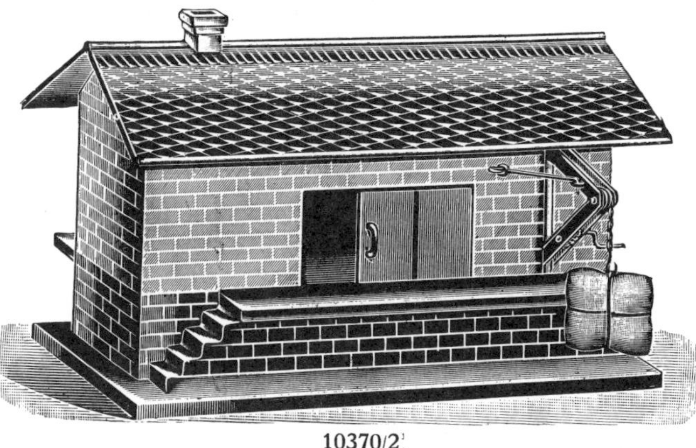
10370/2

10361 **Goods Station** with sliding door and loading platform, fine polychrome japanning. $10^1/_2$ in. long, 6 in. wide, 6 in. high. . . . . each **3/8**

10370/2 **Goods Station,** plastically stamped (imitation brickwork), with stamped roof, with 2 sliding doors, 2 loading platforms and 1 moveable crane, actually working. $10^5/_8$ in. long, $6^1/_4$ in. wide, $6^3/_4$ in. high each **10/4**

10370/3 **Goods Station** plastically stamped (imitation brickwork), stamped roof, 4 sliding doors, 2 loading platforms and 1 moveable crane, actually working, with bales and cases, elegantly finished throughout. $13^1/_2$ in. long, $5^1/_2$ in. wide, $7^3/_4$ in. high each **15/6**

Cranes.

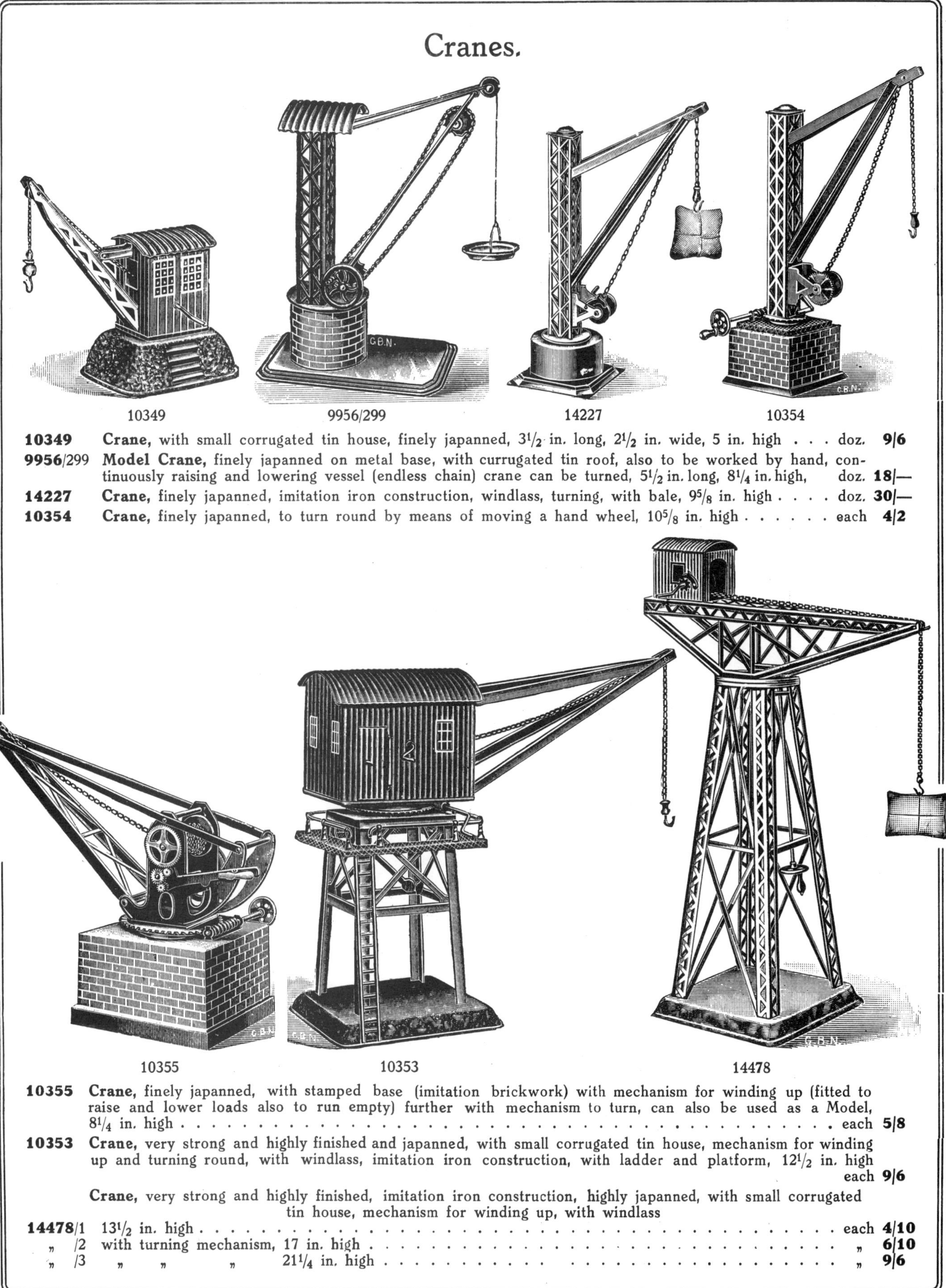

10349 9956/299 14227 10354

10349 **Crane,** with small corrugated tin house, finely japanned, 3½ in. long, 2½ in. wide, 5 in. high . . . doz. **9/6**

9956/299 **Model Crane,** finely japanned on metal base, with currugated tin roof, also to be worked by hand, continuously raising and lowering vessel (endless chain) crane can be turned, 5½ in. long, 8¼ in. high, doz. **18/—**

14227 **Crane,** finely japanned, imitation iron construction, windlass, turning, with bale, 9⅝ in. high . . . . doz. **30/—**

10354 **Crane,** finely japanned, to turn round by means of moving a hand wheel, 10⅝ in. high . . . . . . each **4/2**

10355 10353 14478

10355 **Crane,** finely japanned, with stamped base (imitation brickwork) with mechanism for winding up (fitted to raise and lower loads also to run empty) further with mechanism to turn, can also be used as a Model, 8¼ in. high . . . . each **5/8**

10353 **Crane,** very strong and highly finished and japanned, with small corrugated tin house, mechanism for winding up and turning round, with windlass, imitation iron construction, with ladder and platform, 12½ in. high each **9/6**

Crane, very strong and highly finished, imitation iron construction, highly japanned, with small corrugated tin house, mechanism for winding up, with windlass

14478/1 13½ in. high . . . . each **4/10**

„ /2 with turning mechanism, 17 in. high . . . . „ **6/10**

„ /3 „ „ „ 21¼ in. high . . . . „ **9/6**

Railway Accessories.

13699

14118

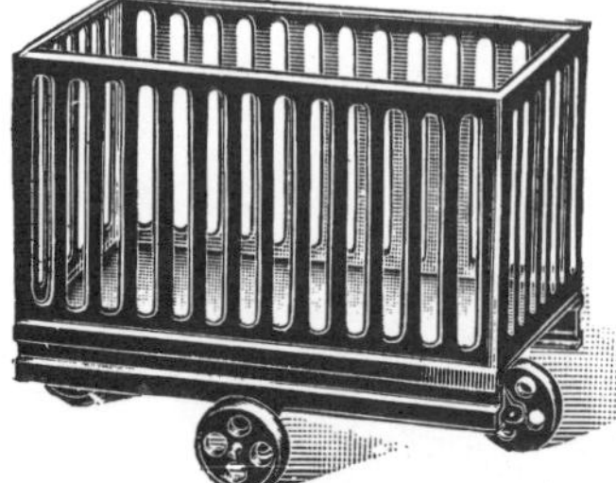

14119

13699 **Trolley,** finely japanned, $5^3/_4$ in. long . . . . doz. **6/4**

14118 „ „ „ $5^1/_2$ „ „ . . . . „ **17/6**

14119 „ „ „ $4^7/_8$ „ „ . . . . „ **17/6**

10202

10203

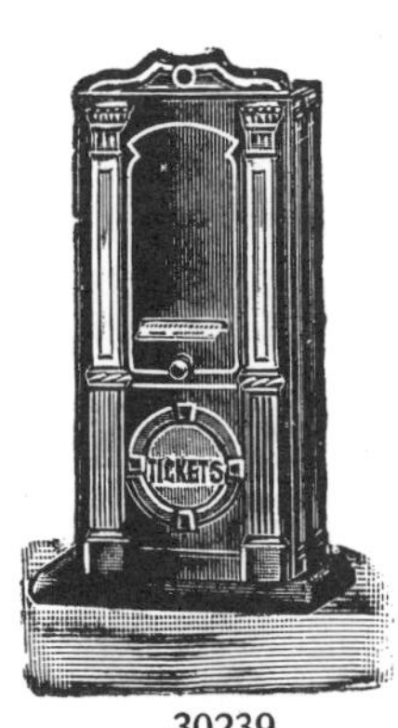

30239

10202 **News Paper Stall,** finely japanned, plastically stamped with miniature news papers and figure, $3^1/_8$ in. wide, $4^3/_4$ in. high . . . . doz. **31/6**

10203 **Station Bar** (Refreshment Stall), finely japanned, plastically stamped, provisions made of sweets, with figure, $3^1/_8$ in. wide, $4^3/_4$ in. high . . . . doz. **38/—**

30239 **Ticket-Automat,** finely japanned, 7 in. high, with 24 tickets . . . . „ **17/6**

8105 **Extra Tickets** . . . . gross **—/10**

14085/2

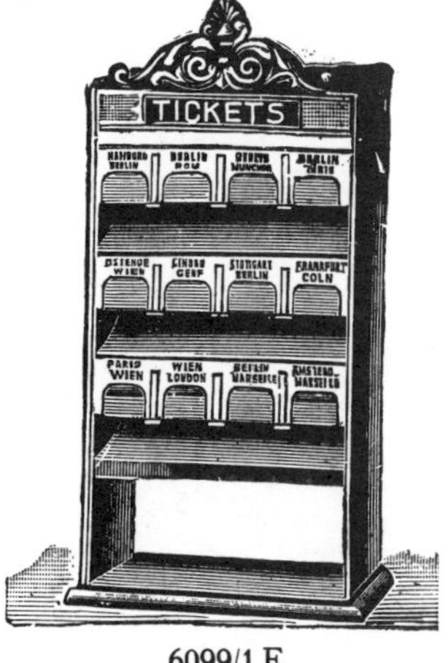

6099/1 E

32421
von
Berlin
nach
Paris
über
Hannover
Düsseldorf
Aachen
Verviers
I. Classe
D-Zug.

8108

14085/2 **Booking Office,** stamped in imitation brickwork and finely japanned, with 2 ticket windows and ticket automat with 24 tickets, detachable roof and fitted for lighting with candles, $6^1/_4$ in. long, $6^1/_2$ in. wide, $7^1/_8$ in. high . . . . each **5/—**

6099/1 E **Railway Ticket Office,** finely japanned, with 12 divisions and 144 Railway tickets for 12 different English routes. Every ticket can be taken out separately, $8^1/_4$ in. high, $5^1/_4$ in. wide . . . . each **4/10**

6099/0 same as above with 9 divisions . . . . doz. **39/—**

8108 **Railway Tickets,** 1 assortment consisting of 144 tickets of 12 various routes . . . . gross **1/—**

Indicators.

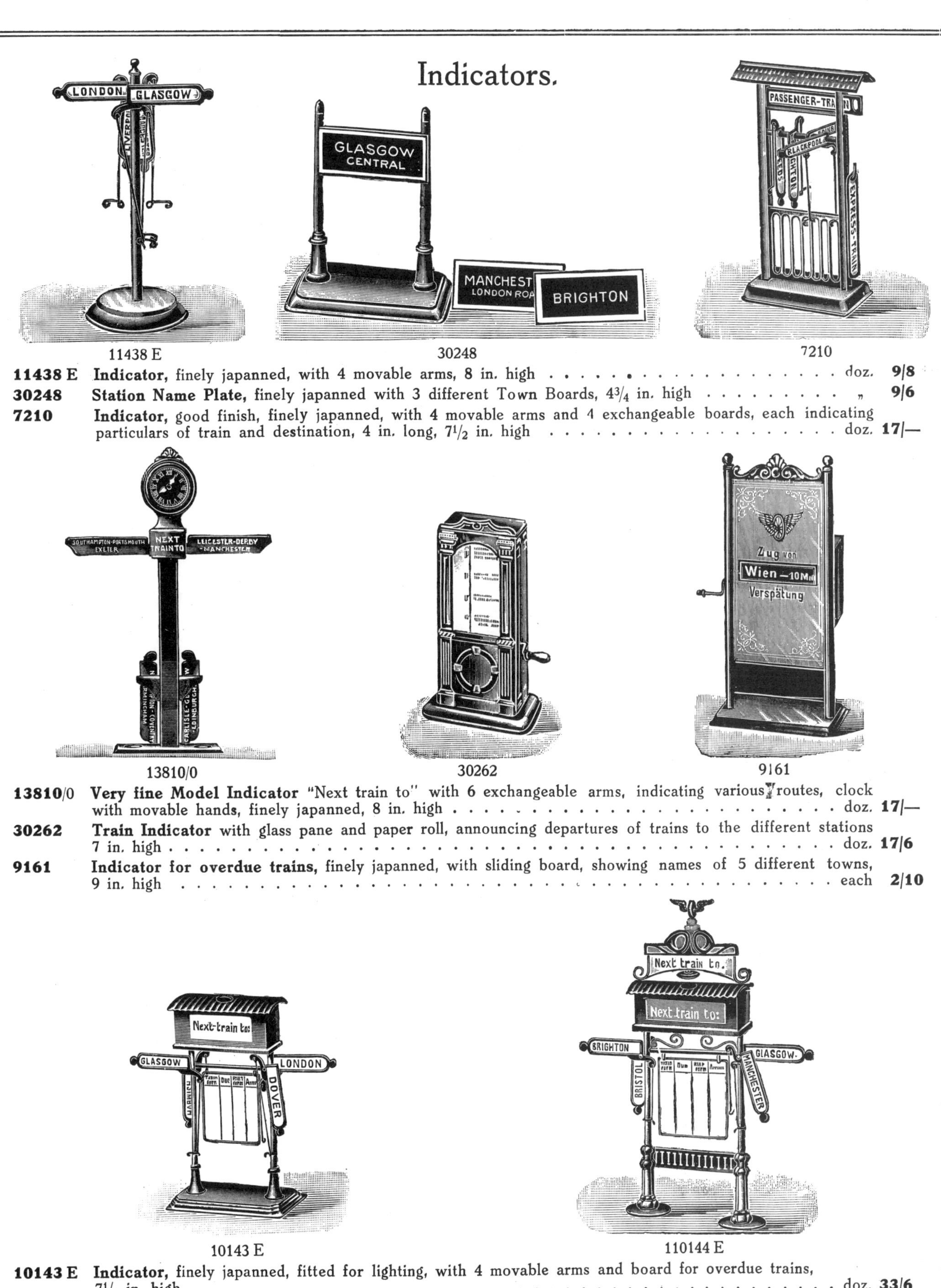

11438 E — 30248 — 7210

11438 E **Indicator,** finely japanned, with 4 movable arms, 8 in. high . . . . doz. **9/8**

30248 **Station Name Plate,** finely japanned with 3 different Town Boards, $4^3/_4$ in. high . . . . „ **9/6**

7210 **Indicator,** good finish, finely japanned, with 4 movable arms and 4 exchangeable boards, each indicating particulars of train and destination, 4 in. long, $7^1/_2$ in. high . . . . doz. **17/—**

13810/0 — 30262 — 9161

13810/0 **Very fine Model Indicator** "Next train to" with 6 exchangeable arms, indicating various routes, clock with movable hands, finely japanned, 8 in. high . . . . doz. **17/—**

30262 **Train Indicator** with glass pane and paper roll, announcing departures of trains to the different stations 7 in. high . . . . doz. **17/6**

9161 **Indicator for overdue trains,** finely japanned, with sliding board, showing names of 5 different towns, 9 in. high . . . . each **2/10**

10143 E — 110144 E

10143 E **Indicator,** finely japanned, fitted for lighting, with 4 movable arms and board for overdue trains, $7^1/_8$ in. high . . . . doz. **33/6**

10144 E **Indicator,** finely japanned, fitted for lighting, with 4 movable arms and board for overdue trains, $11^1/_2$ in. high . . . . each **4/—**

Buffers.

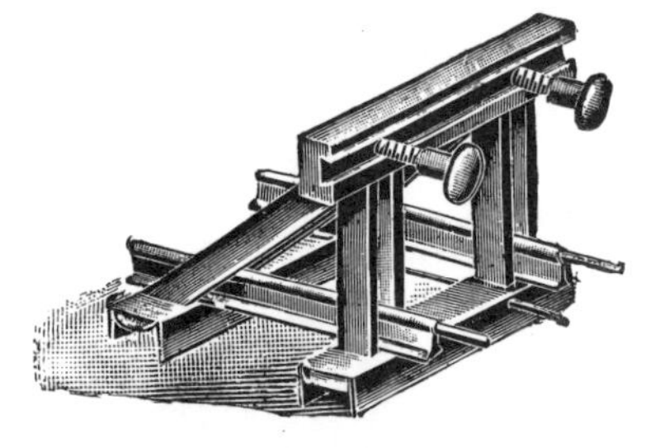

14086

8790

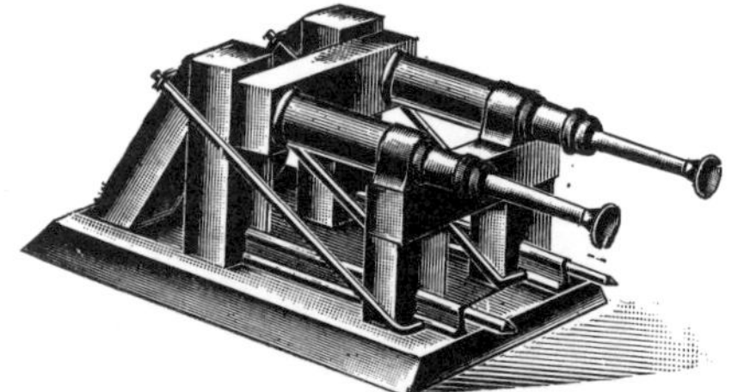

13801

14086/0 **Stop Ends,** plain finish, spring buffers . . . . Gauge 0 = $1^3/_8$ in. doz. **9/8**
„ /1 „ „ „ „ „ „ . . . . „ 1 = $1^7/_8$ „ „ **13/8**
8790/0 „ „ finely polychrome japanned, with spring buffers . . . . „ 0 = $1^3/_8$ „ „ **17/6**
„ /1 „ „ „ „ „ „ „ „ . . . . „ 1 = $1^7/_8$ „ „ **25/4**

Stop Ends, very strong finish, fine grey iron-japanning, with nickelled spring buffers (imitation hydraulic buffers)
13801/0 . . . . Gauge 0 = $1^3/_8$ in. each **3/4**
„ /1 . . . . „ 1 = $1^7/_8$ „ „ **4/—**

Signal Bells.

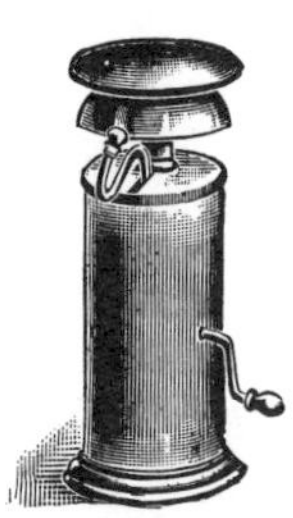

8405/0

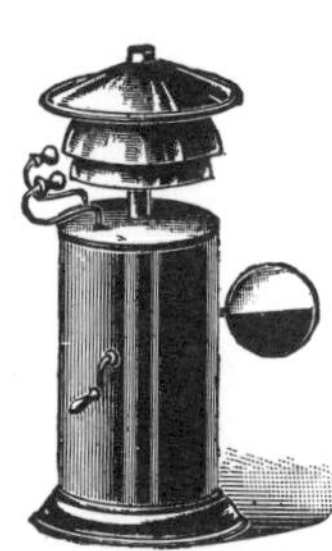

8405/1

9919

8405/0 **Signal Bell,** finely japanned, with single tone, handle to turn, 4 in. high . . . . doz. **11/4**
„ /1 „ „ „ „ „ double „ „ „ „ $4^3/_4$ „ „ . . . . „ **21/—**
9919 „ „ „ „ „ „ „ „ „ „ $6^3/_4$ „ „ . . . . each **3/10**

10291

13403/1

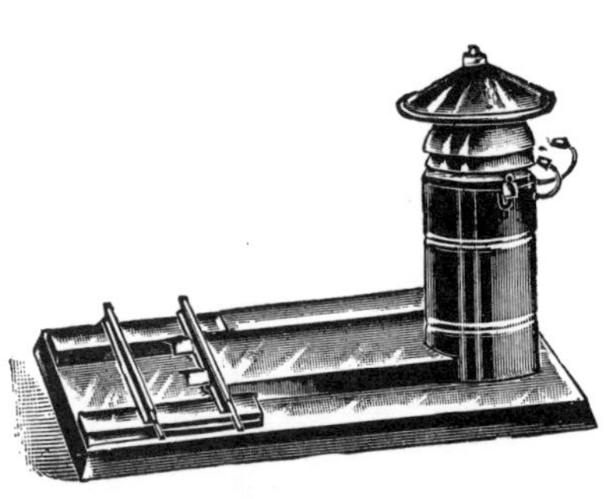

8353

10291/0 **Automatic Signal Bell** with rail contact with strong clockwork-movement, fitting Gauge 0 = $1^3/_8$ in. each **3/10**
„ /1 „ „ „ „ „ „ „ „ „ adjustable, „ „ 0 = $1^3/_8$ „ and Gauge 1 = $1^7/_8$ in. with double tunes . . . . each **5/4**
13403/1 **Automatic Signal Bell** with rail contact with strong clockwork-movement, fitting Gauge I—IV = $1^3/_8$, $1^7/_8$, $2^1/_8$, $2^5/_8$ and 3 in. with double tunes . . . . each **9/2**

As soon as the train touches the contact, the clockwork is released and the bell will sound; wen the train has passed the clockwork is disconnected.

8353/0 **Automatic Signal Bell** with rail contact, fitting Gauge 0 = $1^3/_8$ in. . . . . each **4/10**
„ /1 „ „ „ „ „ „ „ „ I—IV = $1^7/_8$, $2^1/_8$, $2^5/_8$ and 3 in. . . . . „ **5/10**

As soon as the train passes the signal bell and touches the contact, the bell will ring with double tunes.

Bridges.

10346/0

Railway Bridge with rails

realistic finish; middle piece with large arch, imitation ironwork.

10346/0 Gauge 0 = $1^3/_8$ in., $31^3/_4$ in. long, $4^1/_4$ in. wide . . . . each **2/10**

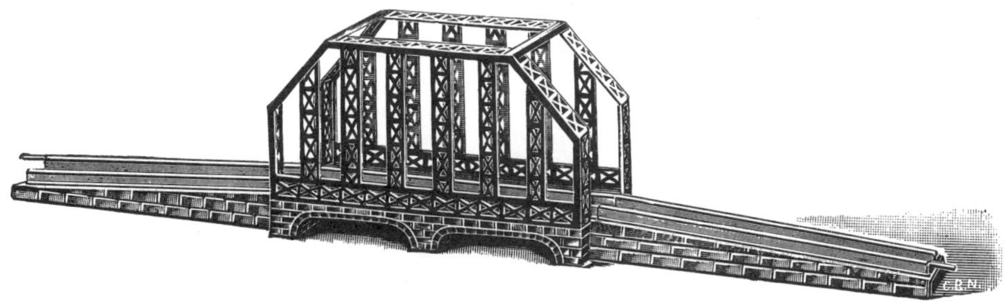

10347/0

Railway Bridge with rails

new and realistic finish; middle piece imitation ironwork.

10347/0 Gauge 0 = $1^3/_8$ in., $31^3/_4$ in. long, $4^1/_4$ in. wide . . . . each **3/10**

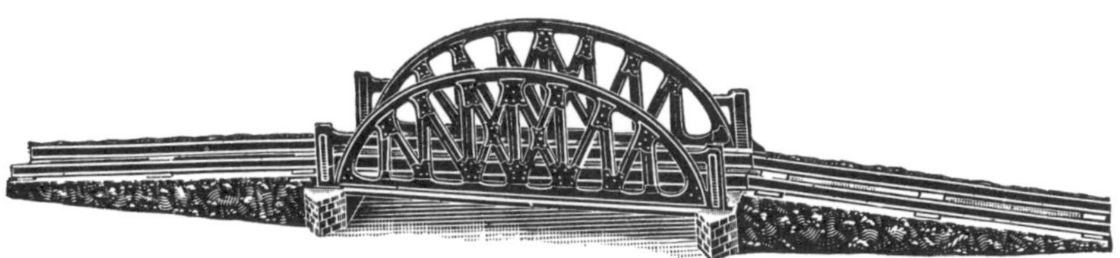

11435

Railway Bridge with rails

realistic finish; middle piece imitation ironwork.

11435/1 Gauge 1 = $1^7/_8$ in., $31^3/_4$ in. long, $5^3/_4$ in. wide . . . . each **4/4**

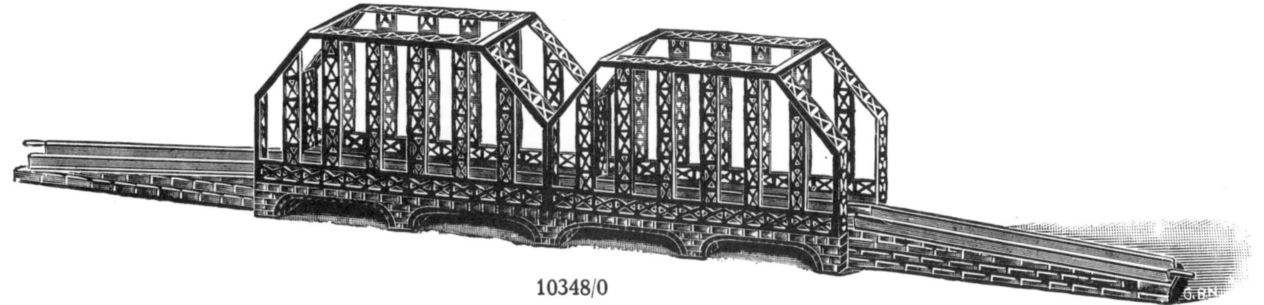

10348/0

Railway Bridge with rails

in a new realistic finish; middle piece with 2 arches, imitation ironwork.

10348/0 Gauge 0 = $1^3/_8$ in., 42 in. long, $4^1/_4$ in. wide . . . . each **6/8**

Bridges.

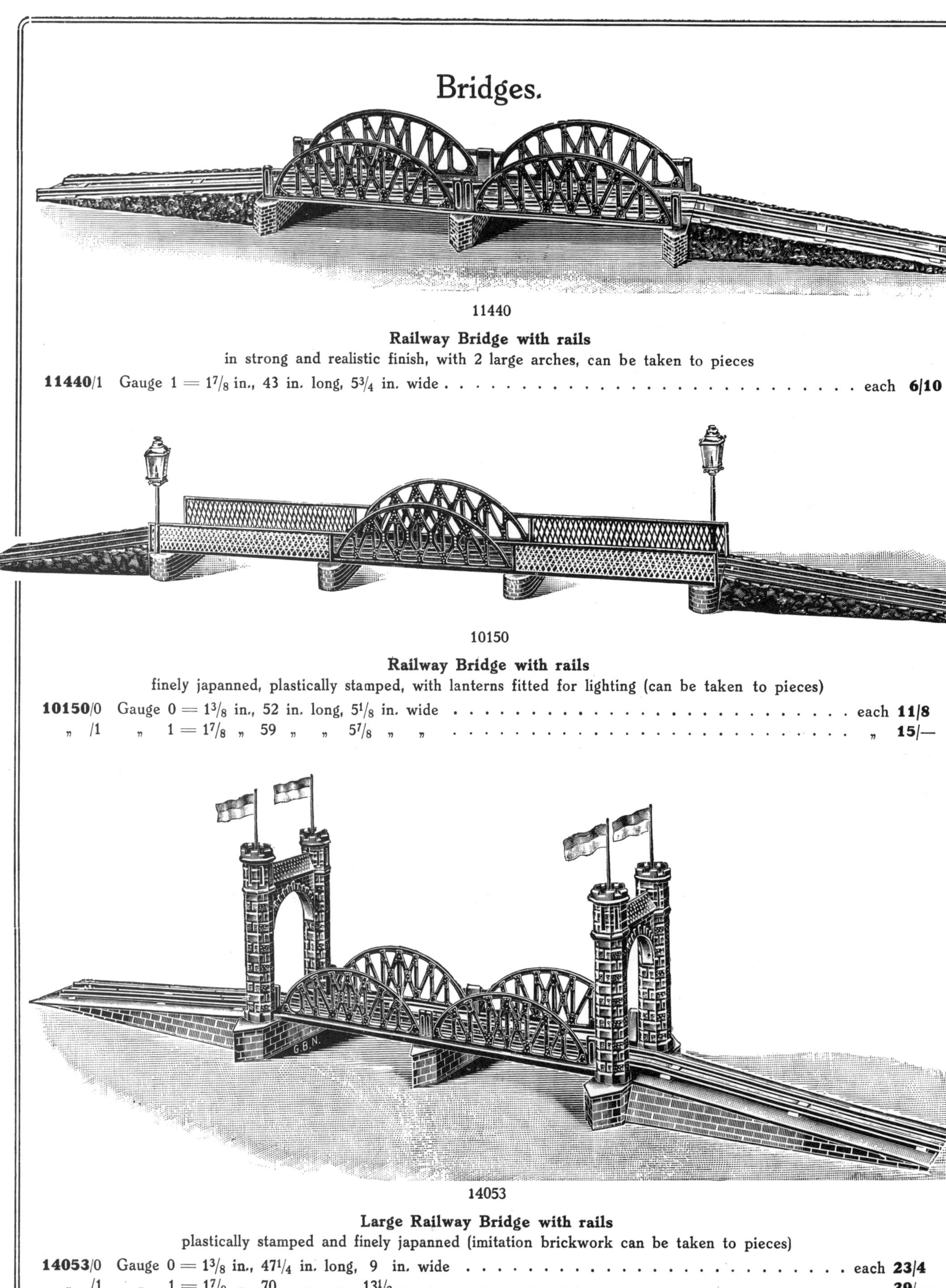

11440

Railway Bridge with rails

in strong and realistic finish, with 2 large arches, can be taken to pieces

11440/1 Gauge 1 = $1\frac{7}{8}$ in., 43 in. long, $5\frac{3}{4}$ in. wide . . . . each **6/10**

10150

Railway Bridge with rails

finely japanned, plastically stamped, with lanterns fitted for lighting (can be taken to pieces)

10150/0 Gauge 0 = $1\frac{3}{8}$ in., 52 in. long, $5\frac{1}{8}$ in. wide . . . . each **11/8**

„ /1 „ 1 = $1\frac{7}{8}$ „ 59 „ „ $5\frac{7}{8}$ „ „ . . . . „ **15/—**

14053

Large Railway Bridge with rails

plastically stamped and finely japanned (imitation brickwork can be taken to pieces)

14053/0 Gauge 0 = $1\frac{3}{8}$ in., $47\frac{1}{4}$ in. long, 9 in. wide . . . . each **23/4**

„ /1 „ 1 = $1\frac{7}{8}$ „ 70 „ „ $13\frac{1}{2}$ „ „ . . . . „ **39/—**

Tunnels

in Realistic Plastic Finish, finely painted.

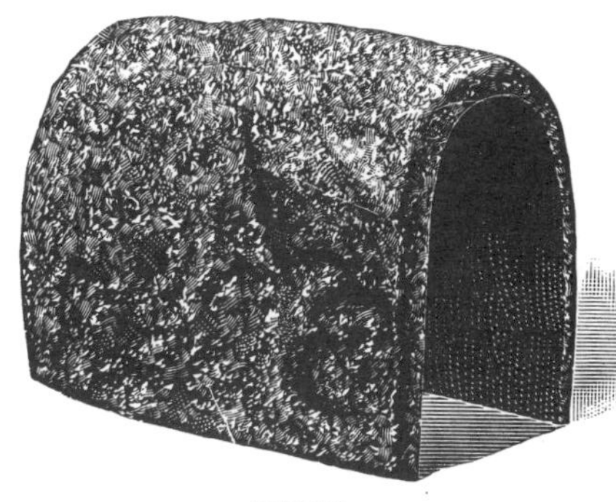

13929/0

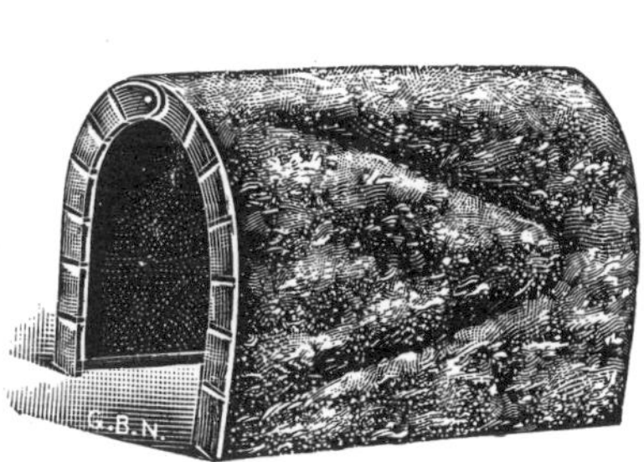

14095/0

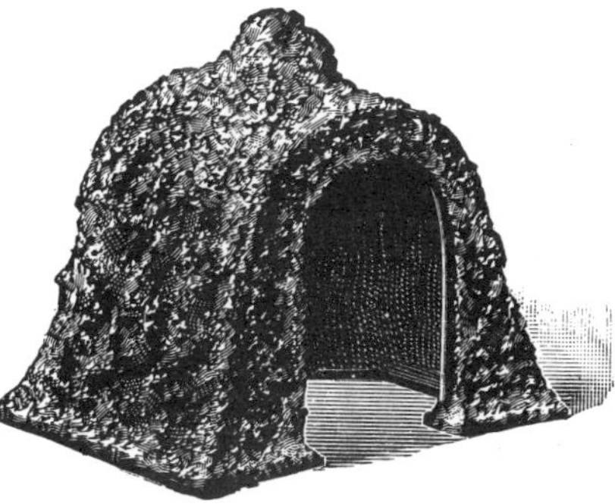

10298/0

Tunnel, plastically finished and finely painted

13929/0	fitting Railways Gauge 0 = $1^3/_8$ in., $6^7/_8$ in. long, $6^1/_4$ in. high	. . . .	doz.	**7/10**
„ /1	„ „ „ 1 = $1^7/_8$ „ 10 „ „ $8^3/_4$ „ „	. . . .	„	**18/—**
„ /2	„ „ „ 2 = $2^1/_8$ „ $11^3/_4$ „ „ 9 „ „	. . . .	„	**34/—**

Tunnel, folding, plastic finish, finely painted

14095/0	fitting Railways Gauge 0 = $1^3/_8$ in., $7^3/_4$ in. long, $5^1/_4$ in. high	. . . .	doz.	**13/8**
„ /1	„ „ „ 1 = $1^7/_8$ „ $10^1/_2$ „ „ 8 „ „	. . . .	„	**23/—**

Tunnel, Plasterwork in plastic finish, finely painted

10298/0	fitting Railways Gauge 0 = $1^3/_8$ in., $8^5/_8$ in. long, 9 in. high	. . . .	doz.	**18/—**

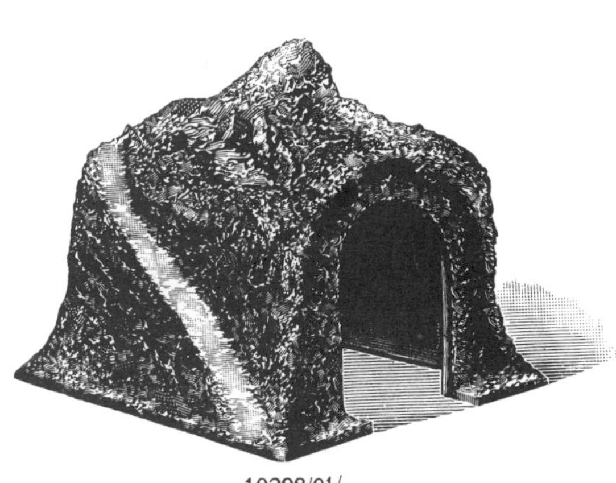

10298/$0^1/_2$

10298/1

Tunnel, Plasterwork in plastic finish, finely painted

10298/$0^1/_2$	fitting Railways Gauge 0 = $1^3/_8$ in. and 1 = $1^7/_8$ in., 12 in. long, $9^1/_2$ in. high	. . . .	each	**2/4**
„ /1	„ „ „ 0 = $1^3/_8$ „ „ 1 = $1^7/_8$ „ with foot-passage at side, 12 in. long, $14^1/_4$ in. high,		„	**4/6**

Tunnels

in Realistic Plastic Finish, finely painted.

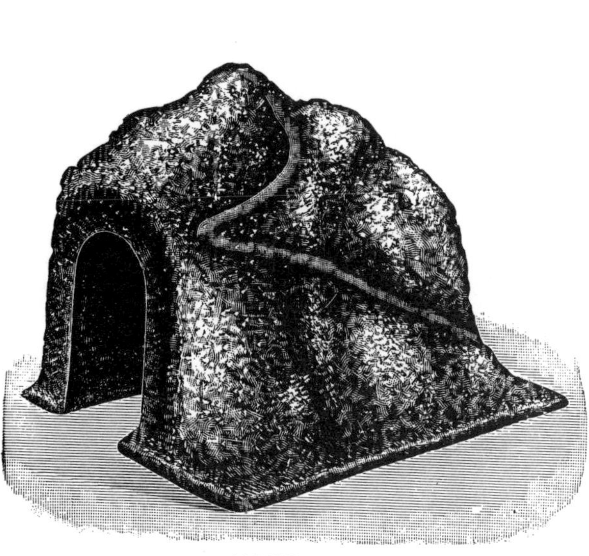

10298/2

10298/3—4

10298/2 plastic finish, finely painted, fitting Railways gauges 1 and 2, $15^3/_4$ in. long, $16^1/_2$ in. high . . . . . . each **7/—**
„ /3 „ „ „ „ „ „ „ 1 „ 2, $21^1/_2$ „ „ 19 „ „ . . . . . . „ **12/—**
„ /4 „ „ „ „ „ „ „ 1 „ 2, $27^3/_4$ „ „ $17^1/_2$ „ „ . . . . . . „ **17/—**

10440

10440 A Model of the St. Gotthard Tunnel and Axenstrasse (Switzerland), plastic finish, finely painted, fitting Railways Gauge 1 and 2, $27^1/_2$ in. long, 17 in. high . . . . each **24/6**

English Railway Signals.

Designed after original drawings.

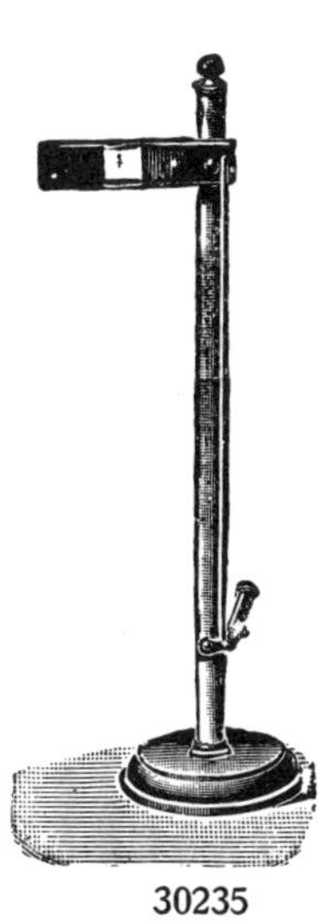
30235

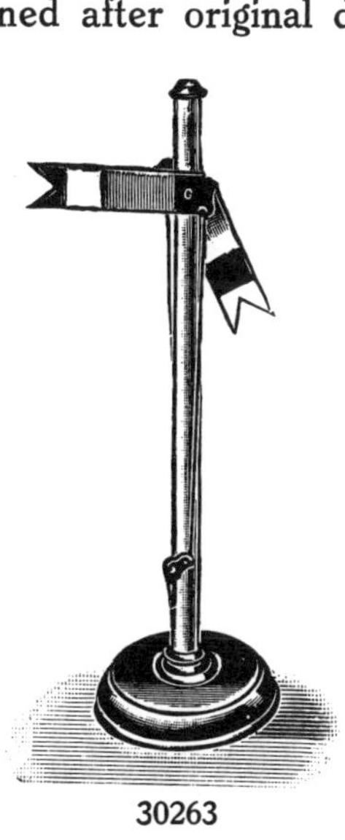
30263

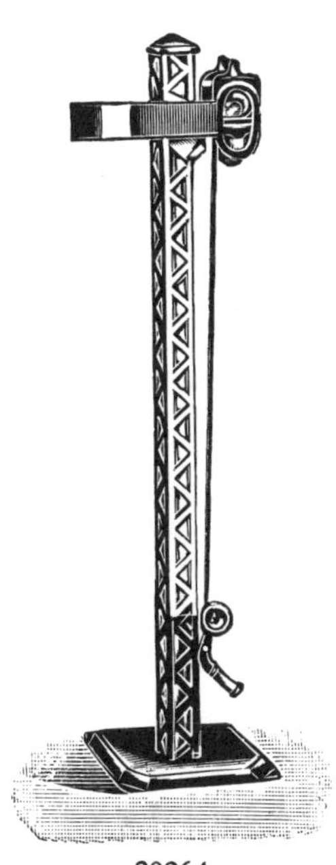
30264

30235 **Signal,** finely japanned, with movable arm, $7^{3}/_{4}$ in. high . . . . doz. **5/10**

30263 „ with 2 movable signal arms, finely japanned, best value, correct colours . . . . „ **9/8**

30264 „ Girderwork post with 1 movable signal arm, 1 lamp to light up, finely japanned, correct colours, 14 in. high . . . . doz. **19/—**

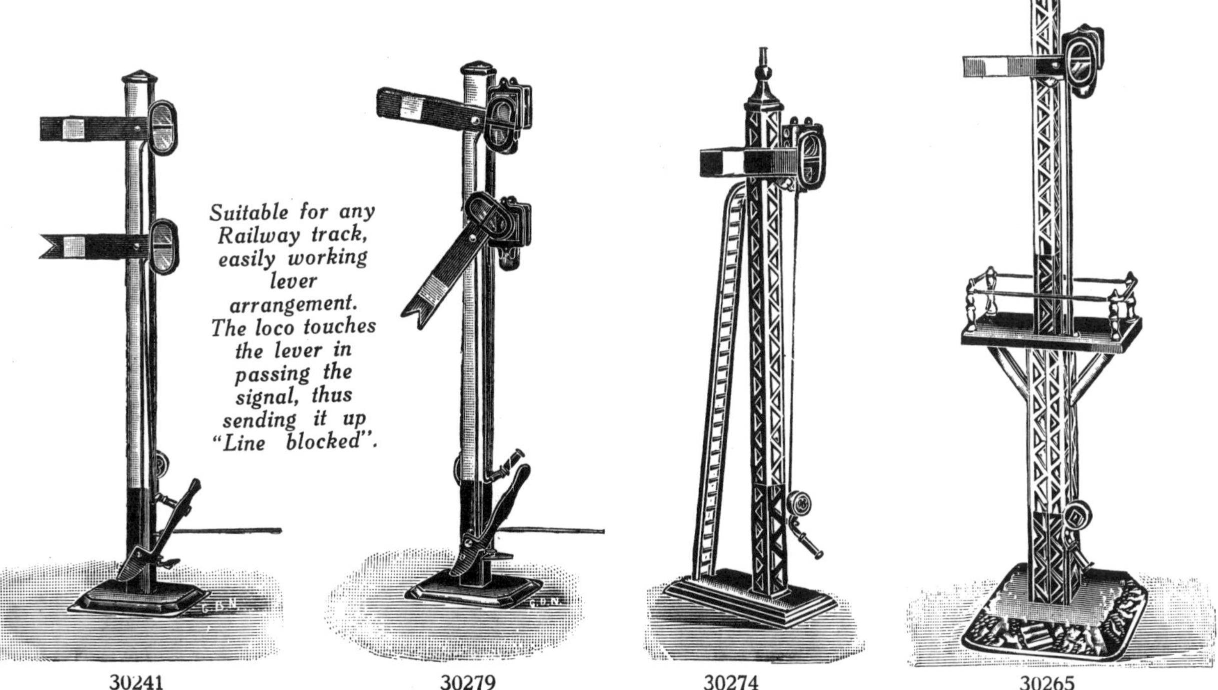

Suitable for any Railway track, easily working lever arrangement. The loco touches the lever in passing the signal, thus sending it up "Line blocked".

30241 30279 30274 30265

30241 **Automatic Signal,** finely japanned with 2 signal arms, one working automatically and one by hand. 14 in. high doz. **18/—**

30279 **Same with 2 lamps to light,** 14 in. high . . . . „ **25/6**

30274 **Signal,** finely japanned, imitation ironwork, with 1 arm, lamp fitted for burning with oil, with red and green glasses and ladder, $14^{3}/_{4}$ in. high . . . . doz. **30/—**

30265 **Signal** in fine polychrome japanning, with railed platform, 1 signal arm and 1 lamp, 18 in. high . . . „ **35/6**

English Railway Signals. Designed after original drawings.

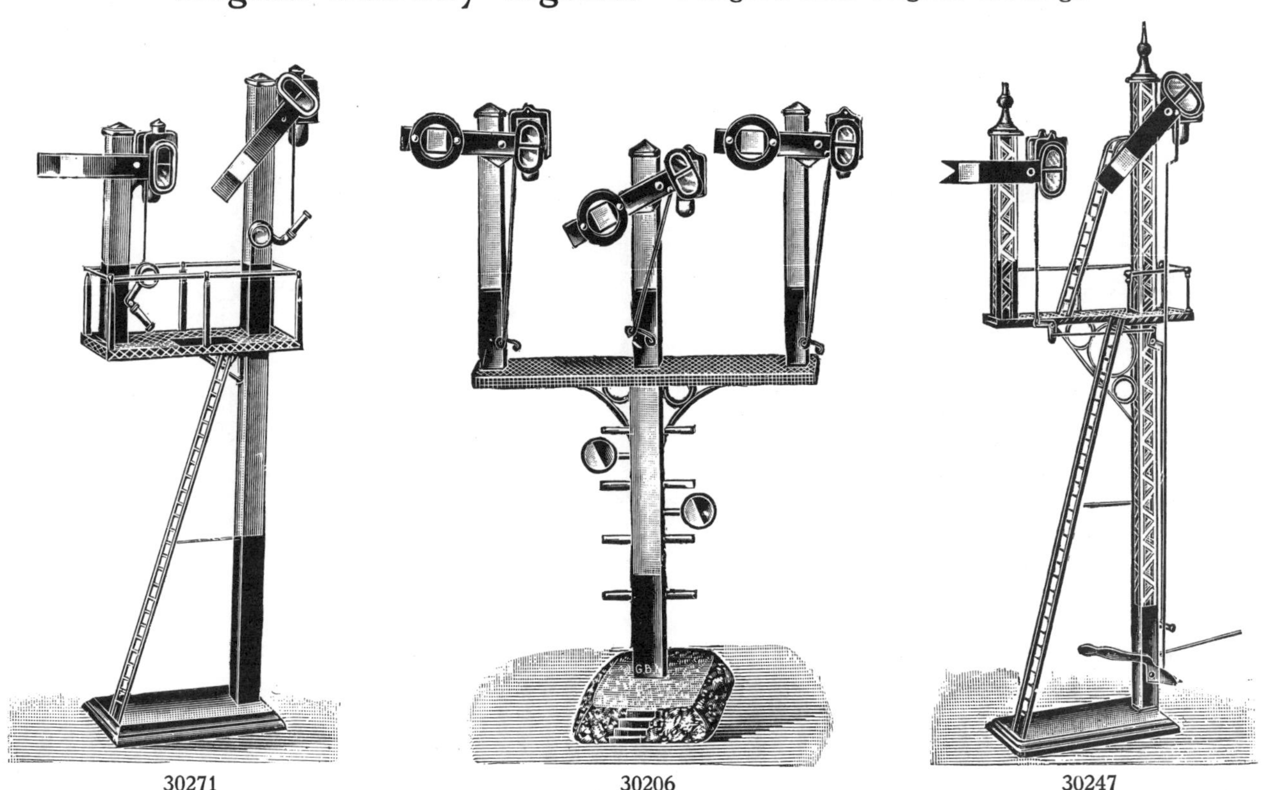

30271 30206 30247

30271 **Bracket Signal** for Main and Branch Lines, finely japanned, with 2 Signals and lamps to light, with red and green spectacles. $17^{1}/_{4}$ in. high . . . . each **5/—**

30206 **Bracket Signal,** on weighted base in fine polychrome japanning, with 3 signals on platform, signals with lamps, fitted for burning with oil, red and green glasses, with signal discs and spikes, 16 in. high, $9^{1}/_{2}$ in. wide . . each **5/10**

30247 **Bracket Signal, fine Model, correct Design,** imitation girderwork, finely japanned, with 2 signal arms one working automatically and one by hand, with 2 ladders and 2 lamps fitted for lighting, with red and green glasses, with railed platform. $19^{3}/_{4}$ in. high . . . . each **7/8**

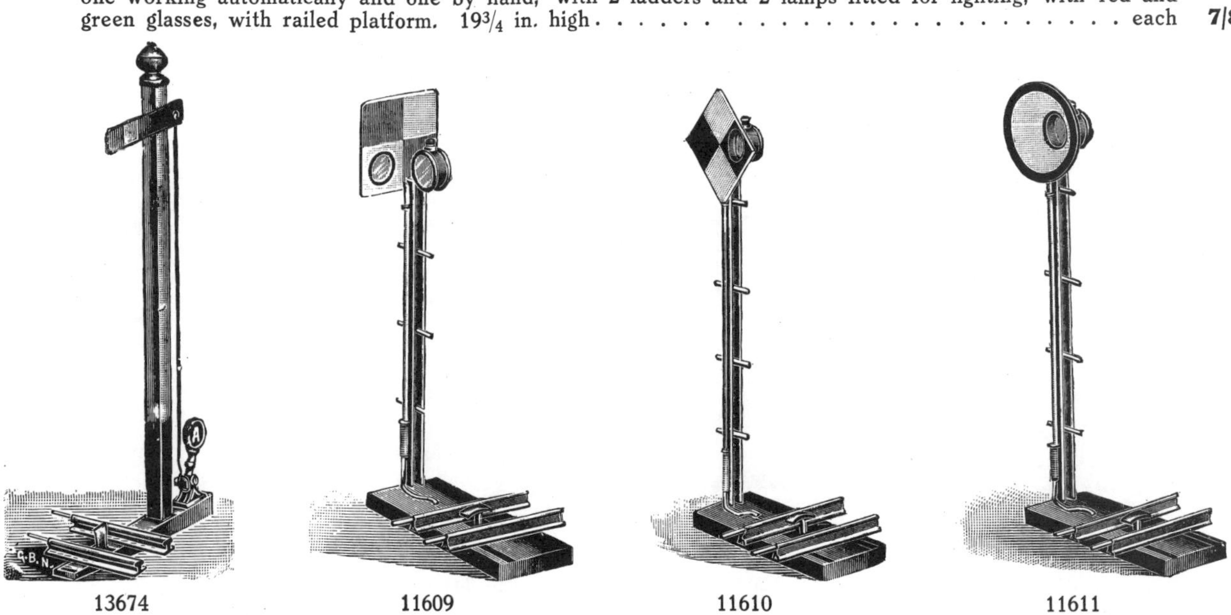

13674 11609 11610 11611

Signals connected with brake rail suitable for clockwork locomotives with brake

13674/0 to fit Gauge 0 = $1^{3}/_{8}$ in., $11^{3}/_{4}$ in. high . . . . doz. **18/—**
„ /1 „ „ „ 1 = $1^{7}/_{8}$ „ $12^{1}/_{2}$ „ „ . . . . „ **28/4**

Automatic Blocksignals, automatically working, when the train touches the rail contact, rails adjustable for all gauges.

11609 $10^{5}/_{8}$ in. high . . . . each **3/—**
11610 $10^{5}/_{8}$ „ „ . . . . „ **3/—**
11611 $10^{5}/_{8}$ „ „ . . . . „ **3/—**

Signal Gantries.

30269

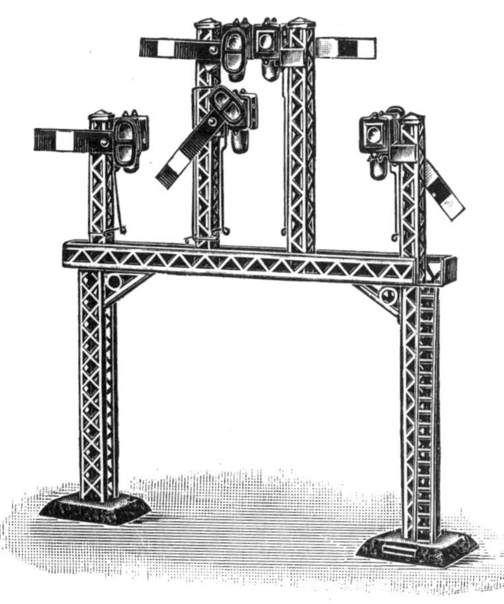

30275

30269 **Model Signal Gantry,** all imitation girderwork, finely japanned, with 2 posts, 3 signals and 3 burning lanterns, with red and green spectacles, 15 in. long, 16 in. high . . . . each **5/—**

30275 **Model Signal Gantry,** all imitation girderwork, finely japanned, with 4 posts, 5 signals and 5 burning lanterns, with red and green spectacles and ladder, $11^1/_2$ in. long, 16 in. high . . . . each **9/—**

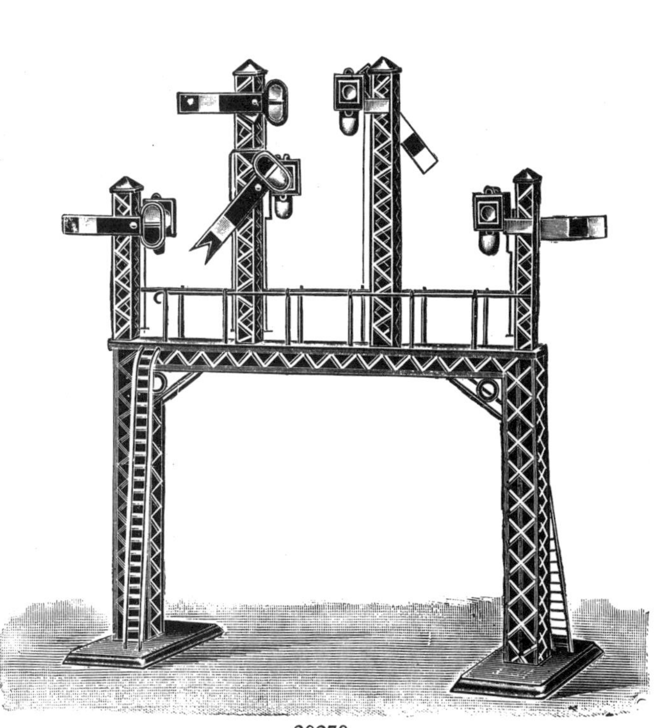

30270

30244

30270 **Model Signal Gantry,** all imitation girderwork, with 2 ladders, 4 posts, 5 signals and 5 burning lanterns, with red and green spectacles, 19 in. high, $16^1/_2$ in. long . . . . each **12/—**

30244 **Gantry Signal,** correct Design and exact colouring, extra strong finish, finely japanned, imitation girderwork, with 4 signal posts and 6 movable signal arms, 6 ladders and 6 lanterns, fitted for lighting, with red and green glasses, $18^1/_4$ in. long, $21^1/_4$ in. high . . . . each **17/—**

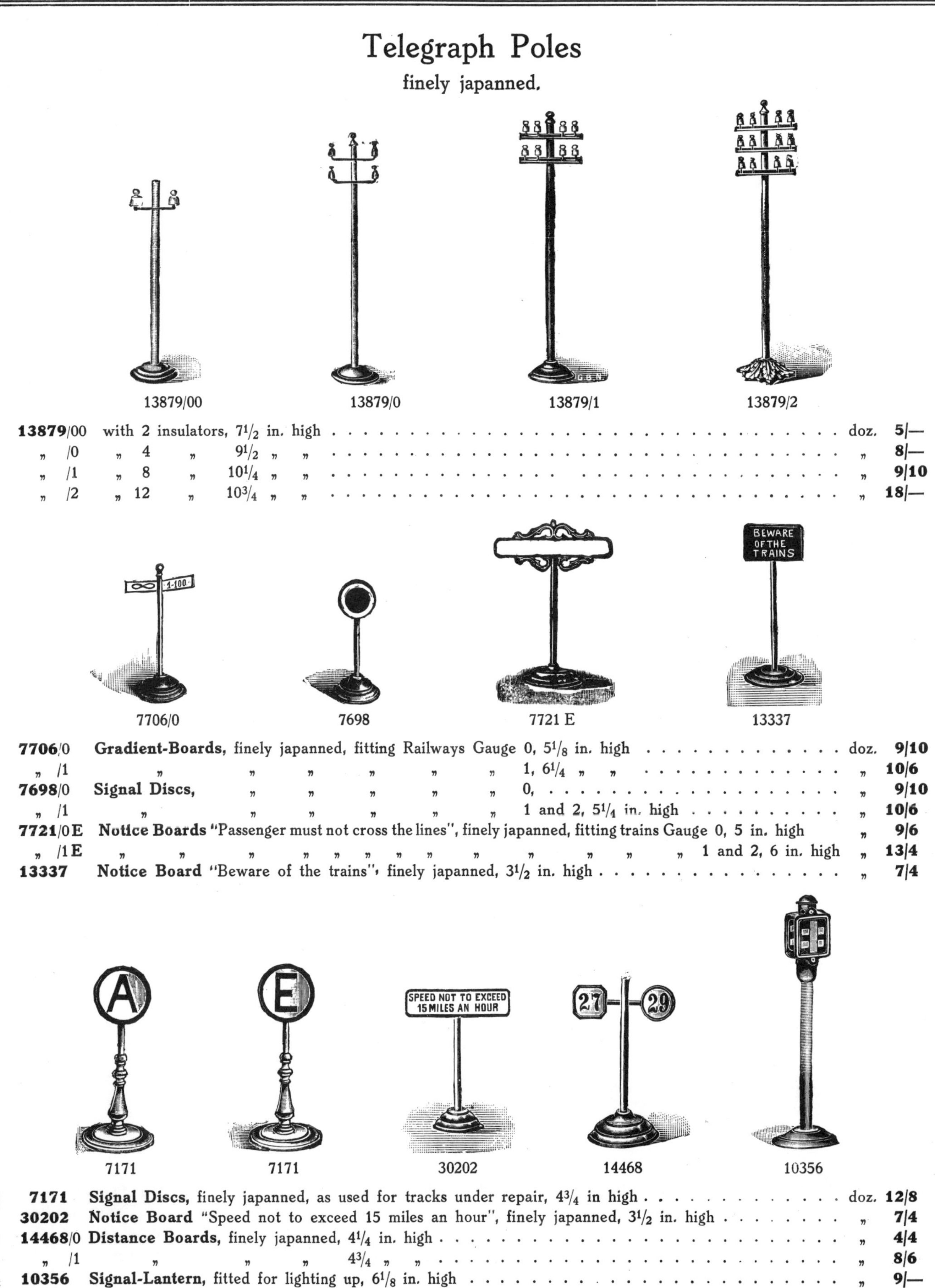

Telegraph Poles

finely japanned.

13879/00 13879/0 13879/1 13879/2

13879/00	with 2 insulators, 7½ in. high	doz.	**5/—**
„ /0	„ 4 „ 9½ „ „	„	**8/—**
„ /1	„ 8 „ 10¼ „ „	„	**9/10**
„ /2	„ 12 „ 10¾ „ „	„	**18/—**

7706/0 7698 7721 E 13337

7706/0	**Gradient-Boards,** finely japanned, fitting Railways Gauge 0, 5⅛ in. high	doz.	**9/10**
„ /1	„ „ „ „ „ „ 1, 6¼ „ „	„	**10/6**
7698/0	**Signal Discs,** „ „ „ „ „ 0,	„	**9/10**
„ /1	„ „ „ „ „ „ 1 and 2, 5¼ in. high	„	**10/6**
7721/0E	**Notice Boards** "Passenger must not cross the lines", finely japanned, fitting trains Gauge 0, 5 in. high	„	**9/6**
„ /1E	„ „ „ „ „ „ „ „ „ „ „ 1 and 2, 6 in. high	„	**13/4**
13337	**Notice Board** "Beware of the trains", finely japanned, 3½ in. high	„	**7/4**

7171 7171 30202 14468 10356

7171	**Signal Discs,** finely japanned, as used for tracks under repair, 4¾ in high	doz.	**12/8**
30202	**Notice Board** "Speed not to exceed 15 miles an hour", finely japanned, 3½ in. high	„	**7/4**
14468/0	**Distance Boards,** finely japanned, 4¼ in. high	„	**4/4**
„ /1	„ „ „ 4¾ „ „	„	**8/6**
10356	**Signal-Lantern,** fitted for lighting up, 6⅛ in. high	„	**9/—**

Arc Lamps.

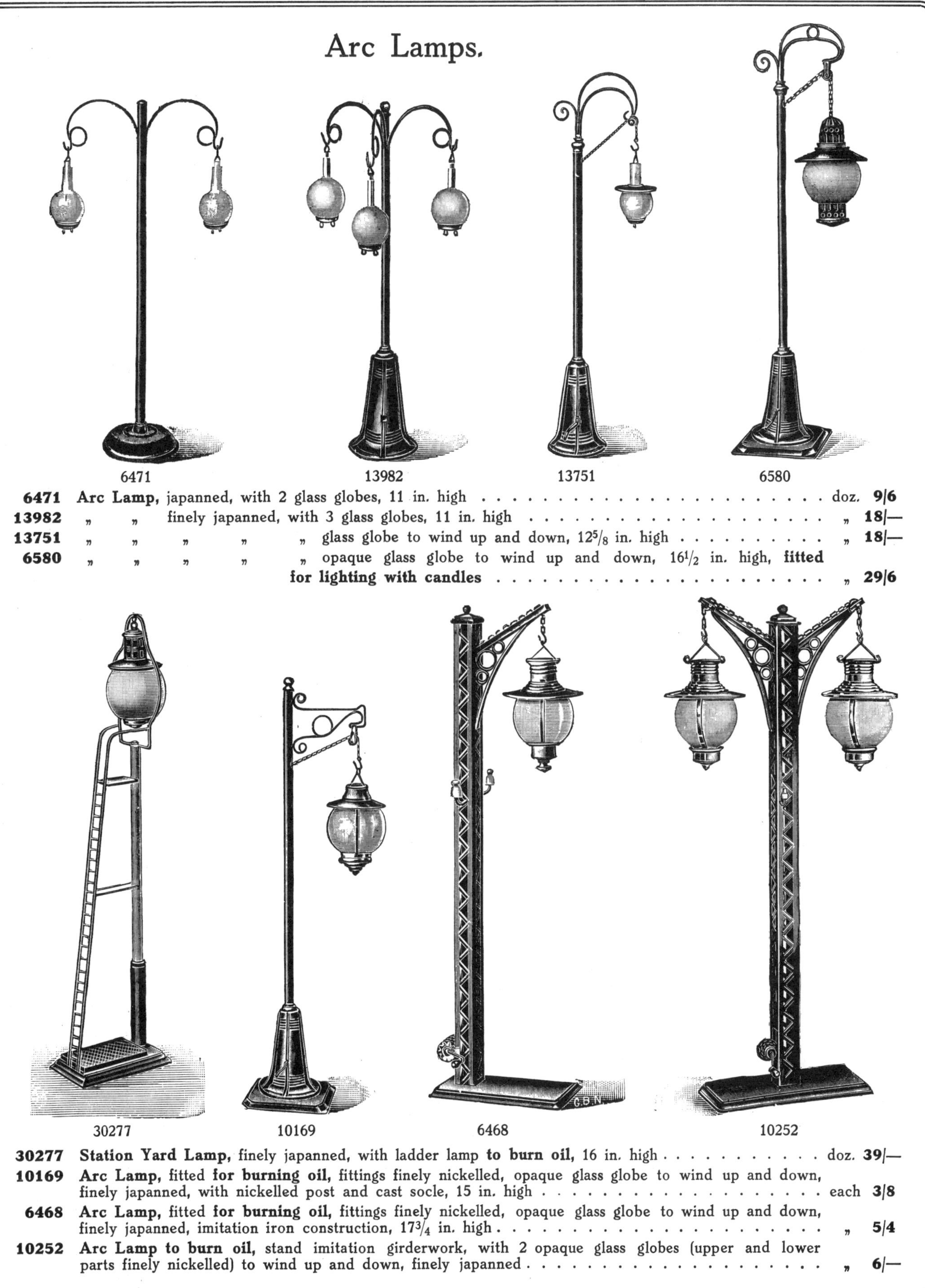

6471 **Arc Lamp,** japanned, with 2 glass globes, 11 in. high . . . . doz. **9/6**

13982 „ „ finely japanned, with 3 glass globes, 11 in. high . . . . „ **18/—**

13751 „ „ „ „ „ glass globe to wind up and down, $12\frac{5}{8}$ in. high . . . . „ **18/—**

6580 „ „ „ „ „ opaque glass globe to wind up and down, $16\frac{1}{2}$ in. high, **fitted for lighting with candles** . . . . „ **29/6**

30277 **Station Yard Lamp,** finely japanned, with ladder lamp **to burn oil,** 16 in. high . . . . doz. **39/—**

10169 **Arc Lamp,** fitted **for burning oil,** fittings finely nickelled, opaque glass globe to wind up and down, finely japanned, with nickelled post and cast socle, 15 in. high . . . . each **3/8**

6468 **Arc Lamp,** fitted **for burning oil,** fittings finely nickelled, opaque glass globe to wind up and down, finely japanned, imitation iron construction, $17\frac{3}{4}$ in. high . . . . „ **5/4**

10252 **Arc Lamp to burn oil,** stand imitation girderwork, with 2 opaque glass globes (upper and lower parts finely nickelled) to wind up and down, finely japanned . . . . „ **6/—**

Street Lamps.

9702/1
for oil

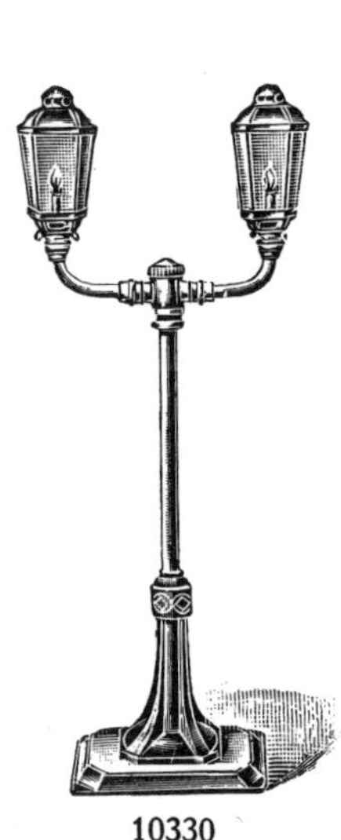
10330
for oil

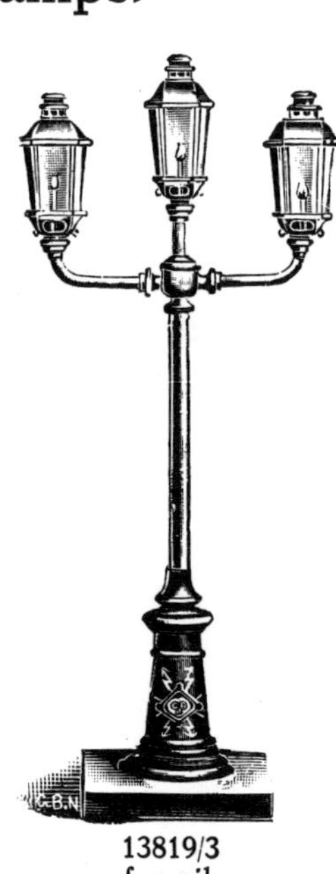
13819/3
for oil

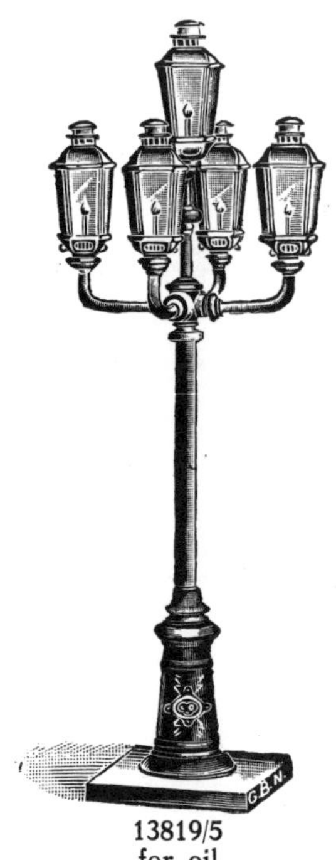
13819/5
for oil

9702/1 **Street Lamp,** to burn oil, strong cast column, with finely nickelled fittings, $7\frac{1}{4}$ in. high . . . . . . doz. **18/—**

10330 **Double Street Lamp,** to burn oil, finely japanned, on cast column, fittings nickelled, with 2 lamps, 11 in. high . . . . each **3/2**

13819/3 **Street Candelabra,** to burn oil, on japanned cast column, fittings finely nickelled, with 3 lamps, 13 in. high . . . . each **8/—**

13819/5 **Street Candelabra,** to burn oil, on japanned cast column, fittings finely nickelled, with 5 lamps, 14 in. high . „ **10/6**

Electric Arc Lamps and Street Lamps.

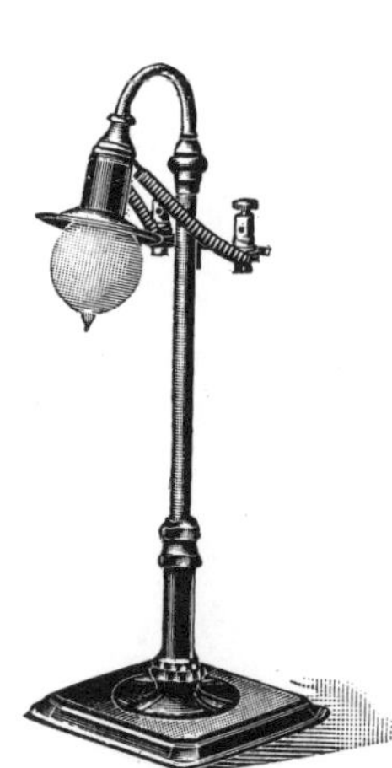

10240
for electric light

14094/1
for electric light

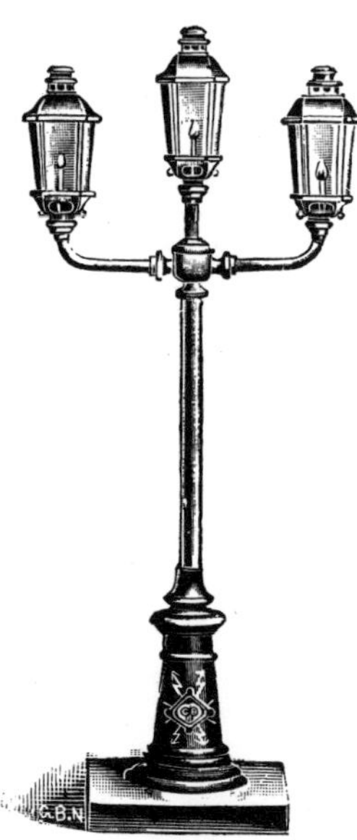
10308
for electric light

10309
for electric light

10240 **Electric Arc Lamps,** 4 Volt, finely japanned, with 1 electric incandescent lamp, $8\frac{3}{4}$ in. high . . . each **4/10**

14094/1 **Electric Street Lamp** for low current, finely japanned, with 1 electric incandescent lamp for 4 Volt, $7\frac{1}{2}$ in. high . . . . each **3/4**

10308 **Electric Street Candelabra** on finely japanned column, fittings finely nickelled, with 3 electric incandescent lamps for 4 Volt, $12\frac{3}{4}$ in high . . . . each **12/8**

10309 **Electric Street Candelabra** on finely japanned column, fittings finely nickelled, with 5 electric incandescent lamps for 4 Volt, $14\frac{1}{4}$ in. high . . . . each **19/—**

Electric Arc Lamps.

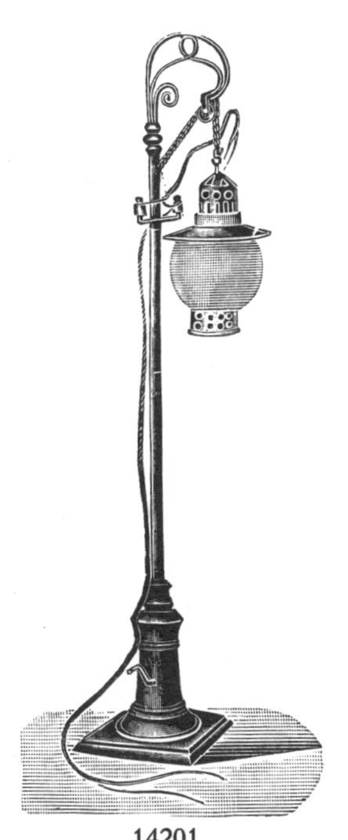
14201

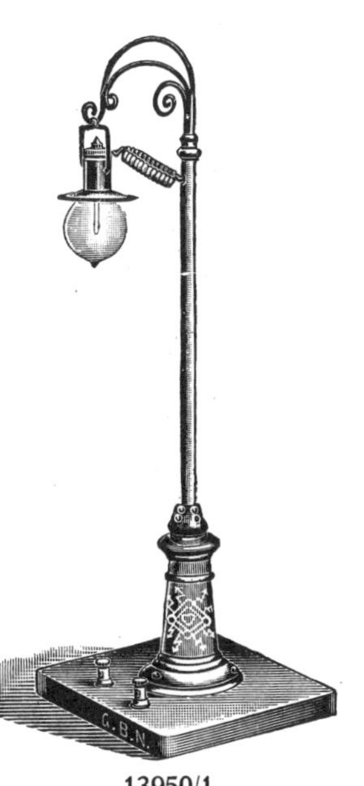
13950/1

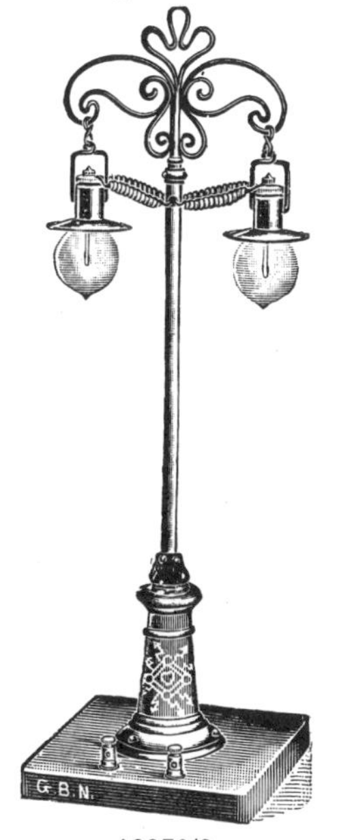
13950/2

13951/1

Electric Arc Lamps

14201	finely japanned, to wind up and down, with	1	electric incandescent lamp for	4	Volt,	$16^1/_4$	in. high	each	**4/10**
13950/1	„ „	1	„ „ „	4	„	$13^1/_2$	„ „	„	**4/10**
„ /2	„ „	2	„ „ „	4	„	14	„ „	„	**8/—**
13951/1	„ „	1	„ „ „	4	„	14	„ „	„	**6/6**

13951/2 13951/4

Electric Arc Lamps

wood base, finely polished, stand highly nickelled

13951/2 with 2 lamps each for 4 Volt, 14 in. high . . . . each **8/—**

13951/4 with 4 lamps each for 4 Volt, 14 in. high . . . . each **16/4**

Electric Arc Lamps for High Current.
For connection with the electric main of other than 110 Volt tension the globe will have to be exchanged for one fitted for the tension required.

13952 for High Current 10292 for High Current

Electric Arc Lamps for High Current

stand imitation girderwork, finely japanned on wood base, to wind up and down the lamp, which is of opaque glass in ball shape, for 110 Volt, fitted with miniature thread.

13952 $18^3/_4$ in. high each **10/6**

stand imitation girderwork, finely japanned on wood base, to wind up and down the 2 lamps, which are of opaque glass in ball shape, for 110 Volt, fitted with miniature thread.

10292 $19^1/_2$ in. high each **17/—**

Single Incandescent Lamps

fitting electric Arc Lamps, Street Lamps &c.

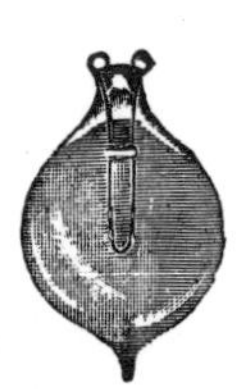
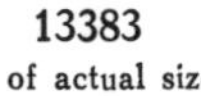

13383
$^{2}/_{3}$ of actual size

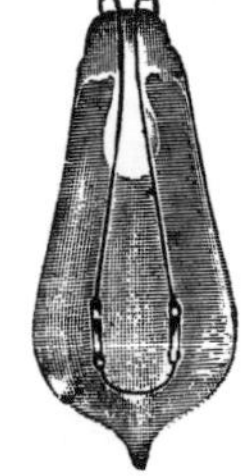

13384
$^{2}/_{3}$ of actul asize

14379/1
actual size

14379/2
$^{2}/_{3}$ of actual size

13383	**Ball-shape** with strong eyes, for $^{1}/_{2}$—10 Volt assorted	doz.	**14/—**
13384	**Pear-shape** with eyes, for $^{1}/_{2}$—10 Volt „	„	**17/—**
14379/1	**Ball-shape** with miniature thread, for 4 Volt	„	**11/6**
„ /2	„ „ „ „ „ 4 „	„	**13/8**

Sundry Accessories for Railways.

9222

9093

8581

8584

8562

8563

9222/0	**Train Tail Lights,** black japanned, with red glass, fitting Railways Gauge 0 = $1^{3}/_{8}$ in.	doz.	**4/6**
„ /1	„ „ „ „ „ „ „ „ „ 1 = $1^{7}/_{8}$ „	„	**7/4**
9093	**Discs,** finely japanned	gross	**13/6**
8581/0	**Corridor Joints** for corridor cars, cloth with metal rims, fitting Gauge 0 = $1^{3}/_{8}$ in.	doz.	**6/—**
„ /1	„ „ „ „ „ „ „ „ „ „ 1 = $1^{7}/_{8}$ „	„	**8/6**
„ /2	„ „ „ „ „ „ „ „ „ „ 2 = $2^{1}/_{8}$ „	„	**9/—**
„ /3	„ „ „ „ „ „ „ „ „ „ 3 = $2^{5}/_{8}$ „	„	**10/—**
„ /4	„ „ „ „ „ „ „ „ „ „ 4 = 3 „	„	**10/6**
8584/0	**Figures** in sitting position (passengers, engine drivers, guards, post officials &c.), about $1^{1}/_{2}$ in. high . .	gross	**18/—**
„ /1	„ „ „ „ „ „ „ „ „ „ „ „ 2 „ „ . .	„	**26/—**

12232/2

8562/00	**Clockwork Keys,** fitting locos Gauge 0 = $1^{3}/_{8}$ in. . . .	doz.	**1/10**
„ /0	„ „ „ „ 0 = $1^{3}/_{8}$ „ . . .	„	**3/—**
„ /1	„ „ „ „ 1 = $1^{7}/_{8}$ „ . . .	„	**4/—**
8563	**Point Lamp** in polycrome finish	„	**5/4**

Railway Figures.

solid pewter, finely japanned figures, sewn in fine covered box.

12232/1	containing 10 figures, box $8^{1}/_{2}$ in. long, $7^{1}/_{2}$ in. wide, doz. boxes	**19/—**
„ /2	„ 16 „ „ $10^{1}/_{2}$ „ „ $8^{5}/_{8}$ „ „ „ „	**31/6**
„ /3	„ 13 solid figures, box 11 in. long, $8^{1}/_{4}$ in. wide, complete per doz. boxes	**63/—**

Ticket Sets.

M 2964

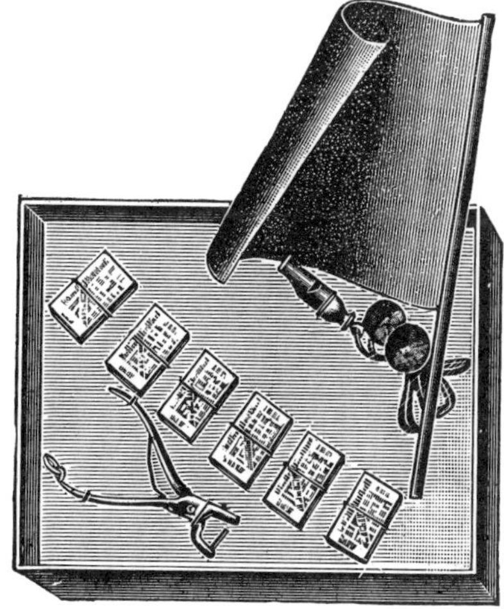

M 3301

M 596

M 2964 **Ticket Set** consisting of: bell punch, with 8 ass. tickets, sewn on card 8×6 in. . . . . doz. **9/8**

M 3301 **Conductor Set** consisting of: finely nickelled iron punch, nickelled whistle with cord and tassels, green flag and 36 tickets, sewn on card, each piece packed in strong cardboard box . . . . doz. **17/6**

M 596 **Omnibus Set** consisting of: nickelled bell punch, nickelled plate with number, and 24 tickets with various routes, packed in strong cardboard box . . . . doz. **18/—**

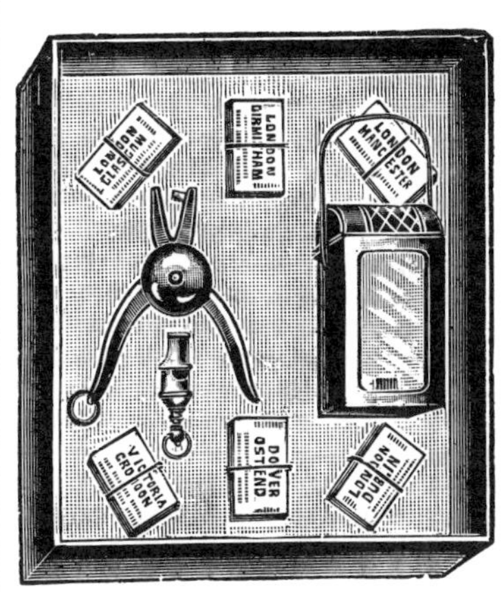

M 3112

M 3427

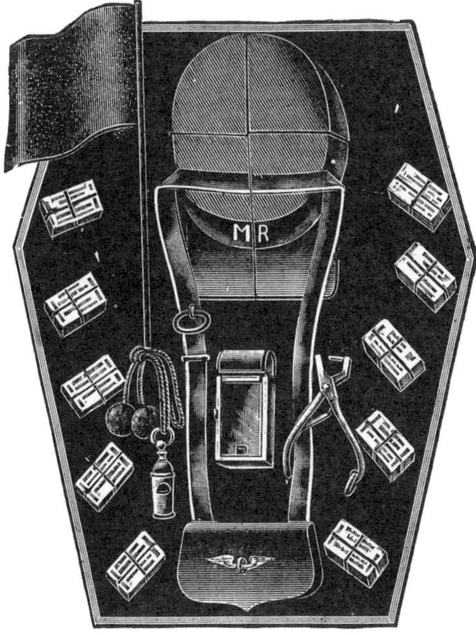

M 3300

Reliable Line. All parts of good quality.

M 3112 **Guard's Set** consisting of bell punch, lantern for candles and 24 tickets with various English routes, 9 in. long, $7^1/_2$ in. wide . . . . doz. **18/—**

M 3427 **Guard's Set** consisting of: cloth cap with initials of Railway, 1 green and 1 red flag, black japanned lamp for oil, nickelled whistle with cord and tassels sewn in red strong cardboard box . . . . each **4/—**

M 3300 **Conductor Set** consisting of cloth cap with initials of Railway, flag, black japanned lamp for candles, nickelled whistle with cord and tassels, guard's lamp, guard's pouch of imitation patent leather, nickelled iron punch and 100 tickets with various routes, all sewn on strong red cardboard . . . . each **4/6**

Guards Outfits.

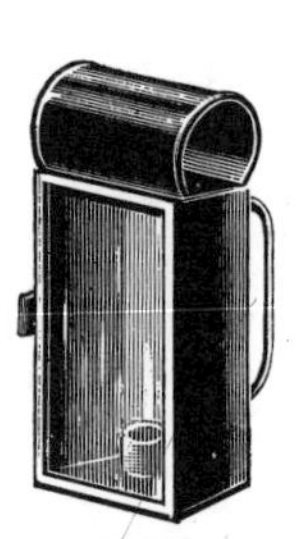
2067/22

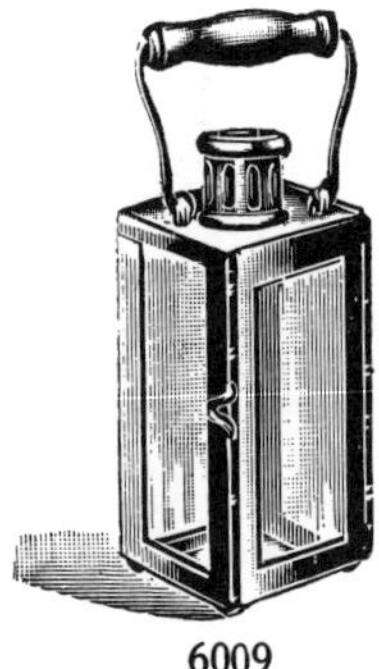
6009

7839/1 and 2

7839/3

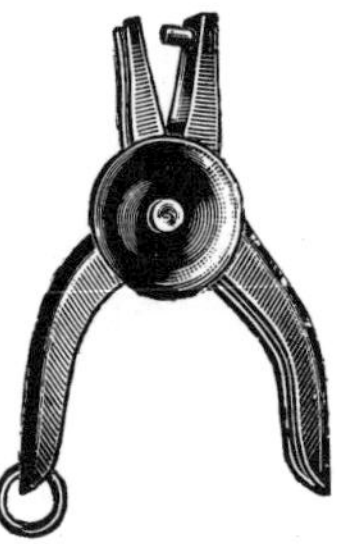
M 3183

2067/22	**Guards lamp** finely japanned, with 1 candle	doz.	**7/—**
6009	„ „ japanned, for candles, with red and green glasses	„	**9/8**
7839/1	**Ticket Punchers,** polished iron $4^1/_4$ in. long	„	**7/—**
„ /2	„ „ nickelled „ $4^1/_4$ „ „	„	**9/8**
„ /3	„ „ tinned „ $4^1/_2$ „ „	„	**3/6**
M 3183	**Bell Punch,** $4^1/_2$ „ „	„	**7/6**

8573

8190/15

8108 E

8573	**Guard's Pouch** fine red leather, strap adjustable	doz.	**10/—**
8190/15	**Guard's Whistle** finely nickelled	„	**1/10**
8108 E	**Railway Tickets**	gross	**1/—**

6817/1

"The little Railway Engineer."

an illustrated Pamphlet, showing in detail how to put together various rail formations from the simple circle to the most complicated Railway System.

The extensive track material in connection with the points, crossings, barriers and stations, watchmen's houses, signals etc. afford the child an excellent opportunity, to develop its combination talent with the help of this pamphlet.

6817/0	for Railways Gauge 0 = $1^3/_8$ in.	doz.	**5/—**
„ /1	„ „ „ 1 = $1^7/_8$ „	„	**8/6**

For orders of not less than 100 "The little Railway Engineer" can be supplied with the name of the customer, at an extra charge of 5.— per %.

CINEMATOGRAPHS

FILMS
MAGIC LANTERNS
SLIDES
STEREOSCOPES

Cinematographs.

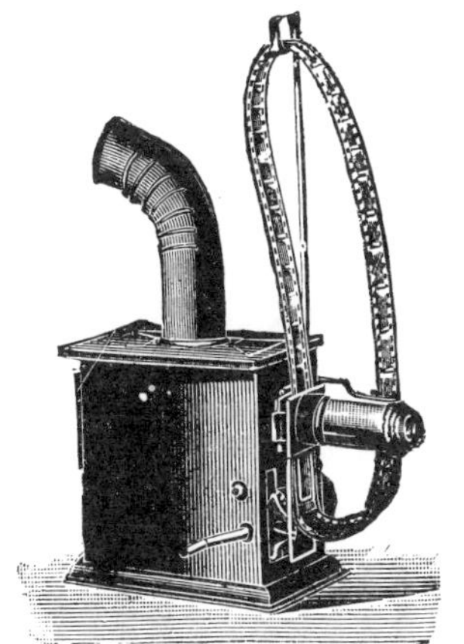

222/40 and 41/2½

Our Cinematographs are manufactured with the very best machinery and tools, which enable us to supply the mechanical parts accurately and **most reliably finished.** We further make it a special point, to use for our apparatus only the very best optics and to supply them with films of excellent effect. Owing to these advantages and the good finish and careful packing our apparatus are considered **exceptional value** throughout.

Several D. R. G. M. and D. R. Patents.

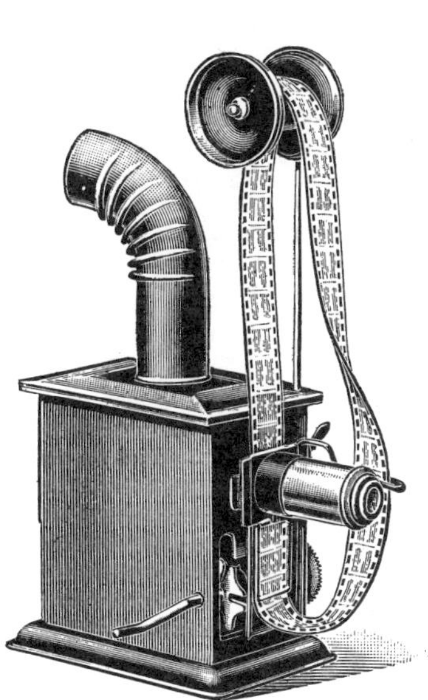

222/42/2½

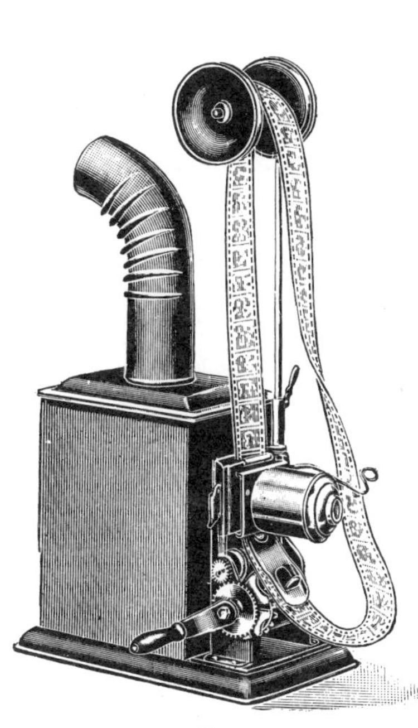

222/44/3

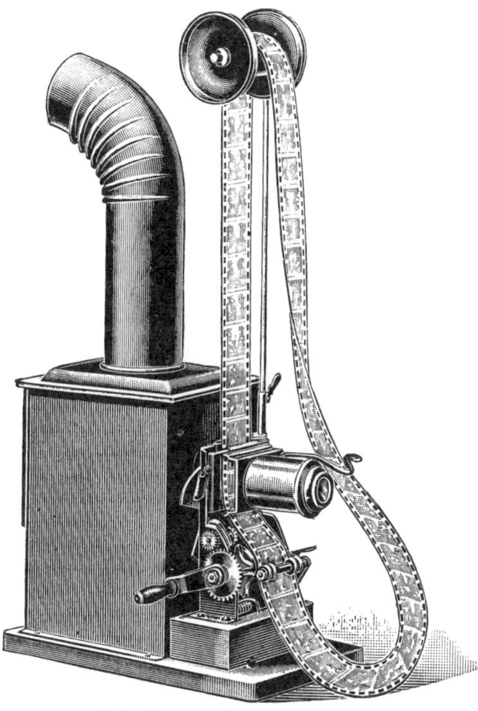

222/45/3 and 3½

with excellent optical effect, reliable film transporter, suitable for all films with "Edison Perforation" can also be used as Magic Lantern. Objective finely nickelled with condenser and 2 finely cut lenses with reflector.

No.	width for glass slides	width for wooden framed slides	Burner of the Paraffine lamp	Films supplied with each Cinematograph	Glass slides supplied with each Cinematograph	each
222/40/2½	1 in.	—	2''' flat burner	1 black film	—	**4/—**
„ /**41**/2½	1 „	—	3''' „ „	3 „ „	3 glass slides	**4/8**
„ /**42**/2½	1 „	—	2''' „ „	3 „ „	3 long „	**4/10**
„ /**44**/3	1⅛ „	—	3''' „ „	3 „ „	3 „ „	**6/10**
„ /**45**/3	1⅛ „	—	3''' „ „	3 coloured „	6 „ „	**8/6**
„ /3½	1⅜ „	—	3''' „ „	3 „ „	6 „ „	**10/6**

Cinematographs

new, excellent and reliable construction.

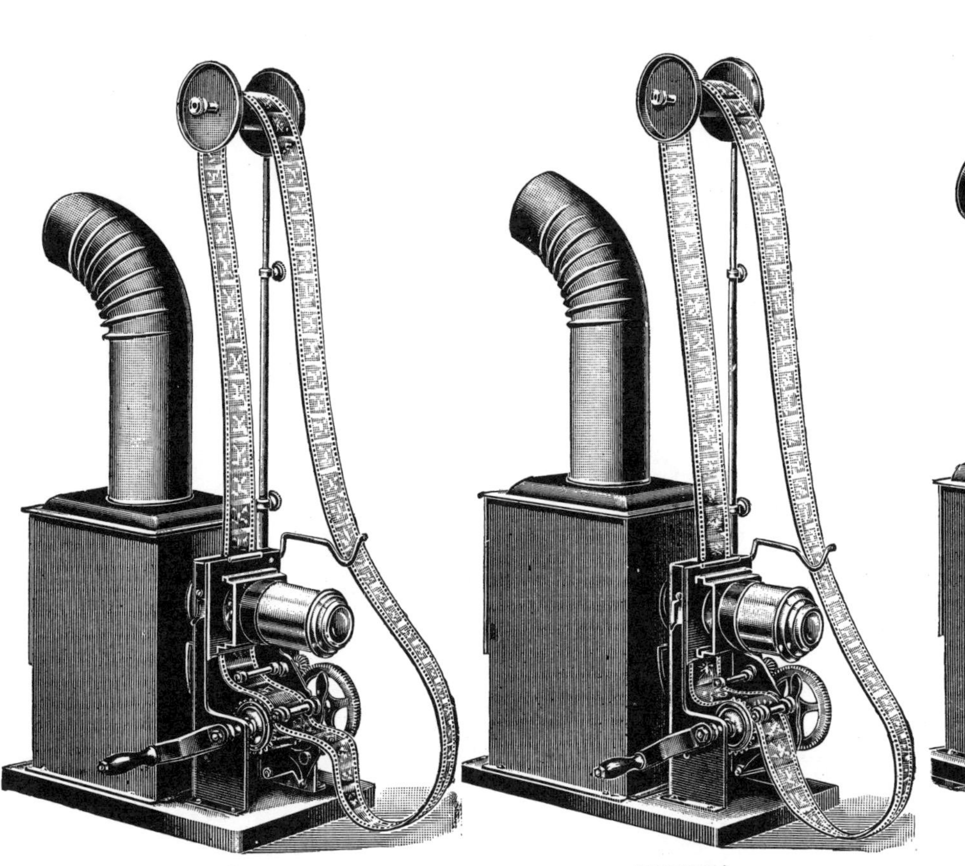

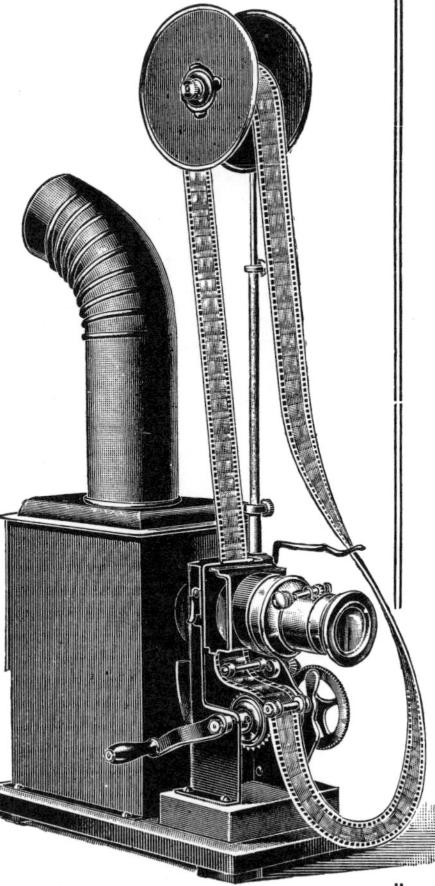

222/47/4

222/47/4½

222/47/5—7
with rack and pinion movement for focusing

with improved Dog Action Film Mechanism, almost noiselessly working, with excellent optical effect, reliable film transporter, for all films with "Edison Perforation"; can also be used as Magic Lantern.

Camera made of fine Russian iron, objective finely nickelled, with condenser, finely cut lenses with reflector, Nos. 5, 6 and 7 with rack and pinion movement for focussing.

No.	width for glass slides	width for wooden framed slides	Burner of the petroleum lamp	Films supplied with each Cinematograph	Glass slides supplied with each Cinematograph	each
222/47/4	1 9/16 in.	1 3/8 in.	5''' flat burner	2 short coloured and 1 long coloured films	12 long glass slides	**14/4**
„ /4½	1¾ „	1 9/16 „	8''' „ „	2 short coloured and 2 long coloured films	12 „ „ „	**17/2**
„ /5	2 „	1¾ „	8''' round „	6 long coloured films	12 „ „ „	**23/2**
„ /6	2⅜ „	2 „	10''' „ „	6 long coloured films 1 Photobing films	12 „ „ „	**29/—**
„ /7	2¾ „	2⅜ „	12''' „ „	6 long coloured films 3 Photobing films	12 „ „ „	**34/—**

Cinematographs

new excellent reliable construction.

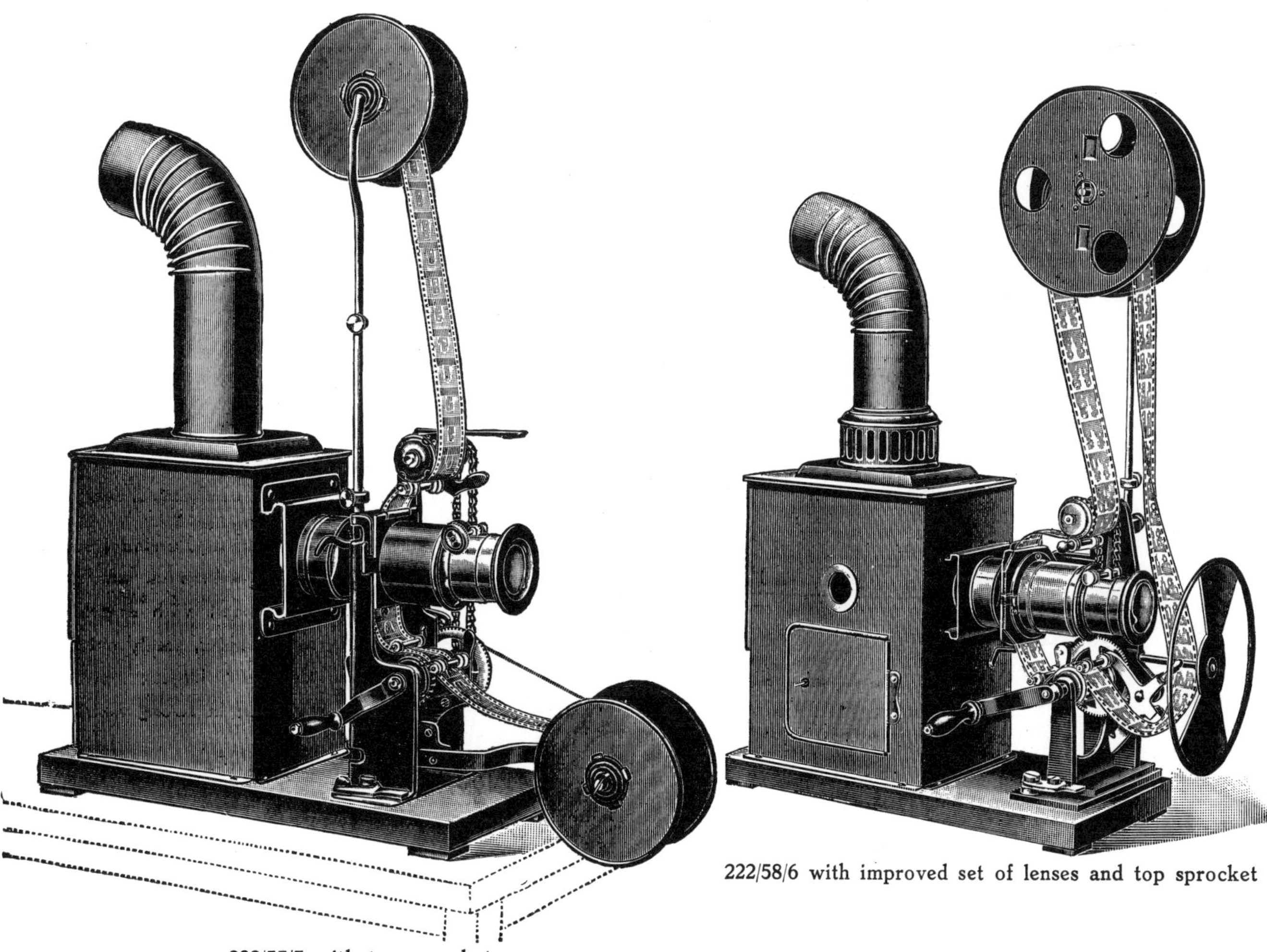

222/58/6 with improved set of lenses and top sprocket

222/57/7 with top sprocket

with improved Dog Action Mechanism, alsmost noiselessly working, with top sprocket (facilitating the smooth working of the transporter and saving the film considerably), with excellent optical effect, reliable film transporter, for all films with "Edison Perforation", with spools for winding up the films; can also be used as Magic Lantern. Camera made of strong Russian iron, objective brass finely polished, with rack and pinion movement for focussing, finely cut lenses, with reflector.

No.	width for glass slides	width for wooden framed slides	Burner of the Paraffine lamp	Films supplied with each Cinematograph	Glass slides supplied with each Cinematograph	each
222/57/7	$2^3/_4$ in.	$2^5/_{16}$ in.	12''' round burner	6 long coloured films 3 Photobing films	12 long Glass slides	**46/—**

Fine Cinematograph

with cast iron base, fine fittings, excellent construction, with improved Dog Action Mechanism, almost noiselessly working film transporter, fine objective with rack and pinion movement for focussing with double condenser 2 in. diam., and shutter.

No.	width for glass slides	width for wooden framed slides	Burner of the Paraffine lamp	Films supplied with each Cinematograph	Glass slides supplied with each Cinematograph	each
222/58/6	$2^5/_{16}$ in.	2 in.	14''' round burner	6 long coloured films 3 Photobing films	12 long Glass slides	**68/—**

222/58/7 with improved set of lenses and top sprocket.

Cinematographs

excellent reliable construction, elegant finish.

High class Cinematograph

suitable for all films with "Edison Perforation" can also be used as a Magic Lantern, for glass slides $2^3/_4$ in. wide, or wooden framed slides $2^3/_8$ in. wide, with Dog Action Mechanism, top sprocket and almost noiselessly working film transporter, with 2 large film spools, and shutter.

With 6 coloured films, 3 fine Photobing-films and 12 fine glass-slides.

Camera made of strong Russian iron, objective fine brass with rack and pinion movement for focussing, with double condenser, $2^5/_{16}$ in. diameter, finely cut objective lenses and 12''' Duplex petroleum-lamp. Packed in strong box.

222/58/7 complete . . . . . each **85/—**

222/360—363/7 with improved set of lenses and top sprocket.

High class Cinematograph

suitable for all films with "Edison Perforation", can also be used as a Magic Lantern (Projection Apparatus) for glass slides $2^3/_4$ in. wide, or wooden framed slides, $2^3/_8$ in. wide. Mechanism of cinematograph (D. R. G. M.) of new improved construction with top sprocket almost noiselessly working, with large spool for films with double condenser, $2^5/_{16}$ in. diameter and 3 finely cut objective lenses, shutter, with 6 coloured films, 3 fine Photobing films and 12 fine glass slides, finely nickelled objective with rack and pinion movement for focussing, with objective cover. Camera made of strong Russian iron. Packed in strong box.

222/361/7 with petroleum lamp (12''' duplex lamp) . each **89/—**
„ /**362**/7 with incandescent Gas lamp . . . . each **95/—**
„ /**363**/7 with electric light. „ **93/—**
„ /**360**/7 without lamp . . . „ **86/—**

Cinematographs.

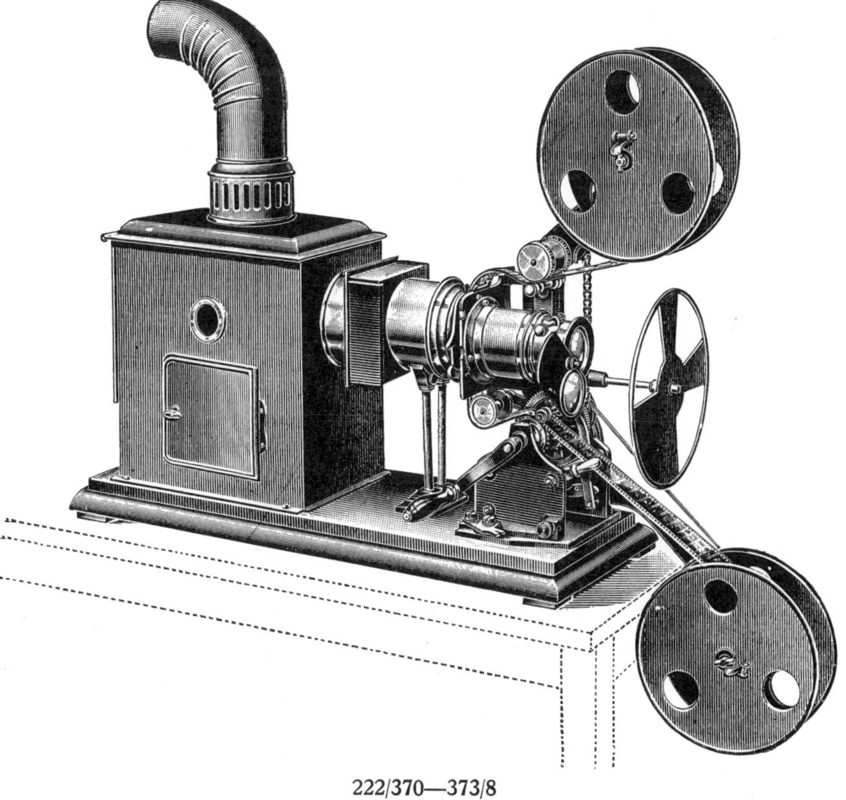

222/370—373/8

Superior Cinematograph

suitable for all films with "Edison Perforation", fitted at the same time as a Magic Lantern (Projection-Apparatus) for slides $3^{1}/_{8}$ in. wide. Mechanism of Cinematograph of new improved construction, almost noiselessly working with spool for long films, with double condenser, $2^{3}/_{4}$ in. diameter, with finely cut objective lenses, top sprocket, shutter, with 6 coloured films, 1 photo-film and 12 covered glass slides, Camera made of best Russian iron, objective finely nickelled with rack and pinion movement for focussing, with objective cover.

222/371/8 with petroleum lamp (with powerful Duplex lamp 10''') . . . each **108/—**

222/372/8 with incandescent gas each **110/—**

222/373/8 with electric light each **110/—**

222/370/8 without lighting arrangement . . each **100/—**

222/380—382/9

Superior Cinematograph

suitable for all films with "Edison Perforation" fitted at the same time as a Magic Lantern (Projection-Apparatus) for slides $3^{1}/_{2}$ in. wide. Mechanism of Cinematograph of new improved construction, almost noiselessly working with automatical arrangement to wind films up and down, with double condenser, $3^{1}/_{8}$ in. diameter, with finely cut objective lenses, shutter, with 6 coloured films, 1 photo-film and 12 covered slides, Camera made of best Russian iron, mounted on fine polished wooden table, objective finely nickelled, with rack and pinion movement for focussing, with objective cover.

222/381/9 with petroleum lamp (with powerful Duplex burner 12''') . . each **140/—**

222/382/9 with incandescent gas each **150/—**

222/380/9 without lighting arrangement . . each **135/—**

Cinematographs.

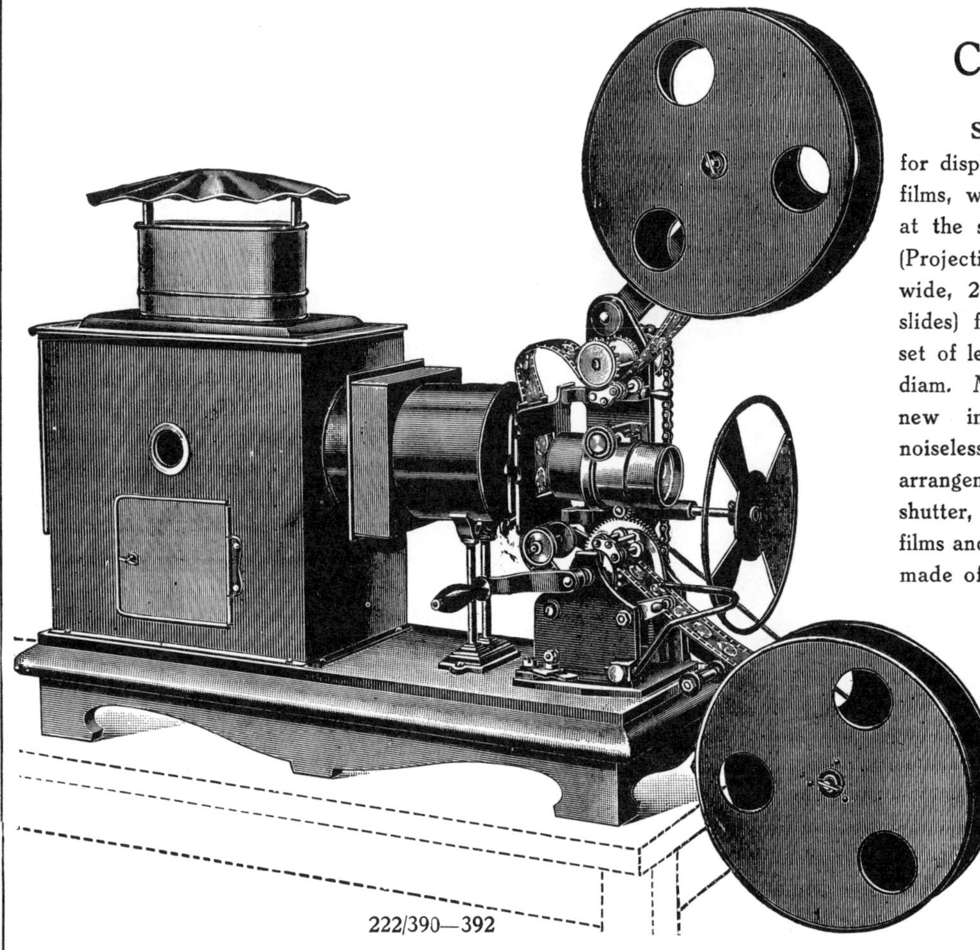

222/390—392

Superior Cinematograph

for display on a larger scale, fitting all films, with "Edison Perforation", fitted at the same time as a Magic Lantern (Projection Apparatus) for slides $3^7/_8$ in. wide, 2 objectives (one for films and slides) finely finished with achromatic set of lenses, double condenser, $3^1/_2$ in. diam. Mechanism of Cinematograph of new improved construction, almost noiselessly working, with automatical arrangement to wind films up or down, shutter, with 6 coloured films, 3 photo-films and 12 covered glas slides. Camera made of best Russian iron, mounted on polished wooden table.

222/391/10
with petroleum lamp, powerful Duplex burner 14'''
each **200/—**

222/392/10
with gas lamp, each **206/—**

222/390/10
without lighting arrangement
each **192/—**

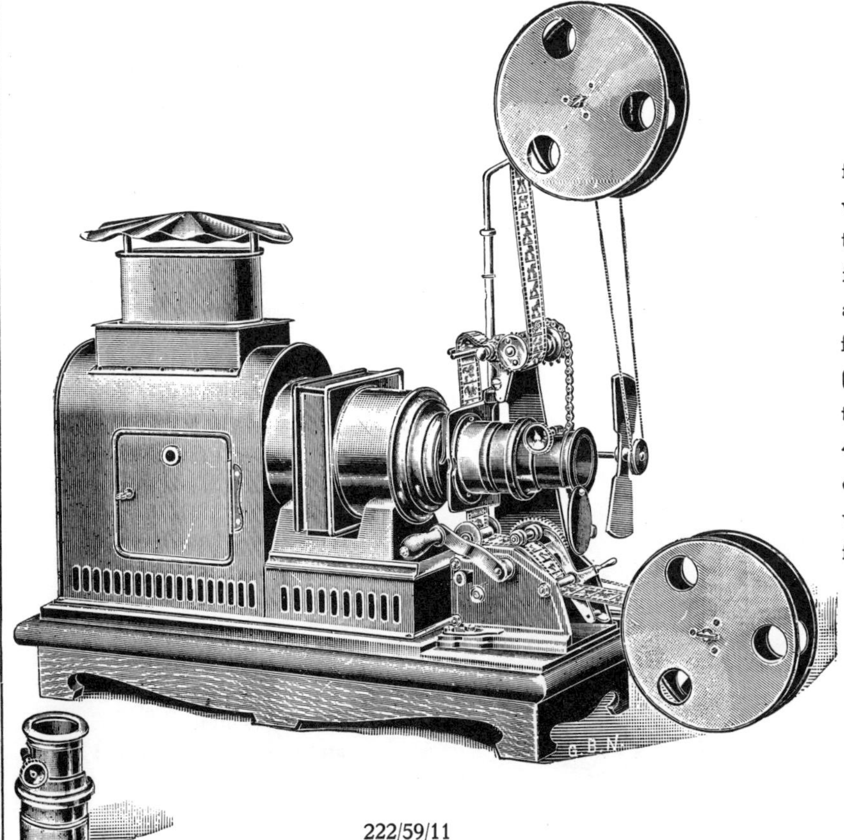

222/59/11

Superior Cinematograph

for display on a larger scale fitting all films, with "Edison Perforation" fitted at the same time as a Magic Lantern (Projection Apparatus) for slides or Photogramms $4^3/_8$ in wide, with adjustable brass front piece, 2 objectives, finely finished, with achromatic set of lenses (1 objective each for the Cinematograph and the Projection Apparatus), double condenser 4 in. diameter, Mechanism of the cinematograph of new improved construction, almost noiselessly working, with mechanical arrangement to wind films up and down, without lighting arrangement, without films and without slides.
each **266/—**

For lighting fittings see pages 246—251 and following.

Cinematographs.

222/95

Superior Cinematograph (only suitable for moving pictures not for the projection of slides) very strong and reliable finish, large lantern body of extra strong sheet iron, objective with very good sets of lenses, Mechanism of the cinematograph (D. R. G. M.) of new improved construction, with automatic arrangement to wind films up and down, fitting all films with "Edison Perforation".

222/95 with double condenser, $2^3/_4$ in. diam. (without illuminant and without films) . . . . each **108**/—

„ /96 same Cinematograph but larger, superior finish with achromatic set of lenses, with double condenser, $3^1/_2$ in. diam. (without illuminant, without films) . . . . each **163**/—

Extra Large Theatre Cinematograph.

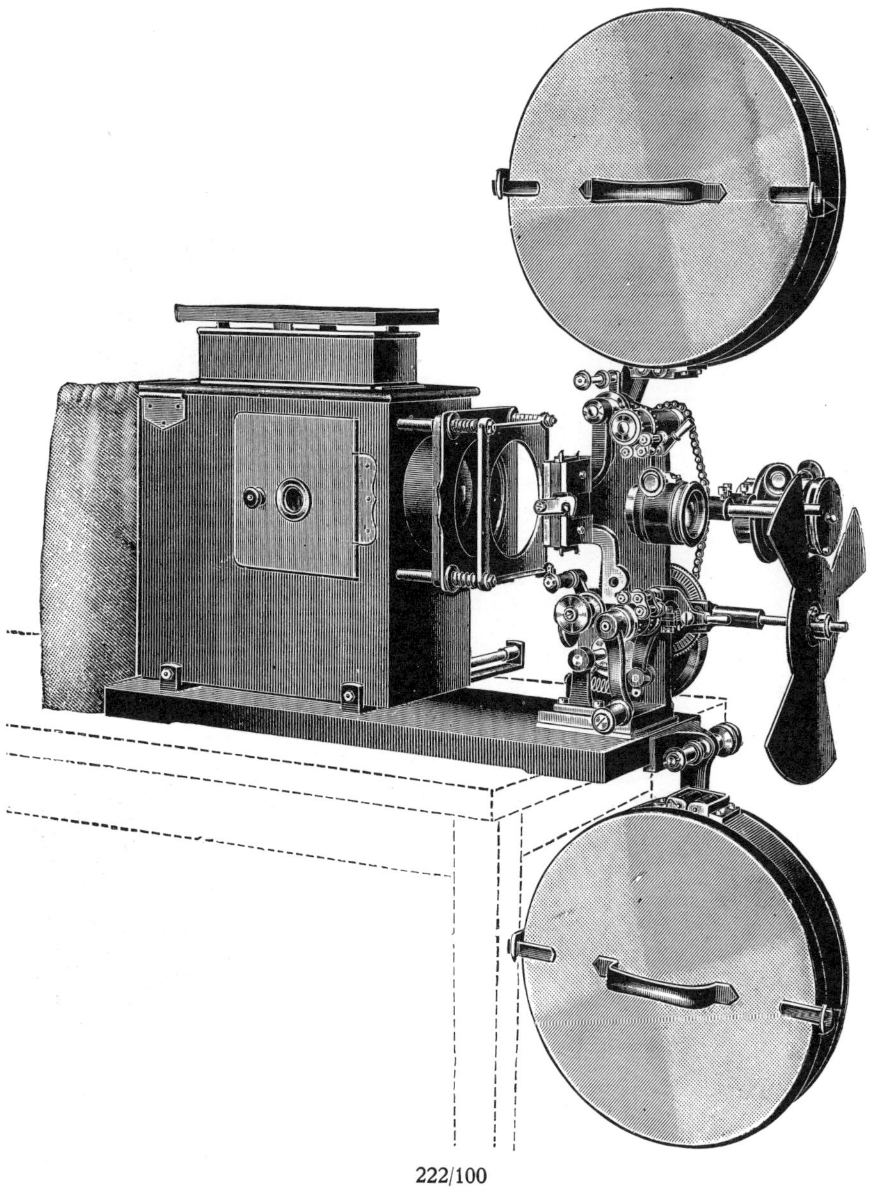

222/100

Cinematograph of excellent workmanship, suitable for projecting glass slides, $3^1/_4 \times 3^1/_4$ in., equally well suited for travelling exhibitors as well as schools, clubs and home use. — Lantern body of strong sheet iron welded together, sliding on 2 runners to centre it either with cinematograph mechanism or magic lantern lenses; permitting the projection of films or lantern slides in quick succession. Condenser 4 in. diameter, perfectly aircooled, solid stage of cast iron plates. Mechanism of the Chinematograph-Apparatus (transporter) is of the best make throughout. All spindles are made of highgrade steel and ground into bearings of sufficient size to give maximum wear. A heavy flywheel (with groove for belt if motor is used) insures an even, steady running of the machine. The propulsion of the film is controlled by the wellknown dog-action, which has proved itself as being the simplest and most substantial action of its kind, exerting the least possible wear on the film. The working is almost noiseless in spite of the rapidity with which the film is pulled down. The masking of the film, by means of a micrometerscrew, may be done while the machine is running. The film is secured to the sprocket wheels by double sets of jockey rollers. Top and bottom film spools are encased in fireproof sheetiron spool boxes. The film and lantern objectives are both fitted with an achromatic set of lenses, easily removable; the focal length of the former is $3^1/_8$ in., that of the latter is $7^1/_8$ in. At a distance of abt. 16 ft. from the screen pictures of about 7 ft. size are obtained. — Further details, sketches and measurements may be had on application.

222/100	without illuminant	each	**416/—**
12548/10	Apparatus for winding or rewinding of the film	„	**19/—**

222/502

222/502 Extra large

Theatre Cinematograph

with electric motor.

This apparatus is especially designed for use in permanent electric theatres. It is fitted to a perfectly rigid frame, constructed of steel girders. The cinematograph mechanism and magic lantern objective are conveniently arranged on this table. The lantern body of strong welded sheet iron is suitable for any kind of illuminant. The quick conversion of the cinematograph into a magic lantern is facilitated by a sliding arrangement which easily permits the centering of the body with the **cinematograph or the magic lantern objective.** The film mechanism is mounted on a solid cast iron base and is driven by an electric motor situated under the table, the speed of which may be regulated as desired, by a resistance.

Two sets of **achromatic objectives** will be fitted to suit the wishes of the buyer with respect to size of picture and distance of projection.

It is absolutely essential to state voltage and kind of current when ordering.

Detailed sketches and measurements may be obtained on application.

Special advantages:

1. Quickest possible "pull down", consequently flickerless pictures.
2. Absolutely rocksteady pictures.
3. Least possible wear of film.
4. Perfectly smooth running.
5. Easy handling.
6. Minimum amount of friction in all working parts.

No apparatus leaves the factory without having stood a test of 6 hours continuous working.

Price complete as per description without illuminant . . . . each **762/—**

For illuminants fitting above apparatus see pages 224—228 of this list.

Prices of single parts:

12548/1	**Operating stand,** rigid steel frame, wooden top	each	**136/—**
„ /2	**Lantern body,** with condenser and stage	„	**76/—**
„ /3	**Cinematograph** with supply and take-up sprockets, objective and filmtrap	„	**380/—**
„ /4	**Objective** for **magic lantern**	„	**47/6**
„ /5	**Electro motor** for high current	„	**57/—**
„ /6	**Resistance** for motor	„	**30/6**
„ /9	**Spool box,** extra large, with safety rollers	„	**19/—**
„ /10	**Rewinding apparatus**	„	**19/—**

Special quotations for films on application.

Cinematographs

in connection with Electric Motor to work the film transporter; with excellent optical effect, reliable film transporter, suitable for all films with "Edison Perforation" fitted at the same time as Magic Lantern. — Film transporter with new dog-action mechanism, working almost noiseless, objective with rack and pinion, with condenser, 2 finely cut objective lenses with reflector, with Petroleum lamp (round burner) and fitted for electric light by means of dry battery.

No.	Width of glass slides	Width of wooden framed slides	Burner of Petroleum lamp	Price each
222/401	2 in.	$1^3/_4$ in.	8''' round burner	**38/—**
„ **/402**	$2^3/_8$ in.	2 in.	10''' round burner	**47/—**
„ **/403**	$2^3/_4$ in.	$2^3/_8$ in.	12''' round burner	**58/—**

Additions:

to No. 222/401 6 long coloured films and 12 long glass slides
„ „ „ /402 6 long coloured films, 1 Photobing film and 12 long glass slides
„ „ „ /403 6 long coloured films, 3 Photobing films and 12 long glas slides

The Dynamograph

A Cinematograph with a Dynamo attached,

automatically generating its own light.

A small **high capacity Dynamo** is mounted next to the Film Mechanism and is connected with it by means of a very fast High-Speed Cogwheel Gear. By turning the handle of the Film Mechanism the Dynamo is worked, thus generating with the aid of a Metallic Filament Bulb an intensive, white light.

For focussing and other purposes a small auxciliary battery is fitted into the base of the apparatus and this battery can be used, whenever the handle of the mechanism is not being turned.

Suitable for all Films with "Standard Edison Perforation". The Apparatus can also be transformed into a Magic Lantern, in which case **the Dynamo also provides the necessary light.**

222/300 **"Dynamograph"**, with fine objective with cog wheel for focussing, 6 coloured films, 12 glass slides, 2 in. wide, **metal filament** electric lamp, 4 Volt, 0,3—0,4 ampère . . . . each **52/—**

222/303 **Same Apparatus, but larger,** with strong mechanism superior workmanship, fine objective and large film spool, 6 Photobing Films, 1 original photographic film, 1 series (3 slides of Photobing slides, $2^3/_8$ in. wide, fitted for wooden framed slides of 2 in. width), **metal filament** electric lamp, 5 Volts, 0,3—0,4 ampère and with 2 large film spools, lower and upper spool for automatically winding up the film . . . . . . each **98/—**

222/303

10207/4 **Spare lamp with metallic filament,** fitting 222/300; 4 Volt, 0,3—04 ampère . . . . . . doz. **17/—**

„ /5 „ „ „ „ „ „ 222/303; 5 „ 0,3—04 „ . . . . „ **21/8**

New Series of Films

with "Edison Perforation", fitting all Cinematographs.

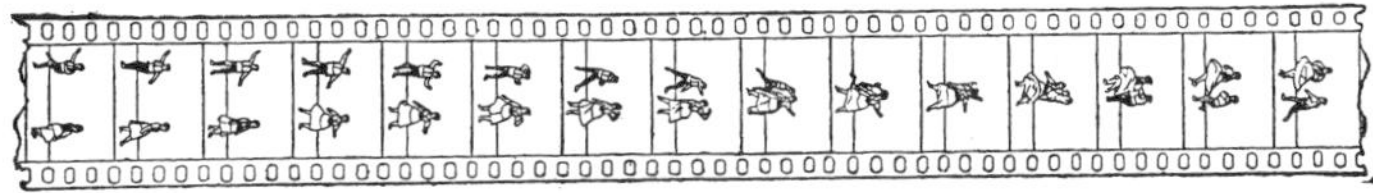

6663 Black (lithographed) Films

abt. 22 in. long, with "Edison Perforation" (1 series = 3 strips) . . . . per doz. series **9/10**

Series I.
1. Dancer and Dancing Girl
2. Comedian
3. Conjurer

Series II.
1. Boxer
2. Performing Dogs
3. Gymnast

Series III.
1. Child with Cat
2. Lady Conjurer with Pigeon
3. Dancing Girl

Series IV.
1. Cuirassier
2. Wrestler
3. Rope-Walker

Series V.
1. Conjurer and Lady
2. Children with Cat
3. Street Scene

Series VI.
1. Steerable airship flying
2. Ski-runner
3. Girl playing Diabolo

Series VII.
1. Clown.
2. Horse racing on the ski-rink
3. Boxer

Series VIII.
1. Recruit
2. The stupid dog
3. Monkey at Breakfast

Series IX.
1. Man balancing a hat
2. Gymnastics on a horse
3. Circus.

Series X.
1. The inattentive pupil
2. Boys on see-saw
3. Magician with bird-cage

Series XI.
1. The interrupted Tea
2. Throwing Bricks
3. Comical Street Cleaner

Series XII.
1. Professional Pianist
2. Fencer on horse-back
3. Loading stones

Series XIII.
1. Cyclist
2. Nigger Dance
3. Too much of a good thing

Series XIV.
1. Athletes
2. Teasing
3. In the Air

Series XV.
1. Balloon Ascent
2. Exercises
3. A Mishap

Series XVI.
1. Fencing
2. Breakable
3. Sleigh Ride

Series XVII.
1. The clumsy Clown
2. The little needle-eye
3. Hard Wood

Series XVIII.
1. Keep to be right
2. Sport on the Ice
3. Journey in an Airship

6666 Fine coloured Films

each abt. 22 in. long, with "Edison Perforation" (1 series = 3 strips) . . . . per doz. series **13/—**

Series I.
1. The Rehearsal
2. The Dancer
3. The Merry Clowns

Series II.
1. Marionette
2. Magician with Flowerpot
3. Performing Dogs

Series III.
1. Acrobats.
2. Serpentine Dancer
3. Child with Cat

Series IV.
1. Shortsighted Seamstress
2. Magician
3. Children with Cats

Series V.
1. Magician with Egg
2. Spanish Dancer
3. Somersault

Series VI.
1. Steerable airship in movement
2. Clown-Tricks
3. Ski-runner

Series VII.
1. Professional Pianist
2. Teasing at the fountain
3. Throwing Bricks

Series VIII.
1. Girl playing diabolo
2. Fencing lesson
3. Lady conjurer with birdcage

Series IX.
1. The disturbed Tea-party
2. Loading stones
3. Circus

Series X.
1. Boys on see-saw
2. Comical street-cleaner
3. Monkey having breakfast

Series XI.
1. Gymnastics on the horses
2. Ski-racing with horse
3. Boxer

Series XII.
1. Pierette
2. Fencer on horse-back
3. Clown

Series XIII.
1. Magician
2. Nigger Comedian
3. Bleriots Trial flight

Series XIV.
1. In a Motor Car
2. Tyrolese Dance
3. Flying Week in Rheims

Series XV.
1. The large Drum
2. Hurdle Race
3. Russian Dance

Series XVI.
1. Ring o' Roses
2. Airship Z VII over the Royal Train
3. A Bet for an Apple

Series XVII.
1. Boxing his ears
2. The Juggler
3. The Recruit

Series XVIII.
1. Tapping the barrel
2. Niggers dancing
3. A Cycle Tour

Films can neither be taken back nor exchanged

6638 Fine long, coloured Films

each **abt. 3½ ft. long,** with Edison Perforation . . . . per series = 6 films doz. box. **50/—**

Series I.
1. The Rehearsal
2. The Magic Head
3. The Merry Clowns
4. Approaching Train
5. Dancer
6. Children with Cats

Series II.
1. Battleship
2. Jumping artists
3. Boys at the Spring
4. Acrobats
5. Magician with Flowerpot
6. Child with Cat

Series III.
1. Skater
2. Magic Performance
3. Tramway
4. Hard Work
5. The Shortsighted Seamstress
6. Living Wheelbarrow

Series IV.
1. Clown Tricks
2. Carriage Drive
3. Marionette
4. Spanish Dancer
5. Winter Games
6. Monkey at Breakfast

Series V.
1. Somersault
2. Performing Dogs
3. The industrious Cooper
4. Pierette
5. Card-players
6. Magician with Rabbit

Series VI.
1. Magician with Egg
2. Playing Ball on the Ice
3. Throwing Bricks
4. Serpentine Dance
5. Boys Bathing
6. Somersaults

Series VII.
1. Boxer
2. Lady conjurer with bird-cage
3. Baker and Professor
4. Gymnastics on the horse
5. The stupid dog
6. Horse racing on the ski-rink

Series VIII.
1. Ski-race
2. Hare chasing
3. Fencing lesson
4. A Bet for an apple
5. Comical street cleaner
6. Loading stones

Series IX.
1. Training
2. Ski-runner
3. Professional pianist
4. Circus
5. Steerable airship in the air
6. Motor race

Series X.
1. Leaving the Ski-course
2. Teasing at the fountain
3. Tobogganing
4. The clumsy waiter
5. Balloon race
6. Cycling

Series XI.
1. The Recruit
2. Man balancing top hat
3. Clown
4. The inattentive pupil
5. The vain cook
6. Boys on see-saw

Series XII.
1. Winter sport
2. Pantomime
3. Fencer on horse-back
4. The disturbed Tea-party
5. Girl playing diabolo
6. Kettle-drummer

Series XIII.
(Aeronautic Series.)
1. The Airship Fleet leaving the port
2. Blériot's Trial Flight
3. Zeppelin's Flight
4. Parceval III and Zeppelin III
5. Flying Week at Reims
6. Zeppelin flying over the Imperial Train

Series XIV.
1. Discovery of the North Pole
2. Hunting Polar Bears
3. Returning from the North Pole
4. Cake Walk
5. Quick Artist
6. Box on the Ears

Series XV.
1. Bavarian Beer
2. The strong Athlete
3. On the Spree
4. Caravan
5. Officers Race
6. Tyrolese Dance

Series XVI.
1. Playing round the Tree
2. Sailing Yacht in a Storm
3. Ring o' Roses
4. Russian Dancer
5. Morocco Horseman
6. The Magic Matchbox

Series XVII.
1. At the Magicians
2. The Astronomer
3. Theet extracted
4. The bewitched building blocks
5. American Dancer
6. Colour Artist

Series XVIII.
1. Fairy Tale
2. " "
3. " "
4. Coronation Procession I
5. " " II
6. " " III

6667 Photo-Bing-Films

directly produced from Original Photographs, **about 43 in. long,** finely finished, with Edison Perforation. . doz. box **32/—**

Excellent Substitute for Photofilms especially suitable for Cinematographs with Petroleum lamps.

Special value **Per Series = 3 Films.** ***Excellent effect.***

Series I.
1. Fine Tobacco
2. Mimic
3. Hunger ist the best sauce

Series II.
1. Still-life
2. In the Joiner's Workshop
3. Smoke Artists

Series III.
1. Mandoline Player
2. Good conversation
3. A bad Cigar

Series IV.
1. Minstrel
2. In the Barber's shop
3. A pick-pocket

Series V.
1. Mimic
2. Knife grinder
3. Sack-race

Series VI.
1. In mortal fear
2. Sand-thrower
3. Gardener

Series VII.
1. The impudent servant
2. Great friends
3. Having a drop

Series VIII.
1. Quarelling rag-pickers
2. A wealthy aunt
3. Winter-sport

Series IX.
1. The Battle of Snowballs
2. Winter Sport with Horse
3. The perfect Cook

Series X.
1. The refreshing Drink
2. The clean Rabbit
3. Dancer betaing the Drum

Series XI.
1. Ski Runner
2. Exciting Telephone Conversation
3. Gymnast on horse-back

Series XII.
1. Accrobatic Tricks
2. Grandfather sneezing
3. The Professor's Speech

Series XIII.
1. The merry Tailor
2. Lady with Dog
3. A bad Drink

Series XIV.
1. Ballet Scene
2. Hurdle Race
3. Five o'clock Tea

~~~~~~ ***Films can neither be taken back nor exchanged.*** ~~~~~~
~~~~~~

Original Photographic Films

in tin boxes.

8861 Original Photo-Films

(produced from original photographs), endless band of **abt. 39½ in. length,** with "Edison-Perforation" . . . . . each **2/—**

List of pictures for photographic films 8861 of 39½ in. length

1. Playing Children
2. Somersaults
3. Bewitched
4. Good Dog
5. Ring ó Roses
6. Punished naughtines
7. Sweethearts
8. Lady tobogganing
9. Punished Treachery
10. Monkey as Gymnast
11. Disturbed idyllic scene
12. For Love
13. The Magician
14. Merry Dance
15. Infantry Parade
16. Dangerous Ride
17. Drill on Board
18. Tobogganing
19. Cross-country ride
20. Start of a Caravan
21. Magic Basket
22. Good Wind (sailing boat)
23. Family-Ball
24. Blue-Jackets' Boat race

Trickfilms:

25. The bewitched Building blocks I.
26. „ „ „ „ II.
27. Match game (Housebuilding)
28. Match game (Scales)
29. „ „ (The Gnome)
30. Lightning Artist
31. Obstinate horse
32. Somersaults
33. Jumping Dog
34. Rococo Dance
35. The magic cloth
36. The large Hat

This Collection is continually enlarged. Rights for alteration of the subjects reserved.

8862 Original Photo-Films

endless band of **abt. 2 meters length,** 1 meter = 39½ in., with "Edison Perforation" . . . . each **4/—**

1. Bull fight
2. A Dance on board
3. The punished Water photograph
4. A Boxer Rising
5. Baby drinking
6. Schinkenklopfer
7. Afternoon tea
8. The idyllic swan scene
9. Our St. Bernhard dog
10. Parseval Balloon
11. The merry Blue Jackets
12. A Record flight

8865 Original Photo-Films

abt. 5 meters long, (1 meter = 39½ in.), finely finished, with "Edison Perforation" . . . . each **10/—**

1. Swimming School (header)
2. On the Müggelsea
3. Balloon drive
4. African Dance
5. Steam Boat on the Seine
6. Departure of a Life Boat
7. Panorama of Blankenese
8. In Japan (comical)
9. On the Skittle ground (comical)
10. Cavalry
11. Railway
12. Contortionist

8870 Original Photo-Films

abt. 10 meters long, finely finished, with "Edison Perforation" (1 meter = 39½ in.) . . . . each **22/6**

1. Macurka
2. Ballet out of "Stradella"
3. Hunting scenes
4. Surprised (detective-picture-piquant)
5. Swimming School (header)
6. Arrival of a Train in Dar-es-Salaam
7. Rescue of ship wrecked persons
8. The first Cigarette
9. In the open bath
10. On the Sprea

8915 Extra long, fine Original Photo-Films

(produced from Original photographs)

abt. 15—30 meters long, with "Edison Perforation" (per meter = 39½ in.) . . . . per meter **2/—**

1. Naval Battle . . . . abt. 16 meters
2. Torpedo-Attack . . . . „ 17 „
3. Funny Story . . . . „ 18 „
4. Incendiary (tragical). . . . . „ 18 „
5. Watering the Streets (comical) . . . . . „ 18 „
6. Caught in a trap (comical) . . . . . . abt. 19 meters
7. Bewitched Jun (comical) . . . . „ 29 „
8. Battle Ship in stormy sea . . . . „ 23 „
9. Carneval-Procession . . . . „ 16 „

8940 Second Hand Films: New (not worn out) films, sections out of long theatre films abt. 5, 10, 15, 20 and 25 meters long, rich assortment in humoristical films, nature scenery, scenes of theatre pieces (Dramas) in tin boxes . . . . per meter **—/8**

In ordering these sections please state the length required per meter Regarding the subjects particular wishes will be considered, as far as the stock permits.

Films can neither be taken back nor exchanged

Lighting Fittings (Illuminants)

for Cinematographs, Magic Lanterns, Projection Apparatus.

One of the most important part of a Cinematograph, Magic or Post Card Lantern is the Illuminant. The clearness, stereoscopic effect and the size of the pictures all depend upon the Illuminant. It is of course a well known fact, that at a given distance from the screen, a strong light will produce much better results, than a relatively weak light. We wish to call special attention to the fact, that with Cinematographs, where only the oblong section out of the circular set of lenses comes into play, the pictures are only $^1/_2$ or $^1/_3$ as large, if compared with the round pictures shown by the same apparatus when used as a Magic Lantern.

For table regarding the use of the single illuminants see page 251.

Petroleum Lighting.

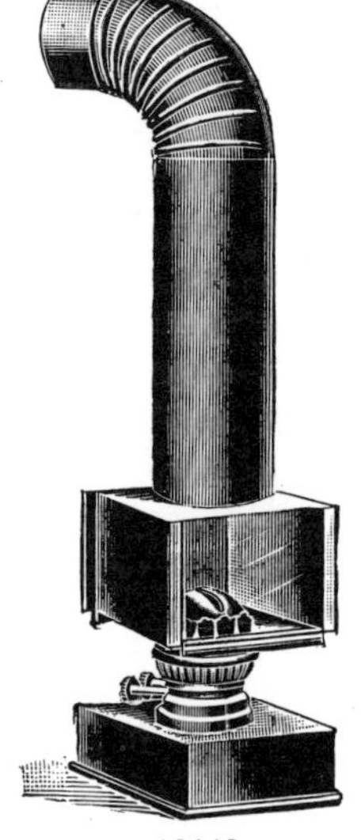

10168

For Magic Lanterns and Sciopticons of middle size the petroleum light is most suitable, less however for larger Cinematographs. The size, which may be obtained with slides ranges up to abt. 2 meter diameter; with a cinematographic projection abt. 1,20 meter. The lighting power of the following petroleum lamps varies according to kind and size, with proper use of the reflector from 60 to 100 candle power.

Duplex Petroleum Power Lamp with 2 flat wicks, each to be moved separately

10168/10	with 10''' duplex burner	each	**8/—**
„ /12	„ 12''' „ „	„	**9/6**
„ /14	„ 14''' „ „	„	**11/8**

Triplex Petroleum Power Lamp with 3 flat wicks, each to be moved separately

10455		each	**22/8**

Wicks extra fitting above lamps

6444/10	10'''	per doz. meter (1 meter = abt. 39$^1/_2$ in.)	**4/10**
„ /12	12'''	„ „ „ (1 „ = „ 39$^1/_2$ „)	**5/8**
„ /14	14'''	„ „ „ (1 „ = „ 39$^1/_2$ „)	**6/8**
6709/8	Triplex lamp wick	„ „ „ (1 „ = „ 39$^1/_2$ „)	**5/8**

Hard glasses extra fitting above lamps

6445/10	fitting 10168/10	doz.	**2/6**
„ /12	„ „ /12	„	**3/—**
„ /14	„ „ /14	„	**4/—**

Incandescent Gas Light.

This kind of illuminant is more suitable (like the petroleum light) for displays in smaller circles and does not come into consideration for displays on a larger scale. Trough the intense white light the pictures when using incandescent gas light will come out somewhat clearer than with petroleum light. The size of picture obtainable is abt. 2 meter diameter for slides; for cinematographic projection about 1,20 meter.

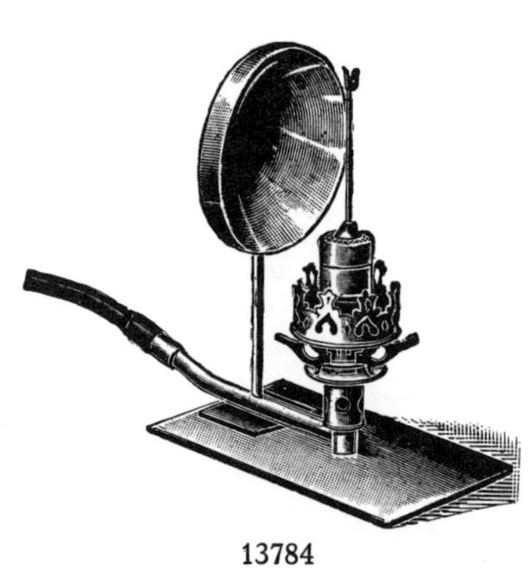

13784

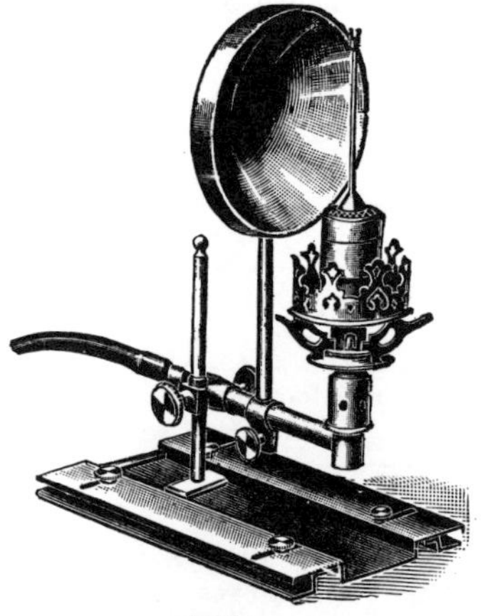

13778

13784 **Incandescent Gas Lamp** for projection purposes, not adjustable, mounted on tin base (3$^7/_8$ in. wide, long 4$^3/_4$ in. long) without glass chimneys or incandescent mantle . . . each **9/6**

13778 **Fine Incandescent Lamp** for projection purposes, finely finished and nickelled burner and reflector adjustable in every direction. Bottom plate adjustable for width, without glass chimney or incandescent mantle . . each **17/6**

Illuminants.

Electric Incandescent Lamp.

The usual incandescent lamps having only small candle power are not very well suitable for projection purposes; particularly the usual incandescent bulbs as used in the household do not suit the purpose well, in consequence of the arrangement of the filaments. It is therefore advisable to use for projecting purposes lamps of from 32—100 c. p. and either use the special Focuslamps stocked by us or good Metallic filament lamps.

10245

"Universal Lamp"

to fit into the chimney socket of cinematograph and projection apparatus for electric bulb, adjustable reflector, with set screw, screw and plug connection and about 7 ft. flexible wiring

10245 without bulb . . . . each **9/2**

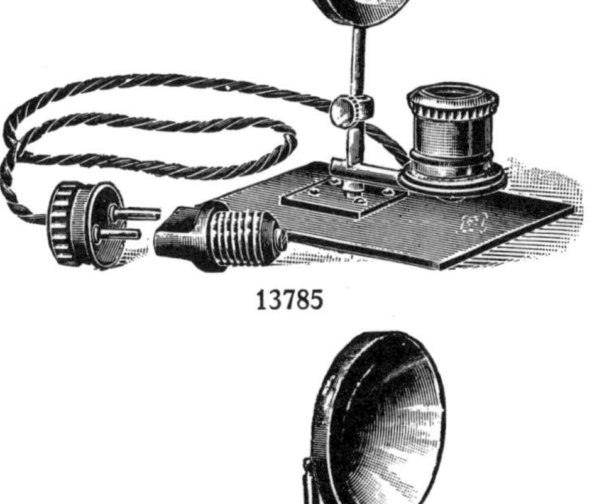

13785

Electric Incandescent Lamp

for Magic Lanterns and Cinematographs adjustable to any height with reflector finely nickelled on japanned metal base with abt. 7 feet flexible wiring, with screw and plug contact

13785 without globe . . . . . . each **7/10**

Fine Electric Incandescent Lamp

for projection, finely finished and nickelled, with abt. 7 feet flexible wiring and screw contact. The width of the bottom plate can be altered the reflector is adjustable. The lamp can be raised or lowered and fixed at any distance from the condenser

13779 without globe . . . . . . each **20/8**

13779

13788/110 **Extra Globes** (Focus Lamps) specially suitable for projection purposes for 110 Volt . . . . each **2/8**

„ **/220** „ „ „ „ „ „ „ „ „ „ 220 „ . . . . „ **2/8**

"Nernst Lamps".

These Lamps are specially suitable for projection purposes on account of their very intensive white and concentrated light and give a capacity of about 50 candlepowers and more.

Electric „Nernst Lamp", most excellent projection lamp, clear, white and very intensive light, with reflector and abt. 7 feet flexible wiring.

13068/110 for continuous current, 110 Voltage . . . . each **27/4**
„ **/220** „ „ „ 220 „ . . . . „ **27/4**
10172/110 „ „ „ 110 „ . . . . „ **27/4**
„ **/220** „ „ „ 220 „ . . . . „ **27/4**

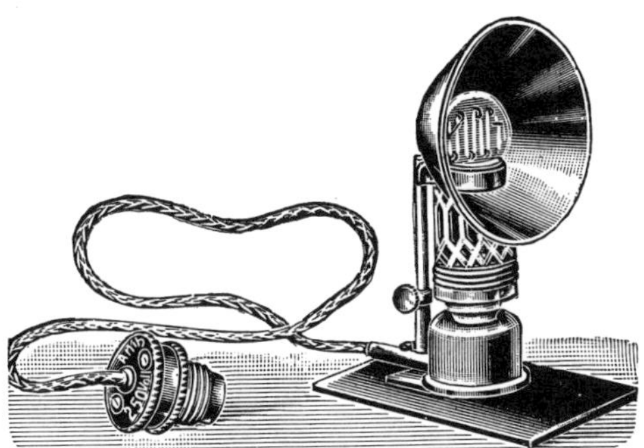

13068 and 10172

10190 **Electrical Lighting Outfit** with dry battery and metallic filament bulb, 4 Volt, to raise or lower, as the height of the objective may require, suitable for small and middle sized projection apparatus and cinematographs . . . . each **5/2**

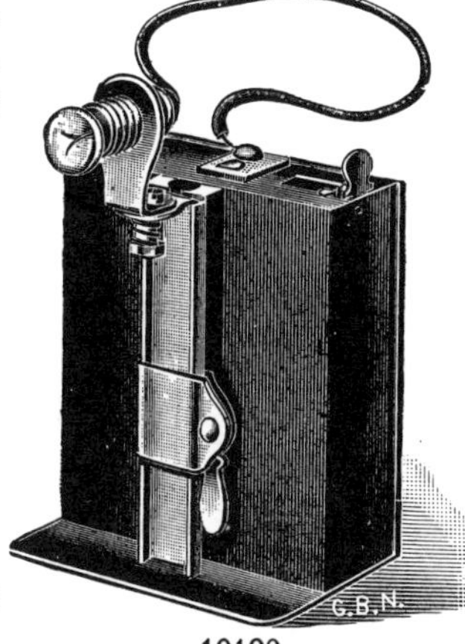

10190

Illuminants

for Cinematographs and Projection Apparatus.

Acetylene Light.

Acetylene-illuminants are particularly suitable for projection purposes of any kind on acct· of their very intensive white and concentrated light. The size of pictures obtainable ranges for fixed projection up to $2^3/_4$ yards for cinematographic projection up to abt. $1^1/_3$ yards — $1^2/_3$ yards. The construction of the lamp is such, that it can be considered quite safe.

10213 13066

Acetylene Lamp for projection purposes, intensive white light, absolutely safe and easy to handle, strong reliable workmanship throughout, finely nickelled, adjustable to the height required, with acetylene generator.

10213/1 approximate burning time, if fitted with abt. $1^1/_2$ oz. of carbide abt. $1^3/_4$ hours, capacity abt. 45 candlepowers each **7/10**

„ /2 approximate burning time, if fitted with abt. 2 oz. of carbide abt. $1^3/_4$ hours, capacity abt. 100 candlepowers with double burner . . . . each **16/6**

13066 **Acetylene Lamp** with double burner, perfectly white light. Easy to handle, absolutely safe, consisting of: water-reservoir, acetylene generator, adjustable burner with reflector and rubber-tube approximate burning time abt. $1^3/_4$ hours, if fitted with $2^1/_2$ oz of carbide, capacity abt. 120 candlepowers . . . . each **28/6**

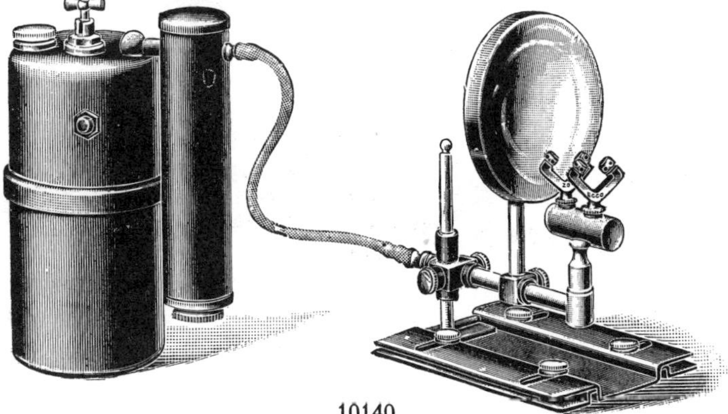

10140

10140 **New Acetylene Lamp** with quadruple flame, **Acetylene Generator,** very strong absolutely safe and easy to handle, complete with adjustable burner, rubber tube, burning time about $1^1/_2$ hours, if filled with 9 oz of carbide, capacity ca. 200 c. p. . . . . each **50/—**

High Pressure Methylated Spirit Gas Light

These lamps, burning with extremely intensive light are very well suitable for large Projection Apparatus. The capacity is equal to 250—300 c. p. The size of the pictures obtainable ranges up to abt. $9^1/_2$ feet diameter, for cinematographic production up to 5—$6^2/_3$ feet.

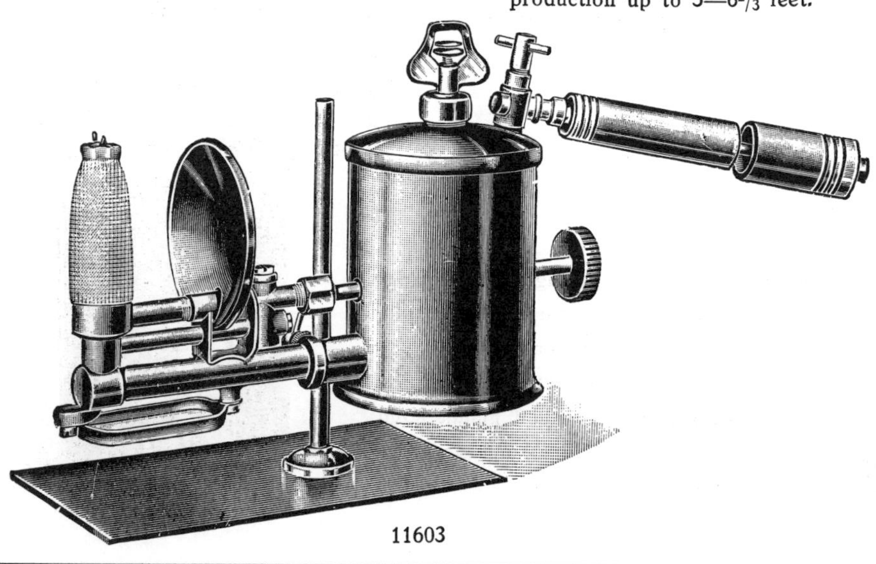

11603

11603 **High Pressure Methylated Spirit Gas Lamp,** specially suitable for large Projection Apparatus and Cinematographs. The capacity of the basin is about 1 pint, approximate burning time, continually for abt. $2^1/_2$—3 hours, when filled with abt. $^4/_5$ pint of methylated spirit. The lamp is very easy to handle and when fitted with a suitable incandescent mantle the lamp will give a light of 250—300 c. p. The reflector fitted between fuel container and flame will protect the former from the radiating heat of the burner, and so do away with any danger of explosion each **58/—**

Illuminants. Electric Arc Light.

Electric Arc Light is the ideal illuminant for projection purposes on account of its enormous intensity of ligth (up to 25000 c. p.) and its concentrated flame.

Owing however to the considerable heat produced by the electric flame and to the special construction of the illuminant it can only be used with large size apparatus.

These lamps may be connected direct with the electric main. Continuous current will produce better results than alternating current.

As the Voltaic arc (electric flame between the 2 carbon poles of the arc lamp) consumes only about 40 Volt, the difference between the tension of the electric main and this voltage has to be absorbed by a suitable resistance. If for instance the tension of the electric current amounts to

65 Volt 25 Volt have to be absorbed
110 „ 70 „ „ „ „ „
220 „ 180 „ „ „ „ „

Such a resistance can either be supplied fitted for current of a certain capacity or adjustable for different ampèrages.

When ordering an electric arc lamp, the following details have to be stated:

1. Intensity of the current in ampères (A).
2. Tension „ „ „ „ Volts (V).
3. Nature „ „ „ whether continuous or alternating current.

The intensity of the light increases with the intensity of the current. The various c. p. of our lamps are:

when using	4	6	10	12	15	20	25 ampères
	500	700	1200	1400	1800	5000	8—10000 c. p.

If continuous current is used the carbon forming the positive pole of the lamp will be consumed by the electric flame twice as quickly as that of the negative pole.

In order to avoid this and the consequent change of the position of the electric arc, a thicker carbon is being used for the plus pole than for the minus pole.

This however is not the case if alternating current comes into question when 2 carbons of equal thickness may be used.

According to the intensity of the current carbons of the following thickness had best be chosen.

	Ampères	4	6	8	10	15	20	30	40	50
Continuous Current	Diameter of upper carbon	5/16	5/16	7/16	9/16	5/8	3/4	3/4	7/8	1 in.
	Diameter of lower carbon	1/4	1/4	5/16	3/8	7/16	1	9/16	5/8	11/16 in.
Alternating Current	Diameter of lower carbon	1/4	5/16	3/8	3/8	9/16	5/8	11/16	3/4	7/8 in.

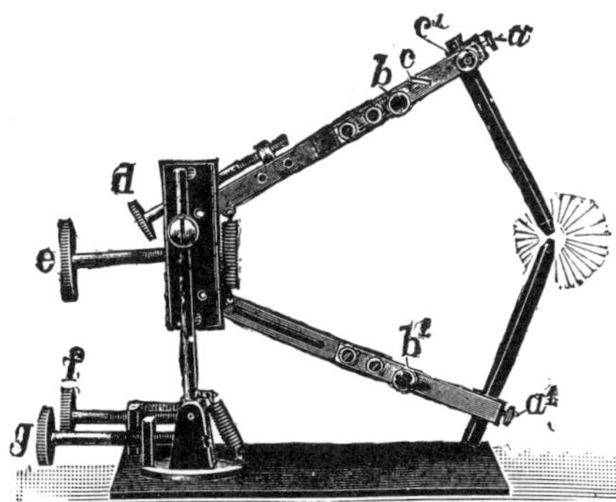

14755 with hand regulation

14756 (and 14757) automatic regulation

Electric Arc Lamp with Hand-regulation, for continuous and alternating current, suitable for distances of over 30 feet with intensive white, ball-shaped light, noiselessly burning, the light can be easily regulated by means of screws, complete **with resistance** and cable about $4^1/_2$ yards long for direct connection with the main, with carbons.

14755/110 for 110 volt . . . . each **68/—**
„ /220 „ 220 „ . . . . „ **84/—**

Electric Arc Lamp with Automatic Regulation, patented (Inherent Steady-light). The lamp regulates itself automatically as soon as the carbons burn away and maintains the same intensity of the light exactly; complete **with resistance,** carbons and cable about 3 meters long for direct connection with the main (3 Ampères).

14756/110 for continuous current of 110 volt (complete with 6 pairs of carbons) . . . . each **102/—**
14757/110 „ alternating „ „ 110 „ „ „ 6 „ „ „ . . . . „ **102/—**

Illuminants.

12548/7

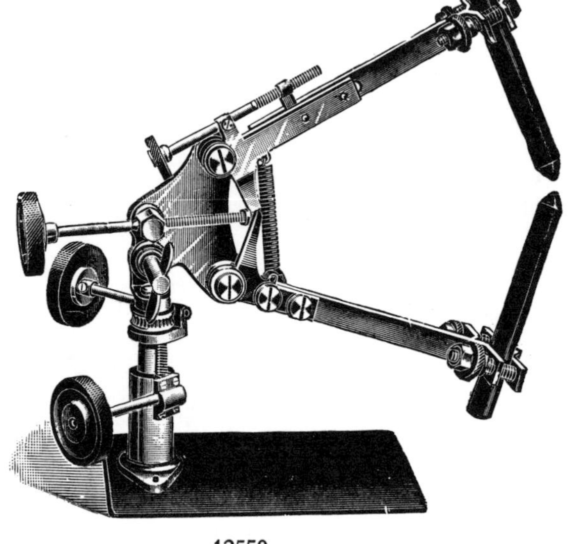

12550

12548/7 **Electric Arc Lamp** (High Current Projection Lamp) for continuous or alternating current of 110 or 220 Volt and up to 100 Ampères. Strong workmanship, elegant finish, simple, safely working mechanism; all movements by means of set screws; adjustable carbon-holder up to $1^1/_8$ in. diameter, good insulated arms, metal parts finely nickelled, with 5 different regulating arrangements, carbons to be fixed at any angle required, a quick exchange of carbons is facilitated by means of the regulating screws.

without resistance each **232/—**

Regulating Resistance

suitable for above arc lamp, adjustable to 5 graduations (10; 12,5; 15; 20; 25 Ampères)

12551/110 for 110 Volt . . . . each **146/—**

„ **/220** „ 220 „ . . . . „ **206/—**

12550 **Electric Arc Lamp** (High Current Projection Lamp) for continuous or alternating current of 110 or 220 Volt and up to 40 Ampères. Strong workmanship, elegant finish, simple, safely working mechanism; all movements by means of driving screws; adjustable carbon-holder up to $^7/_8$ in. diameter, good insulated arms, metal parts finely nickelled with micrometer stand, without resistance . . . . each **118/6**

Regulating Resistance

suitable for above arc lamp, adjustable to 5 graduations (10; 12,5; 15; 20; 25 Ampères)

12551/110 for 110 Volt . . . . each **146/—**

„ **/220** „ 220 „ . . . . „ **206/—**

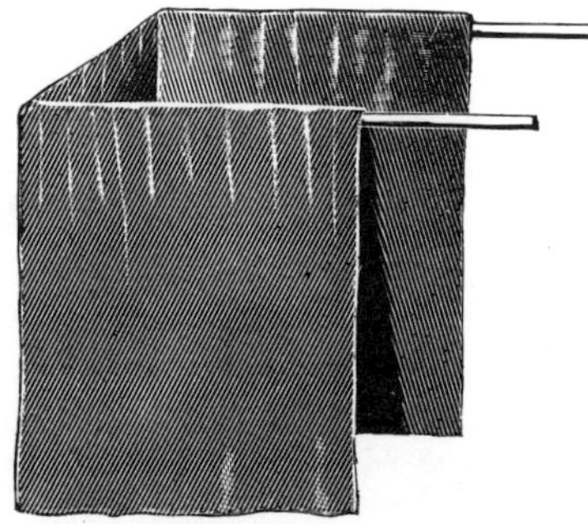

10171

Black Curtain

10171 for covering the body of the apparatus when using more intensive illuminations i. e. arc lamps &c., with black cloth, elastic wire for connection with the apparatus . . . . each **17/4**

List of Illuminants of page 246 up to page 251 and how they fit the various Cinematographs, Magic Lanterns and Projection Apparati.

Illuminants No.	fitting	Greatest possible distance from the screen, **about**	Largest possible approximate size of pictures	
			Glass slides	**Film**
10168/10	222/47/5—6, 222/57/7, 222/58/6—7, 222/95—96 222/370/8, 3150/8—10	*abt. 79 in. abt. 118—138 in.	abt. 39 in. „ 79 „	20×27 in. —
10168/12	222/58/6—7, 222/370/8, 222/380/9, 222/95—96 3150/8—10, 3160/11	*abt. 79 in. abt. 138 „	abt. 39 in. „ 79 „	20×27 in. —
10168/14	222/380/9, 222/390/10, 222/95—96 3150/9—10, 3160/11, 3600/11	*abt. 100 in. abt. 158 „	abt. 51 in. „ 87 „	24×33¾ in. —
13784	222/47/5—6, 222/57/7, 222/58/6—7, 222/370/8, 222/380/9, 222/390/10, 222/95—96 1250/6—8, 3150/8—10, 3160/11, 3600/11	*abt. 79 in. abt. 118—158 in.	abt. 39 in. „ 79 „	20×27 in. —
13778	222/57/7, 222/58/6—7, 222/370/8, 222/390/10, 222/380/9, 222/95—96 1250/8, 3150/8—10, 3600/11, 3160/11	*abt. 79 in. abt. 118—158 in.	abt. 39 in. „ 79 „	20×27 in. —
11603	222/390/10, 222/59/11, 222/100, 222/95—96 3150/10, 3160/11, 3600/11	*abt. 118 in. abt. 237—276 in.	abt. 55 in. abt. 118—138 in.	27×38 in. —
10213/1	222/47/5—6, 222/57/7, 222/58/6—7, 222/370/8 1250/5—8, 875/4—8, 930/4—8, 3150/8—10, 3160/11	*abt. 79 in. abt. 118 „	abt. 39 in. „ 79 „	20×27 in. —
13066 10213/2	222/47/6, 222/57/7, 222/58/6—7, 222/370/8, 222/380/9, 222/390/10, 222/59/11, 222/95—96 930/7—8, 875/7—8, 1250/5—8, 3160/11, 3150/8—10, 3600/11	*abt. 79—118 in. abt. 118—158 „	abt. 39—59 in. „ 79—100 „	20×27 in. up to 27×38 in. —
10140	222/58/6—7, 222/370/8, 222/380/9, 222/95—96, 222/390/10, 222/59/11 1250/8, 3150/8—10, 3160/11, 3600/11 and bigger size	*abt. 118—158 in. abt. 197 in.	abt. 59—75 in. abt. 99 in.	27×38 in. up to 36×49 in. —
10245	222/47/4—6, 222/57/7, 222/58/6—7, 222/370/8, 222/380/9 875/6—8, 930/6—8, 1250/5—8, 3150/8—10	*abt. 79 in. abt. 118 „	abt. 39 in. „ 71 „	20×27 in. —
13785 13779	222/47/4—6, 222/57/7, 222/58/6—7, 222/370/8, 222/380/9, 222/390/10, 222/95—96 930/7—8, 875/7—8, 3150/8—10, 3160/11, 3600/11 &c.	*abt. 79 in. abt. 158 „	abt. 39 in. „ 79 „	20×27 in. —
13068 10172	222/47/6, 222/57/7, 222/58/6—7, 222/370/8, 222/380/9, 222/390/10, 222/59/11, 222/95—96 1250/5—8, 930/8, 875/8, 3150/8—10, 3160/11, 3600/11 &c.	*abt. 118—158 in. abt. 197 in.	abt. 59—75 in. abt. 99 in.	27×38 in. up to 36×49 in. —
14755	222/390/10, 222/59/11, 222/100, 222/380/9, 222/95—96 1250/8, 3150/8—10, 3160/11, 3600/11 &c.	*abt. 237 in. abt. 395 „	abt. 119 in. „ 197 „	57×79 in. —
14756 14757	222/390/10, 222/59/11, 222/100, 222/502 222/95—96, 3150/10, 3160/11, 3600/11 &c.	*abt. 237—316 in. abt. 395 in.	abt. 118—158 in. abt. 197 in.	57×79 in. up to 79×107 in.
12550	222/390/10, 222/59/11, 222/100, 222/502 222/95—96, 3150/10, 3160/11, 3600/11 &c.	according to the power of the current up to 27—33 yards		
12548/7	222/502 &c. all better kinds of Sciopticons	according to the power of the current up to 54 yards.		

Cinematographs marked * may, if used as Magic Lantern or Projection-Apparatus, also be shown at still larger distances from the screen, thus making still larger pictures.

Kinographone-Apparatus Name registered.

Cinematograph-show combined with Talking-Machine

Complete Kinographone Outfit

consisting of: Cinematograph, Synchron-Apparatus "Kinographon" and Talking Machine.

Our largest cinematographs of page 235—239 may at the same time be used in connection with a talking machine and by means of a socalled Synchron-Apparatus, talking and singing pictures may be produced. The necessary connecting arrangement consisting of Differential Gear and a flexible axle each for the cinematograph and the talking machine will be easily fixed to the Cinematograph as well as the talking machine. The Apparatus suits any talking machine on the market.

We supply films and discs fitting this apparatus as stated below. By the ingenuous construction of this Synchron-Apparatus it is possible, to abtain Kinographone displays at home, i. e. pictures, which will be reproduced by the cinematograph in natural movements and will be accompanied in words or music by the talking machine.

226/100 **Synchron-Apparatus,** single, easily to be fixed to the film-transporter of the cinematographs, complete with 2 spirals for connecting the cinematograph with the talking machine . . . . each **13/—**

Synchron Films with the corresponding **Synchron-Disc-Records** (1 meter = abt. $39^1/_2$ in. long)

227/100	subject	1.	Laughing family (Berlin dialect — comical)	abt. 12	meters long incl. disc Record each	**18/—**
„	„	2.	At the dentist (comical)	„ 25	„ „ „ „ „ „	**35/—**
„	„	3.	Service-regulations lesson (comical)	„ 23	„ „ „ „ „ „	**35/—**
„	„	4.	At the baracks (comical)	„ 23	„ „ „ „ „ „	**35/—**
„	„	5.	Tramp taking leave of his native village (illustr. song),	„ 22	„ „ „ „ „ „	**35/—**
„	„	6.	Good night, my darling child (serenade)	„ 29	„ „ „ „ „ „	**37/6**
„	„	7.	The music comes (music hall piece)	„ 34	„ „ „ „ „ „	**40/—**
„	„	11.	Distributing Christmas-boxes	„ 24	„ „ „ „ „ „	**35/—**
„	„	12.	Musical clown	„ 24	„ „ „ „ „ „	**35/—**
„	„	13.	Minuet-waltz (Rococo children's scene)	„ 25	„ „ „ „ „ „	**35/—**
„	„	15.	The forge in the forest	„ 28	„ „ „ „ „ „	**37/6**
„	„	17.	Mad freaks (Trompeter's duet)	„ 25	„ „ „ „ „ „	**35/—**
„	„	18.	The two little finches (Piccolo duet)	„ 25	„ „ „ „ „ „	**35/—**
„	„	19a.	La Musette (french)	„ 12	„ „ „ „ „ „	**18/—**
„	„	19b.	„ „ „	„ 24	„ „ „ „ „ „	**35/—**
„	„	20.	La Matchiche (dance)	„ 24	„ „ „ „ „ „	**35/—**
„	„	21.	La petite Mariée (french)	„ 31	„ „ „ „ „ „	**35/—**
„	„	22.	La Cigale et le fourmi (french)	„ 21	„ „ „ „ „ „	**28/—**
„	„	23.	Un mariage de muets (french)	„ 26	„ „ „ „ „ „	**35/—**
„	„	25.	Any Rags	„ 24	„ „ „ „ „ „	**35/—**
„	„	26.	The Drum Major	„ 24	„ „ „ „ „ „	**35/—**
„	„	31.	Xylophone	„ 26	„ „ „ „ „ „	**35/—**
„	„	32.	Mute Musician in court of law	„ 26	„ „ „ „ „ „	**35/—**
„	„	33.	Schnadahüpfl (bavarian mountain people's dance)	„ 23	„ „ „ „ „ „	**35/—**
„	„	34.	Peasants Wedding	„ 24	„ „ „ „ „ „	**35/—**
„	„	35.	With Zeppelin (comical couplet)	„ 24	„ „ „ „ „ „	**35/—**

Cinematograph Mechanisms.

240/45/3 and $3^1/_2$

240/47/4—$4^1/_2$

240/47/6—7
240/57/7 with double spools
and tops procket

240/58/6
with cast stand and top sprocket

No.		Width for Glass slides	Width for wood framed slides		each
240/45/3	with Maltese Cross Movement	$1^1/_8$ in.	—	objective plain, nickelled	**4/8**
„ „ /$3^1/_2$	„ „ „ „	$1^3/_8$ „	—	„ „ „	**5/8**
„ **47**/4	with Dog action Mechanism	$1^9/_{16}$ „	$1^3/_8$ in.	„ „ „	**8/6**
„ „ /$4^1/_2$	„ „ „ „	$1^3/_4$ „	$1^9/_{16}$ „	„ turned „	**9/6**
„ „ /5	„ „ „ „	2 „	$1^3/_4$ „	„ „ „	**11/6**
„ „ /6	„ „ „ „	$2^5/_{16}$ „	2 „	objective turned, with rack and pinion	**13/6**
„ „ /7	„ „ „ „	$2^3/_4$ „	$2^5/_{16}$ „	do.	**15/—**
„ /**57**/7	„ „ „ „	$2^3/_4$ „	$2^5/_{16}$ „	do. and double spools (see also illustration of No. 222/57/7) page 235	**23/—**
„ /**58**/6	fine cast stand with Dog action Mechanism	$2^5/_{16}$ „	2 „	objective with rack and pinion	**45/6**

Cinematograph Mechanisms.

240/58/7

240/371/8 and 381/9

With arrangement for winding up the film as it comes through the machine

240/58/7	with lower and upper spools (stand of 222/58/7 page 236)	each	**57/—**
„ /**371**/8	„ „ „ „ „ („ „ „ /371/8 „ 237)	„	**76/—**
„ /**381**/9	„ „ „ „ „ („ „ „ /381/9 „ 237)	„	**76/—**
„ /**391**/10	„ „ „ „ „ („ „ „ /391/10 „ 238)	„	**114/—**
„ /**100**	„ „ „ „ „ („ „ „ /100 „ 240)	„	**304/—**
12548/3	„ „ „ „ „ („ „ „ /502 „ 241)	„	**380/—**

Film Winder

consisting of 2 spools, on japanned iron stand to be screwed on a table, lower spool fitted with handle to turn.

(The films, which are wound up when the cinematograph plays, in opposite direction can be easily rewound by this simple, cheap apparatus in the right order, suitable for fresh display.)

Diameter of spools $5^7/_8$ in., suitable for films of about 70—80 meters length.

12549 . . . . each **5/2**

12549

Magic Lanterns.

$71/2^1/_2$

110/3

150/3

Magic Lantern

good, cheap Magic Lantern with oil lamp and 1 glass slide, packed in a box.

71/$2^1/_2$ Width for glass slides 1 in., diameter of lense 1 in. . . . . doz. **9/8**

Magic Lantern

well japanned red or black, with oil lamp, mounted on wooden board, packed in strong box.

110/3 Width for glass slides $1^1/_8$ in., diameter of lense 1 in., with 6 glass slides . . . . doz. **17/8**

150/3 „ „ „ „ $1^1/_8$ „ „ „ „ 1 „ „ 6 „ „ . . . . „ **23/—**

Magic Lanterns.

850/2½

Packing of Magic Lantern 875

875

Strong Magic Lantern, made of Russian Iron with paraffin lamp and open burner.

850/2½	with 3 glass slides, width of glass slides 1 in., diameter of lenses ¾ in.	doz.	**18/—**
„ /3	„ 6 „ „ „ „ „ „ 1⅛ „ „ „ „ 1 „	„	**28/6**

Superior Magic Lantern with paraffin lamp, with socalled Vienna flat-burner with glass chimney, with 12 fine glass slides (slides in separate grooved box) packed in elegant card board box.

No.	width for glass slides	width for wood framed slides	diameter of lense		Price
875/3	1⅛ in.	—	1 in.	each	**3/1**
„ /3½	1⅜ „	—	1⅛ „	„	**4/—**
„ /4	1 9/16 „	1⅜ in.	1⅜ „	„	**5/6**
„ /4½	1¾ „	1 9/16 „	1 9/16 „	„	**6/4**
„ /5	2 „	1¾ „	1¾ „	„	**7/10**
„ /6	2⅜ „	2 „	2 „	„	**9/—**
„ /7	2¾ „	2⅜ „	2⅛ „	„	**12/10**
„ /8	3⅛ „	2¾ „	2⅜ „	„	**14/10**

1703/3

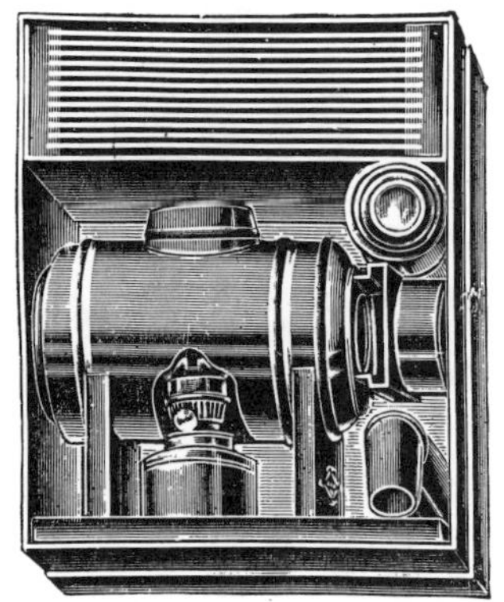
Packing of Magic Lantern 250

250

Magic Lantern, red or black japanned; with oil lamp, mounted on wooden board, packed in strong cardboard box.

170/3 width of glass slides 1⅛ in., diameter of lense 1 in., with 12 glass slides . . . . each **2/6**

Magic Lantern, finely red or black japanned, with paraffin lamp, mounted on wooden board, packed in elegant cardboard box (very practical packing) with 12 fine glass slides (slides in separate grooved box).

No.	width for glass slides	width for wooden framed slides	diameter of lense	Price
250/3	1⅛ in.	—	1 in.	**3/10**
„ /3½	1⅜ „	—	1⅛ „	**4/6**
„ /4	1 9/16 „	1⅜ in.	1⅜ „	**5/8**
„ /4½	1¾ „	1 9/16 „	1 9/16 „	**7/—**
„ /5	2 „	1¾ „	1¾ „	**8/4**
„ /6	2⅜ „	2 „	2 „	**10/8**
„ /7	2¾ „	2⅜ „	2⅛ „	**13/2**
„ /8	3⅛ „	2¾ „	2⅜ „	**15/10**

Magic Lanterns.

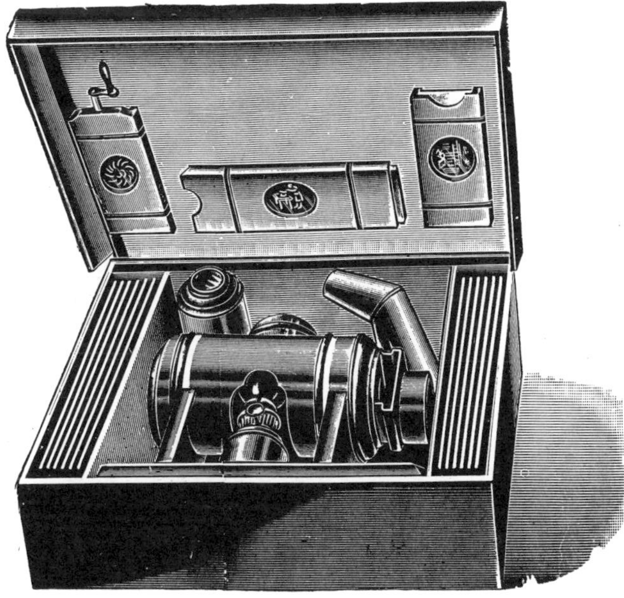

350

Magic Lanterns

finely japanned red or black, with paraffin lamp, 12 fine glass slides, 1 Chromotrope, 1 movable landscape and 1 comical moving picture in wooden frame, packed in fine covered box

350/4	Slides $1^{9}/_{16}$ in. wide, wooden framed slides $1^{3}/_{8}$ in. wide, lens $1^{3}/_{8}$ in. diam. . . . . each	**6/10**
„ /$4^{1}/_{2}$	Slides $1^{3}/_{4}$ in. wide, wooden framed slides $1^{1}/_{2}$ in. wide, lens $1^{1}/_{2}$ in. diam. . . . . each	**8/8**
„ /5	Slides 2 in. wide, wooden framed slides $1^{3}/_{4}$ in. wide, lens $1^{3}/_{4}$ in. diam. . . . . each	**10/4**
„ /6	Slides $2^{3}/_{8}$ in. wide, wooden framed slides 2 in. wide, lens 2 in. diam. . . . . . . each	**13/6**

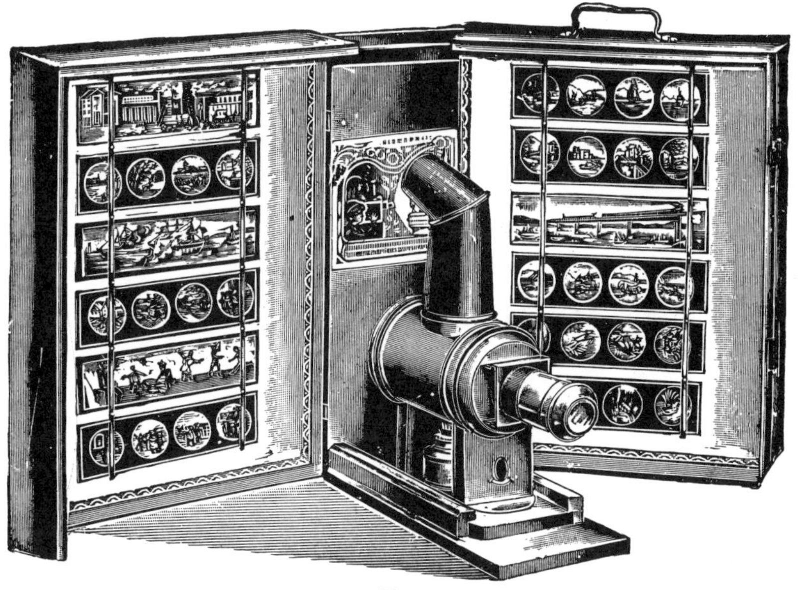

450

Magic Lantern

finely japanned red or black,
with paraffin lamp
and 12 fine glass slides,
well packed and practically arranged
in elegant wooden box with flap doors

450/$3^{1}/_{2}$	Glass slides $1^{3}/_{8}$ in. wide, wooden framed slides	— in.,	lens $1^{1}/_{4}$ in. diam.	. . . . each	**7/—**
„ /4	„ „ $1^{5}/_{8}$ „ „ „ „	$1^{3}/_{8}$ „	„ $1^{3}/_{8}$ „ „	. . . . „	**8/6**
„ /$4^{1}/_{2}$	„ „ $1^{3}/_{4}$ „ „ „ „	$1^{5}/_{8}$ „	„ $1^{5}/_{8}$ „ „	. . . . „	**9/10**
„ /5	„ „ 2 „ „ „ „	$1^{3}/_{4}$ „	„ $1^{3}/_{4}$ „ „	. . . . „	**12/—**
„ /6	„ „ $2^{3}/_{8}$ „ „ „ „	2 „	„ 2 „ „	. . . . „	**15/4**

Magic Lanterns.

"Scio"

(Registered Name).

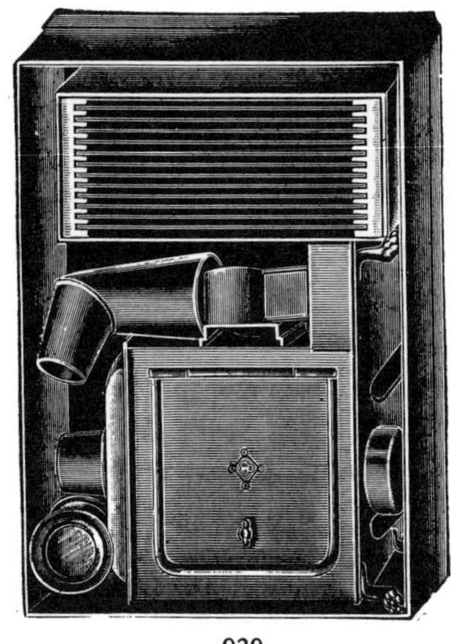

930

930

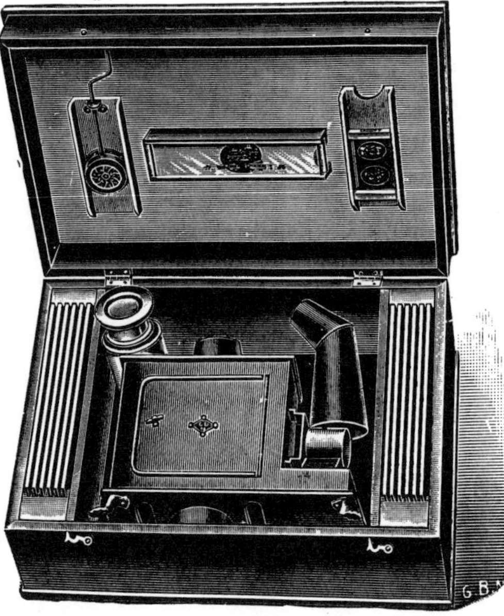

970

A Series of Superior Quality Lanterns constructed on the lines of full sized Magic Lanterns.

Very fine Magic Lantern

elegant shape, **polished Russian iron,** with paraffin lamp and 12 fine glass slides in practical packing (slides in separate grooved box), packed in fine strong cardboard box

No.	glass slides, in. wide	wooden framed slides, in. wide	lens, in. diam.		Price
930/$3\frac{1}{2}$	$1\frac{3}{8}$	—	$1\frac{1}{8}$	each	**5/—**
„ /4	$1\frac{9}{16}$	$1\frac{3}{8}$	$1\frac{3}{8}$	„	**7/4**
„ /$4\frac{1}{2}$	$1\frac{3}{4}$	$1\frac{9}{16}$	$1\frac{9}{16}$	„	**8/—**
„ /5	2	$1\frac{3}{4}$	$1\frac{3}{4}$	„	**9/6**
„ /6	$2\frac{3}{8}$	2	2	„	**11/2**
„ /7	$2\frac{3}{4}$	$2\frac{3}{8}$	$2\frac{1}{8}$	„	**13/8**
„ /8	$3\frac{1}{8}$	$2\frac{3}{4}$	$2\frac{3}{8}$	„	**16/6**

Superfine Magic Lantern

elegant shape, **polished Russian iron,** with paraffin lamp and 12 fine glass slides, packed in **elegant box,** with grooved picture holder

No.	glass slides, in. wide	wooden framed slides, in. wide	lens, in. diam.		Price
960/$3\frac{1}{2}$	$1\frac{3}{8}$	—	$1\frac{1}{8}$	each	**6/4**
„ /4	$1\frac{9}{16}$	$1\frac{3}{8}$	$1\frac{3}{8}$	„	**8/6**
„ /$4\frac{1}{2}$	$1\frac{3}{4}$	$1\frac{9}{16}$	$1\frac{9}{16}$	„	**9/2**
„ /5	2	$1\frac{3}{4}$	$1\frac{3}{4}$	„	**11/2**
„ /6	$2\frac{3}{8}$	2	2	„	**13/2**
„ /7	$2\frac{3}{4}$	$2\frac{3}{8}$	$2\frac{1}{8}$	„	**15/2**
„ /8	$3\frac{1}{8}$	$2\frac{3}{4}$	$2\frac{3}{8}$	„	**18/6**

Superfine Magic Lantern

elegant shape, **polished Russian iron,** with paraffin lamp, 12 fine glass slides, 1 chromotrope, 1 moving landscape, 1 comical moving picture in wooden frame, packed in elegant grooved boxes

No.	glass slides, in. wide	wooden framed slides, in. wide	lens, in. diam.		Price
970/$4\frac{1}{2}$	$1\frac{3}{4}$	$1\frac{9}{16}$	$1\frac{9}{16}$	each	**12/2**
„ /5	2	$1\frac{3}{4}$	$1\frac{3}{4}$	„	**14/2**
„ /6	$2\frac{3}{8}$	2	2	„	**16/6**
„ /7	$2\frac{3}{4}$	$2\frac{3}{8}$	$2\frac{1}{8}$	„	**19/—**
„ /8	$3\frac{1}{8}$	$2\frac{3}{4}$	$2\frac{3}{8}$	„	**22/—**

Magic Lanterns.

1170

Superfine Magic Lantern

with excellent optics fitted with **double condenser,** objective with **3 lenses,** very elegant shape, lantern made of **polished Russian Iron,** with paraffine lamp with **round burner** and **12 finely finished long glass slides, 1 chromotrope, 1 comical moving picture,** and **1 moving landscape,** packed in elegant wooden box.

	slides	wooden framed pictures	diam. of lens	round burner	
1170/$4\frac{1}{2}$	$1\frac{3}{4}$ in.	$1\frac{3}{4}$ in.	$1\frac{1}{2}$ in.	8'''	each **18/6**
„ /5	2 „	2 „	$1\frac{3}{4}$ „	8'''	„ **20/—**
„ /6	$2\frac{3}{8}$ „	$2\frac{3}{8}$ „	2 „	10'''	„ **25/4**
„ /7	$2\frac{3}{4}$ „	$2\frac{3}{4}$ „	$2\frac{3}{16}$ „	10'''	„ **29/6**
„ /8	$3\frac{3}{16}$ „	$3\frac{3}{16}$ „	$2\frac{3}{8}$ „	12'''	„ **34/—**
„ /9	$3\frac{1}{2}$ „	$3\frac{1}{2}$ „	$2\frac{9}{16}$ „	12'''	„ **41/—**

1250

Superfine Magic Lantern

polished Russian iron, with powerful **duplex burner, 12 fine covered glass slides, 1 chromotrope, 1 comical moving picture, 1 moving landscape** in wooden frame, fine adjustable brass objective with rack and pinion and double condenser.

	slides	wooden framed slides	diam. of lens	
1250/5	2 in.	2 in.	$1\frac{3}{4}$ in.	each **26/4**
„ /6	$2\frac{3}{8}$ „	$2\frac{3}{8}$ „	2 „	„ **32/6**
„ /7	$2\frac{3}{4}$ „	$2\frac{3}{4}$ „	$2\frac{1}{8}$ „	„ **38/—**

3150

Sciopticon

polished Russian iron with fine set of lenses, objective with rack and pinion

3150/8 with powerful duplex lamp, **condenser $2\frac{3}{4}$ in. diam.,** fitting glass slides and wooden framed slides $3\frac{1}{8}$ in. wide . . each **39/—**

3150/9 with powerful duplex lamp, **condenser $3\frac{1}{8}$ in. diam.,** fitting glass slides and wooden framed slides $3\frac{1}{2}$ in. wide . . each **53/—**

3150/10 same as above with **condenser $3\frac{1}{2}$ in. diam.** and **achromatic set of lenses,** fitting glass slides and wooden framed slides $3\frac{7}{8}$ in. wide . . . . each **65/—**

Sciopticons.

3160/11

Fine Sciopticon

made of the best polished Russian iron, with fine achromatic set of lenses, objective with rack and pinion

3160/11 with powerful duplex lamp, condenser 4 in. diam., fitting glass slides and wooden framed slides of $4^3/_8$ in. width . . . . each **94/—**

Extra fine Sciopticon

polished Russian iron,
adjustable objective and picture frame,
with brass fittings
and extra fine brass objective, achromatic,
with rack and pinion
condenser $4^1/_8$ in. diam., with American 3 burner
petroleum lamp, very intensifying,
with 24 fine covered square glass slides,
1 picture transporter, 1 chromotrope,
1 comical moving picture and 1 movable
landscape in wooden frame

3600 . . . . each **180/—**

3600

Slide-Carriers

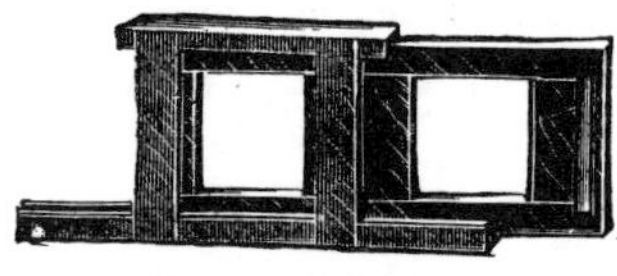

9067 and 9060

suitable for short glass slides and photograms for Sciopticon pictures 4 in. wide

9067/1	for pictures $3^3/_8 \times 3^3/_8$ in.	each	**4/4**
„ /2	„ „ $3^3/_8 \times 4$ „	„	**4/4**

for Sciopticon pictures, $4^5/_{16}$ in. wide

9060/1	for pictures $3^3/_8 \times 3^3/_8$ in.	each	**4/4**
„ /2	„ „ $3^3/_8 \times 4$ „	„	**4/4**

Megascopes

or

Post Card Lanterns.

Apparatus for projecting **opaque articles.** — With these apparatus any photograph, coloured opaque picture, **picture-postcards,** coins, insects, the works of a watch &c. can be produced on the screen greatly magnified.

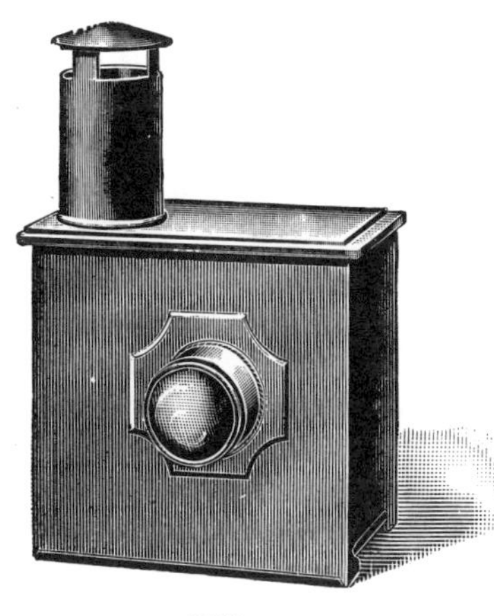

2960

2952

2960 **Megascope for postcards** very strong and nicely finished, lamp with flat burner, 8 in. long, $4^1/_2$ in. deep 12 in. high incl. chimney . . . . each **3/10**

2952 **Same as above** size 8 in. long, $5^1/_4$ in. deep, $13^1/_4$ in. high incl. chimney . . . . each **9/—**

Post Card Lantern

and

Magic Lantern

combined.

2961

2962

2961 **Megascope, combined with Magic Lantern,** finely japanned, very strong and nicely finished, with 12 fine glass slides $2^3/_8$ in. wide, lamp with flat burner, with reflector to be moved from outside; $7^3/_4$ in. long, $5^1/_2$ in. deep, $12^3/_4$ in. high incl. chimney . . . . each **12/8**

2962 **Megascope, combined with Magic Lantern,** finely japanned, very strong and nicely finished, with 12 fine glass slides $2^3/_4$ in. wide, with 2 lamps with round burners, with frame adjustable for all size cards &c., $10^1/_2$ in. long, 6 in. deep, $17^1/_2$ in. high incl. chimney . . . . each **30/6**

Glass Slides for Magic Lanterns.

When ordering extra glass slides or pictures in tin or wooden frames to any Lantern or Apparatus kindly note:

The line numbers of the **glass slides** and **pictures in tin frames No. 7254** correspond with the line numbers of all Magic Lanterns. For instance all glass slides size 5 will fit the Lanterns size 5 etc.

On the other hand the **pictures in wooden frames** and of the chromotropes in tin frames do not always correspond with the line numbers of the Lanterns, and when ordering such pictures in wooden frames it is necessary to give the exact width of these pictures as stated in the description of Magic Lanterns.

All the following Lantern Slides (with the exception of the photographic series page 268 and 269) we deliver also

as Gelatine Pictures

being specially suitable for export to countries in which high duty is charged on heavy articles.

Please see page 271.

Long Glass Slides

finely finished with striking effect of colour in 10 different series of 12 slides (series I—X, series I is given with the Lanterns).

These series comprise a rich assortment of objects and views such as:

Children's scenes, comical pictures, heads of animals, landscapes, sport pictures, fire brigade, ships, north pole scenes, the seasons, carricatures etc.

out of serie III

out of serie IV

(Series I, II, III, IV, V, VI, VII, VIII, IX, X, series I is given with the lanterns)

size	$2\frac{1}{2}$	3	$3\frac{1}{2}$	4	$4\frac{1}{2}$	5	6	7	8	9	10	11	
slides	1	$1\frac{3}{16}$	$1\frac{3}{8}$	$1\frac{9}{16}$	$1\frac{3}{4}$	2	$2\frac{3}{8}$	$2\frac{3}{4}$	$3\frac{3}{16}$	$3\frac{1}{2}$	4	$4\frac{3}{8}$	in. wide
	4	$4\frac{1}{4}$	5	6	7	$7\frac{1}{4}$	8	$8\frac{3}{4}$	$9\frac{1}{2}$	11	12	12	in. long
7695 without cover glass p. doz. series	**8/4**	**9/6**	**13/8**	**17/10**	**23/2**	**29/6**	**42/—**	**54/6**	**71/6**	**90/6**	each series. **10/6**	**11/8**	
7696 with " " per "				**2/4**	**3/4**	**4/2**	**5/4**	**6/4**	**8/—**	**10/10**	**15/4**	**16/10**	

New series of long glass slides for Magic Lanterns

comical children's scenes

finely finished with striking effect of colour, very humourous.

Table 6

Table 11

size	3	$3\frac{1}{2}$	4	$4\frac{1}{2}$		5	6	7	8	9	10	11	
slides	$1\frac{1}{8}$	$1\frac{3}{8}$	$1\frac{1}{2}$	$1\frac{3}{4}$		2	$2\frac{3}{8}$	$2\frac{3}{4}$	$3\frac{1}{8}$	$3\frac{1}{2}$	4	$4\frac{3}{8}$	in. wide
	$4\frac{3}{8}$	$5\frac{1}{8}$	$5\frac{7}{8}$	$6\frac{5}{8}$		$7\frac{1}{16}$	$7\frac{7}{8}$	$8\frac{5}{8}$	$9\frac{1}{2}$	11	$11\frac{7}{8}$	$11\frac{7}{8}$	in. long
6950 without cover glass doz. series	**9/6**	**13/8**	**17/10**	**23/2**	serie	**2/8**	**3/6**	**4/8**	**6/—**	**7/8**	**10/6**	**11/8**	
6951 with " " per "			**2/4**	**3/4**		**4/2**	**5/4**	**6/4**	**8/—**	**10/10**	**15/4**	**16/10**	

New Fairy Tale Pictures.

6458 and 6459

6964 and 6965

Assortment comprising 12 slides = 48 pictures of Fairy Tales:
The poem of the Bell, The fight with the Dragon, The story of Aladdin with the wonderful lamp, with striking effect of colours.

		3	$3\frac{1}{2}$	4	$4\frac{1}{2}$	5	6	7	8	9	10	11 cm
	slides	$1\frac{1}{8}$	$1\frac{3}{8}$	$1\frac{1}{2}$	$1\frac{3}{4}$	2	$2\frac{3}{8}$	$\frac{3}{4}$	$3\frac{1}{8}$	$3\frac{1}{2}$	4	$4\frac{3}{8}$ in. wide
6458	without cover glass per doz. series	**12/8**	**16/10**	**21/—**	each **2/4**	**3/2**	**4/4**	**5/4**	**6/10**	**9/6**	**12/2**	**14/2**
6459	with „ „ per series	—	—	**2/8**	**3/8**	**4/10**	**5/10**	**6/10**	**9/—**	**11/8**	**16/4**	**17/4**

New Fairy Tale Pictures comprising the most popular fairy tales (Hansel and Gretel, Little Snow-white, Red Riding Hood &c.); new pictures with striking effect of colours.

		3	$3\frac{1}{2}$	4	$4\frac{1}{2}$	5	6	7	8	9	10 cm
	slides	$1\frac{1}{8}$	$1\frac{3}{8}$	$1\frac{1}{2}$	$1\frac{3}{4}$	2	$2\frac{3}{8}$	$2\frac{3}{4}$	$3\frac{1}{8}$	$3\frac{1}{2}$	4 in. wide
6964	without cover glass **per doz. series**	**12/8**	**16/10**	**21/—**	**each ser. 2/4**	**3/2**	**4/4**	**5/4**	**6/10**	**9/6**	**12/2**
6965	with „ „ **per series**	—	—	**2/8**	**3/8**	**4/10**	**5/10**	**6/10**	**9/—**	**11/8**	**16/4**

Fairy Tales.

Little Snow-white

Red Riding Hood

comprising 48 pictures of Fairy Tales: **Red Riding Hood, Little Snow-white, Hop o'my thumb, Hansel and Gretel, Sleeping Beauty, Cinderella,** 2 slides for each story, with reading, an excellent series of striking colours finely finished.

		size 3	$3\frac{1}{2}$	4	$4\frac{1}{2}$	5	6	7	8	9
	slides	$1\frac{1}{8}$	$1\frac{3}{8}$	$1\frac{1}{2}$	$1\frac{3}{4}$	2	$2\frac{3}{8}$	$2\frac{3}{4}$	$3\frac{1}{8}$	$3\frac{1}{2}$ in. wide
		$4\frac{3}{8}$	$5\frac{1}{8}$	$5\frac{7}{8}$	$6\frac{5}{8}$	$7\frac{1}{16}$	$7\frac{7}{8}$	$8\frac{5}{8}$	$9\frac{1}{2}$	11 in. long
9275	without cover glass **per doz. series**	**11/6**	**16/6**	**20/6**	**27/4 each ser.**	**3/—**	**4/2**	**5/2**	**6/8**	**9/2**
9278	with „ „ **per series**	—	—	**2/6**	**3/8**	**4/6**	**5/8**	**6/10**	**8/8**	**11/6**

Fairy Tales.

New Series.

Assortment comprising 12 slides 48 = pictures of Fairy Tales:
Cinderella, The Table, The Mysterious Barber, The Nymph of the Well, Story of the young King Zein Alasmon and the King of the Ghosts, The Fisher and the Genius.
An excellent series of striking colours, with reading.

		size 4	$4\frac{1}{2}$	5	6	7	8	9
	slides	$1\frac{1}{2}$	$1\frac{3}{4}$	2	$2\frac{3}{8}$	$2\frac{3}{4}$	$3\frac{1}{8}$	$3\frac{1}{2}$ in. wide
		$5\frac{7}{8}$	$6\frac{5}{8}$	$7\frac{1}{16}$	$7\frac{7}{8}$	$8\frac{5}{8}$	$9\frac{1}{2}$	11 in. long
6974	without cover glass **per doz. series**	**20/6**	**27/4**	**each ser. 3/—**	**4/2**	**5/2**	**6/8**	**9/2**
8337	with „ „ **per series**	**2/6**	**3/8**	**4/6**	**5/8**	**6/10**	**8/8**	**11/6**

Long Glass Slides for Magic Lanterns.

Original Drawings by famous Artists.

Excellent finish, very humorous, Children's scenes of striking colours.

Slide 1

Slide 5

Slide 7

Slide 9

Series No. I.

1 series = 12 different slides of 4 pictures each

	size	3	$3\frac{1}{2}$	4	$4\frac{1}{2}$		5	6	7	8	9	10	11	
	pictures	$1\frac{1}{8}$	$1\frac{3}{8}$	$1\frac{1}{2}$	$1\frac{3}{4}$		2	$2\frac{3}{8}$	$2\frac{3}{4}$	$3\frac{1}{8}$	$3\frac{1}{2}$	4	$4\frac{3}{8}$	in. wide
		$4\frac{3}{8}$	$5\frac{1}{8}$	$5\frac{7}{8}$	$6\frac{5}{8}$		$7\frac{1}{16}$	$7\frac{7}{8}$	$8\frac{5}{8}$	$9\frac{1}{2}$	11	$11\frac{7}{8}$	$11\frac{7}{8}$	in. long
6787	without cover glass **doz. series**	**11/6**	**16/6**	**20/6**	**27/4**	**each ser.**	**3/—**	**4/2**	**5/2**	**6/8**	**9/2**	**12/2**	**13/8**	
6788	with „ „ **per serie**	—	—	**2/6**	**3/8**	„ „	**4/6**	**5/8**	**6/10**	**8/8**	**11/6**	**16/4**	**18/4**	

Slide 6

Slide 10

Slide 11

Slide 12

Series No. II.

1 series = 12 different slides of 4 pictures each

	size	3	$3\frac{1}{2}$	4	$4\frac{1}{2}$		5	6	7	8	9	10	11	
	slides	$1\frac{1}{8}$	$1\frac{3}{8}$	$1\frac{1}{2}$	$1\frac{3}{4}$		2	$2\frac{3}{8}$	$2\frac{3}{4}$	$3\frac{1}{8}$	$3\frac{1}{2}$	4	$4\frac{3}{8}$	in. wide
		$4\frac{3}{8}$	$5\frac{1}{8}$	$5\frac{7}{8}$	$6\frac{5}{8}$		$7\frac{1}{16}$	$7\frac{7}{8}$	$8\frac{5}{8}$	$9\frac{1}{2}$	11	$11\frac{7}{8}$	$11\frac{7}{8}$	in. long
8753	without cover glass **doz. series**	**11/6**	**16/6**	**20/6**	**27/4**	**each ser.**	**3/—**	**4/2**	**5/2**	**6/8**	**9/2**	**12/2**	**13/8**	
8754	with 1 „ **per** „	—	—	**2/6**	**3/8**		**4/6**	**5/8**	**6/10**	**8/8**	**11/6**	**16/4**	**18/4**	

Soldier Pictures.

Representing troops of the most important Nations:

(England, Germany, Austria, Italy, France, Spain, Russia, Turkey, Greece, Japan and North America) in 48 pictures = 12 slides, with reading.

	size	$3\frac{1}{2}$	4	$4\frac{1}{2}$		5	6	7	8	
	slides	$1\frac{3}{8}$	$1\frac{1}{2}$	$1\frac{3}{4}$		2	$2\frac{3}{8}$	$2\frac{3}{4}$	$3\frac{1}{8}$	in. wide
		$5\frac{1}{8}$	$5\frac{7}{8}$	$6\frac{5}{8}$		$7\frac{1}{16}$	$7\frac{7}{8}$	$8\frac{5}{8}$	$9\frac{1}{2}$	in. long
7158	without cover glass . . . . **doz. series**	**16/4**	**20/6**	**27/4**	**each ser.**	**3/—**	**4/2**	**5/2**	**6/8**	
7159	with „ „ . . . . **per** „	—	**2/6**	**3/8**		**4/6**	**5/8**	**6/10**	**8/8**	

Landscapes.

Travels round the world, 12 glass slides.

	size	$2\frac{1}{2}$	3	$3\frac{1}{2}$	4	$4\frac{1}{2}$	5	6	7	8	9	
	slides	1	$1\frac{1}{8}$	$1\frac{3}{8}$	$1\frac{1}{2}$	$1\frac{3}{4}$	2	$2\frac{3}{8}$	$2\frac{3}{4}$	$3\frac{1}{8}$	$3\frac{1}{2}$	in. wide
7682	without cover glass **doz. series**	**8/4**	**9/6**	**13/8**	**17/10**	**23/2**	**29/6**	**42/—**	**54/6**	**71/6**	**90/6**	
7683	with „ „ **per series**	—	—	—	**2/4**	**3/4**	**4/2**	**5/4**	**6/4**	**8/—**	**10/10**	

Pictures of the Nile.

Tropical Landscapes.

Natural Phenomena, Ice Regions, Views of the Nile and Tropical Landscapes

(3 slides each with 4 pictures) an excellently finished and richly coloured series of 12 glass slides = 48 pictures

	size	3	$3\frac{1}{2}$	4	$4\frac{1}{2}$	5	6	7	8	9	
	slides	$1\frac{1}{8}$	$1\frac{3}{8}$	$1\frac{1}{2}$	$1\frac{3}{4}$	2	$2\frac{3}{8}$	$2\frac{3}{4}$	$3\frac{1}{8}$	$3\frac{1}{2}$	in. wide
		$4\frac{3}{8}$	$5\frac{1}{8}$	$5\frac{7}{8}$	$6\frac{5}{8}$	$7\frac{1}{16}$	$7\frac{7}{8}$	$8\frac{5}{8}$	$9\frac{1}{2}$	11	in. long
8845	without cover glass **doz. series**	**11/6**	**16/10**	**20/10**	**27/4**	each ser. **3/—**	**4/2**	**5/4**	**6/8**	**9/2**	
8846	with „ „ **per series**	—	—	**2/6**	**3/8**	**4/6**	**5/10**	**7/—**	**8/8**	**11/6**	

Views of Munich.

Celebrated Churches.

Swiss Views, Royal Castles, Celebrated Curches, Views from Munich and Vienna (3 slides each with 4 pictures) an excellently finished and richly coloured series of 12 glass slides = 48 pictures with text.

	size	3	$3\frac{1}{2}$	4	$4\frac{1}{2}$	5	6	7	8	9	
	slides	$1\frac{1}{8}$	$1\frac{3}{8}$	$1\frac{1}{2}$	$1\frac{3}{4}$	2	$2\frac{3}{8}$	$2\frac{3}{4}$	$3\frac{1}{8}$	$3\frac{1}{2}$	in. wide
		$4\frac{3}{8}$	$5\frac{1}{8}$	$5\frac{7}{8}$	$6\frac{5}{8}$	$7\frac{1}{16}$	$7\frac{7}{8}$	$8\frac{5}{8}$	$9\frac{1}{2}$	11	in. long
8847	without cover glass **doz. series**	**11/6**	**16/10**	**20/10**	**27/4**	each ser. **3/—**	**4/2**	**5/4**	**6/8**	**9/2**	
8848	with „ „ **per series**	—	—	**2/6**	**3/8**	**4/6**	**5/10**	**7/—**	**8/8**	**11/6**	

Travels round the world, interesting views from different countries including:
Rhineland, Paris, Bull Fights in Spain, North Pole, Venice, Naples, New York, Niagara Falls, China, Japan, India, Africa etc.
Fine series of 48 artistic pictures with description on 12 long glass slides.

	size	4	$4\frac{1}{2}$	5	6	7	8	9	10	
	slides	$1\frac{1}{2}$	$1\frac{3}{4}$	2	$2\frac{3}{8}$	$2\frac{3}{4}$	$3\frac{1}{8}$	$3\frac{1}{2}$	4	in. wide
		$5\frac{7}{8}$	$6\frac{5}{8}$	$7\frac{1}{16}$	$7\frac{7}{8}$	$8\frac{5}{8}$	$9\frac{1}{2}$	11	$11\frac{7}{8}$	in. long
6610	without cover glass **per doz. series**	**20/10**	**27/4**	each ser. **3/—**	**4/2**	**5/4**	**6/8**	**9/2**	**12/2**	
6620	with „ „ **each series**	**2/6**	**3/8**	**4/6**	**5/10**	**7/—**	**8/8**	**11/6**	**12/6**	

Travels through Switzerland, Harz and on the Rhine

interesting and picturesque views in excellent finish, richly coloured (series of 48 pictures on 12 glass slides).

	size	4	$4\frac{1}{2}$	5	6	7	8	9	
	slides	$1\frac{1}{2}$	$1\frac{3}{4}$	2	$2\frac{3}{8}$	$2\frac{3}{4}$	$3\frac{1}{8}$	$3\frac{1}{2}$	in. wide
		$5\frac{7}{8}$	$6\frac{5}{8}$	$7\frac{1}{16}$	$7\frac{7}{8}$	$8\frac{5}{8}$	$9\frac{1}{2}$	11	in. long
6846	without cover glass **per doz. series**	**20/10**	**27/4**	each ser. **3/2**	**4/2**	**5/4**	**6/8**	**9/2**	
6847	with „ „ **each series**	**2/6**	**3/8**	**4/6**	**5/10**	**6/10**	**8/8**	**11/6**	

Landscapes.

Trip round the world

representing a trip, leaving Bremerhaven for Gibraltar, Suez Canal, India, Japan, Australia, Cape Colony and returning via England.

Countries and inhabitants illustrated by a series of 48 artistic pictures with description on 12 long glass slides

	size	4	$4\frac{1}{2}$		5	6	7	8	9	10	
	slides	$1\frac{1}{2}$	$1\frac{3}{4}$		2	$2\frac{3}{8}$	$2\frac{3}{4}$	$3\frac{1}{8}$	$3\frac{1}{2}$	4	in. wide
		$5\frac{7}{8}$	$6\frac{5}{8}$		$7\frac{1}{16}$	$7\frac{7}{8}$	$8\frac{5}{8}$	$9\frac{1}{2}$	11	$11\frac{7}{8}$	in. long
9436	without cover glass **doz. series**	**21/—**	**27/4**	**each ser.**	**3/2**	**4/2**	**5/4**	**6/8**	**9/2**	**12/2**	
7209	with „ „ **per series**	**2/8**	**3/8**		**4/6**	**5/10**	**7/—**	**8/8**	**11/6**	**16/8**	

Life in the United States of America with text

fine series comprising 12 long glass slides with 4 scenes each = 48 pictures

	size	4	$4\frac{1}{2}$		5	6	7	8	9	10	
	slides	$1\frac{1}{2}$	$1\frac{3}{4}$		2	$2\frac{3}{8}$	$2\frac{3}{4}$	$3\frac{1}{8}$	$3\frac{1}{2}$	4	in. wide
		$5\frac{7}{8}$	$6\frac{5}{8}$		$7\frac{1}{16}$	$7\frac{7}{8}$	$8\frac{5}{8}$	$9\frac{1}{2}$	11	$11\frac{7}{8}$	in. long
7190	without cover glass **doz. series**	**21/—**	**27/4**	**each ser.**	**3/2**	**4/2**	**5/4**	**6/8**	**9/2**	**12/2**	
7191	with „ „ **per series**	**2/6**	**3/8**		**4/6**	**5/8**	**7/—**	**8/8**	**11/6**	**16/8**	

Religious pictures.

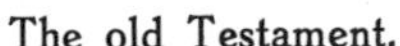

The old Testament.

The new Testament.

The old Testament, the new Testament, the Passion and Views from Palastine

(3 slides each with 4 pictures), with text.

An excellently finished and finely coloured series of 48 pictures on 12 slides

	size	3	$3\frac{1}{2}$	4	$4\frac{1}{2}$		5	6	7	8	9	
	slides	$1\frac{3}{16}$	$1\frac{3}{8}$	$1\frac{9}{16}$	$1\frac{3}{4}$		2	$2\frac{3}{8}$	$2\frac{3}{4}$	$3\frac{3}{16}$	$3\frac{1}{2}$	in. wide
		$4\frac{3}{8}$	5	6	$6\frac{3}{4}$		7	8	$8\frac{3}{4}$	$9\frac{1}{2}$	11	in. long
8841	without cover glass **doz. series**	**11/6**	**16/10**	**21/—**	**27/4**	**each ser.**	**3/2**	**4/2**	**5/4**	**6/8**	**9/2**	
8842	with „ „ **per series**	—	—	**2/6**	**3/8**		**4/6**	**5/10**	**7/—**	**8/8**	**11/6**	

Scientific pictures.

Natural History Pictures (Mammalia)

A series of 48 artistically finished pictures on 12 glass slides, with text

	size	4		$4\frac{1}{2}$	5	6	7	8	9	10	
	slides	$1\frac{1}{2}$		$1\frac{3}{4}$	2	$2\frac{3}{8}$	$2\frac{3}{4}$	$3\frac{3}{16}$	$3\frac{1}{2}$	4	in. wide
		$5\frac{7}{8}$		$6\frac{3}{4}$	7	8	$8\frac{3}{4}$	$9\frac{1}{2}$	11	12	in. long
6621	without cover glass **per doz. series**	**21/—**	**each series**	**2/4**	**3/2**	**4/2**	**5/4**	**6/8**	**9/2**	**12/2**	
6622	with „ „ **each series**	**2/6**		**3/8**	**4/6**	**5/10**	**7/—**	**8/8**	**11/6**	**16/8**	

Natural History Pictures, representing:

Sea animals (amphibia, whales, seals, corals, star-fishes etc.) and **butterflies** with their **caterpillars.**

Highly interesting and instructive series, comprising 12 long slides with 4 pictures each.

		size	4	$4\frac{1}{2}$		5	6	7	8	9	10	
		slides	$1\frac{1}{2}$	$1\frac{3}{4}$		2	$2\frac{3}{8}$	$2\frac{3}{4}$	$3\frac{3}{16}$	$3\frac{1}{2}$	4	in. wide
			$5\frac{7}{8}$	$6\frac{3}{4}$		$7\frac{1}{8}$	$7\frac{7}{8}$	$8\frac{3}{4}$	$9\frac{1}{2}$	11	$11\frac{3}{4}$	in. long
6632	without cover glass	**p. doz. series**	**21/—**	**27/4**	**each series**	**3/2**	**4/2**	**5/4**	**6/8**	**9/2**	**12/2**	
6637	with „ „	**per series**	**2/6**	**3/8**		**4/6**	**5/10**	**7/—**	**8/8**	**11/6**	**16/8**	

Natural History Pictures, representing:

Birds and Amphibia.

Highly interesting and instructive series, comprising 12 long glass slides with 4 pictures each.

		size	4	$4\frac{1}{2}$		5	6	7	8	9	10	
		slides	$1\frac{1}{2}$	$1\frac{3}{4}$		2	$2\frac{3}{8}$	$2\frac{3}{4}$	$3\frac{1}{8}$	$3\frac{1}{2}$	4	in. wide
			$5\frac{7}{8}$	$6\frac{5}{8}$		$7\frac{1}{16}$	$7\frac{7}{8}$	$8\frac{5}{8}$	$9\frac{1}{2}$	11	$11\frac{7}{8}$	in. long
6473	without cover glass	**p. doz. series**	**21/—**	**27/4**	**each series**	**3/2**	**4/2**	**5/4**	**6/8**	**9/2**	**12/2**	
6474	with „ „	**per series**	**2/6**	**3/8**		**4/6**	**5/10**	**7/—**	**8/8**	**11/6**	**16/8**	

New Airship Series

6522

6521

Various Airship, showing the development of aeronautics, finely finished,
48 artistically finished pictures on 12 glass slides with text

			3	$3\frac{1}{2}$	4		$4\frac{1}{2}$	5	6	7	8	cm
		slides	$1\frac{3}{16}$	$1\frac{3}{8}$	$1\frac{1}{2}$		$1\frac{3}{4}$	2	$2\frac{3}{8}$	$2\frac{3}{4}$	$3\frac{3}{16}$	in. wide
6522	without cover glass	**doz. series**	**12/8**	**16/10**	**21/—**	**each series**	**2/6**	**3/2**	**3/10**	**5/4**	**6/10**	
6524	with „ „	**doz.** „	—	—	**32/—**	„ „	**3/6**	**4/6**	**5/10**	**7/8**	**9/6**	

Latest Aeroplanes and their inventors, showing the most celebrated types of modern Flying Machines, finely finished
24 artistically finished pictures on 6 glass slides with text

			3	$3\frac{1}{2}$	4	$4\frac{1}{2}$	5		6	7	cm
		slides	$1\frac{3}{16}$	$1\frac{3}{8}$	$1\frac{1}{2}$	$1\frac{3}{4}$	2		$2\frac{3}{8}$	$2\frac{3}{4}$	in. wide
6521	without cover glass	**doz. series**	**8/6**	**10/6**	**12/8**	**16/10**	**21/—**	**each series**	**2/2**	**3/2**	
6523	with „ „	**doz. series**	—	—	**16/10**	**23/2**	**32/—**		**3/2**	**4/2**	

New socalled "Photobing" Slides

produced from real photographs, finely finished; specially suited for Magic Lanterns with petroleums lamps.

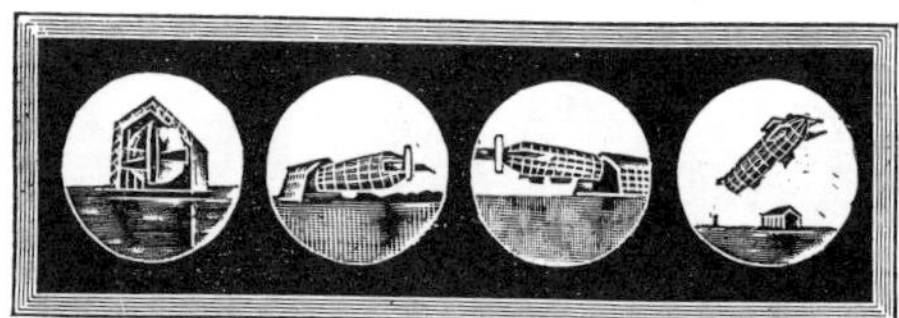

Zeppelin Airship Serie, 3 strips of 4 pictures each

7800/3	$3^1/_2$	4	$4^1/_2$	5	6 cm	
width of slide $1^1/_8$	$1^3/_8$	$1^5/_8$	$1^3/_4$	2	$2^3/_8$ in.	
without cover glass **doz. series 8/6**	**10/6**	**12/8**	**19/—**	**21/— each series**	**2/2**	each series of 3 strips

out of Series I

out of Series II

out of Series III

Industrial Pictures, 3 different series, **Photographs taken from Factories,** with descriptive text

Series I — Manufacture of Celluloid; Series II — Steel and iron Works; Series III — Manufacture of Porcelain

7802/3	$3^1/_2$	4	$4^1/_2$	5	6
width of slide $1^1/_8$	$1^3/_8$	$1^5/_8$	$1^3/_4$	2	$2^3/_8$ in.
doz. series of 3 strips **8/6**	**10/6**	**12/8**	**19/—**	**21/—**	**25/4**

Fine Photographic Magic Lantern-slides

(Photograms).

Zeppelin landing in Munich, Göppingen and Nuremberg, 12 different series of highly finished **original photographs** on 3 glass slides of 4 pictures each, with cover glass

6485/4	$4^1/_2$	5	6	7	8
slides $1^1/_2$	$1^3/_4$	2	$2^3/_8$	$2^3/_4$	$3^1/_8$ in. wide
per series of 3 strips **2/6**	**2/10**	**3/4**	**3/8**	**4/8**	**5/4**

a) Emergency-Landing at Göppingen
(Württbg.).

1. The airship lying at anchor, after its front being considerably damaged by knocking against a pear tree
2. The damaged front under repair
3. Troops watching the airship under repair
4. The airships front being repaired

b) Landing at Munich.

5. The airship on its flight near Munich
6. The airship approaching the landing place
7. Shortly before the landing
8. The airship lying at anchor

c) Landing at Nuremberg.

9. Approaching the landing place
10. The airship lowering for landing
11. Ready to anchor
12. The airship lying at anchor.

High Class Magic Lantern Glass Slides.

Original Photograms

Navy Pictures, 12 different series of highly finished original photographs on 3 glass slides of 4 pictures each with cover glass.

6488/4	$4^1/_2$	5	6	7	8	
slides $1^1/_2$	$1^3/_4$	2	$2^3/_8$	$2^3/_4$	$3^1/_8$	in. wide
per series 2/6	**2/10**	**3/4**	**3/8**	**4/8**	**5/4**	

1. Sailing yachts ("Germania" and "Meteor" on the start
2. Special-Yachts, in the foreground (No. 30) Yacht of the Crownprince of Germany
3. Race
4. Yacht "Germania"
5. H. M. Yachts, "Meteor" and "Hamburg"
6. Torpedoboat
7. Torpedoboat G. 111
8. H. M. S. "Bismarck"
9. H. M. S. "Kaiser Barbarossa"
10. H. M. Cruiser "Scharnhorst"
11. H. M. Armoured Cruiser "Braunschweig"
12. H. M. Cruiser "York" in the Kaiser Wilhelm-Kanal

out of series I

out of series II

Military Pictures, 12 different series each of 6492 and 6493 of highly finished original photographs on 3 glass slides of 4 pictures each with cover glass.

6492/4	$4^1/_2$	5	6	7	8	
slides $1^1/_2$	$1^3/_4$	2	$2^3/_8$	$2^3/_4$	$3^1/_8$	in. wide
series 2/6	**2/10**	**3/4**	**3/8**	**4/8**	**5/4**	per series = 3 strips

6493/4	$4^1/_2$	5	6	7	8	
slides $1^1/_2$	$1^3/_4$	2	$2^3/_8$	$2^3/_4$	$3^1/_8$	in. wide
series 2/6	**2/10**	**3/4**	**3/8**	**4/8**	**5/4**	per series = 3 strips

Series I (No. 6492)

1. Infantry on the march
2. Cavalry Parade
3. Quick firing gun section on the march
4. Artillery in fighting position
5. Marine-Artillery Parade
6. Quick firing gun section in action
7. Officers of the Staff
8. Operating the Heliograph (optical signal)
9. Infantery under cover
10. Infantry in action
11. Infantry in action under cover
12. Artillery in battle-position

Series II

1. Sappers building a pontoon bridge
2. Watering the horses
3. Taking water
4. Erecting the tents
5. In the Camp
6. Rest
7. Aerial Corps with balloon
8. Military balloon ready for starting
9. Military balloon on its flight scouting
10. The Kaiser with foreign Officers
11. The Kaiser in his Motor
12. The Kaiser on horseback

Short Glass Slides with Cover Glass

for Dissolving View Apparatus and Sciopticons.

6040

6040/8½ Glass pictures with cover glass, **finely coloured,** 3⅜ in. long, 3⅜ in. wide, size of picture 2⅜ in. diam. The assortment comprises 11 series of 12 pictures each . . . . per series each **4/4**

The assortment contains the following subjects:

Series I. 12 pictures =
4 pictures Punishment for stealing dainties.
4 „ Winter sports.
4 „ Summer sports.

Series II. 12 pictures =
4 pictures Modern means of conveyance.
4 „ Punishment for teasing.
4 „ Landscape.

Series III. 12 pictures =
4 pictures Landscapes in Switzerland.
4 „ New Landscape.
4 „ Boy and dog.

Series IV. 12 pictures =
4 pictures Motor-accident.
4 „ The naughty Poodle.
4 „ Teasing.

Series V. 12 pictures =
4 pictures Revenge of a painter.
4 „ Waiter's misfortune.
4 „ The naughty monkey.

Series VI. 12 pictures =
4 pictures Children's Scenes.
4 „ The two stout ones.
4 „ The wearisome sun.

Series VII. 12 pictures =
4 pictures The air pump.
4 „ Negro and goose.
4 „ Negro types.

Series VIII. 12 pictures =
4 pictures Children's Scenes.
4 „ Misfortune.
4 „ Children's Scenes.

Series IX. 12 pictures =
4 pictures Goose rider, Cat's spite.
4 „ Gazing in the air, Naughty Boys.
4 „ Lost balance, The unequal ones.

Series X. 12 pictures =
4 pictures Lubberland, Nutcracker.
4 „ Animals' pictures.
4 „ Animals' Scenes.

Series XI. 12 pictures =
4 pictures Children's Scenes.
4 „ Children's Games,
4 „ Children's Jokes.

for Dissolving View Apparatus and Sciopticons.

6630/8½ **Glass Slides finely coloured, well finished,** size 3¼×3¼ in., size of picture 2¾×2¾ in.
This assortment consists of 24 sets of pictures each set contains 12 separate pictures with words
Price per set of 12 pictures **4/4**

Subjects.

No. 1. 12 Slides The Old Testament.
„ 2. 12 „ The New Testament.
„ 3. 12 „ The Passion.
„ 4. 12 „ Paul and Virginia.
„ 5. 12 „ Life in Africa.
„ 6. 12 „ The Polar Regions.
„ 7. 12 „ Hunting and Animal pictures.
„ 8. 12 „ Wild Hunstman.
„ 9. 12 „ Land, Sea and Mountain Views.
„ 10. 12 „ Little Muck.
„ 11. 12 „ Caliph Stork.
„ 12. 12 „ Dwarf Nose.
„ 13. 12 „ Phantom Ship.
„ 14. 12 „ Discovery of America.
„ 15. 12 „ Reynard the Fox Part I, without text.
„ 16. 12 „ Robinson Crusoe.
„ 17. 12 „ Reynard the Fox Part II, without text.
„ 18. 12 „ Don Quixotte.
„ 19. 12 „ = { 6 Slides Red Ridinghood. / 6 „ Puss in Boots.
„ 20. 12 „ = { 6 „ Little Brother and Sister. / 6 „ Hansel and Gretel.
No. 21. 12 Slides = { 6 Slides Cinderella. / 6 „ Sleeping Beauty.
„ 22. 12 „ = { 6 „ Wolf and the Goats. / 6 „ Hare and the Hedgehog.
„ 23. 12 „ = { 6 „ Snow-white. / 6 „ Hop o' my thumb.
„ 24. 12 „ Palastine.
„ 25. 12 „ Max and Moritz, Boxer and Children's Scenes without text.
„ 26. 12 „ Natural Phenomena.
„ 27. 12 „ Egypt and the Nile.
„ 28. 12 „ New Landscapes, without text.
„ 29. 12 „ Different interesting pictures.
„ 30. 12 „ Switzerland.
„ 31. 12 „ Celebrated Buildings and Royal Castles in Munich.
„ 32. 12 „ Celebrated Buildings in Vienna and Prague.
„ 33. 12 „ Celebrated Churches.
„ 34. 12 „ The last of the Mohicans.
„ 35. 12 „ The brave little Tailor.
„ 36. 12 „ The Table, the Ass and the Stick.

Particulars for each subject to be had on application.

Development of aerial navigation

1 long Slide (celluloid film) for Magic Lanterns with 16 finely coloured pictures of the various means of aerial locomotion. Very interesting and up-to-date novelty.

10170/6 with frame 2⅜ in. wide . . . . per film incl. frame doz. **9/6**

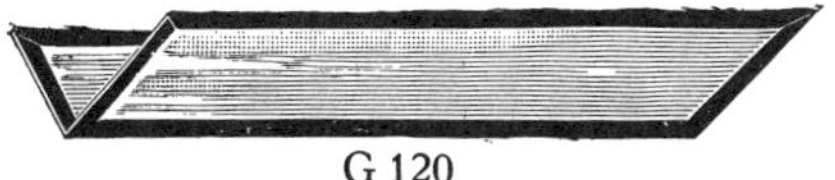

G 120

Gelatine Slides.

When ordering Gelatine slides, please always put "G" before the number. — If required we also deliver glass frames connected by hinges (see illustration) for showing the pictures in the lantern. It is however to be considered, that the Gelatine slides differ in width from the ordinary glass slides (they are abt. $\frac{3}{16}$ in. — $\frac{3}{8}$ in. smaller). But if they are used in connection with the above glass frames, they correspond exactly to the width of the ordinary glass slides.

Number of the **Gelatine slides**	corresponding No. of the glass slides	Description on page	Width of glass slides and glass frames												
			size	$2\frac{1}{2}$	3	$3\frac{1}{2}$	4	$4\frac{1}{2}$	5	6	7	8	9	10	11
			width	1	$1\frac{1}{8}$	$1\frac{3}{8}$	$1\frac{1}{2}$	$1\frac{3}{4}$	2	$2\frac{3}{8}$	$2\frac{3}{4}$	$3\frac{1}{8}$	$3\frac{1}{2}$	4	$4\frac{3}{8}$ in.
G 7695	**7695**	262	doz. ser.	**8/4**	**9/6**	**13/8**	**17/10**	**23/2**	**29/6**	each **3/6**	dz. **54/6**	**71/6**	**90/6**	each **10/6**	each **11/8**
G 6950	**6950**	262	" "		**9/6**	**13/8**	**17/10**	**23/2**	each **2/8**	series **3/6**	ser. **4/8**	**6/—**	**7/8**	series **10/6**	series **11/8**
G 9275	**9275**	263	" "		**11/6**	**16/6**	**20/6**	**27/4**	series **3/—**	**4/2**	**5/2**	**6/8**	**9/2**		
G 6974	**6974**	263	" "				**20/6**	**27/4**	" **3/—**	**4/2**	**5/2**	**6/8**	**9/2**		
G 6787	**6787**	264	" "		**11/6**	**16/6**	**20/6**	**27/4**	" **3/—**	**4/2**	**5/2**	**6/8**	**9/2**	**12/2**	**13/8**
G 8753	**8753**	264	" "		**11/6**	**16/6**	**20/6**	**27/4**	" **3/—**	**4/2**	**5/2**	**6/8**	**9/2**	**12/2**	**13/8**
G 7158	**7158**	264	" "			**16/4**	**20/6**	**27/4**	" **3/—**	**4/2**	**5/2**	**6/8**			
G 8845	**8845**	265	" "		**11/6**	**16/10**	**20/10**	**27/4**	" **3/—**	**4/2**	**5/4**	**6/8**	**9/2**		
G 8847	**8847**	265	" "		**11/6**	**16/10**	**20/10**	**27/4**	" **3/—**	**4/2**	**5/4**	**6/8**	**9/2**		
G 6610	**6610**	265								**4/2**	**5/4**	**6/8**	**9/2**	**12/2**	
G 6846	**6846**	265	" "				**21/—**	**28/—**	" **3/2**	**4/2**	**5/4**	**6/8**	**9/2**		
G 7682	**7682**	265	" "	**8/4**	**9/6**	**13/8**	**17/10**	**23/2**	dz. ser. **29/6**	**42/—**	dz. **54/6**	**71/6**	**90/6**	each **10/6**	**11/8**
G 9436	**9436**	266	" "				**21/—**	**27/4**	ser. **3/2**	**4/2**	each **5/4**	**6/8**	**9/2**	**12/2**	
G 7190	**7190**	266	" "				**21/—**	**27/4**	" **3/2**	**4/2**	series **5/4**	**6/8**	**9/2**	**12/2**	
G 8841	**8841**	266	" "		**11/6**	**16/10**	**21/—**	**27/2**	" **3/2**	**4/2**	**5/4**	**6/8**	**9/2**		
G 6621	**6621**	266	serie				**1/9**	**2/4**	**3/2**	**4/2**	**5/4**	**6/8**	**9/2**	**12/2**	
G 6632	**6632**	267	doz. ser.				**21/—**	**27/4**	ser. **3/2**	**4/2**	**5/4**	**6/8**	**9/2**	**12/2**	
G 6473	**6473**	267	" "				**21/—**	**27/4**	" **3/2**	**4/2**	**5/4**	**6/8**	**9/2**	**12/2**	
G 6522	**6522**	267	doz.		**12/8**	**16/10**	**21/—**	each **2/6**	**3/2**	**3/10**	**5/4**	**6/10**			
G 6521	**6521**	267	doz. ser.		**8/6**	**10/6**	**12/8**	**16/10**	**21/—**	ser. **2/2**	**3/2**				
G 6040	**6040**/$8\frac{1}{2}$	270	Series 1—11, 1 series consisting of 3 slides of 4 pictures each, $13\frac{1}{4}$ in. . . . . per series												**4/4**
G 6630	**6630**/$8\frac{1}{2}$	270	" 1—18 and 24—36, 1 series each of 3 slides of 4 pictures each, $13\frac{1}{4}$ in. " "												**4/4**
			" 19—23, 1 series each of 4 slides of 3 pictures each, 10 in . . . . . . " "												**4/4**

G 120 **Glass Frames,** fitting Gelatine slides

size	3	$3\frac{1}{2}$	4	$4\frac{1}{2}$	5	6	7	8	9	10	11
with	$1\frac{1}{8}$	$1\frac{3}{8}$	$1\frac{1}{2}$	$1\frac{3}{4}$	2	$2\frac{3}{8}$	$2\frac{3}{4}$	$3\frac{1}{8}$	$3\frac{1}{2}$	4	$4\frac{3}{8}$ in.
gross	**24/2**	**30/6**	**34/8**	doz. **3/10**	**4/4**	**5/2**	**6/—**	**7/—**	**8/10**	**9/8**	**11/8**

Moving Pictures in Wood and Tin Frames.

☞ It is important when ordering pictures in wooden frames, to remember that they sometimes differ in width from the glass slides (see description of Lanterns); therefore please give the respective width of the frames, as stated in description of Magic Lanterns. The width of the tin frames corresponds with that of the glass slides.

Chromotropes with Cog-wheel gear in 12 different designs.

	size	$3\frac{1}{2}$	4	$4\frac{1}{2}$	5	6	7	8
	width in.	$1\frac{3}{8}$	$1\frac{9}{16}$	$1\frac{3}{4}$	2	$2\frac{3}{8}$	$2\frac{3}{4}$	$3\frac{1}{8}$ in.
6910 in tin frames	doz.	**4/6**	**5/—**	**6/—**	**7/—**	**8/—**	**11/—**	**13/6**

	size	$3\frac{1}{2}$	4	$4\frac{1}{2}$	5	6	7	8	9	10
	width in.	$1\frac{3}{8}$	$1\frac{9}{16}$	$1\frac{3}{4}$	2	$2\frac{3}{8}$	$2\frac{3}{4}$	$3\frac{1}{8}$	$3\frac{1}{2}$	4 in.
6958 in wood frames	doz.	**8/6**	**9/—**	**10/—**	**12/8**	**15/10**	**19/6**	**22/2**	**25/4**	**30/6**

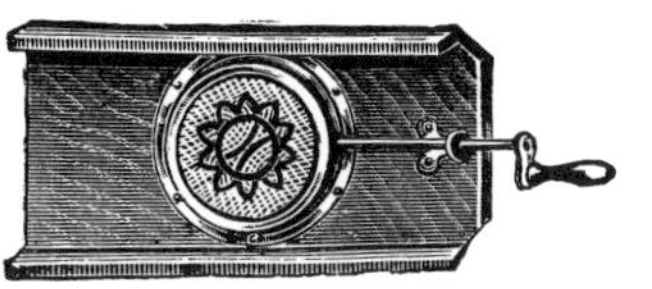

6958 and 8344

Cromotropes with Cog-wheel gear (Hand-Painted) **in wood frame,** in 36 designs.

8344/4	$4\frac{1}{2}$	5	6	7	8	9	10
width $1\frac{9}{16}$	$1\frac{3}{4}$	2	$2\frac{3}{8}$	$2\frac{3}{4}$	$3\frac{1}{8}$	$3\frac{1}{2}$	4 in.
doz. **11/6**	**13/8**	**15/6**	**20/—**	**24/2**	**28/4**	each **2/10**	**3/4**

Moving Pictures in Wood and Tin Frames.

☛ It is important when ordering pictures in woden frames, to remember that they sometimes differ in width from the glass slides (see description of Lanterns); therefore please give the respective width of the frames, as stated in description of Magic Lanterns. The width of the tin frames corresponds with that of the glass slides.

7296

New Revolving Pictures, in **wood frame,** in 6 Subjects:

1. Windmill.
2. Water Mill.
3. Soap Bubbles.
4. Aquarium with Fishes.
5. Conjurer.
6. Clown with 8 Heads.

7296/4	4½	5	6	7	8	9	
width 1 9/16	1 3/4	2	2 3/8	2 3/4	3 1/8	3 1/2	in.
doz. **9/6**	**11/6**	**14/—**	**16/4**	**17/10**	**20/10**	**23/8**	

9030

New Lever Pictures, in **wood frame,** in 6 Subjects:

1. Mother and Child.
2. Butterfly Hunting.
3. The Painter.
4. Cat and Clock.
5. Punch and the Devil.
6. Ship in Stormy Sea.

	9030/4	4½	5	6	7	8	9	10	
width	1 9/16	1 3/4	2	2 3/8	2 3/4	3 1/8	3 1/2	4	in.
doz.	**10/6**	**11/6**	**13/8**	**15/6**	**20/6**	**22/6**	**26/4**	**30/—**	

New Fixed Landscapes, in **wood frame,** in 12 Subjects:

7297

1. Axen Street on the Lake of the four Forest Towns.
2. Grand Canal in Venice.
3. Ambros Castle in the Tyrol.
4. Miramare Castle.
5. The Memnon Columns near Thebes
6. Akka on the Mediterranean Sea.
7. Corfu Island.
8. Niagara Falls.
9. Yellowstone Park.
10. Northern Landscape with the Midnight Sun.
11. Berg Castle on Lake Starnberg.
12. Carlstein Castle (Bohemia).

	7297/5	6	7	8	9	10	
width	2	2 3/8	2 3/4	3 1/8	3 1/2	4	in.
doz.	**8/8**	**10/—**	**11/—**	**13/2**	**13/10**	**16/10**	

New comical changing Pictures, in Tin frame, 12 Subjects.

7254

1. Vagabond and Swell.
2. Professor bathing.
3. Sleeping Postillon.
4. Peasant and Locomotive.
5. Newly painted seat.
6. Tourist and Crocodile.
7. Peasant and Goat.
8. Disappointed Fisherman.
9. Chimney-sweep and Baker,
10. Courageous Lady Cyclist.
11. Forgetting his part.
12. The Cooper's bad luck.

	7254/3½	4	4½	5	6	7	8	9	10	
width	1 3/8	1 9/16	1 3/4	2	2 3/8	2 3/4	3 1/8	3 1/2	4	in.
doz.	**3/—**	**3/6**	**4/2**	**4/10**	**6/4**	**7/10**	**10/—**	**11/8**	**13/—**	

New comical changing Pictures, in wood frame

12 Subjects.

7221

1. Vagabond and Swell.
2. Professor bathing.
3. Sleeping Postillon.
4. Peasant and Locomotive.
5. Newly painted seat.
6. Tourist and Crocodile.
7. Peasant and Goat.
8. Disappointed Fisherman.
9. Chimney-sweep and Baker.
10. Courageous Lady Cyclist.
11. Forgetting his part.
12. The Cooper's bad luck.

7221/4	$4\frac{1}{2}$	5	6	7	8	9	10
width $1\frac{9}{16}$	$1\frac{3}{4}$	2	$2\frac{3}{8}$	$2\frac{3}{4}$	$3\frac{3}{16}$	$3\frac{1}{2}$	4 in.
doz. **6/4**	**7/10**	**8/8**	**10/—**	**12/10**	**15/10**	**18/4**	**20/6**

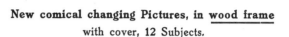

New comical changing Pictures, in wood frame

with cover, 12 Subjects.

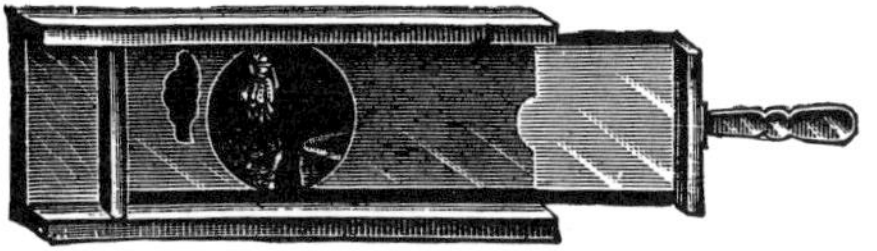

7255

1. The Mountaineer.
2. Conjurer.
3. Pupil and Teacher.
4. Juggler.
5. Horseman.
6. Mysterious Basket.
7. Clown and Dog
8. Gallant Railway Conductor.
9. The unlucky Doll
10. Unlucky Cyclist.
11. Highway-man.
12. Good night.

7255/4	$4\frac{1}{2}$	5	6	7	8	9	10
width $1\frac{9}{16}$	$1\frac{3}{4}$	2	$2\frac{3}{8}$	$2\frac{3}{4}$	$3\frac{3}{16}$	$3\frac{1}{2}$	4 in.
doz. **8/8**	**9/6**	**10/10**	**13/2**	**15/10**	**17/10**	**21/—**	**24/—**

New Landscapes with sliding Figures, in wood frame

12 Subjects.

7268

1. The Flood (comical).
2. Herdsman's cottage with Cattle.
3. Houses of Parliament in Berlin, with tram.
4. St. Peters Church, Rome, a procession.
5. A Balloon.
6. Lighthouse and Ships.
7. Mosque in Cairo with Caravan.
8. St. Gotthards Railway with train and bridge.
9. Conflagration and Fire Brigade.
10. Gondolas in Venice.
11. Bridge in St. Petersburg with Sledge Party.
12. Rhine Landscape with sailing Boats.

7268/4	$4\frac{1}{2}$	5	6	7	8	9	10
width $1\frac{9}{16}$	$1\frac{3}{4}$	2	$2\frac{3}{8}$	$2\frac{3}{4}$	$3\frac{1}{8}$	$3\frac{1}{2}$	4 in.
doz. **8/8**	**9/6**	**11/6**	**13/2**	**16/10**	**17/10**	**21/6**	**25/2**

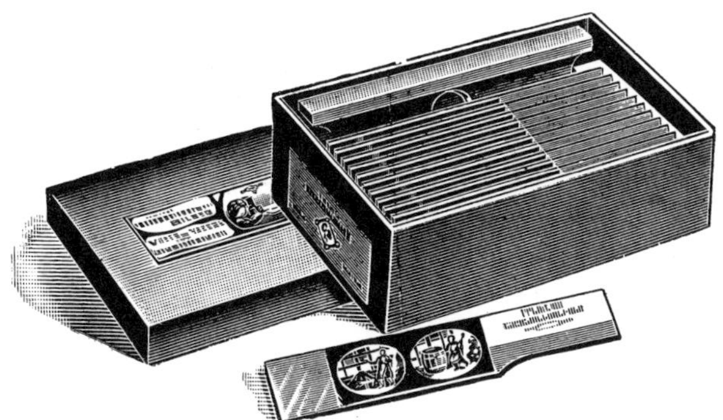

7364

7364 New comical moving Pictures

very practically packed

with **1 wooden frame and 12 exchangeable changing pictures.**

By this new arrangement it is possible — by using only one wooden frame for all moving pictures — to supply a larger number of pictures at a comparatively cheap price.

7364/$3\frac{1}{2}$	4	$4\frac{1}{2}$		5	6	7	8	9	10
width $1\frac{3}{8}$	$1\frac{9}{16}$	$1\frac{3}{4}$		2	$2\frac{3}{8}$	$2\frac{3}{4}$	$3\frac{1}{8}$	$3\frac{1}{2}$	4 in.
doz. boxes **22/2**	**27/4**	**31/6**	each	**3/2**	**4/4**	**5/4**	**6/8**	**8/—**	**9/4**

3500

Camera Obscura

(Drawing Apparatus)

finely japanned, with lens, mirror, frosted glass and movable hood.

3500/0	6 in. long, $5^1/_4$ in. wide, $5^1/_4$ in. high	each	**6/4**
„ /1	$6^1/_2$ in. long, 6 in. wide, 6 in. high	each	**8/6**
„ /2	$8^1/_4$ in. long, 7 in. wide, 7 in. high	each	**10/—**

2959

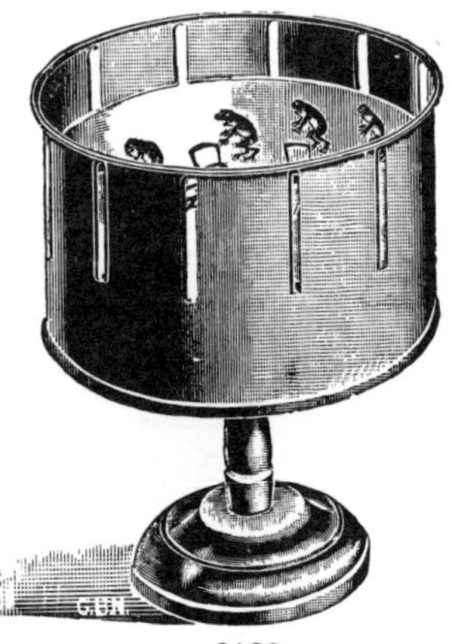

9192

Zoetropes (Wheels of life)

Russian Iron, with strong wooden stand and 6 strips of pictures = 12 pictures.

9192/1	$4^1/_4$ in. diam.		doz.	**10/6**
„ /2	$5^3/_8$ „	„	„	**17/—**
„ /3	$6^3/_8$ „	„	„	**25/4**
„ /4	$7^3/_8$ „	„	each	**3/—**
„ /5	$9^1/_2$ „	„	„	**4/8**

Zoetropes Pictures

one serie consisting of 6 strips = 12 pictures.

8914/1	2	3	4	5
per doz. ser. **5/2**	**7/—**	**8/8**	**13/6**	**20/—**

Zoetropes as Models for Steam Engines see page 81.

Megagraph (Projection and Drawing Apparatus).

Apparatus for Projecting opaque Articles; any photograph coloured opaque pictures, picture postcards, can be produced on the wall greatly magnified or on the table for drawing by means of the mirror.

2959 **Megascope** (Megagraph) very strong and elegantly finished, adjustable with stand $6^1/_4$ in. wide, $16^1/_8$ in. high incl. chimney $4^3/_8$ in. deep . . . each **15/4**

Caleidoscopes.

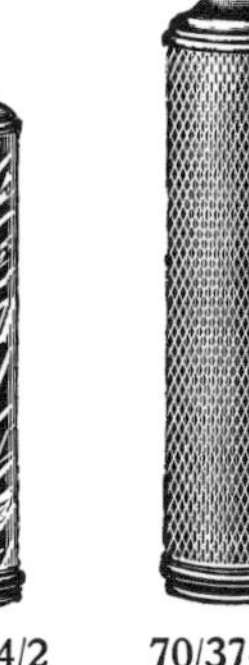

70/374/00—1 70/374/2 70/374/3 70/375/1 70/375/2 70/376 9488

70/374/00	**Caleidoscopes** (Chromotrope) coloured tin printed,	$4^1/_4$ in. long,	1 in. diam.	gross	**17/—**
„ /0	„ „ „ „	5 „ „	$1^1/_8$ „ „	„	**24/—**
„ /1	„ „ „ „	$6^3/_8$ „ „	$1^1/_2$ „ „	doz.	**3/4**
„ /2	„ „ „ „	$8^3/_4$ „ „	$1^3/_4$ „ „	„	**4/10**
„ /3	„ „ „ „	$10^1/_4$ „ „	$2^3/_8$ „ „	„	**9/2**

Fine Caleidoscopes (Chromotrope) with ornamental glass and nickelled metal mounting.

70/375/1	5 in. long, $2^1/_4$ in. diam.	doz.	**17/2**
„ /2	8 „ „ $2^1/_4$ „ „	each	**2/2**

Caleidoscope with original photographs (children scenes) with nickelled metal mounting.

70/376 5 in. long, $2^1/_4$ in. diam. . . . doz. **19/6**

Very fine Caleidoscope (Chromotrope) on finely polished wooden stand, with various magnificent designs.

9488 very strong finish, $12^1/_4$ in. high, $10^3/_4$ in. long . . . each **10/6**

Stereoscopes

in excellent, strong and elegant finish with best optic lenses.

For Stereoscope-pictures see page 278

(with exception of No. 362, stereoscop pictures size $3^1/_2 \times 7^1/_8$ in. are fitting these sterescopes).

362 358/00 358/1

362	**Miniature Stereoscope**, lenses 1 in. diam., with 3 miniature stereoscope pictures	doz. **9/10**
358/00	**Stereoscope**, with 2 prisms 1×1 in. sliding picture holder and fixed wooden handle, dull finish	„ **18/—**
„ /1	„ with 2 prisms 1×1 in. „ „ „ „ folding wooden handle, alder wood dull finish, with sliding picture holder	„ **27/4**

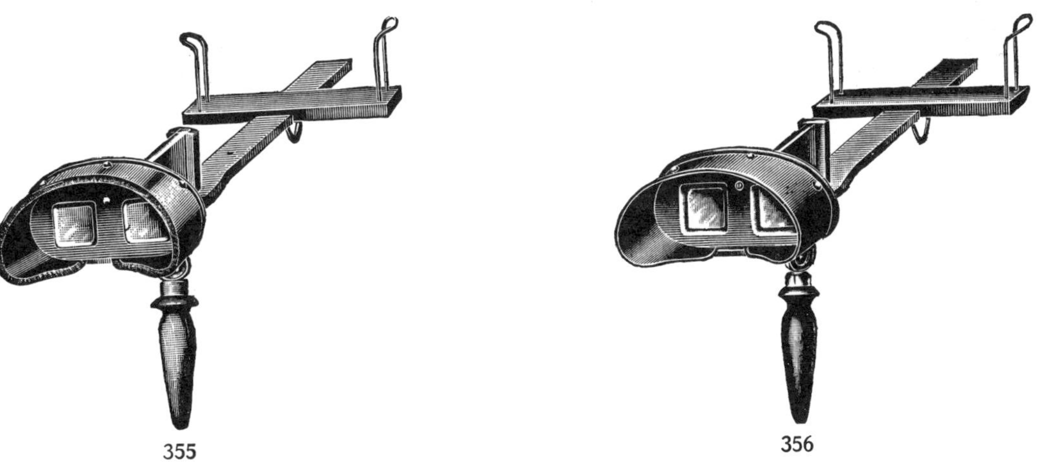

355 356

Stereoscopes with sliding picture holder and folding wooden handle

prisms $1^1/_4 \times 1^3/_8$ in.

355/0	Alder wood, plain	each **2/8**
„ /1	Real walnut, plain, with plush border	„ **3/—**
„ /1½	„ „ „	„ **3/6**
„ /2	„ „ finely polished	„ **5/—**
„ /2½	„ mahogany, finely polished	„ **5/—**
„ /3	Finely black polished	„ **5/8**

Stereoscopes with sliding picture holder, folding wooden handle

prisms $1^1/_2 \times 1^1/_2$ in.

356/0	Alder wood, plain	each **3/—**
„ /1	Real walnut, plain, with plush border	„ **3/6**
„ /1½	„ „ „	„ **3/10**
„ /2	„ „ finely polished	„ **5/4**
„ /2½	„ mahogany, finely polished	„ **5/4**
„ /3	„ Finely black polished	„ **6/—**

Stereoscopes

in excellent, strong and elegant finish with best optic lenses.

317 and 348
with aluminium shade

American Stereoscopes

with aluminium shade, plush border, sliding picture holder and folding wooden handle.

prisms: $1^1/_4 \times 1^3/_8$ in.

317/0	Alder wood, dull finish	each	**3/6**
„ /1	Real walnut, dull finish	„	**3/10**
„ /1½	„ „ „ „ with plush border	„	**4/2**
„ /2	„ „ polished „ „ „	„	**5/8**

prisms: $1^9/_{16} \times 1^9/_{16}$ in.

348/0	Alder wood, dull finish	each	**3/10**
„ /1	Real walnut, „ „	„	**4/2**
„ /1½	„ „ „ „ with plush border	„	**4/6**
„ /2	„ „ polished „ „ „	„	**6/—**

350

352/1

522/1

Stereoscopes straight form, with prisms $1^1/_4 \times 1^3/_8$ in., flap with tin-foil reflector and frosted glass back

350 Mahogany-polished wood $7^3/_4$ in. long, $6^3/_4$ in. high . . . . . each **5/2**

Stereoscopes curved form, with 2 prisms $1^1/_4 \times 1^3/_8$ in. and frosted glass back $7^3/_4$ in. long, $6^3/_4$ in. high

352/1 Real Mahogany, finely polished, flap with mirror . . . . . each **6/8**

Stereoscopes curved form, with 2 prisms $1^9/_{16} \times 1^9/_{16}$ in., frosted glass back and flap with mirror $7^1/_2$ in. long, $6^7/_8$ in. high

522/1 Real Mahogany finely polished . . . . . each **7/—**

353

523

Stereoscopes, with 2 oculars, diameter of lens $1^1/_4$ in., flap with mirror, with frosted glass back, $7^3/_4$ in. long, 6 in. high

353/1	Real Mahogany, finely polished	each	**8/—**
„ /2	„ American walnut, finely polished	„	**8/—**

Stereoscopes, with 2 oculars, diameter of lens $1^1/_4$ in., flap with mirror, with frosted glass back, **with adjustable oculars,** $7^1/_4$ in. long, $6^1/_4$ in. high

523/1	Real Mahogany, finely polished	each	**14/4**
„ /2	„ American walnut, finely polished	„	**14/4**

Stereoscope-Revolving-Apparatus.

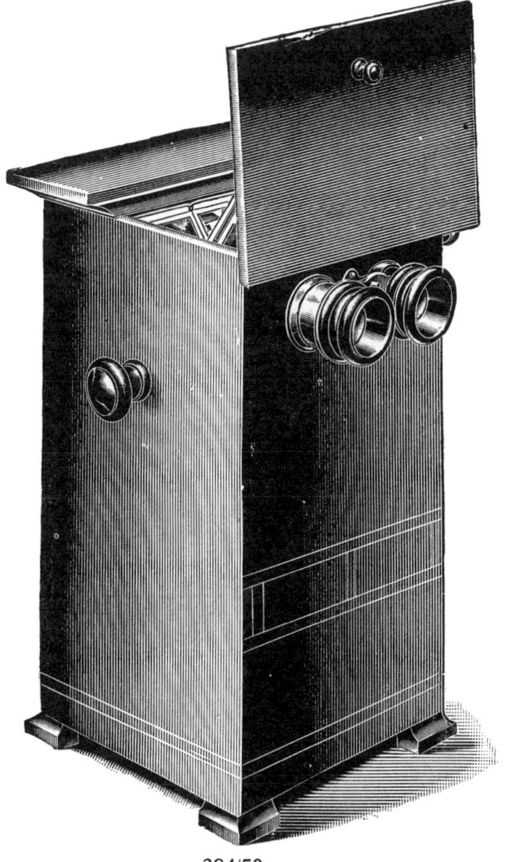

384/50

Fine mahogany-polish

383/50 with best oculars, adjustable in the longitudinal direction, for 50 pictures, $19^3/_4$ in. high (without pictures) . . . . each **68/—**

Real mahogany, finely polished and decorated

384/50 with best oculars, adjustable in the longitudinal direction, for 50 pictures, $19^3/_4$ in. high (without pictures) . . . . each **80/—**

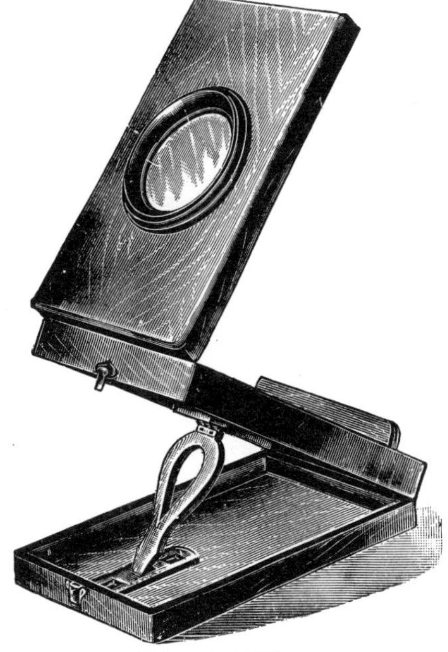

370 and 371

373 and 374/4

Apparatus for magnifying Photographs and picture postcards.

(Microphores).

Microphores, with sliding picture holder, very strongly and elegantly finished, with best optic lenses.

370	Wood, fine mahogany-polished,	lens $2^1/_2$ in. diam.,	6 in. long,	$3^1/_2$ in. wide	each **3/4**
371	„ „ „ „	lens 3 in. diam.,	$8^1/_4$ „ „	$4^3/_4$ „ „	„ **5/—**
372	Real mahogany, finely polished,	lens $3^3/_8$ in. diam.,	$8^1/_4$ „ „	$5^1/_4$ „ „	„ **9/2**
373	„ „ polished, with stand,	lens $3^3/_8$ in. diam.,	9 „ „	$5^3/_4$ „ „	„ **14/4**
374/4	„ „ „ „ „	lens $4^1/_8$ in. diam.,	10 „ „	$6^3/_4$ „ „	„ **19/—**

Pictures for Stereoscopes.

Excellent finish.

9216/6

Fine Original-Photographs in bromide of silver print.

9216/6 packed in envelopes, containing 1 serie of 10 pieces . . . . each serie **2/6**

The pictures are sold in complete series of 10 pieces only.

Collection of Pictures and Series.

1 Series containing 10 pictures.

Series	
1—7	Rhine
8—11	Dresden
17—20	Giant mountains
25—26	Franconian Switzerland
27—34	Bavarian Highlands
47—48	On the Baltic
50—51	Imperial Manoeuvres
52	Prague
54—55	Valley of the Ziller, Lake Achen
56—62	Rome
71—72	Bologna, Naples, Pompeii
73—74	Venice
75—76	Paris, Louvre Museum
77—82	Paris
89—90	Versailles
92	French Castles
94—97	Berlin-Charlottenburg-Potsdam
98—100	Black Forest
105—106	Taunus
107	Frankfurt on Main
109—110	Harz
111—112	Brussels
113—118	Switzerland

Series	
123—128	Riviera
139	Warsaw
143	Moscaw
145	Petersburg
147—150	Vienna
155—156	Nuremberg
157—158	Lake Constance
160—162	Munich
163—165	Bavarian Royal Castles
171	Upper Egypt
173—175	Cairo
181—182	Saxon Switzerland
183—184	Bing Cave*
187	Eisenach
189—191	Hamburg
194	Hannover
205—206	Ascending Montblanc
207—208	High Tauern
214—215	Budapest
219—220	Sweden
224—226	Norway
229—230	Antwerp
231	Bruges
233	Ostend

Series	
235	Caucasia
237	Athens
242—243	Himalaya, India
247—248	Constantinople
249—251	Japan
254—255	South-Sea Coast
260	Victoria-Avenue in Berlin
262—266	Children's Scenes
267—268	At the sea-side
269	Fairy Tales (Hansel and Gretel)
270	Family scenes
271	Coast of Pola—Abazzia
272	Dalmatien
274	The Dolomites
279	Alhambra
285—286	Aëroplane
287—289	Seaside Places at the North Sea
290	Sellin (Baltic Seaside place)
291	Blue Jackets at the seaside
292—294	Zoological Garden in Berlin
295—297	The Netherlands
298	Zeppelin Airship

*) newly discovered, highly interesting stalactite cave in Franconian Switzerland, Germany's largest and finest stalactite gallery-cave.

10393 New fine **coloured Stereoscope** pictures, Original **photographic reproductions in natural colours** (after Lumière's system) high class printing, very plastic effect in series . . . . each consisting of 6 pieces **2/—**

Series	
1	Landscapes, Flowers, Family Scenes
1a	„ „ „ „
2	At the Lake of Garda
2a	Winter Scenery, Palm Gardens
3	Western Dolomites

Series	
3a	Flower Beds
4	Rome
5	„
6	Pompeii
7	Berlin

Series	
8	Amalfi and Sorrent
9	Capri
10	Winter Landscapes
11	Meran

The Collection will be continually enlarged by new reproductions.

9216/7 **Miniature Stereoscope pictures,** fitting Stereoscope 362 Landscapes, views of towns &c. . . . doz. series **8/6**

9216/7

Series	
2	Family Scenes
4	Rome, Venice &c.
6—8	Rome
9—12	Paris

Series	
13	Hamburg
14—15	The Baltic and German Ocean
16—17	Baltic Sea
18	The Rhine

Series	
19	Capri
20—23	Bavarian Highlands
24	Views of Harbours

These Miniature Stereoscope pictures can only be sold in series of 25 pictures.

Magnifying and Reading Glasses.

7008

9029

7009

Reading Glasses
with nickelled mountings and black wood handle

7008/30	1 in. diam.	doz.	**3/2**
„ /35	1 1/4 „ „	„	**3/10**
„ /40	1 1/2 „ „	„	**5/2**
„ /45	1 3/4 „ „	„	**5/10**
„ /50	2 „ „	„	**8/6**
„ /57	2 1/4 „ „	„	**11/8**

Reading (magnifying) Glasses
sewn on cards, superior quality, with **finely nickelled** brass mountings and **finely nickelled** solid handles

9029/1 1/2 with **good** lenses, 4 each of size 1, 1 3/16, 1 3/8 in., sewn on card, per card **8/6**

9029/2 1/2 with **best** lenses, 4 each of size 1 3/16, 1 3/8, 1 9/16 in., sewn on card, per card **11/8**

Reading Glasses
with finely nickelled brass mountings and polished wood handle

7009/35	1 1/4 in. diam.	doz.	**12/8**
„ /45	1 3/4 „ „	„	**14/2**
„ /50	2 „ „	„	**15/10**
„ /55	2 1/4 „ „	„	**17/10**
„ /65	2 1/2 „ „	„	**20/—**

Optical Lenses and Stereoscopic Glasses.

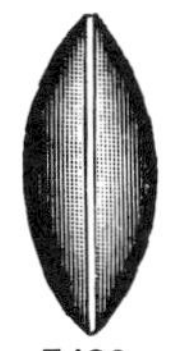

7420
biconvex

7421 and 7428
planconvex

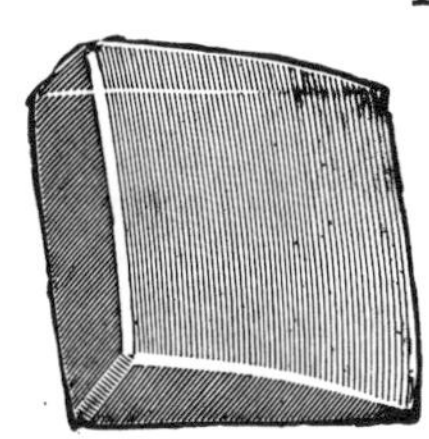

7423

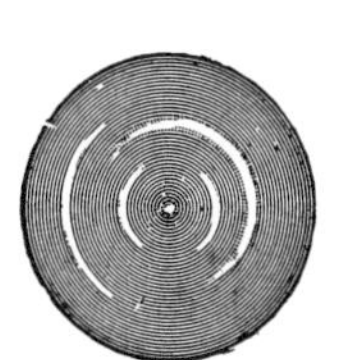

7439

Stereoscopic Glasses

Biconvex Lenses with rounded rims and short focus

7420/15	20	25	30	35	40	45	50	55	60	65	70
9/16	3/4	1	1 1/8	1 1/4	1 1/2	1 3/4	2	2 1/4	2 3/8	2 1/2	2 3/4 in. diam.
Focus 2 1/2	2 1/2	3	3	3 1/2	3 1/2	4	4	4 1/2	4 1/2	5	5"
gross **13/8**	**27/4**	doz. **2/10**	**3/10**	**6/2**	**6/4**	**7/8**	**9/8**	**13/2**	**19/—**	**22/8**	**27/10**

Plano Convex Lenses with rounded rims and long focus

7421/40	45	50	55	60	65	70
1 1/2	1 3/4	2	2 1/4	2 3/8	2 1/2	2 3/4 in. diam.
Focus 7	8	8	9	9	10	10"
doz. **3/6**	**5/10**	**6/4**	**8/8**	**10/10**	**15/4**	**19/4**

7428/35	40	45	50	55	60	65	70	80	90	103
1 1/4	1 1/2	1 3/4	2	2 1/4	2 3/8	2 1/2	2 3/4	3 1/8	3 1/2	4 1/8 in. diam.
Focus 4 1/2	5	7	7	7	7	7	7	7	8	8"
doz. **4/10**	**6/4**	**6/4**	**6/10**	**10/2**	**12/8**	**19/6**	each **2/6**	**2/8**	**3/6**	**5/2**

Stereoscopic Glasses, prismatic cut

7423/0	0 1/2	1
1×1	1 1/4×1 3/8	1 1/2×1 1/2 in.
doz. pairs **6/2**	**10/2**	**15/2**

Stereoscopes Lenses, round

7439/25	33	40
1	1 5/16	1 5/8 in. diam.
doz. pairs **3/6**	**5/2**	**7/4**

Sundry Parts for Magic Lanterns.

Objectives.

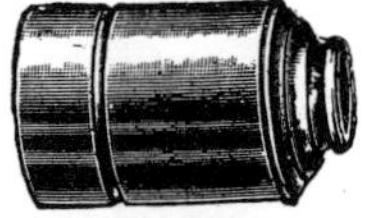

plain finish

turned

with rack and pinion

No. of the Objective:	**10410**/1	2	3	4	5	6	7	8	9
No. of the Apparatus:	222/42	47	47	47	47 47 57	58 58	360—363	370—373	380—382
Size of the Apparatus:	2½	4	4½	5	6 7 7	6 7	7	8	9
Price of the Objective:	doz. **8/6**	**14/6**	**17/6**	**each 5/—**	**6/—**	**7/6**	**9/—**	**10/—**	**16/—**

No. of the Objective:	**10411**/1	2	3	4	5	6	7	8	9
No. of the Apparatus:	70 850 — —	110 850 150 875 170 — 250 —	250 450 875 —	250 350 450 875	250 350 450 875	250 350 450 875	250 350 450 875	250 350 875 —	250 350 875 —
Size of the Apparatus:	2½	3	3½	4	4½	5	6	7	8
Price of the Objective:	doz. **5/6**	**8/6**	**14/6**	**17/6**	**20/—**	**24/6**	**30/6**	**39/—**	**—/—**

No. of the Objective:	**10412**/1	2	3	4	5	6	7	8
	930 960 — —	930 960 — —	930 960 970 1170	930 960 970 1170	930 960 970 1170	930 960 970 1170	930 960 970 1170	930 960 — —
Size of the Apparatus:	3½	4	4½	5	6	7	8	9
Price of the Objective:	doz. **17/6**	**21/6**	**26/—**	**30/6**	**each 3/—**	**3/6**	**4/6**	**5/6**

Condensors.

No. of the Condensor:	**10408**/1	2	3	4	5	6	7	8	9	10	11	12	13
No. of Apparatus:	930—960—970							1170 —	1170 1250	1170 1250	1170 —	1170 —	1170 —
Size of the Apparatus:	3½	4	4½	5	6	7	8	4½	5	6	7	8	9
Price of the Condensor:	doz. **5/—**	**6/—**	**7/6**	**9/6**	**11/6**	**16/—**	**21/6**	**17/6**	**20/—**	**26/—**	**34/6**	**each 4/—**	**5/—**

No. of the Condensor:	**10408**/9	10	12	14	15	16
No. of the Apparatus:	222/47	47 58	47 57 360—363 58	370—373	380—382	390—392
Size of the Apparatus:	5	6 6	7	8	9	10
Price of the Condensor:	doz. **20/—**	**26/—**	**each 4/—**	**each 8/—**	**each 10/—**	**each 12/—**

Reflectors.

No. of the Reflector:	**10409**/1	2	3	4
No. of the Apparatus:	1170 930 930 — 960 960 — — —	930 930 960 960 — —	1170 930 960	1170 1170 930 — 960 —
Size of the Apparatus:	5 3½ 4½	5 6	7	8 9
Price of the Reflector:	gross **18/—**	**30/—**	doz. **7/6**	**9/6**

Sundry Parts for Cinematographs and Magic Lanterns.

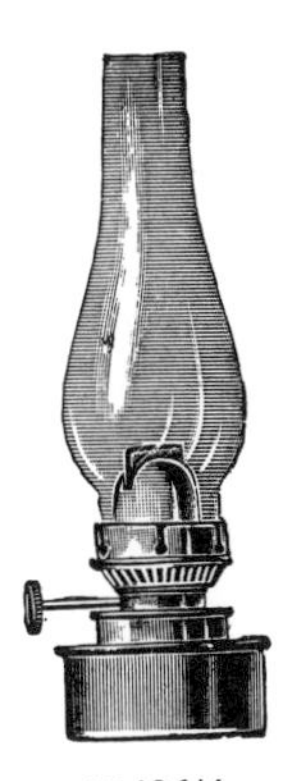
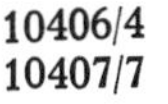
10406/4
10407/7

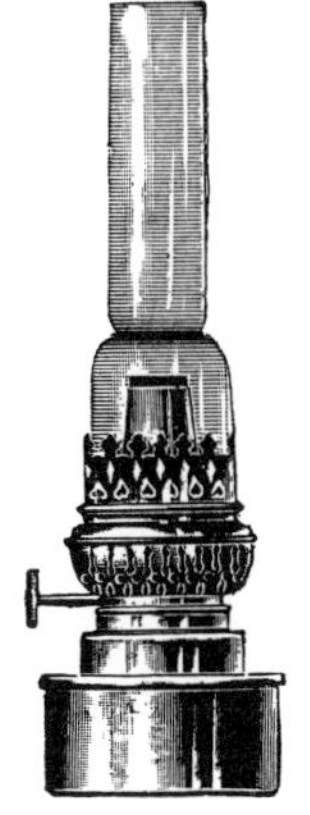
10406/6
10407/11

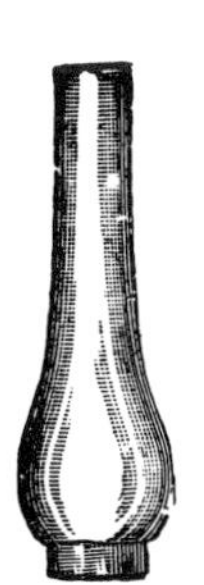
6672/3

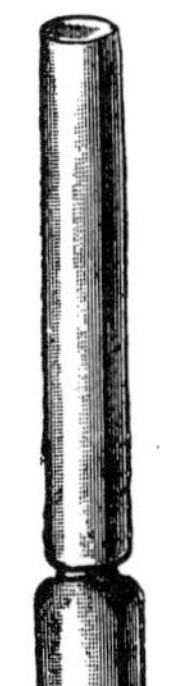
6680/10

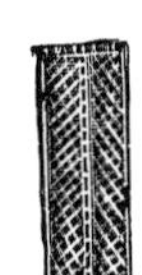
6682

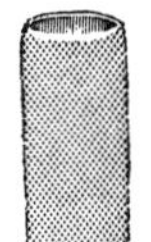
6709

Lamps for Cinematographs.

No. of the Lamp:	**10406**/1	2	3	4	5	6
No. of the Apparatus:	222/42	44 45	47	47	47	47
Size of the Apparatus:	$2\frac{1}{2}$	3 $3\frac{1}{2}$	4	$4\frac{1}{2}$	5	6
Price of the Lamp:	doz. **8/6**	**13/—**	**13/—**	**17/—**	**33/6**	**38/6**

No. of the Lamp:	**10406**/7	8	9	10	11	12
No. of the Apparatus:	222/47 „ /57	48 58	48 and 58 360—363	370—373 —	380—382 —	390—392 —
Size of the Apparatus:	7	6	7	8	9	10
Price of the Lamp each	**4/—**	**5/—**	**5/6**	**12/—**	**13/6**	**14/—**

Lamps for Magic Lanterns.

No. of the Lamp:	**10407**/1	2	3	4	5	6
No. of the Apparatus:	70 110 — 150 — 170	850 850 — — — —	875 — —	250 250 250 222/45 — 875 — — 930	875 930 —	250 — —
	$2\frac{1}{2}$ 3	$2\frac{1}{2}$ 3	3	3, $3\frac{1}{2}$ 4, $4\frac{1}{2}$	5—6	6
Price of the Lamp:	doz. **2/—**	**6/—**	**7/6**	**8/6**	**11/6**	**14/6**

No. of the Lamp:	**10407**/7	8	9	10	11	12
No. of the Apparatus:	875 930	250 —	250 —	1170 —	1170 —	1170 —
Size of the Apparatus:	7—8	7	8	$4\frac{1}{2}$—5	6—7	8—9
Price of the Lamp:	doz. **17/6**	**20/—**	each **2/—**	**3/—**	**3/6**	**4/—**

Chimneys for flat burners.

	6672/2	3	5	8‴
diam. of rim about:	1	$1\frac{5}{16}$	$1\frac{3}{8}$	$1\frac{5}{8}$ in.
gross	**8/6**	**9/—**	**10/6**	**12/—**

Chimneys for round burners.

	6680/8	10	12	14
diam. of rim about:	$1\frac{3}{8}$	$1\frac{1}{2}$	$1\frac{11}{16}$	$1\frac{15}{16}$ in.
gross	**11/6**	**12/—**	**14/—**	**15/6**

Wicks for Lamps for Magic Lanterns and Cinematographs.

Flat Burner Wicks.

	6682/2	3	5	7‴
per meter: doz.	**—/10**	**1/10**	**2/4**	**3/2**

Round Burner Wicks.

6709/8	10	12	14‴
5/8	**6/10**	**9/—**	**10/8**

Duplex Burner Wicks.

6444/12	14‴
5/8	**6/8**

ELECTRIC MOTORS
DYNAMOS

INDUCTION APPARATUS
GEISSLER TUBES

WIRELESS TELEGRAPHY SETS

BATTERIES ACCUMULATORS
EXPERIMENT BOXES

Instructive Electrical Toys.

The interest of the youth for Electrical Toys has grown in proportion to the rapid extension of the technical electric sciences; indeed there are hardly **any better scientific means for instruction than to experiment with electrical or electro-physical apparatus.** The models which we manufacture are specially suitable for this purpose viz: to show the **fundamental ideas of transforming the electrical current into force** by the motor or **to generate light and power** by the dynamo engine.

The Ruhmkorff Apparatus, Experiment Boxes &c., are also very much valued, as **instructive and entertaining Toys** for growing lads.

The **Wireless Telegraph Apparatus** in connection with the **Wireless Distance Switch** as a scientific Toy, is extremely popular with the youth of to-day. The utility of these Apparatus in real use has been manifested on many occasions and the keenest interest is taken in their development.

No apparatus leaves our works without having been tested most conscientiously; but it is natural, that fine mechanical articles may get out of order through the slightest damage and it is therefore necessary, that the apparatus are treated most carefully when being unpacked and the best attention is to be paid to their correct treatment. For customers who have not yet dealt in these electrical goods we give herewith some descriptions and the most important instructions regarding the treatment of these articles which we request you to kindly make a note of.

Instructions for the Treatment of Instructive Electrical Toys.

Electric Motors.

Electric Motors are apparatus which generate motoric power **by means of the electric current.** To work these Electric Motors only **bichromate batteries or accumulators** with an electromotive force of 3,5—4 Volt can be used. Other batteries such as Sal Ammoniac batteries are not suitable to work these Electric Motors, as too large a number of them would be necessary.

The current generated by the batteries or accumulators is conducted by means of insulated wires of at least 1 mm = $^1/_{25}$ in. diameter to both terminals and from here to the brushes on the collector. These **brushes must always touch** the collector (commutator), **very gently** in order not to interrupt the current. We specially mention this, as very often through carelessness (when cleaning or dusting the motor) these contact springs are bent off so that the Motor cannot work any more.

Electric Motors for high current to be connected with the main are fitted with carbon brushes instead of the spring brushes. The same care must be taken with these carbons as with the above spring brushes. Regarding the use of the high current motors for the different currents please compare the special instructions sent out with these motors.

Induction Coils.

Induction Coils (Electrifying Apparatus) and **Ruhmkorff Induction Coils** are apparatus to generate a current with a very large number of alternations and a relatively high power; this is attained by the use of the well known Wagner's or Neef's oscillating Hammer which, when the current is closed, is alternately attracted by the iron core of the coil and repulsed again by the elastic spring of the hammer. This hammer is the most important part of the induction apparatus and specially to be protected against damage. By means of a small screw the hammer can be regulated viz. either placed nearer to the iron core or drawn away from it, but the hammer must not touch the iron core.

The **Induction coils** are used for electrifying persons; according to the construction and prices these coils have either primary or primary and secondary current. In the latter case this is **specially** noted on the fundamental board.

The **Ruhmkorff Induction Apparatus** are principally used to light Geissler Tubes. These tubes generate the most interesting and effective lights. The tubes are very much evacuated, i. e. they contain highly rarefied gases; it is therefore necessary that the tubes, especially on both ends, are not damaged in any way. These Ruhmkorff Induction Coils are also used for lighting Röntgen Tubes and for the generation of electric waves for Wireless Telegraphy.

Dynamos.

Dynamos are apparatus through which **electricity is generated for lighting** by the use of motoric power &c. These Dynamos are therefore specially suitable for instruction and for experimenting. Small incandescent lamps can be illuminated by these dynamos; besides there are a series of other apparatus for experimenting in connection with these machines.

General remarks.

When working Electric Motors the **utmost cleanliness** is the main principle. They are to be cleaned very cautiously after use and to be kept in a clean state.

It must not be omitted **to oil** the frictional parts, specially the bearings of the armature, but too much oiling must also be avoided.

Only the Collector (commutator), on which the brush slide **must never be oiled.**

Bichromate batteries work for a comparatively short time only. If used continually a bichromate battery will last ¼ to ½ hour. Then the battery begins to be exhausted in which case it can be revired by pouring in a few drops of sulphuric acid. If the bichromate batteries are only used for short periods, they last a great deal longer. It is however absolutely necessary that at every interruption the **coal** and **zinc** must be **taken out** of the battery, else the latter would exhaust itself without being worked.

Accumulators are most suitable for a long run. According to their capacity it is possible to obtain power by these up to 24 hours. Details will be found with the Accumulators.

Electric-Motors for Low Current

with triple T anchor, starting in every position of their own accord, mounted on fine wooden bases to be worked by bychromate batteries or accumulators.

10178

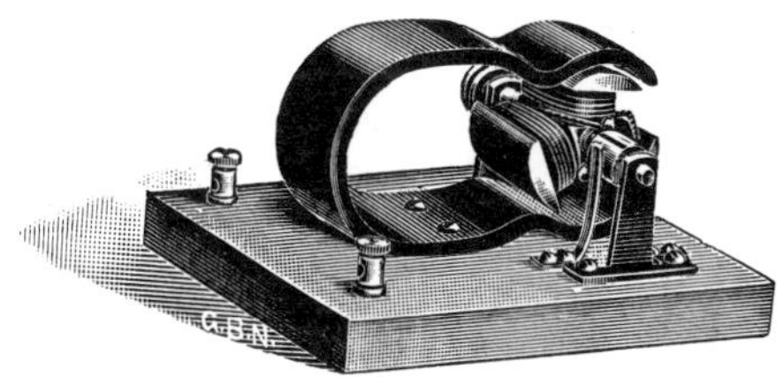

10179
With permanent magnets
(absorbing very little current).

No.	Long	Wide	High		Price
10178/1	4 in. long,	$3^{1}/_{8}$ in. wide,	$3^{1}/_{4}$ in. high	each (without battery)	**2/6**
„ /2	$4^{1}/_{2}$ „	„ $3^{3}/_{4}$ „	„ $4^{3}/_{8}$ „ „	„ „ „	**3/2**
„ /3	$5^{1}/_{8}$ „	„ $4^{3}/_{8}$ „	„ $4^{1}/_{2}$ „ „	„ „ „	**4/10**
10179/1	4 „	„ $3^{1}/_{8}$ „	„ 2 „ „	„ „ „	**3/6**
„ /2	$4^{1}/_{2}$ „	„ $3^{3}/_{4}$ „	„ $2^{3}/_{8}$ „ „	„ „ „	**5/4**
„ /3	$5^{1}/_{8}$ „	„ $4^{3}/_{8}$ „	„ 3 „ „	„ „ „	**8/6**

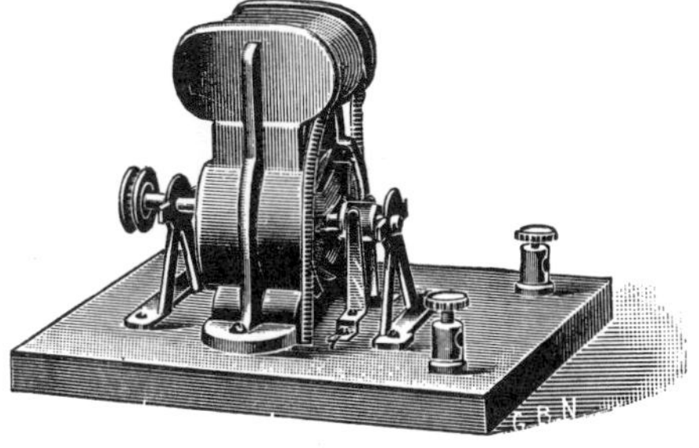

10136

13795/2

10136/1	**Cast iron,** finely japanned, 4 in. long, $3^{1}/_{8}$ in. wide	each (without battery)	**5/4**
„ /2	„ „ „ „ $5^{1}/_{8}$ „ „ $4^{3}/_{8}$ „ „	„ „ „	**6/8**
„ /3	„ „ „ „ $5^{1}/_{2}$ „ „ $4^{3}/_{4}$ „ „	„ „ „	**9/4**
13795/2	**Electric-Motor** with triple T anchor, starting in every position of its own accord, mounted on fine wooden base, $4^{3}/_{4}$ in. long, $3^{1}/_{2}$ in. wide	each (without battery)	**5/4**

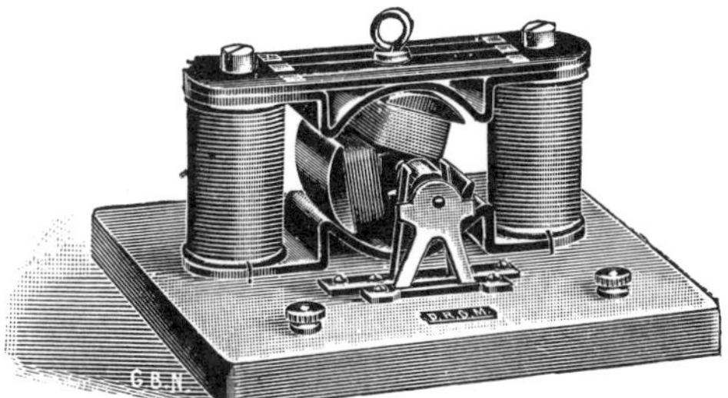

10137 with finely nickelled fittings

14382 with reversing gear

No.	Long	Wide	High		Price
10137/1	$4^{1}/_{2}$ in. long,	$3^{3}/_{4}$ in. wide,	$2^{1}/_{2}$ in. high	each (without battery)	**7/—**
„ /2	$5^{1}/_{8}$ „	„ $4^{3}/_{8}$ „	„ $2^{3}/_{4}$ „ „	„ „ „	**8/6**
„ /3	$5^{1}/_{2}$ „	„ $4^{3}/_{4}$ „	„ $3^{5}/_{16}$ „ „	„ „ „	**12/8**

14382 **Electric-Motor** with triple T anchor, starting in every position of its own accord, with **reversing gear** and switch for cutting off current entirely, on finely polished wooden base, $5^{1}/_{4}$ in. long, $3^{1}/_{4}$ in. wide, $2^{1}/_{4}$ in. high . . . . . each (without battery) **8/4**

10180/1

Electric-Motors for Low Current

with triple **T**-anchor, starting in every prosition of their own accord to be worked by bychromate batteries or accumulators (see pages 316 and 317)

10334

Electric-Motors (Enclosed Type) very powerful, elegantly finished on fine wooden base

10180/1	$4^3/_8$ in. long,	$3^1/_2$ in. wide,	$3^1/_2$ in. high	each without battery	**6/8**
„ /2	$4^3/_4$ „ „	4 „ „	$4^1/_8$ „ „	„ „ „	**8/6**
„ /3	$5^1/_2$ „ „	$4^3/_8$ „ „	$4^3/_4$ „ „	„ „ „	**10/6**

New Electric-Motors, very powerful, finely japanned, on Aluminium base

10334/1	$3^3/_4$ in. long,	$3^3/_4$ in. wide,	$3^3/_4$ in. high	each without battery	**8/6**
„ /2	$4^1/_8$ „ „	$4^1/_8$ „ „	$4^1/_2$ „ „	„ „ „	**10/6**

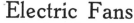

10335

New!

Very powerful Motors!

10336

Electric-Motor, very powerful finely japanned, on Aluminium base

10335/1	$3^3/_4$ in. long,	$3^3/_4$ in. wide,	$4^1/_8$ in. high		each without battery	**10/6**
„ /2	$4^1/_8$ „ „	$4^1/_8$ „ „	$4^7/_8$ „ „		„ „ „	**13/4**
10336/1	$3^3/_4$ „ „	$3^3/_4$ „ „	$4^1/_8$ „ „	in cast iron casing	„ „ „	**15/6**
„ /2	$4^1/_8$ „ „	$4^1/_8$ „ „	$4^7/_8$ „ „	„ „ „ „	„ „ „	**20/6**

Electric Fans

for Low Current

with triple **T**-anchor starting in every position of its own accord, for low current only, to be worked by batteries or accumulators with very small consumption of current, mounted on fine wooden bases, fittings and fan finely nickelled, with protecting guard

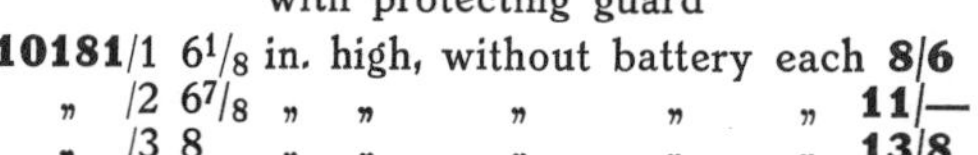

10181/1	$6^1/_8$ in. high,	without battery each	**8/6**
„ /2	$6^7/_8$ „ „	„ „ „	**11/—**
„ /3	8 „ „	„ „ „	**13/8**

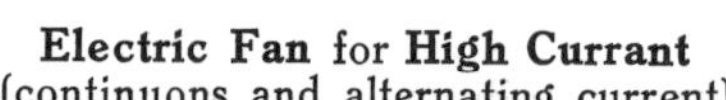

Electric Fan for **High Currant**

(continuons and alternating current)

very reliably working, with regulation resistance, suitable for tensions of 65—220 Volt if continuous current is used and for tensions of 110 to 220 Volt when using alternating current with triple T-anchor starting in every position of its own accord, blades made of aluminium with protecting guard $12^3/_4$ in. high, diam. of propeller $10^1/_4$ in.

10296 . . . . each **34/—**

10181/1

10296

Electric-Motors for High Current

for direct connection with the electric main.

The motors are wound for 110 Volts in such a way that they can be connected direct with the main, no matter if same is alternating or continuous current. It is not necessary to fit in an incandescent lamp or any other resistance. If a higher voltage than 110 is used, a resistance is necessary, in order to reduce the existing voltage to 110. The resistance is to be fitted in according to the special directions, supplied with the motors; it is advisable, to use an incandescent lamp of 16—32 c. p. with a voltage equal to that of the main i. e. for a tension of 220 Volt a lamp of 220 Volt is required.

13126 and 13127

13128

Electric-Motor for High Current (110 Volt) with triple T anchor, starting in every position of its own accord, with best coal contacts, mounted on fine wooden base

13126 $4^{1}/_{2}$ in. long, $3^{1}/_{8}$ in. high, $3^{3}/_{4}$ in. wide . . . . each **21/—**

13127 $5^{1}/_{8}$ „ „ $3^{3}/_{4}$ „ „ $4^{1}/_{4}$ „ „ . . . . „ **30/6**

Electric-Motor for High Current (110 Volt) with triple T anchor, starting in every position of its own accord, with best coal contacts, mounted on fine wooden base, finely finished

13128 $5^{1}/_{8}$ in. long, $3^{3}/_{4}$ in. high, $4^{1}/_{4}$ in. wide . . . . each **33/8**

13355

10405

Electric-Motor for High Current (110 Volt) drum shape, with triple T anchor, starting in every position of its own accord, with new improved coal contacts, mounted on fine wooden base

13355/1 diameter of the drum 3 in., wooden board $4^{3}/_{4}$ in long . . . . each **29/—**

„ /2 „ „ „ „ 4 „ „ „ 6 „ „ . . . . „ **38/—**

Electric-Motors for High Current (110 Volt) extra heavy, powerful Motors for continuous working, with triple T-anchor, starting in every position of its own accord, black japanned with cut and polished edges, extra strong contact-brushes (adjustable) with permanent oiler

10405/1 diameter of the drum-casing 3 in. . . . . each **22/6**

„ /2 „ „ „ „ $3^{1}/_{2}$ in. . . . . „ **34/—**

„ /3 „ „ „ „ $4^{5}/_{16}$ in. . . . . „ **57/—**

Induction- or Electrifying Apparatus.

Latest patterns, very much improved and elegantly finished; considerably reduced prices.

To work Inductions-Apparatus bichromate or good dry batteries with a discharging current of 2—4 Volt are used by connecting the clamps on the wooden base marked + and — with the battery. As soon at the current is closed, the hammer (interrupter) commences to work. If necessary, the hammer can be adjusted by means of the contact screw, either bringing it nearer to the iron core or drawing it away from it. However, the hammer must never touch the iron core entirely. The secondary current is the stronger and the primary the weaker current; for primary and secondary current the respective pole clamps are marked with *P* or *S* respectively. By drawing out the moderator the current can be intensified.

Induction Apparatus

to electrify persons, with moderator, pole clamps and fittings, brass lacquered, with 2 handles and conducting cords, coil of transperent celluloid, mounted on finely polished wooden base.

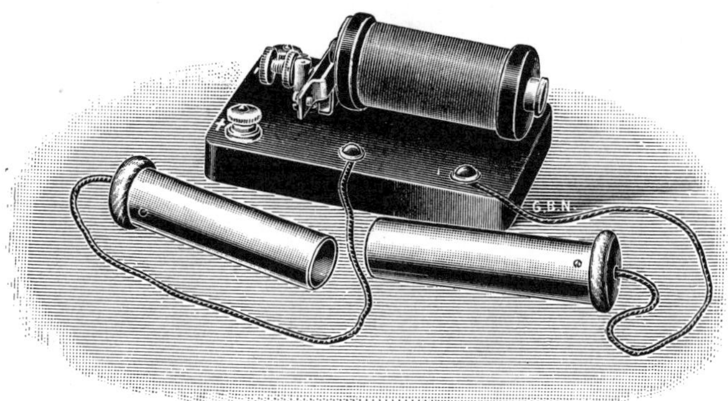

10209/1

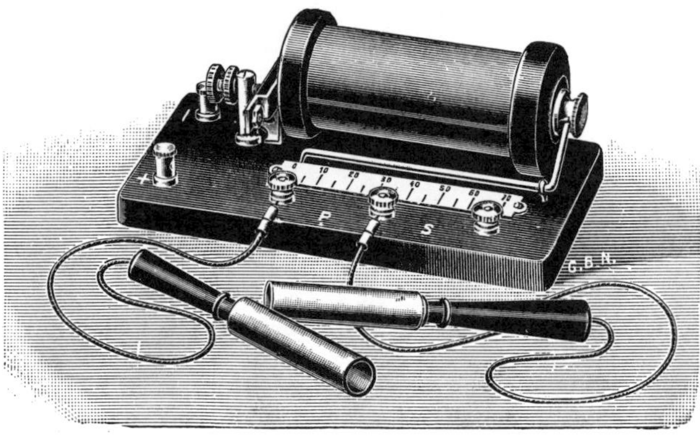

10209/4

10209/1	Length of coil $2^3/_8$ in., wooden base 4 in. long, $2^5/_8$ in. wide	each (without battery)	**3/8**
„ /2	„ „ „ $2^3/_4$ „ „ „ $5^1/_4$ „ „ $2^3/_4$ „ „	„ „ „	**5/2**
	With primary and secondary current:		
„ /3	Length of coil $3^1/_8$ in., wooden base $5^1/_8$ in. long, $2^3/_4$ in. wide	each (without battery)	**6/4**
„ /4	„ „ „ $3^1/_2$ „ „ „ $5^1/_2$ „ „ $3^1/_8$ „ „ base with scale . .	„ „ „	**7/4**
„ /5	„ „ „ 4 „ „ „ 6 „ „ $3^1/_2$ „ „ „ „ „ . .	„ „ „	**8/6**

Induction Apparatus in boxes

to electrify persons, with moderator, spool finely light polished, with black cover, poleclamps and fittings fine brass lacquered, in elegant wooden box, with 2 handles and conducting cords.

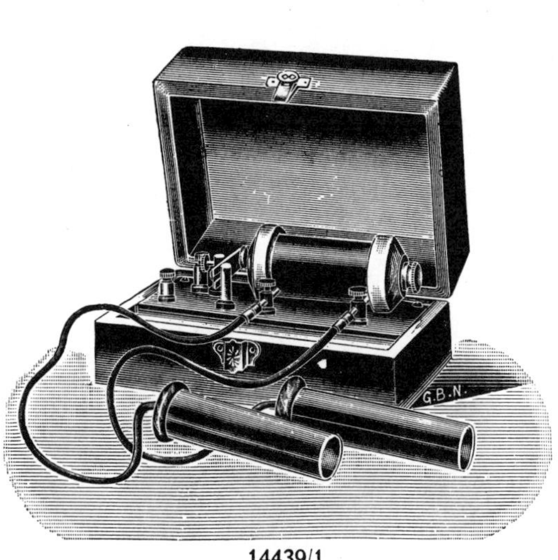

14439/1

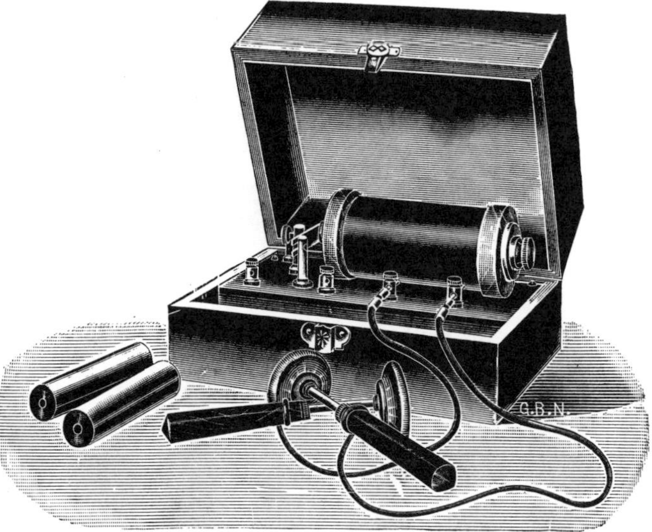

14439/3

14439/1	Length of spool $2^3/_4$ in., box $5^1/_8$ in. long, $3^1/_2$ in. wide	each	**9/2**
„ /2	„ „ „ $3^1/_8$ „ „ $5^1/_2$ „ „ 4 „ „ with Tampons*	„	**11/6**
„ /3	„ „ „ $3^1/_2$ „ „ $5^7/_8$ „ „ $4^5/_{16}$ „ „ „ „	„	**13/8**

*) The Tampons (for electrifying parts of the body) and the handles can be exchanged with each other.

Ruhmkorff Induction Coils.

In new improved finish on finely polished wooden socle, to be worked by bichromate batteries or accumulators of not more than 2 Volt.

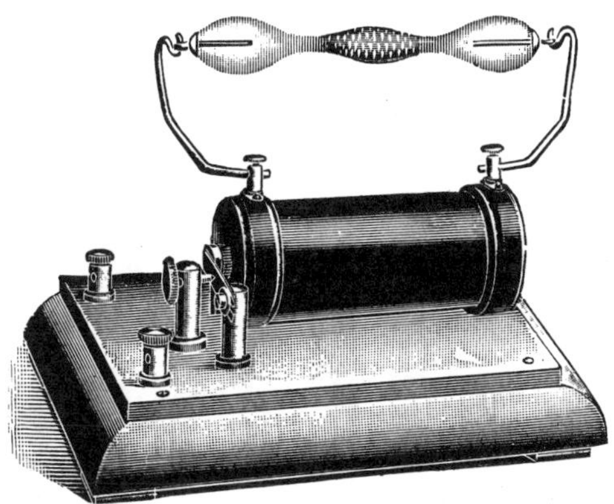

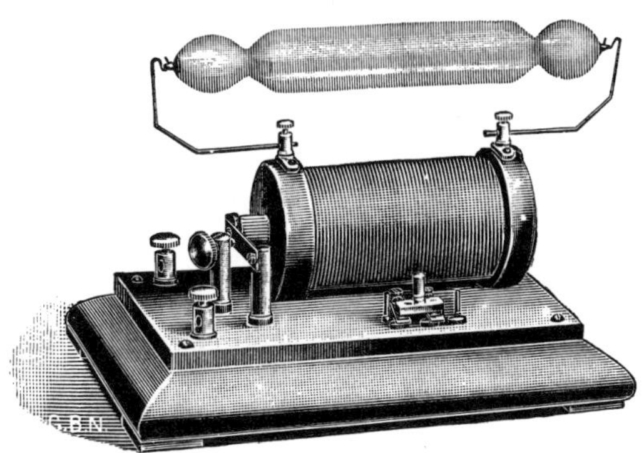

The Spark Inductors are suitable for a large series of highly interesting electro-physical experiments. Such experiments depend of course upon the size of the inductors chosen, or rather on the length of the sparks of the apparatus. The greater the length of the spark, the more intense and effective the experiments will be and the larger sparks are required, the larger must be the current producers, viz. the bichromate batteries or accumulators. The most beautiful and effective experiments can be made by means of the spark inductors with the so called **Geissler Tubes;** larger apparatus can also be used for experiments with Röntgen Rays and for Wireless Telegraphy.

No.	Sparks	Base		without tube
14397/1	$^1/_8$ in.	$4^3/_4 \times 3$ in.	. . . .	each **9/6**
„ /2	$^1/_5$ „	$5^3/_4 \times 3^1/_2$ „	. . . .	„ **11/8**
„ /3	$^1/_4$ „	$6^1/_2 \times 4$ „	. . . .	„ **15/4**
„ /4	$^1/_3$ „	$7^5/_8 \times 5^1/_4$ „	. . . .	„ **22/8**
„ /5	$^1/_2$ „	$8^1/_2 \times 5^3/_4$ „	With commutator to reverse current	„ **30/6**
„ /6	$^3/_4$ „	$9^1/_4 \times 6^1/_8$ „	„ „ „ „ „	„ **38/—**

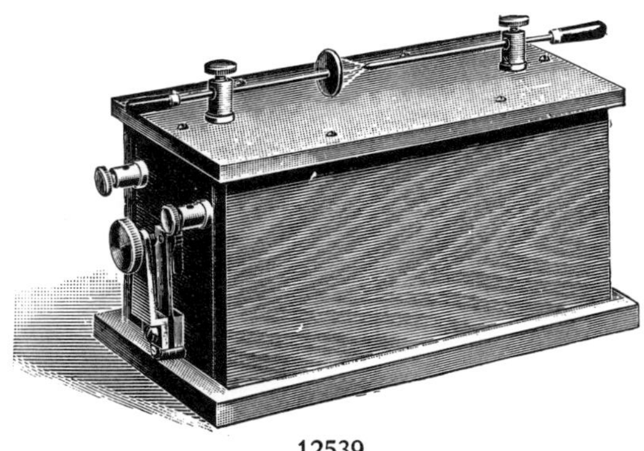

12539

Large Ruhmkorff Induction Apparatus new finish, induction coil in finely polished wood box; spark $1^1/_4$ in. long, with 2 Electrodes (point and plate, the latter for distributing the sparks).

12539 Wood box $8^3/_4$ in. long, $4^3/_8$ in. wide, $5^1/_2$ in. high very powerful inductor . . . . each **76/—**

Ruhmkorff Induction Coils.

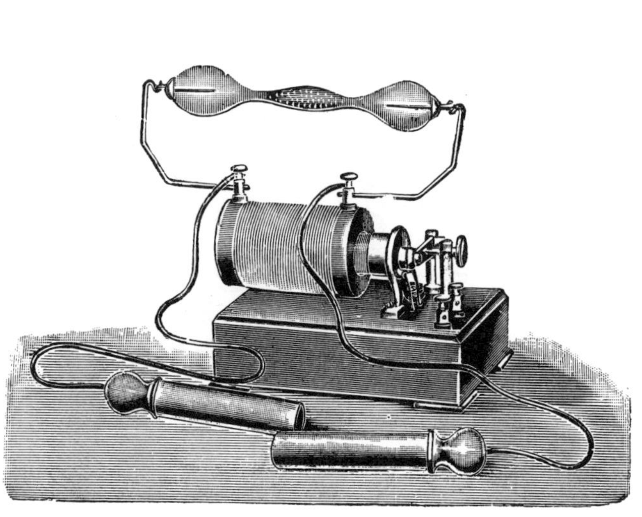

13375

13895

13375 **Ruhmkorff Induction Coil** for illuminating Geissler Tubes, at the same time fitted for electrifying persons, finely finished, with Moderator, on strong, finely polished wooden base, with 2 handles and conducting cords. Length of Sparks about $^1/_4$ in., $4^3/_4$ in. long, $3^1/_8$ in. wide . . . . . . each (without Geissler Tube) **15/10**

13895 **Ruhmkorff Induction Coil** in connection with an Electro Motor for the revolution of Geissler Tubes. The Geissler Tubes form when revolving an illumination rosette of magnificent effect. The whole apparatus is mounted on finely polished wooden base. Length of Sparks from the Induction apparatus about $^5/_{16}$ in., $8^3/_4$ in. long, $4^3/_4$ in wide . . . . each (without Geissler Tube) **37/4**

Electro-Magnetic Inductions Apparatus

working without battery.

Simply by turning the handle the induction current is generated, the apparatus is therefore always ready for use.

10197

13937/1

10197 with 2 handles, mounted on fine wooden base, $3^3/_4$ in. long, 3 in. wide, 3 in. high. . . . . each **5/—**

13937/1 new improved finish, with 2 handles with moderator, mounted on fine wooden base, $4^3/_4$ in. long, $3^3/_8$ in. wide, $3^3/_4$ in. high . . . . „ **9/10**

Geissler and Vacuum Tubes.

13377/8

13377/9

13377/10
11626/10

13377/12
11626/12

Geissler Tubes
best quality
with strong brass rings, assorted in various designs

13377/8	$3^1/_8$ in. long		doz.	**7/—**
„ /9	$3^1/_2$ „ „		„	**7/—**
„ /10	4 „ „		„	**9/—**
„ /12	$4^3/_4$ „ „		„	**9/10**
11626/10	4 „ „	same as above but coloured glass	„	**12/6**
„ /12	$4^3/_4$ „ „	„ „ „ „ „ „	„	**15/6**

13378/18

Geissler Tubes with Uran-glass, very effective, best quality
with extra strong brass rings

13378/8	$3^1/_8$ in. long	doz.	**9/10**
„ /12	$4^3/_4$ „ „	„	**12/8**
„ /18	$7^1/_8$ „ „	„	**17/—**

13379/13

13379/17

Geissler Tubes, filled with coloured liquid, very effective
superior quality, with extra strong brass rings

13379/8	$3^1/_8$ in. long	doz.	**9/10**
„ /10	4 „ „	„	**11/8**
„ /13	$5^1/_8$ „ „	„	**15/—**
„ /17	$6^3/_4$ „ „	„	**17/10**

14364

Geissler Tubes, filled with phosphorescent substance, very effective

14364/10	4 in. long	doz.	**16/4**
„ /12	$4^3/_4$ „ „	„	**21/—**
„ /16	$6^1/_4$ „ „	„	**28/6**

11627

14972

14361

14743

11627/12	**Tubes with fluorescent minerals** (very effective), $4^3/_4$ in. long	doz.	**27/—**
„ /16	„ „ „ „ „ „ $6^1/_4$ „ „	„	**33/6**
14972	**Geissler Tube** with interrupted light, very interesting, $7^7/_8$ in. long	„	**32/6**
14361	**Tubes with Shells and Minerals** good effect, $4^3/_4$ in. high	each	**3/6**
14743	**Vacuum Tube,** socalled Cross shadow-tube. (The Cross lighted by the negative pole [cathode] produces a shadow on the glass cell which retains this shadow for some time after the cross has been removed), $6^1/_4$ in. long	each	**4/10**

Vacuum Tubes.

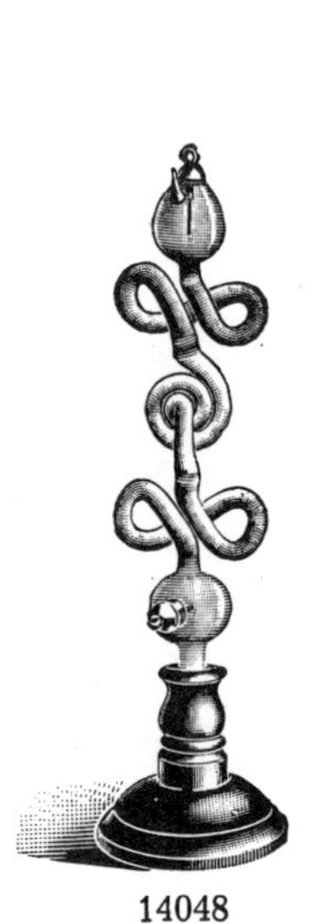
14048

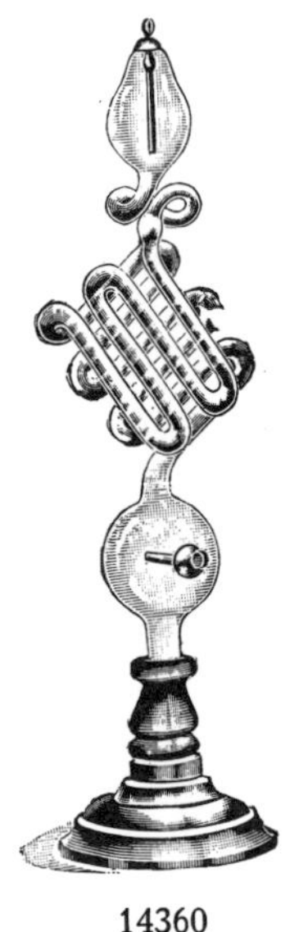
14360

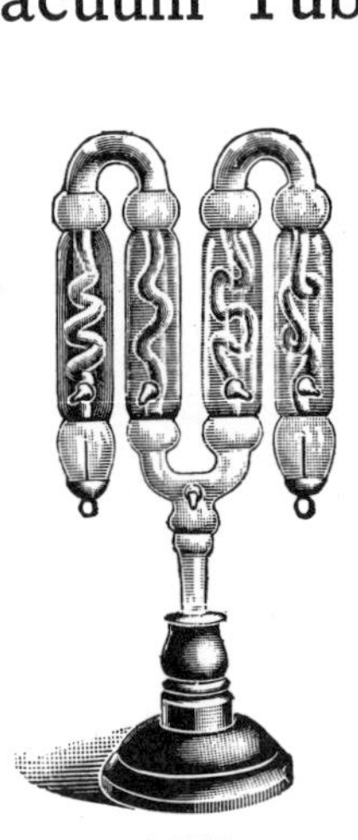
14260

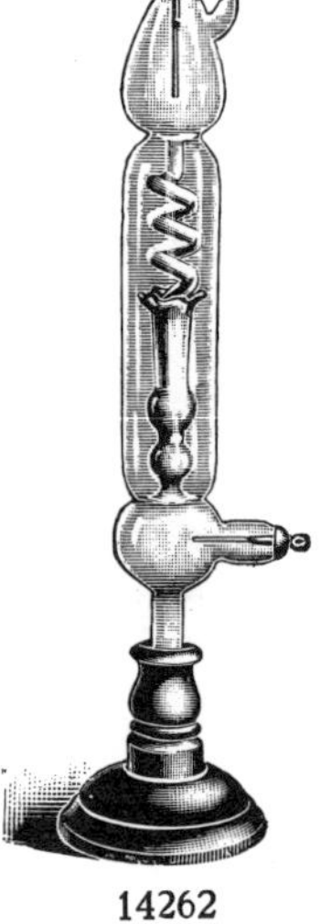
14262

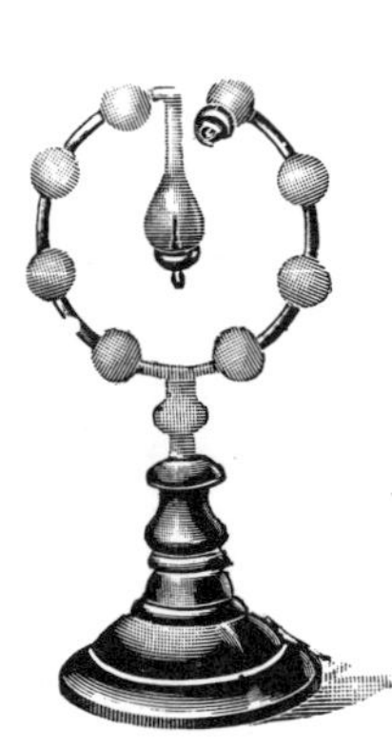
11628

Effective Vacuum-Tubes on wooden stands.

14048	**Geissler Tube,** 7½ in. high	doz.	**18/—**
14360	„ „ very effective, 8 in. high	„	**37/6**
14260	„ „ 4 tubes with coloured liquids, 8 in. high	each	**5/4**
14262	„ „ 1 tube „ „ „ (Uran-glass) inside, 9½ in. high	doz.	**32/6**
11628	**Lighting Wreath** (Tube of Glass in various colours), 6⅛ in. high	„	**38/—**

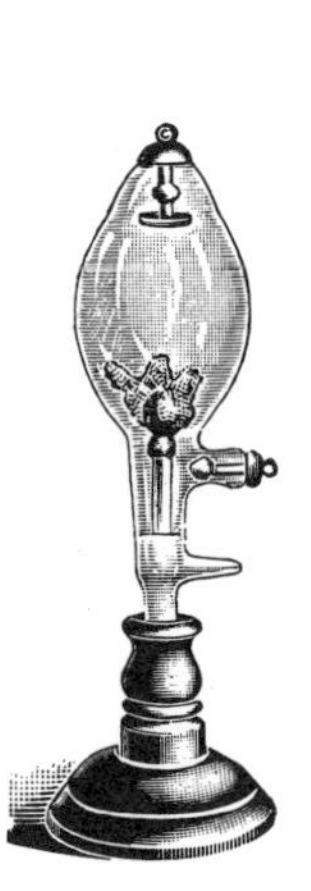
14258

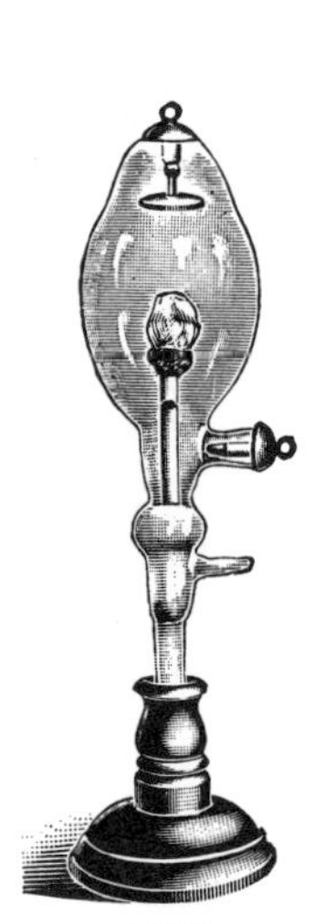
14359

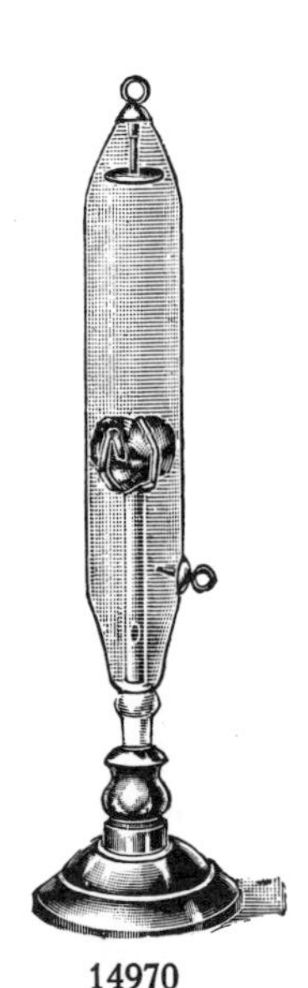
14970

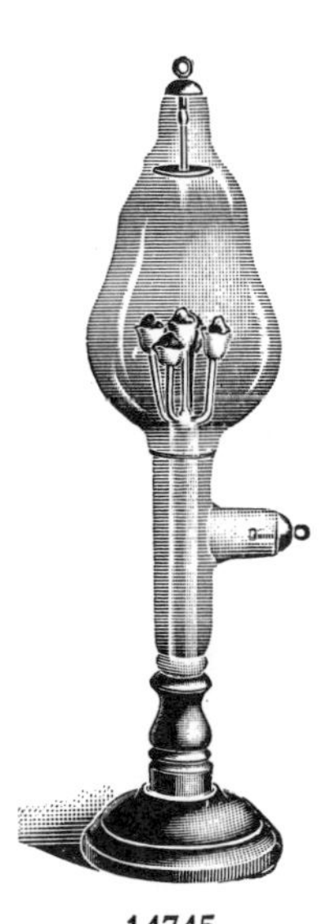
14745

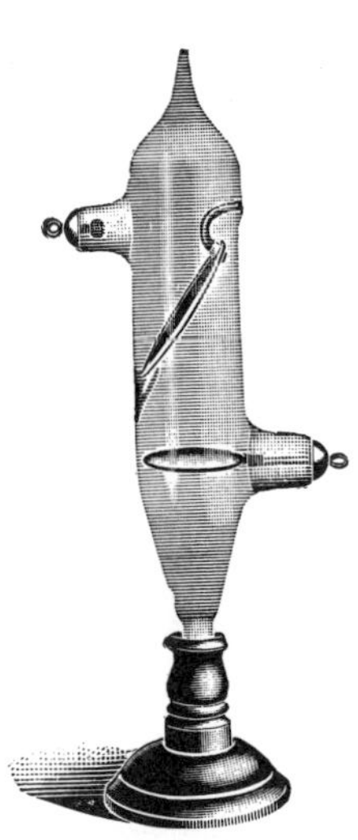
14744

Effective Vacuum tubes on wooden stands.

14258	**Geissler Tubes,** with coral, violet light, 7 in. high	doz.	**40/—**
14359	„ „ „ chalk, red „ 8¼ „ „	„	**40/—**
14970	„ „ „ stone, green „ 12 „ „	„	**40/—**
14745	„ „ „ 4 minerals, 9 „ „	each	**6/10**
14744	**Vacuum** „ for Cathode-Rays (socalled electric lamp) new and very original, (light bright enough to read by), 9 in. high	each	**6/4**

Vacuum Tubes.

14363 14395/1 14395/2 14395/3 14362 14396/1 14396/2

Effective Vacuum Tubes on wooden stands

14363	with lighting flower, $11^{3}/_{4}$ in. high	doz.	**40/—**
14395/1	„ „ branch of roses, $8^{3}/_{4}$ in. high	each	**4/10**
„ /2	„ „ bird, $8^{3}/_{4}$ in. high	„	**4/10**
„ /3	„ „ beetle, $8^{3}/_{4}$ in. high	„	**4/10**
14362	„ „ butterfly, $8^{3}/_{4}$ in. high	„	**4/10**
14396/1	„ „ rose, $10^{1}/_{4}$ in. high	„	**6/4**
„ /2	„ „ forget-me-not, $10^{1}/_{4}$ in. high	„	**6/4**

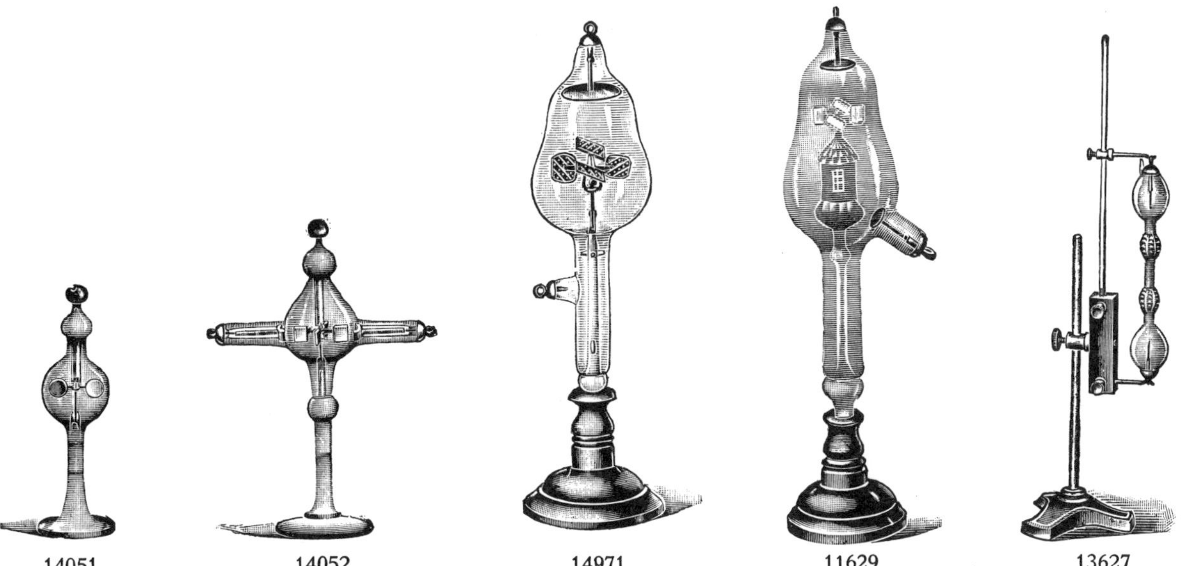

14051 14052 14971 11629 13627

14051	**Radiometer** with 2 discs inside, which revolve under the influence of the light, 4 in. high	each	**2/8**
14052	„ „ 4 „ „ „ „ „ „ „ „ electric currents, $8^{3}/_{4}$ in. high	„	**5/—**
14971	„ for induction apparatus, with 4 discs, lighting in different colours, very brilliant and effective, $10^{3}/_{4}$ in. high	„	**4/4**
11629	**Windmill** (with Radiometer) for induction apparatus, mill lighting in colours, $12^{3}/_{4}$ in high	„	**7/8**
13627	**Stand** for Geissler Tubes with adjustable connecting rod, highly finished with nickelled accessories, fitting Geissler Tubes up to the length of $7^{1}/_{2}$ inch. (without Geissler Tube)	„	**8/—**

Dynamo-Engines.

10210
with metallic filament lamp

10211 and 10212
with carbon filament lamp

Dynamos with permanent Magnets, with Gear Wheels and incandescent lamp to be worked by motors (as a model to be connected with a steam engine) and also to be worked by hand, very easy to turn, with little expenditure of force; mounted on strong wooden base, capacity about 4 volt 0,25 Ampères.

10210	4 in. long, $3^1/_8$ in. wide, $3^5/_{16}$ in. high with metallic filament lamp			each	**9/10**
10211	5 „ „ $3^1/_4$ „ „ $3^1/_2$ „ „ „ carbon „ „			„	**16/4**
10212	6 „ „ $4^1/_4$ „ „ $3^7/_8$ „ „ „ „ „ „			„	**21/—**

10461/1—2

10461/3—4

10329

Dynamos with permanent Magnets, specially suitable for connection with Model Steam Engines on aluminium base.

10461/1	Capacity abt. 3,5 volt, $2^5/_{16}$ in. high	each	**5/8**
„ /2	„ „ 3,5 „ 3 „ „	„	**7/6**
„ /3	„ „ 3,5 „ $3^3/_4$ „ „	„	**9/6**
„ /4	„ „ 3,5 „ $4^5/_{16}$ „ „	„	**13/6**

Dynamos, castings finely mat black japanned, with cut and polished edges, on fine wooden base.

10329/1	Diam. of the casing $2^3/_4$ in., capacity 3,5 volt, 0,8 Ampère if 5000 revolutions per minute are made	each	**17/—**
„ /2	„ „ „ „ $3^1/_4$ „ „ 3,5 „ 1,1 „ „ 5000 „ „ „ „ „	„	**21/—**
„ /3	„ „ „ „ $3^1/_4$ „ „ 3,5 „ 1,2 „ „ 5000 „ „ „ „ „	„	**25/—**

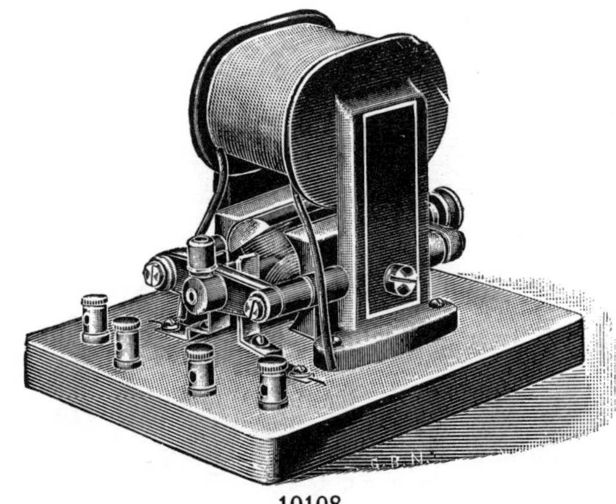

10108

Dynamo with ⊤ anchor, nickelled accessories, finely japanned, mounted on fine wooden base

10108/1 $5^1/_8$ in. long, $4^3/_8$ in. wide, $3^1/_2$ in. high, capacity 6 volt, 0,75 Ampère if 4000 revolutions per minute are made each **18/6**

10108/2 $5^1/_2$ in. long, $4^3/_4$ in. wide, $4^3/_8$ in. high, capacity 8 volt, 1 Ampère if 4500 revolutions per minute are made each **28/6**

10108/3 $6^3/_4$ in. long, $5^7/_8$ in. wide, $5^1/_2$ in. high, capacity 10 volt, 2 Ampère if 4000 revolutions per minute are made each **46/—**

Dynamo-Engines.

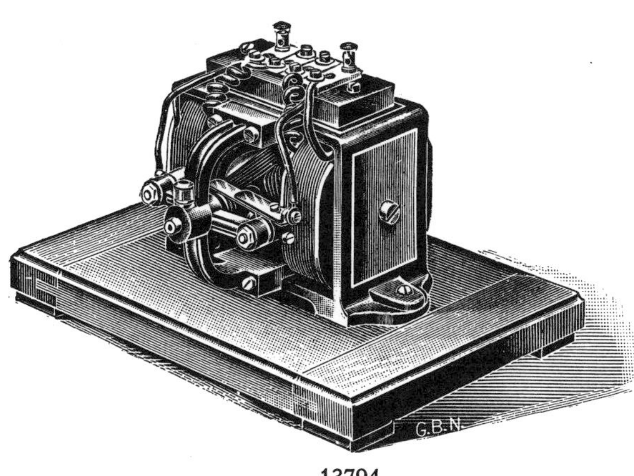

13794

13891

13794 **Dynamo,** with ⊥ anchor, nickelled accessories, pulley of $^7/_8$ in. diam. for round or flat belts, capacity up to abt. 3 Ampères and abt. 8 Volt, if abt. 4500 revolutions per minute are made, finely japanned and exactly finished, on finely polished wooden base, $7^7/_8$ in. long, $6^1/_4$ in. wide, $4^1/_2$ in. high . . . . each **53/—**

13891 **Dynamo,** with drum anchor, nickelled accessories, pulley of $^7/_8$ in. diam. for flat bellts, capacity up to abt. 3,5 Ampères and abt. 15 Volt, by a maximum of 6000 revolutions per minute, finely japanned and exactly finished, mounted on finely polished wooden base, $7^7/_8$ in. long, $6^3/_4$ in. wide, $5^1/_8$ in. high . . . . . each **80/—**

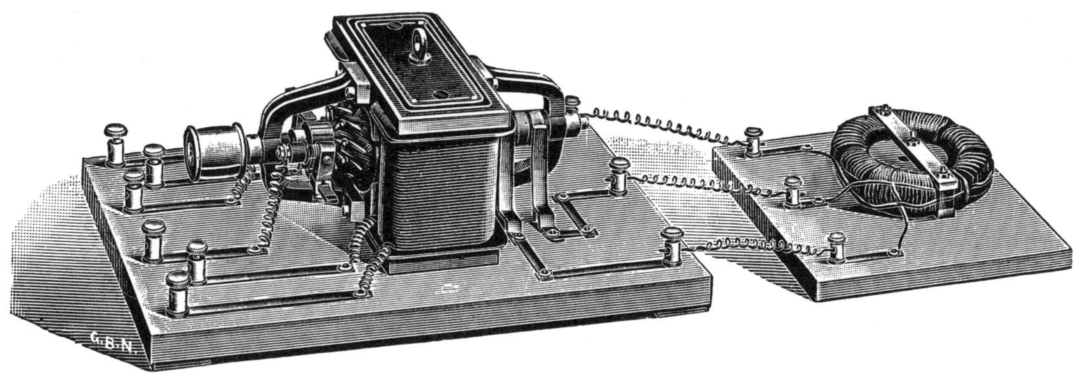

130/960 130/970

130/960 **Dynamo** to generate electric light or electro motoric power, capacity 65 Volt, 0,8 Ampère if 2500 revolutions per minute are made, wires and connection clamps distinctly arranged, specially suitable for instructive purposes, generating either continuous or alternating current, base $11^3/_4$ in. long, $7^7/_8$ in. wide each **140/—**

130/970 **Rotating Electro-magnetic Disc** for experiments in connection with the revolutions made by the dynamo (the induction thereby generated will turn at an increasing speed) very interesting and instructive experiment, base $6^1/_4$ in., $6^1/_4$ in. wide . . . . each **16/—**

Dynamos.

These model dynamos (to be worked by hand) show in an intelligible and instructive manner the production of the electric energy for lighting purposes and for a number of other highly interesting experiments. Induction Coils, Spark Inductors, small Electro Motors, Electric Metallurgy &c., can be supplied with a current, by means of the dynamos; small pocket accumulators can be charged and water decomposed &c. They are therefore qualified in a high degree for instruction and home study. The dynamos produce according to the number of turns, from 0,6 to 2 Ampères, and are provided with a switch, which allows the machine to be used for Intensity as well as Quantity Currents.

Suitable Electric globes on stand see page 315.

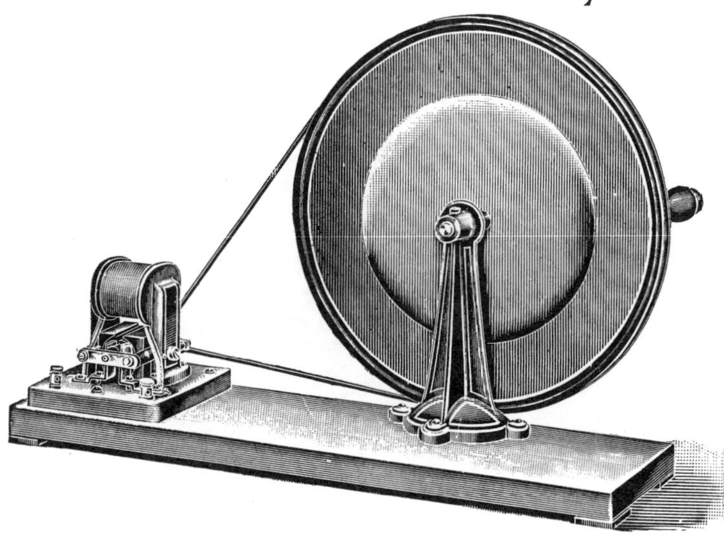

10109/1 und 2

Dynamo with large driving wheel

10109/1 driving wheel $11^3/_4$ in. diameter, capacity abt. 6 Volt, 0,75 Ampère, if 4000 revolutions per min. are made . . . . each **37/6**

„ /2 driving wheel $11^3/_4$ in. diameter, capacity abt. 8 Volt, 1 Ampère, if 4500 revolutions per min. are made . . . . each **48/—**

13365/1 with adjustable leather driving band

13365/1 **Dynamo,** 4—6 Volt, abt. 0,6 to 1 Ampère, $23^1/_2$ in. long, driving wheel $13^3/_8$ in. diameter, height of machine $7^1/_8$ in., height of complete apparatus $16^1/_2$ in., **with adjustable leather driving band and 1 incandescant lamp,** extra strong finish . . . . . . complete each **106/—**

13890

13890 **Dynamo with double connecting gear, driving wheel with flat straps,** capacity 8—10 Volt, abt. 3—4 Ampères, $23^3/_4$ in. long, driving wheel 13 in. diameter, machine 4 in. high, **with adjustable driving band,** height of complete apparatus $15^1/_2$ in. . . . . . complete each **118/—**

Accessories for Wireless Telegraphy.

14076

14076 Coherer, on polished board, with 2 clamps and hammer, 5 in. long, $4^1/_4$ in. . . . . each **6/4**

14071 Oscillator (condensor) on polished board, adjustable, to be used for any, spark gap, 5 in. long, $4^1/_4$ in. wide, each **8/6**

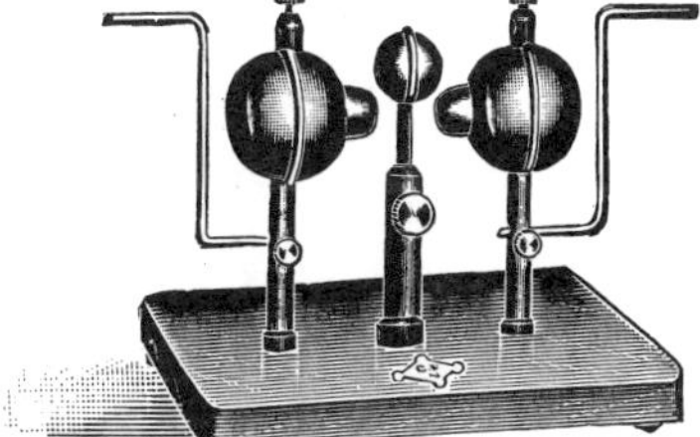
14071

14075

14074

10293

14075 Bell on Stand, for coherer, on polished board with 2 clamps on strong base, $5^1/_8$ in. long, $4^1/_4$ in wide, 5 in. high . . . . each **9/4**

14074 Coherer with Bell, on polished board, consisting of coherer 14076 and bell 14075, $9^1/_2$ in. long, $6^1/_4$ in wide, $6^1/_4$ in. high . . . . each **14/2**

10293 Relay very sensitive, specially adapted for use with Wireless Telegraphy over long distances 4 in. high, „ **15/6**

Wireless Telegraphy Sets.

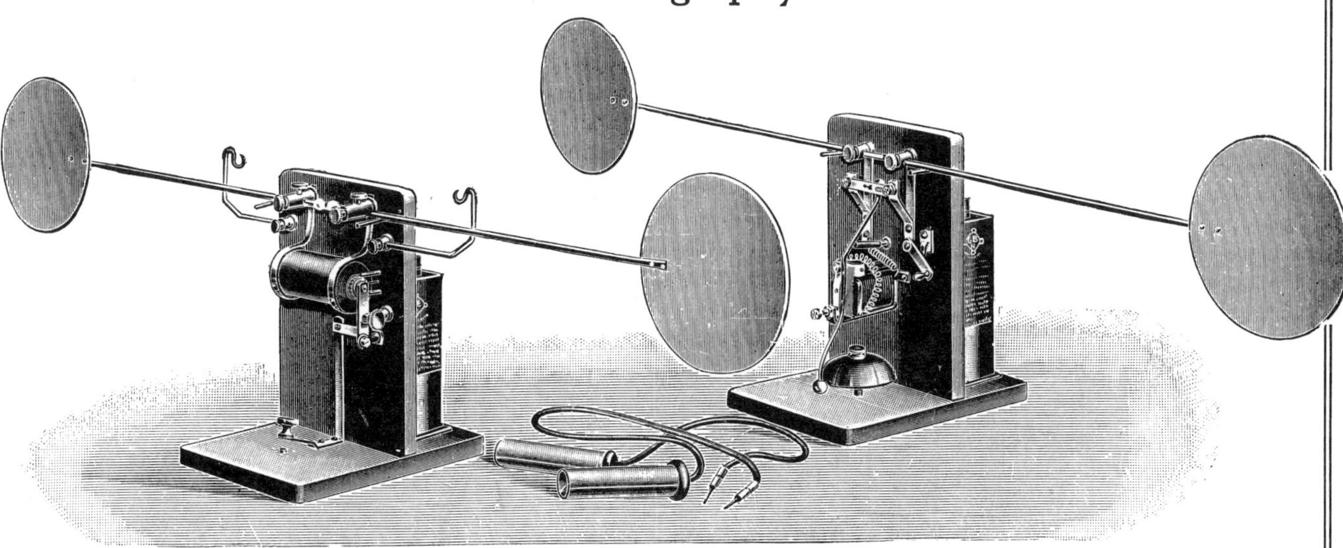
Sender 10250 Receiver

10250 Complete Apparatus for Wireless Telegraphy. Consisting of: **Sender** with Tapping Key, Ruhmkorff Spark Inductor, Condensers and **Receiver** with Coherer, Bell with contact breaker. Both stations with Antennae and aluminium discs, and durable dry batteries. **The Stations will work over a distance of about 10 yards. A pair of handles for electrifying persons** (by means oft he Ruhmkorff coil) and a **pair of brass holders for Geissler Tubes** are included with the Sender . . . . complete set **26/6**

Wireless Telegraphy Sets.

Sender 13757/1 Receiver. 14309

13757/1 **Complete Apparatus for Wireless Telegraphy,** consisting of: **Sender** with Tapping Key, Ruhmkorff-Spark-Inductor, Condenser, Durable Dry Battery, Air Wire and **Receiver** with Coherer, **Relay,** Electric Bell, Disconnector, Air Wire and Dry Battery and clamps, to be connected with a Morse Writing Apparatus. Everything finely finished, mounted on polished wooden bases and packed in strong box, working excellently over a distance of about 20 yards, with an explicit and interesting description of Wireless Telegraphy . . . . each **38/—**

14309 **Morse-Writing-Apparatus,** finely finished, with excellent clockwork, stop key, complete with ink-pad wheel, paper drum, mounted one fine wooden base, fitting Wireless Telegraphy Apparatus 13757/1 each **10/6**

10251

10251 **Apparatus for Wireless Telegraphy complete with Morse Writing Apparatus,** consisting of: **Sender** with Tapping Key and Ruhmkorff Spark Inductor and Condensers; **Receiver** with Coherer, Relay, Bell with contact breaker; **Morse Writing Apparatus** with clockwork and stop key. Both Stations with Antennae and large aluminium discs and durable dry batteries.

This Apparatus will work over a distance of about 15 to 20 yards.

With explicit and interesting description . . . . complete set **63/—**

Wireless Telegraphy Sets.

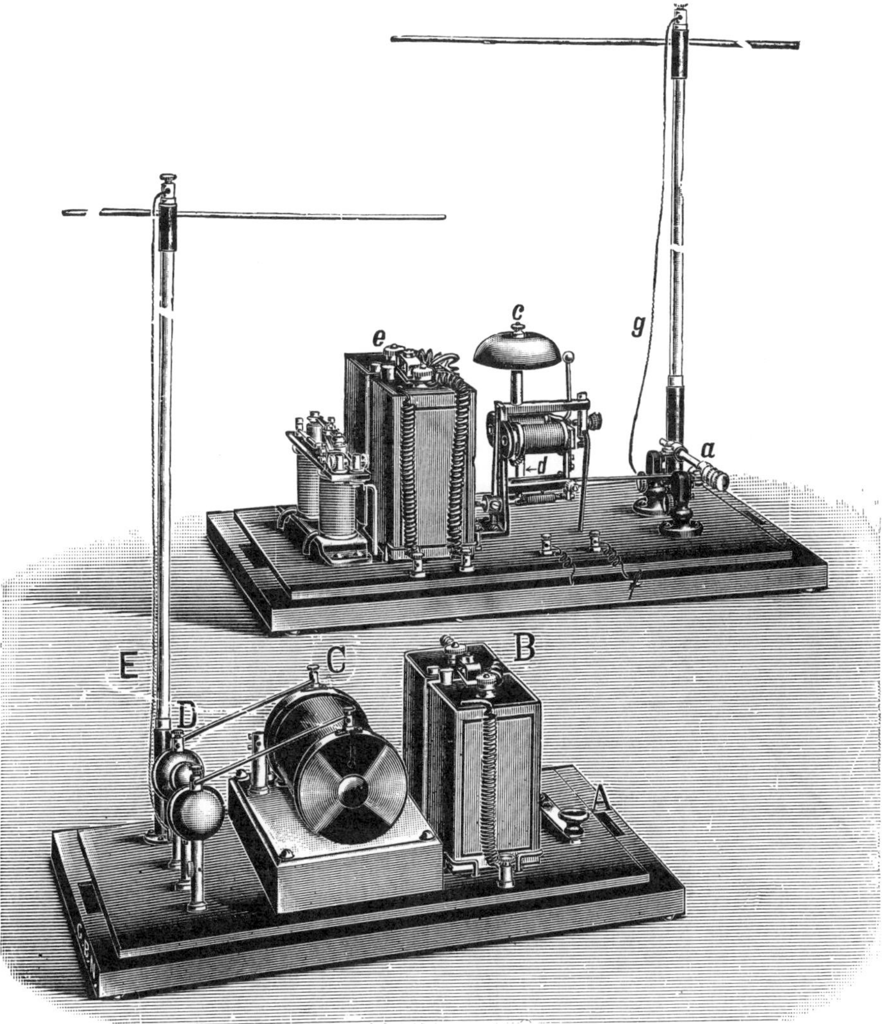

10201

Antennae.

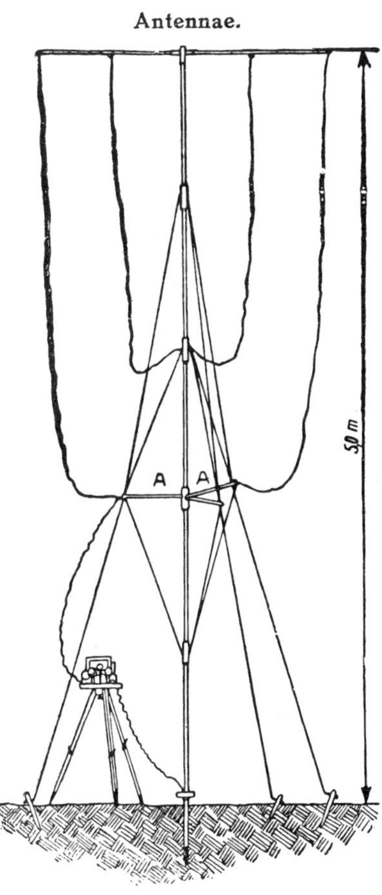

10206

10201 **Complete Apparatus for Wireless Telegraphy, consisting of Sender and Receiver.** Sender with Tapping Key, Ruhmkorff Spark Induktor, Condenser, Air Wire and 2 durable Dry Batteries. Receiver with Coherer, Relay of new, improved construction (absolutely reliably working), Bell, Air Wire, 2 durable Dry Batteries and connecting screw for a Morse Writing-Apparatus (see pages 301/302 of this Catalogue). Everything of strong and high class finish, working most accurately over distances of about 75 yards, mounted on finely polished wooden base (with screw-thread in bottom, suitable for using with tripods, same as used for cameras, etc.) packed in elegant polished cases with lock and key, furnished with explicit and interesting description . . . . apparatus complete each **152/—**

10460 **Same Apparatus** as above 10201 but without batteries when using more powerful batteries or accumulators the capacity of the above apparatus may be increased . . . . each **132/—**

10206 **Special Outfit (air wires) for longer distances,** fitting Wireless Telegraph Apparatus 10201 and 10460, consisting of pole abt. 16 feet high, with iron ground-post, telescopic rods, stays with iron fastening pegs and air wires. By means of these special poles the Wireless Telegraph Apparatus 10201 attains the capacity of transmitting telegraphic signs through a space of abt. 500 ft. and of giving bell signals over a distance of abt. 670 ft. . . . . per set of 2 each **76/—**

A set consists of 2 masts, one each for Sender and Receiver.

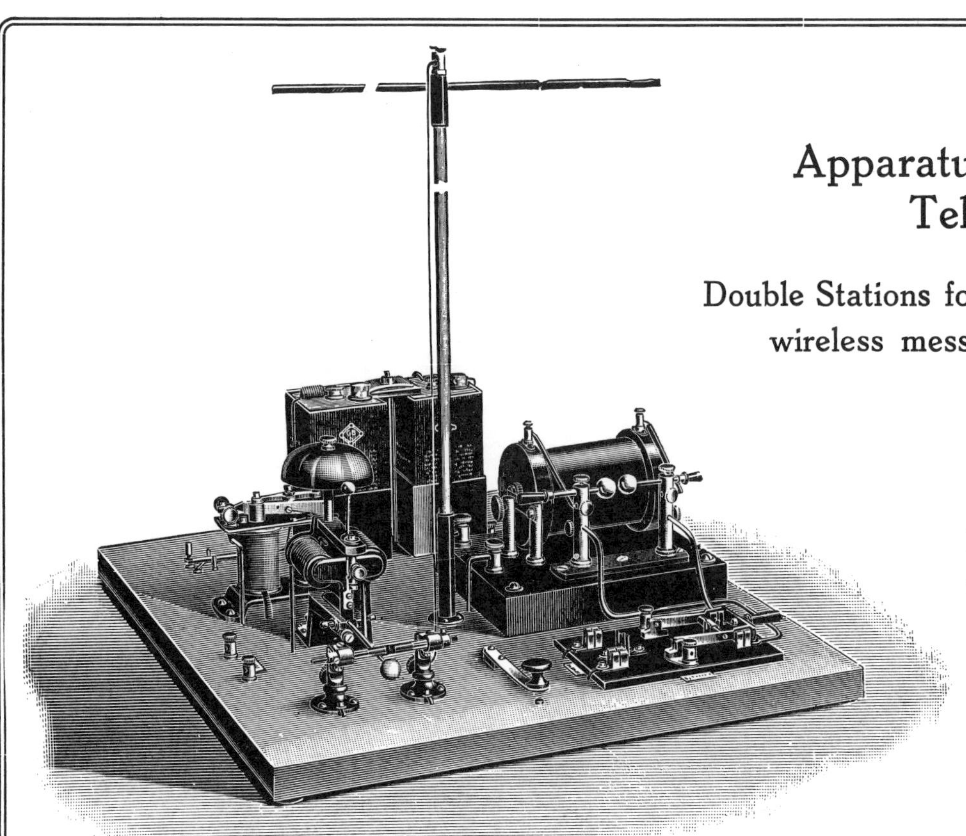

Apparatus for Wireless Telegraphy.

Double Stations for sending and receiving wireless messages at both ends.

Each Station is fitted with a switch to use it either as sender or receiver.

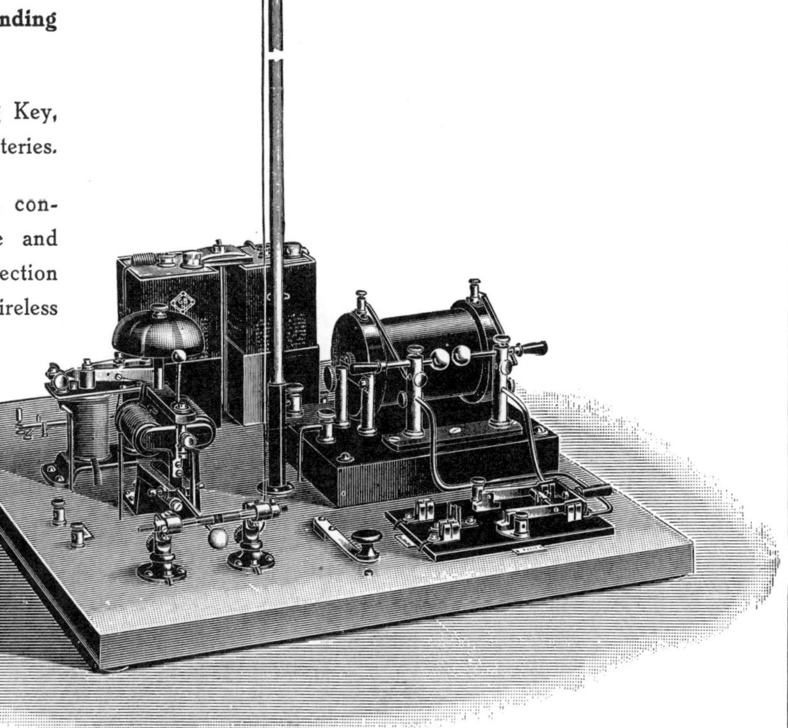

10326 Complete Apparatus for Wireless Telegraphy. Consisting of **2 complete stations for sending and receiving wireless messages.**

Sender with Ruhmkorff Spark Inductor, Tapping Key, Condenser, Antennae and 2 durable dry batteries.

Receiver with Coherer, Relay of new improved construction, reliably working, bell, Antennae and 2 durable dry-batteries, with pole clamps for connection with a Morse Writing Apparatus or a Wireless Distance Switch No. 10141, with switch for sending off or receiving wireless messages.

All parts high class, strong finish, to work over a distance of about 75 yards, mounted on finely polished wood base (with screw thread in bottom, suitable for using with tripods, same as used for Cameras &c.) packed in handsome case with lock and key, with interesting and explicit description . . . . complete set **326/—**

For Morse Apparatus, suitable for above stations please refer to No. 13805 page 302. Large Outfits of Antennae for long distances will be found on page 299.

Apparatus for Wireless Telegraphy.

10141 Wireless Distance Switch.

10141

This apparatus is connected with both the receiver of a wireless telegraphy station and with any other objective such as Electromotor, Incandescent Lamp, Electric Bell &c. These Apparatus can be worked or disconnected through the electric waves from the sender by means of the receiver of the Wireless Station; also suitable for setting electric Railways to work.

Very original and interesting, fitted for 5 connections, on polished wooden base, $5^1/_8$ in. long, $4^3/_8$ in. wide . . each **10/—**

10167

14309

10331 fine

10167 Morse-Writing-Apparatus, Model to practice telegraphing, with Tapping Key on the apparatus for easy teaching of the system; excellent clockwork with stop key, complete with ink-pad, paper wheel &c., mounted on elegant wooden base, $7^1/_4$ in high . . . . each **9/6**

14309 Morse-Writing-Apparatus, excellent clockwork, with stop key, complete with ink-pad, paper wheel &c., mounted on elegant wooden base, $7^1/_4$ in. high . . . . each **10/6**

10331 Fine Morse-Writing-Apparatus, with excellent regulated clockwork, with brass platines and stop key, complete with ink pad, paper wheel, mounted on elegant wooden base, $9^3/_4$ in. high . . . . each **28/4**

Apparatus for Wireless Telegraphy.

13805 Superior Model

13805 **Morse Writing Apparatus,** finely finished and accurately constructed, (Apparatus as used in the post-offices) with excellent regulated clockwork, with stop key and glass cover, complete with Ink-Pad Wheel, Paper Drum etc., mounted on fine wooden base, fitting Apparatus for Wireless Telegraphy No. 10201 . . . . each **65/—**

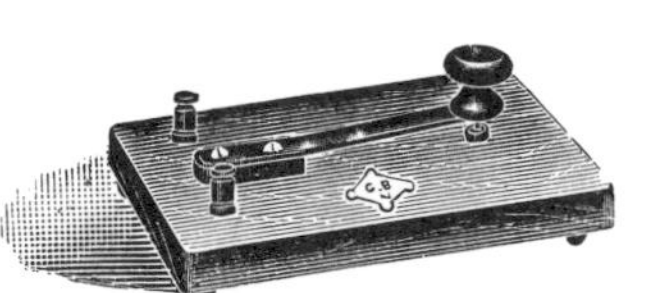

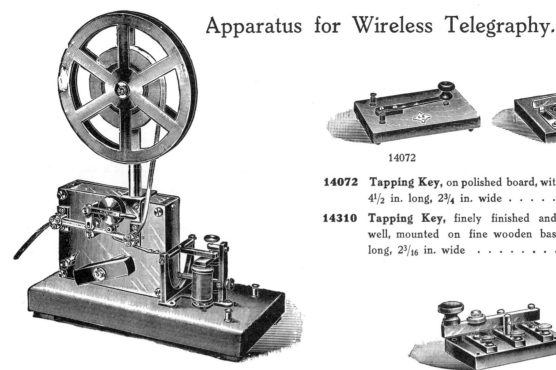

14072

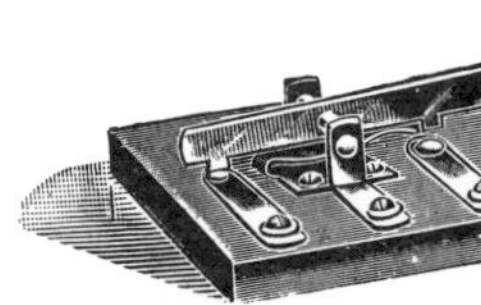

14310

14072 **Tapping Key,** on polished board, with 2 clamps $4^1/_2$ in. long, $2^3/_4$ in. wide . . . . each **4/—**

14310 **Tapping Key,** finely finished and working well, mounted on fine wooden base, $3^1/_8$ in. long, $2^3/_{16}$ in. wide . . . . doz. **19/—**

6304

6304 **Tapping Key for Morse-Apparatus** 13805, highly finished and accurately working, mounted on polished wooden base, length of the Tapping Key $3^1/_2$ in. . . . . each **4/—**

13829

Very interesting and instructive toy for the youth.

13829 **Complete Double-Telegraph-Station** consisting of:

2 Morse Stations with 1 Tapping Key each. Battery and electric wire for a distance of 10 yards. Morse Apparatus with strong regulated clockwork and stop key, ink-writer, paper roll, strong tapping key and dry battery and also with waxed wire 10 yards long in 2 different colours.

By connecting both stations by means of the wire, a complete telegraph-line can be set to work over a distance of about 10 yards and telegraphic signs according to the Morse Alphabet can be sent from one station to the other. By using stronger wires and larger batteries both stations are suitable for longer distances. An explicit description including the Morse Alphabet is enclosed with above apparatus.

Complete Apparatus each **40/—**

New Physical Experiment Boxes.

The numerous and ingenious inventions of the last few years have developed the interest in the laws of physical science to such an extent that we think we are meeting a popular demand in bringing out a set of physical experimental boxes which in a simple and yet most interesting and attractive manner demonstrate the main fundamental laws of physical science. Especially the growingboy find them a welcome means to get acquainted with the laws which regulate the phenomena of nature and the principles underlying the most important modern inventions.

The new experimental apparatus which are made up in attractive boxes in a handy manner, are of superior quality throughout. **Each box contains a manual with explicit instructions and explanatory illustrations.**

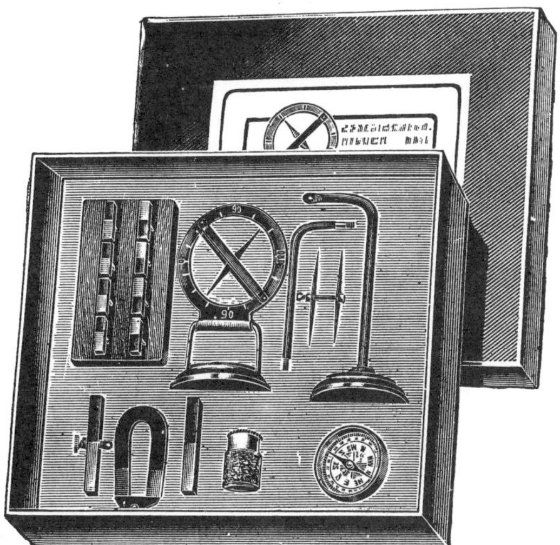

12503 Experiment Box: — "Magnetism"

1. Stand with support.
2. Support, extra.
3. Apparatus to demonstrate molecular magnetism
4. Astatic System,
5. Compass.
6. Gelatine Sheet.
7. Jar of Ironfilings.
8. Horseshoe Magnet with Keeper.
9. 2 Bar Magnets.
10. Inclinatorium.

In strong, handsome box
$10^3/_4$ in. long, 9 in. wide, $2^3/_4$ in. high, with manual
complete each **9/6**

12504 Experiment Box: — "Electromagnetism"

1. Bar Magnet.
2. Apparatus to ascertain the magnetic influence of a continuous current flowing through a straight conductor of electricity.
3. do. through a single looped conductor of electricity.
4. Solenoid.
5. Apparatus to demonstrate electric induction.
6. Galvanometer Coil.
7. Compass.
8. Electric Bell.
9. Electro Magnet with Keeper, on support.
10. Electric Coil with iron core suspended from spiral spring.

In strong, handsome box, $13^1/_2$ in long, 13 in. wide, $2^3/_4$ in. high, with manual . . . . complete each **27/4**

Physical Experiment Boxes.

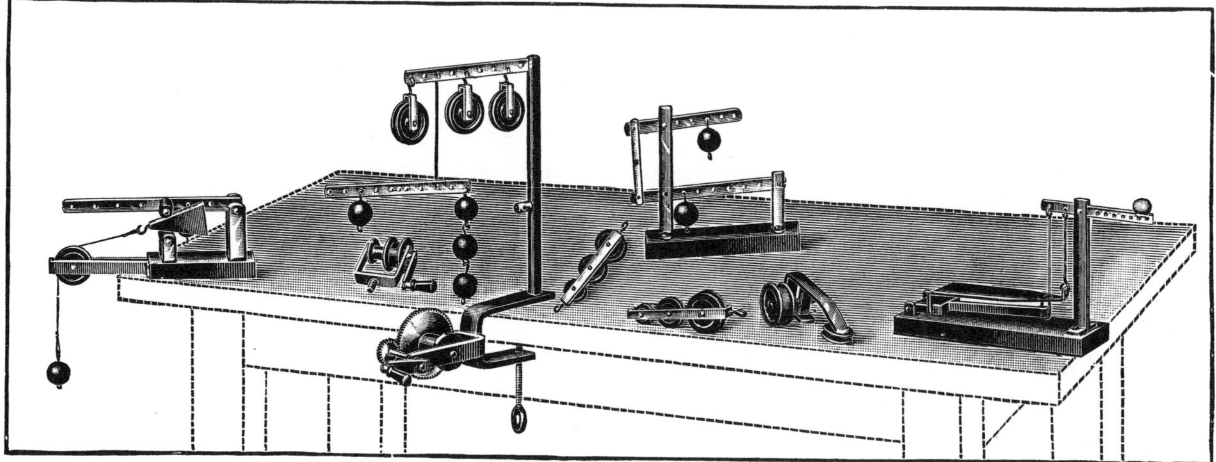

12501 Experiment Box: — "Mechanical Laws, simply explained"
containing:

1. Stand with Clamp to screw on table.
2. Simple levers.
3. 6 Weights.
4. 3 Pulleys.
5. Set of Pulleys.
6. Differential Gear.
7. Windlass.
8. Apparatus to demonstrate the action of a screw.
9. Double lever arrangement.
10. Decimal Weighing Scale.
11. Apparatus to demonstrate the action of wedges.

In strong, handsome box 14 1/4 in. long, 13 1/4 in. wide, 3 1/4 in. high, with manual . . . . complete each **23/2**

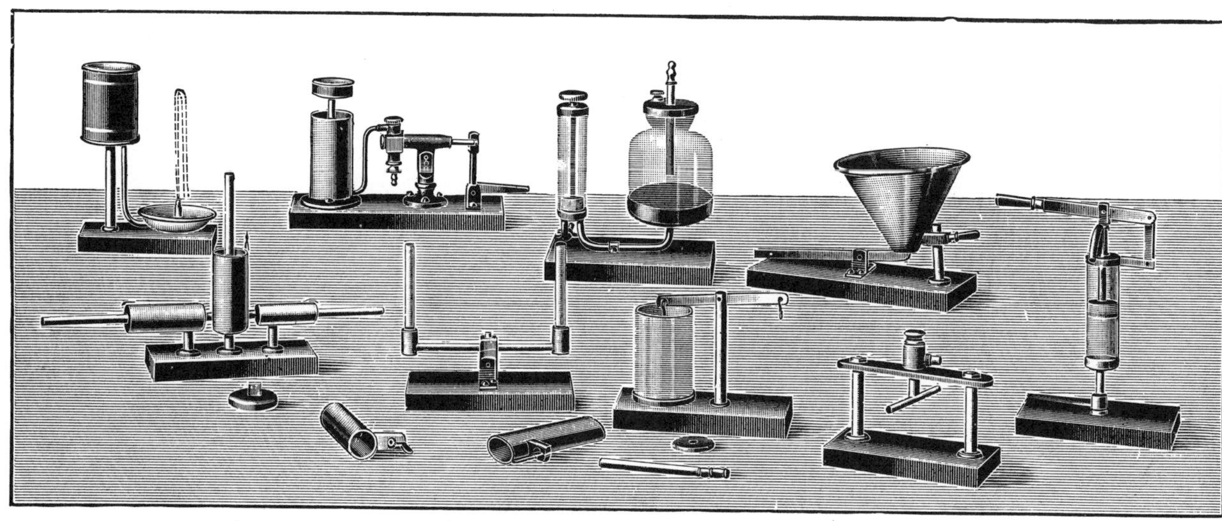

12502 Experiment Box: "The Laws of Liquids and Gases, simply explained"
containing:

1. Apparatus to ascertain Specific Gravity.
2. Apparatus to demonstrate lateral pressure.
3. Fountain.
4. Suction Pump.
5. Hydraulic Press.
6. Force Pump and Herons Ball
7. Apparatus to demonstrate vertical pressure.
8. Communicating tubes.
9. Turbine.

All pump valves and motions are shown under glass, wherever possible to facilitate the demonstrations.

In strong, handsome box 18 in. long, 13 1/2 in. wide, 3 1/4 in. high, with manual . . . . complete each **46/—**

Physical Experiment Boxes.

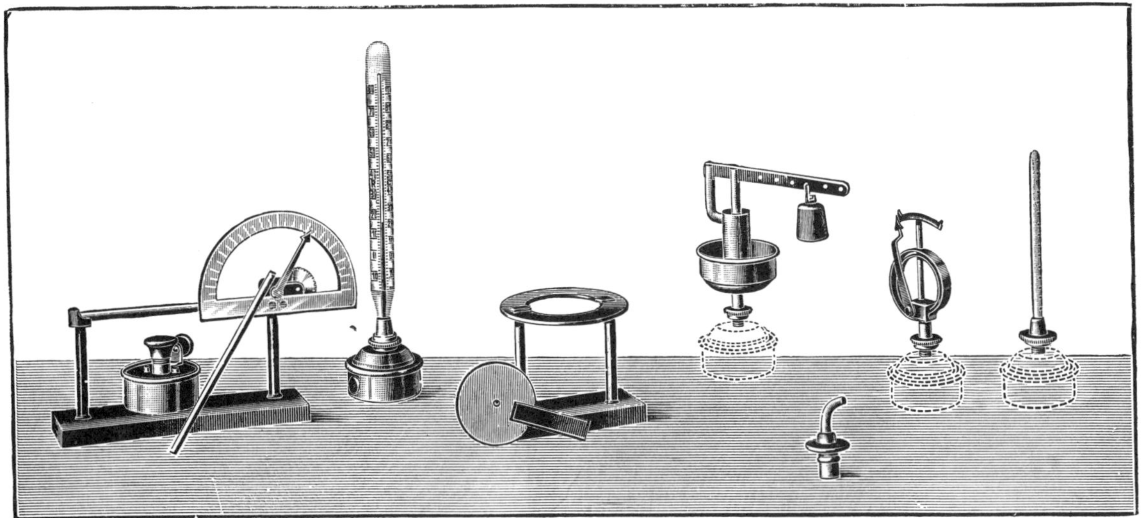

12505 Experiment Box: — "The Laws of Heat, simply explained"
containing:

1. Apparatus to demonstrate the expansion of solid bodies. (Tripod with metal rim and plate).
2. Indicator to ascertain the expansion of various metals.
3. Zinc Bar.
4. Iron Bar.
5. Brass Bar.
6. Spirit Vapour Lamp (2 burners).
7. Evaporator Basin. } to be screwed in
8. Thermometer. } to be screwed in
9. Glass Tube with Scale. } to be screwed in
10. Pressure Gauge, shown open.
11. Apparatus to demonstrate the effects of expansion and condensation of steam.

In strong, handsome box, 13 in. long, 11 in. wide, 3¼ in. high, with manual . . . . complete each **19/—**

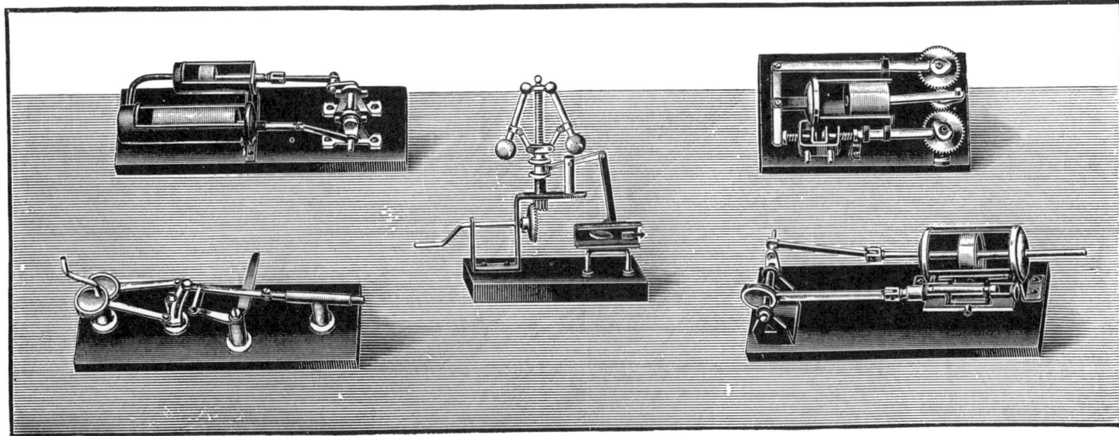

12506 Experiment Box: — "The Laws of Heat, practically applied"
containing:

1. Model of Steam Cylinder with Valve Motion shown in section to demonstrate the action of the Steam Engine.
2. Governor as generally applied to regulate the supply of steam to the cylinder (shown in section).
3. Linkmotion Reversing Gear (shown in section).
4. Hot Air Engine (Caloric Engine) (shown in section).
5. Model of Petrol Motor as used in Motor Cars, Motor Boats &c. (shown in section to demonstrate its action).

In strong, handsome box, 13½ in. long, 13 in. wide, 3¼ in, high, with manual . . . . complete each **28/6**

Physical Experiment Boxes.

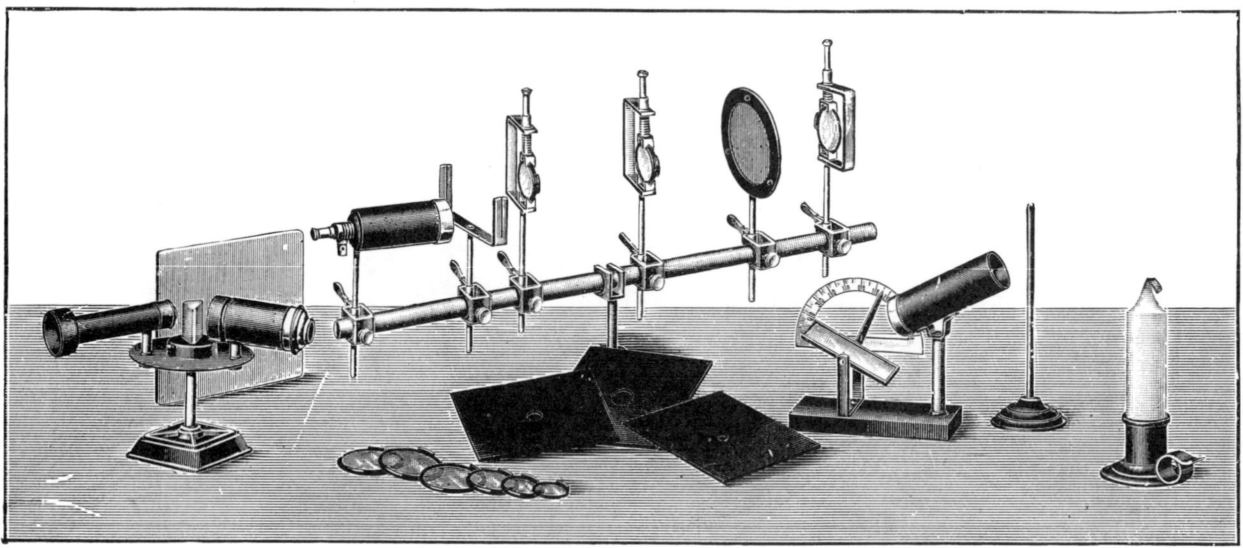

12507 Experiment Box: — "The Laws of Optics".

Containing:

1. Optical Outfit, consisting of:
   3 Lensholders
   1 Electric Illuminant with Screen
   1 Screenholder.
   1 Screen for photometric experiments.
2. 1 Set of Lenses of various focuses and diameters.
3. Apparatus to demonstrate the refraction of light.
4. 1 Standard candle.
5. 1 Upright for the comparison of shadows.
6. Screen for the comparison of shadows.
7. Diaphragms of various sizes.
8. Spectroscope.

In strong, handsome box, 18 in. long, 13½ in. wide, 3¼ in. high, with manual . . . . complete each **23/2**

12508 Experiment Box: — "Applications of the Laws of Optics".

Containing:

1. Magnifying Glass.
2. Microscope.
3. Galilei's Telescope.
4. Terrestric Telescope.
5. Astronomic Telescope.
6. Stereoscope with picture.
7. Camera Obscura.
8. Magic Lantern.
9. Searchlight.
10. Lanternslide.

In strong, handsome box, 18 in. long, 13½ in. wide, 4 in. high, with manual . . . . complete each **28/6**

Experiment Box: "Acoustics".

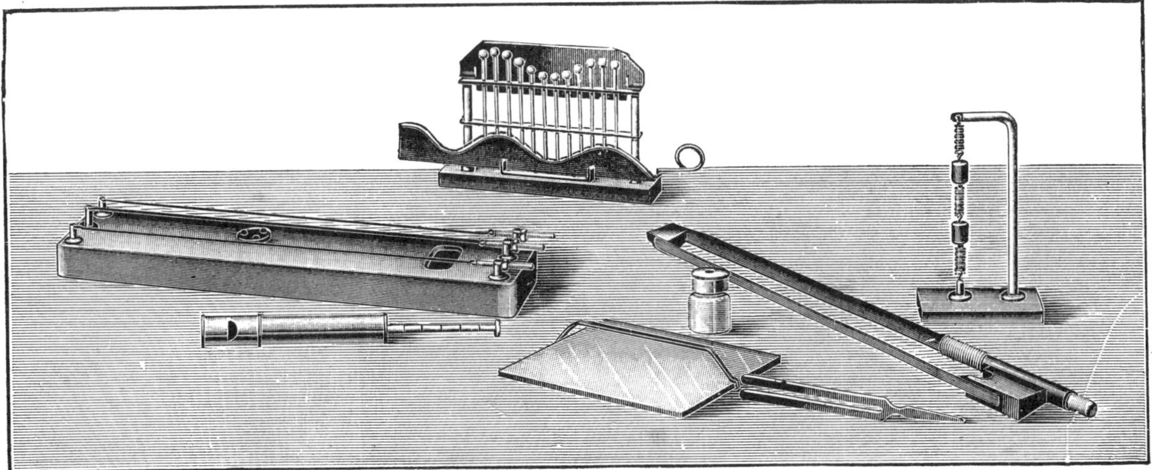

12509 Experiment Box: — „Acoustics"

containing:

1. Apparatus to demonstrate sound waves.
2. Apparatus to demonstrate longitudinal vibrations.
3. Glassplate to produce designs by sound.
4. Jar of sand.
5. Whistle with variable sounds.
6. Tuning Fork.
7. Sounding box with Strings and tuning attachment.
8. Violin Bow.

In strong, handsome box: 18 in. long, 13½ in. wide, 2½ in. high, with manual . . . . complete each **19/—**

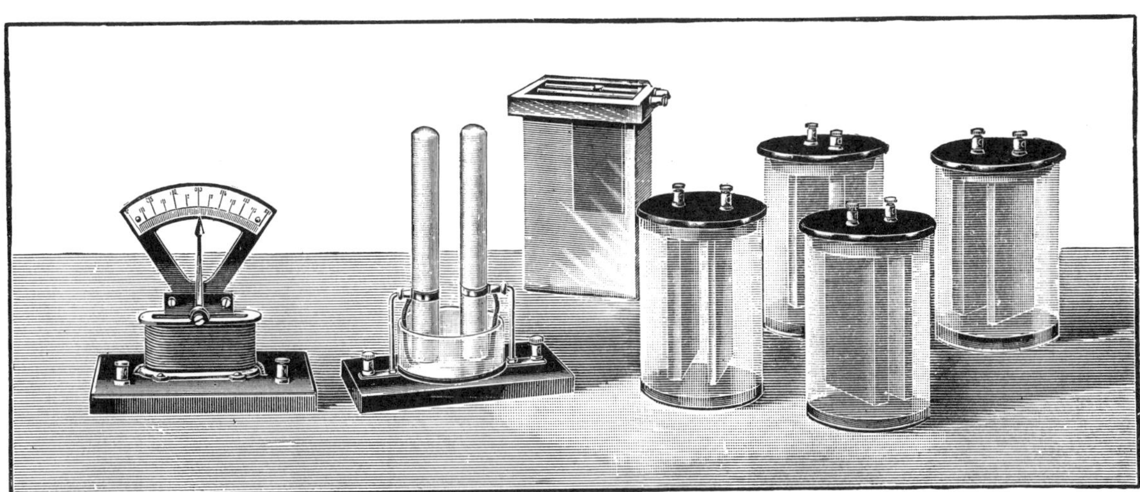

12510 Experiment Box: — "Galvanic Electricity" (Electro Plating)

containing:

1. 4 Bichromate Batteries
2. Apparatus for the electrolysis of water
3. Galvanometer with double winding.
4. Electroplating Apparatus.

In strong, handsome box: 18 in. long, 13½ in. wide, 2⅜ in. high, with manual . . . . complete each **23/2**

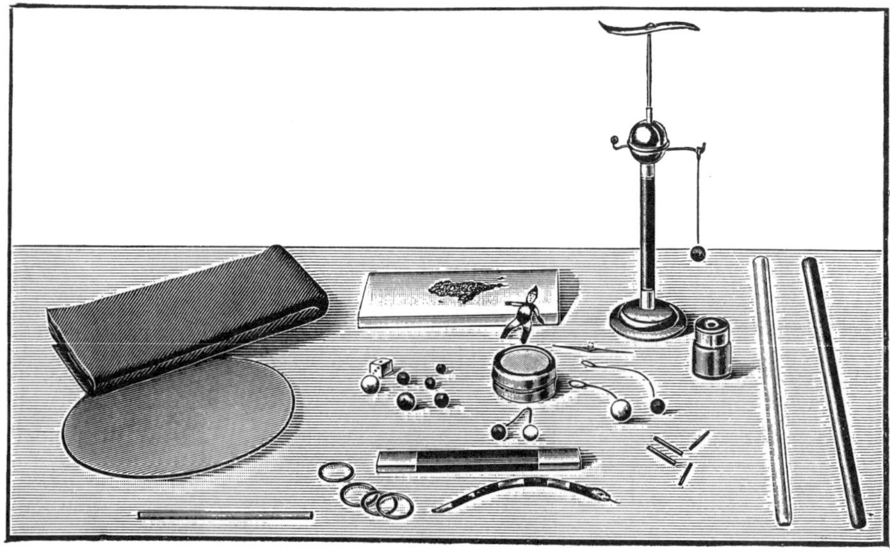

Experiment Boxes.

12511/0 **Experiment Box: "Magnetism"** and **"Friction Electricity"**, containing:

1. Permanent Magnet.
2. Bottle of iron dust.
3. Rings and Wirepieces of soft iron.
4. Strainer.
5. Paper Table.
6. Magnetic Needle with point.
7. Piece of Steel Wire.
8. Stand with insulated foot.
9. Piece of flannel.
10. Vulcanite Rod.
11. Glass Rod.
12. Couple of Pendulum Balls } made of pith.
13. Two light Balls } made of pith.

In strong, handsome box, $8^5/_8$ in. long, $5^7/_8$ in. wide, 2 in. high with manual . . . . complete each **10/6**

12511/1

Experiment Box: "Friction Electricity"

containing:

1. Electrophore with vulcanite plate, cover and flannel.
2. Stand.
3. Pith Ball Pendulum.
4. Electric Whirl.
5. Paper Tufts.
6. Leyden Jar.
7. Glass Rod.
8. Vulcanite Rod.
9. Discharger.
10. Athlete (with pith balls).
11. Pith Snake.
12. Pith Cube.
13. Brass Chain.
14. Electroscope.

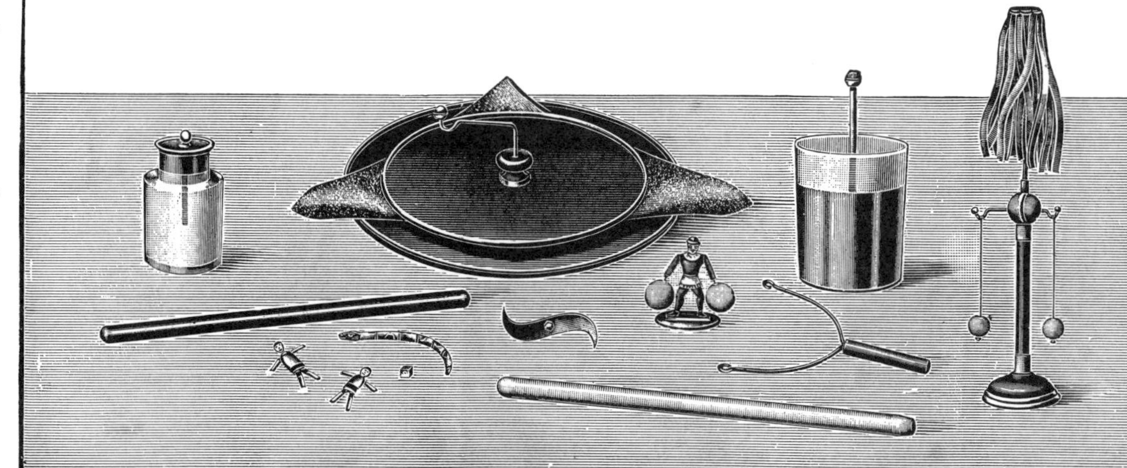

In strong, handsome box 17 in. long, 11 in. wide, $2^3/_4$ in. high with manual . . . . complete each **16/—**

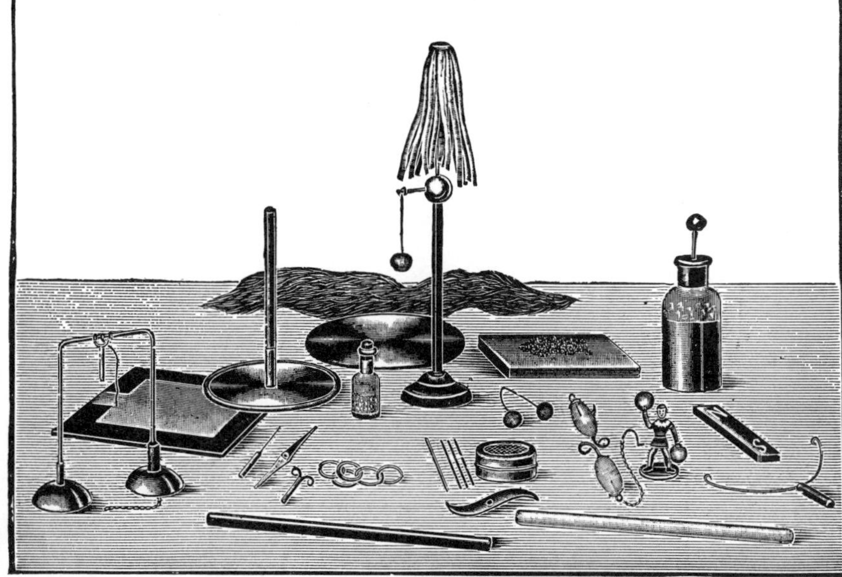

12511/$1^1/_2$ **Experiment Box:**

"Magnetism" and **"Friction Electricitv"**

containing:

1. Permanent Magnet.
2. Bottle of iron dust.
3. Rings and Wire Pieces of soft iron.
4. Strainer.
5. Paper Table.
6. Magnetic Needle with point.
7. Piece of Steel wire.
8. Vulcanite Electrophore covered [with staniol.
9. Fox Tail.
10. Metal Cover with vulcanite handle.
11. Metal Stand with insulated foot.
12. Paper Tufts.
13. Chimes.
14. u. 15. 1 Vulcanite- and 1 Glass Rod.
16. Dancing Balls with various objects.
17. Athlete made of pith.
18. Electric Pendulum.
19. Electric Whirl with point.
20. Leyden Jar and Discharger.
21. Geissler Tube.

In strong, handsome box $16^1/_4$ in. long, 9 in. wide, $3^1/_8$ in. high with manual . . . . complete each **30/6**

Experiment-Boxes.

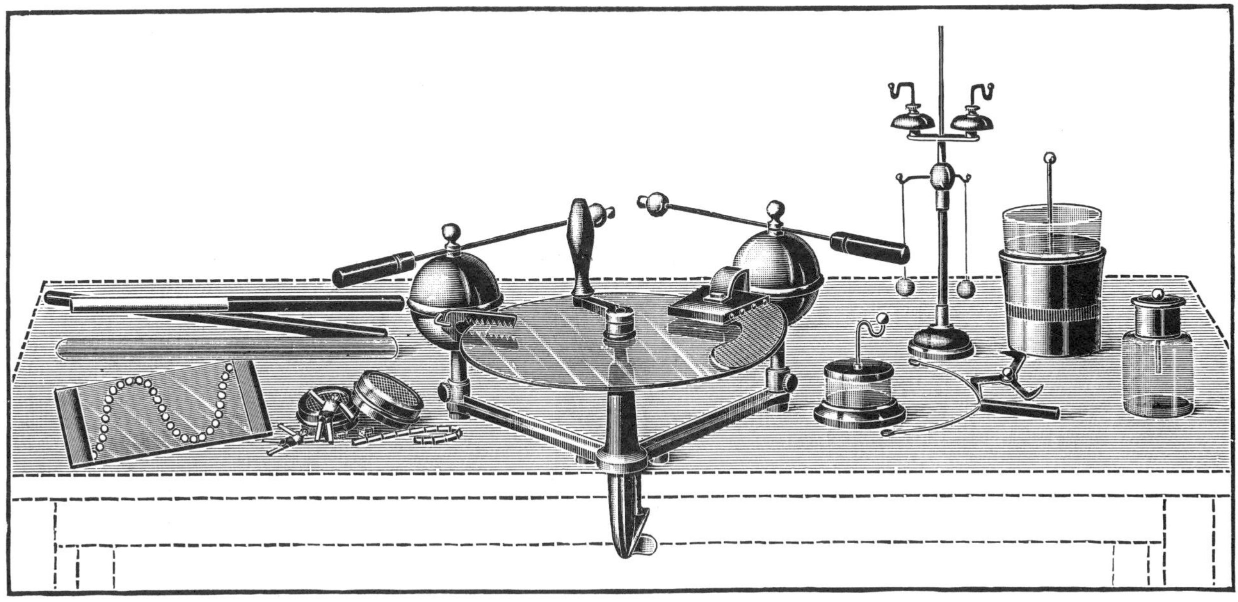

12511/2 Experiment Box: — "Friction Electricity II"

1. Influence Electric Machine.
2. Stand.
3. Bell.
4. Pendulum.
5. Paper Tufts.
6. El. Whirl.
7. Glass Rod.
8. Vulcanite Rod.
9. Lightning Plate.
10. Leyden Jar.
11. Surface Discharge.
12. Discharger.
13. Athlete.
14. Dancing Balls.
15. Electroscope.

In strong, handsome box: 22 in. long, 13½ in. wide, 5 in. high, with manual . . . . complete each **38/—**

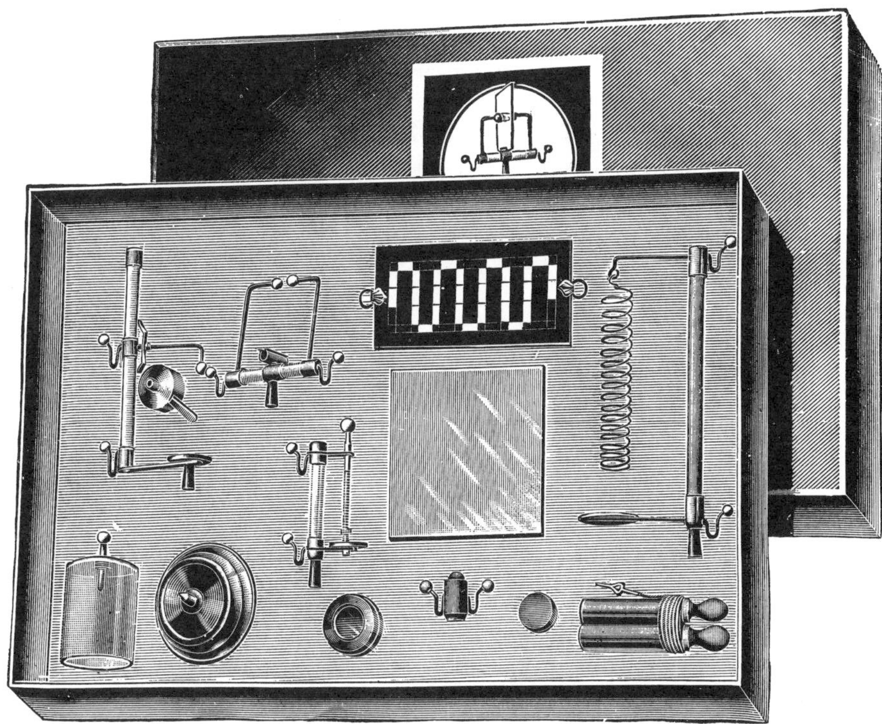

12513 Experiment Box: "Influence Electricity"

Supplementary Box 1 for 12511/2, containing:

1. Lightning Plate.
2. Smoke Condensing Apparatus.
3. Incense Candles.
4. Ignition Apparatus.
5. 1 Box of Amorces.
6. Ozon Apparatus.
7. Glass Plate.
8. Electric catapult.
9. Jonasitor.
10. Spirit Lamp.
11. Electric Spiral Spring.
12. 1 Pair of Handles.
13. Stand.

In strong box: 21 in. long, 13½ in. wide, 4$^{5}/_{16}$ in. high, with manual . . . . each **23/2**

Experiment Boxes.

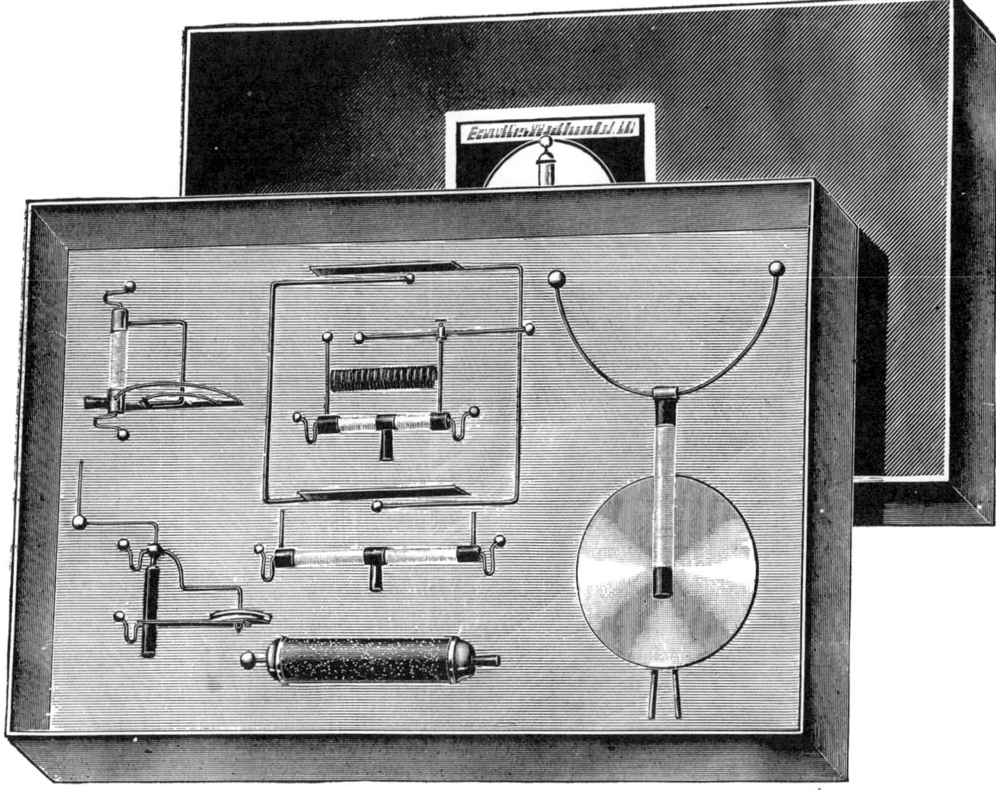

12514 Experiment Box: "Influence Electricity" Supplementary Box II, containing:

1. Model of a Lightning conductor.
2. St. Elmo's fire.
3. Lightning tube.
4. Electric field.
5. 2 Sound Producers.
6. Self-Induction.
7. Discharger.
8. Stand

In strong box, 21 in. long, $13^1/_2$ in. wide, $3^1/_4$ in. high, with manual . . . . complete each **23/2**

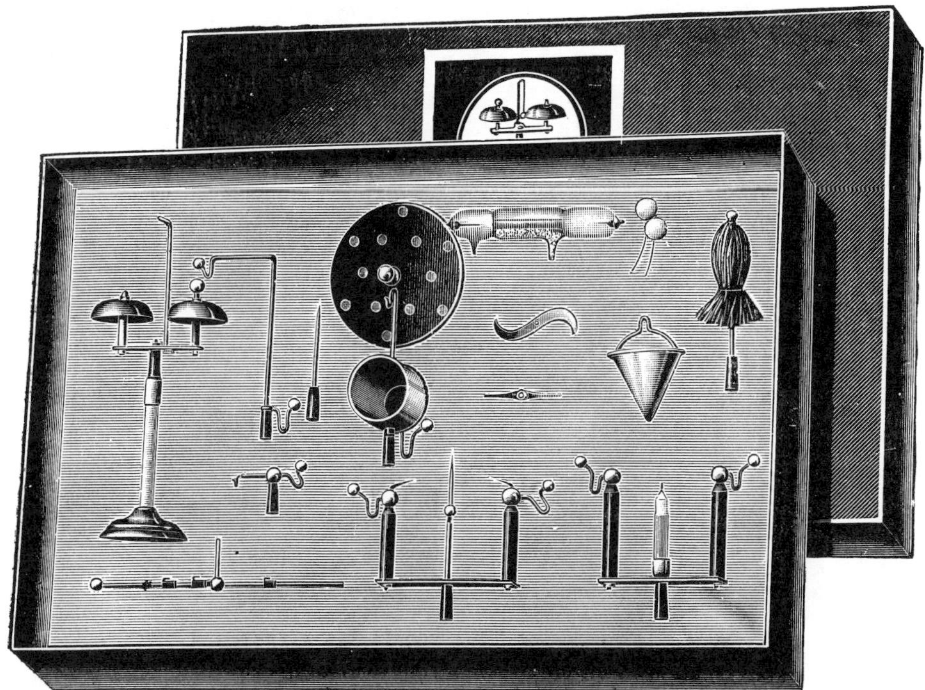

12515 Experiment Box: "Influence Electricity" Supplementary Box III, containing:

1. Electric Bell
2. Sand Apparatus
3. Paper Tufts
4. Pith Balls
5. Electric Whirl.
6. Magnetic Needle.
7. Rotating Disc
8. Tube to ascertain electric charges.
9. Candle.
10. Candle apparatus.
11. Geissler Tube.
12. Stand.
13. Pin for electric whirl and magnetic needle.
14. Electric Rod and Pith balls.

In strong, handsome box, 22 in. long, $13^1/_2$ in. wide, $2^1/_2$ in. high, with manual . . . . complete each **26/6**

Experiment Boxes.

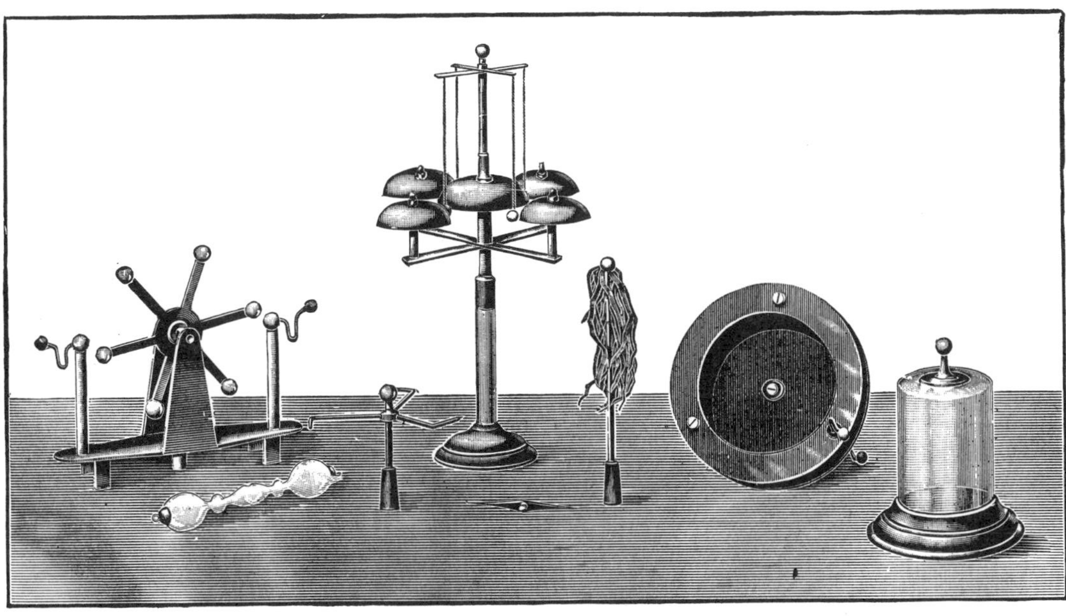

12516 Experiment Box: — "Influence Electricity"

Supplementary Box IV, containing:

1. Electric Bells.
2. Paper Tufts.
3. Dancing Balls.
4. Rotating Wheels.
5. Motor.
6. Upright.
7. Geissler Tube.
8. The bewitched ball.
9. Pith balls.
10. Magnetic Needle.
11. Stand.

In strong, handsome box: 22 in. long, 13½ in. wide, 3½ in. high, with manual . . . . complete each **26/6**

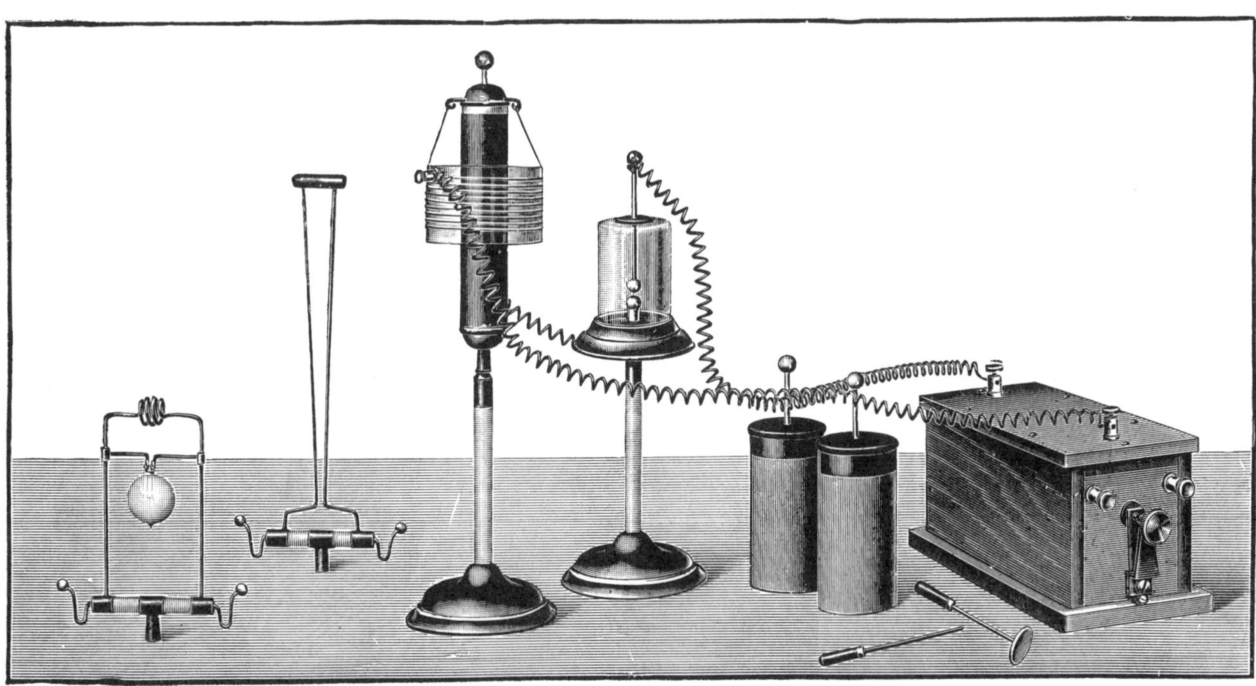

12512 Experiment Box: — "High Frequency Electric Currents"

(Tesla Experiments)

1. Large Induction Apparatus (spark length 1⅕ in.).
2. Electrodes for same (plate and point).
3. 2 Leyden Jars.
4. Electric Incandescent Lamp.
5. Apparatus to demonstrate self induction.
6. Spark Bridge.
7. 2 Stands.
8. Tesla transformator with primary spool.
9. " " " secondary spool.
10. Forked Lightning Conductor.

In strong, handsome box: 21 in. long, 13½ in. wide, 4½ in. high, with manual . . . . complete each **114/—**

Single Physical Experiment-Apparatus.

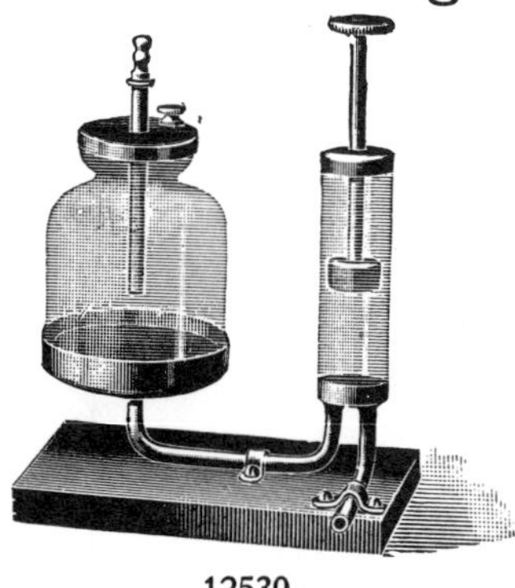

12530

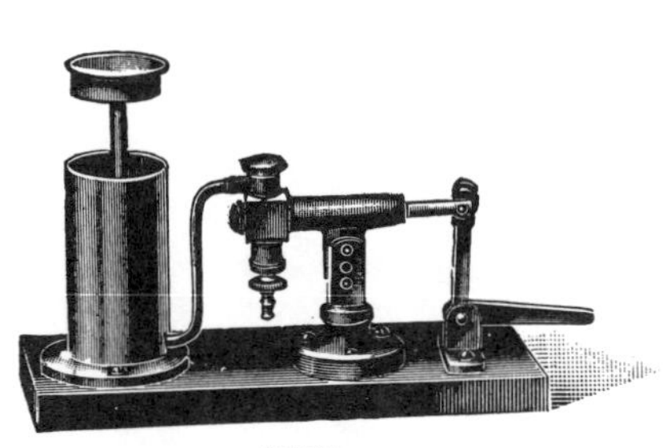

12531

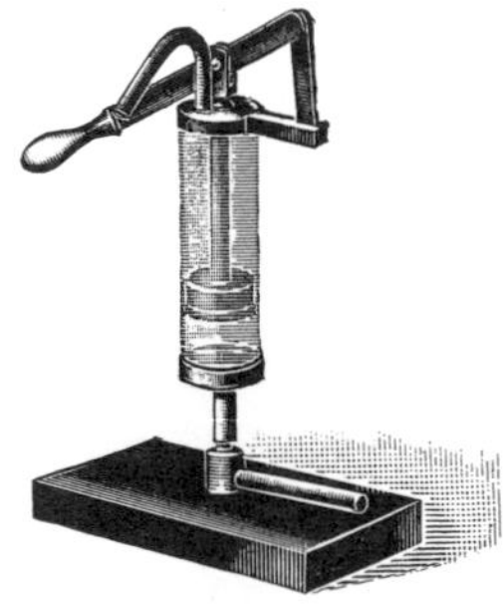

12532

12530 **Pressure Pump,** Demonstration Model for observing the valve work and transit of water under glass containers . . . . each **6/10**

12531 **Hydraulic Press,** Apparatus for producing high-pressure by compression of liquids . . . . „ **9/6**

12532 **Suction Pump,** Demonstration Model for observing valve work and transit of water and in use as building pump under glass container . . . . „ **5/2**

12533

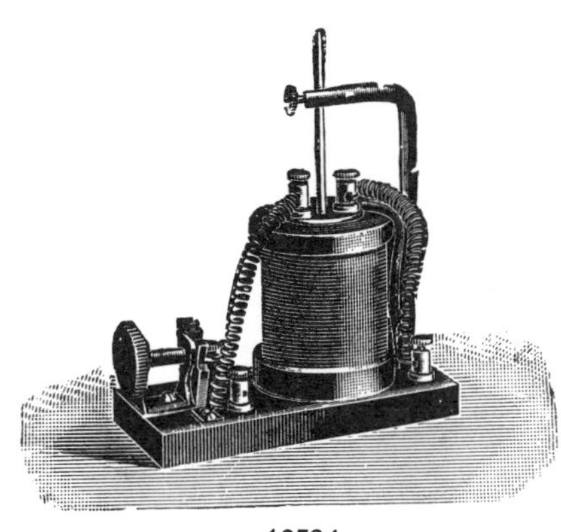

12534

12535

12533 **Inclinator,** Apparatus for ascertaining the locality with compass . . . . each **3/10**

12534 **Inductor,** with primary and secondary coil for indicating induction currents . . . . „ **7/10**

12535 **Apparatus** for ascertaining the expansion of metals, with indicating arrangement of great sensitiveness, including gas generating spirit lamp . . . . „ **6/8**

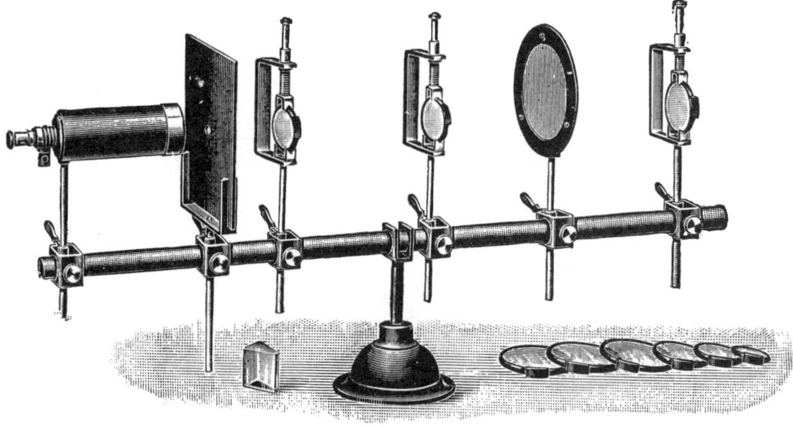

12536

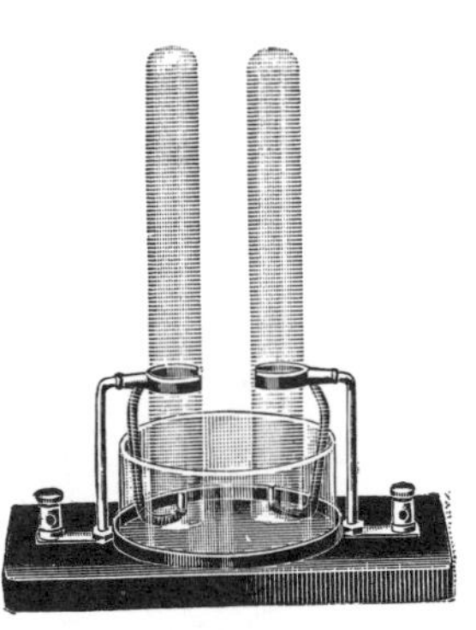

12537

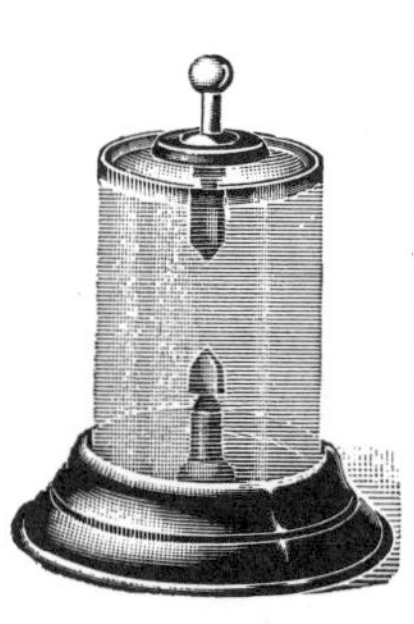

12546

12536 **Optical Outfit,** for studying the course of rays with lenses, mirrors etc., also for measuring the power of light; including set of lenses . . . . each **15/4**

12537 **Apparatus for decomposition of water;** by connection with a galvanic battery, water is decomposed into hydrogen and oxygen . . . . „ **3/2**

12546 **Smokeconsuming Apparatus;** in this apparatus the smoke disappears immediately if it is brought into connection with the pole of an electrical machine . . . . „ **4/10**

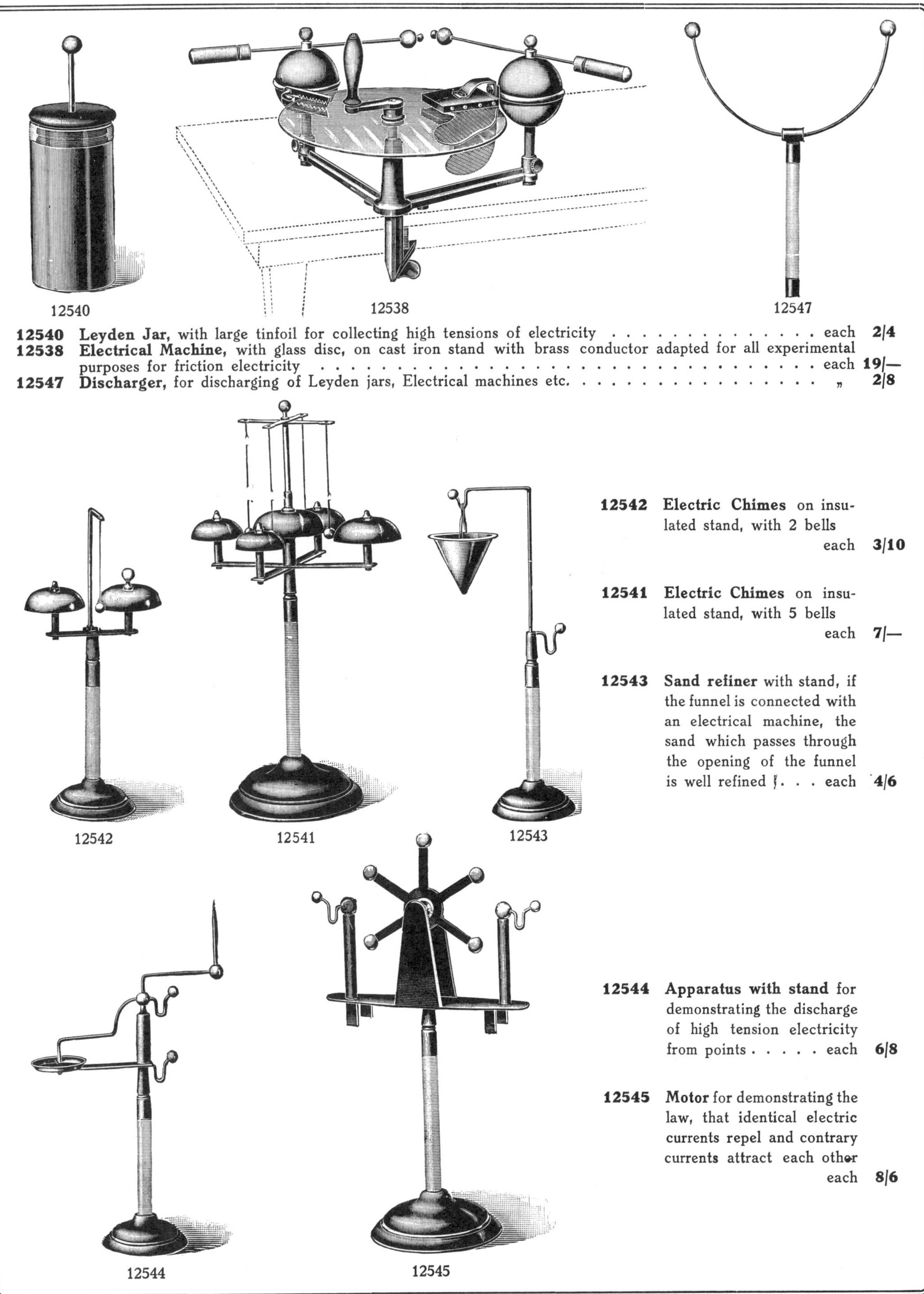

12540 Leyden Jar, with large tinfoil for collecting high tensions of electricity . . . . each **2/4**
12538 Electrical Machine, with glass disc, on cast iron stand with brass conductor adapted for all experimental purposes for friction electricity . . . . each **19/—**
12547 Discharger, for discharging of Leyden jars, Electrical machines etc. . . . . „ **2/8**

12542 Electric Chimes on insulated stand, with 2 bells each **3/10**

12541 Electric Chimes on insulated stand, with 5 bells each **7/—**

12543 Sand refiner with stand, if the funnel is connected with an electrical machine, the sand which passes through the opening of the funnel is well refined . . . each **4/6**

12544 Apparatus with stand for demonstrating the discharge of high tension electricity from points . . . . . each **6/8**

12545 Motor for demonstrating the law, that identical electric currents repel and contrary currents attract each other each **8/6**

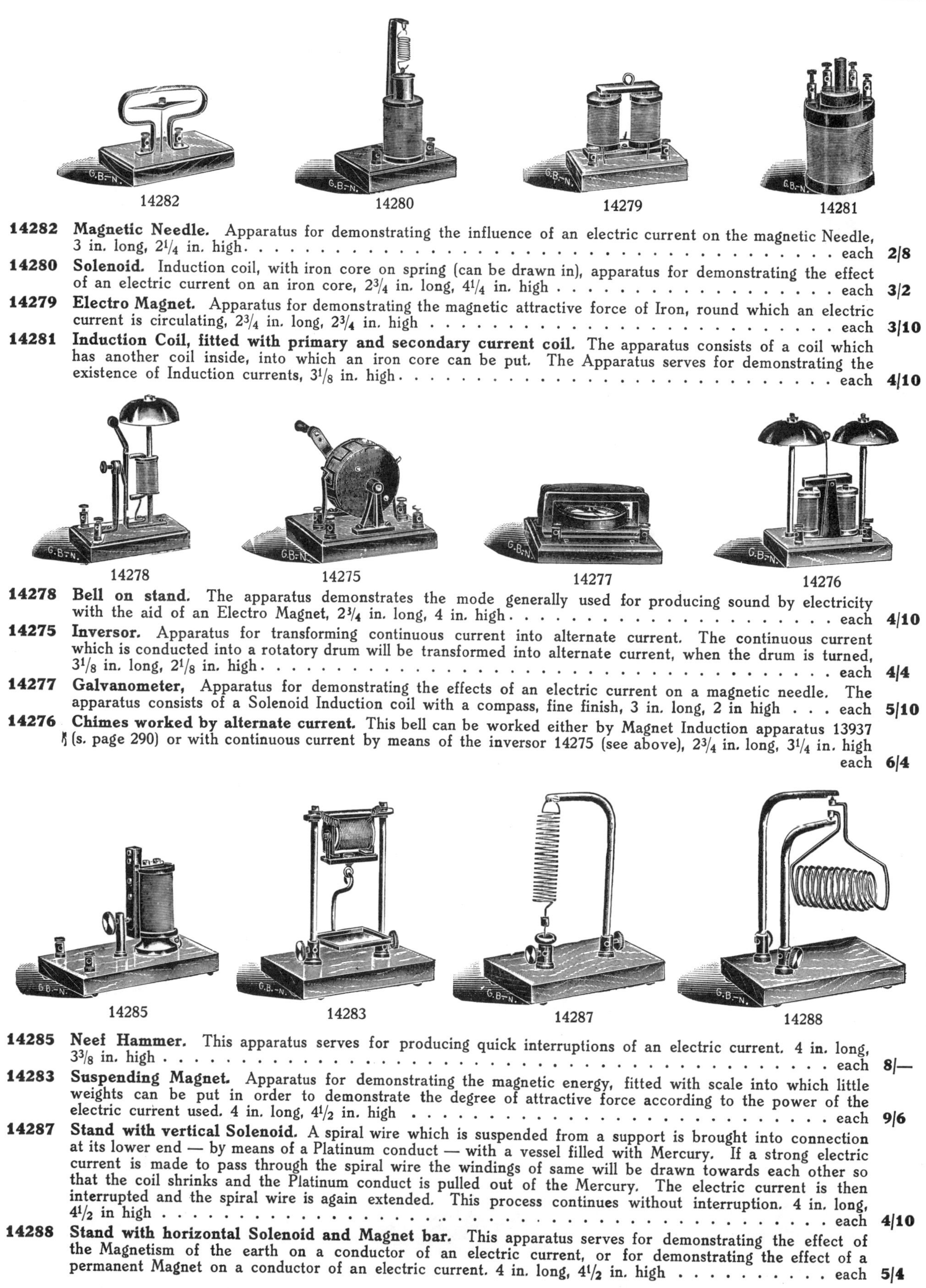

14282 14280 14279 14281

14282 Magnetic Needle. Apparatus for demonstrating the influence of an electric current on the magnetic Needle, 3 in. long, $2^1/_4$ in. high . . . . each **2/8**

14280 Solenoid. Induction coil, with iron core on spring (can be drawn in), apparatus for demonstrating the effect of an electric current on an iron core, $2^3/_4$ in. long, $4^1/_4$ in. high . . . . each **3/2**

14279 Electro Magnet. Apparatus for demonstrating the magnetic attractive force of Iron, round which an electric current is circulating, $2^3/_4$ in. long, $2^3/_4$ in. high . . . . each **3/10**

14281 Induction Coil, fitted with primary and secondary current coil. The apparatus consists of a coil which has another coil inside, into which an iron core can be put. The Apparatus serves for demonstrating the existence of Induction currents, $3^1/_8$ in. high . . . . each **4/10**

14278 14275 14277 14276

14278 Bell on stand. The apparatus demonstrates the mode generally used for producing sound by electricity with the aid of an Electro Magnet, $2^3/_4$ in. long, 4 in. high . . . . each **4/10**

14275 Inversor. Apparatus for transforming continuous current into alternate current. The continuous current which is conducted into a rotatory drum will be transformed into alternate current, when the drum is turned, $3^1/_8$ in. long, $2^1/_8$ in. high . . . . each **4/4**

14277 Galvanometer, Apparatus for demonstrating the effects of an electric current on a magnetic needle. The apparatus consists of a Solenoid Induction coil with a compass, fine finish, 3 in. long, 2 in high . . . each **5/10**

14276 Chimes worked by alternate current. This bell can be worked either by Magnet Induction apparatus 13937 (s. page 290) or with continuous current by means of the inversor 14275 (see above), $2^3/_4$ in. long, $3^1/_4$ in. high each **6/4**

14285 14283 14287 14288

14285 Neef Hammer. This apparatus serves for producing quick interruptions of an electric current. 4 in. long, $3^3/_8$ in. high . . . . each **8/—**

14283 Suspending Magnet. Apparatus for demonstrating the magnetic energy, fitted with scale into which little weights can be put in order to demonstrate the degree of attractive force according to the power of the electric current used. 4 in. long, $4^1/_2$ in. high . . . . each **9/6**

14287 Stand with vertical Solenoid. A spiral wire which is suspended from a support is brought into connection at its lower end — by means of a Platinum conduct — with a vessel filled with Mercury. If a strong electric current is made to pass through the spiral wire the windings of same will be drawn towards each other so that the coil shrinks and the Platinum conduct is pulled out of the Mercury. The electric current is then interrupted and the spiral wire is again extended. This process continues without interruption. 4 in. long, $4^1/_2$ in high . . . . each **4/10**

14288 Stand with horizontal Solenoid and Magnet bar. This apparatus serves for demonstrating the effect of the Magnetism of the earth on a conductor of an electric current, or for demonstrating the effect of a permanent Magnet on a conductor of an electric current. 4 in. long, $4^1/_2$ in. high . . . . each **5/4**

Single Physical Experiment-Apparatus.

14286

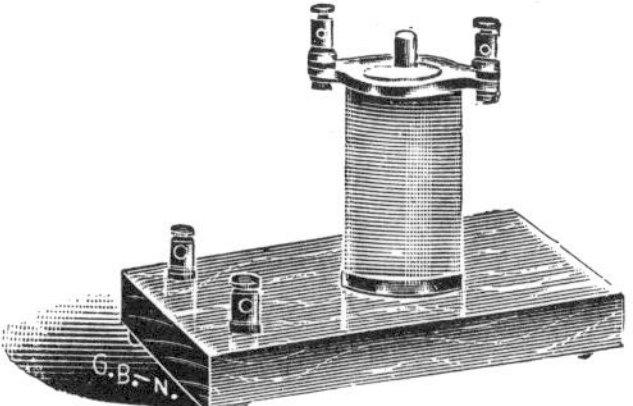

14284

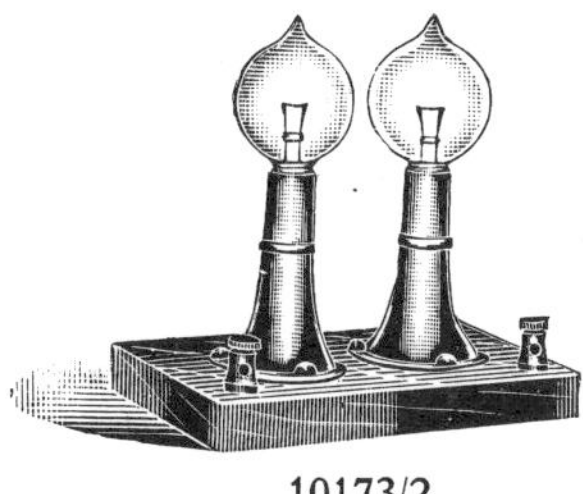

10173/2

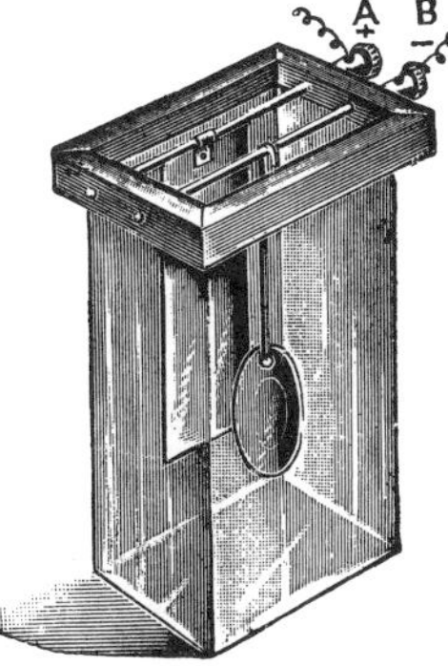

13432

14286 Galvanometer. Apparatus for demonstrating the effect of an electric current on a magnet. The apparatus consists of an Induction coil and a compass, very fine finish, with bevelled glass lid, 4 in. long, 1¾ in. high, each **8/—**

14284 Double Induction Coil. The apparatus consists of one coil contained inside another, into which an iron core can be put. When opening and closing the electric circuit in the first i. e. "Primary Coil", induction currents will be produced within the "Secondary Coil" which is inside. This takes place, no matter if the iron core is put into the secondary coil or withdrawn. The existence of the induction currents can be proved by means of the Galvanometer 14277 and 14286, 4 in. long, 3⅛ in. high . . . . each **8/—**

Incandescent Lamps to be connected with Dynamos 4 Volt, mounted on wooden base

10173/1 3⅛ in. long, 2½ in. wide with 1 Incandescent Lamp . . . . each **3/2**

„ /2 4⅛ „ „ 2⅜ „ „ „ 2 „ . . . . „ **5/4**

13432 Galvanizing Battery (plating bath), consisting of: Glass bath with hard wood frame and two conducting rods, incl. 1 pure nickel anode . . . . complete each **3/—**

13434 Best nickel salt, ready prepared . . . . per doz. packets **8/6**

13435 Pure nickel anodes, extra . . . . doz. **6/2**

Very original. ***Instructive Toy.***

10123

10123 New electric Crane for low current very original and instructive, with switch, with Electro Magnet for lifting Metal objects (iron pieces, railway trucks &c.) lifting capacity up to 2 lbs. Electric Switch-board for lifting, lowering and turning of the crane in every direction, to be worked by Bichromate Batteries or Accumulators. The whole set, ready for connection, mounted on fine wooden base. 17¼ in. high each (without battery) **22/8**

Bichromate Batteries

for Motors, Electric Trains etc.

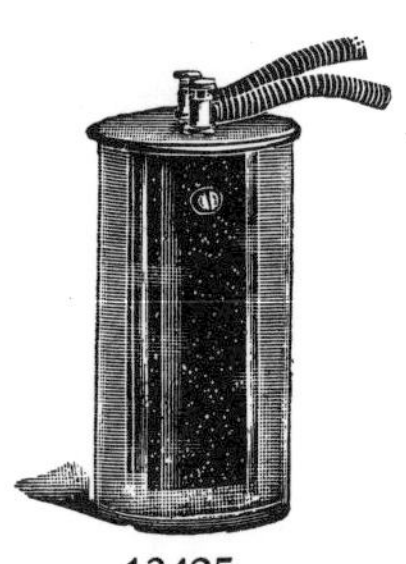
13425

13426

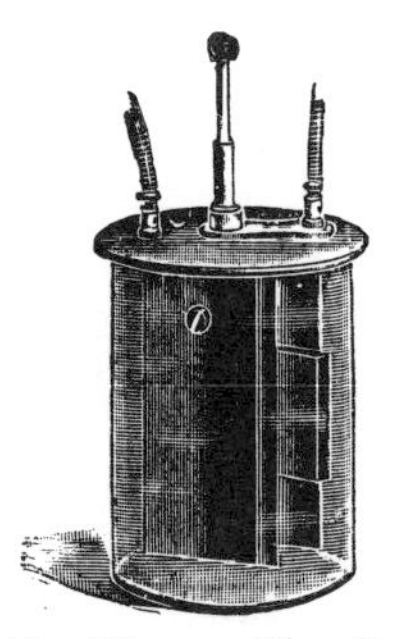
13395 Glass with adjuster

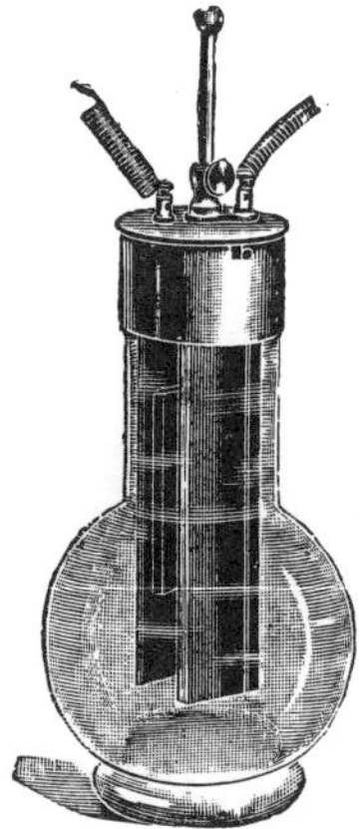
13446

13425	**Bichromate Batteries,** round shape, $2^1/_4$ in. diam., $4^7/_8$ in. high	each	**2/8**
13426	„ „ square „ $3^1/_8$ „ „ $2^1/_4$ „ wide, $5^1/_8$ in. high	„	**3/4**
13395	„ „ (Immersion Batteries) round shape, $3^3/_8$ in. diam., 6 in. high	„	**4/10**
13446/1	„ „ (Grenet Immersion Batteries) Pear shape, $1^3/_4$ in. diam., 7 in. high	„	**3/8**
„ /2	„ „ „ „ „ „ „ 2 „ „ 9 „ „	„	**4/10**

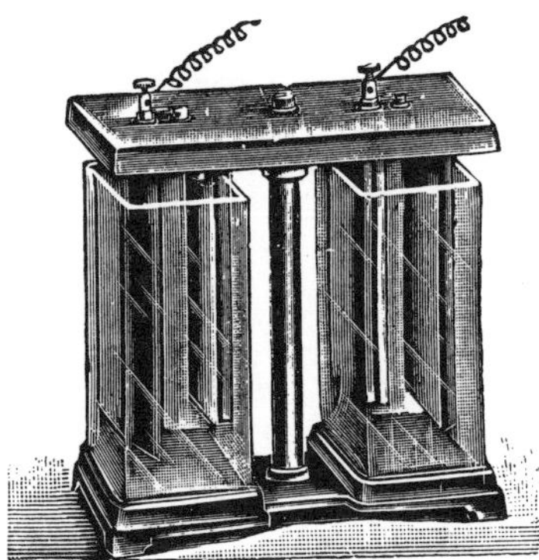
13427

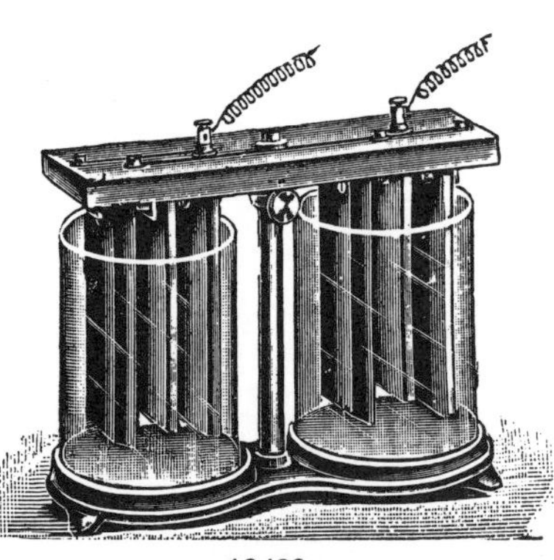
13429

13428

13427 **Bichromate Batteries,** (Bichromate Immersion Batteries with adjuster); double, square glass cells with strong wood lid and adjuster, on japanned iron frame, 6 in. long, $3^1/_4$ in. wide, $6^3/_4$ in. high . . . . each **11/6**

13429 **Bichromate Batteries,** double, 2 round glass cells with strong wooden lid and adjuster, on japanned iron frame, $3^1/_8$ in. diam. each, 8 in. long, $6^1/_4$ in. high . . . . „ **11/6**

13428 **Bichromate Batteries,** quadruple, 4 oblong glass cells, with strong wooden lid and adjuster, on japanned iron frame, 8 in. long, $4^3/_4$ in. wide, $6^1/_4$ in. high . . . . „ **19/—**

Dry Batteries and Pouch Batteries.

10219/2

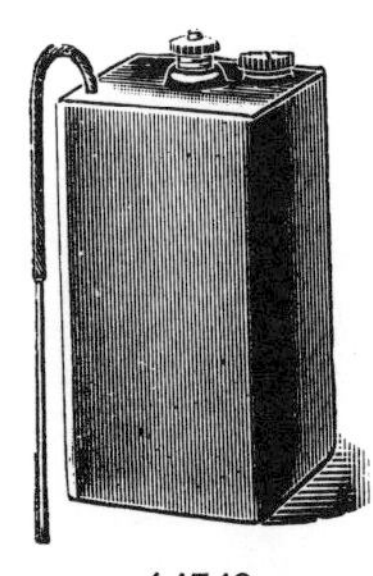
14749

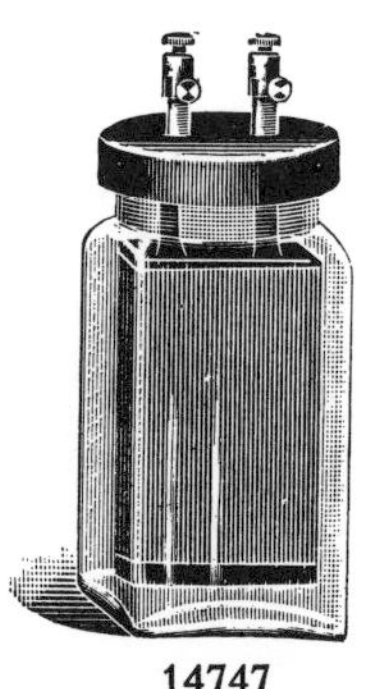
14747

10219/2 **Dry Batteries** (socalled Pocket Batteries) ready for use, capacity abt. 4 Volt . . doz. **14/—**

Dry Batteries (socalled Storage Batteries)

14749/1 square $1^3/_4$ in. wide, 4 in. high . . . each **2/8**

„ /2 „ $2^3/_8$ „ „ $4^3/_4$ „ „ . . . „ **4/—**

The stock-batteries can be kept in stock for an unlimited ime, have to be filled with water before use and are then able to supply current.

14747 **New Filling Batteries (Pouch Batteries) „Aceden"** with prepared plates in glass cell with lid square $5^1/_2$ in high. $2^3/_8$ in. wide . . . . each **5/4**

14748 **Single Reserve Plates** . . . . „ **3/—**

These new batteries have a very great capacity and the current is most intensive and durable. After being exhausted, the battery can be charged again so that these batteries can be compared with accumulators.

Transportable Accumulators.

To work Electric Motors, Induction Apparatus or Electric Trains and to light Incandescent Lamps etc. ***for a longer period, accumulators*** *are mostly used. The working durability and capacity of these accumulators is stated on every single one. The meaning of the word "Capacity" in Ampère hours is that when using 1 Ampère the accumulator can be worked a certain time, with respect to its capacity. If a smaller capacity than 1 Ampère is required of the accumulator, same can of course be worked for a relatively longer time; the durability therefore of the accumulator can be calculated as follows:*

An accumulator which has a duration of 4 Ampère-hours can work for 4 hours, if 1 Ampère is used; if only $^1/_2$ *Ampère is used, same can work about 8 hours (as* $\frac{4}{0,5} = 8$*) and so on. The maximum discharging current, stated on the accumulators, must not be exceeded in any case.*

The accumulators are supplied "not charged", and have to be charged according to the scheme enclosed with every accumulator. The accumulator must be filled with pure chemical sulphuric acid of $24^0/_0$ *Beaumé and then connected with a* ***continuous current*** *light supply or some other current producer, using for the resistance an Incandescent Lamp which reduces the current to the right strength indicated on the accumulator. It would be as well to use the charging resistance No. 14057 page 351.* ***Alternating current cannot be used for charging accumulators but only continuous current.***

Accumulators can neither be exchanged nor taken back.

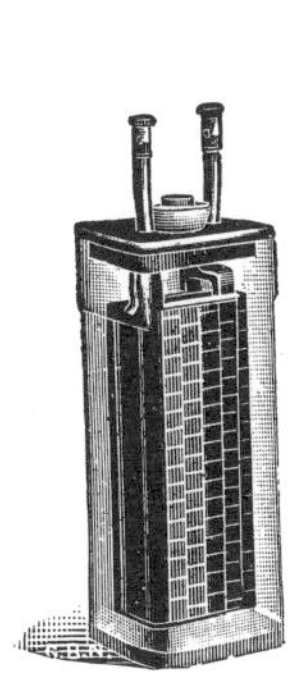

14039

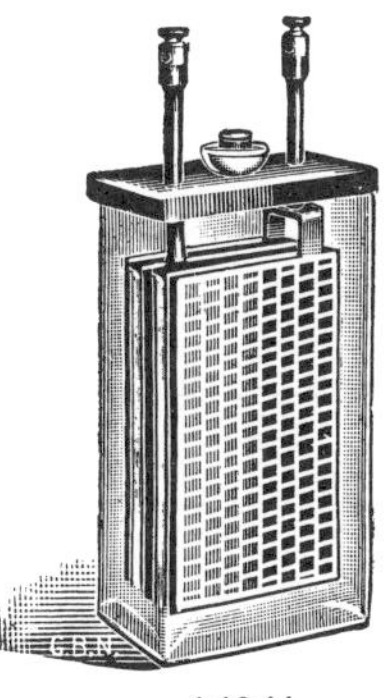

14041

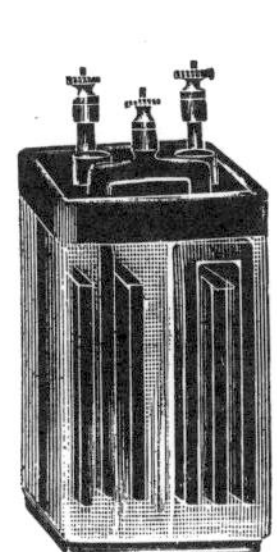

14770—14773

11642—11645 having 2 cells
11646—11647 having 3 cells

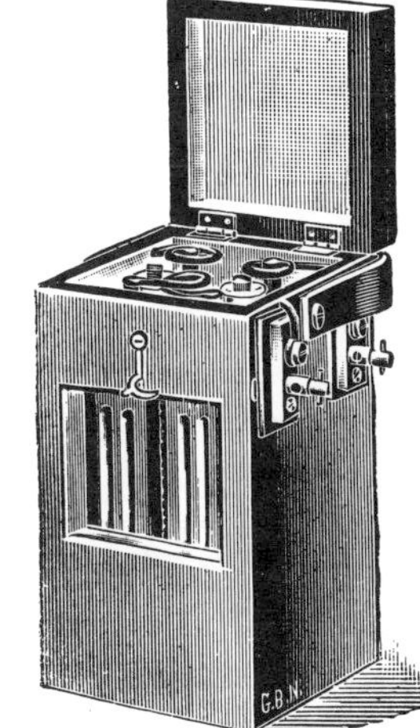

14044—14045
with lid

Transportable Accumulators in glasses, ready mounted in strong glasses, **best quality** (not charged).

No.	with 1 cell = **2 Volt**					with 2 cells = **4 Volt**			
	14038/1	**14039**	**14040**	**14041**	**14041a**	**14770**	**14771**	**14772**	**14773**
Capacity in Ampères-hours	4	6	8	14	25	2	4	8	14
Charging current maximum in Ampères	0,6	0,8	1,25	1,8	3,5	0,5	0,6	1,25	1,8
Discharging „ „ „ „	1	1	2	3	4	0,5	1,0	2,0	3,0
Outside Dimensions: Height	$5^1/_8$ in.	$6^1/_4$ in.	$5^1/_8$ in.	$6^7/_8$ in.	$6^7/_8$ in.	$3^3/_4$ in.	$5^1/_2$ in.	$5^1/_4$ in.	$7^1/_8$ in.
Width	$1^1/_2$ „	$1^1/_2$ „	$1^3/_8$ „	$1^3/_4$ „	$2^3/_4$ „	$1^5/_8$ „	2 „	$3^1/_2$ „	$3^1/_2$ „
Length	$1^3/_4$ „	$1^3/_4$ „	$3^1/_2$ „	$3^1/_2$ „	$3^1/_2$ „	$2^3/_8$ „	$3^1/_8$ „	$3^1/_2$ „	$3^1/_2$ „
each	**5/—**	**6/6**	**8/6**	**10/—**	**16/—**	**6/4**	**8/6**	**15/—**	**20/—**

No.	with 2 cells = **4 Volt** in wooden box without lid				with 2 cells = **4 Volt** in oak wooden boxes with lid		with 3 cells = **6 Volt** in wooden box without lid	
	11642	**11643**	**11644**	**11645**	**14044**	**14045**	**11646**	**11647**
Capacity in Ampères-hours	4	6	14	25	14	25	14	25
Charging current maximum in Ampères	0,6	0,8	1,8	3,5	1,8	3,5	1,8	3,5
Discharging „ „ „ „	1	1	3	5	3	4	3	4
Outside Dimensions: Height	$6^1/_8$ in.	$7^1/_4$ in.	$8^1/_4$ in.	$8^1/_4$ in.	9 in.	9 in.	$8^1/_4$ in.	$8^1/_4$ in.
Width	$2^3/_4$ „	$3^1/_8$ „	$4^3/_4$ „	$4^7/_8$ „	$4^7/_8$ „	$4^7/_8$ „	$4^7/_8$ „	$4^3/_4$ „
Length	$4^1/_2$ „	$4^1/_8$ „	$4^3/_4$ „	$6^7/_8$ „	5 „	$6^7/_8$ „	$6^7/_8$ „	$9^7/_{16}$ „
each	**12/6**	**17/—**	**24/6**	**35/6**	**38/—**	**44/—**	**38/—**	**50/—**

For Resistances see page 351.

Single Accessories for Electric-Motors and Electric Railways.

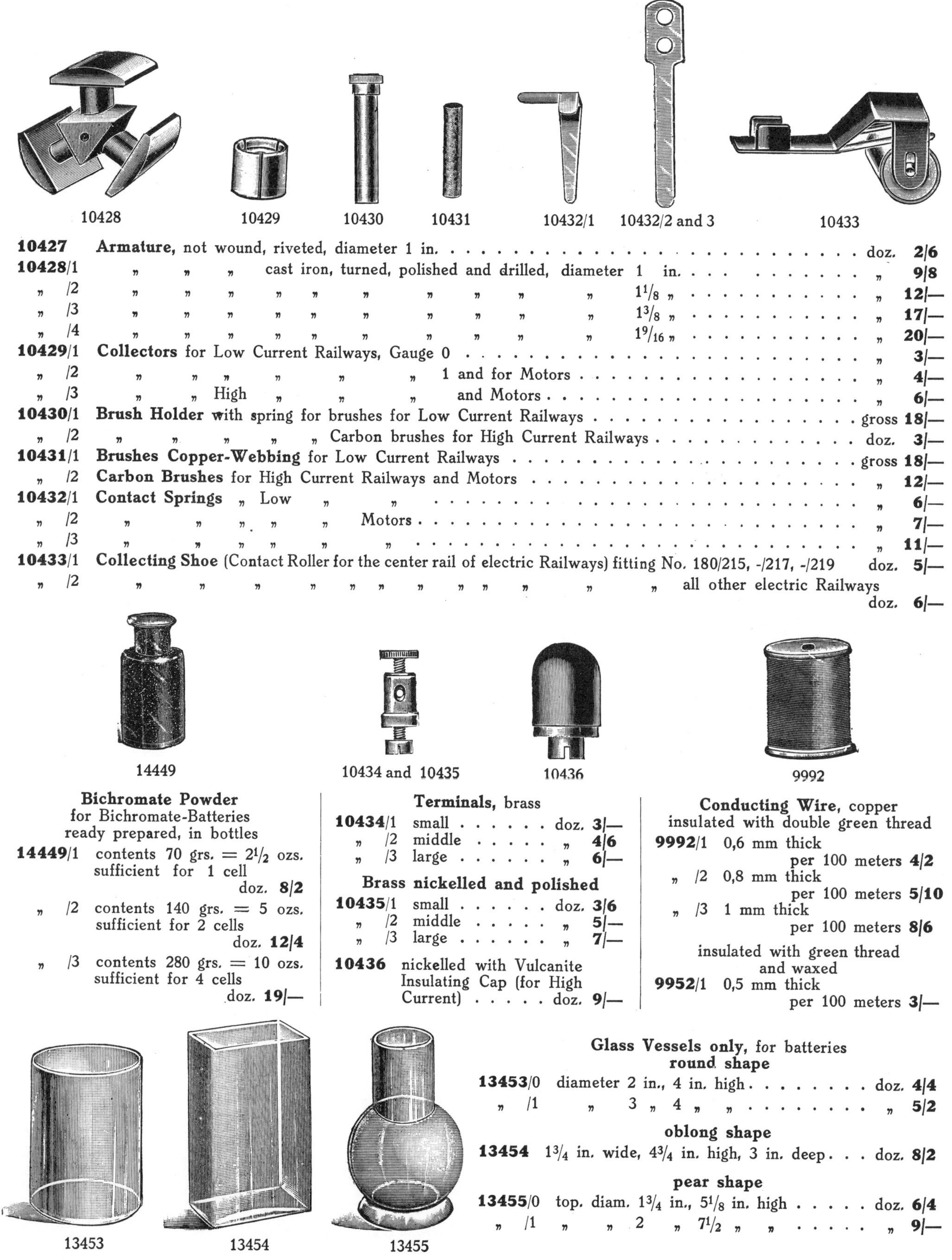

10428 10429 10430 10431 10432/1 10432/2 and 3 10433

10427	**Armature,** not wound, riveted, diameter 1 in.	doz.	**2/6**
10428/1	„ „ „ cast iron, turned, polished and drilled, diameter 1 in.	„	**9/8**
„ /2	„ „ „ „ „ „ „ „ „ „ $1\frac{1}{8}$ „	„	**12/—**
„ /3	„ „ „ „ „ „ „ „ „ „ $1\frac{3}{8}$ „	„	**17/—**
„ /4	„ „ „ „ „ „ „ „ „ „ $1\frac{9}{16}$ „	„	**20/—**
10429/1	**Collectors** for Low Current Railways, Gauge 0	„	**3/—**
„ /2	„ „ „ „ „ „ 1 and for Motors	„	**4/—**
„ /3	„ „ High „ „ „ and Motors	„	**6/—**
10430/1	**Brush Holder** with spring for brushes for Low Current Railways	gross	**18/—**
„ /2	„ „ „ „ „ Carbon brushes for High Current Railways	doz.	**3/—**
10431/1	**Brushes Copper-Webbing** for Low Current Railways	gross	**18/—**
„ /2	**Carbon Brushes** for High Current Railways and Motors	„	**12/—**
10432/1	**Contact Springs** „ Low „	„	**6/—**
„ /2	„ „ „ „ „ Motors	„	**7/—**
„ /3	„ „ „ „ „	„	**11/—**
10433/1	**Collecting Shoe** (Contact Roller for the center rail of electric Railways) fitting No. 180/215, -/217, -/219	doz.	**5/—**
„ /2	„ „ „ „ „ „ „ „ „ „ „ all other electric Railways	doz.	**6/—**

14449 10434 and 10435 10436 9992

Bichromate Powder
for Bichromate-Batteries
ready prepared, in bottles

14449/1 contents 70 grs. = $2\frac{1}{2}$ ozs. sufficient for 1 cell doz. **8/2**

„ /2 contents 140 grs. = 5 ozs. sufficient for 2 cells doz. **12/4**

„ /3 contents 280 grs. = 10 ozs. sufficient for 4 cells doz. **19/—**

Terminals, brass

10434/1 small . . . . . . doz. **3/—**
„ /2 middle . . . . . „ **4/6**
„ /3 large . . . . . . „ **6/—**

Brass nickelled and polished

10435/1 small . . . . . . doz. **3/6**
„ /2 middle . . . . . „ **5/—**
„ /3 large . . . . . . „ **7/—**

10436 nickelled with Vulcanite Insulating Cap (for High Current) . . . . . doz. **9/—**

Conducting Wire, copper
insulated with double green thread

9992/1 0,6 mm thick per 100 meters **4/2**
„ /2 0,8 mm thick per 100 meters **5/10**
„ /3 1 mm thick per 100 meters **8/6**

insulated with green thread and waxed

9952/1 0,5 mm thick per 100 meters **3/—**

13453 13454 13455

Glass Vessels only, for batteries

round shape

13453/0 diameter 2 in., 4 in. high . . . . doz. **4/4**
„ /1 „ 3 „ 4 „ „ . . . . „ **5/2**

oblong shape

13454 $1\frac{3}{4}$ in. wide, $4\frac{3}{4}$ in. high, 3 in. deep . . . doz. **8/2**

pear shape

13455/0 top. diam. $1\frac{3}{4}$ in., $5\frac{1}{8}$ in. high . . . . . doz. **6/4**
„ /1 „ „ 2 „ $7\frac{1}{2}$ „ „ . . . . . . „ **9/—**

ELECTRIC TRAINS

AND

ACCESSORIES

Electric Trains.

Electric Trains are made in 3 ways:

1. **for Low Current, with permanent Magnet** Motors for use with Batteries or Accumulators, fitted for reversing by reversing the current, which is effected by means of a reversing switch connected with the rails,
2. **for Low and High Current,** with Field Magnet Motors for use with Batteries or Accumulators; some of these are also reversing, special lever in cab, but not all (see description of the various items). — These Railways can also be used with High Current-Supply, especially with alternating Current; a resistance must be used for reducing the voltage of the Electric Main Supply,
3. **for High-Current only.** These Railways are specially suitable for Show pieces and Window Attractions. They are fitted for alternating and continuous Current. The conditions for connection are stated with each article; further with each Train explicit instructions and a plan for fitting up are supplied.

1. Electric Trains for Low Current

with permanent Magnet Motors, fitted for reversing by means of a reversing switch.

Below is a table, showing the Accumulators and Bichromate Batteries suitable for the respective train and the **approximate** running time (in hours) of each battery in connection with the respective train. Proper charging of the accumulators and correct treatment of the batteries is indispensable. With every train about 2 yards of green insulated copper wire is supplied.

No.	**Accumulators**								**Bichromate-Batteries**			
	2 Cells in glass case				in wooden box				2 pieces	2 pieces	1 piece	1 piece
	14770	**14771**	**14772**	**14773**	**11642**	**11643**	**11644 14044**	**61645 14045**	**13425** in series	**13426** or **13395** in series	**13427** or **13429**	**13428**
fitting Trains	approximate running time in hours								approximate running time in hours			
179/45 and /50	5	10	—	—	—	—	—	—	4	5	—	—
179/7/00	5	10	—	—	—	—	—	—	4	5	—	—
179/9/0½	5	10	—	—	—	—	—	—	4	5	—	—
180/210/0	2½	5	10	18	5	8	18	32	2	3¼	3¼	6
„ /**211**/0	2½	5	10	18	5	8	18	32	2	3¼	3¼	6
„ /**213**/0	2½	5	10	18	5	8	18	32	1½	3	3	6
„ /**215**/0	2	4	8	14	4	6	14	25	—	2½	2½	5
„ /**217**/0	1½	3½	7½	13½	3½	5½	13½	24½	—	2	2	4½
„ /**219**/0	1½	3½	7½	13½	3½	5½	13½	24½	—	2	2	4½
„ /**221**/0	1¼	3	7	13	3	5	13	24	—	1½	1¾	4
„ /**223**/0	1¼	3	7	13	3	5	13	24	—	1½	1¾	4
„ /**131**/0	2½	5	10	18	5	8	18	32	2	3¼	3¼	6
„ /**133**/0	1½	3½	7½	13½	3½	5½	13½	24½	—	2	2	4½
„ /**35**/00	2½	5	10	18	5	8	18	32	2	3¼	3¼	6
„ /**37**/0	2	4½	8½	14½	4½	6½	14½	25½	1½	3	3	5½
„ /**39**/0	1½	3½	7½	13½	3½	5½	13½	24½	—	2	2	4½
„ /**53**/0	1½	3½	7½	13½	3½	5½	13½	24½	—	2	2	4½
181/213/0	1½	3½	7½	13½	3½	5½	13½	24½	—	2	2	4½
„ /**214**/0	1½	3½	7½	13½	3½	5½	13½	24½	—	2	2	4½
„ /**215**/0	—	2½	5	9	2½	4	9	16	—	—	—	3
„ /**217**/0	—	2	4½	8½	2	3½	8½	15½	—	—	—	3
„ /**219**/0	—	2	4½	8½	2	3½	8½	15½	—	—	—	3
„ /**223**/0	—	1½	4	8	1½	3	8	15	—	—	—	2½
„ /**131**/0	1½	3½	7½	13½	3½	5½	13½	24½	—	2	2	4½
„ /**133**/0	—	2½	5	9	2½	4	9	16	—	—	—	3
„ /**37**/0	1½	3½	7½	13½	3½	5½	13½	24½	—	2	2	4½
„ /**39**/0	—	2½	5	9	2½	4	9	16	—	—	—	3
„ /**53**/0	—	2½	5	9	2½	4	9	16	—	—	—	3
190/217/0	—	2	4½	8½	2	3½	8½	15½	—	—	—	2
„ /**219**/0	—	2	4½	8½	2	3½	8½	15½	—	—	—	2
„ /**221**/0	—	1½	4	8	1½	3	8	15	—	—	—	2
„ /**223**/0	—	1½	4	8	1½	3	8	15	—	—	—	2
180/460/0	1½	3½	7½	13½	3½	5½	13½	24½	—	1½	1¾	4
191/217/0	—	1¼	3½	7	1¼	2½	7	12	—	—	—	—
„ /**219**/0	—	1¼	3½	7	1¼	2½	7	12	—	—	—	—
„ /**223**/0	—	1	3	6	1	2	6	10	—	—	—	—

Electric Trains for Low Current

with permanent Magnet Motors.

Gauge = $1^1/_8$ in.

179/7/00 **Cheap electric Train,** with small gauge rails, fitted for reversing, consisting of Locomotive, Tender, 2 passenger cars and rail cirle consisting of 4 curved rails incl. connecting rail (without battery or reversing switch) each **4/2**

Length of Locomotive	Length of Tender	Length of Car	Length of Train	Rail Formatation	Highest Voltage	Consumption of Current
$4^1/_4$ in.	$2^1/_4$ in.	$3^1/_4$ in.	$15^3/_4$ in.	1 circle = 4 curved Rails	2—4 Volt	abt. 0,6 Ampère

Gauge = $1^1/_8$ in.

179/9/$0^1/_2$ **Electric Train,** with small gauge rails, fitted for reversing, consisting of Locomotive, Tender, 2 passenger cars and oval set of rails 6 pieces incl. connecting rail . . . (without battery or reversing switch) each **5/4**

Length of Locomotive	Length of Tender	Length of Car	Length of Train	Rail Formation	Highest Voltage	Consumption of Current
$5^1/_8$ in.	$3^1/_4$ in.	$3^1/_4$ in.	$18^1/_4$ in.	1 oval set of rails = 4 curved and 2 half straight rails	2—4 Volt	abt. 0,6 Ampère

Gauge 0 = $1^3/_8$ in.

180/210/00 **Electric Train,** fitted for reversing consisting of Locomotive, Tender, 1 long passenger car and cirle of rails (4 curved rails incl. connecting rail) . . . . (without battery or reversing switch) each **5/8**

Length of Locomotive	Length of Tender	Length of Car	Length of Train	Rail Formation	Highest Voltage	Consumption of Current
$5^1/_8$ in.	$3^1/_4$ in.	2 in.	$14^1/_4$ in.	1 circle = 4 curved rails	3—4, 5 Volt	abt. 0,7 Ampère

Gauge 0 = $1^3/_8$ in.

180/211/0 **Electric Train,** fitted for reversing, consisting of Locomotive, Tender, 2 cars and oval set of rails, incl. connecting rail . . . . (without battery or reversing switch) each **7/6**

Length of Locomotive	Length of Tender	Length of Car	Length of Train	1 oval set of rails = 4 curved and 2 straight rails	Highest Voltage	Consumption of Current
$5^1/_8$ in.	$3^1/_4$ in.	4 in.	$19^1/_4$ in.		3, 5—5 Volt	abt. 0,7 Ampère

Electric Trains for Low Current

with permanent Magnet Motors.

Gauge 0 = $1^3/_8$ in.

180/213/0 **Electric Railway** fitted for reversing, consisting of Locomotive, Tender, 2 long passenger cars with oval set of 6 rails incl. connecting rail . . . . (without battery or reversing switch) each **9/6**

Length of Locomotive	Length of Tender	Length of Car	Length of Train	Rail Formation	Highest Voltage	Consumption of Current
$5^7/_8$ in.	$3^3/_8$ in.	$4^3/_4$ in.	$21^1/_2$ in.	1 oval set of rails = 4 curved and 2 straight rails	3,5—5 Volt	abt. 0,7 Ampère

Electric Railways for Low Current

with Electric Head Light.

10217 **Metallic filament lamp** with standard thread, 4 Volt, 0,25 Ampère, fitting the following electric Trains as head lights . . . . doz. **17/—**

Gauge 0 = $1^3/_8$ in.

180/215/0 **Electric Train,** fitted for reversing, Locomotive with connecting rods and **electric head light,** Tender, 2 long passenger cars with oval set of rails incl. connecting rail (without battery or reversing switch) each **13/8**

Length of Locomotive	Length of Tender	Length of Car	Length of Train	Rail Formation	Highest Voltage	Consumption of Current
$7^1/_8$ in.	$3^3/_8$ in.	$5^1/_2$ in.	$24^1/_2$ in.	1 oval = 4 curved and 2 straight rails	3,5—5 Volt	abt. 1,2 Ampère

Gauge 0 = $1^3/_8$ in.

180/217/0 **Electric Railway,** fitted for reversing, Locomotive with connecting rods, with **electric head light** (metallic filament lamp), Tender, 3 fine long passenger cars, with oval set of rails (10 pieces) incl. connecting rail . . . . (without battery and reversing switch) each **16/—**

Length of Locomotive	Length of Tender	Length of Car	Length of Train	Rail Formation	Highest Voltage	Consumption of Current
$7^1/_8$ in.	$3^1/_4$ in.	$5^1/_2$ in.	31 in.	1 oval = 6 curved and 4 straight rails	3,5—5 Volt	abt. 1,25 Ampère

Electric Trains for Low Current

with permanent Magnet Motors.

Gauge 0 = $1^3/_8$ in.

180/219/0 **Electric Train,** fitted for reversing, Locomotive with electric head light (Metallic filament lamp), Tender 2 fine long passenger Cars and 1 fine long luggage van, with oval set of rails (10 pieces) incl. connecting rail . . . . (without battery or reversing switch) each **18/—**

Length of Locomotive	Length of Tender	Length of Car	Length of Train	Rail Formation	Highest Voltage	Consumption of Current
$7^1/_8$ in.	4 in.	$6^1/_8$ in.	$33^1/_4$ in.	1 oval = 6 curved and 4 straight rails	3,5—5 Volt	abt. 1,35 Ampère

Gauge 0 = $1^3/_8$ in.

180/221/0 **Electric Train,** fitted for reversing, consisting of Locomotive, with electric head light (metallic filament lamp), Tender, 2 fine long passenger cars, 1 fine long luggage van, with oval set of rails (10 pieces) incl. connecting rail . . . . (without battery or reversing switch) each **25/6**

Length of Locomotive	Length of Tender	Length of Car	Length of Train	Rail Formation	Highest Voltage	Consumption of Current
$8^7/_8$ in.	$4^3/_4$ in.	$6^3/_4$ in.	38 in.	1 oval = 6 curved and 4 straight rails	3,5—5 Volt	abt. 1,35 Ampère

Gauge 0 = $1^3/_8$ in.

180/223/0 **Electric Train** (Express Train) fitted for reversing consisting of Locomotive, with electric head light (metallic filament lamp), Tender and 2 long fine Express Cars (Dining and Sleeping Car), with oval set of rails (10 pieces) incl. connecting rail . . . . (without battery or reversing switch each **29/—**

Length of Locomotive	Length of Tender	Length of Car	Length of Train	Rail Formation	Highest Voltage	Consumption of Current
$8^1/_4$ in.	$4^3/_4$ in.	$8^5/_8$ in.	$34^1/_2$ in.	1 oval = 6 curved and 4 straight rails	3,5—5 Volt	abt. 1,35 Ampère

10217 **Metallic filament lamp** with standard thread, 4 Volt, 0,25 Ampère fitting the above Trains as head lights . . . . doz. **17/—**

Electric Trains for Low Current

with permanent Magnet Motors.

Gauge 1 = $1^7/_8$ in.

181/213/00 **Electric Train,** fitted for reversing, consisting of Locomotive, Tender, 2 passenger cars and **a** circle of rails (8 pieces) incl. connecting rail . . . . (without battery or reversing switch) each **19/—**

Length of Locomotive 8 in.	Length of Tender $4^7/_8$ in.	Length of Car $5^1/_8$ in.	Length of Train 27 in.	Rail Formation 1 circle = 8 curved rails	Highest Voltage 3,5—5 Volt	Consumption of Current abt. 1,25 Ampère

Gauge 1 = $1^7/_8$ in.

181/214/0 **Electric Train,** fitted for reversing, consisting of Locomotive, Tender, 2 long passenger cars and oval set of rails (10 pieces) incl. connecting rail . . . . (without battery or reversing switch) each **22/10**

Length of Locomotive 8 in.	Length of Tender $5^1/_2$ in.	Length of Car $7^5/_8$ in.	Length of Train $32^5/_8$ in.	Rail Formation 1 Oval = 8 curved and 2 straight rails	Highest Voltage 3,5—5 Volt	Consumption of Current abt. 1,25 Ampère

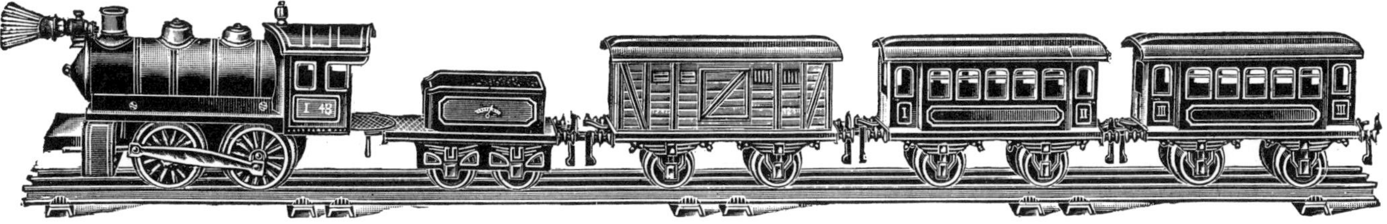

Gauge 1 = $1^7/_8$ in.

181/215/0 **Electric Train,** fitted for reversing, Locomotive with electric head light (metallic filament lamp), Tender, 2 long passenger cars and 1 luggage van with oval set of rails (10 pieces) incl. connecting rail (without battery or reversing switch) each **31/—**

Length of Locomotive $9^1/_2$ in.	Length of Tender $5^1/_2$ in.	Length of Car $7^5/_8$ in.	Length of Train 43 in.	Rail Formation 1 Oval = 8 curved and 2 straight rails	Highest Voltage 3,5—5 Volt	Consumption of Current abt. 1,25 Ampère

10217 Metallic filament lamps with Standard thread, 3,5 Volt, 0,25 Ampère, fitting Railway 181/215/0 . . doz. **17/—**

Electric Trains for Low Current with permanent Magnet Motors.

Gauge 1 = $1^7/_8$ in.

181/217/0 Electric Train, fitted for reversing, Locomotive with head light (metallic filament lamp), Tender, 2 extra long passenger cars, 1 extra long luggage van, with oval set of rails (12 pieces) incl. connecting rail . . . . (without battery or reversing switch) each **34/—**

Length of Locomotive	Length of Tender	Length of Car	Length of Train	Rail Formation	Highest Voltage	Consumption of Current
$9^3/_8$ in.	$5^1/_2$ in.	$8^1/_4$ in.	$44^1/_2$ in.	1 oval = 8 curved and 4 straight rails	3,5—5 Volt	abt. 1,5 Ampère

Gauge 1 = $1^7/_8$ in.

181/219/0 Electric Train, fitted for reversing, with electric head lights (2 metallic filament lamps) Tender, 3 Express cars with fittings, with oval set of rails (12 pieces) incl. connecting rail . . . . (without battery or reversing switch) each **51/—**

Length of Locomotive	Length of Tender	Length of Car	Length of Train	Rail Formation	Highest Voltage	Consumption of Current
$10^7/_8$ in.	$6^1/_4$ in.	$9^1/_2$ in.	51 in.	1 oval = 8 curved and 4 straight rails	3,5—5 Volt	abt. 1,5 Ampère

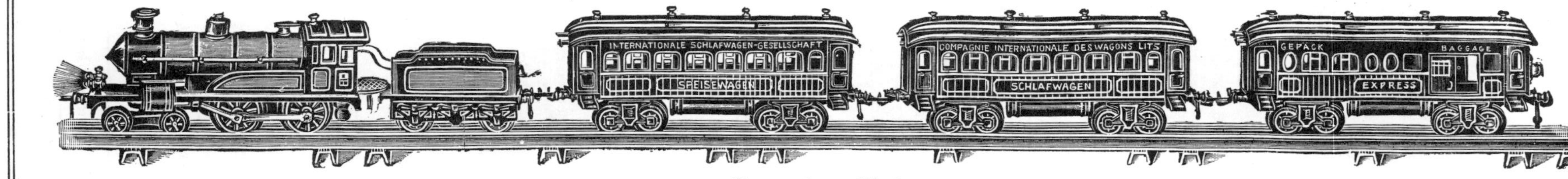

Gauge 1 = $1^7/_8$ in.

181/223/0 Electric Train (Express Train), fitted for reversing, Locomotive on 4 axles = 8 wheels, with 2 electric head lights (metallic filament lamps), 3 long Express cars (without fittings), with oval set of rails (16 pieces) incl. connecting rail . . . . . . (without battery or reversing switch) each **66/—**

Length of Locomotive	Length of Tender	Length of Car	Length of Train	Rail Formation	Highest Voltage	Consumption of Current
12 in.	$6^1/_4$ in.	$13^1/_2$ in.	64 in.	1 oval = 8 curved and 8 straight rails	3,5—5 Volt	abt. 1,5 Ampère

Electric Trains with Field Magnet Motors

suitable for Low as well as High Current (specially Alternating Current).

(For Alternating Current a resistance No. 10415 has to be used, see page 327.)

With carbon filament lamp 4 Volt 0,25 Ampère for Low Current and 1 spare lamp 12 Volt 0,5 Ampère for use with High Current.

14379/1	**Spare Carbon filament lamps,** with Standard thread as head light, fitting the following electric trains, 4 Volt 0,25 Amp. for Low Current . .	doz.	**11/6**
10218/12	„ „ „ „ „ „ „ „ „ „ „ „ „ „ „ 12 „ 0,5 „ „ High „ . .	„	**13/—**

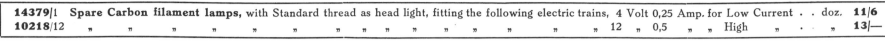

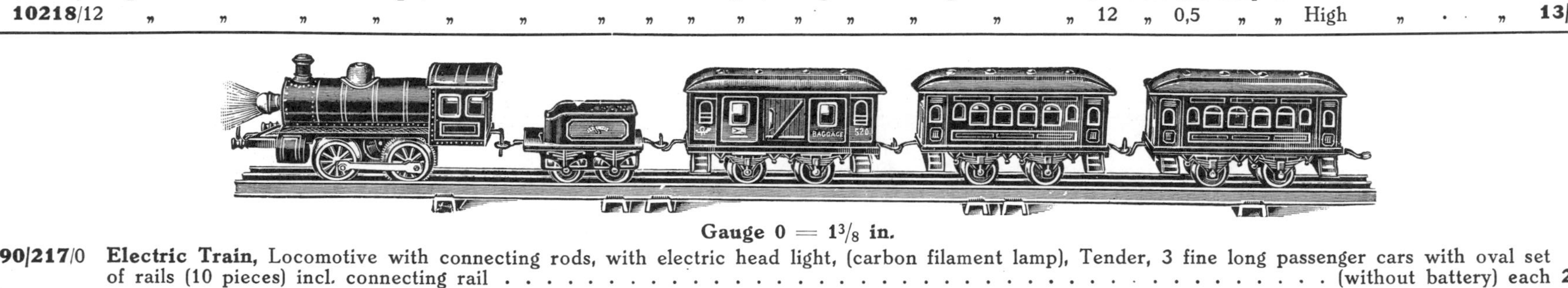

Gauge 0 = $1^3/_8$ in.

190/217/0 **Electric Train,** Locomotive with connecting rods, with electric head light, (carbon filament lamp), Tender, 3 fine long passenger cars with oval set of rails (10 pieces) incl. connecting rail . . . . (without battery) each **21/—**

Length of Locomotive	Length of Tender	Length of Car	Length of Train	Rail Formation	Highest Voltage
$7^1/_8$ in.	$3^3/_8$ in.	$5^1/_2$ in.	31 in.	1 oval = 6 curved and 4 straight rails	4—6 Volt

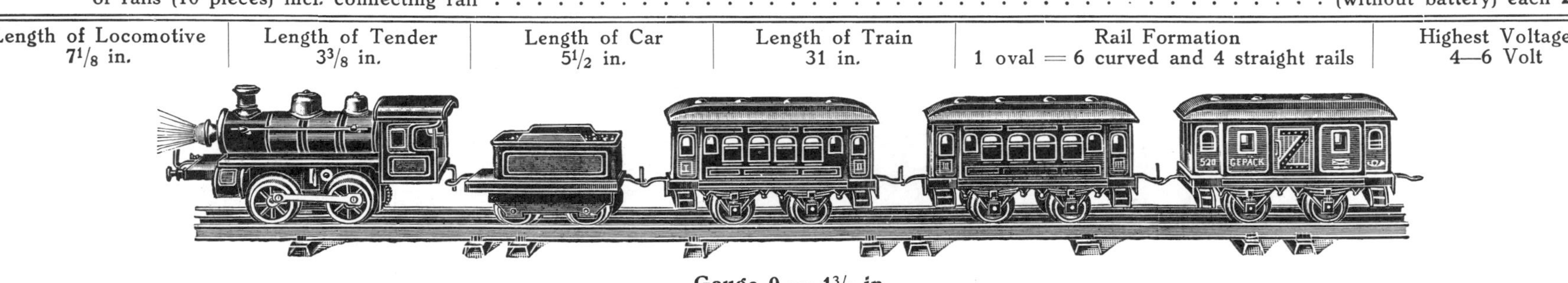

Gauge 0 = $1^3/_8$ in.

190/219/0 **Electric Train,** Locomotive with electric head light (carbon filament lamp), Tender, 2 fine long passenger cars and 1 fine long luggage van with oval set of rails (10 pieces) incl. connecting rail . . . . (without battery) each **23/—**

Length of Locomotive	Length of Tender	Length of Car	Length of Train	Rail Formation	Highest Voltage
7 in.	4 in.	6 in.	$33^1/_4$ in.	1 oval = 6 curved and 4 straight rails	4—6 Volt

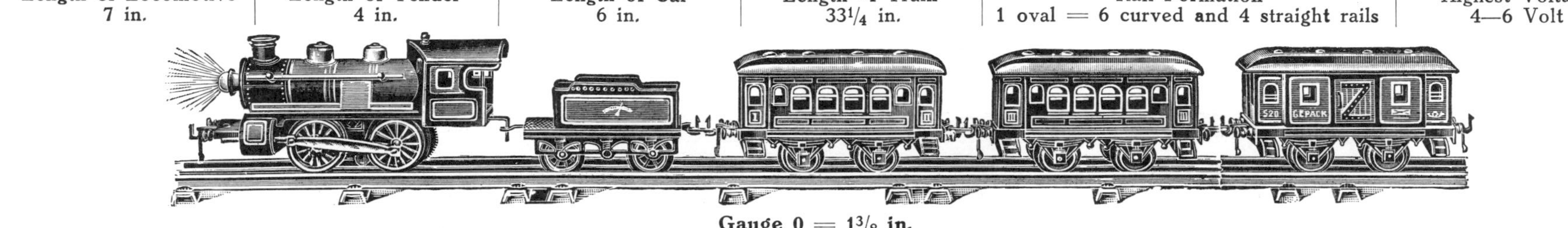

Gauge 0 = $1^3/_8$ in.

190/221/0 **Electric Train,** consisting of Locomotive with electric head light, (carbon filament lamp), Tender, 2 fine long passenger cars and 1 fine long luggage van with oval set of rails (10 pieces) incl. connecting rail . . . . (without battery) each **29/—**

Length of Locomotive	Length of Tender	Length of Car	Length of Train	Rail Formation	Highest Voltage
$8^1/_2$ in.	$4^3/_4$ in.	$6^3/_4$ in.	38 in.	1 oval = 6 curved and 4 straight rails	4—6 Volt

Electric Trains with Field Magnet Motors

for Low and High Current.

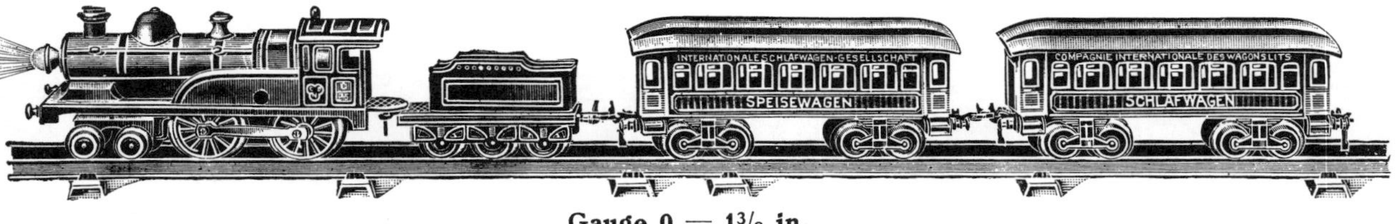

Gauge 0 = $1^3/_8$ in.

190/223/0 **Electric Train** (Express Train), fitted for reversing, with **hand reversing lever** in the Cab of the Locomotive, consisting of Locomotive, with electric head light, Tender and 2 long fine Express Cars (dining and sleeping Car without fittings) with oval set of rails (10 pieces) incl. connecting rail . . . . (without battery) each **34/—**

Length of Locomotive	Length of Tender	Length of Car	Length of Train	Rail Formation	Highest Voltage
$8^1/_4$ in.	$4^3/_4$ in.	$8^5/_8$ in.	$34^5/_8$ in.	1 oval = 8 curved and 4 straight rails	4—6 Volt

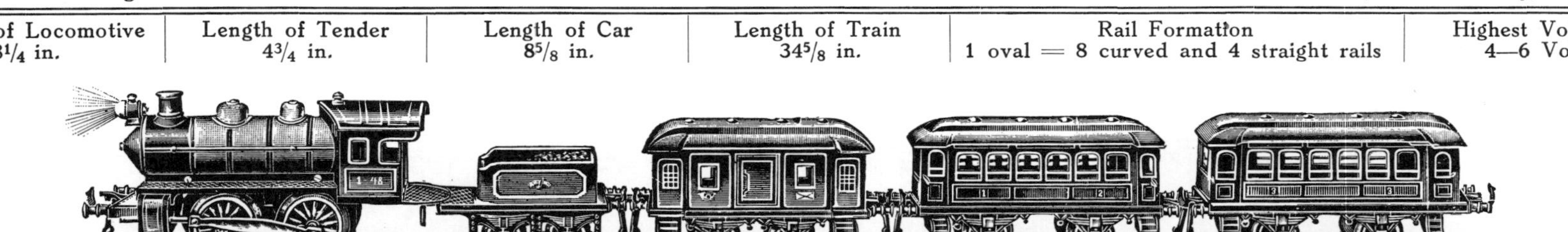

Gauge 1 = $1^7/_8$ in.

191/217/0 **Electric Train,** fitted for reversing, with **hand reversing lever** in the Cab of the Locomotive, Locomotive with electric head light (metallic filament lamp), Tender, 2 extra long passenger cars, 1 extra long luggage van, with oval set of rails (12 pieces) incl. connecting rail . . . (without battery) each **40/—**

Length of Locomotive	Length of Tender	Length of Car	Length of Train	Rail Formation	Highest Voltage
$9^1/_2$ in.	$5^1/_2$ in.	$8^1/_4$ in.	44 in.	1 oval = 8 curved and 4 straight rails	3,5—5 Volt

Gauge 1 = $1^7/_8$ in.

191/219/0 **Electric Train,** fitted for reversing, with **hand reversing lever** in the Cab of the Locomotive, Locomotive with electric head light, Tender, 2 fine long passenger cars with fittings and 1 fine luggage van, with oval set of rails (12 pieces) incl. connecting rail . . . . (without battery) each **53/—**

Length of Locomotive	Length of Tender	Length of Car	Length of Train	Rail Formation	Highest Voltage
$10^1/_2$ in.	$6^1/_4$ in.	$9^3/_8$ in.	51 in.	1 oval = 8 curved and 4 straight rails	4—6 Volt

14379/1 **Carbon filament lamps,** with Standard thread, for head light, fitting above electric Trains, 4 Volt 0,25 Amp. for Low Current . . doz. **11/6**
10218/12 „ „ „ „ „ „ „ „ „ „ „ „ „ 12 „ 0,5 „ „ High „ . . „ **13/—**

Electric Train with Field Magnet Motors

for Low and High Current.

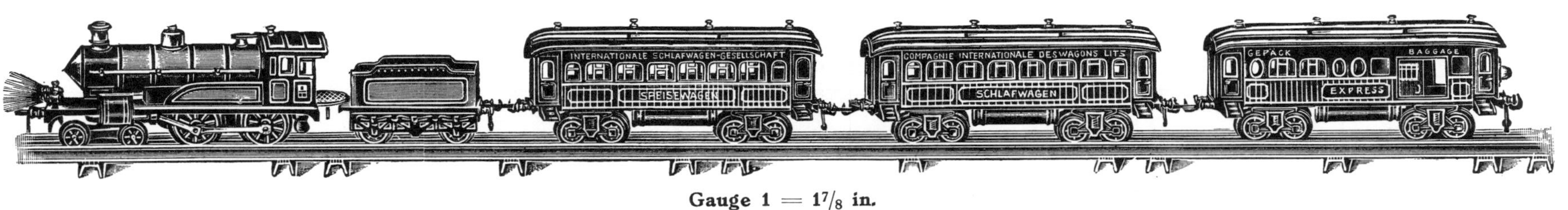

Gauge 1 = $1^7/_8$ in.

191/223/0 **Electric Train (Express Train),** fitted for reversing with **hand reversing lever** in the Cab of the Locomotive, with fine Locomotive on 4 axles, with 2 electric head lights, Tender, 3 long Express cars (without fittings) with oval set of rails (16 pieces) incl. connecting rail (without battery) each **67/—**

Length of Locomotive	Length of Tender	Length of Car	Length of Train	Rail Formation	Highest Voltage
12 in.	$6^1/_4$ in.	$13^1/_2$ in.	64 in.	1 oval = 8 curved and 8 straight rails	4—6 Volt

Carbon metallic filament lamp with Standard thread fitting the above Train as head lights.

14379/1 4 Volt 0,25 Ampère for Low Current . . . . doz. **11/6**

10218/12 12 „ 0,5 „ „ High „ . . . . „ **13/—**

Regulating Resistance

for use with Trains with Field Magnet Motors, when driven from a main supply of **alternating current.**

10415/110 for 110 Volt . . . . each **19/—**

„ **/220** „ 220 „ . . . . „ **21/—**

When running Field Magnet Trains with Low Current (Batteries or Accumulators) of 4—6 Volt it is advisable to make use of a resistance for regulating the speed of the trains. The suitable resistances are No. 14289/0 and 10229 page 351.

Electric Trains for High Current

for Show-purposes

for connection with the main, fitting in a resistance in accordance with the existing Voltage. Explicit direction for use is supplied with every Train.

With electric head light. **Running Forward only.**

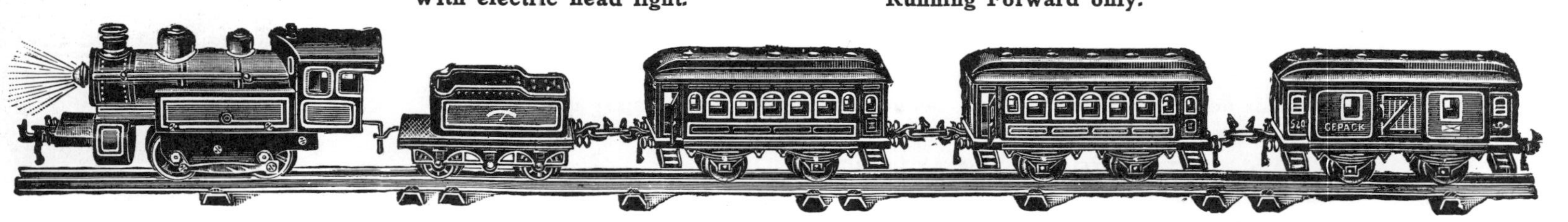

Gauge 0 = $1^3/_8$ in.

200/221/0 **Electric Train** for High Current, consisting of Locomotive, finely polychrome japanned (running forward only) with electric head light, Tender, 2 passenger Cars and 1 luggage van, with oval set of rails (10 pieces) incl. connecting rail . . . . (without resistance) each **43/6**

Length of Locomotive	Length of Tender	Length of Car	Length of Train	Rail Formation	Resistance to be used
$8^5/_8$ in.	$4^1/_2$ in.	$6^3/_4$ in.	38 in.	1 Oval = 6 curved and 4 straight rails	with 110 Volt continuous current 1 lamp at 25 C.P. „ 110 „ alternating „ 1 „ „ 25—32 „ „ 220 „ continuous „ 1—2 „ „ 16—25 „ „ 220 „ alternating „ 1—2 „ „ 16—25 „

Gauge 1 = $1^7/_8$ in.

201/219/0 **Electric Train,** for High Current, consisting of Locomotive, finely hand japanned (running forward only), with 2 electric head lights, Tender, 2 passenger cars and 1 luggage van, with oval set of rails (12 pieces) incl. connecting rail . . . . (without resistance) each **66/—**

Length of Locomotive	Length of Tender	Length of Car	Length of Train	Rail Formation	Resistance to be used
$10^3/_8$ in.	$6^1/_8$ in.	$9^1/_2$ in.	$51^1/_2$ in.	1 Oval = 6 curved and 4 straight rails	with 110 Volt continuous current 1—2 lamps at 16—25 C.P. „ 110 „ alternating „ 2 „ „ 16—25 „ „ 220 „ continuous „ 1—2 „ „ 16—25 „ „ 220 „ alternating „ 2 „ „ 16—25 „

10218/12 **Small spare Carbon filament lamps** with Standard thread fitting the above trains as head lights 12 Volt, 0,5 Ampère . . doz. **13/—**

Electric Trains for High Current

with Electric Head and Tail Light and with Electric Light in the Cars.

Gauge 0 = $1^3/_8$ in.

200/223/0 **Electric Train,** (Express Train), consisting of Locomotive with electric head light, Tender and 3 fine long Express Carriages (Dining, Sleeping- and Luggage Car) completely fitted, with electric light fitted inside each car, with electric tail lamp at the end of the train, with oval set of rails (12 pieces) incl. connecting rail . . . . (without resistance) each **71/—**

Length of Locomotive	Length of Tender	Length of Car	Length of Train	Rail Formation	Resistance to be used:
$8^1/_4$ in.	$4^3/_4$ in.	$8^5/_8$ in.	$44^1/_2$ in.	1 oval = 6 curved and **6** straight rails	with 110 Volt continuous current 1 lamps at 25 C. P. „ 110 „ alternating „ 1 „ „ 25—32 „ „ 220 „ continuous „ 1—2 „ „ 16—25 „ „ 220 „ alternating „ 1—2 „ „ 16—25 „

Gauge 1 = $1^7/_8$ in.

201/223/0 **Electric Train** for High Current, consisting of Locomotive, finely polychrome japanned (forward movement only) with 2 electric head lights, Tender, 3 long Express Carriages completely fitted, with electric light fitted inside each car, with electric tail lamp at the end of the train, with oval rail formation (14 pieces) incl. connecting rail . . . . (without resistance) each **119/—**

Length of Locomotive	Length of Tender	Length of Car	Length of Train	Rail Formation	Resistance to be used:
12 in.	$6^1/_2$ in.	$13^1/_2$ in.	$64^3/_4$ in.	1 oval = 8 curved and 6 straight rails	with 110 Volt continuous current 1—2 lamps at 16—25 C. P. „ 110 „ alternating „ 2 „ „ 16—25 „ „ 220 „ continuous „ 1—2 „ „ 25 „ „ 220 „ alternating „ 2 „ „ 25 „

10218/6 **Small spare Carbon filament lamp,** with Standard thread fitting above trains as head ligths 6 Volt, 0,5 Ampère . . . . doz. **13/—**
„ /6 „ „ „ „ „ „ „ „ „ „ „ „ inside lighting 6 Volt, 0,5 Ampère . . . . . „ **13/—**

Electric Trains for High Current

Reversing-, Slow and Fast Movement

by means of the Universal Resistance, through which alternating and continuous current and voltages of 65—250 Volt are made suitable for these trains.

Gauge 0 = $1^3/_8$ in.

200/369/0 **Electric Train** (Express Train), for High Current, consisting of Locomotive, finely hand japanned (with forward-, backward-, fast- und slow movement) with electric head light, Tender 3 long Express Carriages completely fitted, every car fitted with light inside and electr. tail lamp at the end of the Train, with oval rail formation (16 pieces) incl. connecting rail . . . . (incl. Regulating Resistance) each **111/—**

Length of Locomotive $9^1/_4$ in.	Length of Tender $4^3/_4$ in.	Length of Car $8^5/_8$ in.	Length of Train $45^1/_2$ in.	Rail Formation 1 oval = 16 curved and 6 straight large radius rails	The correct Resistance is supplied with every Railway

Gauge 1 = $1^7/_8$ in.

201/369/0 **Electric Train** (Express Train) for High Current, consisting of Locomotive, finely hand japanned (with forward-, backward-, fast- und slow movement), with 2 electric head lights, Tender, 3 long Express Carriages completely fitted, every car with light inside and electr. tail lamp at the end of the train, with oval rail formation (22 pieces) incl. connecting rail . . . . (incl. Regulating Resistance) each **176/—**

Length of Locomotive $13^1/_2$ in.	Lenght of Tender $7^5/_8$ in.	Length of Car $13^3/_4$ in.	Length of Train $62^1/_2$ in.	Rail Formation 1 oval = 16 curved and 6 straight large radius rails	The correct Resistance is supplied with every Railway

10218/6 **Small spare carbon filament lamps** with standard thread fitting above trains as head lights 6 Volt, 0,5 Ampère . . . . doz. **13/—**
„ /6 „ „ „ „ „ „ „ „ „ „ „ „ inside lighting 6 Volt, 0,5 Ampère . . . . „ **13/—**

Electric Trains for High Current.

Reversing-, Slow and Fast Movement.

By means of the Universal Resistance, through which alternating and continuous current and voltages of 65—220 Volt are made suitable for these trains.

Best Electric Train (Express Train) for High Current, consisting of Locomotive, finely hand japanned, with forward-, backward-, fast and slow movement, with 2 electric head lights, Tender, 3 long Pullmann Carriages, completely fitted, every car fitted with light inside and electric tail lamp at the end of the train.

200/375/0 Gauge 0 = $1^3/_8$ in.

Length of Locomotive	Length of Tender	Length of Car	Length of Train	Rail Formation	The correct Resistance is
$11^3/_8$ in.	$7^1/_8$ in.	$12^3/_4$ in.	58 in.	1 oval = 12 curved and 10 straight large radius rails	supplied with every Railway

incl. Resistance each **166/—**

201/375/0 Gauge = $1^7/_8$ in.

Length of Locomotive	Length of Tender	Length of Car	Length of Train	Rail Formation	The correct Resistance is
15 in.	$8^1/_4$ in.	$19^1/_2$ in.	83 in.	1 oval = 16 curved and 12 straight large radius rails	supplied with every Railway

incl. Resistance each **250/—**

10218/6 Small spare carbon filament lamps with Standard thread, fitting above Railways as head lights, 6 Volt, 0,5 Ampère . . . . doz. **13/—**
„ /6 „ „ „ „ „ „ „ „ „ „ „ „ inside lighting, 6 „ 0,5 „ . . . . „ **13/—**

Electric Trams for Low Current

with permanent Magnet Motors

fitted for reversing by means of a reversing switch. For Batteries and Accumulators kindly refer to pages 316/317. for reversing switches to page 350.

Gauge 00 = 11 in.

Highest voltage 2—3 Volt, Consumption of currant abt. 0,25 Ampère.

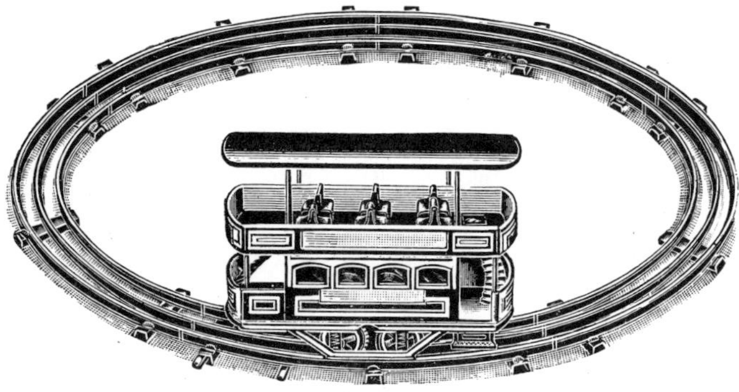

179/45/00

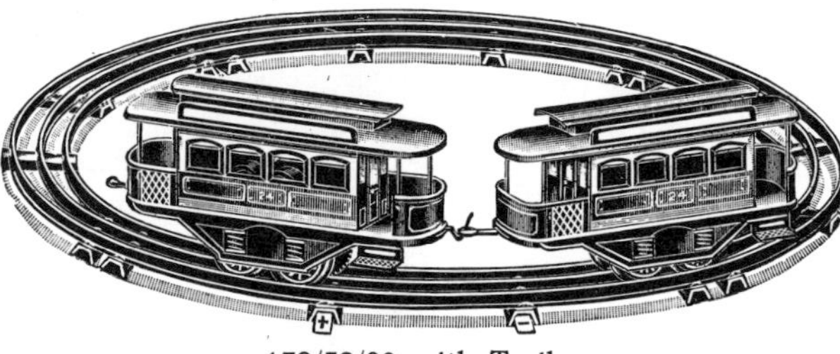

179/52/00 with Trailer
179/50/00 without Trailer

Cheap, electric Trams on small gauge rails, fitted for reversing, with circle of rails incl. connecting rail.

179/45/00	**Tram,** $6^1/_4$ in. long	(without battery and without reversing switch) each	**5/4**
„ **/50**/00	„ without trailer, Tram, $6^1/_4$ in.	„ „ „ „ „ „ „	**5/4**
„ **/52**/00	„ with Trailer, length of train $13^1/_2$ in.	„ „ „ „ „ „ „	**6/10**

Gauge 0 = $1^3/_8$ in.

Highest voltage 3—4,5 Volt, Consumption of current abt. 1 Ampère.

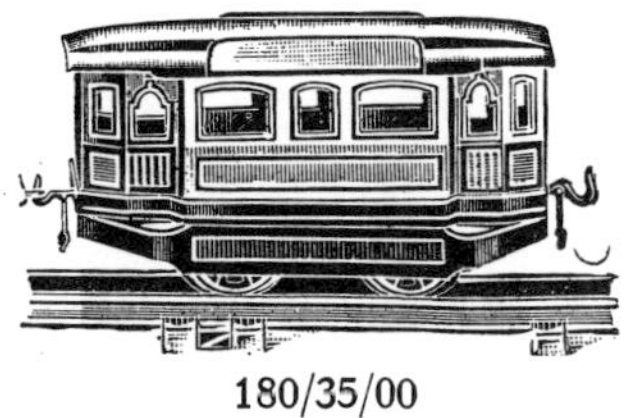

180/35/00

180/37/0

180/35/00 without Trailer, $5^7/_8$ in. long, with circle of rails, (4 curved rails incl. connecting rail)
(without battery or reversing switch) each **9/10**

„ **/37**/0 with 1 Trailer, with oval set of rails, (4 curved, 4 straight rails incl. connecting rail), length of train 13 in.
(without battery or reversing switch) each **14/2**

With Electric Light.

180/39/0 **Tram** with electric head light (metallic filament lamp), with Trailer with electric ligth fitted inside, with oval rail formation, (6 curved, 4 straight rails incl. connecting rail), 14 in. long (without battery or reversing switch) each **20/—**

Highest voltage 3,5—5 Volt, Consumption of current abt. 1,2 Ampère.

10217 Metallic filament lamp with Standard thread, 3,5 Volt, 0,25 Ampère, fitting above tram . . . . doz. **17/—**

Gauge 1 = $1^7/_8$ in.

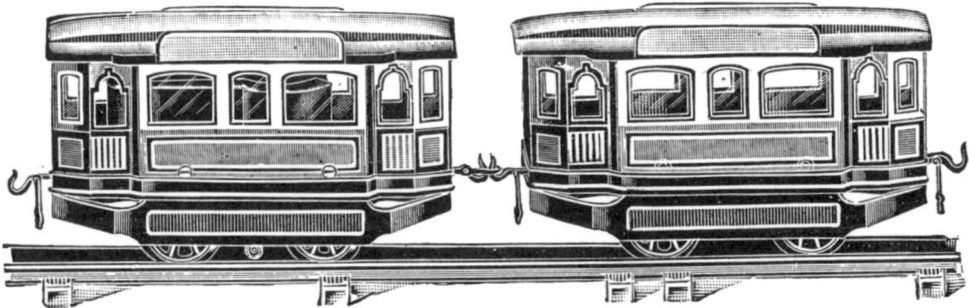

181/37/0 with 1 Trailer and oval set of rails (8 curved, 4 straight rails incl. connecting rail) length of train $16^1/_2$ in. (without battery or reversing switch) each **23/—**

Highest voltage 3,5—5 Volt, Consumption of current abt. 1,2 Ampère.

With Electric Light.

181/39/0 **Train** with electric head light (metallic filament lamp) trailer with electric light fitted inside the car, with oval rail formation (8 curved and 4 straight rails) incl. connecting rail, length of train 17 in. (without battery or reversing switch) each **28/6**

10217 **Metallic filament lamps,** with Standard thread, 3,5 Volt, 0,25 Ampère, fitting above . . . . doz. **17/—**

Electric Railways for Low Current (Underground Railways)

with Electric Lights (metallic filament lamps).

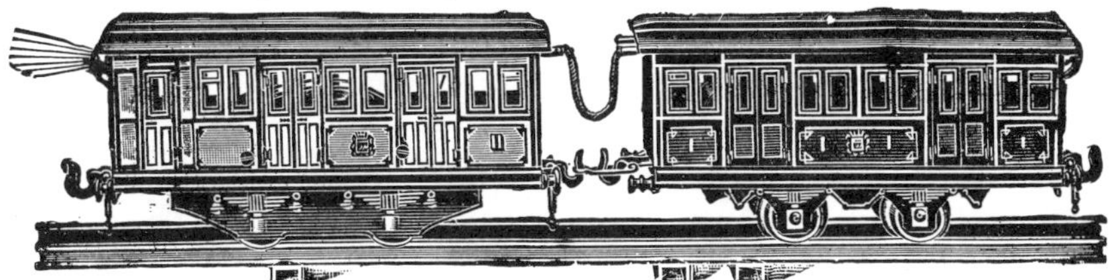

Gauge 0 = $1^3/_8$ in.

180/53/0 Motor with **2 electric head lights** (metallic filament lamps), trailer with electric light fitted inside the car, with oval rail formation (6 curved and 4 straight rails incl. connecting rail) length of train $13^7/_8$ in. (without battery or reversing switch) each **24/8**

Highest voltage 3,5—5 Volt, Consumption of current abt. 1,2 Ampère.

Gauge 1 = $1^7/_8$ in.

181/53/0 Motor Car with **2 electric head lights** (metallic filament lamps), trailer with electric ligth fitted inside the car, with oval rail formation (8 curved and 4 straight rails incl. connecting rail) length of train $19^3/_4$ in. (without battery or reversing switch) each **33/—**

10217 **Metallic filament lamp,** with Standard thread, 3,5 Volt, 0,25 Ampère, fitting above trains . . doz. **17/—**

Electric Trains for Low Current

fitted for reversing.

Gauge 0 = $1^3/_8$ **in.**

180/131/0 **Electric Train,** consisting of Locomotive and 2 long passenger Cars with oval rail formation (6 pieces) incl. connecting rail (without battery or reversing switch) . . . . each **13/4**

Length of Locomotive $6^1/_4$ in.	Length of Car $4^3/_4$ in.	Length of Train $17^3/_4$ in.	Rail Formation 1 Oval = 4 curved and 2 straight rails	Highest voltage 3,5—5 Volt	Consumption of current abt. 1 Ampère

Gauge 1 = $1^7/_8$ **in.**

181/131/0 **Electric Train,** consisting of Locomotive and 2 long passenger cars, with oval rail formation (10 pieces) incl. connecting rail (without battery or reversing switch) . . . . each **27/4**

Length of Locomotive $8^1/_4$ in.	Length of Car $7^5/_8$ in.	Length of Train $25^3/_4$ in.	Rail Formation 1 Oval = 8 curved and 2 straight rails	Highest voltage 3,5—5 Volt	Consumption of current abt. 1,2 Ampère

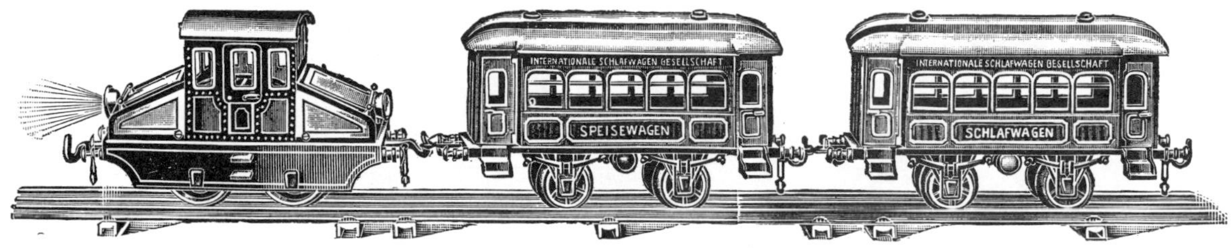

With electric head light (metallic filament lamp)

180/133/0 **Electric Train, (Gauge 0** = $1^3/_8$ **in.)** consisting of Locomotive with electric head ligth (metallic filament lamp) and 2 long passenger Cars, with oval rail formation (10 pieces) incl. connecting rail (without battery or reversing switch) . . . . each **19/—**

Length of Locomotive $6^3/_4$ in.	Length of Car $5^1/_2$ in.	Length of Train $19^3/_4$ in.	Rail Formation 1 Oval = 6 curved and 4 straight rails	Highest voltage 3,5—5 Volt	Consumption of current abt. 1,2 Ampère

181/133/0 **Electric Railway, (Gauge 1** = $1^7/_8$ **in.)** consisting of Locomotive with electric head light (metallic filament lamp) and 2 long passenger cars, with oval set of rails (12 pieces) incl. connecting rail (without battery or reversing switch). . . . . each **31/—**

Length of Locomotive $8^1/_4$ in.	Length of Car $9^3/_8$ in.	Length of Train $29^1/_2$ in.	Rail Formation 1 Oval = 8 curved and 4 straight rails	Highest voltage 4—6 Volt	Consumption of current abt. 1,3 Ampère

10217 Metallic filament lamp with Standard thread 3,5 Volt, 0,25 Ampère fitting above Railways as head ligths . . . . doz. **17/—**

Electric Locomotives for Low Current

with permanent Magnet Motors, fitted for reversing.

Gauge 0 = $1^3/_8$ in.

180/2510

180/2513

180/2517

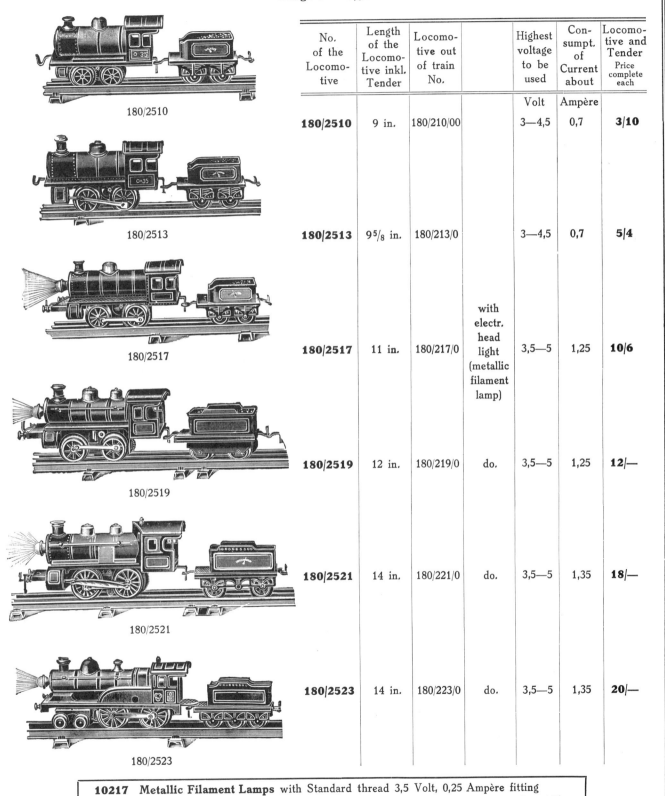

180/2519

180/2521

180/2523

No. of the Locomotive	Length of the Locomotive inkl. Tender	Locomotive out of train No.		Highest voltage to be used	Consumpt. of Current about	Locomotive and Tender Price complete each
				Volt	Ampère	
180/2510	9 in.	180/210/00		3—4,5	0,7	**3/10**
180/2513	$9^5/_8$ in.	180/213/0		3—4,5	0,7	**5/4**
180/2517	11 in.	180/217/0	with electr. head light (metallic filament lamp)	3,5—5	1,25	**10/6**
180/2519	12 in.	180/219/0	do.	3,5—5	1,25	**12/—**
180/2521	14 in.	180/221/0	do.	3,5—5	1,35	**18/—**
180/2523	14 in.	180/223/0	do.	3,5—5	1,35	**20/—**

10217 Metallic Filament Lamps with Standard thread 3,5 Volt, 0,25 Ampère fitting above Locomotives as head lights . . . . doz. **17/—**

Electric Locomotives for Low Current

with Magnet Motors, fitted for reversing.

Gauge 1 = $1\frac{7}{8}$ in.

181/2513

181/2517

181/2519

181/2523 big Express Locomotive

No. of the Locomotive	Length of the Locomotive incl. Tender	Locomotive out of Train		Highest Voltage to be used	Consumpt. of Current about	Locomotive and Tender Price complete each
				Volt	Ampère	
181/2513	$12\frac{1}{2}$ in.	181/213/0 and 181/214/0		3,5—5	1,25	**13/6**
181/2517	16 in.	181/217/0	with electric head light (metallic filament lamp)	3,5—5	1,5	**26/—**
181/2519	18 in.	181/219/0	do.	3,5—5	1,5	**31/—**
181/2523	$20\frac{1}{2}$ in.	181/223/0	with 2 head lights	3,5—5	1,5	**36/—**

10217 Metallic filament lamps, with Standard thread 3,5 Volt, 0,25 Ampère, fitting above Locomotives as head lights . . . . doz. **17/—**

Electric Locomotives with Field Magnet Motors

suitable for Low Current.

Gauge 0 = $1\frac{3}{8}$ in.

190/2517

190/2519

No. of the Locomotive	Length of the Locomotive	Locomotive out of Train		Highest Voltage to be used	Consumpt. of Current about	Locomotive and Tender Price complete each
				Volt	Ampère	
190/2517	11 in.	190/217/0	with electric head light (Carbon filament lamp)	3,5—5	1,25	**15/—**
190/2519	12 in.	190/219/0	do.	3,5—5	1,25	**17/—**

Electric Locomotives with Field Magnet Motors.

Gauge 0 = $1^3/_8$ in.

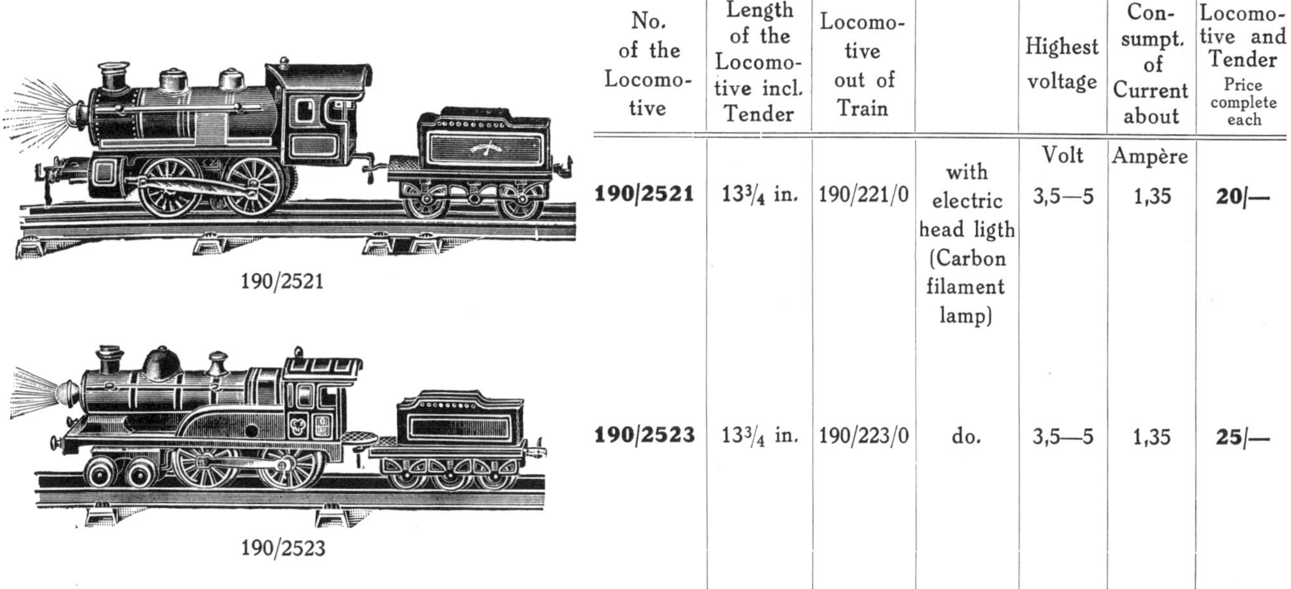

No. of the Locomotive	Length of the Locomotive incl. Tender	Locomotive out of Train		Highest voltage	Consumpt. of Current about	Locomotive and Tender Price complete each
				Volt	Ampère	
190/2521	$13^3/_4$ in.	190/221/0	with electric head ligth (Carbon filament lamp)	3,5—5	1,35	**20/—**
190/2523	$13^3/_4$ in.	190/223/0	do.	3,5—5	1,35	**25/—**

190/2521

190/2523

Carbon Filament lamps with Standard thread fitting above electric Locomotives as head light.
14379/1 4 Volt 0,25 Ampère (for Low Current). . . . . doz. **11/6**

Scale Model, London and North Western Railway

Express Locomotive "George the Fifth" No. 2663

will run over old sharp-radius as well as over new large radius curves.

will run over old sharp-radius as well as over new large radius curves.

M 3453/0

The "George the Fifth" 4—4—0 class of Locomotive is considered to be the "Premier" Locomotive of Englands "Premier" Line and its introduction among our range of Electrically driven Models will no doubt be appreciated by all Model Railway Enthusiasts.

Frames and Superstructure are made of best tinned steel plate, stamped out with powerful press tools.

The Motor is of the Permanent Magnet Type, which can be automatically reversed from the track. Voltage 4—6.

Enamelled and lined in correct L. & N. W. R. colours.

Gauge 0 = $1^3/_8$ in., length of Loco incl. Tender $16^3/_4$ in.

Loco with Tender complet each **13/6**

*NB. This Loco does **not** have to have large radius rails, but will run satisfactorily on the old sharp radius as well as on the new large radius rails.*

Electric Locomotives with Field Magnet Motors.

Gauge 1 = $1^7/_8$ in.

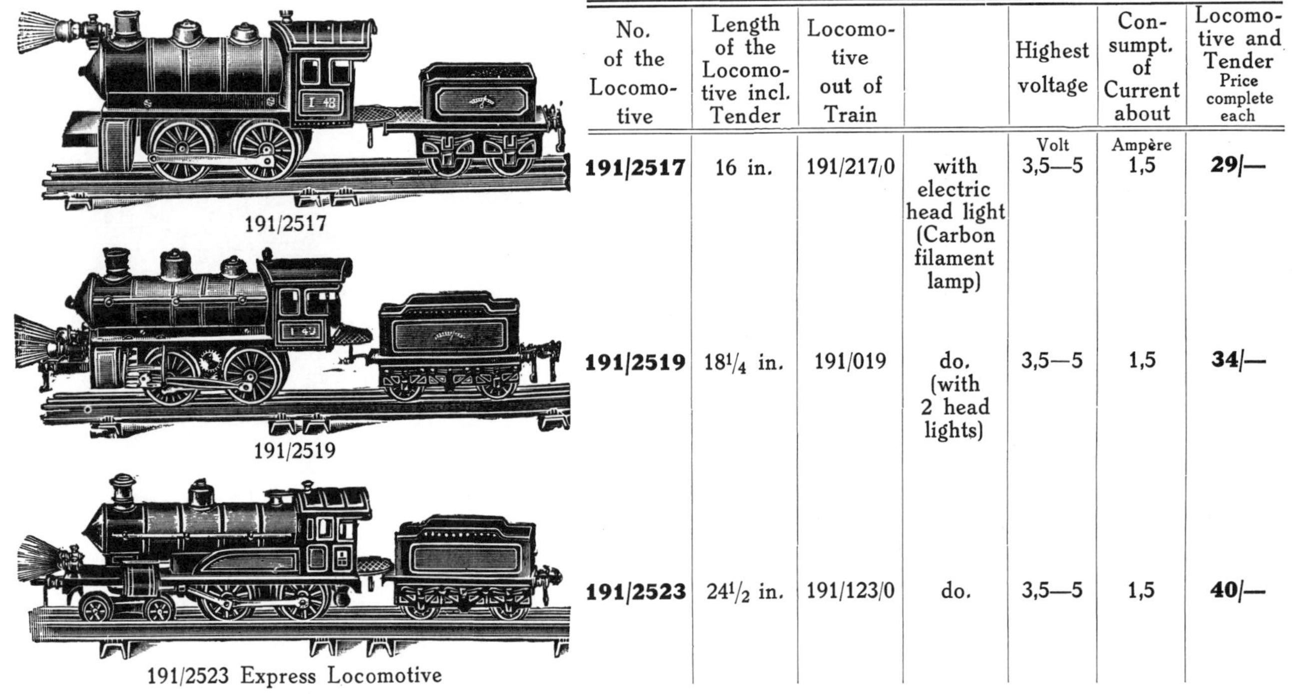

191/2517

191/2519

191/2523 Express Locomotive

No. of the Locomotive	Length of the Locomotive incl. Tender	Locomotive out of Train		Highest voltage	Consumpt. of Current about	Locomotive and Tender Price complete each
				Volt	Ampère	
191/2517	16 in.	191/217/0	with electric head light (Carbon filament lamp)	3,5—5	1,5	**29/—**
191/2519	$18^1/_4$ in.	191/019	do. (with 2 head lights)	3,5—5	1,5	**34/—**
191/2523	$24^1/_2$ in.	191/123/0	do.	3,5—5	1,5	**40/—**

14379/1 **Carbon filament lamps** with Standard thread fitting above electric Locomotives as head light 4 Volt, 0,25 Ampère (for Low Current) . . . . doz. **11/6**

Scale Model London & North Western Railway

Express Locomotive "George the Fifth" No. 2663.

Gauge 1 = $1^7/_8$ in.

will run over old sharp-radius as well as over new large radius curves

will run over old sharp-radius as well as over new large radius curves

M 3453/1

The "George the Fifth" 4—4—0 class of Locomotive is considered to be the "Premier" Locomotive of Englands "Premier" Line and its introduction among our range of Clockwork driven Models will no doubt be appreciated by all Model Railway Enthusiasts.

Frames and Superstructure are made of best tinned steel plate, stamped out with powerful press tools.

The Motor is of the Permanent Magnet Type, which can be automatically reserved from the track. Voltage 4—8.

Enamelled and lined in correct L. & N. W. R. colours.

Gauge 1 = $1^7/_8$ in., length of Loco incl. tender $22^1/_2$ in. . . . Loco with Tender complete each **63/—**

*NB, This Loco does **not** have to have large radius rails but will run satisfactorily on the old sharpradius as well as the new large radius rails.*

Single Locomotives for High Current.

200/2521

200/2523

200/3569

201/2519

201/2523 Express Locomotive

201/3569 Superior Express Locomotive

No. of the Locomotive	Gauge	Locomotive out of Train		Length of the Locomotive incl. Tender	Locomotive and Tender Price complete each
200/2521	0 = $1^{3}/_{8}$ in.	200/221/0	Running forward only with 1 head light	14 in.	**30/—**
200/2523	0 = $1^{3}/_{8}$ in.	200/223/0	Running forward only with 1 head light	14 in.	**34/—**
200/3569	0 = $1^{3}/_{8}$ in.	200/369/0	fitted for reversing with 1 head light	14 in.	**49/—**
201/2519	1 = $1^{7}/_{8}$ in.	201/219/0	Running forward with 2 head lights	$18^{1}/_{4}$ in.	**42/—**
201/2523	1 = $1^{7}/_{8}$ in.	201/223/0	Running forward only, with 2 head lights	$24^{1}/_{2}$ in.	**48/—**
201/3569	1 = $1^{7}/_{8}$ in.	201/369/0	fitted for reversing with 2 head lights	$25^{3}/_{4}$ in.	**76/—**

10218/6 **Small Carbon filament lamps** fitting above Locomotives 6 Volt, 0,25 Ampère . . . . doz. **13/—**
„ /12 „ „ „ „ „ „ 12 „ 0,25 „ . . . . „ **13/—**

Electric Locomotives.

Best Electric Express Locomotive for High Current, fitted for reversing, with fast and slow Movement, with 2 head lights.

200/3575 Gauge 0 = $1^3/_8$ in., length of the Locomotive incl. Tender $21^3/_4$ in., out of Train No. 200/375 . . . each **68/—**
201/ „ „ 1 = $1^7/_8$ „ „ „ „ „ „ „ 29 „ „ „ „ „ 201/375 . . . „ **114/—**

180/540 and 181/540

180/541 and 200/541

New Electric Locomotives (American Type), straight (American) Type with 8 wheels, for **Low Current.**

180/540 Gauge 0 = $1^3/_8$ in., length $9^1/_2$ in. . . . . each **23/2**
181/ „ „ 1 = $1^7/_8$ „ „ $12^1/_4$ „ . . . . „ **35/—**

English Type (also French Type), perfect Model of a Metropolitan Electric Loco on 12 wheels, fitted for reversing, with 1 head light, **for Low Current.**

180/541 Gauge 0 = $1^3/_8$ in., length 11 in. . . . . each **28/6**
181/ „ „ 1 = $1^7/_8$ „ „ $13^1/_2$ „ . . . . „ **38/—**

For High Current, fitted for reversing with 1 head light.

200/541 Gauge 0 = $1^3/_8$ in., length 11 in. . . . . each **48/—**
201/ „ „ 1 = $1^7/_8$ „ „ $13^1/_2$ „ . . . . „ **68/—**

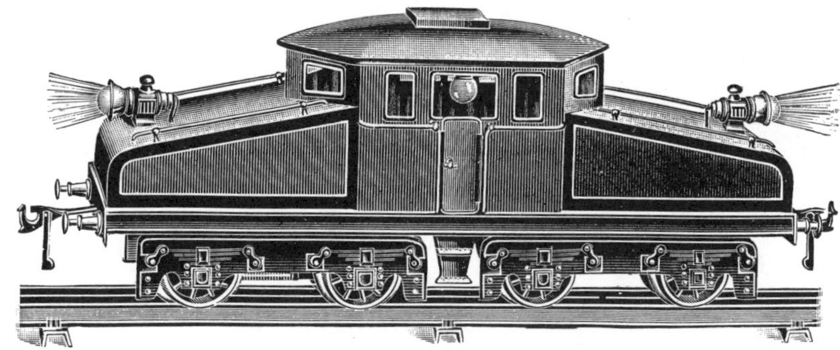

201/551

Gauge 1 = $1^7/_8$ in.

French Type, Loco on 8 wheels for **High Current,** continuous or alternating current, fitted for reversing, Voltage 110—220, with resistance (2 incandescent lamps at 16—32 C. P. each), with 2 head lights.

201/551 $15^1/_2$ in. long . . . . each **89/—**

Head lights fitting above Locomotives, for Low Current:

10217 Metallic filamet lamp with Standard thread, $3^1/_2$ Volt, 0,25 Ampère . . . . doz. **17/—**

for High Current:

10218/6 **Small Carbon filament lamps,** with Standard thread, 6 Volt, 0,5 Ampère . . . . doz. **13/—**
„ /12 „ „ „ „ „ „ „ 12 „ 0,5 „ . . . . „ **13/—**

Electric Underground Locomotives (Electric Haulers).

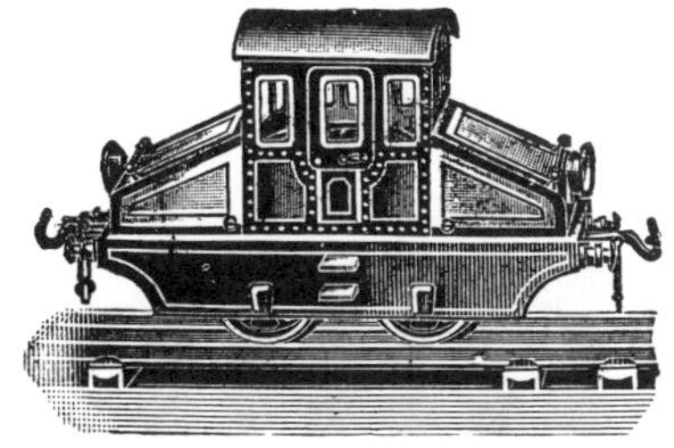

180/531

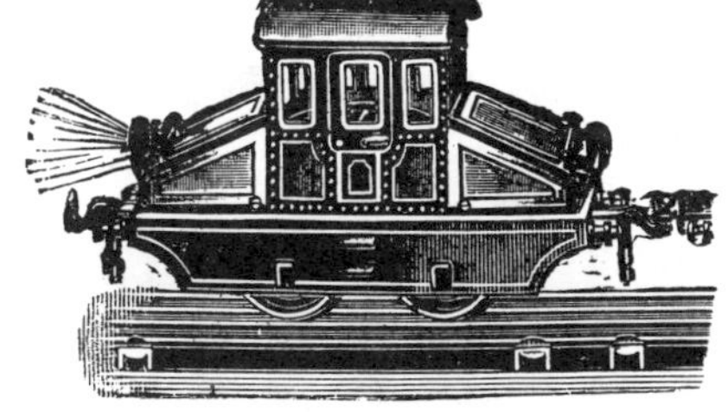

180/1533 with electr. head light

Electric Underground Locomotives for Low Current

180/531	Gauge 0 = $1^3/_8$ in. **fitted for reversing,** $6^1/_4$ in. long	each	**8/—**
181/531	„ 1 = $1^7/_8$ „ „ „ „ $8^1/_4$ „ „	„	**15/4**
180/1533	„ 0 = $1^3/_8$ „ „ „ „ $6^3/_4$ „ „ with head light	„	**13/—**
181/1533	„ 1 = $1^7/_8$ „ „ „ „ $8^1/_4$ „ „ „ „ „	„	**19/—**

10217 **Small spare metallic filament lamps** with small thread, 3,5 Volt, 0,25 Ampère, fitting Locomotives 180/1533 and 181/1533 . . . . doz. **17/—**

Electric Underground Locomotives for High Current

200/2560	Gauge 0 = $1^3/_8$ in., running forward only, with 1 head light $6^3/_4$ in. long	each	**25/—**
201/2560	„ 1 = $1^7/_8$ „ „ „ „ „ 1 „ „ $8^1/_4$ „ „	„	**31/—**
200/2561	„ 0 = $1^3/_8$ „ fitted for reversing, „ 1 „ „ $6^3/_4$ „ „	„	**38/—**
201/2561	„ 1 = $1^7/_8$ „ „ „ „ „ 1 „ „ $8^1/_4$ „ „	„	**46/—**

10218/12 **Small Carbon filament lamp** fitting above Locomotives (for High Current) as head lights, with Mignon thread, 12 Volt, 0,5 Ampère . . . . doz. **13/—**

Electric System of Working Switches.

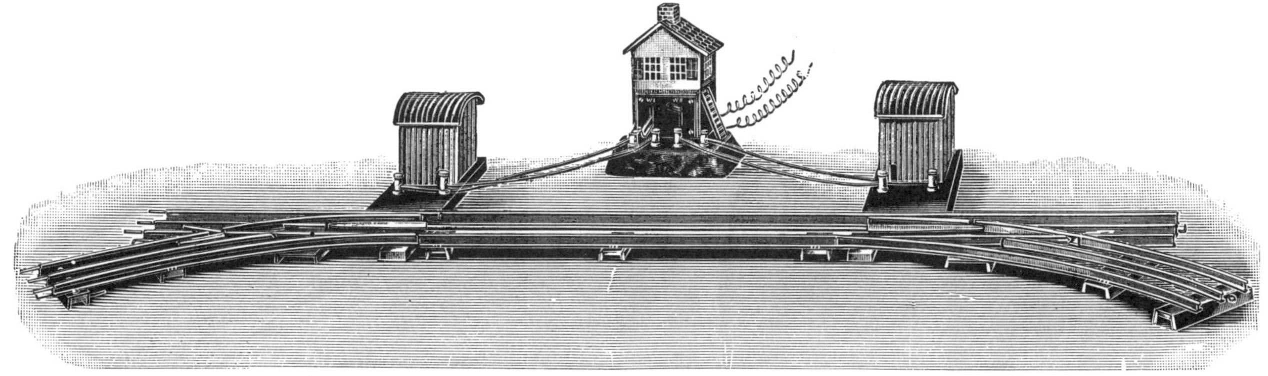

for **Low Current:** Signal Box with 2 Connections

10321	**Signal Box** for 2 connections with electric lamp in house	each	**7/10**

Ordinary Points for above (for Clockwork and Steam Trains)

13024/0	**Left hand point** Gauge 0 to be worked by electricity	„	**6/10**
„ /1	„ „ „ „ 1 „ „ „ „ „	„	**7/4**
13025/0	**Right hand point** „ 0 „ „ „ „ „	„	**6/10**
„ /1	„ „ „ „ 1 „ „ „ „ „	„	**7/4**

Electric Points for above, (for electric Trains)

13106/0	**Left hand point** Gauge 0 to be worked by electricity	„	**9/6**
„ /1	„ „ „ „ 1 „ „ „ „ „	„	**10/6**
13107/0	**Right hand point** „ 0 „ „ „ „ „	„	**9/6**
„ /1	„ „ „ „ 1 „ „ „ „ „	„	**10/6**

Electric Mountain Railway (Rack Railway)

very original, good value.

Electric Railway, consisting of: Locomotive and car, with rail oval in 10 parts including connecting rail, the straight rails with racks, supports of various heights, very strong finish and very well working.

Length of Locomotive	Length of Car	Length of Train	Rail Formation	Highest voltage	Consumption of current
$6^7/_8$ in.	$4^7/_8$ in.	13 in.	1 Oval = 6 curved and 2 long straight rails	4 Volt	abt. 1,75 Ampère

180/460/0 for Low Current . . . . each **23/—**
200/460/0 „ High Current . . . . „ **46/—**

The railway is fitted for a tension of 65—220 volts and in connecting same with the main, it should be specially observed, that a resistance must be fitted in. (14031/1 page 351, or 10290/1, 10317, page 352 of this list) According to the speed the train is required to run, a lamp of 16, or 25 C. P. is to be screwed into the resistance.

Model "Figure 8 Railway", or "Scenic Railway" **with Electric Motor**

for Low Current.

10300

10300 **"Figure 8 Railway" or "Scenic Railway" with Electric Motor** very original, with endless chain and 2 cars. For working this, an **Accumulator** (as shown on page 317 of this List) should be used. The 2 cars are pulled up automatically by means of the chain and are thus continually running along the track. With complete outfit, finely japanned, $15^3/_4$ in. high, length of rails $11^1/_2$ feet . . . . each **30/6**

Rails for Electric Trains

for Low and High Current.

Insulated Single Rails

to transform any ordinary rail at once into an electric rail.

Exceedingly useful novelty, to electrify ordinary systems.

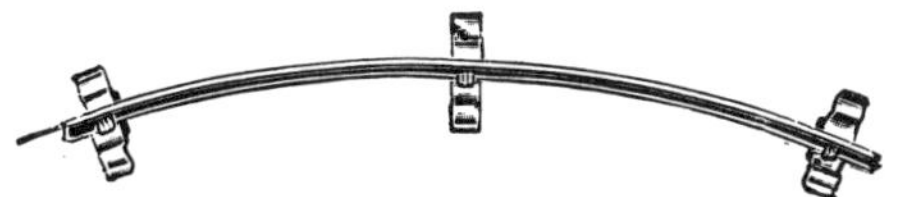

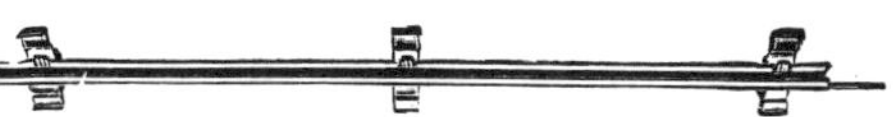

The insulated single rails are inserted by a slight pressure between the ordinary rails as centre rails. They are fixed by a practical arrangement, and form a reliable conductor. An electric track thus produced can be used for low or high current Railways.

13632/0 A	curved centre rails, fitting Gauge 0 = $1^3/_8$ in.	doz.	**2/8**
13633/0 D	straight „ „ „ „ 0 = $1^3/_8$ „	„	**2/8**
13632/1 A	curved „ „ „ „ 1 = $1^7/_8$ „	„	**3/10**
13633/1 D	straight „ „ „ „ 1 = $1^7/_8$ „	„	**3/10**

Electric Rails.

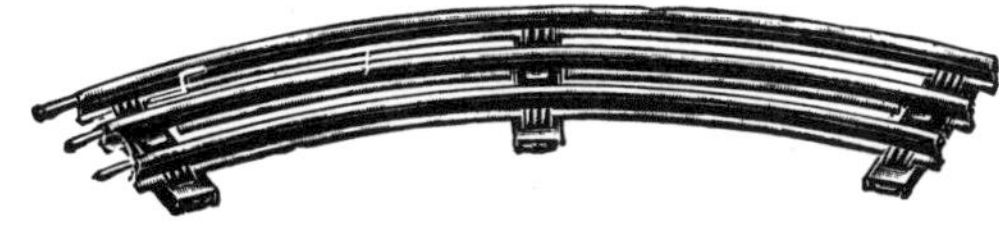

14022

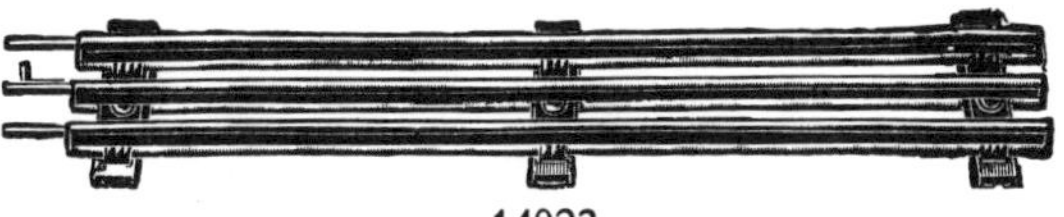

14023

Rails with joining pegs at one end

10174/00 A	curved, Gauge 00 = $1^1/_8$ in.	doz.	**2/10**
14022/0 A	„ „ 0 = $1^3/_8$ „	„	**4/10**
„ /1 A	„ „ 1 = $1^7/_8$ „	„	**6/4**

Rails with joining pegs at one end

10175/00 D	straight, Gauge 00 = $1^1/_8$ in.	doz.	**2/—**
14023/0 D	„ „ 0 = $1^3/_8$ „	„	**4/10**
„ /1 D	„ „ 1 = $1^7/_8$ „	„	**6/4**

Electric Connecting Rails

with 2 terminals, for connection with the currant supply (battery &c.) and joining pegs at one end.

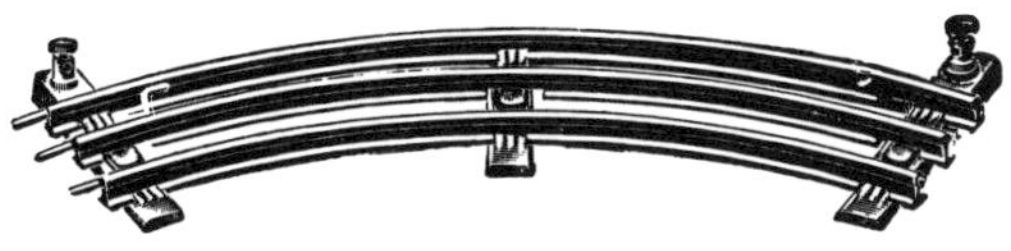

14024

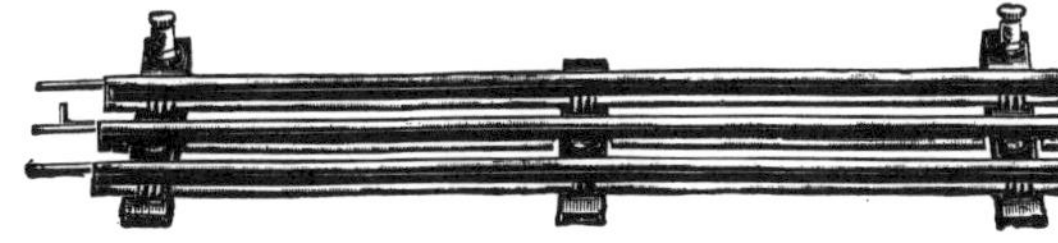

14025

10176/00 A	curved, Gauge 00 = $1^1/_8$ in.	doz.	**3/10**
14024/0 A	„ „ 0 = $1^3/_8$ „	„	**12/8**
„ /1 A	„ „ 1 = $1^7/_8$ „	„	**15/10**

10177/00 D	straight, Gauge 00 = $1^1/_8$ in.	doz.	**3/4**
14025/0 D	„ „ 0 = $1^3/_8$ „	„	**12/8**
„ /1 D	„ „ 1 = $1^7/_8$ „	„	**15/10**

Half und Quarter Electric Rails.

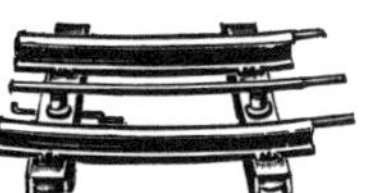

14342

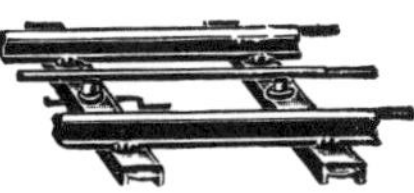

14343

14344

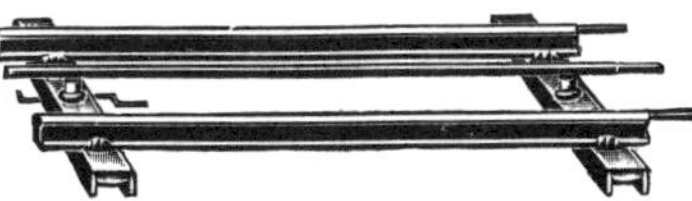

14345

Quarter Rails, curved

14342/0	Gauge 0 = $1^3/_8$ in.	doz,	**2/10**
„ /1	„ 1 = $1^7/_8$ „	„	**3/8**

Quarter Rails, straight

14343/0	Gauge 0 = $1^3/_8$ in.	doz.	**2/10**
„ /1	„ 1 = $1^7/_8$ „	„	**3/8**

Half Rails, curved

14344/0	Gauge 0 = $1^3/_8$ in.	doz.	**3/2**
„ /1	„ 1 = $1^7/_8$ „	„	**4/2**

Half Rails, straight

14345/0	Gauge 0 = $1^3/_8$ in.	„	**3/2**
„ /1	„ 1 = $1^7/_8$ „	„	**4/2**

Electric Crossings.

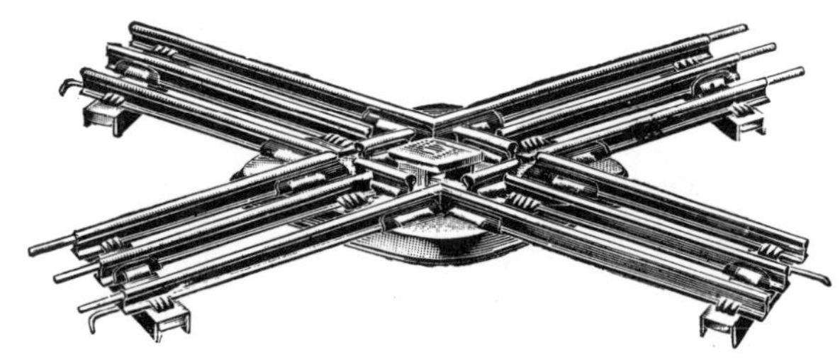

10223/0 and 14026/0

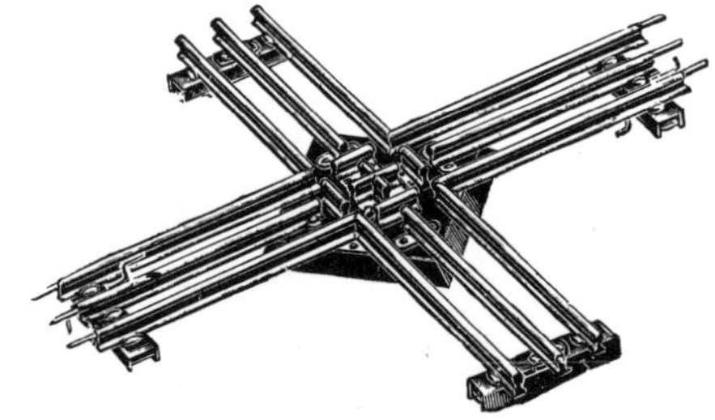

14027

10223/0	**Acute angled Crossings,**	Gauge 0 = $1^3/_8$ in.	each	**2/—**
14026/0	**The same in heaviest quality,**	„ 0 = $1^3/_8$ „	„	**3/8**
„ /1	„ „ „ „ „	„ 1 = $1^7/_8$ „	„	**4/6**
14027/0	**Right angled Crossings,**	„ 0 = $1^3/_8$ „	„	**3/8**
„ /1	„ „ „	„ 1 = $1^7/_8$ „	„	**4/6**

Electric Points.

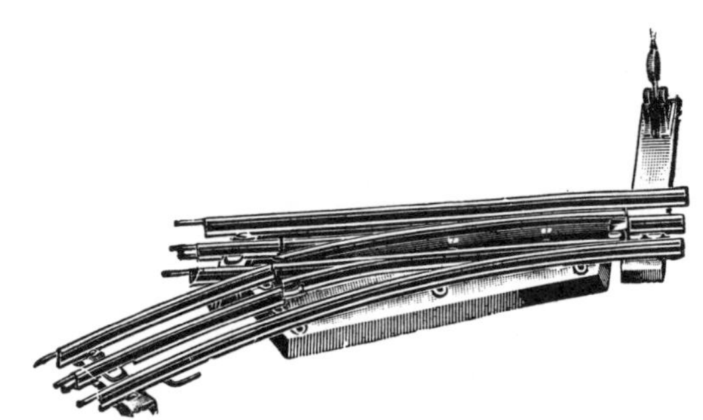

10224/0 and 14028/1

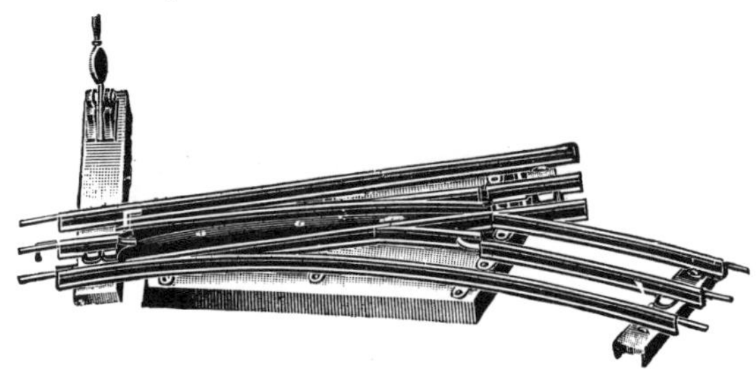

10225/0 and 14029/1

10224/0	**Left hand Points** (with turning lanterns),	Gauge 0 = $1^3/_8$ in.	each	**3/—**
14028/0	**The same in heaviest quality,**	„ 0 = $1^3/_8$ „	„	**7/8**
„ /1	„ „ „ „ „	„ 1 = $1^7/_8$ „	„	**9/—**
10225/0	**Right hand Points** (with turning lanterns),	„ 0 = $1^3/_8$ „	„	**3/—**
14029/0	**The same in heaviest quality,**	„ 0 = $1^3/_8$ „	„	**7/8**
„ /1	„ „ „ „ „	„ 1 = $1^7/_8$ „	„	**9/—**

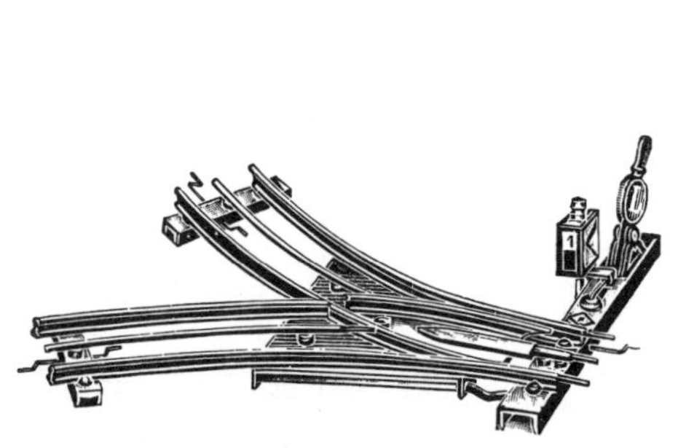

13115

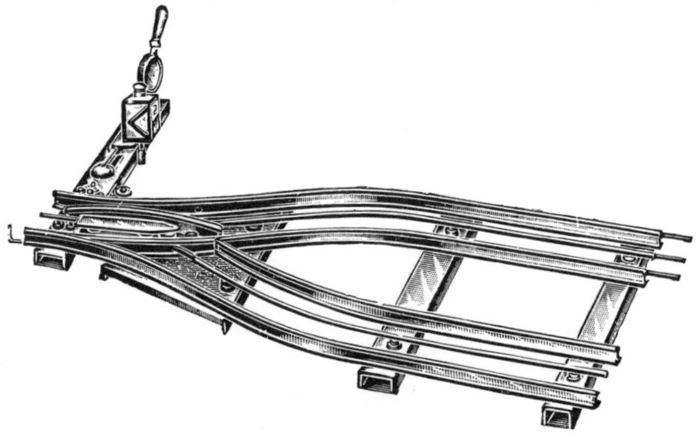

13111

Electric Double Symmetrical Points with 2 curved rails, with 1 turning lantern and 1 lever.

13115/0	Gauge 0 = $1^3/_8$ in.	each	**9/—**
„ /1	„ 1 = $1^7/_8$ „	„	**11/8**

Electric Parallel Symmetrical Points with 1 lever and 1 turning lantern.

13111/0	Gauge 0 = $1^3/_8$ in.	each	**9/—**
„ /1	„ 1 = $1^7/_8$ „	„	**11/8**

Accessories for Electric Railways.

10388

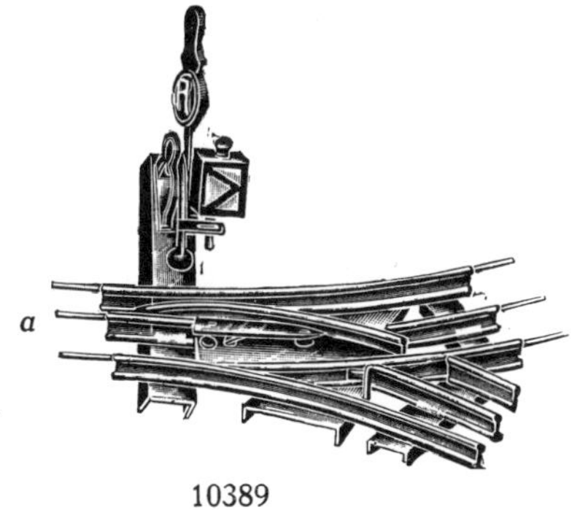

10389

Electric Double Symmetrical Points with 2 curved rails, 1 turning lantern and 1 lever

without joining pegs at the end ***a***

10388/0	Gauge 0 = $1^{3}/_{8}$ in.	each	**4/8**
„ /1	„ 1 = $1^{7}/_{8}$ „	„	**5/8**

with joining pegs at the end ***a***

10389/0	Gauge 0 = $1^{3}/_{8}$ in.	each	**4/8**
„ /1	„ 1 = $1^{7}/_{8}$ „	„	**5/8**

In Connection with bigger Locomotives, resp. Express Trains it is adviseable to make use of our

Electric Rails, Points and Crossings

with extra large Radius, (Standard New Radius).

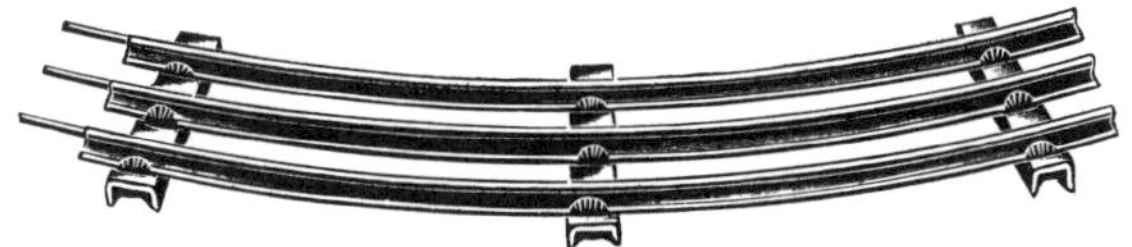

Electric large Radius Rails

10419/0 A	Gauge 0 = $1^{3}/_{8}$ in., curved, 12 pieces to circle, 4 ft. outside diam.	doz.	**6/6**
10420/0 D	„ 0 = $1^{3}/_{8}$ „ straight	„	**6/6**
10419/1 A	„ 1 = $1^{7}/_{8}$ „ curved, 16 pieces to circle, 6 ft. outside diam.	„	**7/6**
10420/1 D	„ 1 = $1^{7}/_{8}$ „ straight	„	**7/6**

Points for the large Radius

10424/0	Gauge 0 = $1^{3}/_{8}$ in., left hand Point	each	**5/8**
10425/0	„ 0 = $1^{3}/_{8}$ „ right „ „	„	**5/8**
10424/1	„ 1 = $1^{7}/_{8}$ „ left „ „	„	**7/—**
10425/1	„ 1 = $1^{7}/_{8}$ „ right „ „	„	**7/—**

Crossings for the large Radius

10421/0	Gauge 0 = $1^{3}/_{8}$ in.	each	**3/8**
10421/1	„ 0 = $1^{7}/_{8}$ „	„	**4/6**

Connecting Rails

10422/0	Gauge 0 = $1^{3}/_{8}$ in. curved	doz.	**14/6**
„ /1	„ 1 = $1^{7}/_{8}$ „ „	„	**16/6**

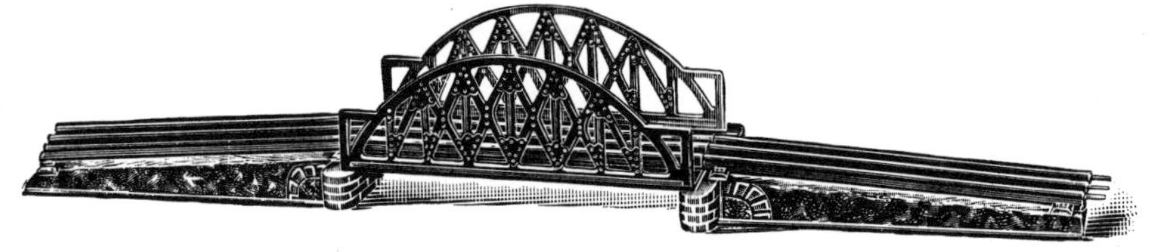

10205

Railway Bridge for Electric Trains
in most realistic, plastic finish, with effective painting, middle piece with large arch, imitation iron work.

10205/0 Gauge 0 = $1^3/_8$ in., 32 in., long, $5^1/_8$ in. wide . . . . each **5/—**
„ /1 „ 1 = $1^7/_8$ „ 32 „ „ $5^3/_4$ „ „ . . . . „ **5/6**

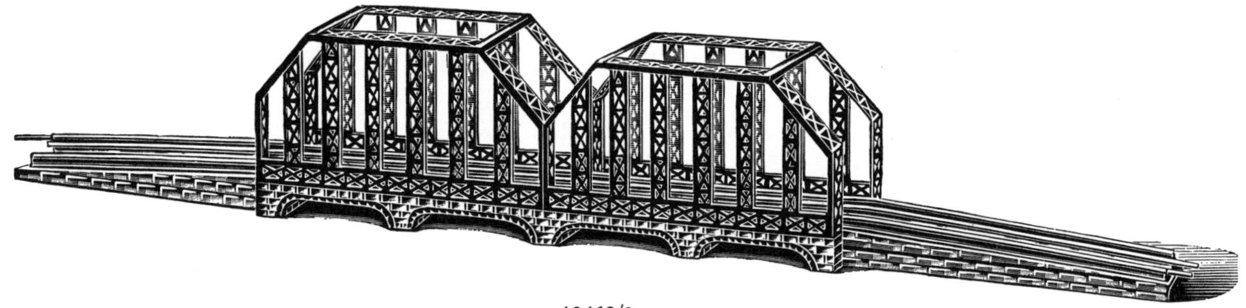

10463/0

Railway Bridge for Electric Trains with 2 arches, imitation iron work.

10463/0 Gauge 0 = $1^3/_8$ in., 42 in. long, $4^1/_4$ in. wide . . . . each **7/8**

11439/1

Railway Bridge for Electric Trains in new realistic finish, with 2 large arches, imitation iron work.

11439/1 Gauge 1 = $1^7/_8$ in., 43 in. long, $5^3/_4$ in. wide . . . . each **8/—**

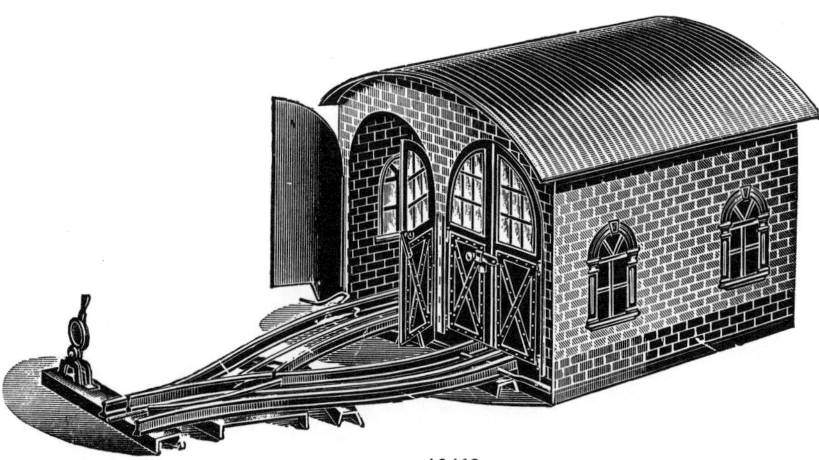

10462

Engine Shed with electric rails

suitable for 2 Locomotives, plastically stamped, imitation brickwork, finely japanned, with swing doors, corrugated roof with parallel symmetrical Point.

10462/0 **Gauge 0 = $1^3/_8$ in.**

Shed, $8^1/_4$ in. long, $8^1/_2$ in. wide, 7 in. high . . . . each **12/6**

10462/1 **Gauge 1 = $1^7/_8$ in.**

Shed, 16 in. long, 11 in. wide, 9 in. high . . . . each **21/8**

Signal with Electric Light

for Low Current.

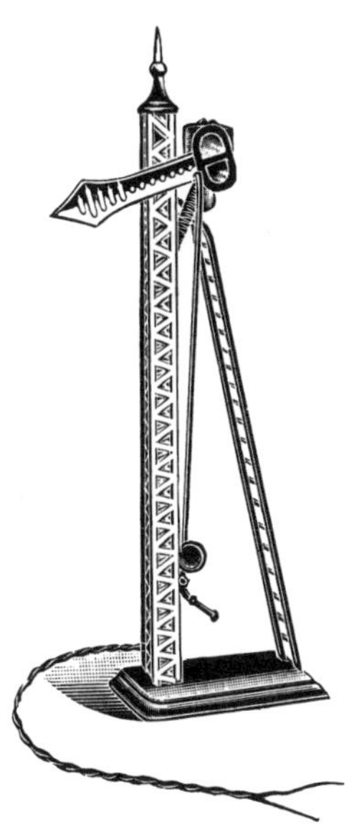

10447 electric

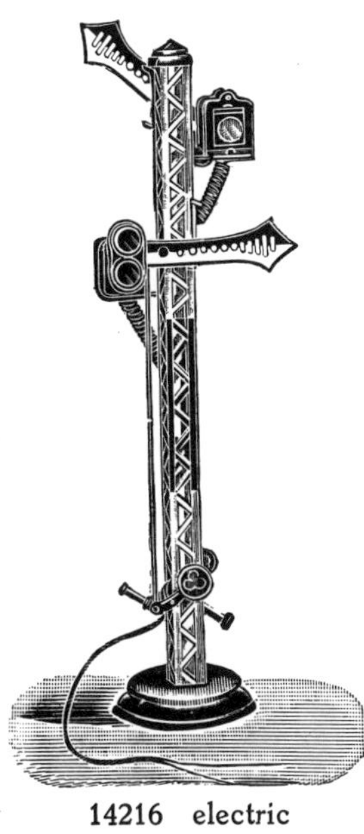

14216 electric

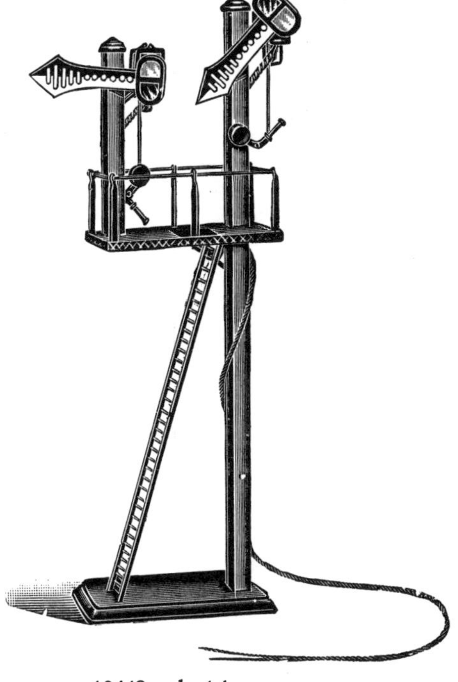

10448 electric

Signals with electric Light,

imitation girder work, electric lamp 4 Volt, with adjustable coloured signal arm and spectacles.

10447	with 1 lamp and ladder, $14^3/_4$ in. high	each	**3/6**
14216	„ 2 lamps, $12^3/_4$ in. high	„	**6/10**
10448	„ 2 „ railed platform and ladder, $17^3/_4$ in. high	„	**8/—**

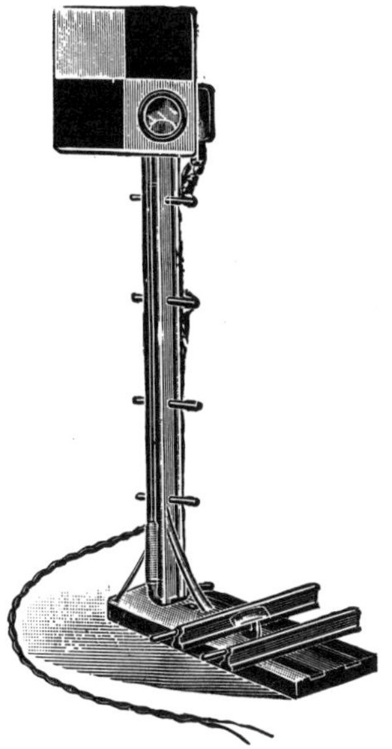

10452 electric

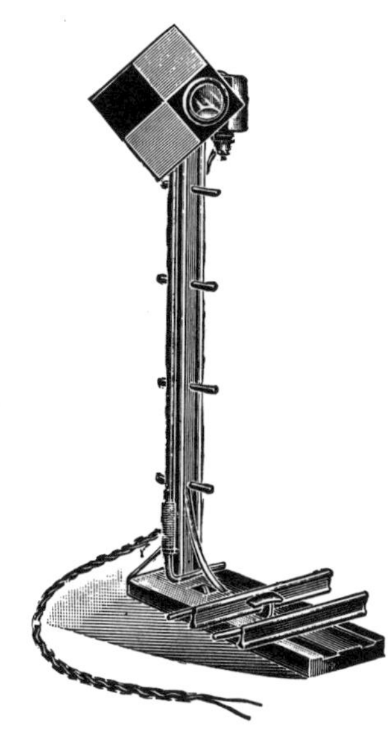

10453 electric

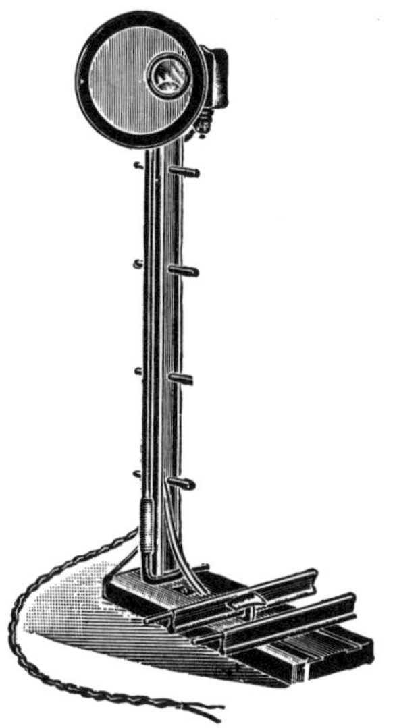

10454 electric

Signals with electric Lights,

working automatically by rail contact, rails adjustable for all gauges.

10452	with square disc., $10^5/_8$ in. high	each	**4/6**
10453	„ „ „ $10^5/_8$ „ „	„	**4/6**
10454	„ round „ $10^5/_8$ „ „	„	**4/6**

Signal Bridges with Electric Light

for Low Current.

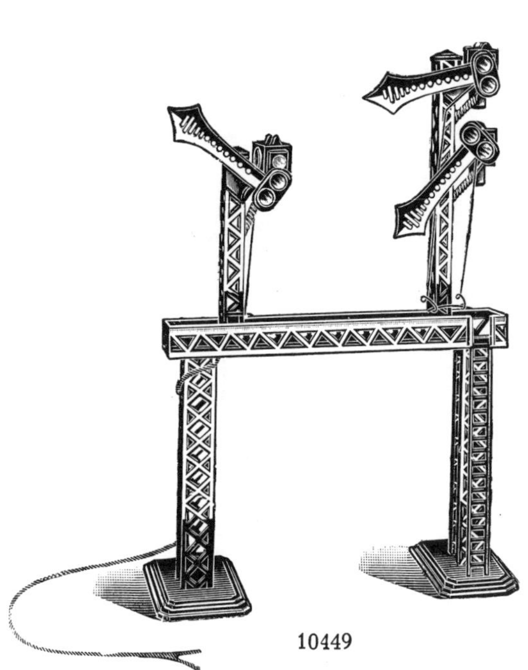

10449

10450

Signal-Bridges with electric lights, imitation girder work, lamps 4 Volt with adjustable coloured signal arms and spectacles

10449	2 Stands with 3 electric lamps, $14^{3}/_{4}$ in. high	each	**9/6**
10450	4 „ „ 3 „ „ $14^{3}/_{4}$ „ „	„	**13/—**

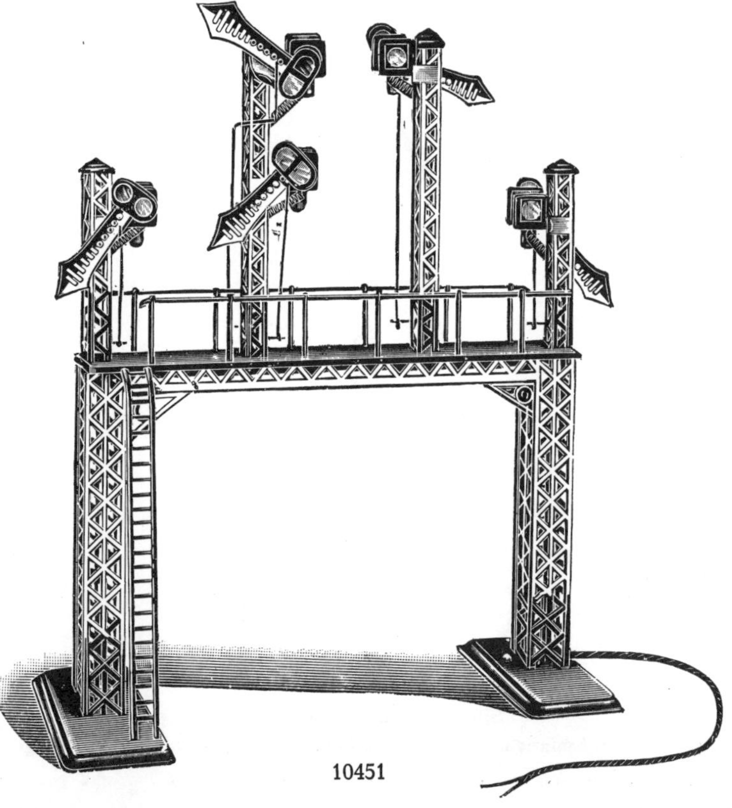

10451

10451 **Signal Bridge with electric lights,** imitation girder work, 4 Columns with 5 electric lamps 4 Volt, with adjustable, coloured signal arms and spectacle, 19 in. . . . . . each **20/—**

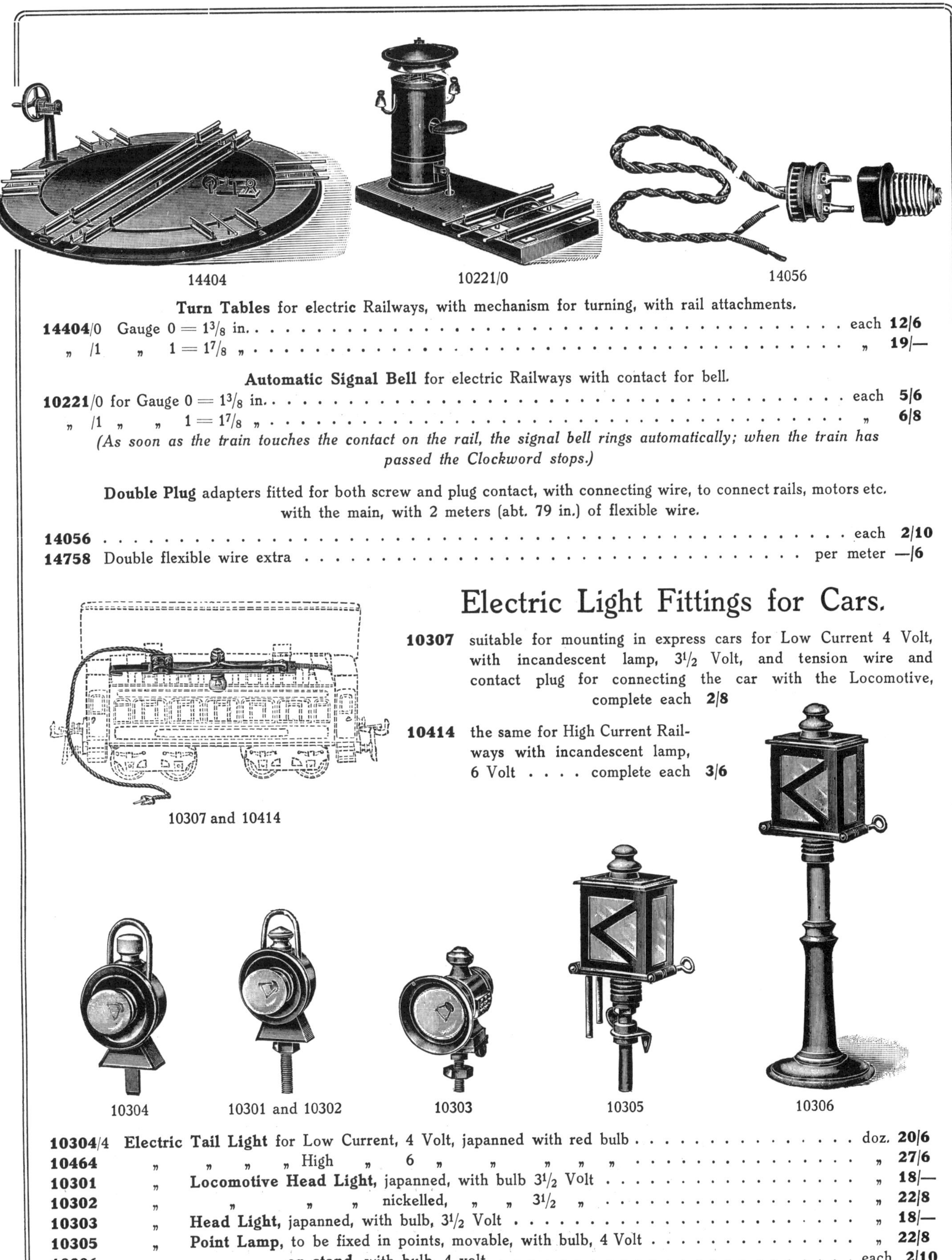

14404 10221/0 14056

Turn Tables for electric Railways, with mechanism for turning, with rail attachments.

14404/0 Gauge 0 = $1^3/_8$ in. . . . . each **12/6**
„ /1 „ 1 = $1^7/_8$ „ . . . . „ **19/—**

Automatic Signal Bell for electric Railways with contact for bell.

10221/0 for Gauge 0 = $1^3/_8$ in. . . . . each **5/6**
„ /1 „ „ 1 = $1^7/_8$ „ . . . . „ **6/8**

(As soon as the train touches the contact on the rail, the signal bell rings automatically; when the train has passed the Clockword stops.)

Double Plug adapters fitted for both screw and plug contact, with connecting wire, to connect rails, motors etc. with the main, with 2 meters (abt. 79 in.) of flexible wire.

14056 . . . . each **2/10**
14758 Double flexible wire extra . . . . per meter **—/6**

Electric Light Fittings for Cars.

10307 and 10414

10307 suitable for mounting in express cars for Low Current 4 Volt, with incandescent lamp, $3^1/_2$ Volt, and tension wire and contact plug for connecting the car with the Locomotive, complete each **2/8**

10414 the same for High Current Railways with incandescent lamp, 6 Volt . . . . complete each **3/6**

10304 10301 and 10302 10303 10305 10306

10304/4 **Electric Tail Light** for Low Current, 4 Volt, japanned with red bulb . . . . doz. **20/6**
10464 „ „ „ „ High „ 6 „ „ „ „ „ . . . . „ **27/6**
10301 „ **Locomotive Head Light**, japanned, with bulb $3^1/_2$ Volt . . . . „ **18/—**
10302 „ „ „ „ nickelled, „ „ $3^1/_2$ „ . . . . „ **22/8**
10303 „ **Head Light**, japanned, with bulb, $3^1/_2$ Volt . . . . „ **18/—**
10305 „ **Point Lamp**, to be fixed in points, movable, with bulb, 4 Volt . . . . . . „ **22/8**
10306 „ „ „ **on stand**, with bulb, 4 volt . . . . each **2/10**

Reversing Switches for Low Current

fitting all electric trains with permanent magnet motors, for reversing or for switching off current entirely.

10214

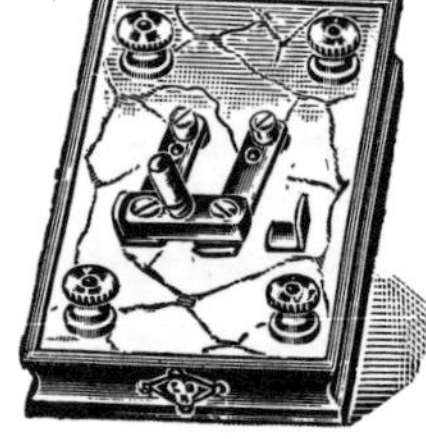
14030/0

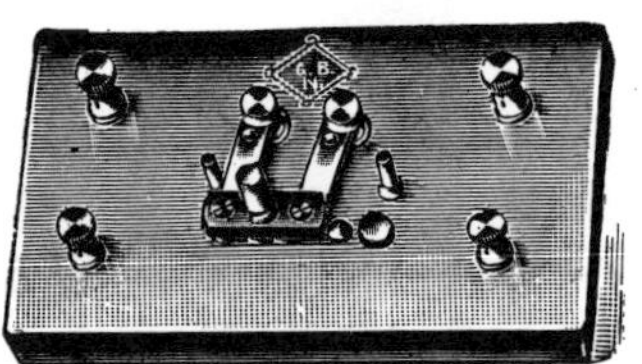
14030/1

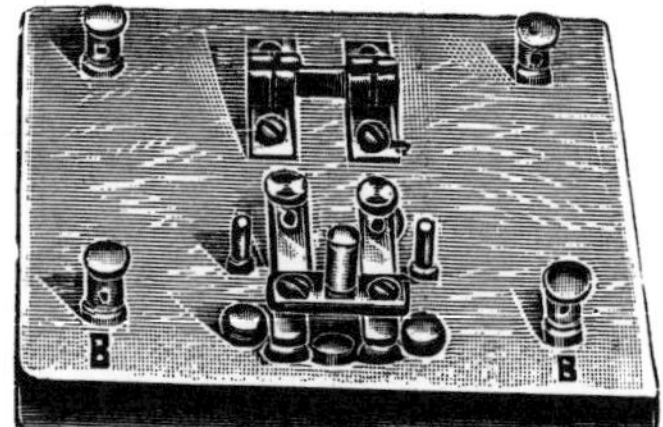
14030/2

10214	$3^3/_8$ in. long, $2^1/_8$ in. wide	doz.	**12/8**
14030/0	$3^3/_8$ „ „ $2^3/_4$ „ „	„	**21/—**
14030/1	4 „ „ $2^3/_8$ „ „	each	**3/2**
14030/2	4 „ „ $2^3/_8$ „ „ with lamella short-circuit fuse	„	**4/10**

10222

10222 **Regulating Resistance** at the same time **Reverser for electric Low Current railways** (controller) with handle, for quick or slow run, brake and reversing, finely polychrome japanned $4^3/_4$ in. high . . . . . each **4/4**

14381

14381 **Switch for Low Current** with finely nickelled case, $1^3/_4$ in. diam., $1^3/_8$ in. high doz. **9/6**

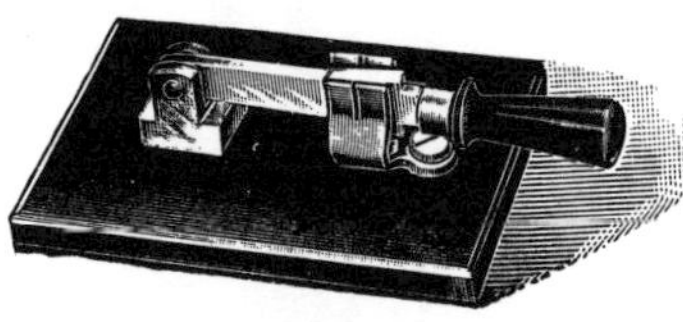

10270/1

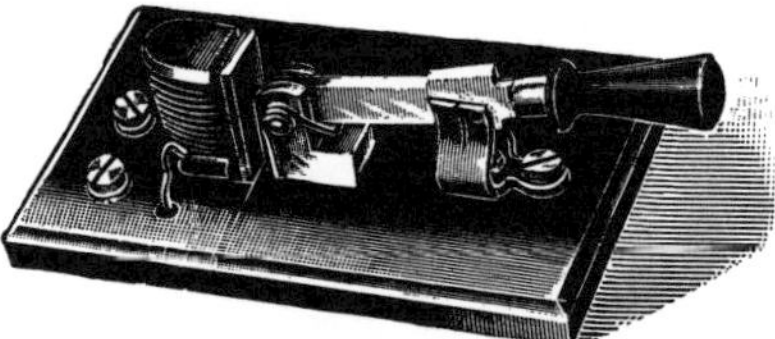
10271/1

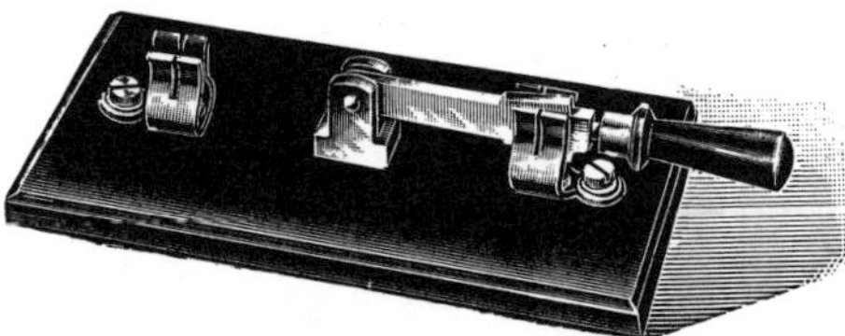
10272/1

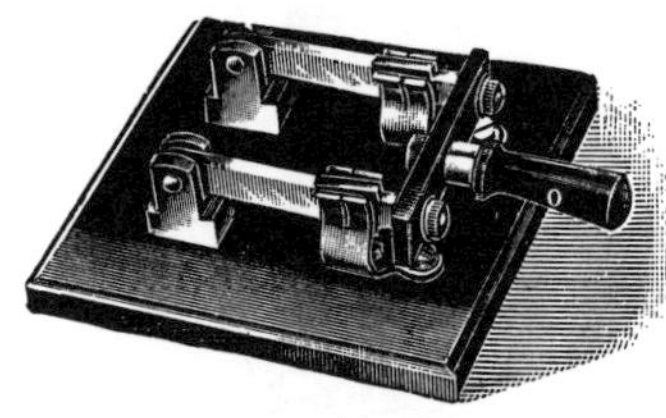
10270/2

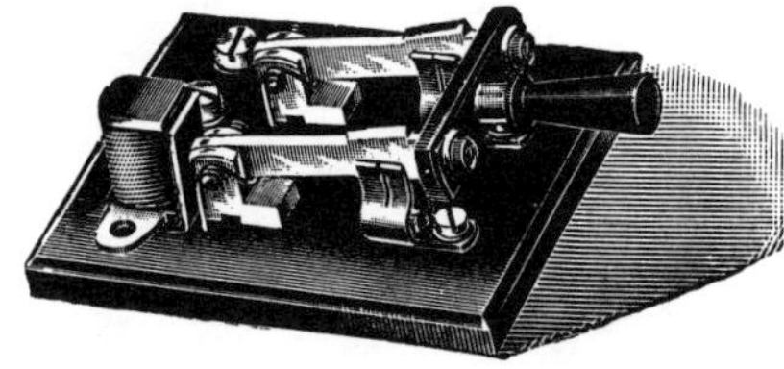
10271/2

10272/2

10270/1	**Lever Switch,** single, on wooden board, $2^3/_4 \times 1^1/_2$ in.	each	**1/4**
„ /2	„ „ double, „ „ „ $2^3/_4 \times 1^3/_4$ „	„	**3/2**
	Automatic Cutouts, Automatically disconnecting in case of short-circuit		
10271/1	single, on wooden board, $3^1/_2 \times 1^3/_4$ in.	each	**3/2**
„ /2	double, „ „ „ $3^1/_2 \times 2^1/_4$ „	„	**5/4**
10272/1	**Lever Reversing and Stopping Switch,** single, on wooden board, $3^1/_2 \times 1^1/_2$ in.	„	**2/4**
„ /2	„ „ „ „ „ double, „ „ „ $3^1/_2 \times 1^3/_4$ „	„	**4/4**

Resistances for Low Current.

14289/0

Resistance (Rheostat)
wire coil, mounted on wood base, for Low Current
$3^1/_2$ in. diam.
14289/0 . . . . doz. **19/—**

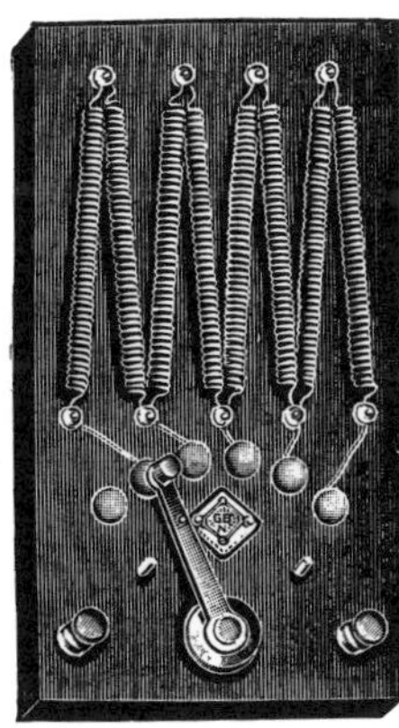

10229

Resistance (Rheostat)
of wire coils, mounted on wooden board
$5^1/_2$ in. long, $3^1/_4$ in. wide
10229 . . . . . each **3/—**

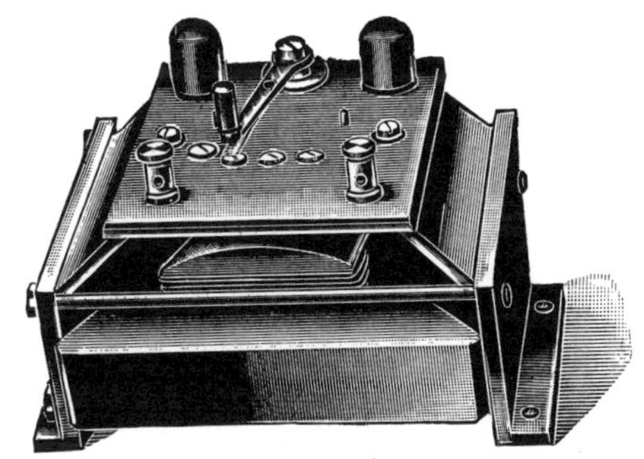

10415

Resistance (Reductor)
to be fitted in with Railways with Field Magnet Motors for use with main supply alternating current, with regulating arrangement
10415/110 for 110 Volt . . . . each **19/—**
„ /220 „ 220 „ . . . . „ **21/—**

Resistance Lamps for High Current.

14031/1

14031/2

Lamp Resistances to fit in, when working Electric Motors and Electric Railways when using the Main.
14031/1 with thread for 1 lamp (Standard Edison thread) and 2 connecting clamps . . . . each **2/—**
„ /2 „ „ „ 2 „ „ „ „ „ 2 „ „ . . . . „ **3/2**
„ /3 „ „ „ 3 „ „ „ „ „ 2 „ „ . . . . „ **5/—**
use with Field magnet Motors in connection with **continuous** current.

For above resistances ordinary incandescent lamps such as are employed for lighting purposes can be used. Care must be taken however that the lamps are correctly chosen with regard to the voltage of the respective supply and that the candle power of the lamps corresponds with those stated in the directions for use of the respective article.

Resistances for Accumulators.

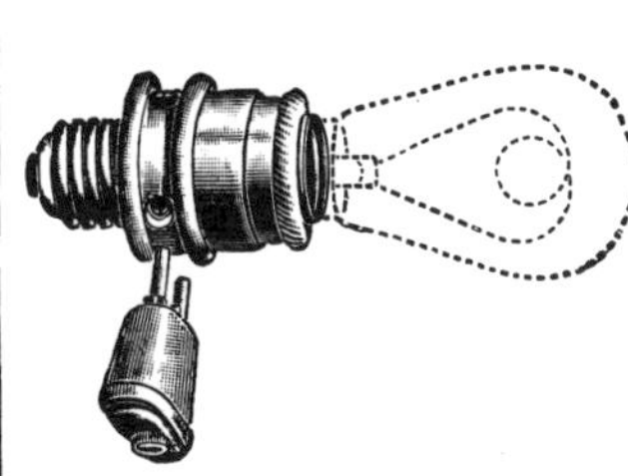

14057

14057 **Charging Resistance** to be used when charging accumulators, suitable for Standard Edison Screw thread. The light is not interrupted, while the accumulator is being charged. Very practical . . . . each **6/4**

For charging the Accumulators No. 14038, 14039, 11642, 11643, 14770, 14771 a lamp of 25 C. P., for No. 14040, 14041, 14772, 14773, 11644, 14044, 11646 a lamp of 32 C.P. and for Nos. 14041a, 11645, 14045, 11647 lamps of 32 up to 50 C.P. are to be used.

14758 **Double Connecting** cable for above . . per each meter (1 mtr. = abt. 39 in. **—/6**

Regulating Resistances for High Current (for continuous or alternating current)

with Nickelin-wire resistance, mounted on a slate base.

10290/1

10290/2

10290/1 for 1 lamp, suitable for high current electric railways, gauge 0 reversing, and gauge 1 not reversing, base 6 in. long, $4^3/_4$ in. wide . . . . each **11/6**

„ /2 for 2 lamps, suitable for high current electric railways, gauge 1, reversing, base $6^3/_4$ in. long, $6^1/_4$ in. wide each **15/—**

„ /3 for 3 lamps, suitable for high current electric railways, gauge 1, reversing, with Cars with 2 incandescent lights and Locomotives with 3 head lights, base $9^1/_2$ in. long, $6^1/_4$ in wide . . . . each **19/—**

10316

10318

Lamp Resistances for high current electric railways, mounted in Signal Boxes

(to be used as the above Nos. 10290/1 and —/2)

10316 finely japanned, with 1 lamp, $8^1/_2$ in. high, $9^3/_4$ in. long . . . . each **8/6**

10317/1 Corrugated Tin house, finely japanned, with 1 lamp, $6^3/_4$ in. high, 7 in. long } to be regulated with . „ **15/8**

10318/1 „ „ „ „ „ „ 2 „ $6^3/_4$ „ „ $10^1/_4$ „ „ } Nickelin-wire resistance . „ **20/—**

7763/0

Self Producing Influence Electrical Machines

System Wimshurst,

with two oppositely revolving vulcanite discs, Fittings finely nickelled, mounted on Iron stand, packed in wooden boxes, with directions and explanations. Very reliable working, without changing poles.

7763/0	Vulcanite discs	$7^1/_8$ in. diam.,	**length of sparks**	$2—2^3/_8$ **in.**	compl. each	**29/—**
/1	„ „	8 „ „	„ „ „	$3^1/_2$—4	„ „ „	**40/—**
/2	„ „	$9^7/_8$ „ „	„ „ „	4—5	„ „ „	**62/—**
/3	„ „	$11^3/_4$ „ „	„ „ „	5—6	„ „ „	**114/—**
/4	„ „	$13^7/_8$ „ „	„ „ „	6—7	„ „ „	**168/—**

Experiment Boxes

excellent finish, suitable for above Electrical Machines.

7781/1 **Experiment box,** containing:

1. Stand with insulated base.
2. Geissler Tube.
3. Electrical Fly-wheel.
4. Electrical Chimes.
5. Glass disc with Tin-foil.
6. Paper Bush.
7. Hand Cylinders.
8. Vulcanite plate with Tin-foil.
9. Various pith objects.
10. 1 Pair of Chains.

per box complete, each **17/4**

7781/1

Experiment Boxes

excellent finish, suitable for above Electrical Machines.

7781/2 **Experiment box,** containing:

1. Univeral Stand.
2. Paper Bush.
3. Chimes with 2 Bells.
4. Dancing Balls.
5. Fly- wheel.
6. Holder for Geissler Tubes and Lightning [plate.
7. Geissler Tube.
8. Lightning plate.
9. Lightning Tube.
10. Balls.
11. Smoke Apparatus.
12. 1 Pair of hand Cylinders.
13. Leyden Jar, $5^1/_8$ in. cylindrical.
14. Discharger.
15. 1 Pair of Chains.
16. Explanations and directions.

packed in elegant box.

per box complete, each **33/8**

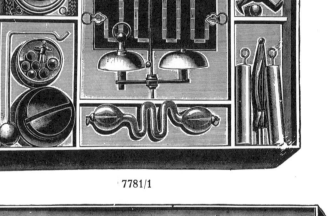

7781/2

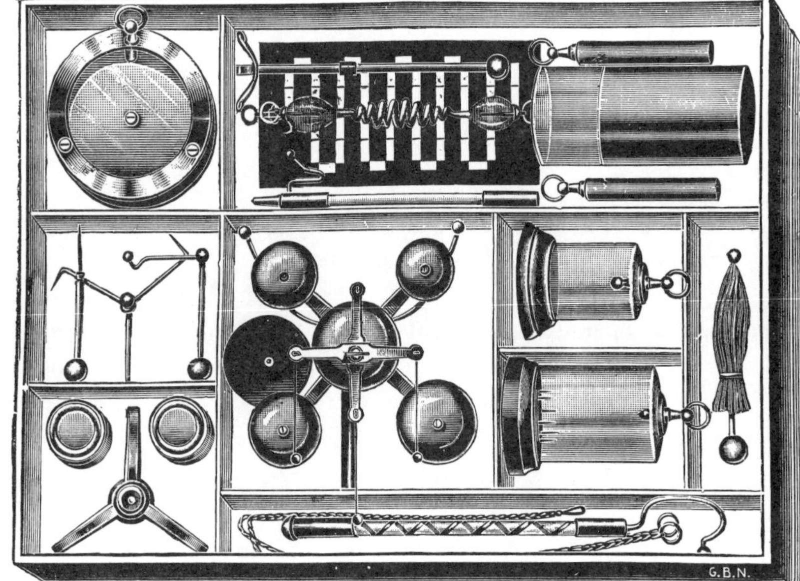

7781/3

Experiment Boxes,

excellent finish.

All Apparatus in extra large finish,

7781/3 **Experiment box,** containing:

1. Universal Stand.
2. Paper Bush.
3. Chimes with 5 Bells.
4. Dancing Balls.
5. Fly-Wheel.
6. Holder for Geissler Tubes and Lightning plate.
7. Geissler Tube.
8. Lightning plate.
9. Lightning Tube.
10. Balls.
11. Smoke apparatus (very interesting).
12. 1 Pair of hand cylinders.
13. Leyden Jar, $5\frac{1}{4}$ in., cylindrical.
14. Discharger with vulcanite handle.
15. 1 Pair of Chains.
16. Illustrations and Directions.

packed in elegant box,

per box complete each **66/—**

Experiment Boxes,

excellent finish,

new collection of interesting Apparatus, extra large finish.

7781/4 **Experiment box,** containing:

1. Universal Stand.
2. Motor for Influence Electricity.
3. Apparatus for Electrical Breath Pictures.
4. Sand Apparatus.
5. Quadrant Electrometer.
6. Electrical Mortar.
7. Surface Apparatus.
8. Candle Apparatus.
9. Rotating disc.
10. Irradiation Apparatus.
11. Lightning Conductor.
12. Illustrations and Directions.

packed in elegant box,

per box complete each **84/—**

Experiment box 7781/4 is very suitable as supplement box for 7781/1—3.

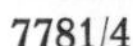

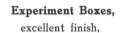

7781/4

Fine Experiment Boxes for Roentgen-Experiments

by means of Wimshurst Electrical Machines.

7788/1 **Roentgen-Collection,** containing: Roentgen Focus Tube (suitable for Wimshurst-Machines No. 7763/0—2), Stand, Fluoroscope 3—4 in. large, chains and directions, packed in elegant cardboard box per box complete, each **46/—**

7788/2 **Roentgen-Collection,** containing: larger Roentgen Focus Tube (suitable for Wimshurst Machines No. 7763/2—4), Stand, chains and directions, packed in elegant cardborad box . per box complete, each **76—**

Very good pictures can be produced on photographic plates with above Roentgen Apparatus.

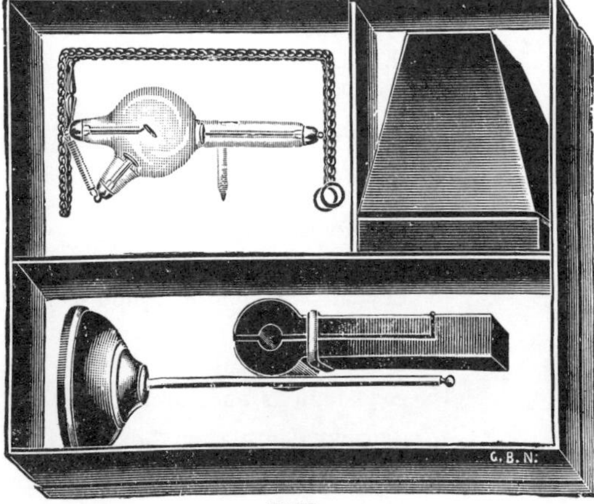

7788

Alphabetical Index.

H

I

K

L

M.

N

O

P

Q

Numerical Index.

LOCOMOTİVES A VAPEUR

TRAİNS A VAPEUR

Locomotives à vapeur avec cylindres oscillants

Locomotives à surforce, avec cylindre oscillant en cuivre et transmission à crémaillère augmentant le rendement de la machine.

Ecartement 0 = 35 mm.

160/520 Ecartement 0 = 35 mm

160/520 **Locomotive à vapeur** avec cylindre oscillant, bien vernie polychrome, avec chaudière en cuivre poli et soupape de sûreté, long. 19 cm . la pièce **frs. 6.—**

160/530 Ecartement 0 = 35 mm

160/530 **Locomotive à vapeur** avec cylindre oscillant, bien vernie polychrome, avec chaudière en cuivre poli et soupape de sûreté, longueur tender inclus 27 cm . . . . . la pièce **frs. 8.—**

160/540 Ecartement 0 = 35 mm

160/540 **Locomotive à vapeur** avec cylindre oscillant, bien vernie polychrome, avec chaudière en cuivre poli et soupape de sûreté, longueur tender inclus 30 cm . . . . . la pièce **frs. 10.—**

avec 2 cylindres oscillants en cuivre nickelé.

160/1569 et **160/1571** Ecartement 0 = 35 mm

160/1569 **Locomotive à vapeur** avec cylindres oscillants, chaudière patinée bleu acier, cylindres et armatures nickelés, long. tender inclus 29 1/2 cm, avec marche simple . . . . la pièce **frs. 15.50**

160/1571 la même, avec marche avant et arrière. . . . . la pièce **frs. 20.—**

160/1573 et **160/1575** Ecartement 0 = 35 mm

160/1573 la même, avec bielles, long. tender inclus 33 1/2 cm. . . . la pièce **frs. 22.—**

160/1575 la même, avec marche avant et arrière . . . . la pièce **frs. 25.—**

Locomotives à vapeur à cylindres fixes.

Ecartement 0 = 35 mm.

160/1580 Ecartement 0 = 35 mm

160/1580 **Locomotive à vapeur,** avec chaudière patinée bleu acier, armatures nickelées avec lampe à gaz d'alcool, **marche avant et arrière;** la machine fonctionne en avant ou arrière sans leviers de marche suivant la direction ou elle a été poussée, longueur tender inclus 35 cm . . . . la pièce **frs. 33.**—

160/1585 Ecartement 0 = 35 mm

160/1585 **Locomotive à vapeur,** avec chaudière patinée bleu acier, armatures bien nickelées avec lampe à gaz d'alcool, marchant en avant et en arrière; changement de marche à coulisse actionné automatiquement par le rail, ou par levier de la plate forme, long. tender inclus 36 cm . . la pièce **frs. 48.**—

160/1593 Ecartement 0 = 35 mm

160/1593 **Locomotive à vapeur,** avec cylindres fixes, chaudière en cuivre laqué, armatures, bien nickelées, huileur continu, lampe à gaz d'alcool, robinet d'arrêt et garde flamme (protégeant la laquè de fondre) marche avant et arrière, avec main-courante, long. tender inclus 38 cm . . . . la pièce **frs. 65.**—

160/1595 Ecartement 0 = 35 mm

160/1595 **Locomotive à vapeur, type moderne,** extra long. forme "Express", exécution supérieure, avec cylindres fixes, quinteur à glissière, robinet d'arrêt, chaudière solide en cuivre laqué, avec lampe à gaz d'alcool et installation complète; long. tender inclus 53 1/2 cm . . . . la pièce **frs. 85.**—

☛ ***Pour ces grandes locomotives à six axces il est nécessaire d'employer des rails courbes à grand rayon, désignés rails "Reforme" fournis sur demande — wagons extra-longs allant avec la locomotive ci-dessus, voir page 347.***

Locomotives à vapeur.

Ecartement I = 48 mm.

161/1569 Ecartement I = 48 mm

Locomotives à vapeur

avec cylindres oscillants, nickelés, chaudière patinée bleu acier et armatures bien nickelées

161/1569 long. tender inclus 36 ½ cm, à marche simple la pièce **frs. 22.—**

avec bielles

long. tender inclus 42 cm

161/1573 marche simple . . . . la pièce **frs. 28.50**

161/1575 „ „ avant et arrière „ „ „ **33.—**

161/1573 et 161/1575 Ecartement I = 48 mm

161/1580 Ecartement I = 48 mm

Locomotives à vapeur

avec cylindres fixes, chaudière patinée bleu acier, armatures bien nickelées

et lampe à gaz d'alcool

161/1580 **marchant avant et arrière,** la machine fonctionne avant ou arrière, sans levier de marche, suivant la poussée avec huileur central continu, long. tender inclus 45 cm, la pièce **frs. 45.—**

161/1585 **marchant avant et arrière,** changement de marche à coulisse, actionné **automatiquement** par le rail ou du levier de la plate-forme, longueur tender inclus 49 cm la pièce **frs. 65.—**

161/1585 Ecartement I = 48 mm
modèle déposée

161/1593 Ecartement I = 48 mm

161/1593 **Locomotive à vapeur,** avec cylindres **fixes,** très bien laquée, avec manette de changement de marche. Chaudière en cuivre laqué, avec **huileur à jet de vapeur, niveau d'eau et manomètre,** avec lampe à gaz d'alcool et garde flamme (protégeant la laque des armatures) avec tuyau de décharge (échappement de la vapeur par la cheminée). **Tender avec imitation charbon. Tender inclus longueur 51 cm, la pièce frs. 110.—**

Locomotives „Express" à vapeur

exécution supérieure.

161/1595

Ecartement I = 48 mm.

161/1595 Locomotive Express, type moderne, extra long, exécution supérieure cylindres fixes de précision avec tiroir distributeur tubulaire et guideur à glissière, mécanisme pour la marche avant et arrière (actionné automatiquement par les rails ou de la plateforme du mécanicien) robinet d'arrêt de la machine, graisseur central, chaudière solide en cuivre bien verni, armatures bien nickelées, niveau d'eau, sifflet forme cloche, avec lampe à gaz d'alcool, échappement de la vapeur par la cheminée, avec rail d'arrêt et un flacon d'huile à machine, longueur tender inclus 73 cm . . . . la pièce **frs. 160.—**

Pour ces grandes locomotives, il est nécessaire d'employer des rails à grand rayon, désignés "rails Réforme" donnant un diamètre plus grand (poir partie des accessoires de chemin de fer).

161/590

Locomotives modernes

bien vernies, exécution très soignée, cylindres fixes de précision avec tiroir distributeur tubulaire, guideur à glissière, mécanisme pour la **marche avant et arrière** (actionné automatiquement par les rails, ou de la plateforme arrière) robinet d'arrêt de la machine, chaudière en cuivre bien verni, armatures nickelées, niveau d'eau, sifflet forme cloche, **pompe alimentaire** (fonctionnement garanti) réservoir d'eau dans le tender, tuyau pour pompe alimentaire, **lampe à gaz d'alcool, garde-flamme amélioré** (empêchant la peinture de brûler), **nouveau graisseur central;** avec tender, 1 rail d'arrêt et 1 flacon d'huile à machine.

161/590	**Ecartement 1 = 48 mm,** long. totale, tender compris: 62 cm, haut. $17\frac{1}{2}$ cm	la pièce	**frs.**	**140.—**
162/590	„ 2 = 54 „ „ „ „ „ 68 „ „ 18	„ „	„	**200.—**
164/590	„ 4 = 75 „ „ „ „ „ 82 „ „ $20\frac{1}{2}$ „			
	avec manomètre	„ „	„	**275.—**

Wagons extra-longs allant avec les locomotives ci-dessus voir partie: Accessoires de chemins de fer.

Chemins de fer à vapeur complets, avec rails

livrés en cartons solides.

Pour les rails détachés et wagons pour compléter les trains, voir partie: „Chemins de fer mécaniques et accessoires“.

Ecartement 0 = 35 mm.

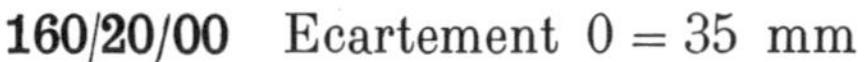

160/20/00 Ecartement 0 = 35 mm

160/30/00 Ecartement 0 = 35 mm

160/20/00 **Chemin de fer à vapeur** comprenant: 1 Locomotive-tender avec chaudière en cuivre poli, cylindre oscillant et soupape de sûreté, 1 wagon de voyageurs et 1 cercle de rails = 4 rails courbes, livrés en carton; locomotive avec tender 19 cm, longueur du wagon $8\frac{1}{2}$ cm, longueur du train 30 cm . . . . .la pièce **frs. 10.—**

160/30/00 **Chemin de fer à vapeur** comprenant: 1 forte locomotive avec chaudière en cuivre poli, cylindre oscillants, soupape de sûreté, 1 tender, 1 wagon de voyageurs et 1 cercle de rails = 4 courbes livrés en carton, locomotive 16 cm, longueur du tender $8\frac{1}{2}$ cm, longueur du wagon 12 cm, longueur du train $40\frac{1}{2}$ cm . . . . .la pièce **frs. 12.50**

160/32/0 Ecartement 0 = 35 mm

160/32/0 **Chemin de fer à vapeur,** comprenant: 1 forte locomotive avec chaudière en cuivre poli, soupape de sûreté, 1 tender, 2 wagons de voyageurs et 1 ovale de rails = 6 rails (4 courbes et 2 droits), livrés en carton solide, longueur de la locomotive $16\frac{1}{2}$ cm, longueur du tender $8\frac{1}{2}$ cm, longueur du wagon 12 cm, longueur du train 56 cm . . . . .la pièce **frs. 15**.—

160/40/0 Ecartement 0 = 35 mm

160/40/0 **Chemin de fer à vapeur,** comprenant: 1 forte locomotive, avec chaudière en cuivre poli et soupape de sûreté, 1 tender, 2 wagons de voyageurs, 1 wagon-poste, 1 ovale de rails = 10 rails (6 courbes et 4 droits) emballés en carton, longueur de la locomotive $19\frac{1}{2}$ cm, longueur du tender $8\frac{1}{2}$ cm, longueur des wagons de voyageurs 14 cm, longueur du wagon-poste 14 cm, longueur du train 74 cm . . . . la pièce **frs. 20.—**

Chemins de fer à vapeur avec rails

soigneusement exécutés.

Ecartement 0 = 35 mm.

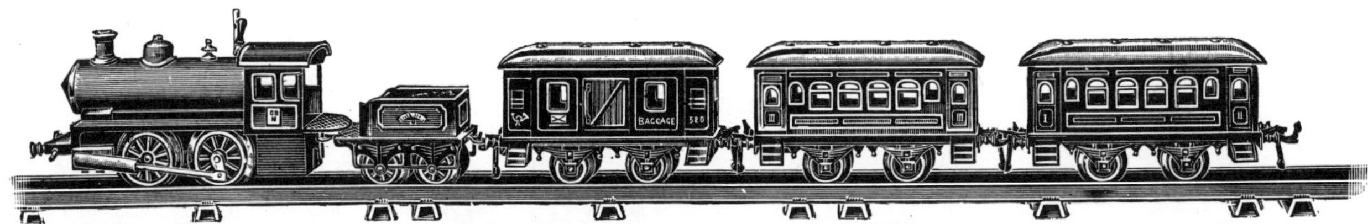

160/169/0 Ecartement 0 = 35 mm

160/169/0 comprenant: une forte locomotive à vapeur, avec **2 cylindres oscillants** en cuivre, tender, 2 wagons de voyageurs et un wagon-poste, avec un ovale de rail = 6 courbes et 4 droits, emballés dans un élégant carton, longueur de la locomotive la 19 cm, longueur du tender 8 ½ cm, longueur du wagon de voyageurs 15 ½ cm, longueur du wagon poste 15 ½ cm, longueur du train 85 cm . . . . la pièce **frs. 27.50**

160/173/0 Ecartement 0 = 35 mm

160/173/0 comprenant: une forte locomotive à vapeur, avec **2 cylindres oscillants** en cuivre, tender, 2 wagons de voyageurs et un wagon poste, avec un ovale de rails = 6 courbes et 6 droits, emballés dans un élégant carton, longueur de la locomotive 20 cm, longueur du tender 11 cm, longueur du wagon de voyageurs 15 ½ cm, longueur du wagon-poste 15 ½ cm, longueur du train 90 cm . . . . la pièce **frs. 35.—**

160/180/0 Ecartement 0 = 35 mm

160/180/0 comprenant: une très forte locomotive à vapeur, avec **2 cylindres fixes** en cuivre, mécanisme **pour marche avant et arrière,** tender, 2 wagons de voyageurs, 1 fourgon, et un ovale de rails = 6 courbes et 4 droits et une brochure „Le petit ingénieur", emballé en élégant carton, longueur de la locomotive 21 ½ cm, long. du tender 12 cm, longueur du wagon de voyageurs 15 cm, longueur du wagon-poste 15 cm, longueur du train 92 cm . . . . la pièce **frs. 51.—**

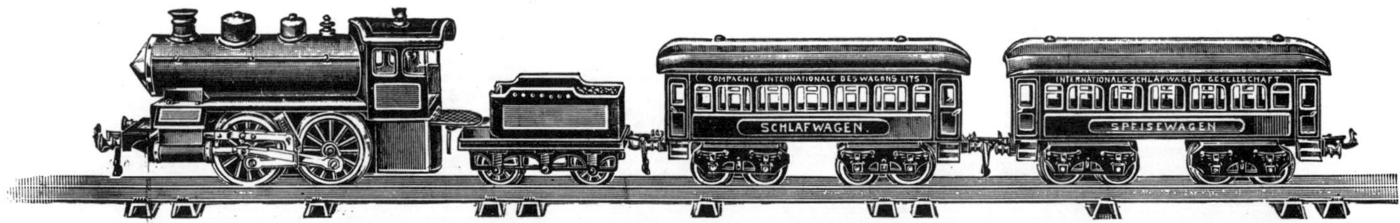

160/185/0 Ecartement 0 = 35 mm

160/185/0 comprenant: une très forte locomotive, avec **2 cylindres fixes de précision et levier à coulisse,** marche avant et arrière, avec **mécanisme automatique** pour changement de marche par les rails, graisseur central, tender, 2 longs wagons de voyageurs, avec 1 ovale de rails = 6 droits et 4 courbes, rail d'arrêt inclus et une brochure „Le petit ingénieur", emballé en élégant carton, longueur de la locomotive 22 ½ cm, longueur du tender 11 cm, longueur des wagons 21 ½ cm, longueur du train 83 cm . . . la pièce **frs. 66.—**

Chemins de fer à vapeur avec rails

soigneusement exécutés.

Ecartement I = 48 mm.

161/169/0 Ecartement I = 48 mm

161/169/0 comprenant: une forte locomotive avec **2 cylindres oscillants** en cuivre, tender, 2 wagons de voyageurs et 1 ovale de rails = 8 courbes et 2 droits livrés dans un carton élégant; longueur de la locomotive 22 cm, longueur du tender 14 cm, longueur des wagons de voyageurs 13 cm, longueur du train 69 cm, la pièce **frs. 36.—**

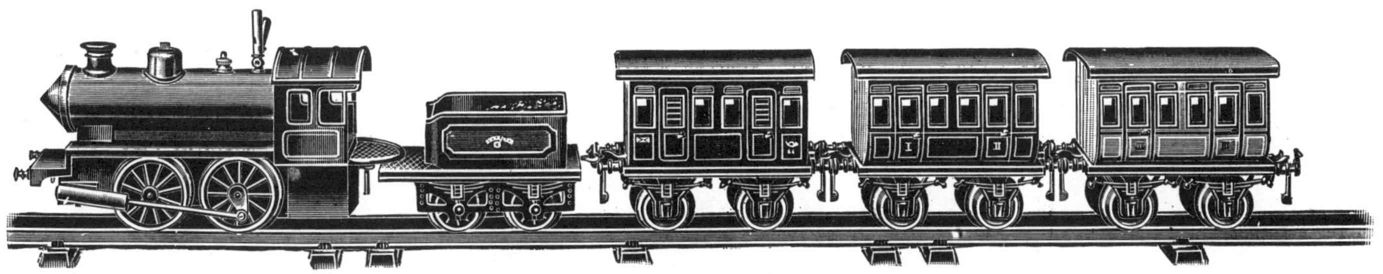

161/170/0 Ecartement I = 48 mm

161/170/0 comprenant: une forte locomotive à vapeur avec **2 cylindres oscillants** en cuivre, tender, 2 wagons de voyageurs, 1 wagon-poste, 1 ovale de rails = 8 courbes et 4 droits, emballés dans un carton élégant, longueur de la locomotive 22 cm, longueur du tender 14 cm, longueur des wagons 15 cm, longueur du train 91 cm la pièce **frs. 42.—**

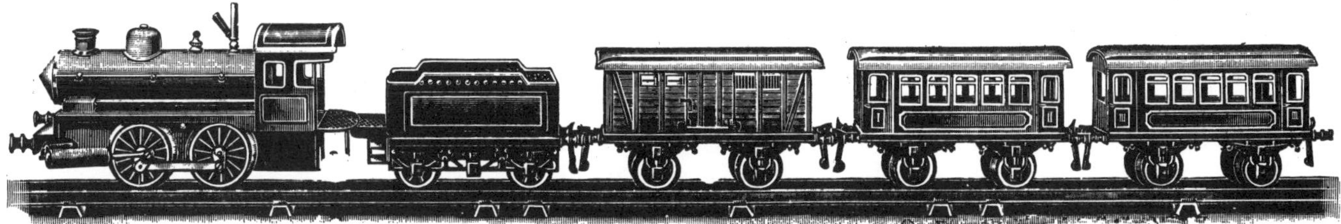

161/173/0 Ecartement I = 48 mm

161/173/0 comprenant: une forte locomotive avec **2 cylindres oscillants** en cuivre, tender, 2 wagons de voyageurs, 1 wagon-bagages et un ovale de rails = 8 courbes et 4 droits (rail d'arrêt compris), emballés dans un carton élégant; longueur de la locomotive 25 cm, longueur du tender 17 ½ cm, longueur des wagons 19 cm, longueur du train 110 cm . . . . la pièce **frs. 49.—**

161/180/0 Ecartement I = 48 mm

161/180/0 comprenant: **une très forte locomotive à vapeur avec 2 cylindres fixes, à marche avant et arrière,** tender, 2 wagons de voyageurs, 1 fourgon, 1 ovale de rails = 8 courbes et 4 droits, emballés dans un carton élégant, longueur de la locomotive 27, longueur du tender 16 cm, longueur des wagons 21 cm, longueur du train 118 cm . . . . la pièce **frs. 68.—**

Chemins de fer à vapeur avec rails,

très soignés.

Ecartement I = 48 mm.

161/185/0 Ecartement I = 48 mm

161/185/0 comprenant: une locomotive avec **2 cylindres fixes de précision, 1 levier à coulisse, marche avant et arrière,** avec changement de marche automatique par le rail, graisseur central, 1 tender, 2 wagons (1 wagon-lits et 1 wagon-restaurant), 1 fourgon, ovale de rails = 8 courbes et 6 droits rail d'arrêt inclus, 2 soufflets et une brochure „Le petit ingénieur", emballés dans un carton élégant, longueur de la locomotive 30 cm, longueur du tender 17½ cm, longueur des wagons 23½ cm, longueur du train 130 cm . . . . la pièce **frs. 108.—**

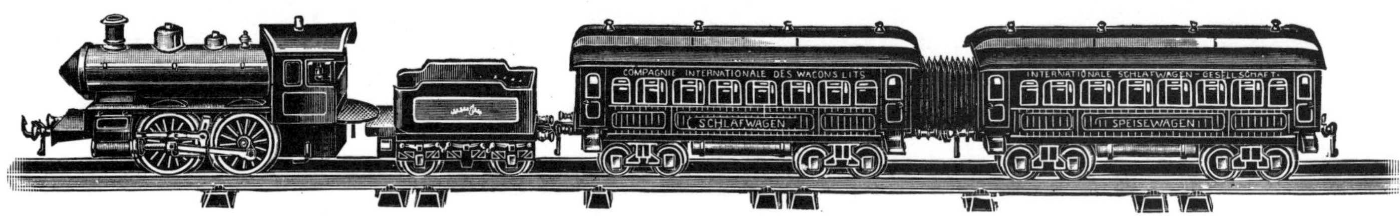

161/186/0 Ecartement I = 48 mm

161/186/0 comprenant: une locomotive avec **2 cylindres fixes de précision, 1 levier à coulisse, marche avant et arrière,** avec changement de marche automatique par le rail, graisseur central, 1 tender, 2 wagons express (1 wagon-lits et 1 wagon-restaurant, complètement agencés), 2 soufflets, 1 ovale de rails = 8 courbes et 4 droits, rail d'arrêt inclus, et une brochure „Le petit ingénieur," emballés dans un carton élégant, longueur de la locomotive 30 cm, longueur du tender 17½ cm, longueur des wagons 35½ cm, longueur du train 124 cm . . . . la pièce **frs. 120.—**

161/90/0 Ecartement I = 48 mm

161/90/0 Chemin de fer à vapeur sur rails, comprenant: 1 locomotive moderne, avec cylindres fixes de précision, tiroirs distributeurs tubulaires et guideur à glissière, **marche avant et arrière,** avec changement de marche automatique par le rail, nouveau graisseur central, tender, 2 wagons express (1 wagon-restaurant, 1 wagon-lits, complètement agencés), soufflet, 1 ovale de rails = 8 courbes et 6 droits, rail d'arrêt niclus, et une brochure „Le petit ingénieur", emballés dans un carton élégant, longueur de la locomotive 37 cm, longueur du tender 24 cm, longueur des wagons 35 cm, longueur du train 137 cm . . . . la pièce **frs. 195.—**

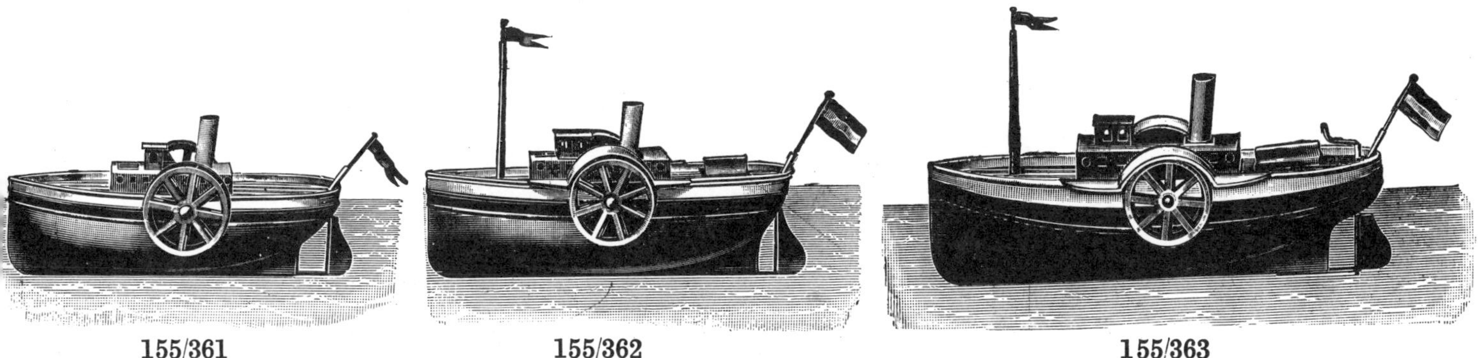

155/361 155/362 155/363

515/361	**Bateaux** (à aubes) **avec ressort solide,** bien verni, longueur 19 cm	la pièce **frs.**	**4.—**
,, /362	,, ,, ,, ,, ,, ,, ,, ,, ,, 22 ,,	,, ,, ,,	**6.—**
,, /363	,, ,, ,, ,, ,, ,, ,, ,, ,, 26 ,,	,, ,, ,,	**9.—**

14299/1

14299/2 et 3

Autobus

bien vernis polychrome, bon mécanisme, essieu de devant mobile **avec** inscription

14299/1	longueur 18 cm, hauteur 11 ½ cm, avec roues en fer blanc	la pièce **frs.**	**2.75**
,, **/2**	,, 25 ,, ,, 14 ,, ,, ,, ,, ,, ,,	,, ,, ,,	**6.—**
,, **/3**	,, 29 ,, ,, 15 ,, ,, ,,caoutchoutées	,, ,, ,,	**9.—**

sans inscription

14299/1 ½	longueur 18 cm, hauteur 11 ½ cm, avec roues en fer blanc	la pièce **frs.**	**2.75**
,, **/2 ½**	,, 25 ,, ,, 14 ,, ,, ,, ,, ,, ,,	,, ,, ,,	**6.—**
,, **/3 ½**	,, 29 ,, ,, 15 ,, ,, ,, caoutchoutées	,, ,, ,,	**9.—**

Chemins de fer mécaniques.

Exécution nouvelle et perfectionnée avec mécanismes solides, très puissants, vernis polychrome, livrés en cartons solides.

169/250/00 Ecartement 00 = 28 mm

169/250/00 Comprenant: locomotive avec **arrêt,** tender, 1 wagon avec fenêtres à jour et cercle de rails oxydés = 5 rails courbes, **écartement 28 mm,** longueur du train 28 cm . . la pièce **frs. 2.75**

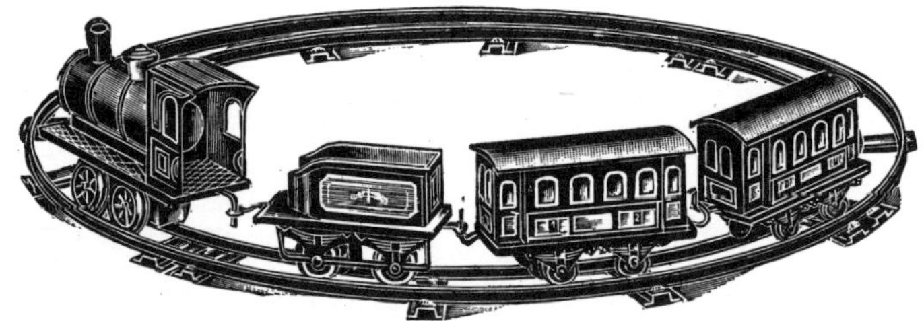

169/253/00 Ecartement 00 = 28 mm

169/253/00 Comprenant: locomotive avec **arrêt,** tender, 2 Wagons et cercle de rails = 4 rails courbes, **écartement 28 mm,** longueur du train 46 cm . . . . la pièce **frs. 3.50**

170/254/00 Ecartement 0 = 35 mm

170/254/00 Comprenant: 1 locomotive avec **frein** (automatique), tender imitation charbon, 1 wagon de voyageurs et un cercle de rails . . . . la pièce **frs. 5.—**

Locomotive 13 cm long.	Tender $8^1/_2$ cm long.	Long. du wagon 10 cm	Long. du train 36 cm	Jeu de rails: 1 cercle = 4 rails courbes (rail d'arrêt compris)

Chemins de fer mécaniques.

Ecartement 0 = 35 mm.

170/256/0½ Ecartement 0 = 35 mm

170/256/0½ comprenant: Locomotive avec frein **automatique,** tender avec imitation charbon avec 2 wagons de voyageurs et un ovale de rails . . . . la pièce **frs. 6.—**

Locomotive long. 13 cm	Tender long. 8½ cm	long. des wagons 10 cm	long. du train 49 cm	Jeu de rails: 1 ovale = 4 courbes et 2 demi-droits (rail d'arrêt compris)

170/260/00 Ecartement 0 = 35 mm

170/260/00 comprenant: Locomotive avec dôme et frein **automatique,** tender imitation charbon avec 2 wagons de voyageurs et cercle de rails . . . . la pièce **frs. 7.25**

Locomotive long. 14½ cm	Tender long. 8½ cm	long. des wagons 10 cm	long. du train 51 cm	Jeu de rails: 1 cercle = 4 courbes (rail d'arrêt compris)

170/257/0 Ecartement 0 = 35 mm

170/257/0 comprenant: Locomotive avec frein et **dispositif pour marche avant et arrière,** tender avec imitation charbon avec 2 wagons de voyageurs et un ovale de rails . . . . la pièce **frs. 8.—**

Locomotive long. 13 cm	Tender long. 8½ cm	long. des wagons 10 cm	long. du train 49 cm	Jeu de rails: 1 ovale = 4 courbes et 2 droits (rail d'arrêt compris)

170/264/0 Ecartement 0 = 35 mm

170/264/0 comprenant: Locomotive avec dôme et frein **automatique,** tender avec imitation charbon, avec 2 wagons de voyageurs et 1 wagon-poste, avec 1 ovale de rails . . . . la pièce **frs. 11.—**

Locomotive long. 14½ cm	Tender long. 8½ cm	long. des wagons 10 cm	long. du train 64 cm	Jeu de rails: 1 ovale = 6 courbes et 4 droits (rail d'arrêt compris)

Chemins de fer mécaniques

Ecartement 0 = 35 mm

170/263/0 Ecartement 0 = 35 mm

170/263/0 comprenant: Locomotive **avec frein, dispositif pour marche avant et arrière,** tender avec imitation charbon, 2 wagons de voyageurs et ovale de rails . . . . compl. la pièce **frs. 11.—**

Locomotive	Tender	Long. des wagons	Long. du train	Jeu de rails: 1 ovale = 6 rails courbes
14½ cm long.	8½ cm long.	10 cm	51 cm	et 2 droits (y compris le rail d'arrêt)

170/166/0 Ecartement 0 = 35 mm

170/166/0 comprenant: Locomotive avec coupe-vent, **frein automatique,** bielles, tender avec intérieur imitation charbon, 2 wagons de voyageurs, 1 fourgon, ovale de rails . . . . compl. la pièce **frs. 14.—**

Locomotive	Tender	Long. des wagons	Long. du train	Jeu de rails: 1 ovale = 6 rails courbes
18 cm long.	8½ cm long.	12 cm	74 cm	et 4 droits (y compris le rail d'arrêt)

170/167/0 Ecartement 0 = 35 mm

170/167/0 comprenant: Locomotive **avec coupe-vent, frein automatique,** bielles, **marche avant et arrière,** changement de marche automatique par le rail, tender avec intérieur imitation charbon, 2 wagons de voyageurs, ovale de rails. . . . . compl. la pièce **frs. 17.—**

Locomotive	Tender	Long. des wagons	Long. du train	Jeu de rails: 1 ovale = 6 rails courbes et 4 droits (y compris le rail pour changement automatique)
18 cm long.	8½ cm long.	12 cm	58 cm	

170/173/0 Ecartement 0 = 35 mm

170/173/0 comprenant: Locomotive **avec coupe-vent, frein automatique,** bielles et mains-courantes, **marche avant et arrière,** changement de marche **automatique** par le rail, tender avec intérieur imitation charbon, 2 grands wagons de voyageurs, ovale de rails . . . . compl. la pièce **frs. 20.—**

Locomotive	Tender	Long. des wagons	Long. du train	Jeu de rails: 1 ovale = 6 rails courbes et 4 droits (y compris le rail pour changement automatique)
18 cm long.	10 cm long.	13½ cm	64 cm	

Chemins de fer mécaniques.

Ecartement 0 = 35 mm

170/175/0 Ecartement 0 = 35 mm

170/175/0 comprenant: Locomotive avec coupe-vent, frein automatique, **marche avant et arrière,** changement de marche **automatique par le rail,** tender avec intérieur imitation charbon, 2 grands wagons de voyageurs, 1 ovale de rails et 1 brochure "Le petit ingénieur des chemins de fer" . . . . . compl. la pièce **frs. 25.—**

Locomotive	Tender	Long. des wagons	Long. du train	Jeu de rails: 1 ovale = 6 rails courbes et 4 droits
22 cm long.	12 cm long.	13½ cm	73 cm	(rail pour changement automatique compris)

170/177/0 Ecartement 0 = 35 mm

170/177/0 comprenant: Locomotive avec coupe-vent, frein automatique, **marche avant et arrière, changement de marche automatique par le rail,** tender avec intérieur imitation charbon, 2 grands wagons de voyageurs, 1 grand fourgon, un ovale de rails extra grand et 1 brochure "Le petit ingénieur des chemins de fer", ... compl. la pièce **frs. 29.—**

Locomotive	Tender	Long. des wagons	Long. du train	Jeu de rails: 1 ovale = 6 rails courbes et 6 droits
22 cm long.	12 cm long.	13½ cm	86 cm	(rail pour changement automatique compris)

170/179/0 Ecartement 0 = 35 mm

170/179/0 comprenant: Locomotive avec coupe-vent, frein automatique, guideur à glissière, **marche avant et arrière, changement de marche automatique par le rail,** tender avec intérieur imitation charbon, 2 wagons de voyageurs extra grands, portes s'ouvrant, 1 ovale de rails et 1 brochure "Le petit ingénieur des chemins de fer" . . . . compl. la pièce **frs. 38.—**

Locomotive	Tender	Long. des wagons	Long. du train	Jeu de rails: 1 ovale = 6 rails courbes et 4 droits
22 cm long.	12 cm long.	17 cm	77 cm	(rail d'arrêt compris)

170/181/0 Ecartement 0 = 35 mm

170/181/0 comprenant: Locomotive avec coupe-vent, frein automatique, **guideur à glissière marche avant et arrière, changement de marche automatique par le rail,** tender avec intérieur imitation charbon, 2 longs wagons d'express et 1 fourgon-poste avec portes s'ouvrant, 1 ovale de rails extra-grand et 1 brochure "Le petit ingénieur des chemins de fer" . . . . compl. la pièce **frs. 40.—**

Locomotive	Tender	Long. des wagons	Long. du train	Jeu de rails: 1 ovale = 6 rails courbes et 6 droits
22 cm long.	12 cm long.	17 cm	96 cm	(rail pour changement automatique compris)

Trains-Express mécaniques

Ecartement 0 = 35 mm

170/191/0 Ecartement 0 = 35 mm

170/191/0 comprenant: Locomotive "Express", montée sur 4 axes, avec bielles, frein **automatique**, marche avant et arrière, changement de marche **automatique** par le rail, tender, 2 grands wagons de voyageurs et 1 ovale de rails. . . . . la pièce **frs. 24.—**

Locomotive	Tender	long. des wagons	long. du train	Jeu de rails : 1 ovale = 6 rails courbes et 4 droits
long. 18 ½ cm	long. 11 cm	13½ cm	69 cm	(rail pour changement automatique compris)

170/193/0 Ecartement 0 = 35 mm

170/193/0 comprenant: Locomotive „Express", montée sur 4 axes, avec bielles, frein **automatique**, mécanisme solide, marche avant et arrière, changement de marche automatique par le rail, avec tender, 2 grands wagons d'express (wagon-lits et wagon-restaurant non garnis), 1 ovale de rails et 1 brochure "Le petit ingénieur des chemins de fer" . . . . la pièce **frs. 33.—**

Locomotive	Tender	long. des wagons	long. du train	Jen de rails : 1 ovale = 6 rails courbes et 4 droits
long. 21 cm	long. 12 cm	22 cm	87 cm	(rail pour changement automatique compris)

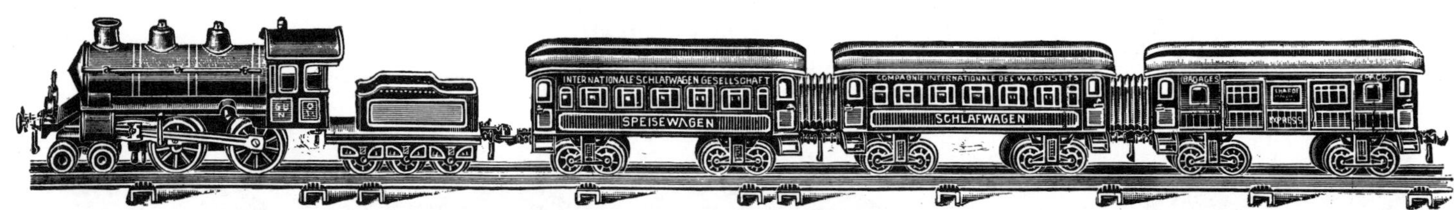

170/395/0 Ecartement 0 = 35 mm

170/395/0 comprenant: très belle locomotive "Express" avec frein automatique, bien vernie à la main, mécanisme de précision, **marche avant et arrière,** changement de marche **automatique** par le rail, tender, 3 grands wagons d'Express (wagon-lits, wagons-restaurant et wagon-bagage avec aménagement à l'intérieur), avec soufflets; très grand ovale de rails, exécution soignée . . . . la pièce **frs. 75.—**

Locomotive	Tender	long. des wagons	long. du train	Jeu de rails : 1 ovale = 12 rails "Réform" courbes et
22 cm long.	long. 12 cm	22 cm	112 cm	4 droits (rail pour changement automatique compris)

Trains Express très bien exécuté, No. 170/397/0, voir **page 148.**

Chemins de fer mécaniques

Ecartement I = 48 mm

171/254/00 Ecartement I = 48 mm

171/254/00 comprenant: Locomotive avec coupe-vent et frein automatique, tender, 1 wagon et un cercle de rails, la pièce **frs. 15.—**

Locomotive long. 20 cm	Tender long. 12½ cm	Long. des wagons 13 cm	Long. du train 51 cm	Jeu de rails: 1 cercle = 6 rails courbes (rail d'arrêt compris)

171/256/00 Ecartement I = 48 mm

171/256/00 comprenant: Locomotive avec coupe-vent, frein automatique et bielles, tender intérieur imitation charbon, avec 1 wagon de voyageurs, un cercle de rails . . . . la pièce **frs. 18.—**

Locomotive long. 20 cm	Tender long. 12½ cm	Long. des wagons 13 cm	Long. du train 51 cm	Jeu de rails: 1 cercle = 8 rails courbes (rail d'arrêt compris)

171/258/0 Ecartement I = 48 mm

171/258/0 comprenant: Locomotive avec coupe-vent, frein automatique et bielles, tender avec imitation charbon, avec 2 wagons de voyageurs, 1 ovale de rails . . . . la pièce **frs. 22.—**

Locomotive long. 20 cm	Tender long. 13 cm	Long. des wagons 15 cm	Long. du train 72 cm	Jeu de rails: 1 ovale = 8 courbes et 2 droits (rail d'arrêt compris)

171/261/0 Ecartement I = 48 mm

171/261/0 comprenant: Belle locomotive avec coupe-vent. frein automatique, marche avant et arrière, changement de marche automatique par le rail, avec bielles, tender intérieur imitation charbon, avec 2 wagons de voyageurs et un grand ovale de rails . . . . la pièce **frs. 24.—**

Locomotive long. 20½ cm	Tender long. 12½ cm	Long. des wagons 13 cm	Long. du train 68 cm	Jeu de rails: 1 ovale = 6 rails courbes et 2 droits (rail pour changement de marche compris)

Chemins de fer mécaniques

Ecartement I = 48 mm

171/263/0 Ecartement I = 48 mm

171/263/0 comprenant: 1 Belle locomotive avec coupe-vent, frein automatique, **marche avant et arrière, changement de marche automatique par le rail,** avec bielles, tender intérieur imitation charbon avec 2 grands wagons de voyageurs et un grand ovale de rails . . . . la pièce **frs. 26.—**

Locomotive long. $20^1/_2$ cm	Tender long. 14 cm	Long. des wagons $19^1/_2$ cm	Long. du train 82 cm	Jeu de rails: 1 ovale = 8 rails courbes et 2 droits (rail pour changement automatique compris)

171/166/0 Ecartement I = 48 mm

171/166/0 comprenant: Locomotive **avec frein automatique** et bielles, tender, 2 wagons de voyageurs, 1 wagon-poste et 1 ovale de rails . . . . compl. la pièce **frs. 30.—**

Locomotive long. $21^1/_2$ cm	Tender long. 14 cm	Long. des wagons 15 cm	Long. du train 90 cm	Jeu de rails: 1 ovale = 8 rails courbes et 2 droits (rail d'arrêt compris)

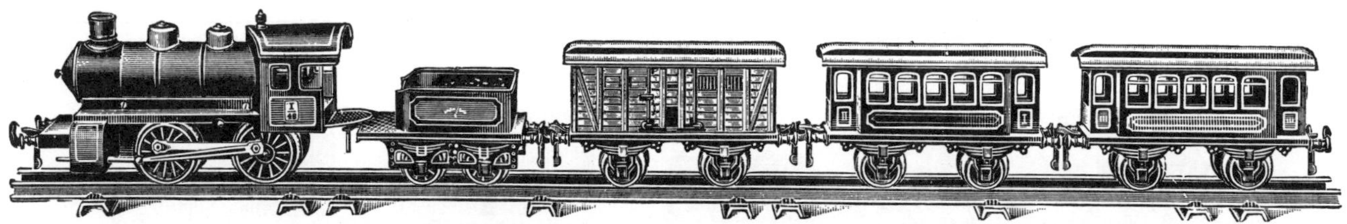

171/267/0 Ecartement I = 48 mm

171/267/0 comprenant: Locomotive avec coupe-vent, frein automatique, **marche avant et arrière, changement de marche automatique par le rail,** avec bielles, tender, intérieur imitation charbon, avec 3 grands wagons et un grand ovale de rails. . . . . la pièce **frs. 40.–**

Locomotive long. 23 cm	Tender long. 14 cm	Long. des wagons $19^1/_2$ cm	Long. du train 108 cm	Jeu de rails: 1 ovale = 8 rails courbes et 4 droits (rail pour changement automatique compris)

Chemins de fer mécaniques

Ecartement I = 48 mm

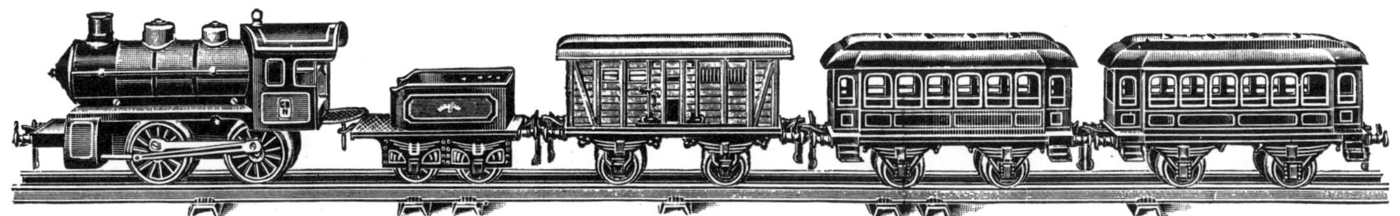

171/275/0 Ecartement I = 48 mm

171/275/0 comprenant: Belle locomotive avec coupe-vent, frein automatique, **marche avant et arrière, changement de marche automatique par le rail,** avec bielles, tender, intérieur imitation charbon, 3 grands wagons et un grand ovale de rails et 1 brochure "Le petit ingénieur des chemins de fer" . . . . la pièce **frs. 50.**—

Locomotive	Tender	Long. des wagons	Long. du train	Jeu de rails: 1 ovale = 8 rails courbes et 4 droits
long. 23 cm	long. 14 cm	21½ cm	112½ cm	(rail pour changement de marche compris)

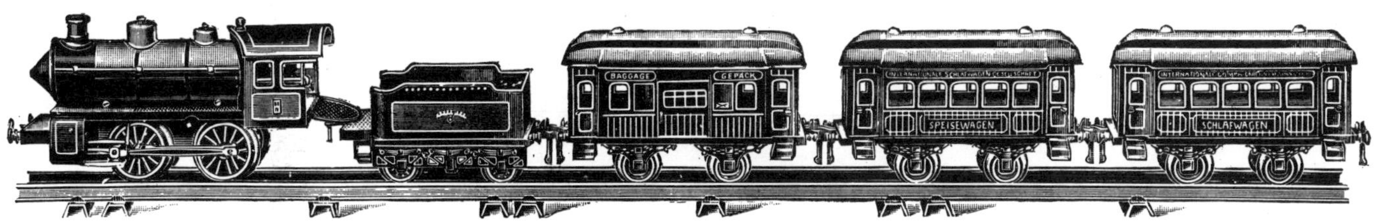

171/277/0 Ecartement I = 48 mm

171/277/0 comprenant: Belle locomotive avec coupe-vent, frein automatique, bielles et mains courantes, guideur à glissière, **marche avant et arrière, changement de marche automatique par le rail,** tender avec intérieur imitation charbon, 3 grands wagons, grand jeu de rails ovale et 1 brochure "Le petit ingénieur des chemins de fer" . . . . compl. la pièce **frs. 66.**—

Locomotive	Tender	Long. des wagons	Long. du train	Jeu de rails: 1 ovale = 8 rails courbes et 6 droits
long. 27½ cm	long. 17½ cm	24 cm	129 cm	(rails pour changement automatique compris)

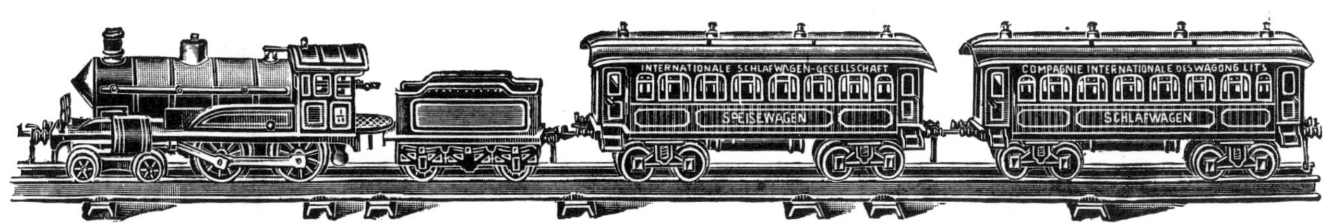

171/293/0 Ecartement I = 48 mm

171/293/0 comprenant: Belle locomotive montée sur 4 axes avec boggie, frein automatique, **marche avant et arrière, changement de marche automatique par le rail,** bielles et mains courantes, tender avec intérieur imitation charbon, 2 grands wagons d'express (1 wagon-restaurant et 1 wagon-lits non garnis) 1 ovale de rails et 1 brochure "Le petit ingénieur des chemins de fer" . . . . compl. la pièce **frs. 83.**—

Locomotive	Tender	Long. des wagons	Long. du train	Jeu de rails: 1 ovale = 8 rails courbes et 4 droits
long. 30½ cm	long. 16 cm	34½ cm	125 cm	(rail pour changement automatique compris)

Locomotives "express", mécaniques supérieures, avec tender.

Ecartement 0 = 35 mm

170/1591

170/1593

170/1591	**Locomotive "Express"**, montée sur 4 axes avec boggie, **frein automatique, marche avant et arrière, changement de marche automatique par le rail,** longueur 19½ cm, tender, longueur 12 cm	la pièce frs.	16.—
6946/0	**Rail pour changement automatique**	„ „ „	1.20
170/1593	**Locomotive "Express"**, montée sur 4 axes avec boggie, **marche avant et arrière, avec changement de marche et frein automatique par le rail,** longueur 21 cm, tender, longueur 12 cm	„ „ „	18.50
6941/0	**Rail pour changement automatique**	„ „ „	1.50

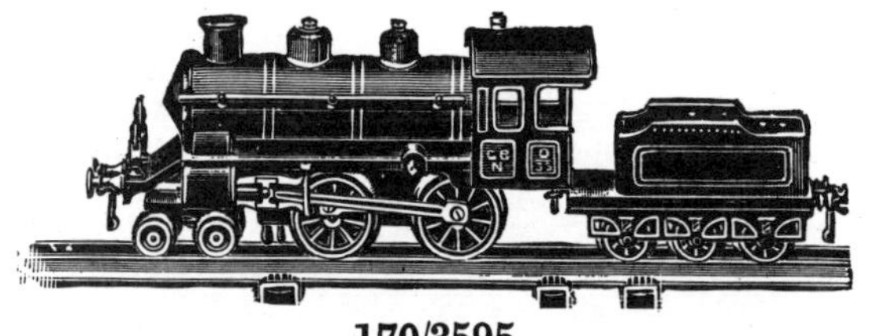

170/3595

170/3595	**Locomotive "Express"** avec tender, bien vernie à la main, avec mécanisme solide, montée sur 4 axes, avec boggie, **marche avant et arrière, changement de marche et frein automatiques par le rail,** très bien exécutée, longueur 34½ cm	la pièce frs.	38.—
6941/0	**Rail pour changement automatique**	„ „ „	1.50

Voir pour belle locomotive „Express" No. 170/3597. Ecartement 0 = 35 mm pag. 152.

Locomotives mécaniques avec tender

bien vernies polychrome.

Ecartement I = 48 mm

171/2554

171/2556

171/2554	**Locomotive** avec coupe-vent, **et frein automatique,** longueur 20 cm	la pièce frs.	8.50
„ /2654	**Tender** allant avec, longueur 12½ cm	„ „ „	8.50
171/2556	**Locomotive** avec coupe-vent, **frein automatique** et bielles, longueur 20 cm	„ „ „	10.45
„ /2656	**Tender** allant avec, intérieur imitation charbon, longueur 12½ cm	„ „ „	10.45

Locomotives mécaniques avec tender

bien vernies polychrome

Ecartement I = 48 mm

171/2563 et 2663

171/1566 et 1666

171/2563	**Locomotive** avec coupe-vent, **frein automatique** et bielles, **marche avant et arrière, changement de marche automatique par le rail,** longueur 20 ½ cm	la pièce	**frs.** 12.—
„ /2663	**Tender** allant avec, intérieur imitation charbon, longueur 12 cm	„ „	„ 1.50
6946/1	**Rail pour changement automatique**	„ „	„ 1.60
171/1566	**Locomotive** avec **frein automatique** et bielles, longueur 22 cm	„ „	„ 10.—
„ /1666	**Tender** allant avec, longueur 12 ½ cm	„ „	„ 1.75

171/2576 et 2667

171/2575 et 2675

171/2567	**Locomotive** avec coupe-vent, **frein automatique,** et bielles, **marche avant et arrière, changement de marche automatique par le rail,** longueur 25 cm	la pièce	**frs.** 25.—
„ /2667	**Tender** allant avec, intérieur imitation charbon, longueur 13 cm	„ „	„ 25.—
6946/1	**Rail pour changement automatique**	„ „	„ 1.60
171/2575	**Locomotive** avec coupe-vent, **frein automatique,** bielles et mains courantes, **marche avant et arrière, changement de marche automatique par le rail,** longueur 25 cm	„ „	„ 28.—
„ /2675	**Tender** allant avec, intérieur imitation charbon, longueur 14 cm	„ „	„ 28.—
6941/1	**Rail pour changement automatique**	„ „	„ 2.40

171/2577 et 2677

171/2593

171/2577	**Locomotive** bien exécutée, avec coupe-vent, **frein automatique** et bielles, **guideur à glissière marche avant et arrière, changement de marche automatique par le rail,** longueur 27 ½ cm	la pièce	**frs.** 39.10
„ /2677	**Tender** allant avec, longueur 17 ½ cm	„ „	„ 39.10
6941/1	**Rail pour changement automatique**	„ „	„ 2.40
171/2593	**Locomotive "Express",** montée sur 4 axes avec boggie, coupe-vent, **frein automatique, marche avant et arrière, changement de marche automatique par le rail,** très belle exécution, longueur 31 cm, **Tender** allant avec, longueur 16 cm	„ „	„ 46.—
6941/1	**Rail pour changement automatique**	„ „	„ 2.40

Locomotives "Express" mécaniques.

Ecartement 0 = 35 mm | **Ecartement I = 48 mm**

171/3595

Locomotive "Express"

Montée sur 4 axes, **avec freins, changement de vitesse, marche avant et arrière, changement de marche automatique par le rail, très bien vernie à la main.**

171/3595 **Ecartement I = 48 mm,** longueur 53 cm tender inclus . . . . la pièce **frs. 75.—**
6941/1 **Rail pour changement automatique** . . . . „ „ „ **2.40**

Locomotive "Express"

type moderne

Montée sur 6 axes, avec freins, **changement de vitesse, marche avant et arrière, changement de marche automatique par le rail, exécution supérieure.**

170/3597 **Ecartement 0 = 35 mm,** longueur 49 cm tender inclus . . . . la pièce **frs. 67.—**
6941/0 **Rail pour changement automatique** . . . . „ „ „ **1.50**
171/3597 **Ecartement I = 48 mm,** longueur 60 cm tender inclus . . . . „ „ „ **140.—**
6941/1 **Rail pour changement automatique** . . . . „ „ „ **2.40**

Funiculaire (chemin de fer à crémaillère)

très original et avantageux.

14460

14460 Funiculaire, comprenant: 1 locomotive avec ressort très solide, 1 wagon, 1 ovale de rails, avec 6 rails ronds et 4 droits, ces derniers à crémaillère, différentes tailles de piliers, construction très solide, fonctionnement irréprochable . . . . complet la pièce **frs. 28.—**

Funiculaire électrique, voir la section "Articles électriques".

Chemin de fer mécanique avec accessoires
disposition avantageuse en boîtes.

10444 **Train complet,** comprenant: 1 locomotive, **écartement 0 = 35 mm** avec ressort et frein, 1 tender, 2 wagons de voyageurs, 1 fourgon, 1 ovale de rails = 6 courbes et 4 droits, 1 gare, 1 tunnel, 1 barrière, 1 sémaphore, 1 lampe à arc, 1 maisonnette de garde-barrière, 1 sonnerie, Carton: longueur 65 cm, largeur 62 cm, par carton **frs. 25.—**

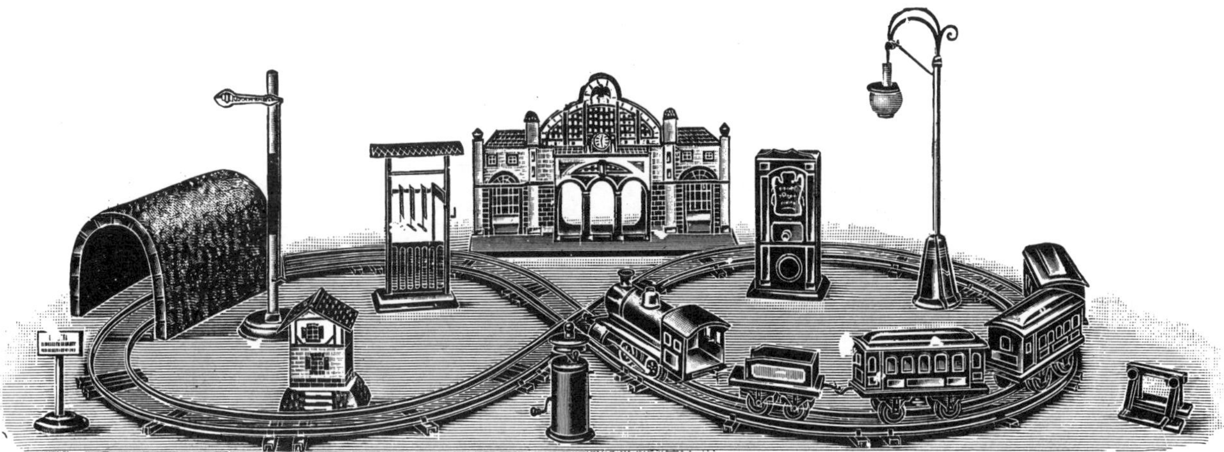

10445 **Train complet,** comprenant: 1 locomotive à ressort, **écartement 0 = 35 mm** avec frein, 1 tender, 2 wagons de voyageurs, 1 fourgon, 1 croisement, 10 rails courbes, 1 gare, 1 tunnel, 1 indicateur de directions, 1 distributeur automatique de billets, 1 buttoir, 1 maisonnette de garde, 1 sémaphore, 1 tableau indicateur, 1 sonnerie, 1 lampe à arc, Carton: longueur 79 cm, largeur 62 cm . . . . par carton **frs. 36.—**

10446 **Train complet,** comprenant: 1 locomotive, **écartement 0 = 35 mm,** avec ressort, frein et changement de marche, 1 tender, 2 wagons de voyageurs, 1 jeu de rails, comprenant 6 rails courbes, 5 droits, 2 aiguilles, 1 plaque tournante, 1 buttoir, 1 gare, 1 indicateur de directions, 1 sémaphore, 1 lampe à arc, 1 sonnerie, 1 tunnel, 1 distributeur automatique de billets, un tableau indicateur, Carton: longueur 80 cm, largeur 65 cm, par carton **frs. 45.—**

Chemin de fer mécanique avec accessoires

disposition avantageuse en boites.

10441 **Train complet,** comprenant: une locomotive à ressort, **écartement 00 = 28 mm,** 1 tender, 2 wagons de voyageurs, 1 cercle de rails = 4 rails courbes, 1 maisonnette de garde, 1 sonnerie, 1 lampe à arc, Carton: longueur 50 cm, largeur 29 cm . . . . le carton **frs. 8.—**

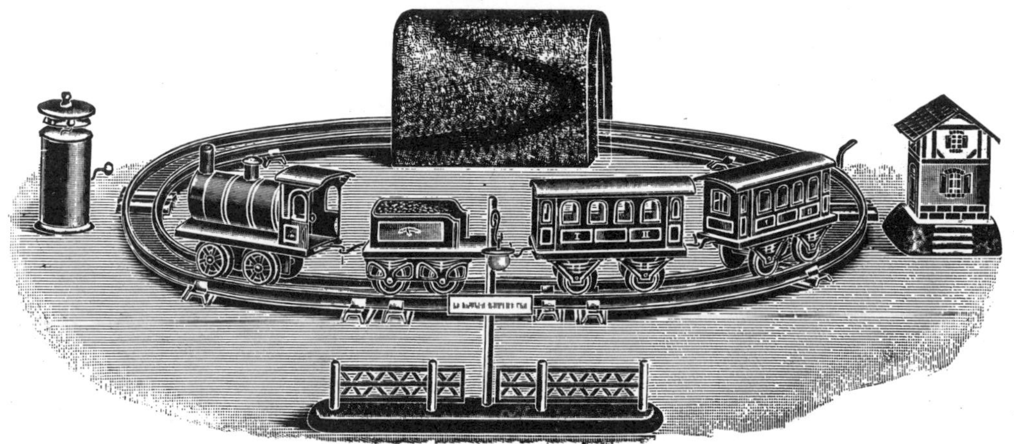

10442 **Train complet,** comprenant: une locomotive à ressort, **écartement 0 = 35 mm** avec frein (fonctionnant par le rail), 1 tender, 2 wagons de voyageurs, 1 ovale de rails = 4 courbes et 2 droits, 1 maisonnette de garde, 1 sonnerie, 1 tunnel, 1 barrière avec lampe à arc simulée, Carton: longueur 54 cm, largeur 45 cm, par carton **frs. 12.—**

10443 **Train complet,** comprenant: 1 locomotive à ressort, **écartement 0 = 35 mm** avec frein (fonctionnant par le rail), 1 tender, 2 wagons de voyageurs, 1 ovale de rails = 4 courbes et 2 droits, 1 gare, 1 maisonnette de garde, 1 sonnerie, 1 signal, 1 lampe à arc, 1 tunnel, Carton: longueur 85 cm, largeur 40 cm, par carton **frs. 19.—**

Trains miniature sans mécanisme

10380/8

disposés en cartons élégants, charmante nouveauté

10380/3	comprenant: locomotive, tender, et 1 wagon, long. du train 21½ cm	la pièce frs.	1.30
,, /4	,, ,, ,, ,, 2 ,, ,, ,, ,, 30 ,,	,, ,, ,,	1.75
,, /5	,, ,, ,, ,, 3 ,, ,, ,, ,, 39 ,,	,, ,, ,,	2.—
,, /6	,, ,, ,, ,, 4 ,, ,, ,, ,, 47 ,,	,, ,, ,,	2.50
,, /8	,, ,, ,, ,, 6 ,, ,, ,, ,, 64 ,,	,, ,, ,,	3.25

Trains solides et bon marché sans mécanisme

bien vernis polychrome, avec roues en fer, livrés dans de jolis cartons.

242/10/2

242/10/2	comprenant: locomotive, tender, et 2 wagons, long. des wagons 9 cm, long. du train 37 cm	la pièce frs.	1.75
,, /12/3	,, ,, ,, ,, 3 ,, ,, ,, ,, 9 ,, ,, ,, ,, 57 ,,	,, ,, ,,	2.75
,, / ,,/4	,, ,, ,, ,, 4 ,, ,, ,, ,, 9 ,, ,, ,, ,, 65 ,,	,, ,, ,,	3.30

242/11/3

242/11/3	comprenant: 1 loco-tender et 3 wagons, long. des wagons 9 cm, long. du train 49 cm	la pièce frs.	2.40
,, / ,,/4	,, ,, ,, ,, 4 ,, ,, ,, ,, 9 ,, ,, ,, ,, 60 ,,	,, ,, ,,	2.75

242/12/6

242/12/6	comprenant: locomotive, tender et 6 wagons, long. des wagons 9 cm, long. du train 88 cm,	la pièce frs.	4.—
,, / ,,/8	,, ,, ,, ,, 8 ,, ,, ,, ,, 9 ,, ,, ,, ,, 110 ,,	,, ,, ,,	5.25
,, / ,,/10	,, ,, ,, ,, 10 ,, ,, ,, ,, 9 ,, ,, ,, ,, 131 ,,	,, ,, ,,	6.50

Trains mécaniques, bon marché et solides

ne fonctionnant pas sur rails.

242/20/4

242/20/1	comprenant: locomotive, tender et 1 wagon, long. des wagons, 9 cm, long. du train 33 cm	la pièce frs.	2.—
,, / ,,/2	,, ,, ,, ,, 2 ,, ,, ,, ,, 9 ,, ,, ,, ,, 44 ,,	,, ,, ,,	2.50
,, / ,,/3	,, ,, ,, ,, 3 ,, ,, ,, ,, 9 ,, ,, ,, ,, 55 ,,	,, ,, ,,	3.—
,, / ,,/4	,, ,, ,, ,, 4 ,, ,, ,, ,, 9 ,, ,, ,, ,, 66 ,,	,, ,, ,,	3.50

Wagons seuls

bien vernis polychrome.

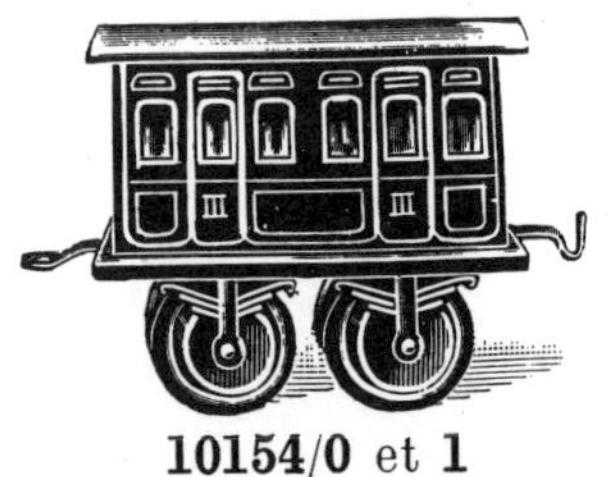

10154/0 et 1

10155/0 et 1

Wagons de voyageurs

10154/0	écart. 0, long. 8 ½ cm	. la pièce frs.	—.65
„ /1	„ I, „ 13 „	. „ „ „	1.75

Wagons à bagages

10155/0	écart. 0, long. 8 ½ cm	. la pièce frs.	—.65
„ /1	„ I, „ 13 „	. „ „ „	1.75

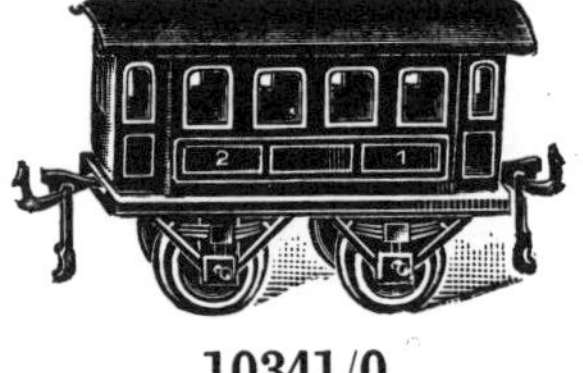

10341/0

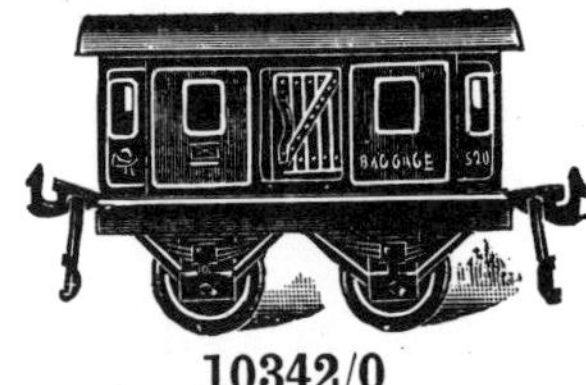

10342/0

Wagons de voyageurs

10341/0	écart. 0, long. 10 cm	. . la pièce frs.	1.—

Wagons à bagages

avec portes à glissières

10342/0	écart. 0, long. 10 cm	. . la pièce frs.	1.—

10341 et 10342 ne sont pas fabriqués en écartement I

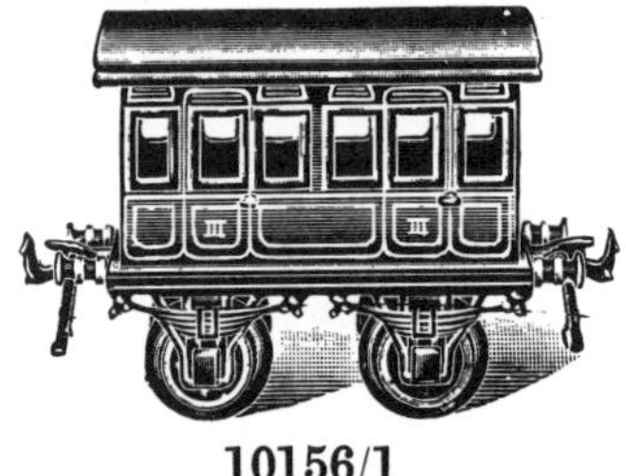

10156/1

10157/1

Wagons de voyageurs

(wagon-coupé).

10156/1	écart. I, long. 15 cm	. . la pièce frs.	2.40

Fourgons-postes

10157/1	écart. I, long. 15 cm	. . la pièce frs.	2.40

10156 et 10157 ne sont pas fabriqués en écartement 0

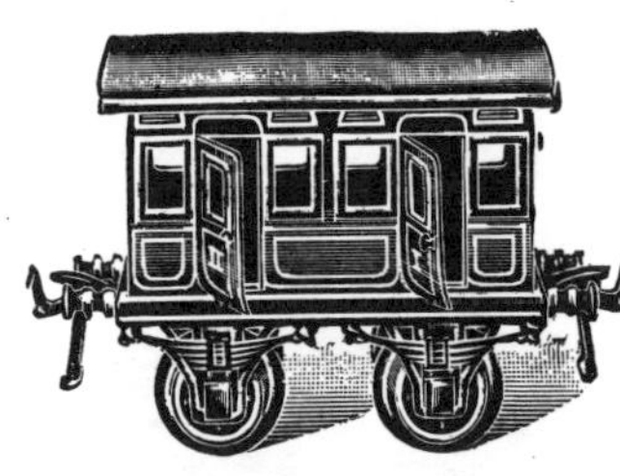

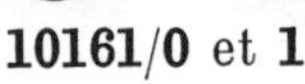

10161/0 et 1

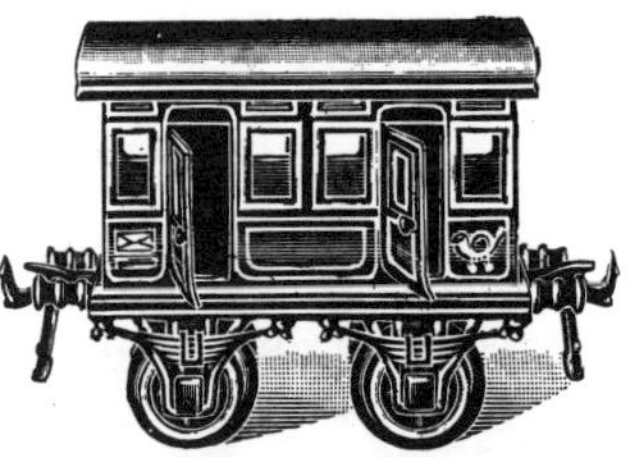

10162/0 et 1

Wagons de voyageurs

portes s'ouvrant.

10161/0	écart. 0, long. 10 cm	. . la pièce frs.	1.30
„ /1	„ I, „ 15 „	. . „ „ „	2.80

Fourgons-postes

portes s'ouvrant.

10162/0	écart. 0, long. 10 cm	. . la pièce frs.	1.30
„ /1	„ I, „ 15 „	. . „ „ „	2.70

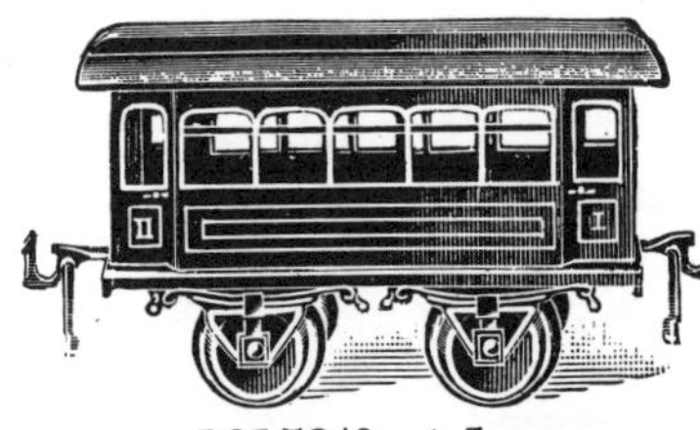

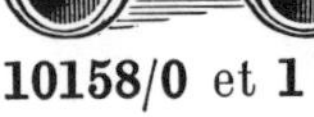

10158/0 et 1

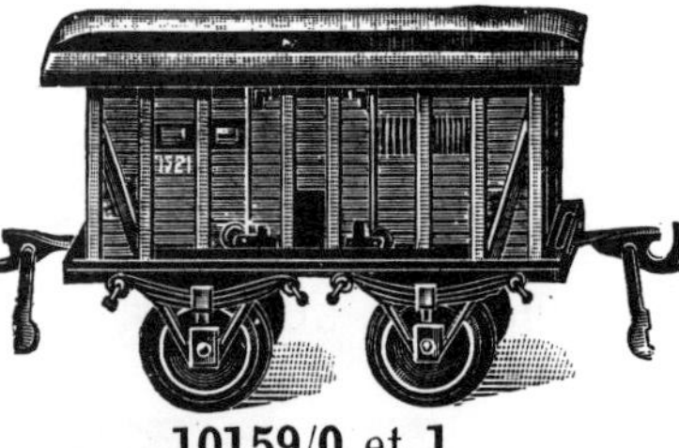

10159/0 et 1

10328/0 et 1

Wagons de voyageurs

10158/0	écart. 0, long. 12 cm	,la pièce frs.	1.20
„ /1	„ I, „ 19 „	„ „ „	3.—

Fourgons à bagages

10159/0	écart. 0, long. 12 cm,	la pièce frs.	1.20
„ /1	„ I, „ 19 „	„ „ „	3.—

Fourgons à bagages

avec portes à glissières.

10328/0	écart. 0, long. 12 cm,	la pièce frs.	1.30
„ /1	„ I, „ 19 „	„ „ „	3.25

Wagons seuls

bien vernis polychrome.

10360

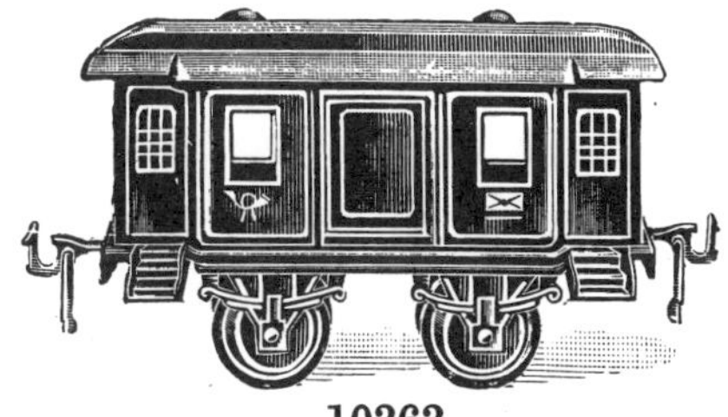

10363

10360/0	**Wagons de voyageurs,** écartement 0 = 35 mm, long. 15 ½ cm, avec portes fermées	la pièce frs.	1.80
„ /1	„ „ „ „ I = 48 „ „ 21 „ „ „ s'ouvrant	„ „ „	3.50
10363/0	**Wagons postes,** écartement 0 = 35 mm, long. 15 ½ cm avec portes ouvrables	„ „ „	2.—
„ /1	„ „ „ I = 48 „ „ 21 „ „ „ „	„ „ „	3.75

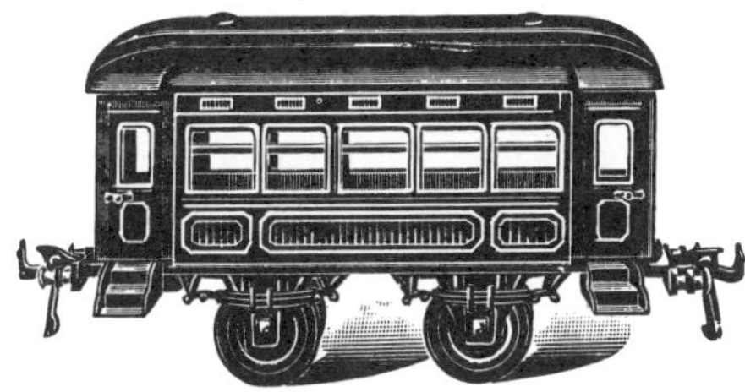

10366/0 et 1

avec portes s'ouvrant

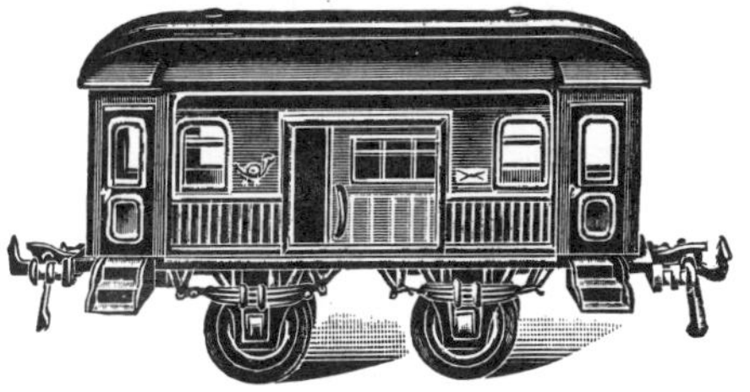

10344/0 et 1

10366/0	**Wagons de voyageurs** avec portes s'ouvrant, écartement 0 = 35 mm, long. 17 cm	la pièce frs.	2.50
„ /1	„ „ „ „ „ „ „ I = 48 „ „ 24 „	„ „ „	4.75
10344/0	**Fourgons-postes** avec portes s'ouvrant, écartement 0 = 35 mm, long. 17 cm	„ „ „	2.75
„ /1	„ „ „ „ „ „ I = 48 „ „ 24 „	„ „ „	5.—

10390 et 10391

avec portes s'ouvrant

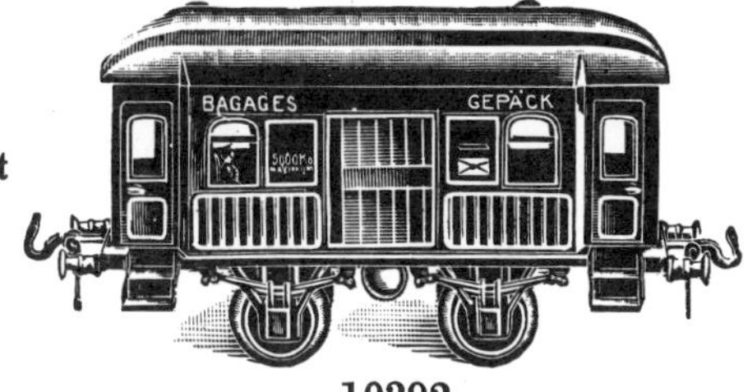

10392

Wagons à couloir (wagons de voyageurs)

avec inscription "Wagons-lits" ou "Wagons-restaurants", avec portes s'ouvrant, sièges et personnages

10390/0	**Wagons-restaurants,** écartement 0 = 35 mm, long. 15 ½ cm	la pièce frs.	3.75
„ /1	„ „ „ I = 48 „ „ 24 „	„ „ „	7.—
10391/0	**Wagons-lits,** écartement 0 = 35 mm, longueur 15 ½ cm	„ „ „	3.75
„ /1	„ „ „ I = 48 „ „ 24 „	„ „ „	7.—

Wagons à couloir (poste et bagages)

avec portes s'ouvrant et à glissières, sièges et personnages (employés)

10392/0	écartement 0 = 35 mm, longueur 15 ½ cm	la pièce frs.	3.75
„ /1	„ I = 48 „ „ 24 „	„ „ „	7.—

Les wagons 10390, 10391 et 10392 peuvent communiquer au moyen de soufflets.

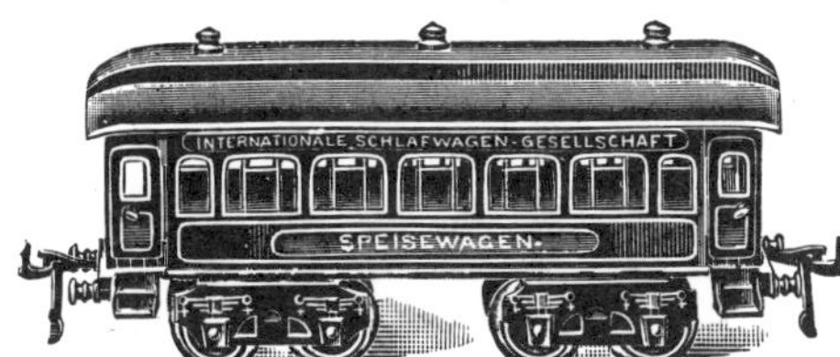

10241/0

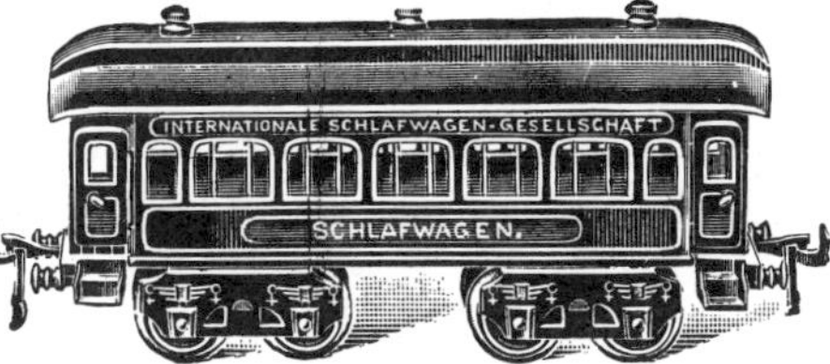

10242/0

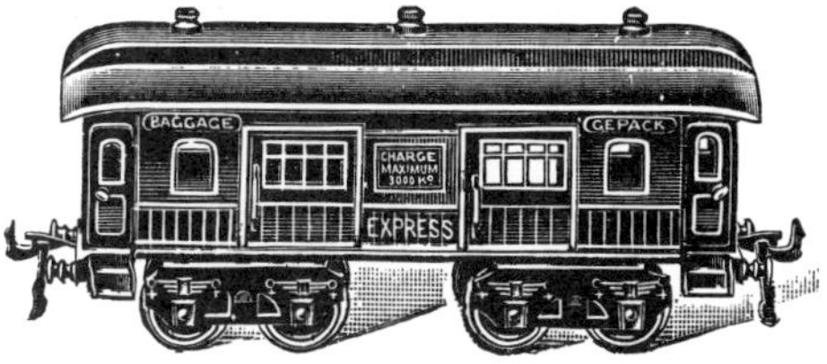

10243/0

Wagons à couloir pour trains express, monté sur 4 axes, sans aménagement intérieur

10241/0	**Wagons-restaurants,** écartement 0 = 35 mm, longueur 22 cm	la pièce frs.	4.75
„ /1	„ „ „ I = 48 „ „ 35 „	„ „ „	10.—
10242/0	**Wagons-lits,** „ 0 = 35 „ „ 22 „	„ „ „	4.75
„ /1	„ „ „ I = 48 „ „ 35 „	„ „ „	10.—
10243/0	**Fourgons-postes,** „ 0 = 35 „ „ 22 „	„ „ „	4.75
„ /1	„ „ „ I = 48 „ „ 35 „	„ „ „	10.—

Les wagons 10241, 10242 et 10243 peuvent communiquer au moyen de soufflets.

Wagons.

13556/1

Wagons à couloir pour trains express (Wagons-restaurants)

avec aménagement intérieur, **bien vernis polychrome**

montés sur 4 axes = 8 roues, avec boggies, avec soufflet, portes s'ouvrant, aménagement intérieur et personnages

13556/0	Ecartement 0 = 35 mm, longueur 22 cm	la pièce	**frs. 7.—**
„ /1	„ I = 48 „ „ 35 „	„ „	„ **15.—**

13638/1

Wagons à couloir (wagons de voyageurs et wagons-lits)

avec garniture, **bien vernis polychrome**

montés sur 4 axes = 8 roues, avec boggies, soufflet, portes ouvrables, avec aménagement intérieur (petits lits et personnages)

13638/0	Ecartement 0 = 35 mm, longueur 22 cm	la pièce	**frs. 7.—**
„ /1	„ I = 48 „ „ 35 „	„ „	„ **15.—**

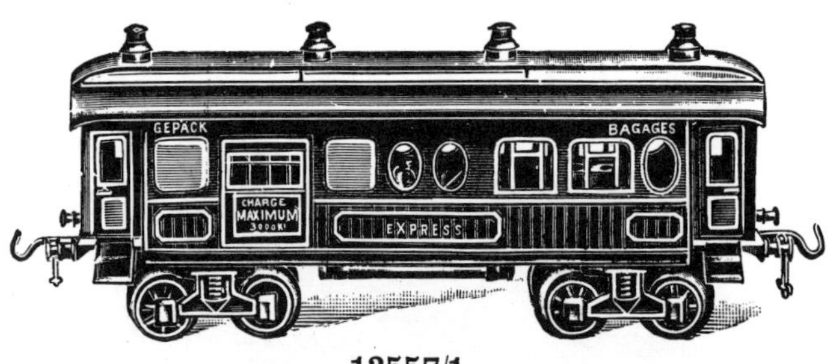

13557/1

Wagons à couloir (postes et bagages)

avec aménagement intérieur, **bien vernis polychrome**

montés sur 4 axes = 8 roues, avec boggies, soufflet, portes ouvrables, avec aménagement intérieur et personnages (employés)

13557/0	Ecartement 0 = 35 mm, longueur 22 cm	la pièce	**frs. 6.—**
„ /1	„ I = 48 „ „ 35 „	„ „	„ **13.50**

Wagons à couloirs pour trains de luxe

très bien vernis à la main

avec boggies, 4 axes, aménagement intérieur (Pullmann-Cars), seulement pour rails à grand rayon

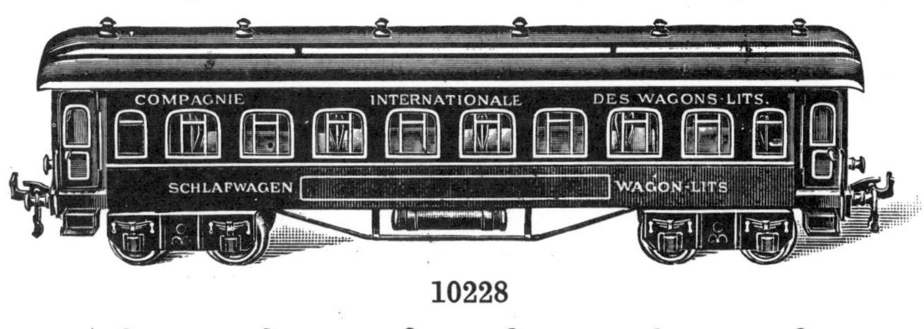

10228

10288

10286/0	Wagons-restaurants,	écartement 0 = 35 mm,	longueur 32 cm	la pièce	frs. 17.—
„ /1	„ „	„ I = 48 „	„ 50 „	„	„ 33.—
10228/0	Wagons-lits,	„ 0 = 35 „	„ 32 „	„	„ 17.—
„ /1	„ „	„ I = 48 „	„ 50 „	„	„ 33.—
10287/0	Wagons-salons	„ 0 = 35 „	„ 32 „	„	„ 17.—
„ /1	„ „	„ I = 48 „	„ 50 „	„	„ 33.—
10288/0	Fourgons-postes,	„ 0 = 35 „	„ 32 „	„	„ 17.—
„ /1	„ „	„ I = 48 „	„ 50 „	„	„ 33.—

Wagons-restaurants et wagons-lits à couloir pour trains de luxe

très bien vernis à la main

Ecartement 0 = 35 mm, I = 48 mm, IV = 75 mm

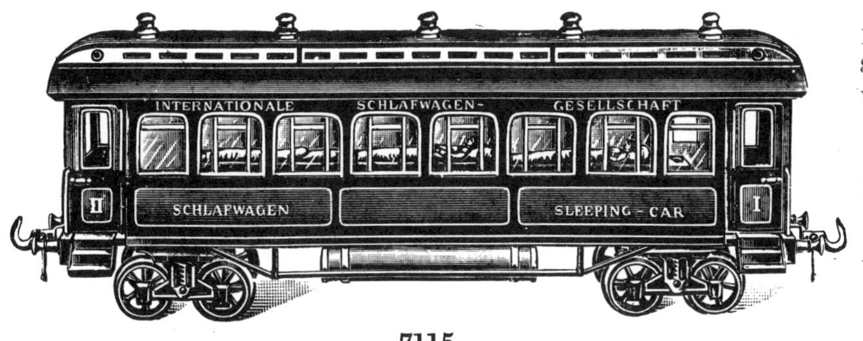

7115

Exécution élégante, montés sur 4 axes = 8 roues, avec boggies, portes s'ouvrant, réservoirs à gaz simulés, soufflets, aménagement intérieur complet et personnages

Ecartement	longueur	wagon-restaurant		wagon-lits	
		No.	la pièce	No.	la pièce
0	22 cm	7114/0	frs. 6.50	7115/0	frs. 12.—
I	35 „	„ /1	„ 12.—	„ /1	„ 22.50
IV	55 „	„ /4	„ 35.—	„ /4	„ 65.—

Wagons à couloir (postes et bagages) pour trains de luxe

très bien vernis à la main

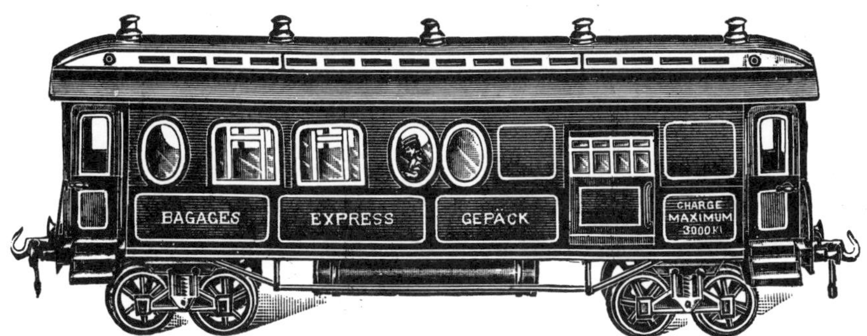

7116

Exécution élégante, montés sur 4 axes = 8 roues, avec boggies, portes s'ouvrant, réservoirs à gaz simulés, soufflets, aménagement intérieur complet, avec personnages

No.	Ecartement	longueur	la pièce
7116/0	0	22 mm	frs. 12.—
„ /1	I	35 „	„ 22.50
„ /4	IV	55 „	„ 65.—

Wagons divers.

Ecartement 0 = 35 mm. **Ecartement I = 48 mm.**

10113/1

10114/1

10118/1

10113/0 **Fourgons** avec cabine de serre-frein et portes à glissières, bien vernis polychrome
écartement 0 = 35 mm, longueur 10 cm . . . . la pièce **frs.** 1.50
„ /1 do. „ I = 48 „ „ 13 ½ „ . . . . „ „ „ 3.—
10114/0 **Wagons de marchandises,** bien vernis polychrome, écartement 0 = 35 mm, longueur 8 ½ cm „ „ „ .90
„ /1 „ „ „ „ „ „ „ I = 48 „ „ 15 „ „ „ „ 2.—
10118/0 do. avec cabine de serre-frein, bien vernis polychrome, écart. 0 = 35 mm, long. 9 ½ cm „ „ „ 1.30
„ /1 „ „ „ „ „ „ „ „ „ „ I = 48 „ „ 15 „ „ „ „

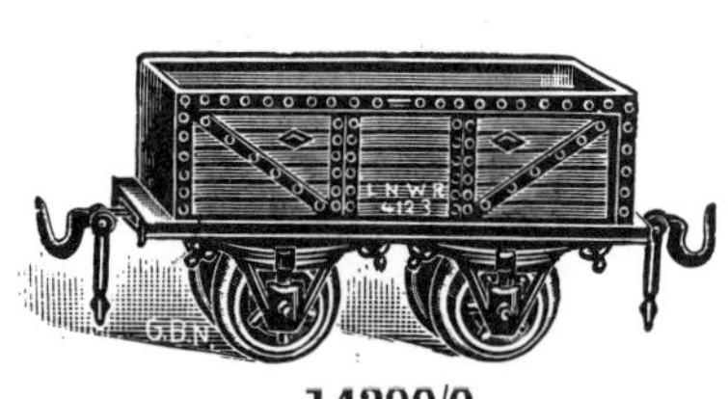

14390/0

10365/1

9681/1

14390/0 **Wagons de marchandises,** bien vernis polychrome, écart. 0 = 35 mm, long. 11 ½ cm . . . la pièce **frs.** 1.15
„ /1 „ „ „ „ „ „ „ I = 48 „ „ 19 ½ „ . . . . „ „ „ 2.40
10365/0 **Wagons-grues,** bien vernis polychrome, écart. 0 = 35 mm, long. 8 ½ cm . . . . „ „ „ 1.50
„ /1 „ „ „ „ „ „ I = 48 „ „ 14 ½ „ . . . . „ „ „ 2.75
9681/0 **Wagons avec bâche,** bien vernis à la main, écartement 0 = 35 mm, longueur 8 ½ cm . . „ „ „ 2.—
„ /1 „ „ „ „ „ „ „ „ „ I = 48 „ „ 15 „ . . . „ „ „ 4.—

9176/0

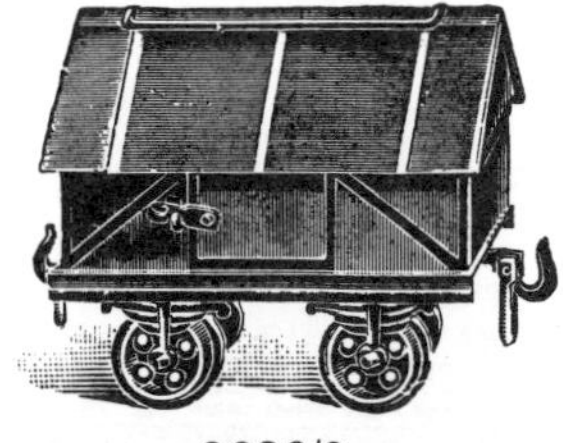

9686/0

9184/1

9176/0 **Wagons à pétrole,** bien vernis à la main, écartement 0 = 35 mm, longueur 8 ½ cm . . . . la pièce **frs.** 2.50
„ /1 „ „ „ „ „ „ „ „ „ I = 48 „ „ 13 ½ „ . . . . . „ „ „ 4.—
9686/0 **Wagons à chaux,** avec toiture à trappe, bien vernis à la main,
écartement 0 = 35 mm, longueur 8 ½ cm . . . . „ „ „ 2.—
„ /1 do. „ I = 48 „ „ 15 . . . . „ „ „ 4.—
9184/0 **Wagons à gaz,** bien vernis à la main, écartement 0 = 35 mm, longueur 8 ½ cm . . . . . . „ „ „ 2.—
„ /1 „ „ „ „ „ „ „ „ „ I = 48 „ „ 13 ½ „ . . . . „ „ „ 3.50

Wagons divers

7084/1

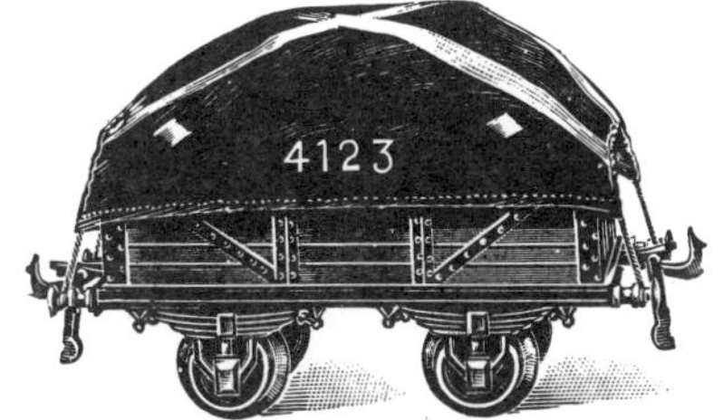

10359/1

7784/0

7084/0	**Wagons à planches,** bien vernis à la main, écartement 0 = 35 mm, longueur 8 ½ cm . . . la pièce **frs.**	2.—
„ /1	„ „ „ „ „ „ „ „ „ I = 48 „ „ 15 „ . . . „ „ „	4.—
10359/0	**Wagons de marchandises,** chargés de sacs, avec bâche, écartement 0 = 35 mm, long. 13 cm „ „ „	2.—
„ /1	„ „ „ „ „ „ „ „ „ I = 48 „ „ 19 ½ „ „ „ „	3.50
7784/0	**Wagons à bois** avec traverse à pivot, et chaîne, vernis polychrome, écartement 0 = 35 mm, longueur 8 ½ cm . . . . „ „ „	1.20
„ /1	do. „ I = 48 „ „ 13 ½ „ . . . . „ „ „	2.—

8356/0

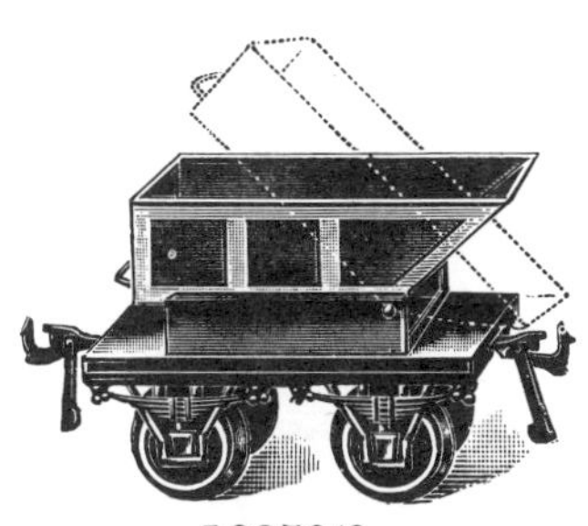
10256/0

10121/1

8356/0	**Wagons-ballast,** avec déversoir amélioré, bien vernis à la main, écartement 0 = 35 mm, longueur 8 ½ cm . . . . la pièce **frs.**	1.90
„ /1	do. „ I = 48 „ „ 13 ½ „ . . . . „ „ „	3.75
10256/0	**Wagons-déversoirs** pivotant et basculant, bien vernis à la main, écartement 0 = 35 mm, longueur 8 ½ cm . . . . „ „ „	2.50
„ /1	do. „ I = 48 „ „ 12 „ . . . . „ „ „	3.75
10121/0	**Wagons à bestiaux,** avec aminaux, bien vernis polychrome, écartement 0 = 35 mm, longueur 8 ½ cm . . . . „ „ „	1.70
„ /1	do. „ I = 48 „ „ 15 „ . . . . „ „ „	3.70

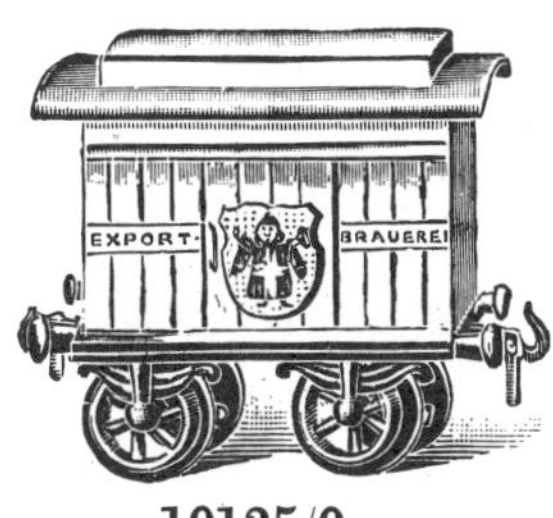

10125/0

9193/0

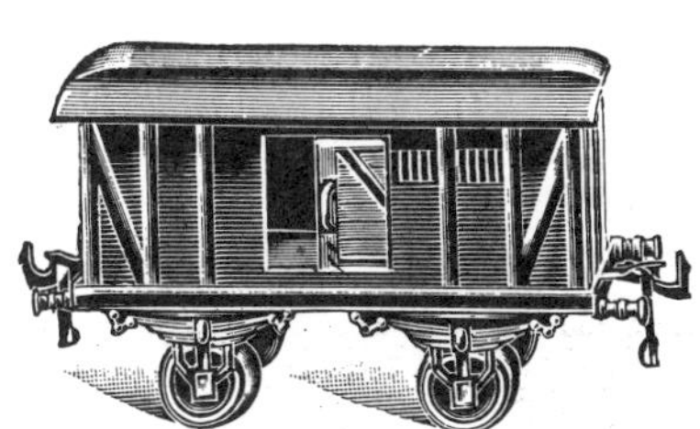
7019 1

10125/0	**Wagons pour bière,** avec portes à glissières, bien vernis polychrome, écartement 0 = 35 mm, longueur 8 ½ cm . . . . la pièce **frs.**	1.50
„ /1	do. „ I = 48 „ „ 19 ½ „ . . . . „ „ „	2.75
9193/0	**Wagons pour meubles,** avec voiture de déménagements, bien vernis à la main, écartement 0 = 35 mm, longueur 8 ½ cm . . . . „ „ „	4.—
„ /1	do. „ I = 48 „ „ 15 „ . . . . „ „ „	6.—
7019/0	**Wagons à chevaux,** avec portes à glissières, garnis, bien vernis à la main, avec 2 chevaux, écartement 0 = 35 mm, longueur 11 ½ cm . . . . „ „ „	4.—
„ /1	do. „ I = 48 „ „ 20 „ . . . . „ „ „	7.—

Wagons divers.

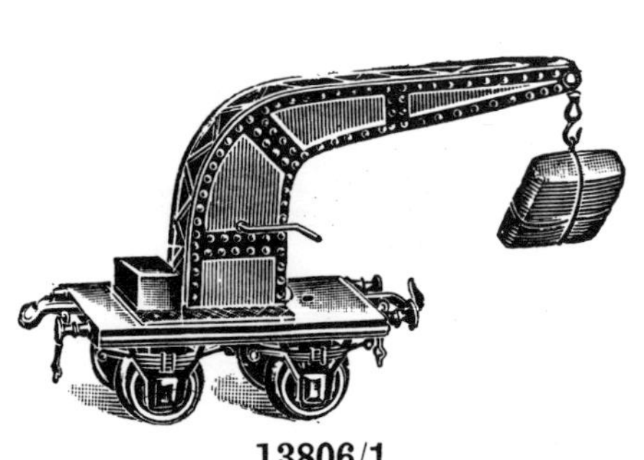

13806/1

10285/0

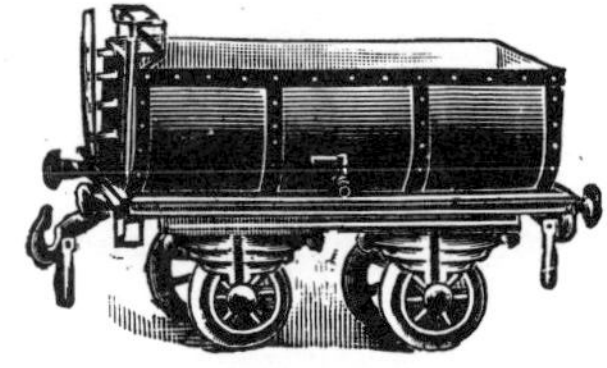

6307/1

13806/0 **Wagons-grues,** avec grue mécanique pivotant, bien vernis à la main,
écartement 0 = 35 mm, longueur 15 cm . . . . la pièce **frs.** 4.25
„ /1 **do.** „ I = 48 „ „ 22½ „ . . . . „ „ „ 6.50
10285/0 **Wagons-grues,** avec grue mécanique tournante, cabine en tôle ondulée, bien vernis à la main,
écartement 0 = 35 mm, longueur 12 cm, hauteur 18 cm . . . . „ „ „ 7.25
„ /1 **do.** „ I = 48 „ „ 17 „ „ 21 „ . . . . „ „ „ 10.—
6307/0 **Wagons-citernes** avec siège de serre frein, avec robinet d'écoulement, bien vernis à la main,
écartement 0 = 35 mm, longueur 12 cm . . . . „ „ „ 3.75
„ /1 **do.** „ I = 48 „ „ 15 „ . . . . „ „ „ 5.75

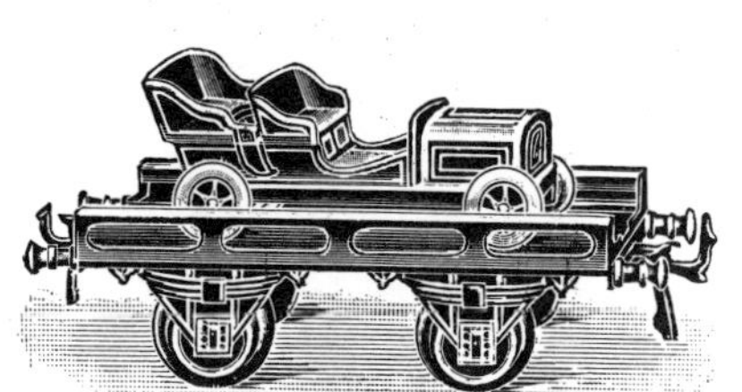

10382/1

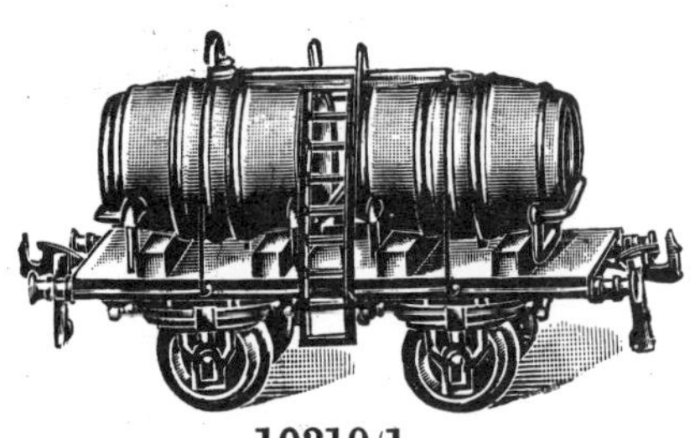

10319/1

10297/1

10382/0 **Wagons pour automobiles,** avec automobile, bien vernis, écart. 0 = 35 mm, long. 11½ cm, la pièce **frs.** 2.50
„ /1 „ „ „ „ „ „ „ „ I = 48 „ „ 21 „ „ „ „ 4.50
10319/0 **Wagons-foudres** avec 2 tonneaux, bien vernis, „ 0 = 35 „ „ 11½ „ „ „ „ „ 5.-
„ /1 „ „ „ 2 „ „ „ „ I = 48 „ „ 19½ „ „ „ „ „ 8.—
10297/0 **Wagons pour acides** avec 4 bombonnes, bien vernis „ 0 = 35 „ „ 11½ „ „ „ „ „ 4.25
„ /1 „ „ „ „ 4 „ „ „ „ I = 48 „ „ 19½ „ „ „ „ „ 7.—

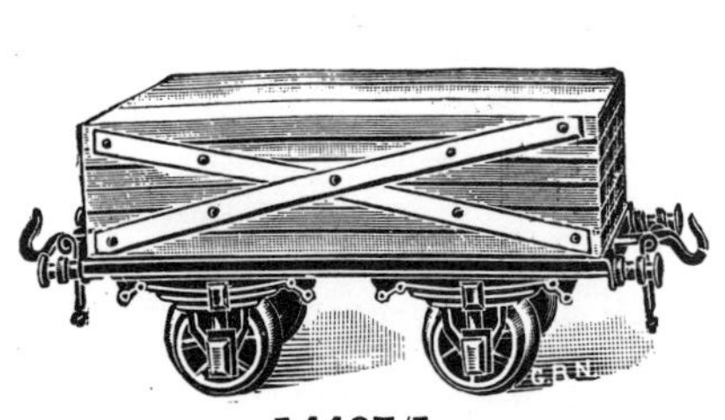

14467/1

14466/1

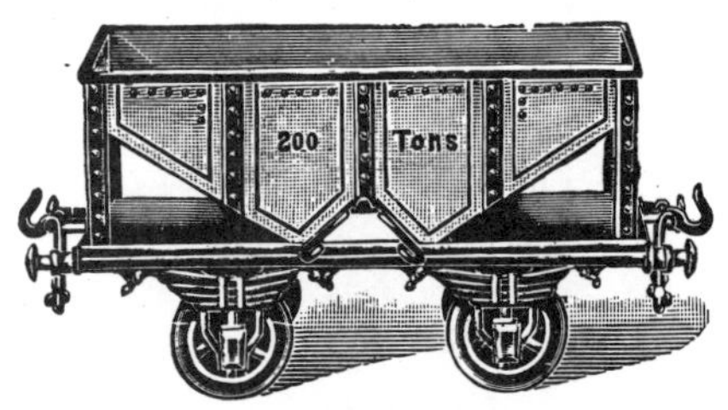

13668/1

14467/0 **Wagons à planches** avec chargement de bois, bien vernis polychrome,
écartement 0 = 35 mm, longueur 11½ cm . . . . la pièce **frs.** 1.50 ✓
„ /1 **do.** „ I = 48 „ „ 20 „ . . . . „ „ „ 3.25 ✓
14466/0 **Wagons à charbons,** intérieur imitation charbon, bien vernis polychrome,
écartement 0 = 35 mm, longueur 11½ cm . . . . „ „ „ 2.40
„ /1 **do.** „ I = 48 „ „ 21 „ . . . . „ „ „ 4.—
13668/0 **Wagons à charbons,** avec 2 trappes, à la partie inférieure, bien vernis à la main,
écartement 0 = 35 mm, longueur 11½ cm . . . . „ „ „ 3.—
„ /1 „ I = 48 „ „ 20 „ . . . . „ „ „ 5.—

Wagons divers

14473/1 14472/0 14465/1

14473/0	**Wagons de secours,** avec cabine de serre frein et grue, portes à glissières, bien vernis à la main, écartement 0 = 35 mm, longueur 16½ cm . . . . la pièce **frs.**	4.25
„ /1	**do.** „ I = 48 „ „ 22 „ . . . . „ „ „	6.50
14472/0	**Wagons à fibre de bois,** garnis, bien vernis à la main, écartement 0 = 35 mm, longueur 16 cm . . . . „ „ „	3.25
„ /1	**do.** „ I = 48 „ „ 25 „ . . . . „ „ „	6.—
14465/0	**Wagons chasse-neige,** avec chasse-neige rotatif, portes s'ouvrant, bien vernis à la main, écartement 0 = 35 mm, longueur 16 cm . . . . „ „ „	5.25
„ /1	**do.** „ I = 48 „ „ 23 „ . . . . „ „ „	10.—

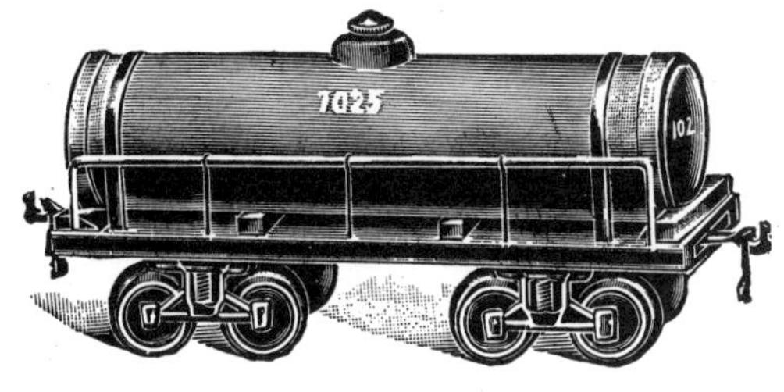

10357/1

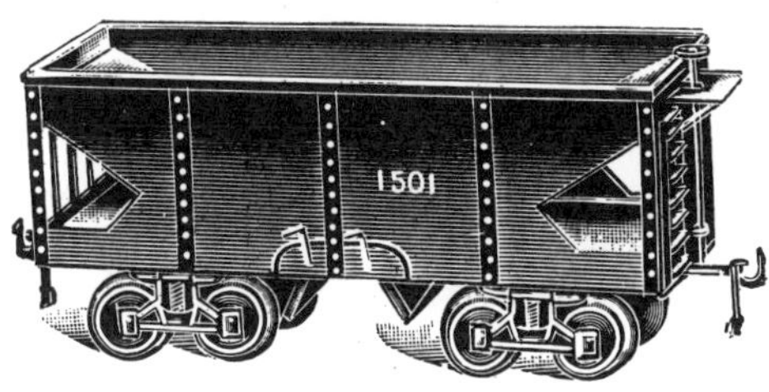

10358/1

10357/0	**Wagons à pétrole,** bien vernis, avec bouchon à vis, écart. 0 = 35 mm, long. 18 cm . . . la pièce **frs.**	5.70
„ /1	„ „ „ „ „ „ „ „ „ „ I = 48 „ „ 26½ „ . . . „ „ „	9.—
10358/0	**Wagons à charbons,** avec trappes à la partie inférieure, écart. 0 = 35 mm, long. 18 cm „ „ „	6.30
„ /1	„ „ „ „ 2 „ „ „ „ „ „ I = 48 „ „ 26½ „ „ „ „	11.—

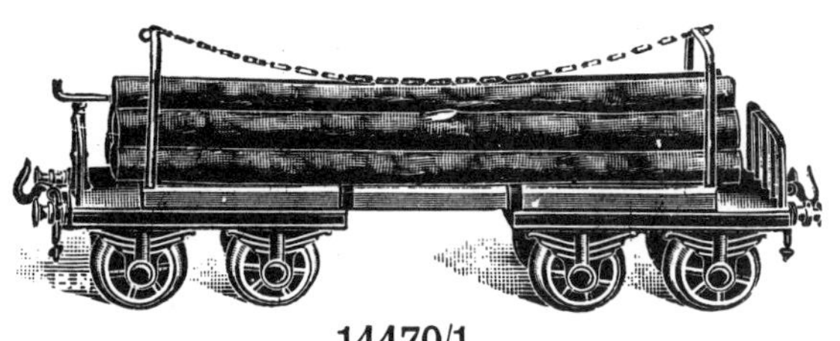

14470/1

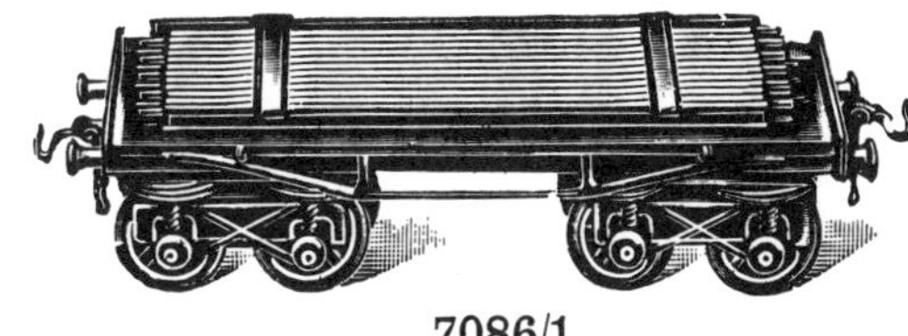

7086/1

14470/0	**Wagons à poutres,** garnis, bien vernis à la main, écart. 0 = 35 mm, long. 20 cm . . . . . la pièce **frs.**	4.50
„ /1	„ „ „ „ „ „ „ „ „ „ I = 48 „ „ 30 „ . . . . . . „ „ „	7.25
7086/0	**Wagons à rails,** garnis, pour la réparation de la voie, bien vernis à la main, écartement 0 = 35 mm, longueur 17½ cm . . . . „ „ „	4.—
„ /1	**do.** „ I = 48 „ „ 25 „ . . . . „ „ „	7.20

Wagons divers

Wagons longs à 4 axes = 8 roues.

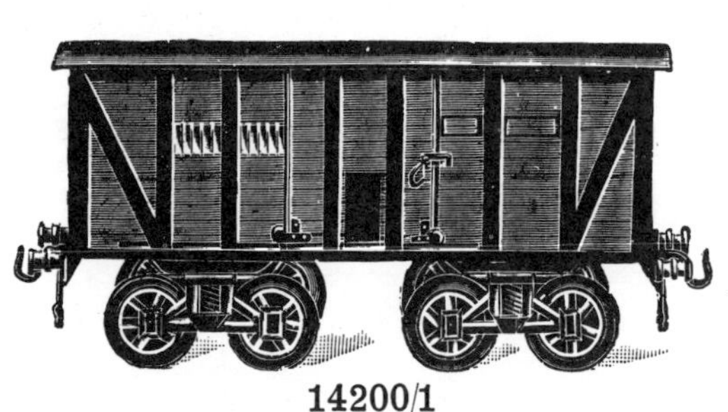

14200/1

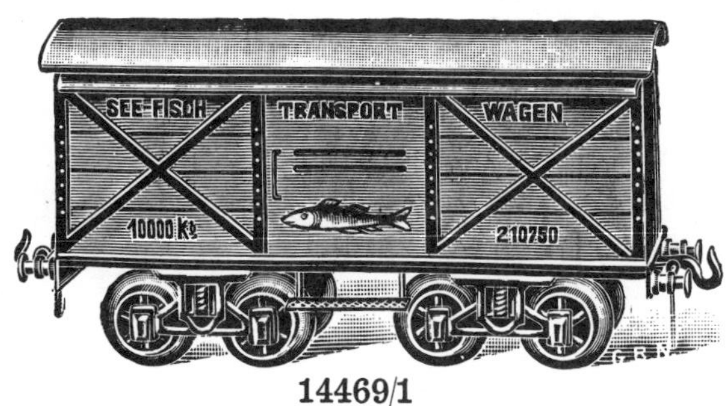

14469/1

14200/0	**Wagons de marchandises,** avec portes fermées, bien vernis polychrome,	
	écartement 0 = 35 mm, longueur 16 ½ cm . . . . la pièce **frs.**	**2.75**
„ /1	**do.** „ I = 48 „ „ 26 „ . . . . „ „ „	**5.75**
14469/0	**Wagons de marée,** portes s'ouvrant, bien vernis à la main,	
	écartement 0 = 35 mm, longueur 22 ½ cm . . . . „ „ „	**6.75**
„ /1	**do.** „ I = 48 „ „ 26 „ . . . . „ „ „	**10.75**

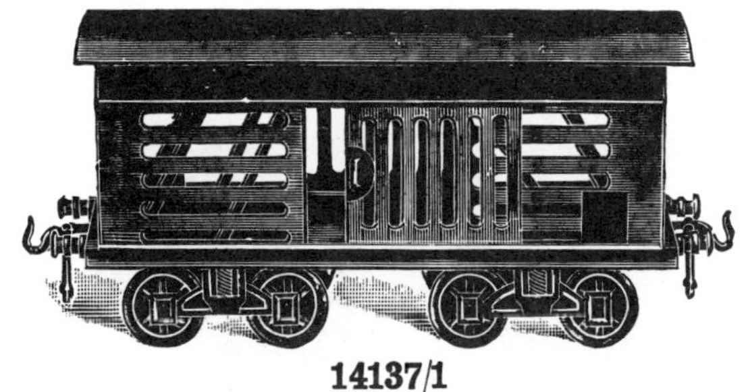

14137/1

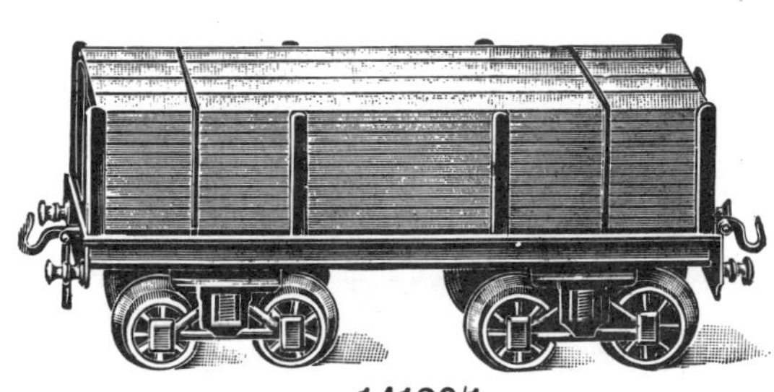

14120/1

14137/0	**Wagons à bestiaux,** portes s'ouvrant, bien vernis à la main,	
	écartement 0 = 35 mm, longueur 22 cm . . . . la pièce **frs.**	**7.—**
„ /1	**do.** „ I = 48 „ „ 26 „ . . . . „ „ „	**10.25**
14120/0	**Wagons à planches,**garnis, bien vernis à la main, écartement 0 = 35 mm, long. 16 cm . . „ „ „	**3.25**
„ /1	„ „ „ „ „ „ „ „ „ „ I = 48 „ „ 25 „ . . „ „ „	**6.25**

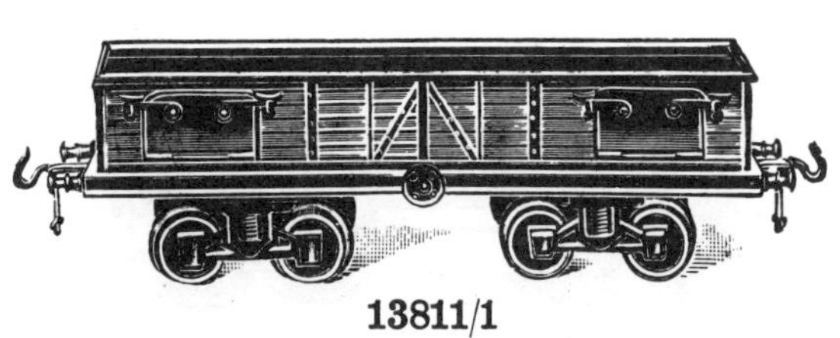

13811/1

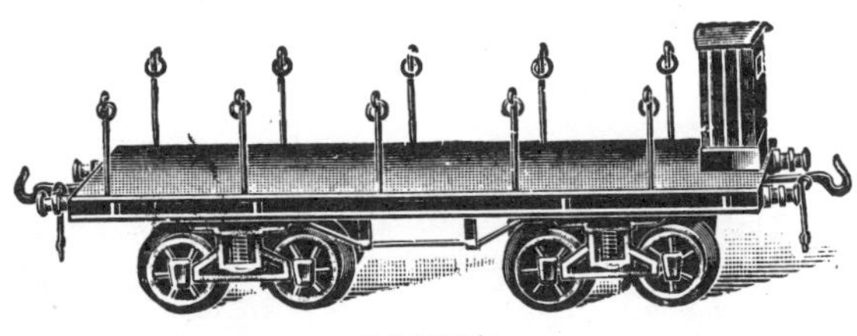

14464/1

13811/0	**Wagons à charbon,** avec portes s'ouvrant, bien vernis à la main,	
	écartement 0 = 35 mm, longueur 24 cm . . . . la pièce **frs.**	**5.25**
„ /1	**do.** „ I = 48 „ „ 30 „ . . . . „ „ „	**7.50**
14464/0	**Wagons plates-formes,** avec cabine de garde frein, bien vernis à la main,	
	écartement 0 = 35 mm, longueur 24 cm . . . . „ „ „	**4.80**
„ /1	**do.** „ I = 48 „ „ 30 „ . . . . „ „ „	**7.50**

Gares de banlieue, bien vernies polychrome.

10371 | **10372**

10371 **Gare** de banlieue, avec 2 pavillons et abri, long. 27 cm, larg. 13 cm, haut. 14 ½ cm . . . . la pièce **frs. 6.**—

10372 **Gare** de banlieue, avec socle en relief et barrière, installation pour l'éclairage à bougies, long. 35 cm, larg. 21 cm, haut. 16 ½ cm, ... la pièce **frs. 10.**—

10373 **Gare** de banlieue, avec 2 pavillons, abri, barrière (mobile) et installation pour l'éclairage à bougies, long. 40 cm, larg. 27 cm, haut. 23 cm . . . . la pièce **frs. 18.**—

Passerelles de chemins de fer.

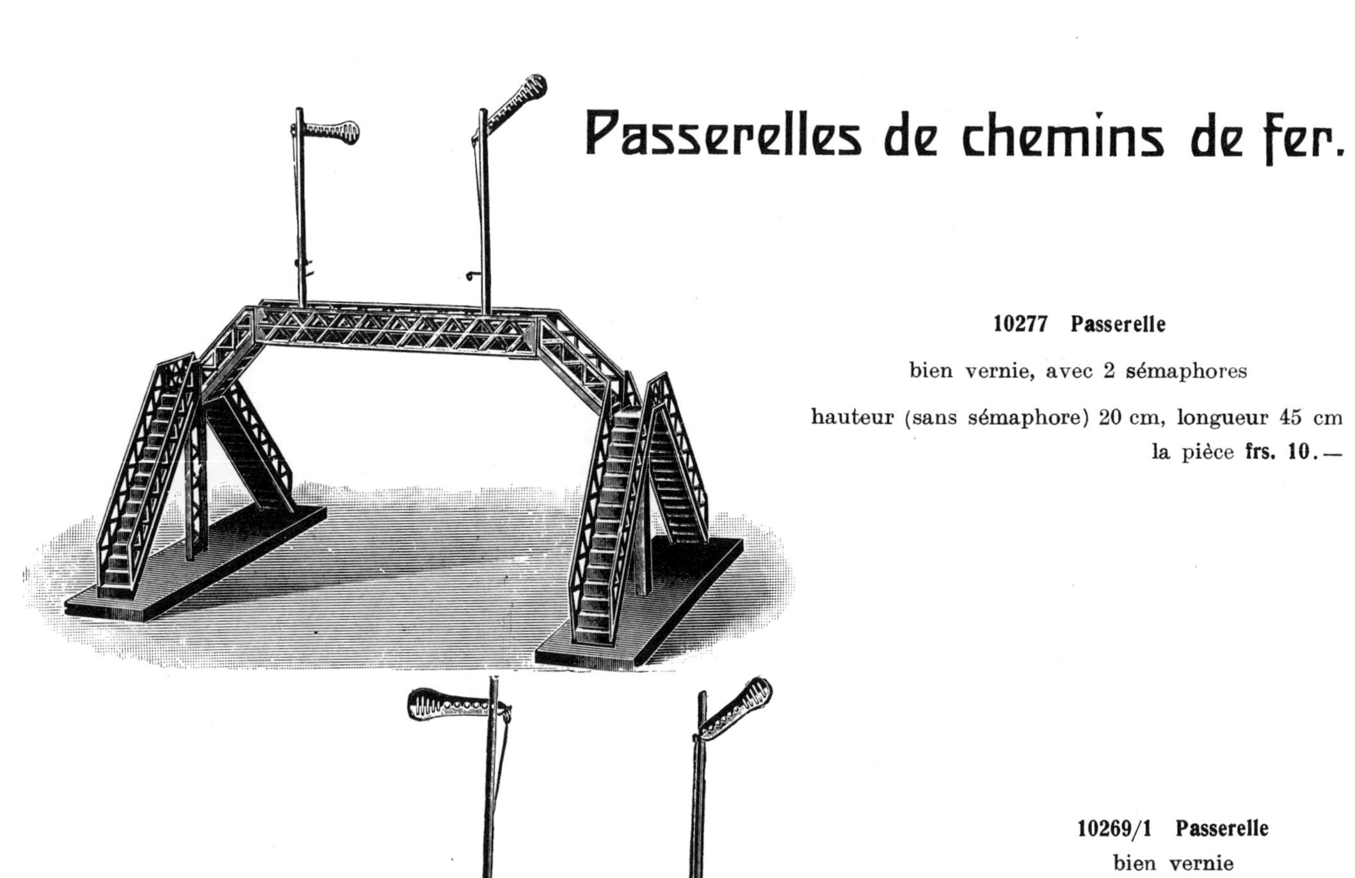

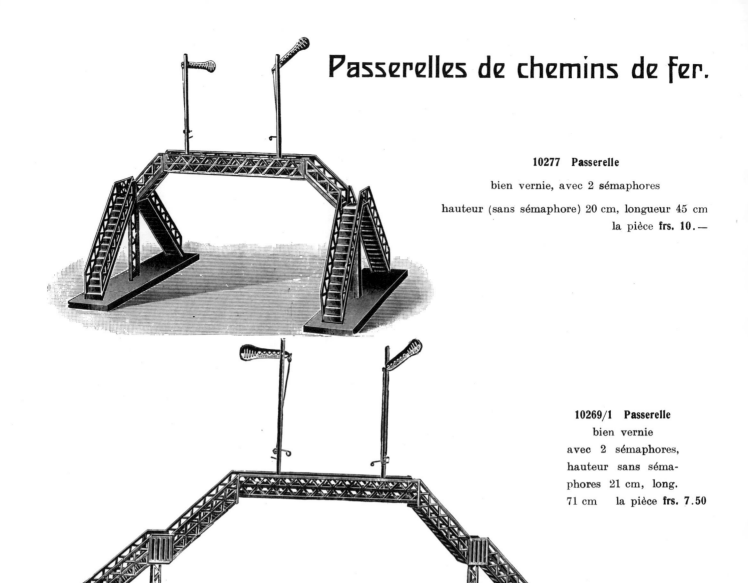

10277 Passerelle

bien vernie, avec 2 sémaphores

hauteur (sans sémaphore) 20 cm, longueur 45 cm

la pièce **frs. 10.—**

10269/1 Passerelle

bien vernie avec 2 sémaphores, hauteur sans sémaphores 21 cm, long. 71 cm la pièce **frs. 7.50**

13409 Passerelle

bien vernie, avec personnages, long. 59 cm, hauteur 21 cm, allant aux trains écartements I et II = 48 et 55 mm, avec 3 sémaphores avec disques colorés mobiles, et une lanterne s'éclairant. . . la pièce **frs. 20.—**

Kiosques, distributeurs automatiques de billets, etc.

10202

10203

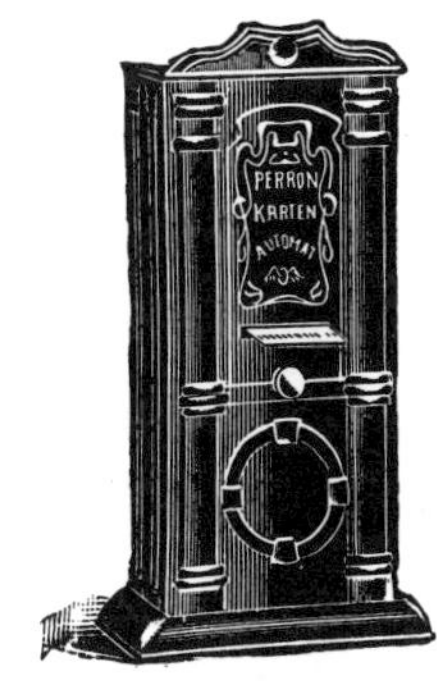

14084/1

10202 **Kiosques à journaux**, bien vernis, estampés en relief, avec journaux en miniature et personnage, largeur 8 cm, haut. 12 cm . . . . la pièce **frs.** 3.75

10203 **Buffets**, bien vernis, estampés en relief, garnis de mets et boissons divers et personnage, larg. 8 cm, haut. 12 cm, la pièce **frs.** 4.—

F 3015 **Distributeurs automatiques de billets de quai,** bien vernis, haut. 17 cm, avec 24 billets . . . . la pièce „ 2.—

8105 **Billets de quai** . . . . la grosse (144) „ 1.35

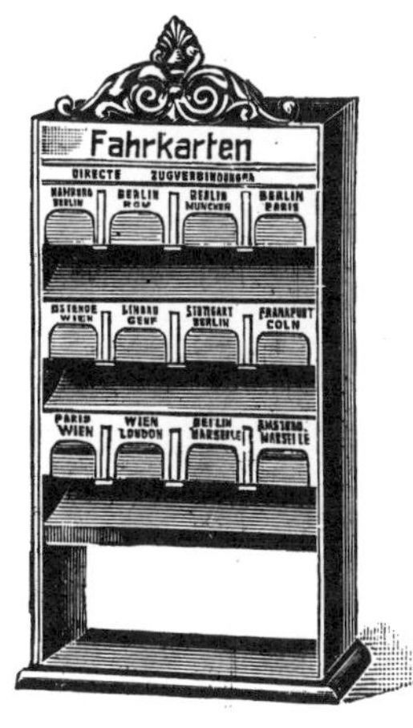

6099/1

14085/1

6099/0 **Armoires à billets,** nouvelle exécution améliorée, très bien vernies, avec 9 casiers et 108 billets pour 12 différents itinéraires; on ne peut retirer qu'un billet à la fois. Hauteur 19 cm, largeur 11,5 cm la pièce **frs.** 5.—

„ /1 **do.** avec 12 casiers et 144 billets, hauteur 25,5 cm, largeur 13,5 cm . . . . la pièce „ 7.50

14085/1 **Guichet en relief façon maçonnerie,** très bien verni; avec 2 guichets et distributeur automatique de billets (avec 24 billets), toit démontable. Installé pour l'éclairage à bougies; long. 16 cm, larg. 16 ½ cm, haut 18 cm, la pièce **frs.** 8.50

8093 **Encre** d'imprimerie (violette) . . . . le flacon „ —.30

8137 Caractères de caoutchouc (17 numéros et 4 blocs) . . . . la série „ 1.35

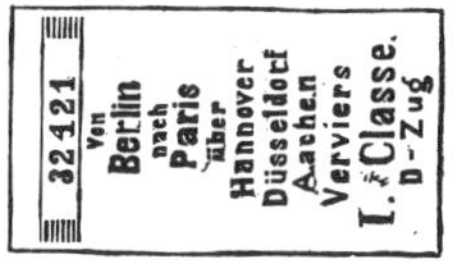

8108

8108 **Billets,** assortiment de 144 billets portant 12 itinéraires différents, ... le jeu **frs.** —.90

Indicateurs de directions.

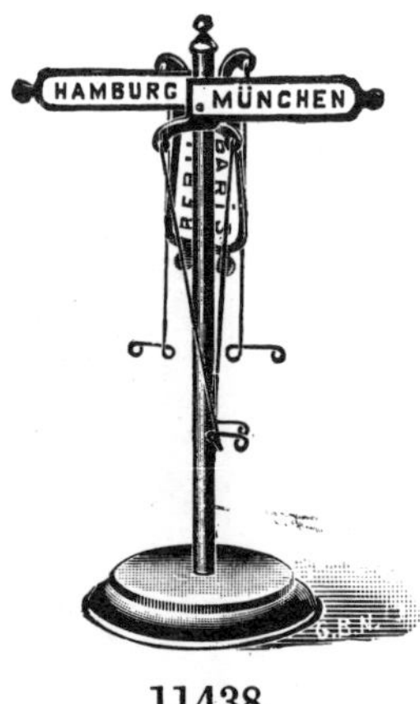

11438

7199

7210

11438 **Indicateurs de directions,** bien vernis, avec 4 bras mobiles, hauteur 20 cm . . . . la pièce **frs.** 1.25

7199 „ „ „ bien vernis, avec 4 plaques indicatrices interchangeables pour les directions et 4 pour les trains; hauteur 19 cm . . . . la pièce **frs.** 1.75

7210 „ „ „ bien vernis, avec 4 plaques indicatrices de directions, mobiles, et 4 interchangeables pour les trains, hauteur 19 cm . . . . la pièce **frs.** 2.—

10143

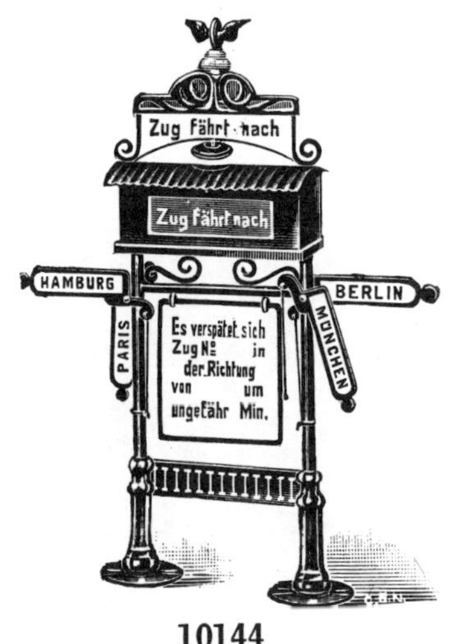

10144

9161

10143 **Indicateurs de directions,** bien vernis, pouvant s'éclairer, avec tableau pour les retards et bras mobiles, hauteur 18 cm . . . . la pièce **frs.** 4.—

10144 „ „ „ bien vernis, pouvant s'éclairer, avec tableau pour les retards et bras mobiles, hauteur 29 cm . . . . la pièce **frs.** 6.—

9161 **Indicateurs de retards,** bien vernis, avec 5 indications différentes hauteur 22½ cm . . . . . . „ „ „ 4.25

14128

14128 **Appareil pour timbrer les billets,** bien verni, sur socle en fer blanc, avec porte-types, rouleaux de couleur et 1 série de caractères (17 numéros et 4 blocs); hauteur 12 cm . . . . la pièce **frs.** 3.30

Signaux.

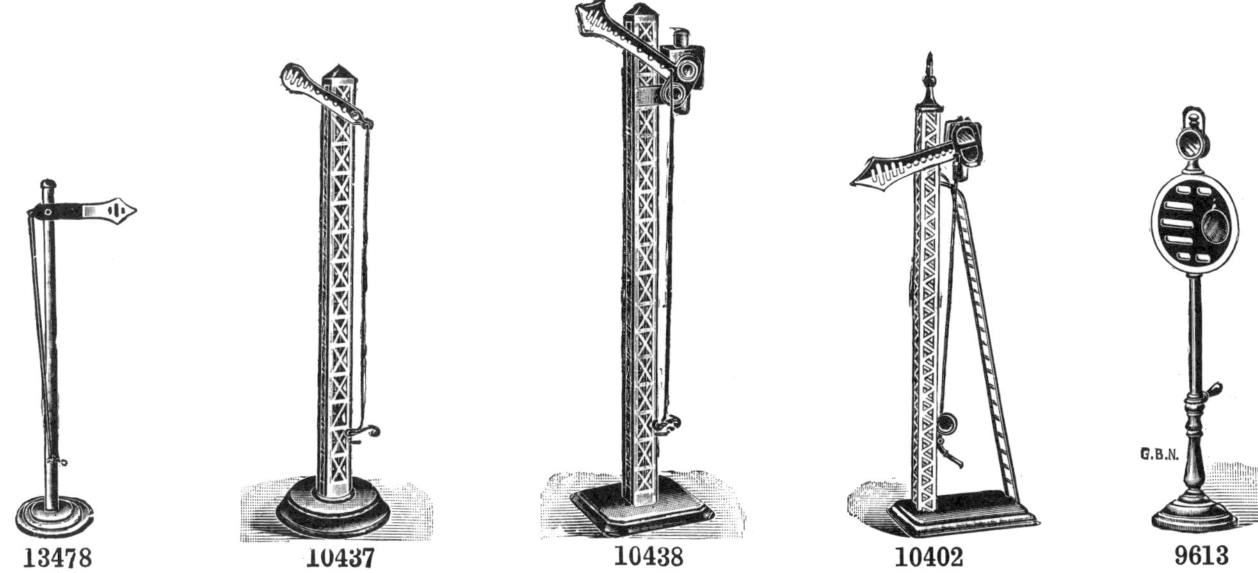

13478	**Sémaphore,** 1 bras, haut. 20 cm . . . . la pièce **frs.**	—.65
10437	„ imitation construction en fer, bien verni, avec 1 bras, haut. 30 cm . . . . „ „ „	1.80
10438	„ **avec éclairage,** imitation construction en fer, bien verni, avec 1 bras, 1 lanterne s'éclairant et disques lumineux colorés, haut. 35 cm . . . . „ „ „	2.50
10402	**Sémaphore avec éclairage,** imitation construction en fer, bien verni, avec 1 bras, 1 lanterne s'éclairant et disques lumineux colorés et mobiles, haut. 37 cm . . . . „ „ „	3.50
9613	**Disque rond,** bien verni, mobile, haut. 23 cm . . . . „ „ „	2.—

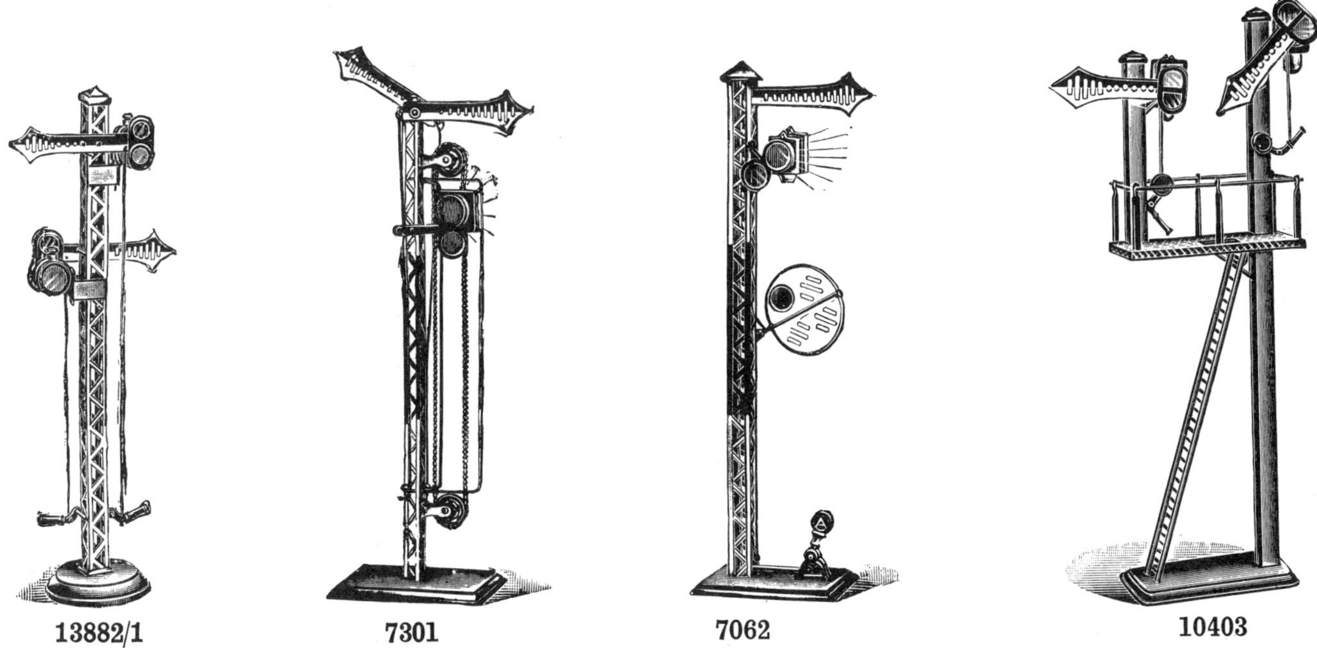

13882/1	**Sémaphore avec éclairage,** imitation construction en fer, bien verni, 1 lanterne s'éclairant, 1 bras, 1 disque signal et disques lumineux colorés et mobiles, haut. 35 cm. . . . . la pièce **frs.**	4.75
7301	**Sémaphore avec éclairage,** imitation construction en fer, bien verni, avec 1 lanterne s'éclairant, disques lumineux colorés et mobiles, 2 bras mobiles et lanterne se descendant, haut. 37½ cm . . „ „ „	7.20
7062	**Sémaphore avec éclairage,** avec 1 signal mobile, 1 lanterne s'éclairant, 1 disque pliant, avec un levier mécanique, haut. 36 cm . . . . „ „ „	8.50
10403	**Sémaphore avec éclairage,** passerelle, 2 signaux mobiles, 2 lanternes s'éclairant et échelle, haut. 45 cm „ „ „	8.50

Signaux automatiques dits "Bloc-système"

Aussitôt que le train touche le contact du sémaphore, le bras se place automatiquement et indique: "Voie fermée".

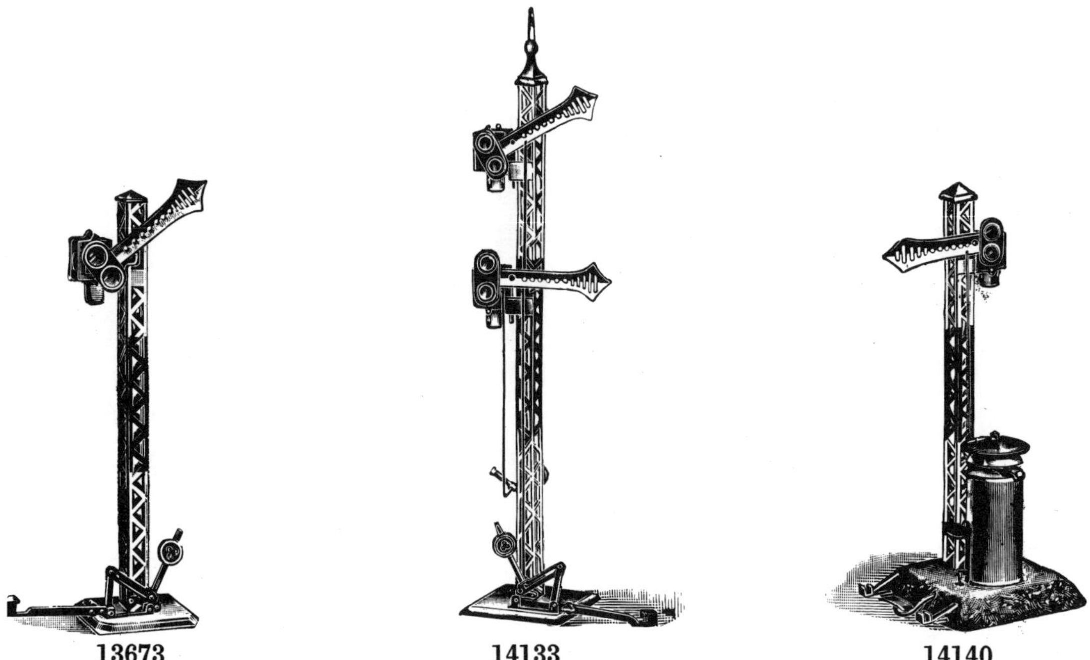

13673 14133 14140

13673 **Sémaphore,** avec éclairage, imitation construction en fer, avec bloc-signal automatique, bien verni, 1 bras, 1 disque mobile rouge et vert et 1 lanterne pouvant s'allumer, hauteur 30 cm . . . . . . la pièce **frs.** **4.50**

14133 **Sémaphore,** avec éclairage etc., comme le précédant, mais avec 1 bras mécanique, 1 bras à déclanchement automatique et 2 lanternes pouvant s'allumer, hauteur 40 cm . . . . la pièce **frs.** **5.50**

14140 **Sémaphore,** avec éclairage, imitation construction en fer, 1 bras avec disque mobile rouge et vert et 1 lampe pouvant s'allumer, sémaphore et sonnerie à **déclanchement automatique** fonctionnant par le rail avec ressort solide; monté sur socle en relief, bien verni, hauteur 30 cm . . . . la pièce **frs.** **8.25**

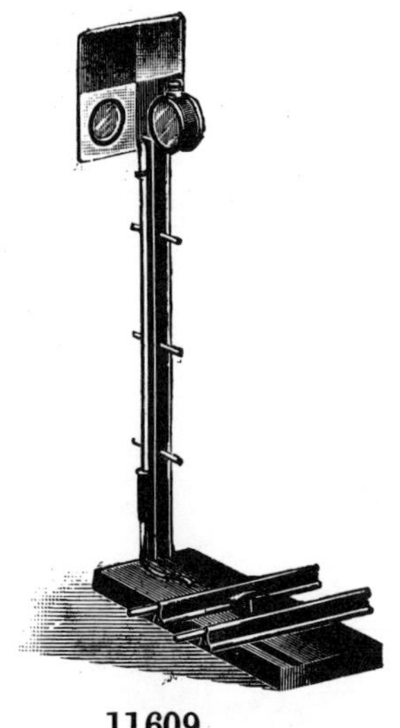

11609

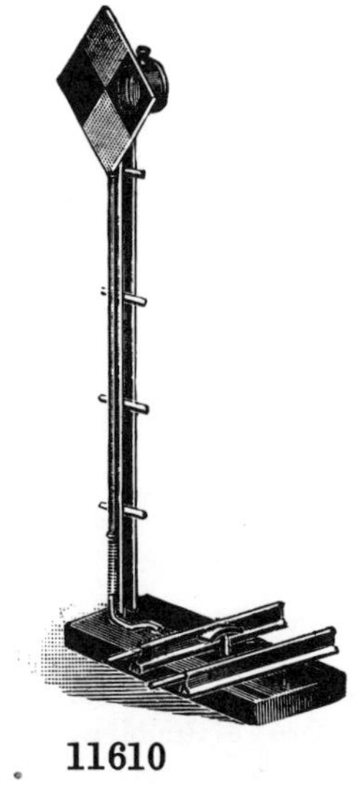

11610

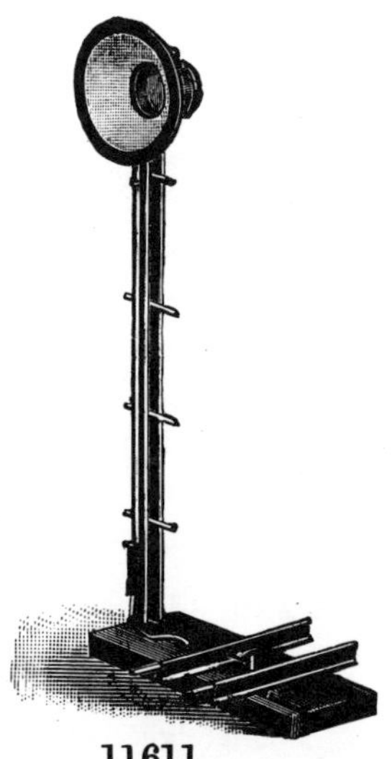

11611

11609	**Signaux automatiques** "Bloc-système", allant à tous les écartements, hauteur 27 cm	la pièce **frs.**	**4.60**
11610	" " " " " " " " " 27 "	" " "	**4.60**
11611	" " " " " " " " 27 "	" " "	**4.60**

Passerelles à signaux

imitation construction en fer, bien verni.

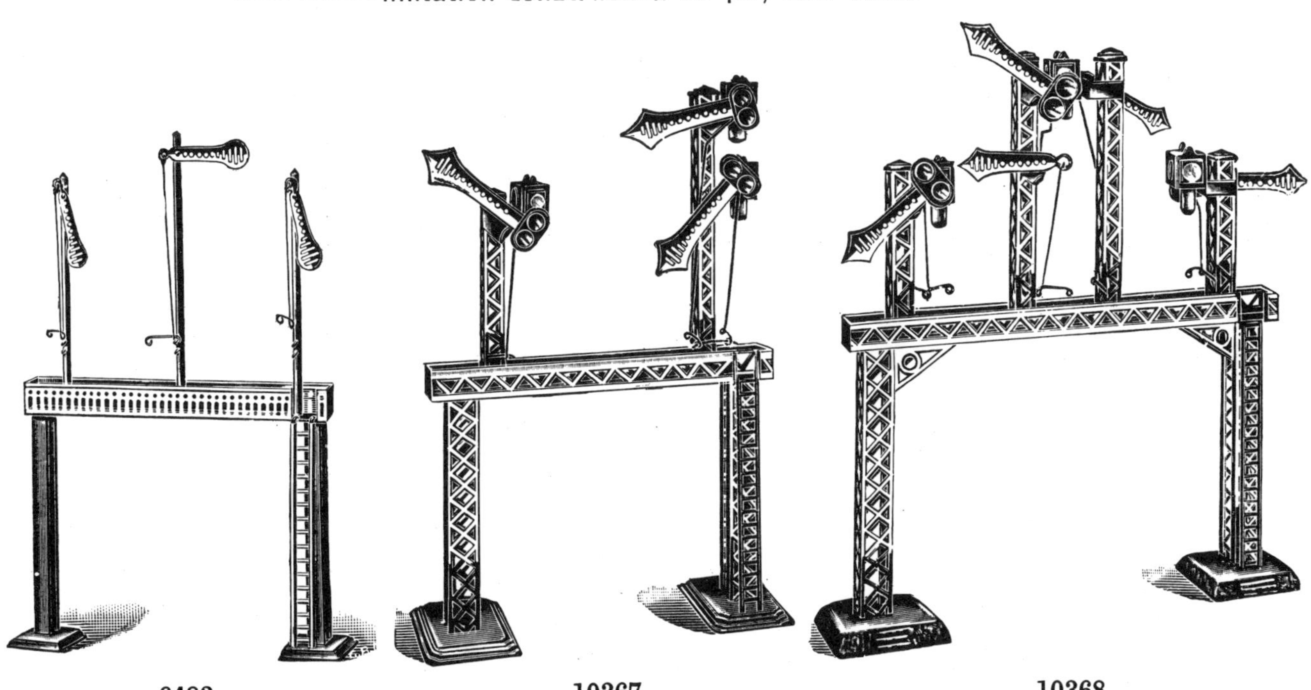

6483 10367 10368

6483 **Passerelle à signaux** avec 3 mâts et 3 signaux, hauteur 34 cm . . . . la pièce **frs. 2.—**
10367 „ „ „ „ 2 „ „ 2 lanternes s'éclairant et 3 bras avec disques colorés, haut. 42 cm „ „ „ **8.50**
10368 „ „ „ „ 4 „ „ 3 „ „ „ 5 „ „ „ „ „ 42 „ „ „ „ **13.—**

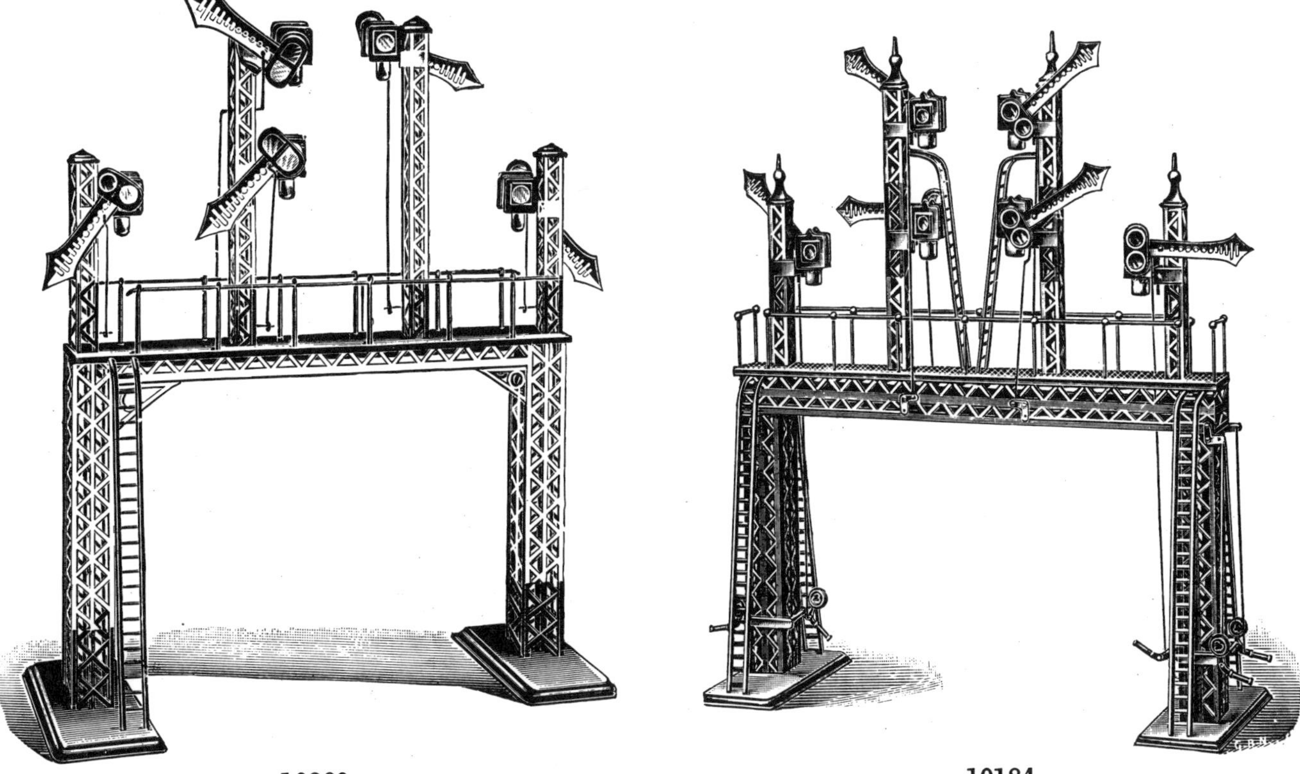

10369 10184

10369 **Passerelle à signaux** avec 4 mâts, 5 lanternes s'éclairant et 5 bras avec disques colorés, hauteur 48 cm,
la pièce **frs. 20.—**
10184 „ „ „ „ 4 „ 6 „ „ „ 6 „ „ „ „ „ 54 cm „ „ „ **30.—**

Passerelles à signaux avec éclairage électrique
pour courant à basse tension.

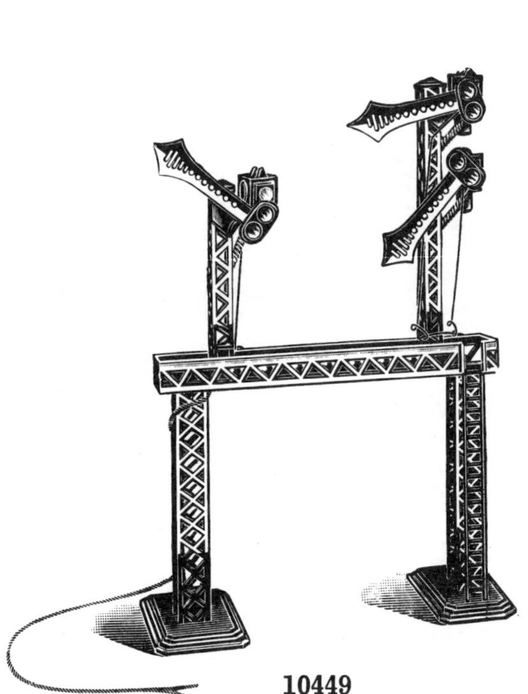

10449

10450

Passerelles à signaux avec éclairage électrique, imitation construction en fer, lanternes avec lampes à incandescence d'une tension de 4 volts, avec disques mobiles colorés.

10449 2 mâts avec 3 lanternes électriques, haut. 42 cm . . . . la pièce **frs. 15.—**

10450 4 „ „ 3 „ „ „ 42 „ . . . . „ **20.—**

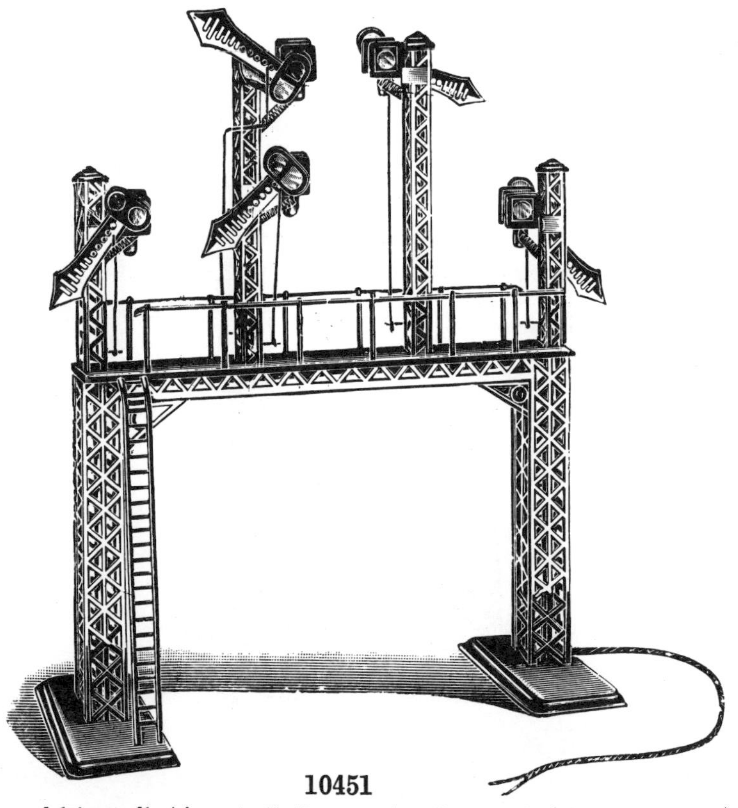

10451

10451 **Passerelle à signaux avec éclairage électrique,** imitation construction en fer, 4 mâts avec 5 lanternes électriques avec lampes à incandescence d'une tension de 4 volts et disques mobiles colorés, hauteur 48 cm . . . . la pièce **frs. 30.—**

BING BROTHERS A.-G.
NUREMBERG

Special Catalogue

of

Plush and Felt Toys

with and without clockwork

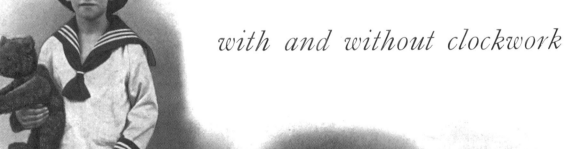

Spezial-Preisliste

über

Filzspielwaren und Plüschtiere

mit und ohne Uhrwerk

Catalogue spécial

de

Jouets en peluche et en étoffe

avec et sans mécanisme

Special catalogue

of

Plush and Felt Toys

with and without clockwork

Catálogo especial

de

Juguetes de peluche y fieltro

con y sin resorte

Haupt-Vorzüge unserer Filz- und Plüsch-Spielwaren:

Beste Qualität der verwendeten Materialien.
Natürliche Formen und lebenswahrer Gesichtsausdruck.
Die nicht beweglichen Filz-Tiere und -Figuren sind weich gestopft.
Die mechanischen Filz-Tiere und -Figuren sind durchwegs mit solidem Uhrwerk von langer Laufdauer versehen.
Unsere sämtlichen Artikel werden in solider Packung geliefert.
Die Kartons der mechanischen Artikel sind mit wirkungsvollen Etiketten versehen.

Avantages de nos jouets en peluche et en étoffe:

Nos matières premières sont de toute 1ère qualité.
Imitations très réussies au point de vue corps et figure.
Les animaux et objects sans mouvement sont bourrés de matières souples.
Les animaux et objets mécaniques sont sans exception, munis d'un ressort solide et d'une longue durée.
Nos marchandises sont emballées en cartons solides et élégamment étiquettées.

Preferences of our felt and plush toys:

The material used is of best quality.
Natural forms and life-like expressions.
All animals and figures without movement are of soft finish.
The mechanical figures and animals are fitted with strong clockwork and with long springs.
All our articles are packed in strong card-board boxes.
The boxes of the mechanical figures have an effective picture on the lid.

Ventajas principales de nuestros juguetes de fieltro y peluche:

Las materias empleadas son de 1ª calidad.
Formas y caras, verdaderas copias del natural.
Los animales y figuras de fieltro sin movimiento, son rellenas suavemente.
Todas las figuras y animales de fieltro mecánicos, son provistos de un resorte sólido de larga duración.
Todos nuestros artículos son librados en embalajes muy bien acondicionados.
En los cartones de los juguetes mecánicos, hay etiquetas de mucho efecto.

Tiere — Animaux **„Trippel-Trappel"** *Animals* — **Animales**

Der hervorragendste Artikel der kommenden Saison! — Nouveauté sensationelle de la Saison!
The most striking attraction of this season! — ¡Artículo de gran atracción de la próxima temporada!

Als Schaustück oder zur Vorführung der „Trippel-Trappel"-Tiere im Verkaufsraum geeignet, bestehend aus 6 Tieren und fein gekleidetem Clown. Antrieb mittels Handrad oder einem Elektromotor

Employé comme pièce d'étalage ou pour la présentation des animaux avec Système „Trippel-Trappel". Comprenant: 6 animaux et un clown bien habillé, marchant ou moyen d'un volant ou d'un moteur électrique

Suitable as showpiece or for showing "Trippel-Trappel" animals in the shop, consisting of 6 animals and finely dressed Clown, to be worked by turning a handwheel or by an electric Motor

Apropiado como pieza de muestra para enseñar el sistema "Trippel-Trappel" en una tienda, compuesto de 6 animales y de un payaso bien vestido, funcionando por medio de una rueda con impulsión manual ó por un electromotor

12340	ganze Höhe hauteur totale *entire height* altura total	85 cm	ganze Breite largeur totale *entire width* anchura total	156 cm	Plattendurchmesser diam. du socle *diam. of the base* diám de la plancha	120 cm	sh 210/-	complet

Tiere und Figuren
Animals and figures

„Trippel-Trappel“

Animaux trottinants
Animales y figuras

D. R.-Patent und ges. gesch. D. R.-G.-M.
Patente in Frankreich, England u. Amerika angemeldet.
Eine sinnreiche Anordnung ohne jedes Federwerk oder sonstigen komplizierten Mechanismus ahmt naturgetreu die Bewegungen der Füße nach.

Breveté S.G.D.G.
Breveté en France, en Angleterre et en Amérique.
Une disposition ingénieuse, sans ressort ou autre mécanisme compliqué, imite le mouvement des pattes.

German patent and registered pattern (D.R.G.M.) patents applied for in France, England and America. By a clever arrangement without any Clockwork or complicated mechanism the natural movement of the animals is exactly imitated.

Patente y modelo registrado. Patente en Alemania, Francia, Inglaterra y en América. Un dispositivo ingenioso, sin resorte ú otro mecanismo complicado, imita de un modo natural el movimiento de las patas.

268/11

Mohairplüsch, weiß, struppig
Pluche de Mohair, blanche, ébouriffée
Mohair plush, white, long haired
Peluche de Mohair blanco, erizado

268/11/1	2	3	4	
ca. 21	25	32	33 cm	lang — long / *long* — largo
„ 16	21	24	26 „	hoch — haut / *high* — alto
sh 4/-	6/4	7/6	10/-	Stück — pièce / *each* — pieza

299/11

Mohairplüsch, weiß, zottig
Pluche de Mohair, blanche, velue
Mohair plush, white, woolly
Peluche de Mohair, blanco afelpado

299/11/1	2	3	4	
ca. 24	28	30	38 cm	lang — long / *long* — largo
„ 18	22	24	27 „	hoch — haut / *high* — alto
sh 5/-	7/6	11/-	14/6	Stück — pièce / *each* — pieza

„Trippel-Trappel"

weiß und braun gefleckt
mouchetée blanc et brun
white and brown mottled
manchado blanco y bruno

260/11	**Lammplüsch** Peluche de laine *Lamb plush* Peluche de lana	22×17 cm	sh 3/6	**Stück** pièce *each* pieza
261/11	**Filz** feutre *Felt* Fieltro	28×21 cm	sh 5/-	**Stück** pièce *each* pieza

braun und dunkel gefleckt
tachetée brun et foncé
brown and dark mottled
manchado bruno y oscuro

262/11	**Sealplüsch** Peluche de Sea *Seal plush* Peluche de Seal	36×23 cm	sh 5/8	**Stück** pièce *each* pieza

261/11, 262/11

Filz, braun — feutre brun
Felt brown — Fieltro, marrón

255/11/1	2		
ca. 30	33 cm	**lang** — long *long* — largo	
,, 18	21 ,,	**hoch** — haut *high* — alto	
sh 3/8	5/3	**Stück** — pièce *each* — pieza	

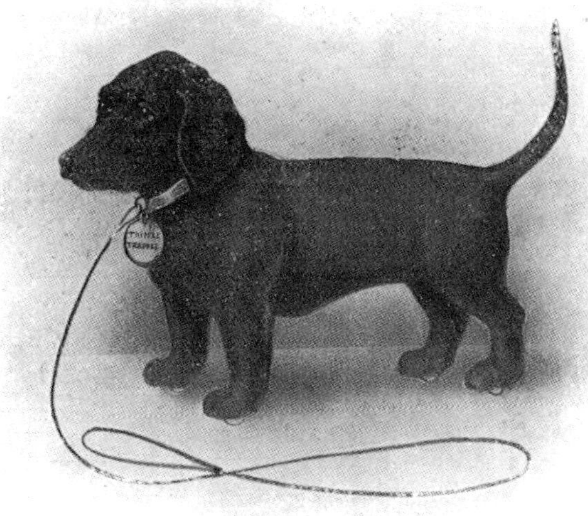

255/11

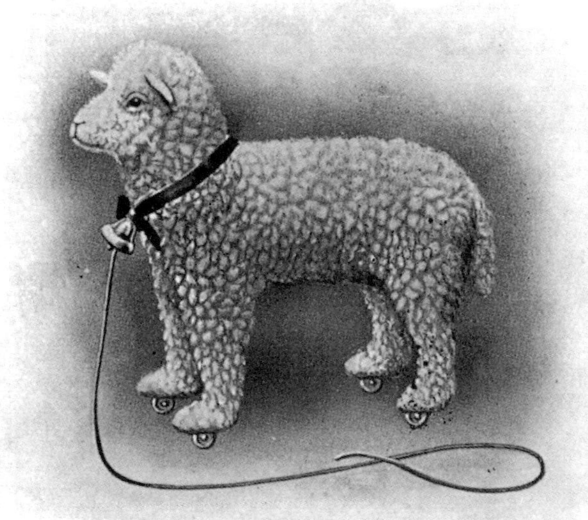

259/11

Mohairplüsch, weiß, mit Glöckchen und Seidenband
Peluche de Mohair, blanche, avec clochette et ruban de soie
Mohair plush, white with bells and silk ribbon
Peluche de Mohair, blanco, con campanilla y cinta de seda

259/11	ca. 28 cm	**lang** long *long* largo	25 cm	**hoch** haut *high* alto	sh 3/8	**Stück** pièce *each* pieza

Tiere / Animaux trottinants „Trippel-Trappel“ Animals / Animales

263/11

Wollplüsch, weiß
Peluche de laine, blanche
Wool plush, white
Peluche de lana blanca

263/11	ca. 27 cm	lang long *long* largo	22 cm	hoch haut *high* alto	sh **6/-**	Stück pièce *each* pieza

264/11

Mohairplüsch, langhaarig, weiß und braun gefleckt mit Lederhalsband und Leitriemen
Peluche de Mohair, à longs poils, tachetée blanc et brun, avec collier et laisse
Mohair plush, long haired, white and brown mottled with leather collar and guide rope
Peluche de Mohair, de pelo largo, manchado blanco y bruno con collar y trailla

264/11/1	**2**	**3**	**4**		
ca. 25	32	37	40	cm	lang — long *long* — largo
„ 18	21	24	27	„	hoch — haut *high* — alto
sh **4/6**	**6/-**	**9/-**	**12/-**		Stück — pièce *each* — pieza

Mohairplüsch, weiß und schwarz gefleckt
Peluche de Mohair, tachetée blanc et noir
Mohair plush, white and brown mottled
Peluche de Mohair, manchado blanco y negro

12493	ca. 35 cm	lang long *long* largo	21 cm	hoch haut *high* alto	sh **6/10**	Stück pièce *each* pieza

12493

Tiere
Animaux trottinants

„Trippel-Trappel"

Animals
Animales

258/11

Filz grau
feutre gris
Felt grey
fieltro gris

ca. 24 cm lang long *long* largo 17 cm hoch haut *high* alto

258/11 sh 4/- Stück pièce *each* pieza

Mohairplüsch, weiß
Peluche de Mohair, blanche
Mohair plush, white
Peluche de Mohair, blanco

ca. 24 cm lang long *long* largo 16 cm hoch haut *high* alto

257/11 sh 4/- Stück pièce *each* pieza

257/11

256/11

Mohairplüsch, braun
Peluche de Mohair, brune
Mohair plush, brown
Peluche de Mohair, bruno

ca. 23 cm lang long *long* largo 16 cm hoch haut *high* alto

256/11 sh 4/- Stück pièce *each* pieza

Tiere mit Rollglocke „Trippel-Trappel“ Animals with rolling bells
Animaux avec timbre roulant Animales con timbre rodando

Mohairplüsch, weiß, mit Lederhalsband und Leitriemen, Glocke vernickelt, Räder bronziert mit Gummireifen
Peluche de Mohair, blanche, avec collier et laisse en cuir, timbre nickelé avec roues bronzées et caoutchoucs
Mohair plush, white with collar-ring of leather and guide rope, nickelled bells, bronced wheels with rubber tyres
Peluche de Mohair blanco, con collar y traílla de cuero, timbres niquelados, con ruedas bronceadas y engomadas

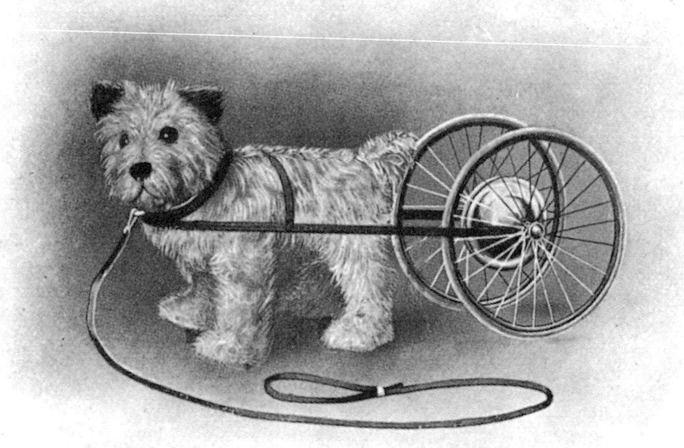

268/12

	268/12/1	2	
ganze Länge / long total / *total length* / largo total	39	42 cm	
Räder / roues / *wheels* / ruedas	$12^1/_2$	17 cm	Durchm. / *diam.*
	sh 5/6	10/6	Stück / pièce / *each* / pieza

ganze Länge / long totale / *total length* / largo total	50 cm	Räder / roues / *wheels* / ruedas	21 cm	Durchm. / *diam.*

299/12 sh 17/- Stück / pièce / *each* / pieza

299/12

258/12

Filz grau, Glocke vernickelt, Räder bronziert, mit Gummireifen
feutre gris, timbre nickelé avec roues bronzées et caoutchoucs
felt grey, nickelled bells, bronced wheels with rubber tyres
fieltro gris, timbres niquelados, con ruedas bronceadas y engomadas

ganze Länge / longueur totale / *total length* / largo total	36 cm	Durchm. der Räder / diam. des roues / *diam. of the wheels* / diám. de las ruedas	$12^1/_2$ cm

258/12 sh 6/4 Stück / pièce / *each* / pieza

Pudel — Caniche — *Poddle* — Perro de aguas
„Trippel-Trappel"

7299/11

Mohairplüsch, weiß, zottig, mit Uhrwerk im Korb, welches den Pudel in Bewegung setzt
Peluche de Mohair, blanche, veloutée, avec ressort dans la corbeille faisant marcher le caniche
Mohair plush, white wooly with clokwork in the basket moving the dog
Peluche de Mohair blanco, velloso, con resorte en el cesto moviendo el perro

7299/11 26 cm lang — long / long — largo; 24 cm hoch — haut / high — alto; sh 13/- Stück — pièce / each — pieza

12498

Filz braun auf lackiertem Automobil mit Uhrwerk
feutre brun, sur automobile vernie avec ressort
Felt brown on japanned Motor Car with clockwork
fieltro bruno, sobre automóvil barnizado con resorte

12498 15 cm lang — long / long — largo; 12 cm hoch — haut / high — alto; sh 20/6 dozen Stück — pièce / each — pieza

„Trippel-Trappel" Bär, als Reittier,

Mohairplüsch braun, mit Trippel-Trappel-Bewegung

Ours „Trippel-Trappel," comme animal se montant
Peluche de Mohair brune, système „Trippel-Trappel"

"Trippel-Trappel" Bear, as a riding animal.
Mohair plush brown, with "Trippel-Trappel" movement

Oso "Trippel-Trappel" como animal de silla,
peluche de Mohair bruno, con movimiento "Trippel-Trappel"

90 cm lang — long / long — largo
60 cm hoch — haut / high — alto

280/100 sh 98/6 Stück — pièce / each — pieza

280/100

Tiere mit Uhrwerk — Animaux avec ressort — *Animals with clockwork* — Animales con resorte

1282/50

Laufende Katzen mit beweglichem Ball
Chat trottant avec balle mobile
Running Cats with moveable ball
Gatos andando con bola movible

			1	2	3	4	
			20	25	30	35 cm	lang / long / largo
1282/50	Lammplüsch, weiß / Peluche de laine, blanche / *Lamb plush, white* / Lama blanca de cordero	sh	2/-	3/-	4/3	5/10	Stück / pièce / *each* / pieza
1282/60	Mohairplüsch, weiß / Peluche de Mohair, blanche / *Mohair plush, white* / Peluche de Mohair, blanco	sh	—	—	—	7/4	Stück / pièce / *each* / pieza

Mohairplüsch, Großer Bär braun, kleiner Bär weiß

Peluche de Mohair, grand ours brun, petit ours blanc

Mohair plush, big bear brown, small bear white

Peluche de Mohair, oso grande de bruno, oso pequeño blanco

8280/67	21 cm	hoch / *high* / haut / alto	sh	6/4	Stück / pièce / *each* / pieza

8280/67

12486

1 großer Hase, Mohairplüsch, weiß, mit Stoffweste und seidenem Halsband, 2 kleine Hasen, Filz, Auto fein lackiert

Grand lapin en peluche de Mohair, blanche avec habit en drap et ruban de soie au cou, 2 petits lapins feutre, automobile bien vernie

1 big Hare, Mohair plush, white, with waistcoat of stuff and collarband of silk, 2 small hares felt, Auto finely japanned

1 conejo grande de peluche de Mohair, blanco, con chaleco de paño y collar de seda, 2 conejitos de fieltro y automóvil, bien barnizado

Hase / lapin / *hare* / conejo	28 cm	hoch, / haut, / *high,* / alto,	Auto / automobile / *auto* / automóvile	29 cm	lang / long / *long* / largo

12486	sh	7/10	Stück / pièce / *each* / pieza

Tiere auf Rollschuhen mit Uhrwerk — Animaux sur patins à roulettes avec ressort
Animals on roller-skating with clockwork — Animales con patines, á resorte

mit originellen Bewegungen, vor- und rückwärts fahrend, D. R.-G.-M.
avec mouvements originaux, marchant en avant et en arrière
with original movements, skating forwards and backwards
con movimientos originales, marchando hacia adelante y hacia atrás

12405

Mohairplüsch, goldgelb
Peluche de Mohair, jaune d'or
Mohair plush, gold yellow
Peluche de Mohair, amarillo de oro

12405 21 cm hoch — haut / *high* — alto sh 4/- Stück — pièce / *each* — pieza

Filz, mit origineller Stoffkleidung
Feutre, avec vêtements originaux, en étoffe
Felt, originally dressed
Fieltro, con vestido original

12497 22 cm hoch — haut / *high* — alto sh 5/8 Stück — pièce / *each* — pieza

12497

12496

Mohairplüsch, mit origineller Stoffkleidung
Peluche de Mohair, avec vêtements originaux, en étoffe
Mohair plush, originally dressed
Peluche de Mohair, con vestido original

12496 22 cm hoch — haut / *high* — alto sh 5/8 Stück — pièce / *each* — pieza

Tiere mit Uhrwerk, originelle Bewegungen

Animaux avec ressort, mouvements originaux

Animals with Clockwork, original movements

Animales con resorte, movimientos originales

12408

hüpfender Affe mit naturgetreuem Gesicht, Mohair braun
Singe sauteur, avec tête parfaitment imité, Mohair brune
Jumping Monkey with lifelike face, Mohair brown
Mono brincando, con cara natural, Mohair bruno

12408 17 cm hoch – haut / *high* – alto sh 4/- Stück / pièce / *each* / pieza

3288/62/1

hüpfendes Känguruh, Mohair braun
Kangourou sauteur, Mohair brune
Jumping Kangaroo, Mohair brown
Canguro brincando, Mohair bruno

3288/62/1 22 cm hoch – haut / *high* – alto sh 5/3 Stück / pièce / *each* / pieza

3294/107

hüpfender Frosch, Filz in natürlichen Farben, mit Stimme im Hut
Grenouille, bondissant, feutre teint couleur naturelle, avec voix dans le chapeau
Jumping Frog, felt in natural colours, with voice in the hat
Rana brincando, fieltro en colores naturales, con grito en el sombrero

3294/107 18 cm hoch – haut / *high* – alto; 24 ,, lang – long / *long* – largo sh 5/3 Stück / pièce / *each* / pieza

Vögel mit origineller Wackel-Bewegung, mit Uhrwerk
Oiseaux avec mouvement original (se dandinant), avec ressort
Birds with original waddling movement, with clockwork
Pájaros con movimiento original (meneando el cuerpo) á resorte

Plüsch, fein farbig — Peluche, jolies taintes — *Plush, finely coloured* — Peluche de colores finos

12404/1	2	
20	25 cm	hoch — haut / *high* — alto
sh 4/-	5/3	Stück — pièce / *each* — pieza

12403/1	2	
14	20 cm	hoch — haut / *high* — alto
20	22 cm	lang — long / *long* — largo
sh 4/-	5/4	Stück — pièce / *each* — pieza

Pudel mit Uhrwerk — Caniche avec ressort — *Poodle with clockwork* — Perro de aguas á resorte

Plüsch, weiß, zottig, sich im Kreise drehend, mit origineller automatischer Abstellvorrichtung

Peluche, blanche, velue, se mouvant en cercle avec arrêt automatique, très original!

Plush, white, woolly, turning in a circle with automatic stopping arrangement

Peluche blanco afelpado, girándose en círculo, con paro automático y original

254/11 30 cm hoch — haut / *high* — alto sh 9/6 Stück — pièce / *each* — pieza

Tiere und Figuren mit Uhrwerk — Animaux et personnages, avec ressort

Animals and Figures with clockwork — Animales y figuras á resorte

lackiertes Blechei, bezw. Kugel im Kreise drehend
faisant tourner en cercle un œuf ou une boule en fer blanc verni
turning in a circle japanned tin egg or ball
volviendo en círculos un huevo ó una bola de chapa barnizada

7281/110

Filz — feutre
felt — fieltro

7281/110	16 cm	hoch haut *high* alto	sh 1/7	Stück pièce *each* pieza
12407	15 cm	hoch haut *high* alto	sh 26/6 dozen	Stück pièce *each* pieza

12407

12490

Filz, gekleidet, sortiert
feutre, habillé, assorti
felt, dressed, assorted
fieltro, vestido, surtidos

15 cm hoch — haut *high* — alto

12490 sh 1/7 Stück pièce *each* pieza

Mohairplüsch, braun
Peluche de Mohair, brune
Mohair plush, brown
Peluche de Mohair, bruno

7280/62/1 21 cm hoch haut *high* alto sh 5/3 Stück pièce *each* pieza

7280/62/1

Tiere und Figuren mit Uhrwerk — Animaux et personnages avec ressort
Animals and Figures with clockwork — Animales y figuras á resorte

Plüsch, gekleidet, Kugel im Kreise rollend
Peluche, habillé, faisant tourner une boule en cercle
Plush, dressed, tourning ball in a circle
Peluche, vestido, volviendo una bola en círculo

12472 24 cm hoch — haut / *high* — alto sh 5/8 Stück — pièce / *each* — pieza

Filz, gekleidet, Koffer vor sich her rollend
Feutre, habillé, roulant une malle
Felt, dressed, turning a trunk
Fieltro, vestido, haciendo rodar un baúl

M 3417 25 cm hoch — haut / *high* — alto sh 7/6 Stück — pièce / *each* — pieza

„Trippel-Trappel"-Bewegung, Schiff mit Uhrwerk — Mouvement „Trippel-Trappel", bateau avec ressort
"Trippel-Trappel" Movement, boat with clockwork — Movimiento „Trippel-Trappel", bote con resorte

12475 27 cm hoch / haut / *high* / alto 35 cm lang / long / *long* / largo sh 8/6 Stück / pièce / *each* / pieza

12488 27 cm hoch / haut / *high* / alto 35 cm lang / long / *long* / largo sh 8/6 Stück / pièce / *each* / pieza

Figuren mit Uhrwerk, Filz, gekleidet — Personnages avec ressort, feutre, habillé
Figures with clockwork, felt, dressed — Figuras con resorte, fieltro, vestido

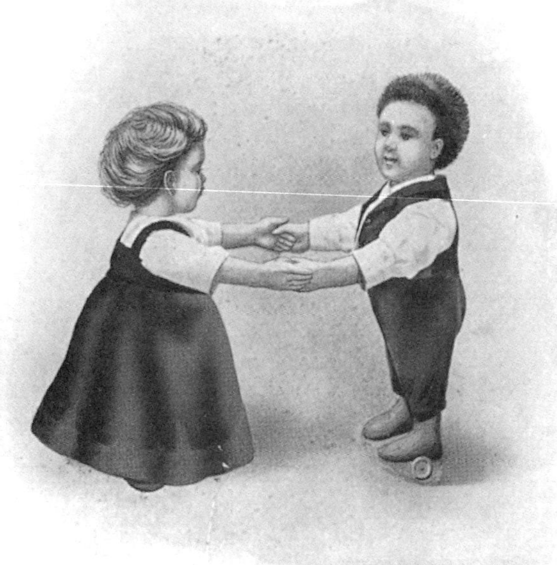

sich im Kreise drehend — se mouvant en cercle — *turning in a circle* — girando en círculos

12406 Knabe — garçon *boy* — muchacho 18 cm hoch haut *high* alto sh 6/10 Stück pièce *each* pieza

12489 Knabe — garçon *boy* — muchacho 25 cm hoch haut *high* alto sh 8/6 Stück pièce *each* pieza

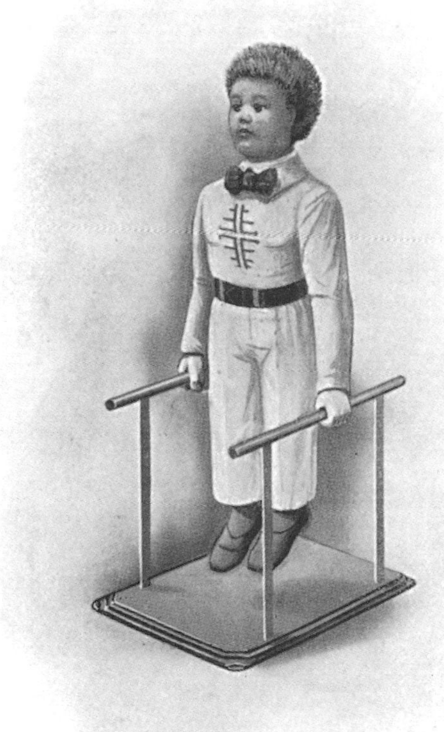

sich am Barren drehend — travaillant au trapèze — *making gymnastics on the bar* — trabajando á la barra

12494 26 cm hoch haut *high* alto sh 3/10 Stück pièce *each* pieza

Clown mit „Trippel-Trappel“-Bewegung, auf einer Schnur vor- und rückwärts gehend, ohne Uhrwerk, Filz, originell bekleidet

Clown avec système „Trippel-Trappel“, allant et venant sur une corde, sans ressort, feutre vêtu, très original!

Clown with "Trippel-Trappel" movement, walking forward and backward on a rope, without clockwork, felt originally dressed

Payaso con movimiento "Trippel-Trappel" caminando hacia adelante y hacia atrás de la cuerda, sin resorte, de fieltro, vestido de un modo original

Clown — Clown
Clown — Payaso
23 cm hoch — haut / *high* — alto

12476 sh 5/6 Stück / pièce / *each* / pieza

12476

Tennisspieler, Ball schleudernd, Filz, fein gekleidet, mit Uhrwerk

Joueur de tennis, lançant des balles, feutre, bien habillé, avec ressort

Tennisplayer, throwing ball, felt, finely dressed, with clockwork

Jugadores de tennis, lanzando la pelota, fieltro, bien vestidos, á resorte

12482 12483

23 cm hoch — haut / *high* — alto

12482	Tennisspieler . . . . Joueur de tennis . . *Tennisplayer* . . . . Jugador de tennis .	sh 8/-	Stück / pièce / *each* / pieca
12483	Tennisspielerin . . . Joueuse de tennis . *Lady playing tennis* . Jugadora de tennis .	sh 8/-	„
12481	Mulatte als Tennisspieler Mulâtre jouant au tennis *Mulatte playing tennis* Mulato como jugador de tennis	sh 8/-	„

„Clown als Trapezkünstler" — „Clown-acrobate"

"Clown as tumbling acrobate" — "Payaso-acróbata"

D. R.-P. und D. R.-G.-M.
brevеté

D. R.-G.-M. patented
patentado

10299

Ohne jede Mechanik! — Durch Schnurzug wird die Figur in den verschiedensten Stellungen und Bewegungen vorgeführt, die originell und überaus komisch wirken. — Figur mit Stoffbekleidung und originell bemaltem Gesicht aus Filz. — Trapez aus solidem Eisengestell, fein lackiert, mit Klammern, am Tisch anzuschrauben.

Sans mouvement d'horlogerie! -- Par un système de cordes et de roulettes on fait exécuter au clown des mouvements les plus amusants. — Personnage habillé genre „clown", figure grotesque. — Le trapèze est solidement monté en tiges de fer finement vernies et peut être fixé à la table à l'aide de crampons.

Without any mechanics! — By pulling the string, the figure will perform various positions and movements, which have an original and comical effect. — Figure with cloth dress and originally painted face of felt. — Trapezium solid iron stand, finely japanned with iron cramps to fasten on the table.

¡Sin mecanismo! — Por medio de cordones y poleas se dá al clown unos movimientos graciosos y originales. — Clown vestido de paño con cara de fieltro pintado. — Trapecio de soportes de hierro, bien barnizado, con grapas para sujetarlo á la mesa.

		10299/1	2	3	
Trapez — Trapèze / *Trapezium* — **Trapecio**		44	55	65 cm	hoch — haut / *high* — alto
Figur — Personnage / *Figure* — **Payaso**		19	23	27 ,,	,,
complet	sh	7/6	11/-	15/-	Stück — pièce / *each* — pieza

Weichgestopfte Plüschtiere — Animaux en peluche, rembourrage souple.

Plush Animals softly stuffed. — Animales de peluche, con relleno suave

		mit Stimme avec voix *with voice* con gruñido			mit automatischer Brummstimme avec voix automatique *with automatic growling voice* con gruñido automático				
		15	17	22	25	28	35	43 cm	Sitzhöhe hauteur assis *high sitting* altura sentados
280/10	**Mohair, weiß** Mohair blanche *Mohair, white* Mohair blanco	sh 2/1	2/9	4/5	6/2	7/6	13/-	20/-	Stück — pièce *each* — pieza
280/11	**Mohair, goldgelb** Mohair jaune d'or *Mohair gold yellow* Mohair amarillo de oro	sh 2/1	2/9	4/5	6/2	7/6	13/-	20/-	Stück — pièce *each* — pieza

Mohair, weiß, mit Patentgliederung und Brummstimme
Mohair blanche, articulé et avec voix
Mohair, white, with patented jointed legs, with growling voice
Mohair blanco, con articulaciones patentadas y gruñido

295/60/2 35 cm lang / long / *long* / largo sh 6/- Stück / pièce / *each* / pieza

Weichgestopfte Plüschtiere mit Stimme

Animaux en peluche avec voix, rembourrage souple

Plush Animals, softly stuffed, with voice

Animales de peluche con relleno suave y voz

Lammplüsch, weiß — Peluche de laine, blanche
Lamb plush, white
Peluche de lana de cordero, blanco

281/50/1	2	3	
8	10	12	cm hoch — haut / *high* — alto
sh 8/6	17/-	20/6	dozen

Mohairplüsch, weiß — Peluche de Mohair, blanche
Mohair plush, white
Peluche de Mohair, blanco

281/160 22 cm hoch — haut / *high* — alto . . sh 4/- Stück — pièce / *each* — pieza

Lammplüsch, weiß — Peluche de laine, blanche
Lamb plush, white
Peluche de lana de cordero, blanco

282/50/2	3	
10	12	cm hoch — haut / *high* — alto
sh 1/5	2/2	Stück — pièce / *each* — pieza

Mohairplüsch, weiß — Peluche de Mohair, blanche
Mohair plush, white
Peluche de Mohair, blanco

282/60/3	4	5	
12	14	17	cm hoch — haut / *high* — alto
sh 2/6	2/10	4/2	Stück — pièce / *each* — pieza

Weichgestopfte Plüschtiere — Animaux en peluche, rembourrage souple

Softly stuffed Plush Animals — Animales de peluche, con relleno suave

in naturgetreuen Formen, mit Stimme — forme naturelle, avec voix
natural forms, with voice — verdaderas copias del natural, con gruñido

Lammplüsch, weiß, rotbraun gefleckt — Peluche de laine, blanche, tachetée rouge-brun
Lamb Plush, white, redbrown spotted — Peluche blanco de lana de cordero, con manchas bruno-rojas

283/50/1	2	3	
17	22	28 cm	hoch — haut / *high* — alto
sh 1/11	3/-	4/6	Stück — pièce / *each* — pieza

Kurzplüsch, grau — Peluche courte, grise — *shorthaired Plush, grey* — Peluche corto, gris

286/74/1	2	3	4	5	
18	20	26	32	39 cm	lang — long / *long* — largo
13	15	20	24	31 ,,	hoch — haut / *high* — alto
sh 2/4	3/2	5/4	8/-	11/8	Stück — pièce / *each* — pieza

Weichgestopfte Figuren „Hasen-Babies“ mit Stimme

Personnages à rembourrage souple, „Lapins façon baby” avec voix

Figures softly stuffed "Hare Babies" with voice

Figuras con relleno suave "Niños-conejos" con voz

Lammplüsch, weiß, mit Stimme — Peluche de laine blanche, avec voix
Lamb Plush, white, with voice — Peluche blanco de lana de cordero, con voz

285/50/1	2	3	
28	34	35	cm hoch — haut / *high* — alto
sh 3/-	3/6	4/6	Stück / pièce / *each* / pieza

Lammplüsch, weiß, mit Mama-Stimme
Peluche de laine blanche, avec voix disant „maman”
Lamb Plush, white, with voice "Mama"
Peluche blanco de lana de cordero, diciendo mamá

285/550/4 42 cm hoch — haut / *high* — alto sh 6/8 Stück / pièce / *each* / pieza

Bären auf Rollen (Reit-Tiere) — Ours sur roues (se montant)
Bears on wheels (as a riding animal) — Osos con ruedas (como animal de silla)

stehend, mit extrastarkem Gestell und soliden Eisenrädern
sur 4 pattes, avec monture extra forte et roues solides en fer
standing on 4 legs with extra strong framed base and strong iron wheels
en pié, con soporte extra-fuerte y ruedas de hierro sólido

Mohairplüsch, braun — Peluche de Mohair, brune — *Mohair Plush, brown* — **Peluche de »Mohair«, bruno**

	mit Druckstimme — avec voix *with voice* — con voz			mit Zugstimme — avec voix grognand *with growling voice* — con voz gruñiendo				
280/200/	17	22	28	35	43	50	60 cm	hoch — haut *high* — alto
	24	30	39	48	62	68	78 cm	lang — long *long* — largo
sh	5/-	8/-	11/6	18/-	27/6	38/-	55/-	Stück — pièce *each* — pieza

Hunde auf Rollen (Reit-Tiere) — Chiens sur roues (se montant)
Dogs on wheels (as a riding animal) — Perros con ruedas (como animal de silla)

Mohairplüsch, weiß, braun gefleckt, mit extrastarkem Gestell und soliden Eisenrädern

Peluche de Mohair, blanche, tachetés brun avec monture extraforte et roues solides en fer

Mohair Plush, white, brown spotted with extra strong framed base and strong iron wheels

Peluche de Mohair, blanco, con manchas brunas con soporte muy sólido y ruedas de hierro fuerte

	mit Druckstimme — avec voix / *with voice* — con voz				mit Zugstimme — avec voix grognant / *with growling voice* — con voz gruñiendo			
270/200/17	22	28	35	42	50	60	cm	hoch — haut / *high* — alto
24	30	39	48	62	68	78	,,	long — long / *long* — largo
sh 4/-	6/6	9/6	15/-	23/-	35/-	51/-		Stück — pièce / *each* — pieza

Menagerie-Wagen — Voiture de Ménagerie — *Menagerie Car* — Carro de fieras

Locomobile mit solidem Uhrwerk, sowie Wagen in feiner Polychromlackierung, Türen zum Öffnen, mit 3 Filztieren, Locomobile und Wagen mit verstellbarer Vorderachse zum Gerade- und Kreisfahren

Locomobile à ressort et wagon vernis polychrome, portes s'ouvrant, avec 3 animaux, locomobile et voiture avec essieu de devant mobile pour marche droite ou circulaire

Traction Engine with good clockwork and car, fine polychrome japanning, car with doors to open, with 3 felt animals, traction engine and car with adjustable front axle for straight and circular run

Locomóvil con resorte sólido y carro bien barnizado al polícromo, abriéndose las puertas, con 3 fieras de fieltro, locomóvil y carro con ruedas delanteras giratorias para marchar recto y haciendo círculos

10196 ganze Länge — longueur total / *total length* — largura total } 41½ cm Höhe — haut / *high* — alto } 12 cm complet sh 4/6 Stück — pièce / *each* — pieza

Nummern-Verzeichnis — Table de numéros
Numerical Index — Indice numérico